Washington Irving by John Wesley Jarvis, 1809.
(Courtesy Historic Hudson Valley, Tarrytown, New York.)

The Original Knickerbocker

The
ORIGINAL
KNICKERBOCKER

The Life of Washington Irving

Andrew Burstein

BASIC
BOOKS

A Member of the Perseus Books Group
New York

Designed by Brent Wilcox

Library of Congress Cataloging-in-Publication Data
Burstein, Andrew.
    Original knickerbocker : the life of Washington Irving / Andrew Burstein.
        p.   cm.
    Includes bibliographical references and index.
    ISBN-13: 978-0-465-00853-7
    ISBN-10: 0-465-00853-4
    1. Irving, Washington, 1783–1859.   2. Authors, American—19th century—
Biography.   I. Title
PS2081.B87   2006
818'.209—dc22
[B]
                                                                    2006029004

10 9 8 7 6 5 4 3 2 1

TO HACKLEY SCHOOL,
Tarrytown, New York,
where the life of the mind has always mattered

Fiction is history that *might* have taken place, and history fiction that *has* taken place. We are, indeed, forced to acknowledge that the novelist's art often compels belief, just as reality sometimes defies it.

—André Gide, from *Lafcadio's Adventures*

Contents

MANHATTANITE

CHAPTER 1

New York's Lost Past

1783–1803

Moonlight walk on the Battery, in serene pomp of heaven from white light of the moon. sails gliding along—slipping along with the tide. ripple of the river with gleam of moonlight on it. voice of seamen—pull of an oar.

—Scattered images recalled from his New York
boyhood, in a notebook Washington Irving
kept while in England, 1818.[1]

W HAT REMNANTS OF THE PAST LIE UNDER THE asphalt, or in the muck just off shore? It is a question that anyone curious about the overbuilt and very vertical City of New York asks at some point. Take away the high-rise apartments, the traffic lights, and the taxis—visualize the city as the equivalent of a middle-sized town. Go back a little further in time to cobblestone and dirt, when there were as many crooked and narrow lanes as perpendicular streets. One could espy longshoremen unloading sailing vessels containing European manufactures and then reloading them with furs, hides, lumber, and wheat. Think of scores of sails visible at any one time. Manhattan, then, would be truly an unfamiliar place, or to use a term Washington Irving liked, *"terra incognita."*

In his 1809 *A History of New York*, the masterful crazy quilt that first made Irving a national celebrity, the author exposed the attitude of an early nineteenth-century Manhattanite: Overdo everything while keeping a straight face, and always pretend to be bigger than you are. As if Jeffersonian democracy were the end, not the beginning, of the national experience, he enlarged the sovereign decades of Dutch New Amsterdam of 150 years past,

3

"those sweet days of simplicity and ease, which never more will dawn on the lovely island of Manna-hata." He gave his hometown a huge and prosperous history, which it never had. He was on his way to composing some of the greatest legends about American history *in* American history.

Readers in other parts of the Union understood him. They understood that without wit and humor, it would be impossible to tell the story of America except in stiff, snobbish, puritanical form. The young country had little to recommend it but its people's expectation that they would amount to something soon enough. By poking fun at pomp and pretense, the resourceful author, a cross-cultural observer of moods and trends, made room for America on the world stage.

At the time he published his farcical *History*, Washington Irving knew more about politics and manners than he let on. As much as he was fascinated by New York's past, he wished to critique its fashionable present garb, too. *A History of New York* is peppered with erudite footnotes in which the mock-serious author seriously mocks the "notorious wise men of Gotham," bloated theorists stumbling over themselves as they tried to imitate European science. In the end, the upstart Irving would outshine the best post-Revolutionary brains because he accepted New York for what it really was—provincial. The modest Manhattanite loved his "Manna-hata" and the view of the world it afforded him.

★   ★

New York's allure was its deep harbor, but its geography had been adapting to settlement since the arrival of the earliest Dutch inhabitants, who saw the island as "a convenient place abounding with grass." A contemporary of Irving's—one of the "wise men of Gotham"—wrote about its natural features and how they were being altered. Samuel L. Mitchill inspected the area's gray granite and observed the "crags and vallies," hills already "dug down"; swamps being "filled up"; knolls being "pared away"; gullies "brought to a level." Thus began the smoothing of old Manhattan, a process that eliminated its local waterways and reshaped its contours, all to accommodate commerce and a growing population.[2]

In a literary sense, Washington Irving would come to "own" the Hudson River. When he was born, the Hudson was as often called the North River, just as the Delaware had once been the South River, names that delineated the unofficial margins of the former colony of New Netherland. From the Dutch to the English to the early American empire, the wide Hudson was thickly occupied by crossing ferries and Albany-bound commercial vessels that paused at landings along the way to pick up passengers. In 1807, two years before Irving's comic *History* emerged, the great inland waterway saw the commercialization of steam with Robert Fulton's *Clermont*. Irving was to experience the age of oar and sail, steam and rail, as he plied the Hudson and gave its towns and byways a storied past; eventually, he would settle on its banks, just below Tarrytown.[3]

The Manhattan he called home until the age of thirty-two is all but impossible for us to picture in its full sensory detail. Imagine a time when no sounds were louder than church bells and sleigh bells. Think of stockyards on the Bowery, or of Astor Place as an expansive garden. Think of men in high hats and loose pantaloons. Think of stables the way we think of parking lots. Think of progress as brightening the shops on lower Broadway with gaslights instead of dim oil lamps.

That was the town Irving first wrote about. Days of commercial movement were followed by nights when family members huddled close. On bitterly cold evenings, a writer's ink might freeze on the nib of the pen, even as he or she was sitting by a fire. Winter sleigh rides had been popular since the time of the Dutch; sleigh bells were mandated because, without them, pedestrians were sometimes blindsided in the quiet of the night, stomped on and run over. That was not the only remnant of Dutch New Amsterdam: Some old houses with distinctive gabled roofs survived, structures with high steps still known as "stoops." Dutch surnames were scattered through the City Register.

The city's institution of higher learning, Columbia College, then located in a garden-like setting a few blocks west of today's City Hall Park, required proficiency in Greek and Latin for admission. Its Faculty of Arts taught moral philosophy, mathematics, astronomy, geography, logic, rhetoric, and belles lettres. Its government in these years was unwieldy (initially under the control of sixty-five regents). Still, it fielded an excellent faculty and added to the city's spirit.

Especially near the wharves and among the markets that predominated there, the bustle that Manhattan would become famous for was already a part of every resident's every day. The East River beat with oceangoing vessels; Pearl and Broad Streets, a bit inland, served as the center of the wholesale trade; William Street, between Fulton and Wall, "elevated and convenient," was the best-known location for retail shops—this was where the Irving family earned its livelihood during Washington's first years. New York was, even then, a vibrant, multiethnic city, with lots of visitors and constant traffic in and out. Blacks were most noticeable on the waterfront, and represented around

15 percent of the population; among whites, there was one person of Dutch or German ancestry for every three of English or Scotch-Irish background.

Yet lower Manhattan remained bucolic. Beyond its wind-worn brick and wooden struts and broad harbor views were a rural landscape and an essential earthiness we are no longer reminded of when we gaze up at today's steel structures. The street grid of the 1780s would probably be recognizable to modern New Yorkers, though it stopped below the old city gates at what is today's City Hall Park. To the north lay grazing land, and a place called the Collect, a roughly circular fresh-water pond, its contents soon to be acknowledged as undrinkable. Strong breezes were not yet diverted around tall buildings, few streets were paved, and, though hard to imagine, hogs, unregimented in their comings and goings, freely consumed the city's plentiful garbage.

That Manhattan is where the life of Washington Irving begins. The year he was born, 1783, witnessed the end of the Revolutionary War. Manhattan Island was on a slow mend, having been caught up in hostilities and left in British hands. Residents had witnessed abuses of power, espionage, plunder, desperate acts of violence and self-preservation, the grievous mistreatment of rebel prisoners, an upsurge in infectious disease—seven years of uncertainty. A disastrous nighttime fire of unknown cause had occurred in 1776, soon after the long occupation began. Almost all the inhabitable properties west of Broadway were scorched when historic Trinity Church burnt down. With peace, little was being done to reclaim what was lost. During the year 1783 alone, some 20,000 British soldiers and 30,000 apprehensive civilians left town. Government was sorely needed to clean up the mess; exiled patriots were poised to reenter the city and to reestablish the promising commercial hub that had existed before the war.

Before long, New York would be that inviting, sea-blue port city all envisioned, marked by its gentle hills and dotted with church spires. But first, a tremendous movement of population would have to take place. The excitement of that year brought an assemblage of strong-minded lawyers to town, many of them groomed for bright careers after service in the officer corps of the Continental Army. Aaron Burr and Alexander Hamilton, among them, opened law offices on Wall Street and began their political careers in the heart of the city. Many like them exchanged war-weariness for a different kind of combat: controlling access to power.

By 1790, the official U.S. census would put the city's population at 33,000, pushing it, once and for all, past that of Philadelphia. Masses had returned to pick up their shattered lives, and many more came from abroad to take their chances. Among the immigrants at the beginning of this topsy-turvy period was a German butcher's twenty-year-old son, John Jacob Astor, who would later play an important role in the life of our subject.[4]

✦ ✦

The active war was over, but the city was in for several more years of rebuilding amid economic hardship when Washington Irving was born to William and Sarah Sanders Irving on April 3, 1783. Parents many times over, they had emigrated from England twenty years before. William and Sarah were fifty-one and not quite forty-five, respectively, when their youngest was born.

From 1762, the year after her marriage, Sarah Irving had produced children every other year: Her first two Williams, one born in England, the other in New York, both died in infancy; the third William, the first to survive, was born in 1766; next came the ill-fated John, in 1768, who lived barely a year; Ann (Nancy) in 1770; Peter in 1772; Catharine in 1774; Ebenezer in 1776; a longer-lived John in 1778; Sarah (Sally) in 1780. Washington, as the eleventh and youngest, was doted on by his seven surviving older siblings. He remained close to all—especially William, Peter, and Ebenezer—and was notably attached to his cheerful, kindhearted mother.

The two-story home where Irving grew up, at 128 William Street, between Fulton (then Partition) and John Streets, was only yards from the North Dutch Church, where Revolutionary prisoners were housed during the war, and a few blocks above Wall Street and the building now called Federal Hall. On one afternoon in November 1783, when the future author was barely six months old, the last of the British occupiers, the staunchest of their civilian allies in tow, glumly marched to the East River and boarded ships. In their wake, General George Washington and some eight hundred of his soldiers, far less well clad than the departing redcoats, paraded down Broadway to the accompaniment of ecstatic cheers and reclaimed the city.

Irving was named for the victorious general, of course, and the uncontested story of his Scottish maidservant Lizzie's encounter with President Washington must be repeated: One day in 1789, while New York was, albeit briefly, the new nation's capital, she spotted the First of Men on the street and followed him into a shop; there she introduced the six-foot-three chief executive to his six-year-old constituent. Irving's writer-nephew and the family's diligent biographer, Pierre Munro Irving, quotes the audacious Lizzie, evidently from his famous uncle's recollection of the family account. "Please your Honor," she is to have said, "here's a bairn was named after you." George Washington then gently laid his hand on the head of his future biographer.[5]

The Father of His Country may or may not have felt a momentary senti-mental attachment, but it seems clear that Washington Irving's biological fa-ther was not a warm individual. Pierre describes him unsympathetically as "a sedate, conscientious, God-fearing man, with much of the strictness of the old Scotch Covenanter in his composition." Deacon William Irving deplored dancing as an irreligious activity. Politically, however, he was unquestionably attached to the Revolutionary cause. He and his growing family rode out most of the war in the occupied city, yet he was able to establish his patriot cre-dentials afterward. A Presbyterian minister who testified to the deacon's loy-alty at the height of the period of retribution against Tories certified that William Irving was "friendly inclined to the liberties of the United States, and greatly lamented the egregious barbarities practised by her enemies on the unhappy sons of liberty, that unhappily fell in their power." Sarah Irving, too, was said to have evidenced her political sentiments—or, at least, her human-ity—by tending to American prisoners.[6]

As the youngest child, Washington received plenty of guidance. His much older siblings and their friends helped to inspire in him a love of language and literature. Brothers William and Peter absented themselves from religious so-ciety, which had a more pronounced effect on his young mind than the stern religiosity of his Presbyterian father, or even the tender Episcopalian faith of his mother. The father's rule was that all his children had to be present for bedtime prayers at nine o'clock. As a teenager, Washington occasionally crawled out of his second-floor bedroom window and scampered off, unbe-knownst to his parents, to enjoy the city's nightlife. He told Pierre these stories when he took his nephew to the old William Street homestead in 1849, just before it was to be torn down.[7]

As a young man in England, Irving's father had been employed on the high seas. After coming to New York in the 1760s, he became a merchant. In the years after his youngest child was born, he encouraged his eldest son to help run his hardware, wine, and sundries business. William, Jr., was already sev-enteen when Washington entered the world. He spent his early adulthood in the fur trade among northern New York's Indian tribes before moving back to the city. The family business was located among the specialty shops on William Street, at number 75, a block from their home in the direction of Wall Street.

When Washington Irving was six—the year he received his blessing from his famous namesake—the state legislature ordered old Fort George on the Battery, at the southern tip of Manhattan, torn down, and Broadway extended south. Fine private homes would rise here during his youth, and Sunday strollers could eye the fashionable crowd. The demilitarized Battery was beautified: Elm trees lined a new walkway. Here, and about the revitalized town, police constables made the rounds in a concerted effort to defend the emerging public parks from insensitive citizens. Fines were imposed for "leaving broken-down carriages . . . or other nuisances" that might damage the roads. Citizens were required to have leather buckets on hand in case of fire. Elsewhere, people planted poplars in front of their houses. Greenwich Street, west of Broadway nearer the Hudson, became the neighborhood of choice for the upwardly mobile middle class.

At the north end of the settlement, above modern City Hall, developers wondered what to do about the Collect, so long the city's fresh water supply. Marshlands bordered it to the west, and Lispenard's meadows lay adjacent. The 1790s would pass before local government resolved to drain and fill in the seventy-acre pond. In the last days of the century, the discovery of a drowned woman in a newly constructed well, and the ensuing murder trial of her lover, would call attention to these mysterious surroundings where in colonial times gentlemen took their dogs and hunting guns and scared out game birds. The city's rapidly expanding population needed places to go.

The 1790s also witnessed pestilential outbreaks. Despite the authorities' warnings, animal carcasses rotted in the streets as yellow fever, presumed to have been imported from the West Indies, caused widespread panic. From 1795 to 1798, late summer and early autumn brought the deaths of many hundreds of New Yorkers, especially the poor, who were carted away and buried in a new potter's field at the site of present-day Washington Square Park.[8]

★ ★

Without straying far from home, young Washington Irving received a proper education. The first school he attended was a three-minute walk for little legs, a kindergarten run by one Ann Kilmaster. He apparently recalled her name years later when he described a real-life U.S. Army officer named Thomas Butler, who was dismissed for refusing to cut his old-fashioned queue in favor of a standard military haircut; in *A History of New York*, the hapless colonel was fictionalized and Dutchified as "Keldermeester." In the early 1790s, one could still hear a good bit of Dutch spoken in the streets of downtown, and Irving himself picked up just enough of the language to twist the city's history into an imaginary world of wonders.[9]

Later, he matriculated at the coeducational school of a Revolutionary War veteran, Benjamin Romaine, located on Partition Street, and scarcely a greater walk from home than Miss Kilmaster's was. Romaine oversaw Irving's education for the next eight years. He was strict, and, as the family historian Pierre wrote, "a man of good sense and sound judgment, but of moderate scholarship." He liked his pupil personally, but he never believed that Irving had much intellectual potential. The fun-seeking student later recounted that he had an early crush on a classmate at Romaine's who stood a head taller than he, a girl who was his opposite in a dramatic performance. She confessed to finding him appealing, too, but his diminutive size proved the ultimate barrier to the consummation of this childhood crush—as if it were not enough to be the youngest in a large family.[10]

In his brief introduction to *The Sketch Book,* Irving referred to this period of his youth. He dreamed of the wider world, he said: "Books of voyages and travels became my passion, and in devouring their contents I neglected the regular exercises of the school." In fair weather, he would stroll to the East River, where cargo-laden vessels were docked, watch as they set sail, and "waft myself in imagination to the ends of the earth!" Pierre records that his uncle was eleven—it was 1794—when he read *Robinson Crusoe,* and then *The World Displayed,* a collection devoted to seafaring adventures. Irving later acknowledged having been "slow" at school; but as a lover of books, he recalled going to a particular inn, where the "old landlord" encouraged the lad to read aloud to him for hours at a time. His parents laid down rules about reading. They would not permit him to read after bedtime, and so he clandestinely lit candles and quietly turned the pages. Romaine caught him during class peering into a pocket-sized travel adventure, which he was trying to hide in his lap, under his desk.[11]

Little has been preserved about Irving's sisters in the years on William Street, other than that Catharine was unsuccessfully courted by John Anderson, who loaned young Washington his drawing books, and whose better-known brother Alexander would later produce engravings for Irving's stories. We do know that the Irving household was full of energy, and that literary curiosity was by no means confined to the youngest child. William, Jr., committed his free hours to the Calliopean Society, a literary club for young men that sometimes met at his home; brothers Peter and John also belonged.

In late 1793, when Washington was ten, William married Julia Paulding, the older sister of a young poet who was set on becoming a novelist and essayist. James Kirke Paulding (1778–1860) would be Washington Irving's early collaborator, valued correspondent, and lifelong friend. Though his literary reputation would never approach that of the youngster who was initially his disciple, Paulding is noteworthy for being the first outside the Irving clan to be considered a confidant, and, as important, the one who introduced Washington Irving to Sleepy Hollow.

The Irvings were of English and Scottish ancestry, and Paulding (originally "Pauldinck") was half Dutch. His boyhood years were spent in the vicinity of Sleepy Hollow, which his young friend, not he, would make famous. Jim Paulding could relate the history of this region from the most direct of connections: His family contained a number of dedicated Revolutionaries who fought and suffered there. The Hudson Valley had been a danger zone known as the "Neutral Ground," which separated British-occupied New York from American forces to the north and west. Residents of uncertain allegiance roamed in small bands, committing highway robbery and worse; and here, in 1780, a few daring souls captured the British spy Major John André, who was in league with the American general Benedict Arnold in the attempt to deliver West Point to the enemy. One of André's captors was Paulding's cousin John.[12]

The twenty-odd miles that separated lower Manhattan from Tarrytown-on-Hudson might as well have been a hundred. Roadways leading north from the city were poorly kept, and in wet weather slow and dangerous. Travel upriver, on the other hand, was becoming accessible, though not yet routine, in the 1790s. Citizens of the republic were keen on "internal improvements," as the extension of a communications infrastructure was termed. The concurrent growth of overland postal routes and cheaper newspaper delivery across state lines and into the interior gradually made people more aware of their distant neighbors. All this contributed to New York's rise as a site for capital investment, retail business, and the dissemination of ideas.[13]

Jim Paulding, a country boy by the standard of the day, moved from his uncle's home in Tarrytown to New York City in 1796. He accompanied his brother-in-law's brother, then just entering his teens, to the theater. The four years that separated them did not mean much, at least not for long. Paulding had a dreamy character comparable to that of his younger friend. Both felt the influence of Oliver Goldsmith's *Citizen of the World*, a pert collection of letters from a fictional Chinese philosopher. Goldsmith imparted sentiment along with irrepressible comedy—in later years, Irving would become Goldsmith's biographer. When Irving was sent north during a yellow fever scare, he and Paulding chatted freely as they hiked through the Hudson Valley. It was at this time that young Irving first glimpsed "Wolfert's Roost" on the banks of the Hudson River, the picturesque estate that would become, by 1836, his Sunnyside home.[14]

That was how Washington Irving's impressions of the world were forming. New Yorkers were reaching out. Of an early overnight voyage up the Hudson, before the steamboat age had commenced, he wrote of the Dutch-speaking river captain and the enslaved black crew who understood his Dutch. In even more memorable fashion, Irving gushed about the scenery:

> What a time of intense delight was that first sail through the Highlands. I sat on the deck as we slowly tided along the foot of those stern mountains, and gazed with wonder and admiration at cliffs impending far above me, crowned with forests, with eagles sailing and screaming around them; or listened to the unseen stream dashing down precipices; or beheld rock, and tree, and cloud, and sky reflected in the glassy stream of the river. And then how solemn and thrilling the scene as we anchored at night at the foot of those mountains, clothed with overhanging forests; and every thing grew dark and mysterious.[15]

Just going upriver was, at this time, a fine adventure.

When Irving was a teenager, his William Street neighbors included milliners, a shipmaster, a shoemaker, a carpenter, and a furrier. He was not raised among the privileged.[16] It was from the East River wharves that he imagined the globe; from Greenwich Street, on the west side of town, that he viewed the northward extension of the fashionable world; and it was in the Hudson Valley, where Jim Paulding made him feel at home, that Irving's mind already wandered—and would wander authoritatively when he became a professional writer.

✦   ✦

At sixteen, and with just a smattering of Latin, Irving joined his Columbia-educated brother John at the law office of Henry Masterton. The two lawyers-in-training bore no great love for the law. John, at this time, preferred theology; Washington, of course, sensed that he ought to be writing with imaginative description, not technical precision. Meanwhile, brother Peter, though trained by Columbia's distinguished medical faculty and called "Dr. Irving" for most of his life, did not care to practice medicine; his passion was politics at this time, and before long he would give Washington his first real opportunity to write and influence—or rather, to write and entertain—the people of New York.

William, the eldest of the brothers, spent years as a leader in the New York literary community, which he used as a stepping-stone to political office. He never lost direction. A realist like his father, he was eventually able to parlay his local reputation into a seat in Congress. Ebenezer, the third oldest brother, was perhaps the true inheritor of his father's business sense. He remained entirely "a regular man of business," as Washington put it. He wrote of Ebenezer feelingly in 1840: "He has all father's devotion and zeal, without his strictness. Indeed, his piety is of the most genial and cheerful kind. . . . I wish to God I could feel like him."[17]

Peter, the second oldest, was unpredictable. The course he took raises questions. Everyone spoke of his potential, but in everything he did, his commitment wavered. His disposition was mild; he was not suited for a tough crowd. It was Peter to whom Washington grew emotionally closest, and that is why his choices matter here. He attended Columbia for three years in the mid-1780s; after dropping out for unknown reasons, he returned and completed a medical degree in 1794. His dissertation on the nature and treatment of influenza was remarkable because few called the contagion by its modern name at this time; most physicians merely isolated the "violent catarrh" that accompanied it. But Peter Irving gave a clear clinical description of the common flu.

He was a physician in name only, as far as anyone can tell. He went by the professional title of "M.D.," and for a time he kept a pharmacy on Broadway. He felt compelled into political activism, but lacked the thick skin to master it. He tied his fortunes to those of the energetic Aaron Burr, editing Burr's New York newspaper for as long as Burr needed such a vehicle—and for as long as Burr's career thrived. Peter did not have William Jr.'s resilience; and so, long before William entered the House of Representatives, he would trade politics for the family business, almost as a last resort, and look to England for opportunity.[18]

For the moment, politics was unavoidable, and the Irving brothers were in the thick of it. The year 1799, the youngest Irving's sixteenth year, was pivotal. In New York, and across America, liberal-minded Republicans clashed with old-school Federalists for state and national offices. Vice President Thomas Jefferson threatened to unseat the incumbent president, John Adams. In Manhattan, one of the most curious figures in all of American history, Aaron Burr, undertook to elect a Republican slate of presidential electors and so pave the way for a Jefferson presidency. Burr's star was rising, and to the Irving brothers who were adept with a pen—William, Peter, and Washington—his success would be good for New York and good for the rising generation.

Burr came from superior stock. He was a graduate of Princeton, and the son of a respected former president of that institution. As New York State attorney general from 1789 to 1791, and a United States senator after that, he was known for his fresh ideas and his agile mind. The workingmen of New York City eagerly embraced his populist proposals to expand the electorate and to extend bank credit beyond the elite families, and yet Burr was able to maintain cordial relations with prominent Federalists. This made him un-usual in a time of bitter partisanship. And threatening to the status quo—the way any free spirit unnerves the power elite.

Then, reports of a sensational murder diverted attention from the single-minded political struggle already under way. In mid-December 1799, as news of George Washington's death traveled north from Virginia, a sweet, unof-fending young woman of marriageable age, the dutiful ward of a Quaker cou-ple, disappeared. It was a season of steady snows, and she was last seen stepping into a sleigh in front of her Greenwich Street boardinghouse. Res-cue efforts went forward in the cold.

Only days after she went missing, Gulielma Sands was found at the bottom of a newly constructed well in Lispenard's meadows. The well provided an al-ternative source of drinking water to the contaminated Collect and it be-longed, coincidentally, to Aaron Burr's fledgling Manhattan Company. Hauled up from the well just after New Year's Day, 1800, her pale corpse was put on public display at the insistence of her relatives—who somehow thought that justice would be better served in this grisly manner.

All eyes focused on a lodger at the unfortunate woman's boardinghouse, her supposed lover, Levi Weeks. He was promptly arrested and taken to the Bridewell prison, on the northern reaches of Broadway, to await trial. The prison was old and dank, but no accused murderer in the early republic was ever so fortunate as Levi Weeks. He had as his defense team New York's most skilled attorneys: Aaron Burr, Alexander Hamilton, and Henry Brockholst Livingston.

The legal world fixated on the Weeks case. Levi's brother Ezra, a builder, supplied wooden pipes for Burr's Manhattan well project, and he was at the same time under contract to construct a new home for Hamilton. It is also possible that the two eldest of the Irving brothers, William Jr. and Peter, knew Ezra through their common activities as Freemasons. Ezra Weeks had politi-cal clout in New York.[19]

Two other Irving brothers, John and Washington, were already a part of the city's small legal community, and could not but have taken an interest in the case that was on everyone's lips. Of Levi's three distinguished counsel, Brock-holst Livingston is least known today, but not then. He was the only one with experience as a defense attorney in a murder case, and it was in Livingston's office that the eighteen-year-old lawyer-in-training Washington Irving would gain six months' experience in the year following the Weeks trial. There was no better proving ground for a young man.

Brockholst Livingston, raised amid conflict, was ripe for this case. The son of New Jersey's wartime governor, he was a man who never shunned political controversy. Throughout the raucous and divisive 1790s, he was an ally of Burr's and, in the course of all-too-human events, embroiled himself in public shouting matches, once taking on the equally intemperate Alexander Hamilton, his co-counsel in the Weeks case. On a separate occasion, Livingston agreed to serve as the second (chief negotiator for one party in a prospective duel) when the Republican James Nicholson challenged the arch-Federalist Hamilton; as Nicholson's second Livingston succeeded in preventing an armed confrontation.

But Livingston, a trustee of Columbia College, was known for his volatility at least as much as for his diplomacy. In 1798, a couple of years before the untested Irving went to work for him, he killed one James Jones in a duel—Burr's stepson having served as his second in that deadly affair. As a published satirist, Livingston had penned a piece for the Republican *New York Argus,* which made light of the Federalist agenda. Jones, a merchant, took offense, and confronted Livingston at the Battery, pulling his nose in a traditional gesture of disdain. No gentleman could let such a provocation stand, and Livingston mortally wounded his opponent by putting a bullet in his groin.[20]

This is all to say that, aside from whatever legal ambition his family might have had for him, Washington Irving grew up in a highly charged political world; he hobnobbed not just with the pen-wielding but also the pistol-wielding men of the founding generation. In such a climate Levi Weeks was tried at Federal Hall (functioning in this instance as City Hall) on Wall Street, in March 1800. Irving was a legal novice, made aware of the activities of Burr, Hamilton, and Livingston by his politically inclined brothers. We have no record of the teenager's thoughts on this occasion, yet he could not but have paid close attention to the proceedings.

Americans have always loved to fixate on crimes of passion, not to mention a circus-like murder trial. The young and attractive defendant was said to have held his head proudly, as a presumably innocent man would: But were the "thousand rumors" true? Did Levi Weeks callously drown the modest young Quaker, after seducing her, because he did not wish to marry her?

The trial was sensationalized in the press. Weeks's attorneys suggested that Elma took her own life because she was depressed. Many of those who squeezed into the courtroom remarked on the powerful opening statement delivered by Aaron Burr, who described his client as "a man of much worth, of mild and amiable manners, and of a very gentle and affectionate disposition." Burr was known for his keen eyes, and his powers of persuasion as a speaker were perhaps unmatched in his generation.[21]

Washington Irving knew all this. A few years hence, he would capture Burr's subtle character for posterity—though he ultimately did less than he could have to rescue Burr's name. Irving was a part of Burr's inner circle, drawn in by his older brothers. They were of the mercantile class, but aimed to better themselves through literary production; Burr was from one of colonial America's most distinguished families, and a war hero to boot. He supported the arts. Since the Irving brothers were trying to establish a name for their family, it made sense to attach themselves to eminent characters. The better one knew Aaron Burr at this time, the more likely he was to know the Irving brothers—they had just set down in the vortex of a political whirlpool.

The trial went through one night and into a second day—an unusual occurrence in the criminal courts of 1800. The defendant with the enviable political connections was found not guilty in the death of Gulielma Sands, though most circumstantial evidence certainly pointed in his direction. The "dream team" of Burr, Hamilton, and Livingston simply overpowered the underdog state prosecutor, Cadwallader Colden. Yet Levi Weeks was a marked man. After his acquittal, he left town because he could not find work in New York. Eventually he turned up in Mississippi Territory, where, like his successful brother before him, he gained local acclaim as a builder.[22]

The case lingered in the minds of New Yorkers,[23] much as melodrama of this kind dominated the literature of 1800. It was not just sensational journalism but a fetishization of the dead that revealed an underlying restlessness among the reading public.[24] Irving absorbed this fact, though by the time he came to deal with death and remembrance in his stories, he would communicate a subtler, more intense, more reflective language that linked him with other writers of the budding Romantic age.

But at this point, largely to please his family, he stood at the beginning of a career in the law. It is hard to say precisely what impact Aaron Burr had on him, but for the next several years, Irving could not ignore Burr. More than once, he would find himself face-to-face with this "mysterious" man, long anathematized by history. Burr was more than a tainted official accused and found not guilty of treason in 1807; more than the "murderer of Hamilton." He was a leading figure in New York (and then national) politics. He was wry and precise and intelligible, and shed an air of quiet confidence. He was no worse and no better than the glorified founders: He indulged with them in political manipulation and ethically questionable land speculation. To the Irvings, he was a potential patron.

Why, then, has history made so much of his supposed bad morals? As a popular figure in New York politics, Burr found himself caught up in several whisper campaigns, more often than not initiated by the talented (but jealous and ungracious) Alexander Hamilton. Burr turned the other cheek, with rare exceptions, and made little attempt to fight back, until 1804, when Hamilton's mouth precipitated their famous duel. He would suffer worse press after killing Hamilton, of course, and everything unraveled from there.

History needs villains. Neither Republicans nor Federalists entirely trusted Burr. Thomas Jefferson called him "a crooked gun," that is to say, unpredictable. But Jefferson was uncomfortable with political independents, and unpredictable does not mean villainous. Burr was a formidable national candidate in 1800, and a trustworthy vice president to Jefferson. Fearful of his chances in future elections, his enemies fashioned him into a villain; an unquestioning posterity followed suit. The truth is that history becomes simplified as time wears on.[25]

Then as now, the press was extremely influential. The politically vulnerable Burr turned to Dr. Peter Irving to state his case to the public. Peter wished to represent the Burr line in the state assembly and was deeply devoted to Burr's cause. But as the embattled editor of the Burrite *Morning Chronicle* he lacked political canniness—and he certainly did not grow rich in the endeavor. He would need his younger brother's help, more than once, to prop him up. Thus Washington Irving would write in support of Burr's political chances, and bear witness to Burr's ultimate political downfall.

The Levi Weeks trial, meanwhile, with its undertones of seduction, violence, and justice denied, remains symbolic not only of the times but of the centrality of the Irving brothers in Manhattan social circles. They knew everyone connected to the high-profile case. They interacted not only with Aaron Burr and Brockholst Livingston, but also with the unsuccessful prosecutor, Cadwallader Colden, a future New York mayor and U.S. congressman. And then there was the ambitious printer-bookseller-attorney David Longworth, compiler of the annual City Directory. Longworth produced the first of three pamphlets on the Weeks case—just hours after the verdict was read. The Irvings knew him familiarly as either "Dark Dave" or "Dusky Davy" when he agreed to publish *Salmagundi*, a series of sarcastic musings authored pseudonymously by Washington and William Irving and James Kirke Paulding. But that, too, was yet to come.

A second pamphlet on the Weeks trial was authored by William Coleman, a protégé of Hamilton's, who was shortly to be named editor of the New York *Evening Post,* in which capacity he would invite Washington Irving to publish political tracts. Coleman would live to see Irving celebrated as America's premier man of letters in the columns of the newspaper he began. His pamphlet on the trial was published by John Furman. The sister of an Irving family friend of the same name was to marry John Irving.[26]

These are all indicators that the Irving brothers' New York was a fairly intimate place as yet, a place where sharp pens assessed every event and every mood. By the turn of the century, the brothers were testing the political waters and building their social connections.

☆   ☆

Washington Irving never expressed fondness for the study or practice of law, though for lack of a better opportunity he was destined to remain in the profession for several years more. In 1801, as the eighteen-year-old went to work for Brockholst Livingston, Aaron Burr was elected vice president of the United States amid an upsurge of Republican sentiment. The office was repayment for Burr's success in seeing New York's Federalists voted out of office. Then, when Irving was only six months in his employ, Livingston was named to the New York State Supreme Court; after only a short time, President Jefferson would appoint him to the U.S. Supreme Court.

None of this high-level political reshuffling immediately altered the youngest Irving's prospects. It did, however, show New York's fluidity: When Brockholst Livingston's New York office closed, Irving went to work not for another Republican but for a prominent Federalist, Josiah Ogden Hoffman (1766–1837). This changed his life. In Hoffman's service he would, for the first time, find a real home in the law; meanwhile, brother Peter intensified his advocacy on behalf of Vice President Burr, who now set his sights on the governorship of New York. Washington Irving's connections kept on tangling: With what political ideology would he finally identify, Hoffman's Federalism or Peter's Burrite program?[27] Of the Irving brothers, Washington alone described himself as a Federalist. But there were various degrees of Federalist affiliation and various kinds of Republicans.

The Federalist in his life, Josiah Ogden Hoffman, was the same age as Irving's eldest brother, William, that is, seventeen years his elder. Hoffman had served as attorney general of the state of New York from 1795 to 1802 (after Burr had held the same office). In New York politics, the morals of many a public figure were called into question, not just Burr's; Irving no doubt knew that

Hoffman had been accused of misusing the power of his office, of taking a bribe to rule in favor of the foreign-controlled Holland Company land venture that served the interests of his Ogden relatives as well as Alexander Hamilton's land-rich Federalist father-in-law. His reputation did not suffer significantly from the suggestion of unethical favoritism, however.

In 1802, just as Irving came to work at his office, the widower Hoffman married a daughter of the late newspaper editor John Fenno, whose paper, the *Gazette of the United States,* had been the principal voice of the Hamiltonians in the early 1790s. Certainly Hoffman's political loyalties lay with the already privileged and powerful. So although Irving remained faithful to his brothers' interests, he attached himself to Hoffman and his family, appreciating their social and economic prospects. The rough and tumble of popular politicking disagreed with Irving's temperament; Hoffman's Federalism seemed to offer a respite from it.

By extrapolating from later statements, one can see that even while writing for Peter's Burrite newspaper, the *Morning Chronicle,* Washington Irving was more comfortable, generally, with a mild Federalist view of the world. He looked critically at Jefferson's commercial philosophy, which theorized an anti-urban, anti-speculative sensibility; and he distrusted the idealistic Jeffersonian design to give the American Everyman political authority equal to that of his traditional social betters. Irving thought that the less educated should yield to their social betters—that was the Federalists' mantra.[28]

The Irving brothers' livelihood owed much to their humorless father's determined commercial enterprise, and several of the siblings, including Washington, would assiduously attend to it over the years. They therefore trusted Burr more than they trusted the agrarian populist Jefferson. If the youngest Irving was a Hoffman Federalist, he was not uncomfortable with the character of Aaron Burr, Republican. Burr was sensitive to a range of New York interests. The institution he founded as the Manhattan Company would eventually be known as the Chase Manhattan Bank.

The balance that Washington Irving maintained (to be both Burrite and Federalist) was possible because there was no singular Republican national platform. New York Republicans were a more diverse lot than, say, the Virginia (Jeffersonian) Republicans. New York political alliances were based upon an identification with one of a few dominant family networks—principally the Clintons and the Livingstons. Both of these families flirted with the Jeffersonians while significantly refusing to burn their bridges to the New York Federalists. The Burrites were different from the land-based Clintons and the old money Livingstons: For one, they were a scrappier lot.

This is how William and Peter Irving so easily identified with them. Burrites negotiated with the Clinton and Livingston clans and their patroon allies without subordinating themselves to one or another of the families. They were independent.

After 1800, the Clinton people became closely associated with Jefferson. And so, even as Jefferson's first-term vice president, Burr received no favored treatment—indeed, Jefferson restricted Burr's power. One likely explanation for the president's behavior is that he had reason to fear that Burr's popularity might hurt the chances of his handpicked successor, fellow Virginian James Madison. As further evidence of this, Burr was replaced on the national ticket in 1805 with George Clinton, a much older man, and never much of a political philosopher, whose best days were behind him.

Thus, even though he was an established attorney, and adept at glad-handing the voters of Albany as well as Manhattan, Aaron Burr was still something of an underdog in national politics. This made him attractive to such enterprising nonconformists as Andrew Jackson of Tennessee. And again, as a connoisseur of literature and a patron of the arts, Burr suited the Irvings' taste.

Washington Irving, law clerk, walked a fine line. He liked the society of interesting men. Politics was bringing him in touch with some of New York's most interesting, Federalist *and* Republican. He knew whom he liked, individually, more than he had a strong party identification. He tolerated (perhaps even admired) Burr more than he approved of Republican Party principles. He preferred the Federalists' notion that good government did not require pandering to the mythic "people"—but he did not run from Burr's republicanism and stand up for all-out Federalist snobbery. Simply put, he gravitated to people of substance.[29]

The point to be made is that, while still in his teens, Washington Irving had formed a political personality distinct from that of his Democratic-Republican brothers.[30] He showed conviction. He would write in support of Burr, and no one would have to twist his arm; but the better model for his political temperament was his new employer, Josiah Ogden Hoffman, who entered Irving's life in 1802.

Like those who preceded him in evaluating young Irving's scholarly worth, Hoffman was apparently less impressed with his brainpower than with his personal amiability. And Hoffman's new wife, Maria, fifteen years younger than her lawyer husband and only two years older than Irving, appreciated the good humor of the outgoing nineteen-year-old, a sentiment entirely reciprocated.

★ ★

Not long after the *Morning Chronicle* began its publication, Washington Irving was writing in its pages pseudonymously as "Jonathan Oldstyle," an individual torn between Republican aspirations and Federalist vanity. Between November 1802 and April 1803, Oldstyle contributed nine pieces. This was the first public collaboration of the two brothers, Peter and Washington, who would grow interdependent as time went on. In letters of later years, Washington would never mention Peter's name without some recollection of their sympathetic understanding of each other or their common labors; it was always "my dear, dear brother Peter," "the companion of my thoughts," or "bosom friend." At a slightly younger age in colonial Boston, Benjamin Franklin had labored as an apprentice at his older brother's newspaper; here he composed his marvelously piquant, pseudonymously authored "Silence Dogood" essays, in which he dangerously dissected language and as dangerously preached tolerance. The difference between Franklin and Irving was that James Franklin was notably jealous of his brother's talent, obliging Ben to flee to Philadelphia, whereas Peter and Washington were mutually supportive. The apprentice had all the freedom he wanted or needed right at home.[31]

As Jonathan Oldstyle, Irving deliberately adopted a Federalist-sounding *nom de plume*. One year earlier, Joseph Dennie's Federalist-leaning *Port Folio* had introduced "Oliver Oldschool," whose demeanor was somewhat pedantic—Irving was playfully piggybacking on Dennie's persona. The noted playwright William Dunlap (a Jefferson partisan) had named one of his characters "Major Oldstyle" in a piece performed in 1801, with which Irving was also unquestionably familiar.

Irving's Oldstyle was also meant to be read another way, as a throwback to the famed *Spectator* essays of the early eighteenth century. *Spectator* was the work of a pair of Oxford-educated literary entertainers, Joseph Addison and Richard Steele, whose "old" style still echoed with a vibrancy and a vitality that time had not impaired. From 1711 to 1714, more than six hundred *Spectator* essays were published. The American founders had honored Addison and Steele for their elegance of thought and pertinacious wit; even after the founding era, every young man of substance read them.

As a quaint, provincial theater critic, Oldstyle remarked on every facet of New York culture that came to mind. Irving knew early, just as Benjamin Franklin had as "Silence Dogood," that "fashion" masked insecurity, and that something stylish could fall out of favor and become absurd. Manhattan's

Park Theater had opened in 1798, at a cost of $130,000, on Park Row, near where a new City Hall was shortly to be built. The four surrounding acres were planted with elms, willows, catalpas, and young poplars. Seven arched doorways led inside. Identifying himself as an "uninterested spectator," Irving's ready critic wondered aloud whether there was ever a time when people did not take themselves too seriously. Gentlemen with powdered hair had, until late, dressed for the theater in "an air of the greatest spruceness and tightness." Then, out of the blue, the male of the species transformed itself, now assuming an air of "the most studied carelessness." He was "lounging along the streets in the most apparent listlessness and vacuity of thought." Minding this creature was the New York "belle," who, strapped into her proper clothes, resembled "a walking bottle." It was she who was obliged to "undergo the fatigue of dragging along this sluggish animal"—the "modern beau"—to the theater. Irving was nudging those who he thought were in on the joke, in effect asking, "Who might we be, after we shed our good manners and drop our pretended courtesies?"[32]

That taste for irony was in *Spectator*, too. Number 17 begins: "Since our persons are not of our own making, when they are such as appear defective or uncomely, it is, methinks, an honest and laudable fortitude to dare to be ugly."[33] For young Irving, theatergoers were an easy group to caricature, as they had been for *Spectator*'s narrator, who defined himself quintessentially as a member of an audience, watching a play.

New Yorkers were taking their places in a new kind of society, an adaptable republican society in which everyone was seeking to fashion his or her own brand of respectability. Liberated ladies and gentlemen put on airs, testing new forms of behavior in the new republic. In contrast, there was the democratic gallery, paying less and demanding more from the experience—and behaving rudely. Irving used his debut as a critic to mock them all.[34]

As for "Jonathan" Oldstyle, he was kin to the "Brother Jonathan" of Revolution-era cartoons, who symbolized the New World's untutored white male, and who was, therefore, American through and through. Jonathan was the youthful ancestor of Uncle Sam, a father figure yet to be born; but unlike the large, outward-looking Sam, Jonathan was a simple countryman who, when he stood before the erudition of the Old World, could be construed as an embarrassment.

Irving's Jonathan was a newcomer to the theater, overwhelmed by city life. In one essay, a naïve Jonathan-type confesses as much to Oldstyle, leading Irving's narrator to explain: "Bye the bye, my honest friend was much puzzled about the curtain itself. He wanted to know why that *carpet* was hung up in the theatre? I assured him it was no carpet, but a very fine curtain." The same fellow's attention is diverted by a copious quantity of *"candle-grease"* dripping from the chandelier; it soils his clothes, that is, his *"bran-new"* coat, Irving tells us, supplying the dialect of poor Jonathan.[35]

Irving-as-Oldstyle took aim at the gallery, which was monitored by constables. From the cheap seats, he wrote, the noises were "somewhat similar to that which prevailed in Noah's ark." Whistling and verbal outbursts were succeeded by "a discharge of apples, nuts & ginger-bread, on the heads of the honest folks in the pit." He himself claimed to have been "saluted aside my head with a rotten pippin." The gentleman beside him urged composure, only to be pelted himself, and still he "bore the blow like a philosopher." A "sharp-faced Frenchman, dress'd in a white coat and small cock'd hat," was less patient, and "jumped upon his seat, shook his fist at the gallery, and swore violently in bad English."

"I find there is no play, however poor or ridiculous from which I cannot derive some entertainment," Irving opened his comic review of *The Tripolitan Prize,* a drama taken from current events. The Jefferson administration was involved in a limited naval war with Tripoli to defend American shipping in the Mediterranean. Just as the on again, off again war itself dragged on, Irving the spectator had to wait, too long, he felt, for the appearance onstage of anyone resembling a fierce North African pirate. Each time a stage direction was given—some bustling backstage, or a roaring thunderstorm—he expected to see that nasty, bewhiskered terrorist appear before him; but instead, invariably, some "pretty behaved young gentry" came on, "a party of village masters and misses taking a walk for exercise." When the battle was at last engaged, there was too much "decency and decorum" for his taste, and the Tripolitan "very politely gave in—as it would be indecent to conquer in the face of an American audience."[36]

Irving's nine short essays in his brother's newspaper mostly dealt with the theater scene and reflected the general excitement over the pricey Park Theater. Despite the outlay in building it, the most expensive seat cost fifty cents, making Irving's varied social commentary possible. His critical ploy was to draw extreme comparisons; yet there was no militancy about him. The blow never smarted. His primary purpose was to deliver good-natured fun.

He loved attending performances at the Park, and his romance with the theater would flourish as the years went by.[37] If he carried himself with a condescending air at this point, the pose was expected of a self-satisfied theater critic (or, for that matter, a dandified nineteen-year-old trying to hide his youth). Anticipating for a moment a more advanced Irving style, what we see already is a taste for burlesque. He wants to make trouble, and he wants it to feel good.[38]

He had hardly had time to develop an original style: "Jonathan Oldstyle" was awfully close to *Spectator*, but it was hard not to emulate brilliance. The attention to history, geography, and manners, a narrator who laughs off his own modest origins—many besides Irving learned their technique from Addison and Steele.[39] None of this detracts from the character of Irving's prose. The eighteenth century was not concerned with originality in the sense that the nineteenth and twentieth centuries were. Neither Franklin nor Irving was seeking to establish himself as an "original" when each started writing for the public. All writers routinely discoursed on body and soul, mind and spirit, and eccentric behavior, whether directly or parenthetically. They wrote to please an audience, but also put that audience off balance, for effect. What distinguished a good writer, or a popular wit, from the mass of writers was the ability to forge a smooth, convivial style, or what the mid-eighteenth century's preeminent rhetorician Hugh Blair called "perspicuity of language" arising from "native genius." Irving understood the game.[40]

★　★

At this point, Washington Irving could not but define himself by his affiliations. His crowd was a book crowd as well as a theater crowd. They met at various places, often in a tavern, to mix words. Theirs was an old Anglo-American institution: a club. Again, the prototype belongs to *Spectator*, which described the idiosyncrasies of friends and acquaintances amid the raillery and ultimate solidarity of those who belonged to literary clubs. The next phase of Irving's career as an author would require collaboration. "Jonathan Oldstyle" was a first attempt; he needed his peers to help him along.

It was Addison who wrote of "those little nocturnal assemblies, which are commonly known by the name of Clubs." He described the self-selected fraternities as innocent, unproductive, and irresistible. The clubs that flourished in the first decade of the eighteenth century in England had such names as the "Hum-drum club" ("made up of very honest gentlemen, of peaceable dispositions, that used to sit together, smoke their pipes, and say nothing, till midnight").[41] Benjamin Franklin began his climb to respectability in Philadelphia in 1727–1728 by forming the Junto, a cooperative of sorts, in which friends met, ordinarily at a tavern, to take up topics of common interest. They downed moral philosophy, or discussed the design of nature, in company with wine. On the eve of the American Revolution, while serving in London as the agent of several colonies, the by now world-famous Dr. Franklin frequented various distinguished clubs, philosophizing, lifting glasses, and singing. The fellowship he imbibed among the ingenious crowd at the Thursday evening "Club of Honest Whigs" in the early 1770s reminded him that the "friends of liberty" enjoyed enlightened support abroad.[42]

The club tradition was very much alive in Irving's New York. From the time he was in grammar school, his brothers William, Peter, and John were, as already noted, active members of the Calliopean Society, named after the Greek muse of the heroic epic. That club, founded on the eve of George Washington's presidency, would still exist in 1830, when Pierre M. Irving became a member. The Federalist newspaper editor and student of the American language Noah Webster, and the early republic's most enthusiastic supporter of the theater, William Dunlap, were members of the Philological Society, begun in 1788, which seems to have merged into the Friendly Club in the early 1790s. At one point, Josiah Ogden Hoffman served as the Philological Society's president.

A sense of literary community sustained the maturing intellects of Irving's New York, young men born too late to partake of Revolutionary glory and requiring some civil means of contributing to republican society. Before there was a national literature to adhere to, and a lucrative market for their productions, they were drawn to one another, and Irving was drawn to them. He did not have the advantages of his older brothers—he did not attend Columbia. But he was already a recognized talent: Club culture, with its ever-growing lending libraries and friendly, often humor-filled, debates, promised to sustain him. The wits who preceded Irving in the literary club scene were all reared on eighteenth-century models: Laurence Sterne, Oliver Goldsmith, and Alexander Pope, in addition to *Spectator*. Irving's brothers, and Paulding, led him to soak up the works of these same authors, and he would one day be among those who helped Sterne and Goldsmith, though perhaps not the older Pope, remain relevant to the Anglo-American scene decades after the height of their popularity.[43]

☆   ☆

What "Jonathan Oldstyle" showed was Washington Irving's audacity. One might say that he was prematurely self-confident as a writer. He was not the most studious of the Irving brothers, as he would have agreed. But he was, early on, and with a less regular education, able to exceed whatever creative genius his older brothers might have possessed. He followed their example, profited from their connections, and before long established himself as their lead writer. The family cohered.

He belonged to a politically engaged family, yet at twenty, Washington Irving cannot be associated with a theory of politics, either Federalist or Republican. Both parties demanded a kind of enthusiasm for the "sport" of politics that he could not muster. But when it came to the "sport" of language, he took a sanguine approach. We need only contrast Joseph Dennie, as "Oliver Oldschool," who was a hardcore Federalist and who broadly condemned the destabilizing effect of popular speech on a proper English language.[44] Irving, younger and no killjoy, and far from desiring a leveling democracy, was not above capitalizing on (or lowercasing) the linguistic novelties he could draw from his middle-class surroundings. He accepted the mutability of language as a good thing.

CHAPTER 2

Early Travels

1803–1806

Thus the whole circle of travellers, may be reduced
to the following heads:
Idle Travellers,
Inquisitive Travellers,
Lying Travellers,
Proud Travellers,
Vain Travellers,
Splenetic Travellers,
Then follow the Travellers of Necessity.
The delinquent and felonious Traveller,
The unfortunate and innocent Traveller,
The simple Traveller,
And last of all (if you please)
The Sentimental Traveller.

—Laurence Sterne, *A Sentimental Journey* (1768)

IRVING KEPT TRAVEL JOURNALS THROUGH MUCH of his life. They offer us a firsthand glimpse of the travel conditions that Americans endured as the nineteenth century progressed. By wagon, wooden barge, sailing ship, stagecoach, steamboat, and train, he traveled farther than almost any other man or woman of his generation. His journals were fodder for his fiction, notes to jog his memory. They add color to a world we can only imagine.

When he was a law clerk, and before he turned twenty-one, Washington Irving made two trips to Johnstown, New York. Sisters Nancy and Catharine had each married upper Hudson men, and Washington, loving adventure, resolved to visit them. In 1800, and again in 1802, he journeyed for two days up the North (or Hudson) River to Albany. From Albany, another long day's wagon ride finally brought him to his family. Although his health was never quite sound in these years (his breathing was often labored, for reasons that were never clear), he experienced en route the enchantment of the still thinly populated Highlands that his imagination, and his active pen, would never tire of capturing.

A noteworthy town in the republic's early history, Johnstown was founded in the 1760s, when Sir William Johnson, unusual in his sympathetic treatment of Indians, sought to establish a protectorate where Indians and white settlers could coexist. Late in the American Revolution, just after (but oblivious to) the British debacle at Yorktown, Virginia, that effectively ended the war, Johnstown was the site of a tense battle in which Colonel Marinus Willett, later one of Aaron Burr's closest political associates, defeated a Loyalist force. By 1800, the town had lost its frontier feel and was on its way to becoming a manufacturing village.

On his 1802 visit, Irving read and composed sketches, and in an effort to deal with his lung complaint went to Ballston Spa, near the town of Saratoga Springs. The mineral springs were in their nascent years; in later life, as centers for literary discussion as well as hydrotherapy, their attraction would grow, and Irving would become a regular visitor.[1] It was on his return to the city that he penned the "Jonathan Oldstyle" essays.

In the summer of 1803, he made the third, and most demanding, of his northern excursions. He traveled with the family of his new employer, Josiah Ogden Hoffman, in a small party that included another New York attorney, Thomas Ludlow Ogden. Cousins Hoffman and Ogden were eager to inspect their lands abutting the St. Lawrence River and British Canada. In March 1801, the New York State Assembly had formally established St. Lawrence County, naming Ogdensburg its seat.

Ogdensburg was at that time still called by its Indian name, Oswegatchie. Part of the controversial Holland Land Company purchase that Josiah Hoffman had purportedly used his authority as state attorney general to benefit, it was approximately the same distance from Montreal, by water transport, as Manhattan was from Albany. The Holland Company investors aimed to bring improvements to the region—roads, mills, and harbors—so as to invite settlement and reap profits on the resale of smaller tracts carved from the hundreds of thousands of acres. Land in the vicinity of Oswegatchie was still a primal environment, recently inhabited by the Six Nations of the Iroquois.[2]

Along with the two men, Irving enjoyed the company of four women: his mentor's new wife, Maria Fenno Hoffman; Martha Hammond (Mrs. Thomas

MAP 2.1   Washington Irving's New York

Ludlow) Ogden; Ann Hoffman, the attorney's thirteen-year-old daughter from his earlier marriage; and an Ogden cousin, Eliza. Together they would spend a month in the wilderness. They would be roughing it, even by the standards of the day.

Irving kept a journal of the expedition, fifty-nine pages worth. It begins with his visit, along with the ladies, to Ballston Spa, while the two attorneys attended court in Albany. Ballston was "intolerably stupid" to him—he did not even like the taste of the restorative springwater. He did, however, enjoy the antics of one Boston-bred parvenue in her fifties, whose "queer dress & manners" made for clandestine conversation and a nice character sketch. The matronly woman, trying to appear half her age, did not know how absurd she appeared to Irving; at the ball they all attended, she wore "a gold ribbon round her waist her hair turnd up" and scented. When Irving puckishly presented her with fresh flowers to enhance the bouquet of artificial ones she carried on her person, she was so pleased that she invited him to accompany her back to Boston. The next day, when the men returned from the state capital, they were regaled with little vignettes about "Queen Sheba"—the nickname Irving now gave her—and were disappointed to learn that the previous night's revelry had taken its toll and made her indisposed.[3]

Heading out, the party rested at Utica, then followed the Black River north. They moved deeper into a wilderness of waterfalls and serpentine rivers. After some days, they joined a marathon deer hunt, helping strangers in a canoe to run down the wounded animal. At the end of a long and comical chase, Irving jumped into the water and grabbed the deer by its ear while Ludlow Ogden clutched its leg. The local hunter, after plunging his knife into the creature, gave Irving's hungry party the haunch as a commission for assisting in the capture. Drenched, the men stripped in the woods and changed into dry clothes. That night, they stayed in tiny Carthage at a tavern run by a Frenchman who had come to America with General Von Steuben to fight in the Revolution. "A dirtier house was never seen," wrote Irving. "We dubbed it 'The temple of Dirt.'" Before their departure, Irving thought himself clever in penciling a couplet above the fireplace:

> Here Sovereign Dirt erects her sable throne,
> The house, the host, the hostess all her own.

A few years later, Judge William Cooper, father of the future novelist James Fenimore Cooper, was with Josiah Hoffman on another trek north, and appended to Irving's lines two more, meant to scold the writer, in absentia, for his uppity attitude:

> Learn hence, young man, and teach it to your sons,
> The wisest way's to take it as it comes.[4]

Thirty years after this, the judge's son would likewise take Irving to task for his writing.

Before they arrived at Oswegatchie, the Hoffman-Ogden party had to endure hard rains, which came on just after one of the wagons stalled with a broken axle. The men chivalrously guided the women to a tiny bark shed, but deep mud and fierce winds hampered repair efforts. They groped for the house they were told was a half-mile ahead. "The rain now fell in the greatest quantity I had ever seen," Irving wrote. The walk to the house was "most painful," and the place turned out to be a crude hut equipped with "three crazy chairs" and several kegs of rum.

The owner was a surveyor. He and two companions were present, one of these "the most impudent chattering forward scoundrel I ever knew." The travelers' trunks, containing fresh clothes, were soaked through. The uncouth men—seeing a cause for celebration in the crowded hut where Irving did not—brought out the alcohol and commenced drinking and card playing. Adding to the confusion, the wagon driver Hoffman and Ogden had hired struck his foot with the axe he was using to chop wood. Irving slept fitfully on one of the "crazy chairs," waking occasionally to hold an umbrella over the women and protect them from the leaky roof.

This was a travel tale typical of the early 1800s. Three more days passed before the party emerged from thick woodlands and reached its destination on the St. Lawrence, "a beautiful & extensive tract of country . . . inconceivably enlivening." The trial of the trail was behind them, and young Irving, despite his ailing lungs and persistent cough, picked up his pen again to record these events. It is amazing to consider that his earliest extant travel journal had survived all that.[5]

By occasionally tagging along when Josiah Hoffman negotiated, the young New Yorker gained knowledge that took him beyond the legal education he cared so little for. At one point, after Oswegatchie and before they made their final push to Montreal, the poised and experienced Hoffman was off conducting some business when Irving found himself at an island encampment of Indian traders. An attractive Indian woman sat intentionally beside him and made apparent advances—Indian cultures were understood to condone sexual openness. But he was unprepared for what happened next. The woman's irate husband, who had been drinking, suddenly knocked Irving to the ground. Wishing to avoid more trouble, Irving scampered off to the boat and left Hoffman's agent to make peace with the Indians.

In a less harrowing encounter farther upriver (and this time with Hoffman himself alongside to watch out for him), Irving was awarded an Indian name. He was singled out, no doubt because of his age, and in a mock ceremony was dubbed "Vomonte," which, he was told, translated as "Good to everybody." This was how he would be characterized in the *beau monde* of later decades when he became famous for making friends in high places. Meanwhile, the naming ceremony would be his last interaction with North American Indians for thirty years.

When Irving reached the civilized center of Montreal, officials of the Northwest Fur Company entertained him warmly. He found himself in the midst of an assemblage of grizzled fur traders who gladly related their "wide and wild peregrinations, their hunting exploits and their perilous adventures and hair-breadth escapes among the Indians." Never would he forget those authentic old trappers and their stories.[6]

Montreal had long been the focal point of the fur trade. Every summer furs arrived from the interior, and merchants from as far away as London showed up. No one matched the entrepreneurial John Jacob Astor, out of New York City. His empire, launched in the 1780s, was built on beaver, raccoon, and muskrat, and required a long summer's work and large warehouses in Montreal.[7] Also in Montreal, Irving met Henry Brevoort, another New Yorker, an Astor operative of Dutch ancestry a few years his junior. He and Brevoort were destined to become great friends, sometimes roommates, and faithful correspondents for decades.

When, out of curiosity, he returned once more to Oswegatchie/Ogdensburg a half-century later, Irving remembered the rigors of the 1803 trip, but in simpler form: "We toiled through forests in wagons drawn by oxen; we slept in hunters' cabins, and were once four and twenty hours without food; but all was romance for me." By then, all he was willing to write of his encounters with the neighborhood Indians was of paddling in their canoes—with the young ladies onboard, of course—on "the limpid waters of the St. Lawrence." The charms of the company and delight of the scenery had made a lasting impression. The passage of time would make the grueling journey a "romance."[8]

★ ★

Peter Irving's embrace of Aaron Burr reached high tide during the New York gubernatorial campaign of spring 1804. The isolated erstwhile vice president, his hands tied in Washington, had hoped to return to New York and do something more rewarding than hold nominal power as the second-highest national executive while being systematically excluded from all major decisions.

With the campaign season getting under way, Burr paid close attention to the *Morning Chronicle*. At the end of 1803, in addition to political news and opinion, Washington Irving wrote two further pieces on the New York theater, picking up where "Jonathan Oldstyle" had left off. This time, however, he was "Dick Buckram," writing to his friend "Andrew Quoz."[9] Ostensibly a "young buck," or man on the make, "Dick Buckram," Irving's actor persona, claims strong masculine attributes. At the same time, *buckram* meant "pretentiousness" or "bombast." He is clearly someone other than the inoffensive "Vomonte," good to everybody.[10]

The continuation of "Oldstyle" in this new form was inspired by a series of performances a Manhattan troupe had given in Albany when Irving was in the vicinity with the Hoffmans and Ogdens. His "Dick Buckram" was a dandy and a "lover," dressed in a "sky colored silk coat, red jacket, green small clothes, and shoes decorated with large plated buckles." He arrived onstage "in a deliberate manner smoking a tobacco pipe," as the Dutch traditionally did, ostensibly trying to appeal to his particular audience, "understanding that the Albanians were of Dutch extraction." But the audience was composed of the same crowd the acting company ordinarily performed for in Manhattan, all of whom had journeyed up the Hudson to escape another summer of yellow fever. The Dutch, meanwhile, were off "feasting on sturgeon."[11]

Vice President Aaron Burr was so impressed with "Dick Buckram" that he sent a sampling of Irving's essays to his daughter Theodosia, who was the same age as Irving and already married. As the identity of the author of "Oldstyle" and the latest "Dick Buckram" continuation had been released only to insiders, Burr could state knowingly that it was "the production of a youth of about nineteen [he was now nearly twenty-one, in fact], the youngest brother of Dr. Peter Irving, of New-York."[12]

Burr was no doubt elated when, at Peter's behest, Washington Irving turned to partisan politics. In dramatic fashion, the youngest Irving openly embraced the cause—Burr's run for governor against the Jefferson-Clinton candidate, Morgan Lewis. The satirist's vehicle was a short-lived sheet called the *Corrector*. Peter ran the *Corrector,* which was printed concurrently with the *Morning Chronicle*, in April 1804, for the singular purpose of answering a series of crude attacks on Burr issuing from the *American Citizen*, another New York City newspaper.

It was a battle of editors: Peter Irving versus James Cheetham. The opponent could have been another Washington Irving invention, but he was not; he was real, born with the name "Cheetham." His short biography sounds implausible, but in truth James Cheetham, who was reared in England, began his unpromising career as a hatter. He immigrated to New York in 1798, at the age of twenty-six, and reinvented himself as a political writer. It was Burr who apparently discovered him, and Burr who helped him to establish his newspaper. Then Cheetham took advantage of—cheated—his patron. When Burr responded unsatisfactorily to his offer to take on Jefferson (and refused to line his pockets), the editor sold his services to the Clintons and, just like that, became a Jefferson partisan, turning the *American Citizen* into an organ of Burr's political destruction. Though he was a hack writer, impertinent and heavy-handed, by 1804 Cheetham had considerably damaged Burr's reputation, necessitating a last-minute countereffort from Peter Irving's *Chronicle*.

But Peter was atypical of the partisan editors of the period. He was too reserved to print obvious lies, or to pass on ugly rumors and pitch abusive words at Burr's enemies. Cheetham derided him by calling him "Miss" Irving, a direct allusion to his sexual identity. Civil Peter knew whom he could turn to for help: Washington resented Cheetham's unprovoked assaults on his brother, including the suggestion (with clear homosexual overtones) that he was merely the slavish follower of a known libertine. If the question was who could more cleverly destroy with a pen, James Cheetham or Washington Irving, the latter proved himself the less callous, but more skillful, attack artist.[13]

Offering a contrast to Peter, a respectable medical doctor by training, he cast James Cheetham as a bumbling physician, and the reader of his rag his hapless patient. Though the editor's medicines sought to accomplish something meaningful, they proved instead to be "powerful promoters of sleep." If taken in too large doses, "they are apt to excite nausea at the stomach," Irving pushed. "The patient will find it difficult to swallow them at first, they generally have to be crammed down the throat by force, and the patient beaten over the head with a club." The three-line headline shouted:

BEWARE OF IMPOSTERS!!
TWENTY YEARS PRACTICE!!
JAMES CHEETHAM—QUACK DOCTOR.[14]

Irving wrote for the *Corrector* until the end of April 1804. Then, in mid-May, owing to his poor health, he took advantage of an opportunity to go to Europe. He went at the behest of his businessmen brothers William and Ebenezer, who walked onto the ship with him before bidding farewell. It was customary to send a loved one on an ocean voyage to clear up a lung ailment—the sea air was meant to do one good when medical treatment had failed. "It is with delight we share the world with you," wrote William. This kind of commitment shows how tightly knit the family was, and how healthy its business was at this time.[15]

Before his departure, Irving had breakfast with Aaron Burr, and they discussed his trip.[16] He also gave his attentions to the Hoffman family. As a talented sketch artist, he had been giving drawing lessons to thirteen-year-old Matilda who, though only a year younger than her sister Ann, had been deemed too young and fragile to join the trek to Oswegatchie the year before. He would not forget Matilda.[17]

★   ★

The *Rising States* set sail from New York harbor, bound for France. On arrival in Bordeaux after thirty-six days on the Atlantic, some of them feverish, Irving began another elaborate journal. He described the French countryside, the narrow streets and stone buildings of the city, and the differences he noted in the behavior of Europeans and Americans. A passport issued by the French justice ministry at this time, a half-century before photography, described his appearance: "Hair chestnut—eyebrows do. [ditto]—eyes gray—nose long—mouth middling—chin large—forehead middling—face oblong—height 5 feet 7 inches."[18]

He found travel in Napoleonic France difficult. He was often assumed to be an Englishman, and therefore subject to official harassment. In Nice, staying at the aptly named Hotel des Étrangers, he discovered that his passport was of the kind carried by "suspected persons." The local official in charge initially threw up his hands, insisting: "It is out of my power." This obliged Irving to seek out two people who could vouch for his character: a business associate of the New Jersey/New York Ogden family, and Stephen Cathalan, the longtime U.S. consul in Marseilles, who had been acting on behalf of American interests ever since Thomas Jefferson, as U.S. minister to France, had enjoyed his company in 1787. The young traveler noted the consul's chief foible in one line: "[He] wants no trumpeter to proclaim his great deeds as long as he has the use of his tongue." To bail himself out of a jam, Irving had to swallow his pride. He had to "prove" himself, through his contacts, to be "peaceably & properly in france," and not a spy.

He confided to his journal the continuing frustrations that arose from most people's ignorance of America's independence:

> I was asked the other day at dinner by a well dressd frenchman whether my *province* (for he took the United States to be a mere province) was not a great wine country and whether it was not in the neighborhood of *Turkey* or *somewhere there about*! Another time I was accosted by a French officer "vous etes Anglais monsieur" said he—"Pardonnez moi" replied I "Je suis des Etats Unis d'Amerique"—"Eh bien—*c'est la même chose*"![19]

Questions of his status resolved, Irving recorded his tour of France with a distinct consciousness of walking in the footsteps of earlier published travelers, most particularly the mid-eighteenth-century novelist Laurence Sterne. On several occasions, he made precious references to Sterne's experience, as immortalized in *A Sentimental Journey Through France and Italy* (1768). He even gave the 233-page notebook the title "Journal of a Tour thro France,

Italy, Sicily." Irving alluded also to Oliver Goldsmith's work of 1762: He spoke of overcoming homesickness as getting past the "damp" that hovered over his spirits so that he might become "more a 'Citizen of the World.'" Again, this time in a letter to brother William, "I am continually more and more sensible that I am not *Citizen of the World* enough to form a Traveller."[20]

Weaned on his elders' caring companionship, he adapted only gradually to his situation: "I want a friend to whom I can impart my sensations with whom I can exchange my ideas and to whom I can look for support and sympathy," he wrote to William. "With admiring grand prospect or a magnificent piece of workmanship, how do I wish that I had some one with me to participate in the enjoyment and to whom I might communicate my feelings." One is reminded, again, of Sterne, who expressed human susceptibility with unprecedented candor, and wrote in *A Sentimental Journey:* "'Tis sweet to feel by what fine-spun threads our affections are drawn together."

The connection between these two world-class raconteurs is hard to resist. Reading Sterne, one cannot but sense a disquieting urgency, which Irving also expressed throughout his career. There is, as well, a combustible combination of snobbery and self-doubt in both writers. Though Irving was not self-destructive in the way Sterne tended to be, both exhibited physical delicacy and emotional softness—the tubercular Sterne insisting that a man should not have to restrain his tears. In their mature fiction, both liked to convey a sense of mystery, and to appear more spontaneous than they really were.[21]

Sterne divided his "travellers" into such arbitrary categories as "inquisitive," "proud," "vain," "splenetic," and, of course, "sentimental." In situating himself among the different types, Irving repeatedly mentioned Sterne's "Smelfungus" (a severe appellation for the author Tobias Smollett), whom Sterne had encountered in one place after another and invariably described as a spoilsport. Here is Sterne's version: "Smelfungus" was a "traveller" who "set out with the spleen and jaundice, and every object he pass'd by was discoloured or distorted." Irving, as the critic who had poked fun at the Bostonian "Queen Sheba" at Ballston Spa, and who could unsparingly satirize "Doctor" James Cheetham in the *Corrector,* as readily found targets for his sharp pen in Europe. In the midst of his French frustrations, he chastised himself for not holding back: "There is nothing I dread more than to be taken for one of the *Smellfungii* of the world."[22]

On the general subject of women, Sterne was famous (or infamous, in some circles) for his suggestive prose. *A Sentimental Journey* ends—really it is a nonending—with his unexpected rendezvous at an inn: He shares a room with a woman and her maid, the three separated only by a thin curtain. Before the account spontaneously breaks off, the narrator explains: "So that when I stretch'd out my hand, I caught hold of the Fille de Chambre's—"; Irving, recounting an incident at a crowded inn halfway between Marseilles and Nice, tells how he confronted the innkeeper on being told that he was to lose his room to more important guests, an engineer and his wife, who had arrived after him. At first, the young traveler invoked his nationality—he was, he said, an *"American gentleman."* Thus: "[I] considered myself *equal at least* to any engineer general in France and would not give up my room to him if he was to come with all his engines and lay seige [*sic*] to it." But this strategy not immediately succeeding, he agreed he was willing to cede half of his room to "the engineer's lady." At this, he retained his quarters. Curiously, either Irving or, more likely, a protective editor of his papers, possibly Pierre, inked out the bawdy Sternean allusion from its appearances both in his journal and in a letter of the same time to his family.[23]

Yet in writing to a young coworker at Hoffman's law office, Irving expressed shock at the sexual openness of the French. Restricting himself from (once again) carrying on a "very dull, *smellfungus like* story," he would withhold, he said, "a recital of my chagrins, my ill humors and my little embarrassments." He described an evening's amusement—a dance performance—and sounded prudish: "The female dancers shew their persons without any modesty and reserve[.] they are dressed in a flesh colored habit that is fitted exactly to the shape and looks like the skin."

Americans of this time were entirely unaccustomed to such displays. Irving admitted that he was "delighted" by the dancers' "agility" and "elegant attitudes," and promptly made an acknowledgment: "My american notions of delicacy & propriety are not sufficiently conquerd for me to view this shameless exposure of their persons." But the combined indifference of older women to such "spectacles" and the utter directness with which Frenchmen discussed their mistresses annoyed him most. As he narrates one conversation he had with "an old gentleman of much respectability," Irving responded to the suggestion that he take a mistress himself:

"What! my good sir," cried I "Is this the advice you give to a poor devil who is travelling for his health and who has a constitution to *get* instead of to *spend?*" "Phoo. Phoo." replied the old genius "I have a girl myself and she don't hurt my constitution—I only play with her"—!!!

Perhaps, in France, "old debauchees with one foot in the grave" could do just fine spending their money on "prostitutes who have the art of awakening faint sparks," but Irving intended to "keep the morals I brought with me from america."[24]

French conditions clearly wore on him. His spirits improved the nearer he got to Italy. The valley of Nice, its population then little more than ten thousand, had many delightful qualities, judging from his journal, but he struggled with the southern dialect, and frequently remarked on the unhygienic conditions and "abominable smells" that "weary travellers" faced. While waiting at Nice for his passport to be reissued, and fighting off mosquitoes and gnats, he took "solitary morning rambles along the sea shore," wishing earnestly to be on the "bosom" of the ocean, and en route to Genoa. The days passed slowly. Before departure, he made a "rugged ascent" into the mountains east of the town and gazed out at the "unruffled Medditeranean speckled here & there with the bark of a fisherman." He believed that crossing into Italian waters would release him from his "troubles."[25]

★　★

Seaborne communications separated him from news of home by at least six weeks. There was uncomfortable intelligence—another yellow fever outbreak in New York, according to the Paris papers—but nothing to counterbalance this news, nothing to put his mind at ease. In fact, a good deal had happened in his hometown in the few months since his departure. He would learn of it from William, but only after he arrived in Genoa.

Vice President Aaron Burr faced an uncertain political future in the spring of 1804. The Jeffersonians had abandoned him, and despite the best editorial efforts of Peter Irving, he would not be New York's next governor. He had carried New York City, but Morgan Lewis soundly defeated Burr statewide. This was politics.

Before May was over, the lame duck vice president had turned his attention to the volatile Alexander Hamilton, whom he had known for more than two decades, and from whom he expected a display of dignity superior to what he expected of a Cheetham. But Hamilton had made personal remarks during the campaign that Burr found insulting and uncalled for. He demanded that Hamilton retract them—and do so in a most public way, as was the custom in affairs of honor.

Hamilton's refusal (or, rather, his combined procrastination and prevarication) led to their notorious duel on July 11, 1804, on the New Jersey side of the Hudson River, while Irving was in France viewing Gothic architecture. On learning of Hamilton's fate that autumn, he confided to his brother William that he had once been "an Admirer" of Hamilton and "a partizan with him in politics," though he felt, along with William and Peter, "a high sense of the merits of B[urr]." Thus, he stated, "your account of the persecution [of] the friends of Col Burr has fairly made my blood boil in my veins."[26]

After the duel, Burr's more vulnerable associates were charged as co-conspirators. Matthew Livingston Davis, an organizer for Burr, was for a time imprisoned; and Washington Irving's close friend Samuel Swartwout, another of the vice president's associates, fled New York to avoid a similar fate. That must have been part of what William meant by "persecution." Peter Irving, who ran as a Burrite for an assembly seat and lost, did not otherwise suffer for his partisanship. As William's letter is not extant, we cannot know whether the "persecution" he relayed to his brother stopped there, or whether William feared that Peter and he might come under fire as well.[27] As Washington reacted to William's information, he struggled to write with evenhandedness:

> Whatever may have been the circumstances of the duel I am satisfied they have been honorable on both sides and the affair should have been treated with delicacy & suffered to sink into silence. The manner in which it has been prosecuted is a melancholy proof to what a rancorous height political animosities are attaining in our country.

At the same time, he made clear that he did not prefer the state of politics in Europe. This was the time of Napoleonic conquest, a time of grave uncertainties—he had encountered *les gendarmes* on the road, and he felt unnerved. From this distance, he wished for civility to adhere to republican politics in America; in light of the Burr-Hamilton duel, he especially lamented that partisanship had grown so deadly. Admitting to his homesickness, he expressed his complex thoughts amid frustrations:

> I shall, I think, never complain against government when I return to america. My fellow countrymen do not know the blessings they enjoy; they are trifling with their felicity and are in fact *themselves* their worst enemies. I sicken when I think of our political broils, slanders & enmities and I think when I again find myself in New York I shall never meddle any more in politicks.[28]

* *

After this, Irving's letters home ceased to dwell on American politics. He had fully exchanged contexts, and became decidedly less homesick. "My health is growing stronger & stronger every day," he wrote home as the months went by. "I do not know when I have felt myself so strong & brisk and I even begin to acquire a little tinge of health in my countenance."[29] From Italy, in October 1804, he wrote of his improved condition to John Furman, one of the clerks in Hoffman's law office and an Irving family friend. He insisted that he had overcome "the effects of that enervating indisposition that rendered me for some time before I left New York, languid, irritable, spiritless, a burthen to my friends and to myself."[30]

Italy was transformative. The voyage from Nice to Genoa had taken three and a half days. Eluding privateers as they left French waters, Irving had sailed past Monaco, "situated on a flat rock that runs into the sea," and viewed the small town of Cogoleto, birthplace of Christopher Columbus, not knowing that he would one day be Columbus's biographer. After a few days in Genoa, he already felt he had seen enough to judge the Italian women superior in beauty to the French: "The[y] are extremely well made," he wrote to William, "have charming countenances and fine black eyes with which they know the art of languishing most bewitchingly."[31]

Irving was immediately made comfortable by the welcome he received from Thomas Hall Storm, a fellow New Yorker he had known when younger, who was doing business in Genoa and (though only one year older than Irving) was shortly to be named a vice consul there. Hall Storm invited Irving to share his elegant quarters and promised to introduce him to the "nobility and Beau monde."[32] Over the next two months, they "rambled," often in the company of fine ladies. When they had fun—generally when socializing with other foreigners—Irving allowed that "the sober Italians stare at us often with surprize and call us the *wild Americans*"—like the English, but for their "higher flow of spirits." He spoke imperfect French and no Italian.

He did grow particularly close to one person. She was Lady Shaftesbury, Barbara Webb, who had married the fifth Earl of Shaftesbury. She was, along with her husband, a prisoner of Napoleon's war, though permitted to live in a grand style; he was an eccentric, the result of a violent fall from his horse that had altered his speech and behavior. Both Shaftesburys admired America, and believed that "we are advancing rapidly to become the first nation in the world." Irving compared Lady Shaftesbury to the young bride Maria Fenno Hoffman ("something in her looks & manner"), and he behaved with her as he had with the woman she resembled, visiting daily and staying for informal meals as though a member of the family.[33]

Writing to a New York theater buddy on the first day of 1805, from aboard a ship heading to Messina, Sicily, Irving showed that he missed the old camaraderie. Infusing his writing with quotes from Shakespeare and Addison, he situated himself in "*outlandish* parts," and looked ahead to "sicily that island of fable & romance"; but he constantly imagined himself back in New York with his friends.

Part of what he wrote about was male-female relations. Uneasy with French sexual license, he said he found something quaint but incomprehensible in Italian courtship behavior. Unmarried girls could not leave their homes unless they were under the eye of a "sage" guardian, unlike in New York, where boys and girls appeared in public together, relaxed and unaccompanied: "The innocent familiarities that prevail between young people of both sexes in America & England is unknown in this country." And concerning the young Italian women themselves: "Were I what is called a *marrying man* I would as soon put my neck into a hempen noose as into the hymenial one, with any of them." He retained, he said, his "national prejudices." His heart, he assured, "still points towards new york." He playfully signed off as "J O," for "Jonathan Oldstyle."[34]

His compulsion, while still at sea, to share his yearnings and spill his thoughts in this way may well have come as the result of a life-threatening incident that had taken place two days before he began this particular letter—day seven of a thirteen-day voyage. He had just heard stories, from the Genoese onboard, of murderous pirates who plied the Mediterranean, when their American vessel, the *Matilda* of Philadelphia, was boarded by a pirate crew one day south of the island of Elba, somewhere between Corsica and the Italian shoreline. It did not matter that they had hoisted their American colors; all nations were fair game for the lawless privateer. No one on the *Matilda* even owned a pistol. They were defenseless.

Irving described the pirate leader as "a tall ragged fellow with his shirt sleeves rolld up to his elbows displaying a most formidable muscular pair of arms." His men were armed with "rusty cutlasses & stilettos." He demanded to see passports and wanted to know what cargo was onboard, and then he insisted that Irving come with him back to his ship, ostensibly to interpret for his French-speaking captain. A Genoese urged Irving not to comply, fearing that separating the passengers was merely the pirates' way to weaken them and slit their throats more easily. Irving went nonetheless.

"A more villainous looking crew I never beheld," he wrote. "Their dark complexions, rough beards and fierce black eyes scowling under enormous bushy eye brows were enough to inspire distrust & apprehension." The captain of the privateer waylaid Irving and the others long enough to facilitate a thorough, uninterrupted search of the *Matilda* for money and valuables. The pirate captain suddenly announced that he was acting in the service of Great

Britain, blockading Genoese shipping; yet Irving could see that his crew consisted of Maltese, Portuguese, Italians, and others. Ransacking the vessel yielded little more than some wine and brandy for the pirates, but now the danger was what might occur after they got drunk.

In the end, the *Matilda* was permitted to pass without further incident. For some confiscated furniture, the Americans were, implausibly, given a receipt meant to be presented to the British consul on Malta. Irving figured that the pirates stopped short of a complete pillage of the vessel out of a desire not to invite retribution from the U.S. government. That night, he had "horrid dreams" about assassins clutching stilettos and hovering over him.[35]

Since he had apparently sailed into the swirl of a naval cat-and-mouse game between England and France, his stay at Messina was short, constrained by political events. Admiral Horatio Nelson was in search of the French fleet, and Irving was able to observe the English champion's well-formed, finely tuned armada performing maneuvers. At Siracusa, on the southeast coast of Sicily, he saw American frigates, and became acquainted with some of the U.S. naval officers who were engaged in taking on the much-trumpeted threat emanating from Tripoli. Excited to be in their company, he left on a ground expedition (there was no military purpose to it) with a South Carolinian, Captain John Hall, and some other sailors. At Catania, a city built on the ruins of one destroyed by an eruption from Mount Etna, he visited the Cathedral of St. Agatha, and had his pocket picked. He saw a lot of "miserable villages," "crater of an old volcano," "birds in the convent," "music & dancing," "men with swords," and he watched the parading of a prisoner turn into an altercation, a chase: the "dastardly nature of a Sicilian mob."[36]

From here he and Captain Hall went on alone along a road uncharted by foreigners. Armed with pistols and swords and accompanied by a servant who carried "at least a half a dozen pistols stuck in his pockets and girdle," they traveled on mules for five days. Irving must have felt he was playing soldier—he was sure to emphasize the armaments in his next letter home. In Palermo, he and the captain said their goodbyes, and Irving sailed to Naples.

As always, he attached himself to his new friends, only to be lost without them—"very lonesome missd Hall exceedingly," he wrote in his journal. But two weeks later, in Naples, he had the further good fortune to meet up with Joseph Carrington Cabell of Virginia. Cabell, five years his elder, would later be instrumental in helping Thomas Jefferson establish the University of Virginia, but for now he was just an intelligent, good-natured young American, and that was quite enough to qualify him to be Irving's new best friend. Cabell had been to Rome, and was as well acquainted with Paris—

where Irving was now pointing himself—and so Irving fell in with Cabell for the long haul.

Finding Cabell and himself "well fitted," with common aims, they soon left Sicily for Rome. Irving's physical health was now "perfectly restored." They reached the ancient city in advance of Holy Week and visited palaces, gardens, famous frescoes, and the Vatican. Irving ran into Washington Allston, the young American painter who would become his close friend in subsequent years. On his twenty-second birthday, April 3, 1805, Irving called at the studio of the eminent neoclassical sculptor Antonio Canova, then at work on a statue of Napoleon that was "to be naked in the style of the ancients." That evening, he and Cabell "rambled" into the countryside and looked upon the city from a perfectly situated hill. After witnessing mass at the Sistine Chapel and other rituals of Holy Week from a closer vantage point ("Never did I see such an ostentatious piece of humility," Irving remarked as a cardinal washed the feet of twelve monks in white robes and gave them each white flowers), Irving and Cabell took one last look at the Roman Forum and then embarked on the road to Paris.[37]

Irving's journal comes alive between Terni and Foligno, in the Apennines, where springtime offered rainbows and dreamlike vistas that the traveler found purifying: "The sun breaking from among the clouds often threw partial gleams of light on the white towers of a village or convent half embowerd among the woods. . . . The fertility of the country is remarkable & the mountains are often coverd half way up with olive trees of an amazing size."[38] Their carriage had to be complemented with oxen to make the steep ascent. Feeling a solitary thrill in the high country, in a wrinkled land dotted with undefined ruins and errant goatherds, Irving let his senses speak for him: a convent bell in the distance; breezes that were flower-scented; itinerant musicians playing their instruments. As he moved from one mountain village to the next, his language climbed with him: "fugitive tints," "elasticity in the air." Arriving in Bologna, he pronounced that he now knew why the Italian countryside was referred to as "the Garden of Europe."[39]

When his brother William, who was funding Irving's travels, learned of these peregrinations, he wrote back expressing "both pleasure and mortification"—pleasure at Washington's restored health, mortification for his decision to "*gallop through Italy*." William had been calculating cost-effectiveness: His brother had tarried eleven weeks in Genoa when two would have sufficed; and then he missed out on the most magnificent sites—"leaving Florence on your left and Venice on your right"—to suit Joseph Cabell's schedule. Cabell may have been an "estimable fellow," William deduced, but meeting him was probably "the most unfortunate occurrence of all your journey." The Virginian appeared to be "flying on the wings of impatience" to get back to Paris, but that should not have directed his companion's movements. "Good company," William chastised, "is the grand desideratum with you."[40]

★   ★

Irving and Cabell crossed the Alps together. "The Scenery of Switzerland surpassed my expectations," the former wrote home. "Rocks pild on rocks lift their stupendous summits into the clouds." Near Luzern, he wrote a poem—Irving was never known for poetry—which was preserved only because Cabell held on to it.

> *Upon the placid bosom of the Lake*
> *I lie and sweetly dream the Hours away.*
> *Anon a Vision of approaching Day*
> *Strikes on my Lids, and I awake*
> *To find 'tis but the Glimmering Ray*
> *Of the false dawn.*[41]

The devious little twist at the end seems to symbolize the chimerical nature of Irving's response to Switzerland. To the Sentimental Traveller, the Swiss people were, like their peculiar country, dignified and independent, displaying a "candor that we may search for in vain among the surrounding nations." It was proof for this American that the "energy of mind" native to an untamed landscape sustained "liberty"; for here he had found something wonderful: "the sublime characteristics of a freeman."

There was misery among the inhabitants of Italy that was entirely absent in Switzerland; there, they could walk anywhere, their "purses open in [their] hands," and not fear molestation: "No part of Europe has interested me as much as this little spot. France speaks to the senses, Italy to the imagination, but Switzerland to the *heart.*"[42]

On May 19, 1805, Irving and Cabell were just beyond the Swiss border, aboard a "diligence," or stagecoach, that would take them to Paris. The "gay" countryside was alive with the songs of skylarks, and Cabell did his best to romance a pretty French girl who rode with them. It was not Irving's way of doing things, but he did not seem to mind. In the diligence, five days from the French capital, he recorded that it was one year to the day since he had left New York.[43]

The year in Europe caused Irving to relish his Americanness. He had recently written in his journal in Basel, after a dinner with a party of Swiss travelers who expressed curiosity about his native land:

It is flattering to an American to perceive, how rapidly his country is increasing in importance and exciting the attention and admiration of the old world. While Europe is wasting its strength in perpetual commotions, the United States, blessed with profound peace and an excellent government, is gaining daily accesses of wealth & power and rising by tranquil yet rapid degrees to take the most conspicuous seat among the nations.[44]

In Paris, Irving cleaned himself up at a floating bathhouse on the Seine, read some American newspapers, strolled through the Jardin des Tuilleries, and attended the theater with the American painter John Vanderlyn, whose patron was Aaron Burr. When writing to his superintending brother William, Irving took more care than he had in Italy, conscious of the expectations placed upon him by his family. Knowing the reputation of Paris, he promised that he would be "guarded" in his behavior. "Travelling has made me better acquainted with myself," he assured. "It has given me a humilliating conviction of my own insufficiency—of my own ignorance and how very much I have to learn." He was tired of hobnobbing with the upper class, he said. "I will never move in any circle where my society is merely tolerated. I have had a complete surfeit of nobility in Italy & Sicily. It makes my blood boil to see a star on a jacket or a ribband in the buttonhole, entitle a blockhead a puppy a scoundrel to rank above the man of worth and merit." Twisting the opening sentence of Sterne's *A Sentimental Journey*, he added: "Thank heavens, we *order these matters* better *in America*."

To his brother Peter, the lapsed lawyer asked to be remembered to Josiah Ogden Hoffman. "Tell him I long for the time when I shall be once more numbered among his disciples." He expressed himself with less enthusiasm, and more a sense of resignation, in a candid letter to one of his fellow law students in Hoffman's employ: "Let me return to America . . . let me *endeavor* to bury myself among the musty authors of the Law and prepare myself for that starving profession with which I am to struggle thro this world."[45]

He remained in Paris through the summer, but he stopped recording his activities. In September, he was in the Netherlands, where he complained more than he delighted: He took a carriage ride with "an uncouth looking old Dutchman" whose pipe smoking "envelloped [them] in a most villainous fog"; he lamented "the sameness in the houses—streets, people, manners &c that in a little time satiates curiosity."

The first week of October, he escaped in a "neat packet . . . under prussian colors," sighting *"Old England"* for the first time from the deck: "The sunrise was beautiful, the atmosphere pure and serene, and I could scarcely believe it was the Island of smoak & fog I saw before me." The countryside he passed by "presented that scene of industrious cultivation that characterizes England." Everything looked "flourishing" and "comfortable." He had eyed the English with distrust, he said, always expecting them to make him, as an American, feel small. But his doubts on this score soon dissipated: "In england I feel my-self a man—in france I was a cypher." It was his removal from despotic gov-ernment to a freer climate that convinced him of the fundamental decency of America's former motherland.[46]

He booked his voyage back to New York in the dead of winter, and as 1806 began, he committed his person to the ship *Remittance*. It would be ten years before he returned to England. In the time between, he would establish him-self as a satirist of uncommon buoyancy.

For fifty-two days, Irving endured a voyage battered by strong headwinds and unsteady sailing. His journal contains a fragmentary record of the time at sea, one particular day's giddy, fatalistic, stream-of-consciousness report after high waves drove the passengers below deck into a crowded cabin:

> [P]oor don Pedro mounted companion way As he peepd out sea broke over & completely sousd him from head to foot—So much the better—he'll have to change his clothes & be clean in spight of himself. tie on my cravat put on cap & once more mount companion ladder Ladies there—Wish them good morning—put my arms round their waists & hug them tight to keep them from falling—What it is to be careful![47]

In the quivering confusion that was a part of many an Atlantic crossing, Wash-ington Irving found himself in dangerously close proximity to exposed women, his fellow captives for nearly two months.

For this uncommitted young man who enjoyed being part of an audience or part of a literary fraternity, the desire for companionship was reflexive. We do not know—we cannot even speculate—whether he succumbed to experi-mentation with women in his twenty-two months abroad; it is enough to say that he regularly alluded to differences in sexual behavior across cultures, as he expressed an honest curiosity about people and places. His tour of the Continent had made him more knowledgeable about the world.

And he was only twenty-two.

CHAPTER 3

Whim-Whams and
a Treason Trial

1806–1807

*Good-nature is our steersman, reason our ballast, whim the breeze
that wafts us along, and MORALITY our leading star.*

—Washington Irving, in *Salmagundi*[1]

AFTER HIS REIMMERSION IN THE LIFE OF THE CITY, it took no time at all for Washington Irving to fall back in with the old crowd, and to indulge in festive frolics that had earlier stimulated the prose of "Jonathan Oldstyle." He had rejoined Hoffman's law firm, to be sure, and was engaged in helping his brother Peter translate from French the forgettable François Depons's *A Voyage to the Eastern Part of Terra Firma*. But when he joined an outspoken fraternity dubbed the "Lads of Kilkenny," or sometimes the "Nine Worthies," his after-work hours seemed to constitute his real life. In the spring of 1806, their recorded activities were supping and drinking in taverns, smoking cigars, talking about women, and composing ditties.

His eldest brother William was forty years old, and by now the father of five (including the future biographer Pierre, who was just turning four). Though William wielded an effective pen, he had too many serious concerns, one presumes, to join in the rowdier aspects of the group's activities. Peter, who sold his newspaper after keeping it alive until the end of 1805, was a thirty-three-year-old bachelor who could find no objection to the sporting life—so he was there to revel with the younger set. Sturdy Ebenezer, who had turned thirty, is counted in their number, but he, even less than William, was one to let loose; he had wed at the end of 1805, and his wife was pregnant.

James Kirke Paulding, living under his brother-in-law William's roof and an intimate of all the Irving brothers, was naturally in the thick of things. He was an early Burrite, besides, and had been a contributor to both the *Morning Chronicle* and the *Corrector*.

When the Lads of Kilkenny were not in the audience of the glamorous Park Theater (bought from William Dunlap by John Jacob Astor and William Beekman in 1805), or at Dyde's Hotel pub next door, Gouverneur Kemble provided them with a retreat on the Passaic River, just outside Newark, which the group styled as "Cockloft Hall" and used as a site for uncensored merriment. Kemble, three years younger than Irving, would be his lifelong friend. He was the descendent of wealthy merchants, and related by marriage to General Thomas Gage, the last British governor-general of Massachusetts at the time of Lexington and Concord. This part of his background only made his circumstances more curious, and it is possible that Mrs. Gage was in fact a spy in the service of patriots. The soon-to-be-famous "Cockloft Hall," also known to the group as "Bachelor's Hall," was a part of Kemble's inheritance, and was ordinarily maintained by a caretaker. Paintings of Kemble's righteous ancestors hung on the walls, and antique furniture gave the home a certain eminence. Kemble, as the property owner of record, was lightheartedly known to the Lads as the "Patroon."

The others who fell into their Kilkenny club circle included Henry Ogden, merchant (about to sail for China); Peter Kemble, Gouverneur's younger brother; Sam Swartwout, Burr's right-hand man; and Henry Brevoort, the good-natured, financially secure, New York-based fur trader Irving had met in Montreal in 1803. There is no record of their talking politics, but numerous references to their evenings of revelry.[2]

Just two months after his return from Europe, Irving received a welcome guest: Joseph Cabell. Irving's traveling companion had sailed into New York harbor before heading home to Virginia, and over the next twelve days allowed his friend to introduce him to his circle: his brothers, Paulding, the rest of the Lads of Kilkenny, the elegant families of Manhattan—Hoffmans, Coldens, Mitchills, and Lewises—an actress or two, and as many unmarried young women as an excited Irving could round up. The Virginia gentleman was pleased by all the attention. He wrote: "Irving who is the favorite of some of the best company in New York, insisted on my going an extensive round with him, which together with the business of seeing the town and its environs, kept me in constant employment." Peter Irving gave Cabell a letter of introduction to Aaron Burr, then in Philadelphia, the young Virginian's next stop.[3]

That is all Cabell relates, but he must have glimpsed the Lads of Kilkenny in their milieu. They may not have been the dissipated pranksters suggested in later reminiscences, but their desire was simple: to stir things up and to laugh loudly, to entertain and to be entertained. At some point, their spirited conversation was molded into a comic composition. One thing led to another, and *Salmagundi* was born, *Or, the Whim-Whams and Opinions of Launcelot Langstaff, Esq. & Others,* as it was subtitled. *Salmagundi* was a joint production by the team of Jim Paulding, Washington Irving, and William Irving, Jr., and built around the make-believe Cockloft Hall, the scene of whim-whams and other antics.

Salmagundi was a legitimate word, defined in the 1813 edition of Johnson's *Dictionary* as "a mixture of chopped meat and pickled herrings, with oil, vinegar, pepper and onions." So it was a mishmash, a hash of opinion and comedy—wider in scope and more unruly than the script of "Jonathan Oldstyle." It contained updated Oldstyle-like commentaries on New York society, measured riffs from Paulding and the younger Irving on the politics of the day, William's lightweight verse, and even a sprinkling of genuine sentiment. In the twelve months during which *Salmagundi* circulated—twenty numbers in all—this odd publication escaped the bounds of New York (to the surprise of the authors), delighting some for its independence and irritating others for its impertinence; it eventually found readers in England.[4]

Paulding appears to have been the real instigator of *Salmagundi,* or at least equal to Washington Irving in its conception. Like Irving, whose personality was ill suited for the legal trade, Paulding was never meant for the drudgery of the federal loan office where he was then employed; all he wanted to do was write, though it was thought highly unlikely at this time that anyone could survive easily on his writing. Even Noah Webster, whose "Blue-Backed Speller" had been a standard teaching tool across America since 1783, did not realize the wealth he thought he warranted from the millions sold because he had signed away copyright.[5] The three Salmagundians signed away theirs, accepting a few hundred dollars in the near term; and when Paulding determined to engineer *Salmagundi's* republication in 1819, his younger partner felt by then that the work was juvenile and unworthy of reissue. For Paulding, though, it was always a darling child. To some it appeared that he was struggling to offset his friend's increasingly greater critical success, forcing Paulding to deny feelings of jealousy: "I never claimed more than an equal share," he said of *Salmagundi* in 1846, still desirous of acquitting himself of the crime of comparison, but at the same time willing to acknowledge that he resented the work's unequal attribution.[6]

There probably would have been no first publication of *Salmagundi* if the Lads of Kilkenny had not spent the better part of a year working up to it—if what they were doing can be considered "working." When Gouverneur Kemble was off in Philadelphia in May 1806, Irving wrote to him in the spirit of their weekend romps. He began, "Since I cannot have the pleasure, my dear fellow, of conversing with you in any other manner, I am determined to have a sociable dish of chat with you every morning upon paper, though I am fearful you will find me very stupid company." Of his life in the workplace, he boasted of not working hard, and instead smoking "a sentimental or rather philosophic segar . . . over the office fire," and "lolling in crazy armchairs," disturbed only by the regular frowns drooping from "the ponderous fathers of the law." He was, then, left to imagine the better world his friend Kemble inhabited, "perhaps sipping in inspiration and champagne; listening to the light joke; enjoying the union of mirth, melody, and sentiment, in a song, or basking in the sunshine of some fair Hunkamunka's eyes."[7]

Irving showed a strong parodic impulse, and he did not shy from painting a carnal picture. By "Hunkamunka," he meant the princess in Henry Fielding's satirical "tragedy" of 1730, *Tom Thumb*. Tom was a miniature giant-killer, an unlikely hero, whom women could not resist. "Fair Hunkamunka" was the imaginative conjuring of a female ready to throw herself at her man. In Fielding's play, sexual desire and jealousy result in a series of passionate (but ludicrous) murders, so that none of the principals survive at the curtain's fall.

The bachelors' bond genuinely absorbed Irving. Another letter to Kemble, two days later, described his options: Was Irving to continue to enjoy "the riotous, roaring, rattle-brained orgies at Dydes," or was he expected to be the "pretty-boy-kind of a fellow as ever graced a tea party"? "God bless the women!" he exclaimed halfheartedly. Four of the Lads—Kemble, Ogden, and Peter and Washington Irving—would never marry.[8]

So this was some of what went through his mind in the months leading up to the publication of *Salmagundi*, a critical phase in Irving's development as a humorist. He would find in literary collaboration not only a release but also a continuation of what he seemed to crave most: readymade community, and a respite from decision. Writing was a *pre*occupation, but what would be his eventual occupation? What would writing lead to? Surely not riches. Would he be a lawyer, like his sturdy brother John? Or become more instrumental in day-to-day operations of the family's business that William and Ebenezer now handled? His travel experience suggested this as a possibility—Peter, no longer publishing, would be heading off to England soon, and would be lost to their writing group just as *Salmagundi* began to simmer. His timing was always poor.

During the second half of 1806, Irving accepted that his clerkship could not go on forever and that he would be admitted to the New York Bar—or fail trying. He acknowledged his preparation as weak, in spite of Hoffman's best efforts. But in November 1806, Hoffman (in his official role as examiner) let him squeak by, and, with his diligent brother John, he took up offices at no. 3 Wall Street—not inconsequentially the former residence of Aaron Burr!

Irving's career as a lawyer would be short, and would be of even less consequence to the people of the City of New York, as John inferred in an 1807 letter. Brothers Washington and Peter, he said, were both averse to "honest industry," and reduced, at this time in their lives, to "genteel beggary."[9]

Salmagundi began its life as an irregular periodical, somewhat haphazard in preparation. Its authors as well as its printer claimed (in print) not to have any interest in making money on the venture. Indeed, during his lifetime, Washington Irving saw to it that *Salmagundi* was excluded from his *Collected Works*. The publication of the first number took place in January 1807, spearheaded by Paulding, who wrote the prefatory remarks and, as "Launcelot Langstaff," the first section; then Irving jumped in with his report from the "New-York Assembly" in the guise of "Anthony Evergreen, Gent." That "Assembly" was not a political conclave but a fashionable ball, the perfect vehicle for Irving's satirizing pen.

Why perfect? Because Irving—all the Irvings—were striving for respectability themselves. The British traveler John Lambert spent time in New York in 1806–1808, and published his findings. He divided the city's society into three (he termed them "distinct") social classes: first, the officers of the government, successful professionals, and merchants—people of property; second, the smaller merchants, retailers, and clerks; and third, the "inferior orders of people." The Irvings hobnobbed, but were only uncertainly a part of that first category.[10]

As Evergreen, Irving feigns subtlety when none is intended; or he evinces the smug self-satisfaction of a "real" fashion critic. He opens by pronouncing himself the "Herschel" of the "firmament of fashion," a reference to the famous English astronomer Sir William Herschel, and demanding equal treatment. From here, he appropriates Laurence Sterne's customary method of overanalyzing everything—in which getting something right does not matter as much as describing it well. As the ball progresses, the comic writer spins:

> Let the grumbling smellfungi of this world, who cultivate taste among books, cobwebs and spiders, rail at the extravagance of the age; for my part I was delighted with the magic of the scene, and as the ladies tripped through the mazes of the dance, sparkling and glowing and dazzling, I, like the honest chinese, thanked them heartily for the jewels and finery, with which they had loaded themselves, merely for the entertainment of the bystanders—and blessed my stars that I was a bachelor.[11]

Exaggerated parts represented the comical whole. For Sterne, objects came at all angles: "Nothing is more dangerous, madam, than a wish coming sideways in this unexpected manner upon a man." For Irving, at the ball: "I was struck with the energy of sundry limbs, which seemed to be flourishing about, without appertaining to any body. After much investigation and difficulty, I at length traced them to their respective owners."[12]

The earnest observer of these years, John Lambert, wrote of New York fashion:

> The dress of the gentlemen is plain, elegant, and fashionable, and corresponds in every respect with the English costume. The ladies in general seem more partial to the light, various, and dashing drapery of the Parisian belles, than to the elegant and becoming attire of our London beauties, who improve upon the French fashions.[13]

For Irving's Evergreen, there was a self-inflated Briton on the scene, "a fellow of infinite verbosity," who stuffs cheese and crackers into his jacket pocket so as to avoid possible injury by "venturing his limbs in the crowd of hungry fair ones who throng the supper-room door." But the French were Evergreen's declared favorites, regardless of the prejudices Irving may have incurred in his European travels: "I love the nation," he writes, "as being a nation of right merry fellows, possessing the true secret of being happy; which is nothing more than thinking of nothing, talking about any thing, and laughing at every thing."[14]

At the fashionable ball, then, the dancers are all Frenchmen. By "the most accurate computation," Irving ratchets up the absurdity:

A frenchman passes at least three-fifths of his time between the heavens and the earth, and partakes eminently of the nature of a gossamer or soap-bubble. One of these jack-o-lanthorn heroes . . . unfortunately wound himself—I mean his foot—his better part—into a lady's cobweb muslin robe; but perceiving it at the instant, he set himself a spinning the other way, like a top; unraveled his step, without omitting one angle or curve, and extricated himself, without breaking a thread of the lady's dress![15]

There is a faint trace of sexual suggestiveness in the momentary mix-up of body parts; Sterne, no doubt, would have approved.

While his more prolific brother was preparing to immortalize the Cockloft family, William Irving, as "Pindar Cockloft," contributed tributary verse. Towed along by his younger brother, he took up some of the same subjects, willingly subordinating himself to whatever Washington led with. William took his own shot at fashionable Frenchmen:

> . . . *this poor town has been woefully* fashed;
> *Has long been be-frenchman'd, be-cockney'd, be-trashed.*

Young men in the eighteenth century revered the ancient Theban lyric poet Pindar (the original of that name), just as Plato and Aeschylus had called him "the Wisest" and "the Great." But let us be honest here: William "Pindar" Irving was entirely satisfied with doggerel.[16]

Absurdity prevails in *Salmagundi*, though one notably solemn and weighty essay, Paulding's "Mine Uncle John," showed a sentimental side that Washington Irving—all good fun—had yet to exhibit. Paulding tallies Uncle John's "loves and disappointments" in a bittersweet tribute to his still-living, fifty-year-old relative. The man in the tale dies a lifelong bachelor ("I dont intend to do the thing in a hurry" is his mantra). Having procrastinated when an accomplished young woman wished to marry him, he goes to his grave a loser at love: "*Tut, boys! I might have had her*" is his final lament.[17]

For Irving, there is yet no suggestion of the wistful writer he will become. His trade is satire. As the *Salmagundi* series progresses over February–March 1807, the imaginary Cocklofts and their friends become more unconventional. Rich in heritage, mock-patriarch Christopher Cockloft has but a small family now, as Irving tells it:

> Having lost most of the children when young, by the excessive care he took to bring them up like vegetables. This was one of his first whim-whams, and

a confounded one it was, as his children might have told had they not fallen victims to his experiment before they could talk. . . . He sprinkled them every morning with water, laid them out in the sun, as he did his geraniums.

Those who survived grow to be "odd, *runty*, mummy looking originals." Mrs. Cockloft, meanwhile, is "a warm admirer of shining mahogany, clean hearths, and her husband."[18]

Of the hapless Cocklofts and their whim-whams, Irving has still more to say. The word *whim-wham* required a history and a complete sociology. Thus the family mansion is as "full of whims and oddities as its tenants," and lets off a "perilous groaning" in the wind that requires the services of a carpenter-physician. The author explains: "Whim-whams are the inheritance of the Cocklofts, and every member of the household is a humorist *sui generis*, from the master down to the footman." The family dog howls at church bells, which one Cockloft insists was "owing to a peculiar delicacy in the organization of his ears," but which the author declares to be "a mere Cockloft whim-wham which the little cur indulges." Sterne delighted in the naughty possibility of language, as readers of *Tristram Shandy* knew only too well, and Irving is at his most Sternean in *Salmagundi*, combining sensory surprises with physical movement and ironic accident. He is only a little less naughty than his predecessor.[19]

Taking the comedic script in a new and politically interesting direction, Paulding introduced a repeating character, implausibly named Mustapha Rub-a-dub Keli Khan, "Captain of a Ketch," and a Tripolitan prisoner.[20] The prototype for the Mustapha letters (there are nine of them in *Salmagundi*) was Goldsmith's *Citizen of the World*, whose Chinese traveler reports home on the strange habits of Europeans. Picturing, for instance, the tightly bound feet of a desirably earthy Chinese bride, he testifies: "The ladies here [England] are horridly ugly . . . red cheeks, big eyes, and teeth of a most odious whiteness . . . and they have such masculine feet, as actually serve *some* for walking!" In Paulding's opening number on this theme, "Mustapha" describes the beauty of the "infidel" women of New York and expresses astonishment at a statistic attributing to one in five of them the existence of a soul, which in his culture is "a monstrous superfluity" for the gentler sex. Some are known to "usurp the breeches," or wear the pants, in the family, and "actually swear!"[21]

The next time Mustapha appears, he descends from the pen of William Irving and describes the government of the United States as a "LOGOCRACY"—a celebrated neologism traditionally awarded to brother Washington, who famously refused to allow words to police him. So it was, in fact, Williamcum-Mustapha who came up with the idea that America's "government of words" (the Greek *logos* means "word") nurtured an at once verbose and militant citizenry: "The country is intirely defended *vi et lingua*, that is to say, by *force of tongues*." Each town has its martial "SLANG-WHANGERS," Mustapha notes, editors by trade, "talking desperados" who conduct a nonstop war of words.[22]

When Mustapha returned two months later, Washington Irving took a crack at the persona. In his hands, the character of Jeffersonian democracy is extended. "The deep shadows of midnight gather around me," Mustapha opens, "and nothing disturbs the holy silence of the hour, save the sound of distant drums, mingled with the shouts, the bawlings, the discordant revelry of his majesty, the sovereign mob." Irving is a brash critic, and he adds something rhythmic to his prose when he tosses out references to "the puffers, the bawlers, the babblers, and the *slang-whangers*"—newspaper editors—"coolly bathing their pens in ink, and rioting in the slaughter of their thousands." Irving's Mustapha finally explains his excitement: "I have seen the great political puppet-show—An ELECTION."

Irving's intent was to show how Jefferson's vaunted democratization could be expected to do little for the republic but enfranchise those unfit to take part in the political process. He had chosen his immediate subject for good reason. Over the first days of May 1807, his New York readers had witnessed just such an election. A number of seats in the New York State Assembly were up for grabs. Josiah Ogden Hoffman was among the contenders, but he—and all the sensible Federalists who ran—went down in defeat. The election-day circus provokes a lively train of words. We witness the difference between the colorful Washington Irving and his two *Salmagundi* colleagues: He does not use a laconic sentence anywhere, and rarely a straightforward one.

An election is the grand trial of strength, the decisive battle when the Belligerents draw out their forces in martial array; when every leader burning with warlike ardour, and encouraged by the shouts and acclamations of tatterdemalians, buffoons, dependents, parasites, toad-eaters, scrubs, vagrants, mumpers, ragamuffins, bravoes and beggars, in his rear, and puffed up by his bellows-blowing slang-whangers, waves gallantly the banners of faction, and presses forward TO OFFICE AND IMMORTALITY!

Writers at this time let their imaginations wander only so far, preferring to hug something solid. But in Irving's style there is already something less forced—or, better said, something pliable, something comparatively unstructured. He has a knack for the absurd. Although he does not digress as far as Sterne does, he certainly tilts in Sterne's direction. It was for Irving, perhaps, as Sterne wrote self-reflectively in *A Sentimental Journey:* "I think there is a fatality in it—I seldom go to the place I set out for."[23]

Irving gave a separate account of the election to a young female acquaintance who had captured his interest during the season when *Salmagundi* was in full production. "We have toiled through the purgatory of an Election," he wrote to Mary Fairlie, whom he fictionalized in *Salmagundi* as "Sophie Sparkle." Lamenting the Federalists' defeat, he explained: "I was as deep in mud & politics as ever a moderate gentleman would wish to be—and I drank beer with the demagogues, and I shook hands with the mob—whom my heart abhorreth."

He had not wanted, had not intended, to descend to the level of the democratic mass. Why would he? But an unexpected rain had driven him indoors, and his chance selection of an old book in a barroom kept him reading in one place, until there he was, in company with some like-minded fellows. They had taken to drinking. And before the storytelling New Yorker knew what was happening, it was as though he were back in Oswegatchie, or Montreal, listening to hardened veterans of the fur trade spin their tales of Indian country. And he had become one with them. Or perhaps he was reliving his encounter with pirates of the Mediterranean, but was no longer the "dude" he had been in their presence. "Oh my friend," he affected the men's swagger, "I have been in such holes & corners—such filthy nooks and filthy corners, sweep offices & oyster cellars!"

He next found himself in the company of a group of blacks because they supported ("by some unaccountable freak") the same Federalists he embraced. "Truly, this serving ones country is a nauseous piece of business," he wrote irreverently to Mary Fairlie. The superior-feeling young Federalist had to poke fun at his own ordinariness in succumbing to the common emotions of a committed citizen of the republic.[24]

However it be said, Irving remained a proud New Yorker. The "antient and venerable city of *Gotham,*" he wrote in the pages of *Salmagundi,* was "renowned and delectable . . . this best of all possible cities." He insisted that his stories would be safe in the hands of "the wise men of Gotham," for theirs was a town filled with curiosity and curiosity-seeking souls.[25]

★ ★

At the time of the May city elections, the first half of the *Salmagundi* essays had gone to press. Out of the blue, Irving was dispatched to Richmond, Virginia, to attend the treason trial of Gotham's own Aaron Burr. Peter Irving was by now in Europe, exploring the tracks laid by his younger brother (foregoing Sicily, and adding Scotland to his itinerary). Whether Peter's timely absence was meant to make his appearance as a witness (or worse, as a suspect) impossible, we cannot know.[26] At any rate, the younger brother's presence in Richmond was meant to be supportive. The Federalist-leaning Washington Irving, in this odd instance, was far more likely to sympathize with the former Republican vice president than would any Republican friend of the Jefferson administration.

In the three years since his defeat in the New York gubernatorial election, after the Hamilton duel, and after his removal from the national ticket, Burr had explored his options in the West. He was Colonel Aaron Burr, after all, who had seen action on the Canadian frontier, and in Manhattan, during the American Revolution. Encouraged by the commander of the U.S. Army, General James Wilkinson, who was based in New Orleans, he visited with such energetic expansionists as the still untested Tennessee militia general Andrew Jackson; they met up in 1805 and again in 1806, and discussed in more than theoretical terms what means might present themselves to rid frontier Americans of perceived threats from the remnants of Spanish imperial power and a resurgent Napoleonic military interest in the Southwest. To men like Burr and Jackson, the decidedly unmartial President Jefferson was not preparing adequately for likely contingencies, and stout-hearted men were needed to step in. Mexico awaited these determined invaders.

Something happened to undermine Burr's plan of readiness—or, if we call it what it really was, a general plan for direct action in the event of the armed conflict many expected. The collaborator who was closest to the theater of operations, General Wilkinson, got cold feet and betrayed Burr by exposing the "plot" to seize Spanish territory. Irving's old friend, the blond, good-looking Lad of Kilkenny Sam Swartwout, was a prominent pawn in the midst of Wilkinson's turnabout; because Swartwout knew too much, Wilkinson ordered him arrested as a courier from Burr who supposedly bore a coded letter, and, with it, treasonous intent. Swartwout was placed in military custody, identified by Jefferson as one of the "principal emissaries of Mr. Burr," and sent to Washington, where he narrowly escaped being prosecuted along with Burr. It has been said that Swartwout's fine physiognomy and innocent appearance contributed to his being exonerated, much as it had saved the accused murderer Levi Weeks in New York. One of Swartwout's supporters, arguing his case before the U.S. Supreme Court, was Francis Scott Key.[27]

General Wilkinson was a notoriously unsavory character with a long history of playing both sides of the street—accepting money from Spanish authorities while holding positions awarded by Washington. He now pretended that Burr was an independent actor, a singular conspirator, and a traitor to his country. Jackson, who had long detested Wilkinson, held his tongue for the moment, but covered his own tracks. He declared his obedience to the Jefferson administration and his surprise that Burr was not what he said he was: an emissary from Washington, or if not quite that, then at least acting with the government's acquiescence."[28]

Early in 1807, President Jefferson pounced: He issued a dramatic proclamation that all but designated his former vice president a traitor. The move smacked of politicking, insofar as Jefferson himself, as well as Secretary of State Madison, knew of the westerners' impulse to seek out more land for America, even if it meant crossing boundaries—previous statements showed them condoning such a posture. But somehow, with the no-longer-trusted Burr involved, the meaning of the transgression changed. Jefferson was orchestrating Burr's life-or-death examination before the public, and prompting his prosecution in a federal court.[29]

Irving reserved comment on the upcoming trial. En route, he paused for several days in Baltimore, Washington, and Fredericksburg, where he wrote to Mary Fairlie of his first impressions of America below the Mason-Dixon line: "The land famous for grog drinking, horse racing and cockfighting; where every man is a colonel or a captain or a Negro, the first title conferred on every man who has killed a rattle snake." As for the nation's capital: "The only great personages I saw there were two Jackasses in a field, kicking at each other." This he equated with "metempsychosis," the passing of one soul (the politician's) into another being (the jackass). The young satirist was still at it.[30]

In Williamsburg, he visited with Joseph Cabell, the Virginia comrade who had shared in his European adventures. Cabell had just recently married an heiress. "He laughed much at my rapid way of courting," Cabell wrote of Irving to a close friend, President Jefferson's personal secretary, Isaac Coles. In that Irving and he had apparently exchanged racy letters, and Irving had seen close up Cabell's methods of entrancing women just a year before, in the backseat of a French stagecoach, the newlywed joked about the conversation they were having now: "'Well, said I, Irving, did you burn my letters, as I requested.' 'Oh, said he, they have gone up the chimney long ago!'" He added of his former traveling companion: "He is a fine little fellow."

As a worldly young Virginian, and now a proper husband, Cabell was also, curiously enough, a member of the grand jury deliberating over Burr's fate.

He would sit in judgment as Sam Swartwout, to whom Irving had introduced him in New York, testified on Burr's behalf, and convinced Cabell, as he convinced others, that General Wilkinson had unfairly maligned them both. Officially, Irving was still a lawyer, having been hired, nephew Pierre Irving tells us, "on an informal retainer from one of the friends of Colonel Burr." Fortunately for Irving, he was not placed in the awkward position of his friend Cabell; for his legal knowledge was minimal, his trial experience nonexistent. The assistance he was meant to provide the defendant was as a skilled writer.[31]

Burr's trial began on May 22, and continued in spurts throughout the summer. All were waiting for the government's chief witness to arrive in Richmond—the morally suspect Wilkinson, whose pomposity matched his girth. The dilatory general kept everyone in suspense—attorneys, the grand jury— as he took his own good time traveling up from New Orleans to testify.

Irving outlined the comic dimension of the scene in a letter to his mentor's wife, Maria Hoffman: "We are now enjoying a kind of suspension of hostilities; the grand jury having been dismissed the day before yesterday for five or six days, that they might go home, see their wives, get their clothes washed, and flog their negroes." He worried about the personal expenses that Burr, who was not a rich man, would be facing as a result of the drawn-out affair. To Irving's mind, the very idea of putting Burr on trial was absurd; he envisioned the principals coming to their senses—or else "a most farcical termination" to the trial.[32]

Wilkinson finally did arrive, in the third week of June, to the accompaniment of more satire. Burr's accuser may have been commander of the U.S. Army, but he in no way overpowered the man he had come to charge. "He still maintains his ground," Irving reported of Burr, in a letter to James Paulding. Remembering Burr as a great New York lawyer, he added that though the tables had turned, he "enters the Court every morning with the same serene and placid air that he would show were he brought there to plead another man's cause, and not his own." The only description history has of the two adversaries' encounter in the courtroom is that crafted by Washington Irving. It gives us a precious caricature of Wilkinson and insight into the comportment of Aaron Burr, of whom history has painted but few, and mainly corrupted, pictures:

> Wilkinson strutted into Court, and took his stand in a parallel line with Burr on his right hand. Here he stood for a moment swelling like a turkey cock, and bracing himself for the encounter with Burr's eye. The latter did not

take any notice of him until the judge directed the clerk to swear in Gen. Wilkinson; at the mention of the name Burr turned his head, looked him full in the face with one of his piercing regards, swept his eye over his whole person from head to foot, as if to scan its dimensions, and then coolly resumed his former position, and went on conversing with his counsel as tranquilly as ever. The whole look was over in an instant; but it was an admirable one. There was no appearance of study or constraint in it; no affectation of disdain or defiance; a slight expression of contempt played over his countenance, such as you would show on regarding any person to whom you were indifferent, but whom you considered mean and contemptible.[33]

It was a look made for the stage. As theater critic, Irving commended the performer. Burr had just demonstrated a mark of distinction, in Irving's eyes, that instantaneously deflated Wilkinson's ballooning air of self-importance.

The foreman of the grand jury, the eccentric Congressman John Randolph of Virginia, called the oversized Wilkinson a "mammoth of iniquity," and noted privately that he didn't think the guilt of Wilkinson would prove the innocence of Burr, nor that the guilt of Burr would prove the innocence of Wilkinson. Irving watched as the duplicitous general explained his reasons for doctoring the letters that would have exposed his central role in the scheme he wanted to convince the jury he had no prior knowledge of—precipitating a war with Spain for the benefit of land-hungry American settlers.

The lawyers battled. The government suggested that Burr was a vile seducer, a man who lied to raise funds and gain conscripts for a quixotic plan. The defense insisted that Burr was "a persecuted patriot," and that the president should be subpoenaed for relevant documents. Both sides hurled invectives. Jefferson's eyes and ears in Richmond, District Attorney George Hay, acknowledged of Burr: "He takes every advantage, denies every position advanced in the prosecution, acquiesces in no decision . . . and while he boldly asserts his innocence, adopts every measure within his power to bar the door to an inquiry."[34]

Yet as strong as Burr appeared to many, when Irving visited him in his jail cell, set on an isolated hill outside Richmond, he saw and sensed something else—something that would stay with him for some time to come. Without judging the defendant's innocence or guilt, he noted how far Burr had fallen. "The last time I saw Burr," he wrote in early July, after leaving Richmond and heading north, "he was then in the Penetentiary—a kind of State Prison. The only reason given for immuring him in his abode of Theieves—Cut throats & incendiaries was that it would save the United States *a couple of hundred dol-*

lars (the charge of guarding him in his lodgings)." Irving was granted admittance after some difficulty, and then was allowed only a brief visit. "Strange measures these!" he protested. And then this:

> Burr seemed in lower spirits than formerly[.] he was composed & collected as usual; but there was not the same cheerfulness that I have hitherto remarked. . . . He had a bad cold which I supposed was occasioned by the dampness of his chamber which had been lately white-washed. I bid him farewell with a heavy heart, and he expressed with peculiar warmth and feeling, his sense of the interest I had taken in his fate—I never felt in a more melancholy mood than when I rode from his solitary prison—such is the last interview I had with poor Burr—and I shall never forget it.[35]

Jefferson was cold-blooded in his consideration of the case. He saw Wilkinson as truthful only because doing so accorded with his deep desire to prosecute Burr. He knew at the same time that the Federalist-dominated judiciary wanted to deny him satisfaction. Indeed, the presiding judge, Supreme Court Chief Justice John Marshall, was as fixated on limiting the president's authority as the president was on weakening the chief justice. District Attorney Hay told Jefferson that the chief justice could be seen gazing at the defendant "with an expression of sympathy & sorrow, as strong as the human countenance can exhibit without *palpable* emotion." In the end, Burr was found not guilty because Marshall had defined treason too narrowly for Jefferson's taste, and the government could not prove its case.[36]

☆   ☆

Irving stayed in Richmond long enough to see the wheels of justice turn, and stall, but he arrived home well before the trial finished. En route, he stopped in Washington, D.C., where Joseph Cabell's friend Isaac Coles, the presidential secretary, provided him with a personal introduction to Thomas Jefferson. Coles soon after complained to Cabell that he did not like the company Irving kept, namely the Burrite Samuel Swartwout. Irving, for his part, left no record of his moment with the third president of the United States.[37]

Back in New York in time for the distribution of the last several numbers of *Salmagundi*, Irving momentously wrote for the eighteenth, published in November 1807, what is today a largely unknown piece: "The Little Man in Black." It is a touching parable, like Paulding's "Mine Uncle John," set in a dreamy past, as "Rip Van Winkle" and "The Legend of Sleepy Hollow" later would be. In the story, a "little village" is "thrown into a grand turmoil" by the appearance of a "mysterious individual." The unnamed "little black looking man" takes up residence in an old building that has the reputation of being haunted, which adds to his discomforting aura. He seeks to remain above the talk and "broils" of the village and seems "lost in meditation."

The people of the village naturally want to see into the unknowable man, to figure him out. Frustrated, they rationalize that he must be bad. Every reader sees what is coming: The little man alienates the younger generation because he does not take part in their "sports." The old are suspicious because he does not practice a trade. Seemingly oblivious, he continues to keep his secrets to himself. And so, as rumor enlarges, the little man is branded a *"witch*—a race of beings at that time abounding in those parts." Irving reminds his reader of human nature: "Suspicion, when once afloat, goes with wind and tide, and soon becomes certainty." Villagers now avoid the little man and refuse to pass by his door.

One winter's night, alerted to a dog's cry, the narrator's grandfather somehow finds himself at the home of the little man. He holds back at first, then overcomes his fear of witchcraft and enters the "desolate abode." He finds the "harmless stranger" in his bed, eyes sunken and sad, and without a fire to warm him, and recognizes that the outcast man is dying of hunger. So he bids a servant go for food, and sits compassionately beside the bed. It is too late, of course. As a final act, the little man presents him with rare volumes constituting the collected wisdom of a certain philosopher: "In me you behold the last descendent of the renowned Linkum Fidelius!" the little man pronounces. The reader and narrator mourn together the "last tear" shed by the lonely little man.[38]

As a story of man's inhumanity to man, and a guide to compassionate behavior, "The Little Man in Black" succeeds. Most readers must have figured that they knew who the subject of the story was. If not a precise depiction of Aaron Burr, he is part Burr and part Irving's imagination. The discredited former vice president, though five foot six inches tall, the same height as Hamilton, and a bit taller than "Little Madison," was often referred to as "Little Burr" in the newspapers. "As to little B," Irving wrote to Gouverneur Kemble from Richmond, "he bears his misfortunes without the least depression." Like the character in Irving's story, Burr had fallen on hard times; he was persecuted, his essential nature commonly misjudged.[39]

Irving had stood witness, as the mysterious man—as the talented Burr would be labeled, without ever contesting the label—was made an outcast by a violent and vindictive society. Though Irving repeatedly claimed not to be as comfortable with Burr's political creed as he was with Federalist society, he certainly spent considerable energy over the years advancing Burr's interests, and feeling Burr's pain. Burr, meanwhile, bore up well in spite of everything, and endured. After the Richmond trial, he accepted an exile in Europe lasting several years, after which time he would return to New York and take up the practice of law.

Even so, Irving was prescient. In an 1825 account, fed to a New York newspaper and used as "filler," some young lawyers on a steamboat heading up the Hudson were engaged in conversation about a pending case. Within earshot was a man wearing a broad-brimmed hat, old-fashioned boots, and "a coat considerably worn," which suggested to them that he might be an upstate farmer. As the stranger revealed "a halo of genius" and proceeded to resolve their legal argument, they stared back in "silent wonder." The article concludes: "All eyes were fixed on the extraordinary stranger—all were desirous to know his name. Inquiry was made—and reader! that stranger was *Aaron Burr.*"[40]

The newspaper could just as well have said of the passenger with the penetrating eye: "That stranger was The Little Man in Black." Although he lived to be eighty, Aaron Burr never erased the mysterious and suspect character with which his political generation determined to brand him.[41]

★   ★

As absorbing as the Burr trial was for American newspaper readers, and New Yorkers especially, in the middle of *Salmagundi*'s run, Washington Irving kept coming back to the inconstancy of his own life. Just a week before "The Little Man in Black" appeared, he was writing sophomorically to the teenager Ann Hoffman about their friends' romantic escapades: "Take warning all ye flinty damsels who, making a business of breaking the hearts of Simple brainless Soft headed young gentlemen . . ." He boasted to her of another two- or three-day gathering of the Lads of Kilkenny at Gouverneur Kemble's New Jersey mansion, where "great devastation" had ensued. This was a fantasy life he did not wish, at twenty-four, to let go of; and then again, perhaps he was simply attempting to escape the vagaries of politics, which provided little satisfaction.[42]

Salmagundi's twenty numbers, recounting the Cocklofts and their world, cannot be read anymore without proper annotation, given the collection's responsiveness to local gossip and issues of momentary concern to the life of the city and the nation—a critique of politics in New York during Jefferson's second term. The fictional Cocklofts caricatured the real Livingstons, and the rival Clintonians were shown as faithless. Their leader, DeWitt Clinton, mayor of New York from 1803 to 1807, possessed unlimited ambition. To temper Clinton, Governor Morgan Lewis, who had defeated Burr (and who was married to a Livingston), replaced Clinton at City Hall with Marinus Willett, a longtime Burrite. This was the political world that the Irving brothers knew, navigated, and that the youngest Irving loathed.[43]

Salmagundi was an ongoing conversation. Many of the essays took swipes at rival editors, Federalist and Jeffersonian, who disparaged the popular series out of jealousy. *Salmagundi* was, without declaring itself so, a Burrite reading of the times. And in this vein, it is worth noting that the most biting personal attacks were those authored by Paulding and William Irving, the more ardent Burrites, and not Washington Irving, whose fun-loving portrait of "Launcelot Langstaff" (Morgan Lewis) in *Salmagundi* no. 8 is temperate and even a little sympathetic.

In Irving's hands, Langstaff/Lewis is a man of "unquestionable veracity," whom Irving decides to paint as a bachelor. He is "exceedingly proud of his personal independence." His "single blessedness" is his political independence, which is easier to profess than to maintain; and so he must bear responsibility for the "mischievous vivacity of his fancy." Irving ends his piece on Lewis by noting that "his are the whim-whams of a courteous gentleman."[44]

In addition to its local political flavor, *Salmagundi* must be read with an eye toward the tradition it comes out of—a style of criticism tied to *Spectator*, and a brand of comic portraiture tied to Sterne, Fielding, and Goldsmith, the last of whom, not coincidentally, included a mysterious character in his *Citizen of the World* called "the man in black."[45] Because the tripartite comic anthology of Paulding and William and Washington Irving was truly a collaborative effort, we cannot know the full extent of the younger Irving's contributions. Those essays containing elements that resonate with his distinct and identifiable style are the ones discussed at length above. In other instances, he may have read and advised, or helped to edit; and we must presume that during his time in Richmond he contributed little.[46]

The publisher of *Salmagundi* was David Longworth, who had been publishing the City Directory for years, and had authored a sensational pamphlet on the Levi Weeks trial. He was an integral part of the original plan for *Salmagundi*—in fact, he was the one who profited most on the shared venture. Though not a writer on the order of Irving or Paulding, "Dusky" had a bit of the joker in him: He had named his bookstore "The Sentimental Epicure's Ordinary," combining incongruous ideas of sentimentality, luxurious living, and drinking.[47] But whatever manner of man he was, he owned enough business sense to take out the copyright on *Salmagundi* in March 1807. Acting as printer-publisher of the series, he saw after the first six weeks, as word spread and sales multiplied, that it would be pointless not to make out on the project. Having professed the same "sublime contempt" for money as the three authors in a prefatory "Publisher's Notice" (appearing at the beginning of the introductory number), Longworth simply had a change of heart. Irving, not realizing what was happening, wrote to Paulding from Richmond two months later asking what arrangements had been made between Longworth and the authors. "I shall stand much in need of a little sum of money on my return," he had said. The authors came to agreement with their publisher, and then went on to other things; Longworth continued to publish reprints of *Salmagundi* for as long as he held the copyright.[48]

Thanks in large measure to Washington Irving and James Kirke Paulding, New York literary culture was beginning to interest more people from more distant places. Its having produced such peculiar, pungent prose added to the city's growing reputation as the major entrepôt for trade and finance in the United States. Irving's next project, just around the corner, promised to give his native city even greater exposure. In fact, his satiric masterpiece *Knickerbocker's History of New York* would catapult him so far above his *Salmagundi* partners that it would be *his* association with the earlier series alone that would sustain the work as an object of literary curiosity.[49] And *his* New York would become known as Knickerbocker New York.

CHAPTER 4

Meet Diedrich Knickerbocker

1808–1809

I am none of those cynics who despise the world, because it despises them: on the contrary, though but low in its regard, I look up to it with the most perfect good-nature, and my only sorrow is, that it does not prove itself more worthy than the unbounded love I bear it.

—Washington Irving, from the final page of
A History of New York, 1809

Thus what was levity, scandal called by a harsher name.

—Oliver Goldsmith, from *The Vicar of Wakefield,* 1766

IRVING OFFICIALLY RESIDED WITH HIS MOTHER ON William Street, but he was spending more time on Greenwich Street, near the Hudson, where his brother William and his friend Paulding and the Hoffmans, his surrogate family, all lived. Tree-lined Greenwich Street was "a fashionable drive," according to one nineteenth-century chronicler. It had been carved out by 1760 as the road to Greenwich (later called "Greenwich Village"). It was the one thoroughfare on the West Side with a significant number of private houses on it before the Revolution—thus the "river-side drive" was known in winter to be "all a-jingle with the bells of sleighs." Signs of the city's growth northward were felt along Greenwich Street perhaps more than anywhere else; after 1794, when Aaron Burr purchased the estate of Richmond Hill, located west of Macdougal Street and extending south to Canal,

Greenwich itself became more attractive. Burr still owned the property on the day he shot Alexander Hamilton.[1]

In the first decade of the nineteenth century, Manhattan's population was double that at war's end, and some seven hundred structures were going up each year. Greenwich Street between Liberty and Chambers was where shoemakers, tailors, butchers, grocers, and watchmakers earned their keep; this was also where James Woods ran a tin and hardware store and Nicholas Lozier practiced medicine.[2] William Irving, Jr., and his growing family resided a block or so north of the infamous boardinghouse where Elma Sands and Levi Weeks had once kept company. The Hoffmans lived south of here, nearer to the stylish homes that extended from Battery Park. They also owned a summer home across the East River at Ravenswood, just below the dangerous waters of Hellgate, where the East River meets the Long Island Sound—today's Astoria, Queens. Here Irving sometimes tied up Henry Brevoort's sailboat, the *Tinker*, and conveniently ferried himself to and from Manhattan.[3]

At the Hoffman home, Irving made known his fondness for the dark-haired Matilda, who was sixteen when *Salmagundi* began circulating. Sixteen was not too young to make important life decisions in the early 1800s. Irving had begun tutoring Matilda in drawing when she was thirteen; later, he read poetry to her, and tried to convey his serious side. And though Matilda's elder sister Ann was the more beautiful, Irving's heart was drawn to the one he called a "timid, shy, silent little being." Over time, and after his long sojourn in Europe, their bond intensified. He was, as he reflected in an undated fragment written many years later, "excessively attached"—yes, he "idolized" her, and by all indications wanted Matilda Hoffman, someday, to be his wife. Josiah Ogden Hoffman would have been pleased; he would eventually have made Irving his law partner even though the younger man admitted to "an insuperable repugnance" for legal studies.[4]

Irving had drawn closer to Henry Brevoort, sometimes referred to by his Kilkenny nickname of "Nuncle," who was now a business associate of John Jacob Astor in the ever profitable fur trade. In the spring of 1808, Irving twisted brother Peter's arm to keep him company on a trip to Montreal, where he arranged to meet up with Brevoort. (He returned home on Robert Fulton's steamboat.) Also, as his literary reputation enlarged, Irving wrote of himself, somewhat facetiously, as a "hero of the tea table," and a regular at parties where he took a willing and able part in social dancing.[5]

Rebecca Gratz was the cultured and captivating daughter of a wealthy Jewish merchant in Philadelphia, an often-heralded beauty and the close friend of Maria Fenno Hoffman. It was at the Hoffmans' that Irving first met her.

When he visited Philadelphia, he lodged at the Gratz home, delighting Rebecca, two years his senior and a devotee of English literature, with his uncommon wit. She, in turn, became taken with Maria's stepdaughter Matilda, who occupied Washington's affections. The outgoing Washington and the engaging Rebecca were fond tea-table companions, warm friends who maintained correct relations. In one letter to Maria, Rebecca expressed her concern for his spirits: "What is the matter with your favorite Washington? I heard he was dejected and in bad health. 'Does he pine in seclusion and let the queen of yellow melancholy prey on his cheek?' . . . I should be the first among his lamenting friends if any serious calamity befell him."[6]

So the gossipy writer from Manhattan flitted here and there, enjoying society as he found it; but he kept returning to the Hoffmans, who had moved again, this time closer to the island's southern tip. Irving was unfocused during the fall of 1808; he was getting by on his charm, and on his clever constructions. Everyone seemed to be enabling his writing vocation.

Yet he was not to be allowed entire ease. A season of deaths diverted his thoughts, beginning with that of his sister Nancy, of Johnstown, who was thirty-eight; and then his seventy-six-year-old father died. Fortunately for his mother, Sarah, several nearby sons made sure she was cared for. But Washington was unprepared for what happened next: His precious Matilda died in April 1809. He was devastated.

As Matilda lost strength that winter, Irving had been at her bedside. She succumbed to tuberculosis before her eighteenth birthday. "I saw her fade rapidly away," he later wrote, "beautiful and more beautiful and more angelical to the very last. . . . I was the last one she looked upon." He retained her Bible and prayer book as keepsakes; these artifacts were close at hand, even in late life. Similarly distraught was Matilda's nineteen-year-old sister Anne, who married the same year and gave birth the following to a daughter she named Matilda. Rebecca Gratz wrote to her friend Maria Hoffman: "The fatal news has just reached us—and our tears mingle with yours over the early grave of our Beloved Matilda, . . . having from her birth indications that the fragile form would soon yield to the power of death."[7]

Irving spent two months trying to mourn in his own way, and to clear his head. The spring of 1809 found him at Kinderhook, New York, one of the earliest Dutch-American settlements, 125 miles north of Manhattan along the Hudson. (In Dutch, the town's name translates as "Children's Corner.") Here Irving resided with the family of William Peter Van Ness, a prominent Burrite, whose estate later became the main residence of another native son of Kinderhook, Martin Van Buren. Irving was thankful to have this "little empire" at his disposal.

Here, too, he took delight in the company of a particular friend of the Van Nesses, "a schoolmaster who teaches the neighborhood—a pleasant good natured fellow," Irving told Brevoort, "with much native, unimproved shrewdness and considerable humour." His new, talkative companion, one year his junior, was Jesse Merwin, whom Irving would later immortalize as "Ichabod Crane."[8]

In June, Irving returned to Manhattan. He was "in better humour with all around him," as he self-diagnosed. He had his portrait painted by John Wesley Jarvis, a young artist who had captured Thomas Paine not long before, and would paint the likeness of many a New York personality. Jarvis's Irving is notable for the dark, sensitive eyes—for a face that bespeaks a quiet intensity (see frontispiece).[9]

For some months now, Washington Irving had been piecing together a mock history containing a stock of wholesome political satire. It must have seemed to him a fit successor to *Salmagundi,* and a way to release more of the nervous energy he had generated in observing the world around him. The new work, a portrait of Jeffersonian America seen through Irving's eyes as New York writ large, was a burlesque, the most meaningful form political writing took in these years.[10]

★   ★

A History of New York, which came to be called as often *Knickerbocker's History,* did not emerge easily—it slowly evolved. As with *Salmagundi* and "Jonathan Oldstyle" that had preceded it, the *History* was largely composed at the old William Street home. In its genesis, it was a joint production of Washington and Peter Irving, a response to the erudite *Picture of New-York,* published in 1807 by the esteemed (and perhaps overly self-satisfied, in the minds of the Irvings) Dr. Samuel L. Mitchill, Columbia medical professor, founding editor of the prestigious *New York Medical Repository,* and United States senator.

When the older Irving brothers attended Columbia, the school's greatest booster was the restless Mitchill, who variously assumed the roles of professor, physician, politician, botanist, geologist, mineralogist, and city historian. His *Picture of New-York* describes Manhattan's rock formations, water currents, and the "fitness" of its natural port. It lays out the laws of the city that had passed since 1787, namely, fines assessed for the destruction of trees; the quantity of gunpowder permitted to be stored in any given place; the means of organizing to fight fires; rules for the inspection of beef and pork; and other fine points of daily life that might appear to some as superfluous intelligence: "Butter must be sold by the pound, and not by the roll or tub." Mitchill craved detail. He jumped at statistics. The two Irvings must have begun their project by joking with one another about this overly serious author's unconcealed pride.[11]

As a Columbia-trained physician, Peter obviously knew Dr. Mitchill. There was no more distinguished person in the entire city. But Peter had no second thoughts about satirizing him. Who, then, was the prime instigator of their work? Was it Washington, always trying to deny his political heart, while able to turn out a satirical product with apparent ease? Or the much older Peter, who had known Mitchill longer and better, but who was supposed "too nice" to launch political attacks? It is hard to say for certain.

At this early stage, while Peter and he were writing down their ideas somewhat roughly, Washington made yet another trip to Montreal. As his nephew Pierre vaguely notes, he was conducting business "for a commercial house in New York," apparently not his own family's business. When he returned, though, to his surprise and dismay, he learned that Peter had embarked for Liverpool without giving a return date. No one had consulted his erstwhile collaborator, Washington, who now did the only thing an inspired writer could: He completely reconceived the *History*, and made it into the masterpiece it probably could not have been if Peter had remained in New York. As Pierre explains, with refreshing honesty, "Peter had not the rich comic vein of Washington; and though his taste was pure and classic, it was a little too nice and fastidious not to have sometimes operated as a drawback upon the genial play of his brother's exuberant humor." Peter remained overseas for the next twenty-seven years.[12]

Consistent with the comic conspiracy present in its pages, *A History of New York* was finally brought to the attention of the public through a calculated piece of trickery. Irving induced his friends Paulding and Brevoort to submit a notice to William Coleman's (Federalist) *Evening Post*. When printed on October 26, 1809, it read as follows:

> *DISTRESSING*
>
> Left his lodgings some time since, and has not been heard of, a small elderly gentleman, dressed in an old black coat and cocked hat, by the name of KNICKERBOCKER. As there are some reasons for believing he is not entirely in his right mind, and as great anxiety is entertained about him, any information concerning him left at the Columbian Hotel, Mulberry street, or at the office of this paper, will be *thankfully* received.

We are left to assume that the editor, William Coleman, an Irving acquaintance, either did not know of the ruse or did not mind terribly when he found out.

Two weeks later a letter to the editor appeared in the same paper, signed by "A TRAVELLER." It suggested that a man fitting the description was seen along the road to Albany; he carried "a small bundle tied in a red bandana handkerchief; he appeared to be travelling northward, and was very much fatigued and exhausted." The plot thickened on November 16, when the landlord of the Mulberry Street hotel where Knickerbocker had lodged wrote in with an update: "Nothing satisfactory has been heard of the old gentleman since; but a *very curious kind of a written book* has been found in his room in his own handwriting." The landlord explained his intention of collecting Knickerbocker's unpaid rent. "Now I wish you to notice him [give him notice], if he is still alive, that if he does not return and pay off his bill, for board and lodging, I shall have to dispose of his Book, to satisfy me for the same." The ploy seemed to be working: A sympathetic New Yorker approached Jack Irving, in his capacity as a lawyer, suggesting that a reward be given to the individual who succeeded in finding the missing man.[13]

The actual author had kept the work secret to this point. He had secured as his publisher the partners Inskeep and Bradford: Inskeep operated the manufacturing end of their enterprise out of Philadelphia, and Bradford sold books at 128 Broadway, in New York. When *A History of New York* was released to the public on December 6, 1809, St. Nicholas Day, Irving's authorship could only be guessed at. St. Nicholas Day was a day on which some Dutch New Yorkers honored the patron saint sometimes referred to as "Sancte Claus." Irving had orchestrated everything perfectly.

The two-volume work was advertised as that "found in the chamber of Mr. Diedrich Knickerbocker," and "published in order to discharge certain debts he has left behind." Its insincere dedication to the as-yet-unproductive New-York Historical Society furthered the fiction that it was a legitimate historical product. The society, founded with the help of Dr. Samuel L. Mitchill, had recently awarded Irving a membership.[14]

As for "Diedrich Knickerbocker," there was a New York Federalist, native to the upper Hudson, named Herman Knickerbocker, who practiced law in Albany. He had entered Congress in March 1809. It appears that Irving did not know Congressman Knickerbocker personally but had simply borrowed his euphonic name. Over the years, they would become warm friends.[15] One must wonder, too, whether Irving ever chuckled in pronouncing the mock-Dutch historian's first name as it can be parsed in English, as one who had "died rich."

Knickerbocker's History would prove a widely read and lucrative book, persuading brothers Peter and Ebenezer that they should cut Washington in as a silent partner in their newly constituted mercantile business, P & E Irving, operating out of New York and Liverpool, where Peter now resided. The Irving family business had gone through permutations during Washington's early writing career: In 1803, William, Sr., and William, Jr., had founded Irving & Smith, on Pearl Street; Ebenezer, along with Jim Paulding's brother Nathaniel, had done well as wine merchants, wholesale and retail, on Front Street near the East River wharves, since 1801, and would remain partners for a few more years. Meanwhile, as a part of P & E Irving, brother Washington was to receive one-fifth of the profits, though he would have no duties other than to pursue his career as a writer.[16]

☆   ☆

With pseudoscientific pomp, *Knickerbocker's History* opens with an explanation of light and darkness. The narration drifts in concern from the earth to the sun as the reader is introduced to its first Dutch luminary, "Professor Von Poddingcoft (or Puddinghead, as the name may be rendered into English)." The good professor had demonstrated why the oceans do not spill into space by swinging a bucket of water around his head, the "ruby red visage" of which successfully stood in for the sun, thus demonstrating centrifugal force. He taught gravity with gravity, then, until an overeager student arrested his swinging arm and sent the "earth" into the "sun," generating new confusion about the fate of the heavenly sphere humans called home. It was Irving's opening salvo in his war against accepted wisdom and moral authority.

Going several steps beyond the all-encompassing natural history provided by Dr. Mitchill, without his academic authority (and thus, in Irving's fractured way of presenting "facts," with a legitimacy equal to *all* established authority), Knickerbocker assumes the mantle of the skeptical historian: "It has ever been the task of one race of philosophers to demolish the work of their predecessors, and elevate more splendid fantasies in their stead, which in their turn are demolished and replaced by the air-castles of a succeeding generation." As a self-proclaimed chronicler of human folly, Irving quickly establishes himself as a parodist of all the historians of the world who have taken themselves too seriously.[17]

We move, then, from eternity to the Western Hemisphere. The America that is wrought by Knickerbocker grudgingly accepts the "vulgar opinion" that Columbus—"Christoval Colon, a Genoese"—should get credit for its discovery. Yet Irving as historian-proper demands a fuller explanation: If he "who has been clumsily nicknamed Columbus," gets credit, as tradition has it, then the land should properly be called "Colonia." Irving as historian-errant returns, and he is not quite ready to deliver over the country to his American, or Colonian, readers:

> Think you the first discoverers of this fair quarter of the globe had nothing to do but go on shore and find a country ready laid out and cultivated like a garden, wherein they might revel in their ease? No such thing: they had forests to cut down, underwood to grub up, marshes to drain, and savages to exterminate.

His is not the heroic model to which the founding generation subscribed. Texts that elevated and mythologized the formation of the Union already existed. Rationalizing the conquest of the Indians' country, these "ponderous tomes . . . so important to the happiness of society" (we may note Irving's bitter sarcasm), accomplished no more than to have left the question of justification obscure. Slowly we learn that "right and title" and "unsullied consciences" are too easily claimed by the first to enjoy a property. (This may be the only indication in any of his writings that Irving was a lawyer.) Because Indians exhibited only "barbarism" and "imbecility," rejecting decent clothes and decent money, they were considered "beneath the human character." Europeans who came to cultivate were invested with the rights of landownership, and those whose lives were "vagabond, disorderly, unrighteous" had no rights.[18]

It was early in American history for this kind of protest. Yet Irving exposed a flawed logic when he extended his radical diatribe: Because the aborigines were overly content with the little they had, they had no rights. Because they behaved with Christian charity and were "sober, frugal, continent, and faithful in their word," without knowledge of religion, they had no rights. But those who expropriated tribal lands gave the Indians "help" in the form of "rum, gin, brandy, and the other comforts of life" so that they might develop desires that could then remain unfulfilled—this was how the Indians were "improved," according to standard histories. As Book 1 ends, the reader is little humored, but deeply cautioned about the arrogance of power.

☆   ☆

We come to the founding of New York, and a very different perspective. Irving's Dutch settlers are not terribly hostile, nor are they by nature a superior people (indeed, a good many of Dutch heritage in 1809 resented the author's depiction of their ancestors as silly and impractical).[19] But because so much of New York's early history had been forgotten, they were clay to be molded by the author's hands.

Diedrich Knickerbocker is less haphazard than he appears. He wishes to restore to the senses something good, something genuine, that history has left behind. In spite of his ranting about frauds perpetrated by dignified historians and philosophers, he wants to believe—Irving wants to believe—that there is a better place to live than the present. Beginning right here, he will have fun with time—he will *displace* time—in order to take us to that lively place. He will do the same over and over during his career.

The complexity of Washington Irving's humor makes his *History* something more than mere whimsy. Scouring libraries, private and public, he pieced together the early- to mid-seventeenth century. He related to the Dutch who dominated the region from 1609 to 1664 because they came as merchants, seeking profit in fur trading, just as brother William and his best friend Brevoort had inclined toward; the Dutch settlers were part of an expanding maritime empire whose true vitality was lost once England seized control of the thirteen colonies' history.

Henry (or Hendrick) Hudson, "of whom we have heard so much, and know so little," had "learned to smoke tobacco under Sir Walter Raleigh." He was "a short, square, brawny old gentleman, with a double chin, a mastiff mouth and a broad copper nose, which was supposed in those days to have acquired its fiery hue from the constant neighborhood of his tobacco pipe." Wherever we look in Irving's tales, we can expect to encounter the long Dutch pipe as a kind of stage direction, its dream-inducing puffs of smoke meant to carry us to the place of suspended disbelief.

The year 1809 was the bicentennial of Hudson's famed voyage, which did not go unnoticed. Yet Irving's commodore was what we would call a hands-off manager, stocking up on "gin and sourcraut" and permitting his men to lounge at their posts "unless the wind blew." Accordingly, his vessel, the *Half Moon,* did not find a Northwest Passage to China, but did sight the island of "Mannahata," whose "hills of smiling green swelled gently, one above another, crowned with lofty trees of luxuriant growth." Hudson excited the people of Old Amsterdam to venture over, and the next boatload of colonists put down roots next to the New Jersey marshes, in Communipaw (variant of a lost Indian word). New York's sleepy "mother settlement" was as low-lying as any Dutch village, and is today's Jersey City. In Communipaw, no metropolis would ever develop; it was too easy a target for the English who might contemplate a raid; and so Communipaw's favorite philosopher-adventurer Oloffe Van Kortlandt, or "Oloffe the Dreamer," sought out "a new seat of empire."

The people of Communipaw were not ordinarily motivated to look beyond their fragrant pipes, but after sailing up the Hudson to the Tappan Zee, an uncertain scouting party returned amid swells and billows; they were scattered in the swirls of Hellgate, and finally shipwrecked on the east side of Manhattan. Here, Oloffe the Dreamer had his vision: "The good St. Nicholas came riding over the tops of the trees, in that self-same wagon wherein he brings his yearly presents to children." The Dutch patron saint (whose importance as a cultural symbol Irving had just begun to exploit) lit his pipe and smoked. As the clouds of smoke spread, he wordlessly indicated to Oloffe that the Dutch should "settle down and build the city here." The people of Communipaw, recognizing Oloffe's good sense, "pronounced him a most useful citizen and a right good man—when he was asleep." What we have here, in Oloffe's primordial Communipaw, is Rip Van Winkle in utero.[20]

The Dutch (in orthodox history, that is) not only wanted to take advantage of trading opportunities with the surrounding Indian tribes but also hoped to squeeze out the English. Thus began four decades of an on-and-off competition that would end in a relatively peaceful transition to English rule. First, Director-General Peter Minuit purchased the island of Manhattan, in 1625, and established "boweries," or farms, north of the core of settlement at the southern tip of the island, where the population numbered in the hundreds only, up to the mid-1640s. One twentieth-century historian perversely referred to Minuit as "a kind of early Dutch Aaron Burr, brilliant, unscrupulous, and embittered by dismissal from his post in New Amsterdam"—just the sort of false erudition Irving, as a skeptic of "great" historians, might have shaken his head over.[21]

Three individuals—three Dutch rulers of New Netherland—act out the plot of Irving's circus history. Before the proficient Pieter Stuyvesant could take charge for the last seventeen years leading to the English takeover, economy and diplomacy were in the hands of two other governors, Wouter Van Twiller and Wilhelm Kieft. Irving makes Van Twiller (his "Walter the Doubter") a habitually lazy man who presides over a "golden age," and Kieft ("William the Testy") a finicky, overeducated incompetent.

Though the real Wouter Van Twiller of seventeenth-century New Amsterdam was militant, impulsive, and ultimately fired for alcoholism and fraud,[22] Irving's Van Twiller is celebrated for his passivity and inaction, which makes his success all the more mystifying.

His face, that infallible index of the mind, presented a

vast expanse, unfurrowed by any of those lines and angles which disfigure the human countenance with what is termed expression. . . . His habits were as regular as his person. He daily took his four scheduled meals, appropriating exactly an hour to each; he smoked and doubted eight hours, and he slept the remaining twelve of the four-and-twenty. Such was the renowned Wouter Van Twiller—a true philosopher, for his mind was either elevated above, or tranquilly settled below, the cares and perplexities of this world.[23]

Van Twiller is Lao Tzu, and he is creating a Tao for the Dutch. Doing nothing, nothing is left undone. By investing "Walter the Doubter" with unimaginable achievement, Irving imagines a world where feelings of harmonious community are self-sustaining. It is the antithesis of American politics.

Jefferson's political creed centered on tapping the citizen's sense of neighborly commitment to attain "harmony and affection" in republican society. Thus, Irving could easily have made Wouter Van Twiller his Jefferson lookalike. But that would have been too sympathetic. He chose instead to portray the mild-mannered and philosophical Jefferson as Wilhelm Kieft, whose surname supposedly meant "*wrangler or scolder.*" Irving toyed with etymology so as to explain how the Kieft family's essential trait led to the governor's being "universally denominated William the Testy."[24]

There was a farcical resemblance, at least in physical appearance. Jefferson, in his mid-sixties, was more than six feet tall, rail thin, with small, grayish eyes; his face, red and sensitive to the sun, peeled easily. Irving's William the Testy was "a brisk, wiry, waspish little old gentleman . . . his cheeks were scorched into a dusky red, by two fiery little grey eyes." Both were inventors whose homes contained examples of ingenious tinkering—in William the Testy's case, "Dutch ovens that roasted meat without fire; carts that went before the horses." They were students of Latin and Greek, and knew just enough metaphysics to "confound." William was a man whose résumé looked impressive but whose performance as a stand-in for the president was pitifully ineffectual.[25]

In the *History*, William the Testy is full of projects, yet bound to be outwitted by the English enemy. He had created a society in which people were increasingly "meddlesome and factious." But he persisted in micromanaging. He noticed the appearance of "faction," and noted that factious people had pipes in their mouths; so he banned pipe smoking, oblivious to the fact that the New Nederlander lived and died by the pipe: "Take away his pipe? You might as well take away his nose!"[26]

Troubles followed. When war with the English seemed imminent, the governor did not beef up the armed forces; instead, he sent his men out "armed to teeth" with "powerful speeches." He was slow to realize that it was in the nature of the "Pilgrims," ever since Plymouth Rock, to expand; for they were "a people who are always seeking a better country than their own." William the Testy had to be replaced—it was the price he paid for his stubbornness in defending the land with "trumpeters and wind-mills."[27]

There is more to all this than meets the eye, of course. Irving's disparagement of Kieft's pronouncements (and Thomas "William the Testy" Jefferson's) is grounded in history. As to the first, a 1649 memorial to the Dutch government recounted the jurisdictional controversy with the English, and Kieft's ineffective warnings to the English settlements in Connecticut:

> Director Kieft has caused several protests to be drawn up, in Latin and in other languages, commanding them by virtue of his commissions from the Lords States General . . . to desist from their proceedings and usurpations. . . . But it was knocking at a deaf man's door, as they did not regard these protests or even take any notice of them.

The principal author of this memorial is presumed to have been Adriaen Van der Donck, an actual individual, whom Irving renders "the great historian Van der Donck"—the person generally credited for giving Manhattan its name. The 1649 memorial may well have been available to Irving, if not in the original, then gleaned from a secondary source.[28]

In Irving's *History*, however, Kieft's response to the "daring aggressions of the Yankees" is Jefferson's embargo threat against the British, which dominated the news in 1807–1808. Irving leads with the heading, "How William the Testy undertook to conquer by proclamation—How he was a great man abroad, but a little man in his own house." Nothing in *Knickerbocker's History* is quite so transparently political as this section of book 4.

"Testy"/Jefferson goes with his instincts. To show his mettle, the speech-wielding "potentate" (president) gathers the "burghers" (Congress) and explains to them the dire situation that the entire Dutch (U.S.) community faces. He presents his solution—not "an infernal machine" to combat the enemy on the ground but "an instrument in writing" instead. Irving has him place it before the committee:

> The burghers gazed at it for a time in silent awe, as a wary housewife does at a gun, fearful it may go off half-cocked. . . . The document in question was a

PROCLAMATION, ordering the Yankees to depart instantly from the territories of their High Mightinesses under pain of suffering all the forfeitures and punishments in such case made and provided. It was on the moral effect of this formidable instrument that Wilhelmus Kieft calculated.[29]

As Irving compiled his *History*, France and England were at war. Neither side respected American neutrality—U.S. vessels risked being sunk on the high seas. Aiming to "starve" the European belligerents, especially Great Britain, Jefferson issued a proclamation asserting the rights of neutrals. Then, at Jefferson's behest, the Republican majority in Congress passed a law forbidding *any* American vessel from carrying its cargo to or from *any* foreign port. Thus international commerce was shut down. To deter smuggling, no ship was permitted to sail even to an American port adjacent to Canada without the president's permission.

The embargo remained until Jefferson left office in 1809, but it had failed miserably. It appears that the Irving brothers were involved in some questionable money transactions to circumvent the embargo in the spring of 1808, when Washington traveled to Montreal—thus the author had a personal stake in what he was writing. Tensions were high along the frontiers, where customs agents and militias inspected and patrolled. From northern New York and Vermont, rafts carried prohibited exports to fellow conspirators in Montreal. Resistance was rife.[30]

Though he conventionally claimed he had no interest in political activism, Irving was annoyed. Jefferson's presidential style—not just his proclamations—irked him. Even before the embargo, even before Burr's trial, something visceral had caused one man of words to disparage an even more famous man of words. The ultimate source of Irving's consternation was that Jefferson apparently felt nothing for New York City.

The Irving brothers' livelihood was bound up in New York's commercial development. Irving had an especially strong commitment to the city's traditions, arts, and culture. Like other moderate Federalists, he distrusted Jefferson's republic; he saw much republican rhetoric but little true dignity. Jefferson the agrarian philosopher, the physiocrat, idealized farming as a vocation and lorded the small cultivator's morals over luxury industries and urban roughness; he disparaged urban American culture while ignoring the outward-looking spirit of enterprise Irving saw about him in New York City and among the respectable families he admired. (Not inconsequentially, the Dutch lacked the tradition of a landed elite; they supported instead a merchant oligarchy from city to city.)[31]

On another level, Irving's anxiety about Jefferson seems odd because Jefferson privileged (and romanticized) a rural idyll, as did Irving. But the Virginian's "tranquil permanent felicity" was a haven for brutish white slave owners, whereas Irving's idyll was the Hudson of his rambles—Kinderhook now, and Sleepy Hollow to come. Irving was not above making racist remarks—his letters contain many such references—but neither was he interested in making excuses for slave owners. If Jefferson appeared to have little feeling for New York, Irving had no feeling for the South. Because he found Jefferson remote, it was easy for him to target the Virginian in his satire.

As for General James Wilkinson, commander of all U.S. forces, Jefferson's ally, and Burr's chief accuser at the Richmond treason trial, Irving's *History* achieves a new height in comic portrayal. "General Jacobus von Poffenburgh," like Wilkinson, was "exceedingly round." But Irving was not just interested in an obvious jab at the general's girth; it was how to translate size into the capacity to blow wind: "Neither did his bulk proceed from his being fat, but windy; being blown up by a prodigious conviction of his own importance, until he resembled one of those bags of wind given by Aeolus, in an incredible fit of generosity, to that vagabond warrior." Von Poffenburgh had "risen to great importance" in the reign of Kieft, commanding "his whole disposable force."

One of Wilkinson's most notorious acts was the prosecution of Colonel Thomas Butler, a Revolutionary War hero and friend of Andrew Jackson's, who had refused to cut or "crop" his hair—the modest queue, reminiscent of Revolutionary days, that was, by the general's decree, no longer tolerated in the army. In one of his most memorable send-ups in the *History,* Irving ridicules the general's campaign against the queue. Referring first to Wilkinson, he writes:

> He was a disciplinarian, too, of the first order. Woe to any unlucky soldier who did not hold up his head and turn his toes when on parade. . . . Now so it happened, that among his officers was a sturdy veteran named Kelder-meester, who had cherished, through a long life, a mop of hair not a little resembling the shag of a Newfoundland dog, terminating in a queue like the handle of a frying pan.

The rest of Irving's vignette follows history closely. Hearing of the general's decision, the colorful veteran lets loose some "soldier-like oaths" and refuses to comply. He is arrested and tried for "mutiny, desertion and all the other list of offences noticed in the article of war. . . . His obstinacy remained unshaken to the very last moment, when he directed that he should be carried to his grave with his eel-skin queue sticking out of a hole in his coffin." The real Colonel Butler was court-martialed in 1805; he died that same year, presumably with his queue still in place. In his letter to James Paulding from Richmond, in 1807, Irving had already lambasted the self-important Wilkinson, who was "swelling like a turkey cock" when he entered the courtroom where Burr was on trial. As good as that description was, the thinly disguised portrait of 1809 was an improvement, and assuredly a salve for the many who recognized Wilkinson as the liar and blowhard he was. The inference, of course, was that President Jefferson was daft to take his general's word in the treason trial of the much-maligned Aaron Burr.[32]

☆   ☆

Despite Irving's reservations about Jeffersonian America, the *History* was not meant to be aggressive, or even half serious. It did not offer concrete solutions to the problems of Jefferson's second term. Furthermore, we need to understand the times: Irving's caricatures do not approach the nastiness of New York's partisan newspapers, which reprinted gossip and smeared without conscience.

Playing fast and loose with history, Irving comfortably models his Jefferson on a Dutch governor who was a city merchant (not a country planter) prior to his elevation. The worst Irving would say about Jefferson-as-Kieft was that he suffered from the politician's disease of artificiality—that his judgments suffered from an engagement with ideas instead of with people. His refusal to maintain a strong navy, his ruinous embargo, and his support for General Wilkinson all pointed to a lack of productivity, an unwillingness to waver from his preconceptions.[33]

Irving's treatment of Pieter Stuyvesant, the last of the Dutch governors, returns the narrative to its historical foundations and releases it from the age of Jefferson. As Knickerbocker explains, Stuyvesant was "the very reverse of his predecessors, being neither tranquil and inert, like Walter the Doubter, nor restless and fidgeting, like William the Testy; but a man, or rather a governor, of such uncommon activity and decision of mind, that he never sought nor accepted the advice of others." In Irving's treatment, he was called "Hardkoppig Piet; or Peter the Headstrong."[34]

The historical Stuyvesant, the only Dutch governor who is at all remembered (save for Irving's *History*), was plucked from the Dutch West Indies in 1647 to solve the crises of New Netherland. In his Caribbean post, he had been ordered to attack the Spanish island of St. Martin, during which engagement a cannonball shattered his right leg. He arrived in New Amsterdam complete with a wooden leg to match his hardheaded policies. He promptly issued city ordinances designed to clean and repair the streets, established speed limits for wagons and carts, personally managed all real estate transactions, and even established the acceptable sizes for loaves of bread. (Sometimes truth is stranger even than Irving's fiction.)

Stuyvesant's foreign policy initiatives were as determined as his domestic orders. In 1653, as word arose that New Englanders planned to attack Manhattan, the governor authorized the construction of a defensive wall at the town's northern limit—the modern Wall Street. Two years went by, Indian raids surprised Long Island, and Stuyvesant turned and attacked New Sweden, the small colony to the west of the Dutch settlement, in retaliation for the Swedes' documented interference with the activities of Dutch merchant traders. The Swedes surrendered without a struggle.

But Stuyvesant's troubles were far from over. In 1664, James, Duke of York, was given a royal patent on lands not just abutting those of the Dutch but running through parts of New Netherland. Since London was tired of dancing around the increasingly outnumbered Dutch, James, to claim his lands, brought an impressive fleet with him. Faced now with an overwhelming force, Stuyvesant prudently hesitated. Connecticut's John Winthrop, Jr., worked out a surrender that protected the commercial interests of the Dutch in New Amsterdam. And though they would hold fast to Dutch culture for some time to come, they soon found themselves members of an English polity known as New York.[35]

In Irving's comical retelling, the same train of events finds Stuyvesant sending General Von Poffenburgh into action against the Swedes. Re-employing the imagery he had used in his letter to Paulding to describe Wilkinson entering the Richmond courtroom, Irving tells us that the opposing generals try to "out-strut and out-swell each other like a couple of belligerent turkey cocks." Ultimately, though, a swarm of mosquitoes, "not a little resembling one of the plagues of Egypt," drive the Swedish leader out of his fortress. And rather than credit Von Poffenburgh, the Dutch people attribute victory to "the miraculous intervention of St. Nicholas."

But the Swedes are not done yet, and as such, a "hunger for martial glory" stirs up the bloodlust of the peg-legged veteran Peter the Headstrong. And so "the most horrible battle ever recorded in poetry or prose" comes to pass, as the Dutch forces charge forward under the call of "St. Nicholas and the Manhattoes!" This time, the Swedes fight fiercely:

And now commenced the horrid din, the desperate struggle, the maddening ferocity, the confusion and self-abandonment of war. Dutchman and Swede commingled, tugged, panted and blowed. The heavens were darkened with a tempest of missives. Bang! went the gun—whack! went the broad swords—thump! went the cudgels—crash! went the musket-stocks—blows—kicks—cuffs—scratches—black eyes and bloody noses, swelling the horrors of the scene!

In Irving's irreverent send-up of the Greek epic histories, "the deities who watched over the fortunes of the Netherlanders . . . left the field and stepped into a neighboring tavern to refresh themselves."

At the height of his battle with the Swedes, the "gallant Peter . . . plunged, sword in hand, into the thickest of the foe." Only one "crafty Swede," a long queue hanging down his back, dares take him on; he drives his sword at the Dutchman's heart, but it glances off and tears open a side pocket containing Stuyvesant's tobacco box, "piously decorated with a portrait of the blessed St. Nicholas," which explains its power to repel the seemingly well-aimed thrust. Furiously, Peter turns on his fleeing attacker. "Ah, whoreson caterpillar!" he cries, slashing the Swede with a blow that might have decapitated him but for "the pitying steel" that "struck short and shaved the queue forever from his crown."

As the battle wears on, Stuyvesant's Swedish counterpart, Governor Risingh, "his faithful troops banged, beaten, and kicked by the invincible Peter," realizes the fight has turned against him. Language being Irving's favorite weapon, Risingh pauses here "to disburden himself of five thousand anathemas." He then strides over to his rival leader, and, after some posturing (shades of Ajax and Hector in the *Iliad*), the two engage in the swordplay equivalent of scratching and clawing until Peter reaches up and clubs the Swede with his wooden leg, knocking him down once and for all. The Swedes give way.[36]

This last vignette was Irving's critique of the culture of the duel, the gentleman's recourse that was meant to be seen as a mark of manliness and a sophisticated form of conflict resolution. A duel was orchestrated to render a private quarrel publicly significant. Irving showed instead that no ritual could make killing noble; men did not prove their worth by dueling with pistols or swords any more than it was glorious to conk a rival on the head with a wooden leg.

At the end of *Knickerbocker's History*, Stuyvesant defends his city "by dint of the strength of his head." But it is clear to his people, if not to him, that history cannot be stopped. For Irving, the British invasion is a denouement; the real pathos comes in the forced retirement of Governor Stuyvesant, wherein we glimpse Irving's Federalist-leaning protest against the Jeffersonian ideal of an educable people, and his admission that as a satirist, he could offer no real solution to the problems facing the republic's leaders:

> The brawling multitude could not but reflect with self-abasement upon their own pusillanimous conduct, when they beheld their hardy but deserted old governor, thus faithful to his post, like a forlorn hope, and fully prepared to defend his ungrateful city to the last.

The story concludes in two ways—first, with measured hope: "Let the reign of the good Stuyvesant show the effects of vigor and decision, even when destitute of cool judgment"; and then, with healthy suspicion: "But at the same time, let it caution against a too ready reliance on the good faith of others."[37]

✯   ✯

What remains to be said about our historian? He has learned that governors (and presidents) are not heroes. Leaders, appointed or elected, are as prone to bad decisionmaking as anyone else; yet, Irving yearns for the exceptional individual possessed of the mind and the will necessary to lead. (This is how he will later portray both Columbus and Washington.)

Knickerbocker is a skeptic, but one given to dreaming. That is his appeal: He is a devout escapist. As Knickerbocker's creator, Irving is interested in making light of the real issues of the day, but only as his secondary object; he is primarily engrossed in booking passage to a more innocent time and place, a fabled America that the forgotten Dutch of New Amsterdam days are in some ways made to represent. But we do not yet know this about Washington Irving—he has not yet found his invincible antihero in Rip Van Winkle.

The world of Diedrich Knickerbocker revolved around a Manhattan where everything was new, and where the simple act of naming was not only meaningful for the moment but also for the future. In writing the way he did, Irving succeeded in giving a kind of immortality to a playful, pipe-smoking, St. Nicholas–venerating generation that had been largely forgotten.

How an author comes up with names can be a window into that author's strategy as well as his personality. Irving tells imaginative stories about naming, as how the Indian name "Manna-hata" refused to die after the adoption of "New Amsterdam"; where we get the name "Kip's Bay" or "Cortlandt Street"; and how the forbidding "Hellgate" originated. This last is particularly interesting: The tides where the East River meets the Long Island Sound could be treacherous; early sailors dubbed the spot "Hellgate," and the name stuck. Irving could not resist footnoting the "numerous rocks, shelves, and whirlpools" when he explained the history of the narrows in his *History*. He so liked the sound, as well as the idea, of "Hellgate," that in handwritten notes to his publisher in 1848 he revised his original footnote to chastise the "mealy-mouthed men, of squeamish consciences, who are loth to give the Devil his due" for softening the word to "Hurl-gate."[38]

In his naming game in the *History*, Irving also looks for excuses to mention people and places that had crossed from reality into his fantasy life. He sends Peter Stuyvesant up the Hudson just to give himself time to wax about its beauty; and he introduces the "Van Nests of Kinderhoeck, valiant robbers of birds' nests, as their name denotes." Then there are the "Van Winkles, of Haerlem . . . they were the first that ever winked with both eyes at once." Of the "Couenhovens," whom he identifies with Sleepy Hollow, he writes: "These gave birth to a jolly race of publicans, who first discovered the magic artifice of conjuring a quart of wine into a pint bottle."

And so, developing his own vocabulary, Irving famously accounts for the family whose renown he is responsible for creating:

KNICKERBOCKERS, of the great town of Scaghtikoke [sic], where the folk lay stones upon the houses in windy weather, lest they should be blown away.

The real Congressman Herman Knickerbocker, living at this time in that town, northeast of Albany, was known among his friends as the "Prince of Schaghticoke."

These derive their name, as some say, from *Knicker*, to shake, and *Beker*, a goblet, indicating thereby that they were sturdy toss-pots of yore; but, in truth, it was derived from *Knicker*, to nod, and *Boeken*, books; plainly meaning that they were great nodders or dozers over books—from them did descend the great writer of this history.

The "toss-pot" is not just an object, but conveys the double meaning of an idea that is easily discarded—or an effort at erudition (or definition) that is entirely immaterial. Irving keeps on saying, "Don't be taken in by the overly studious historian." He looks up from books as he looks for his moral. We also see glimpses of future work, and future fame, with occasional references to "haunted regions of the Kaatskill Mountains," where Rip Van Winkle will go to sleep, perchance to dream.[39]

Like the well-meaning but ponderous Dr. Mitchill before him, Irving could adopt a gazetteer's approach to local history because America was still a young place. The "new" land in Irving's text nurtured an "embryo" New York, an "infant city" and an "infant" culture, causing modern critics to observe that *Knickerbocker's History* is not merely a playful place of playful names and a fabled civilization but an exercise in reconstituting a warm and tranquilizing childhood for its author, a personal escape from responsibility.

There may be some truth in this, but there is also danger in overinterpreting what was a common metaphor of the period. In support of independence, for instance, Thomas Paine's *Common Sense* (1776) alluded more than once to America's "infant" state; and Fourth of July speakers in the 1790s and early 1800s routinely lauded America as an "infant empire." The Republican poet Joel Barlow, in the same year that *Knickerbocker's History* appeared, proclaimed that the welcoming continent made America a "gigantic infant of a nation," able to "look forward to a state of adolescence, with confidence to a state of manhood." So, seizing this familiar trope, Irving is not so much celebrating a fantasy of childhood as he is casting history in terms that the young republic already understands.[40]

He knew he was not the only one who considered the *idea* of America something with enduring sentimental potential. That is why he sought to preserve the Hudson as a place less populous, where nature yielded magnificent secrets and persistent stories of the unexplained preoccupied the rural residents. That is also how the St. Nicholas whom Oloffe the Dreamer consulted struck a chord, leading directly to later American depictions of Santa Claus— it was Washington Irving who first associated this figure with fun. Christmas in America began, in that sense, when Knickerbocker's folk took heart by invoking the blessings of "the great and good St. Nicholas."

Irving was a great publicist. As "the city of New Amsterdam waxed great under the protection of St. Nicholas" and the visionary Oloffe spread his good news, the modern Santa Claus was waiting in the wings. The *History* records: "At this early period was instituted that pious ceremony, still religiously observed in all our ancient families of the right breed, of hanging up a stocking in the chimney on St. Nicholas eve; which stocking is always found in the morning miraculously filled; for the good St. Nicholas has ever been a great giver of gifts, particularly to children."[41]

As yet, America had no recognized Christmas holiday. Irving expressed only the germ of it here. And although no one person "invented" Christmas, we can say that Irving dressed up an idea that had been floating around. The public that loved his *History* simply could not forget his pure and good-humored St. Nick. James Paulding even went on to write *The Book of St. Nicholas.* Something was starting to stir that would gradually evolve into the Christmas we know by the mid-1830s, but it would require still more of Irving's story-spinning for the public to visualize it fully.[42]

We can say, at least, that the St. Nicholas touch was symptomatic of the author's fondness for talismanic themes. There is no doubt that the mock-historian Irving loved the experimental perspective of the living imagination—one might even say "child's play" in deference to the Freudian interpreters of his work. He wrote to create a comic, but inviting, dreamscape.

Irving is present as a narrator throughout his burlesque *History.* He alternates among voices: an absurd arrogance (the title page pronounces his "the only Authentic History of the Times that ever hath been or ever will be published"); a Sternean-style wavering ("My readers must doubtless perceive how completely I have altered my tone and deportment since we first set out together"); and a seductive allegiance to the reader ("The writer of a history may, in some respects, be likened to an adventurous knight"). Irving suggests that chivalry, or gallantry, is his aim as much as enlightenment by painting himself into history as a "meddlesome knight-errant."[43]

In this world of his own creation, the twenty-six-year-old's voice still bears features of the great satirists of the eighteenth century: Jonathan Swift, Henry Fielding, and Laurence Sterne. The historian Knickerbocker's occasional mockery of his own text smacks of Fielding. The whimsical personalities Irving gives his characters are reminiscent of Sterne.[44] But the *History*'s closest relative is Swift's *Gulliver's Travels.* Swift's use of irony is Irving's, as is his wistful time-transcendence and his parodic treatment of violent behaviors. As the literary scholar William Hedges has explained, Swift evinces a clear-cut system of values in his work ("Man alone, blessed with an inventive mind, goes on from discovery to discovery—enlarges and multiplies his powers of destruction"), whereas Irving tries to be subtler, muddling his values, and taking pride in his "mercurial" persona.[45]

All the same, we can see what Irving's values were as a writer. He was not only in command of his research and writing but deeply absorbed in the role of the historian in society; he was keen on setting the terms of his publishing contract (for *A History of New York,* he earned more than any previous American writer of fiction had earned from a single work); he was aware that to be accepted by the city's critical elite he had to be thorough both in his self-education and in his business practices. Indeed, he cared about acceptance.

At the same time, he was taking chances with his pen. He showed an attitude. There was something audacious about Washington Irving that too few have given him credit for. He used his knowledge of historical discourse to shame the real or imagined pedant, and yet he was sentimental enough (as a Sternean) to ask that his periodic confessions of humanity be deemed no less genuine than his adoration of the wild Hudson.

This is why the politics in his book do not overwhelm. This is why Sir Walter Scott, no expert in Jeffersonian politics, would come to appreciate the mock epic: "Our sides have been absolutely sore with laughing," he noted, in concert with his wife and her friends. A writer for the *Monthly Anthology and Boston Review,* in February 1810, observed that the author of *Knickerbocker's History* was "one of those privileged beings, who, in his pilgrimage through the lanes and streets, the roads and avenues of this uneven world, refreshes himself with many a secret smile at occurrences that excite no observation from the dull, trudging mass of mortals." This is exactly what Irving was hoping to communicate.[46]

To draw an intentional paradox, Irving was aggressively congenial as a historian. He was proud of his artfulness as a writer. He served up nervy nonsense, and it came across as a nonconformist's vision. Yet his alienation was also real. He felt a cool (not a burning) desire to peel away layers of so-called polite society while blowing the whistle on all political and intellectual dishonesty. This was the province of youth.[47]

However one regards Irving's *History,* New York was looked upon after 1809 as a city with sound literary credentials. In short, Diedrich Knickerbocker was famous.

CHAPTER 5

Irving Goes to War,
Sort Of

1810–1815

*Indeed, we do not pretend to the rigid precision and dispassionate cool-
ness of historical narrative. Excited as we are by the tone and temper
of the times, and the enthusiasm that prevails around us, we cannot, if
we would, repress those feelings of pride and exultation, that gush
warm from the heart, when the triumphs of our navy are the theme.*

—Washington Irving, in the *Analectic Magazine*, 1814

NO ONE IN THE PUBLIC EYE CAN EXPECT TO BE
immune from judgment. The author of *A History of New York* wished
for calm, and wished in vain.

In the world of the early nineteenth century, at least as much as now, literary culture played directly into political discourse. When Jefferson left office
and retired to Monticello, and Aaron Burr was in exile in England, the Irvings' New York remained a temperamental place. In wondering, after the initial publication of his *History*, "Where do I go from here?" Washington Irving
continued to navigate local and national politics, but felt ill-equipped to manage its meaner aspects. Bound to his politically active brothers, he would
learn that politics invites public persons into uneasy situations. And publishing, too, placed him in a bubble.

Even so, as a political satirist, and an ambitious one at that, Washington Irving did not follow in the tradition of the newspaper scribblers who provoked
so as to defame. He was not a hater, by any means, but he was a trenchant observer. Sometimes when he added spice to his literary concoctions, he wished

he had held back. Usually, when his words were the most peppery, his motive was to defend a friend or a family member. Back in 1804, he had found himself forced to confront James Cheetham, the editor who attacked Burr through brother Peter; and after the appearance of his *History,* he would occasionally be distracted by rival satirists and pressed to come to the defense of one who felt the barbed pen. Doing so, Irving invited reprisal. He was never comfortable with the result. This may be one reason why in subsequent years he depoliticized his texts (and managed his life story).

Around the time he was putting *Knickerbocker's History* to bed, Irving joined his literary allies to hurl one more bit of invective at a critic. One John Rodman had published a pamphlet belittling the activities of Irving's friend, the Scottish educator James Ogilvie, who was making the rounds in New York. Ogilvie was dependent on the opiate laudanum and was, by all accounts, an eccentric—an easy target. Rodman's *Fragment of a Journal of a Sentimental Philosopher* cast the public lecturer as a man of false sensibility, a radical, a clown. The pamphlet included numerous unmistakable references to Irving's circle of acquaintances; the Irving team countered with a onetime issue of the *New-York Review; or Critical Journal,* printed up by the same house that was publishing *Knickerbocker's History.*

Irving had apparently met Ogilvie through Joseph Cabell, his travel companion in Europe. Ogilvie, who had ingratiated himself with Cabell's Virginia neighbor Thomas Jefferson, opened his first American school in the small town of Milton, just below Monticello, where the president went to market. He had as a pupil Jefferson's eldest grandson and namesake. Before taking to the lecture circuit, Ogilvie expanded into Richmond. The orator was in Richmond while Irving was attending the Burr trial in 1806, and they may have crossed paths in Philadelphia as well. So when Ogilvie arrived in New York in 1809, Irving introduced him around. It did not bother him in the least that Ogilvie was an outspoken critic of religion, or that he was a Jefferson partisan and an admirer of William Godwin, the English novelist and freethinker. Something about Ogilvie drew Irving—perhaps his sentimental style—and the Scotsman was apparently responsive to Irving's melancholy in the months after the death of Matilda Hoffman. The most curious part of the calculus is this: Rodman was married to the former Harriet Fenno, the sister of Irving's dear friend, and Matilda's young stepmother, Maria Fenno Hoffman. Rodman had struck a nerve.[1]

Irving may not have been the instigator of the *New-York Review,* but it was his talent at "payback" that repeated his 1804 slashing of the defamatory editor Cheetham. Rodman had, without subtlety, mocked Ogilvie's oratorical "gesticulations" as ludicrous, and he intimated that the anti-Christian pedagogue was ill suited for polite society. This provoked the reviewer(s) to exaggerate Rodman's holier-than-thou lifestyle, to make him appear the complete prig—not to mention "testy," an adjective Irving used once before, and prominently. Rodman was never heard from again, at least not as a critic.[2]

Though Irving made a tidy profit from his *History*, he still feared the future. There was no international copyright understanding as yet, and he had no sequel in mind. His means still derived from the family business, in which his role was secondary at best. So when he or one of his collaborators dismissed Rodman as an ill-bred "ironmonger" (taunting, "If . . . we ever catch him, hawking his hardware . . .") at the same time, the Irvings' hardware and sundries business was in transition, and certainly not booming.

With his future prospects cloudy, he considered politics; yet he hated that scene, and continued to say so. Early in 1810, while tentatively seeking an appointment in the state capital of Albany (strictly for the income it might provide), the unimpressive student of the law protested the vicious and unprofitable character of state politics, and wished he could disappear. Writing at length to the Hoffmans, he lamented the "servility, and duplicity, and rascality I have witnessed among the swarm of scrub politicians who crawl about [Albany]." All he found, he said, were "scenes of intrigue and iniquity." With shrinking determination, he despaired: "I have no prospect ahead, nor scheme, nor air castle to engage my mind withal." So soon after his success, the author of *Knickerbocker's History* seemed to feel that he must roam unproductively. He expected to return to Manhattan with a "great store" of knowledge "of the wickedness of my fellow creatures," he told Maria Fenno Hoffman. "That, I believe, is the only kind of wealth I am doomed to acquire in the world."[3]

★   ★

No American writer of fiction had yet been able to earn a respectable living strictly by writing, and Irving was out of ideas. His sensitive brother Peter, now in England tending to the family's import business, understood Washington's dilemma. Peter was of a similar cast, more man of leisure than slave to a profession; he told his younger brother that they, of the Irvings, were the ones least able to endure "the drudgery of regular business."[4] If Peter, the nonpracticing doctor, was inclined to dream of financial independence while planning to work only halfheartedly at business, Washington was less optimistic. He anticipated a lifetime spent under pressure to make ends meet.

These would be trying years for him. It was not that he relied on family out of laziness—his dynamic dealings with publishers showed that he was intent on squeezing as much legal profit as possible out of his writing. But his brothers' efforts represented his only rational hope for a life of anything approaching ease. And so he took a certain amount of direction from them, and spent less time creating. He continued to read widely—Walter Scott, Lord Byron, Samuel Rogers, whose poem *The Pleasures of Memory* he had especially enjoyed when younger, and Thomas Campbell. Peter Irving, once, long ago, a hero of the New York literary club scene, had become friends with Campbell in England; as a consequence, Washington would shortly help bring together choice examples of Campbell's verse in a single volume, and prepare a eulogistic biographical introduction. This generous act was to serve him well when he met the appreciative poet several years later.

Meanwhile, New York's population was nearing 100,000, and its maritime economy needed to keep growing. William and Ebenezer decided that their brother should go to Washington, D.C., to lobby the nation's decisionmakers on behalf of the merchants' interest. Jefferson's embargo had been succeeded by a piece of legislation that permitted commerce with England and France, but under a watchful eye.

And so Irving left New York on December 21, 1810. In Baltimore, he re-encountered the portrait painter John Wesley Jarvis, who was now "universally passing for a great wit." Then, "struggling through the mud and mire," he rode the final miles to the nation's capital, and arrived on January 9, 1811. Over the next two months, he made friends with important people, and secured a reputation among the nation's leaders—including President James Madison himself—for nonpartisan decency and sober self-assurance.

On the very evening of his arrival in Washington, Irving was able to insinuate his way into a levee ("or drawing room") held by Dolley Madison. He donned his silk stockings, as he wrote to his friend Henry Brevoort, and strode "like a vagabond Knight errant" into the fray. Within ten minutes, he was "hand in glove with half the people in the assemblage." He described Mrs. Madison as "a fine, portly, buxom dame." The president fared less well: "Poor Jemmy! he is but a withered little apple-John." James Madison, physically unimposing, was a giant of a thinker and a forceful legislator before taking on executive responsibilities; Irving's lighthearted choice of a shriveled-up apple as a metaphor for Madison was but a shallow symbol of a first impression meant to entertain the recipient of his letter. Some have made too much of this uncensored characterization. Indeed, Irving would soon after take delight in the personable president's high opinion of his talents—and take in stride Madison's critique of Irving: "that I talkd too much."

Thrown suddenly into capital society, he found a mooring at the home of the former congressman John P. Van Ness, the brother of his Kinderhook friend. He also became fast friends with the gentle New York Federalist he was bound to receive an introduction to—"my cousin the congressman," as he put it—Herman Knickerbocker. Irving also ran into Aaron Burr's close New York ally of years past (and Burr's future biographer), the political junkie Matthew Livingston Davis. "Mat is as deep as usual," Irving wrote sarcastically to Brevoort, "shakes his head & winks through his spectacles at every body he meets." During his two months in Washington, Irving sat in the congressional gallery in an effort to understand the business of the nation firsthand; he also rose good-naturedly to every social occasion.

He took special liking to two dynamic politicians who were bound for oratorical greatness and many controversial years of headline grabbing. They were Henry Clay of Lexington, Kentucky, who would four times seek and fail to win the presidency; and John Randolph of Roanoke, a veritable caricature of the old-fashioned Virginia planter, dreadfully thin, misshapen, and sallow, sexually ambiguous in appearance, but a firebrand in Congress. Irving had first encountered "Jack" Randolph, as he called him, at the Burr trial, where Randolph was foreman of the grand jury. The poker-playing Clay and the hard-drinking Randolph were as literary as any in Irving's New York circle, and quite as theatrical as the classically trained actors Irving had come to know. These two southerners would, some fifteen years later—almost predictably, given their explosive passions—face down one another in a celebrated duel on the banks of the Potomac.

So this was the Washington, D.C., of Irving's second visit. New life had arisen in the four years since Aaron Burr's acquittal. A younger generation, born in the 1770s, had become the leaders of Congress. That body was becoming ever more animated, and the social scene followed suit. Irving moved between the older and younger generations with apparent ease. He told his brother William of a particular triumph: "Mrs. Madison is a sworn friend of mine." It seems that maternal figures of every generation were attracted to him, and he to them. Meanwhile, as the congressional session came to an end in early March 1811, Irving figured he had impressed some stubborn lawmakers. At his most argumentative, he would say, "However *officious* I may be in politics . . . I am on very good terms with all our public officers."[5]

★　　★

Returning to New York, Irving and his best friend, Henry Brevoort, took up lodgings together at 16 Broadway, near fashionable Bowling Green. They had separate bedrooms, ample shelves of books, and a common sitting room where the pair engaged in genial debate and shared laughs. They continued to pay addresses or attend tea parties at the Hoffmans, and from time to time reconnected with the old Lads of Kilkenny, though adult occupations made these gatherings infrequent and incomplete. Sam Swartwout arrived from England, where he had been baby-sitting the exiled Burr; Gouverneur Kemble, the wayward master of "Cockloft Hall," returned from England, too, and Irving was pleased to encounter "the Patroon," as he still referred to him, affable and unaffected by his time abroad—there was a way of thinking among Americans that the Grand Tour changed a person, and not always for the better.

The domestic setup Irving and Brevoort maintained lasted one year, part of which time Brevoort spent in Canada on a fur-trading mission for John Jacob Astor. From one distant outpost, Brevoort sent uplifting news to Irving: "Your History is going the rounds through the Village from the Commandant to the smallest Indian Trader, so that you contribute more to their merriment & pleasure than you probably would if you were here yourself."

Early in 1812, Brevoort left for an extended stay in England: "[I] am completely out of spirits, I do miss you terribly," wrote the one left behind. A year went by, and Brevoort joined Irving in recalling their happy coexistence: "You see, my dear Wash, how much I long to fill the vacant chair on the opposite side of the well recollected Table in our private sanctuary, but let all my remembrance fill the vacancies in your heart as yours most truly does in mine." On Brevoort's return home, the two took out a new lease together, this time at the corner of Greenwich and Rector Streets.[6]

Though geography had distanced them, Irving and Brevoort remained close. The younger man was an emotional substitute for Irving's brother Peter, whom Brevoort visited and reported on sympathetically from England; Brevoort also scoured the country for "old odd Books" that his friend back in New York might enjoy. And it was Brevoort who would most significantly promote Irving's literary career in the coming years—in England when Irving was in New York, and in New York when Irving was in England. He had occasion, while attending lectures at the University of Edinburgh early in 1813, to present *Knickerbocker's History* to the venerable Walter Scott; the poet-novelist gave thanks "for the uncommon degree of entertainment" he had received "from the most excellently jocose history of New York." He added: "I beg you will have the kindness to let me know when Mr. Irvine [*sic*] takes pen in hand again." Brevoort elaborated to his late housemate: "You must understand his words literally, for he is too honest and too sincere a man to compliment any person." No literary light shone brighter than Scott; to be read and appreciated by him would have been an honor for any American.[7]

Yet for several years after his *History* made its splash, Irving did not produce any new writing. He busied himself, off and on, redoing his earlier successful publications. In 1811, he learned that the *History* was being translated into French. That same year, a Londoner acquired a bound copy of *Salmagundi* from "Dusky Davy" Longworth, and released a British edition, favorably judged in the *London Monthly Review*. In 1814, Longworth published "A New and Improved Edition," which included woodcuts by the New York wood engraver Alexander Anderson. Irving might have collaborated with Longworth in this instance because political comments that some readers had found offensive were toned down. Still, as each year passed, he became less interested in touting his association with the *Salmagundi* collection.[8]

In 1812, Bradford & Inskeep brought out the second edition of *A History of New York*. Irving removed inappropriate political references and touched up points of syntax. Meanwhile, Jim Paulding pitched a book idea on the understanding that it would be a collaborative effort; their correspondence shows that Irving signed on, but it never came to pass—even the topic is lost to history.[9]

The hesitant author finally decided to edit a literary journal. In the autumn of 1810, he had turned down one such proposal from John E. Hall, a Princeton-educated lawyer: "I do not wish to meddle with my pen for a long while."[10] But he changed his mind at the end of 1812 when asked to edit *Select Reviews*, published by Moses Thomas of Philadelphia. He presumed the work would be a desultory exercise, but it proved serious, and at times challenging. Under Irving's editorship, through the years 1813 and 1814, the periodical that had been known as *Select Reviews* became the *Analectic Magazine*.

It was a "Miscellany," that is, it collected articles and reviews, literary and political intelligence, from British and French sources. These included samples of poetry by Walter Scott and Lord Byron; Irving, Paulding, and other American writers supplied occasional prose pieces. The *Analectic Magazine* was distributed by Bradford & Inskeep and Collins & Co. in New York, though it reached well beyond, with agents in Boston, New Haven, Trenton, Washington, Richmond, Savannah, and New Orleans.

Aside from standard extracts, the *Analectic* featured Irving essays of 1813 that concerned North American Indians: "Traits of Indian Character" and

"Philip of Pokanoket" (the latter introduced by an epigraph from the poet Campbell). These two pieces would become late additions to Irving's famed *Sketch Book,* in 1820, so he must have thought them significant products of his mind. But as America and Great Britain stepped up their naval warfare along the U.S.-Canadian border, the *Analectic*'s editor gave prominent place to biographies of America's emerging naval heroes.

★ ★

For the better part of a century, the War of 1812 has been presented to students of American history as unexciting, save perhaps for the "bombs bursting in air" in Baltimore harbor. Nothing could be further from the truth. As a conflict much diluted in the historical imagination, the nationalist point of view in this "second American Revolution" has been lost. Jeffersonian Republicans declared their peaceful intent with regard to all nations, but viewed expansion westward across Indian lands as inevitable. They fully expected, one day soon, to annex Canada.

That nationalism needs to be recalled to mind. To provide clearer context, Irving's friend Paulding is an ideal guide. In 1812, he published with Bradford & Inskeep a pseudonymous essay called *The Diverting History of John Bull and Brother Jonathan.* His pen name was "Hector Bull-us."

Paulding's ingenious little parable caricatures the haughty British personality and retells the history of Anglo-American relations with a comic selectivity. The story of continents is reduced to a conflict between a few villages on opposite sides of a great millpond. "Squire Bull sent Jonathan to settle new lands," only to get "handsomely rib-roasted" while "attempting to pick Jonathan's pocket." No one had ever compressed the American Revolution so neatly.

As time went by, Brother Jonathan was suspected of "a sneaking kindness" toward "Little Beau Napperty," that is, Napoleon, of "Frogmore." Being an equal opportunity satirist, Paulding poked fun at the Frenchman's diminutive stature and trademark headgear: "Instead of saying yonder is Beau Napperty with his cocked hat on," people said, "yonder is the cocked hat, with little Beau Napperty under it." The United States was given exclusively a New Yorker's commercial perspective: "Brother Jonathan had in general no great stomach for fighting, was not easily provoked to extremity, and loved profit rather better than honour." Nonetheless, when his pocketbook (America's right, as a neutral country, to trade with anyone it chose) was threatened, Jonathan was roused to anger. And so he sent Squire Bull a "respectful" letter: "Honoured Father, 'Sblood, what d'ye mean, you bacon faced son of a horned cow, by telling me I shant visit Beau Napperty when I please!" As aggressive as Squire Bull was in Paulding's ridiculous morality play, the pamphlet ends with an appeal for mutual restraint: "It is a thousand pities to see father and son fighting and squabbling, when they ought to be a stay and staff to each other in the troubles of this distracted world."[11]

But war came a short time later, egged on by congressional War Hawks such as the declamatory Henry Clay. Clay was joined by other men in their thirties, too young to recall the Revolution and desirous of obtaining a national glory of their own. Irving himself stood on the sidelines for as long as he could. In Washington in 1811, he had taken careful note of feuding legislators and competing demonstrations of patriotic zeal. But as he wrote to William P. Van Ness, he was unmoved by their blank sentiment: "As to talking of patriotism & principle, I've seen enough both of general & state politics to convince me they are mere words of Battle—'Banners hung on the outer walls,' for the rabble to fight by."[12] Once war got under way in June 1812, and even as pro-commercial Federalists shook their heads in disgust, Irving changed his mind and fervently embraced his country's cause.

Like Jefferson's embargo, the conflict stood to deprive New York City of its commercial health, at least temporarily. But this time, Irving was prodded by his eldest brother. William, forty-seven, was a vocal supporter of the campaign to cut the British down to size; he was a naval booster in particular, and, at the close of 1813, was elected to Congress as an ally of the Madison administration in its prosecution of the war. He would be reelected twice, and remained in office until 1819.

Irving had been itching to return to Europe, but he knew he would have to wait out the hostilities. He had not adopted anything like a jingoistic tone since his adventure-filled tour of the Mediterranean. He told Peter six months after war was declared that early naval victories over the vaunted British fleet "were well-timed to save the national spirit from being depressed and humiliated by the paltry war on the frontiers." More pressure to perform was put on a newly aggressive navy when American forts in Detroit fell to the enemy.

Traveling in government circles, Irving had become friendly with a bona fide hero. The short, broad-shouldered Stephen Decatur, keen-eyed hero of the Tripolitan war and more recently captain of the USS *United States*, was honored at a public dinner in New York at the end of 1812, which Irving attended. Unable to banish from memory the long years of British occupation during the Revolution, the city was now on a war footing. "You would scarcely recognize our old peaceful city," Irving advised Peter. "Nothing is talked of but armies, Navies, Battles &c."[13]

The American army, that is, its land-based force, was an unprofessional corps, and it made little headway during the war—thus Irving's characterization of the "paltry war on the frontiers." In his view, and in others' as well, military "quacks" now stood at the command of poorly trained state militias of insufficient size. The navy, on the other hand, was performing exploits that lent themselves to legend making of the kind Irving was most adept at conveying to a reading public hungry for hope. It had begun with Captain Isaac Hull of the USS *Constitution,* who destroyed a British warship in the mid-Atlantic, then Decatur, capturing the HMS *Macedonian* with minimal casualties, and dragging his prize of war back to U.S. shores—New Yorkers lined the East River shore to watch as Decatur's prize glided toward the Battery, its *American* flag prominently flying.[14] Then, hoping to oust the enemy from Detroit, President Madison named Commodore Oliver Hazard Perry to take charge of the Lake Erie theater. Perry's fleet attacked the British in the fall of 1813, sustaining heavy casualties, yet the commodore was able to report: "We have met the enemy and they are ours."

Irving's biographical sketch of Commodore Perry in the *Analectic Magazine* is well written, but does not go much beyond being informative, and is typical of the war propaganda others wrote: "He is of a manly and prepossessing appearance, mild and unassuming in his address, amiable in his disposition, and of great firmness and decision." Symbolizing the ideal American personality, he mixed "native gentility" with "sober dignity," leaving room for "the freedom of intimacy." Perry possessed, in sum, "a character of high moral excellence, of high-minded courtesy, and pure unsullied honour." This kind of portrait was possible only in a nationalistic moment.

Only Irving's concluding thoughts hint at the romance and nostalgic poignancy he will soon turn to in his fiction. After the victory on Lake Erie, his narrative employs a preachy kind of hopefulness: "The peal of war has once sounded on that lake, but probably will never sound again. The last roar of cannonry that died along her shores, was the expiring note of British domination." Projecting the day when Canada and the United States would be united, he placed himself in the future:

> When the shores of Lake Erie will hum with a busy population; when towns and cities shall brighten where now extends the dark and tangled forest; when ports shall spread their arms, and . . . when the present age shall have grown into a venerable antiquity, and the mists of fable begin to gather round its history; then will the inhabitants of Canada look back to this battle we record, as one of the romantic achievements of the days of yore.[15]

Breathless and swollen with pride, Irving's prose reveals his devotion to the cause of liberation (of the human heart) as much as to the cause of national security. This fervency—in writing of the inner spirit—would become his trademark in the coming phase of his career. But for now, he allowed the war to restrict his imagination and redirect his pen.

✻ ✻

As the year 1814 opened, no end to the war was in sight. The British attempted to avenge their losses in the naval campaign of the previous year. Their threefold plan was to march from Montreal and invade northern New York, employ the navy in the Chesapeake and torch Baltimore and Washington, and dispatch a separate fleet from Jamaica to occupy New Orleans. The northern incursion was stopped at Plattsburg, New York, above Lake Champlain. The destruction of Washington went forward, forcing the Madisons to flee as the federal government's most stately buildings went up in flames. Afterward, the editor of the *Analectic Magazine* determined to join the war effort in the most conspicuous way possible, and signed on as an aide de camp to Governor Daniel D. Tompkins of New York (concurrently a New York State militia general).

Daniel Tompkins was born in rural Scarsdale, Westchester County, in 1774, and attended Columbia in the early 1790s, overlapping there with Peter and John Irving. Practicing law in New York, he was an early Burr supporter who worked for Jefferson's election in 1800. After that, he served on the New York State Supreme Court for three years before becoming governor of New York, a position he would hold for a decade. In the topsy-turvy world of New York politics, he was initially put in office as DeWitt Clinton's answer to the supposedly faithless Morgan Lewis, whom Clinton had earlier supported against Burr.

As governor, Tompkins (unlike Irving) supported Jefferson's 1807–1808 embargo. It was only natural that he would approve Jefferson's friend and successor, Madison. He had hoped for a more aggressive U.S. military posture as war impended, but his public statements showed him to be a harmonizer. He sought to maintain good relations with Clinton, but broke with the prickly power broker when the latter challenged Madison for the presidency in 1812.

Seeking reelection as a pro-administration candidate in 1813, Tompkins issued an address to electors decrying the "flagrant iniquity and unhallowed tyranny" of the British aggressor. "It was a war," he said, "not waged to the destruction of the rights of others; but in defense of our own," and necessary to preserve the honor of "the only free people on earth." As 1814 opened,

Tompkins was buoyed by the near-complete electoral sweep by pro-war legislators in the state assembly. With the governor's urging, they called for the enlistment of twelve thousand new militiamen, at attractive salaries.[16]

Irving accepted Madison as a reasonable and thoughtful statesman, and was a particular fan of Governor Tompkins. He wrote to his brother the congressman in the autumn of 1814: "Tompkins is absolutely one of the worthiest men I ever knew. I find him honest, candid, prompt, indefatigable, with a greater stock of practical good sense and ready talent than I had any idea he possessed."

Lieutenant Colonel Irving accompanied the mild-mannered governor/general on inspections of fortifications in Brooklyn, Hellgate, and Ellis Island, and then trudged north with him to Sacketts Harbor, on Lake Ontario near the Canadian border. They were attended by the Iron Greys, the particular unit of the New York State militia to which both Lieutenant Henry Brevoort and Major Samuel Swartwout belonged. At the end of his life, Irving could still recall how his Kilkenny friend Sam "had great bother with his Iron Greys; first this thing was wrong, then that; at one time their guns were too light, then too *heavy*." The Iron Greys were for most of their existence encamped in Greenwich Village, known for the inherited wealth of many of their individual enlistees (they arrived for parade in their coaches), and for the social life that it sponsored.[17] This gives us a truer sense of the war footing on which Colonel Irving really stood—much like Benjamin Franklin, for good reason never pictured with a gun, who was nonetheless named a momentary colonel during the French and Indian War.

At Sacketts Harbor, the United States was feverishly building war vessels in the hope that it would soon have enough to drive off the enemy once and for all. In anticipation of a decisive battle, President Madison ordered Stephen Decatur to lead in the fight. But politics, as usual, played a central role in the tense jockeying for power in the region. Army and navy commanders in upstate New York were accusing each other of standing in the way of victory. In the meantime, the president had written to Governor Tompkins offering him what would seem the irresistible position of secretary of state. The New Yorker turned him down because the pay was insufficient to justify moving his large family to Washington, though he told Madison something different: that he thought he could do more to serve the nation by remaining as war governor. Madison was angry by the refusal, and left the State Department without a head. Given that the secretaryship was a stepping-stone to the presidency, Tompkins's refusal suggests the limits of his ambition—or perhaps the realization that the Virginia dynasty of presidents was not about to allow a northern interloper to forestall the accession to office of James Monroe.[18]

The extant papers from this period show how aide de camp Irving issued written orders in the prosaic language of military bureaucracy, warning, here and there, of impending attack (though he never saw any cannon fired in anger). He had done more to endanger life and limb in his upstate travels with the Hoffman-Ogden party, back in 1803, than during this time of war. In December 1814, when in accordance with the legislative calendar, Tompkins returned to civilian duties in Albany, Irving accompanied him. Weeks later, word arrived that the Treaty of Ghent had been signed. Peace returned to the North American continent.

And so ended Irving's military career. He had been inspired to participate at the highest levels of planning; and despite his general's best effort to lead New Yorkers to the fight, Irving and his mighty pen missed out. After the war, Tompkins remained fortunate as a politician. In 1817, he accepted his reward for diligent service and became vice president under Monroe. Thus, the two most prominent New York Republicans with whom Irving associated closely, Aaron Burr and Daniel Tompkins, saw their careers peak as vice presidents of the United States. A different interpretation would be that the vice presidency was considered powerless, a way of paying lip service to the Republican organization of a large state. In fact, Tompkins was the third New Yorker to serve as vice president under a Virginian, the ineffective, aging George Clinton having succeeded Burr.

Speaking of that prominent family of power brokers, one critic of Mr. Madison's war who was also a critic of the Irving family, and of Washington Irving in particular, was the highly visible, notably egotistical mayor of New York. DeWitt Clinton (1769–1824), an on-again, off-again ally of President Jefferson, had seen his chance to wrest the presidency from James Madison by representing the antiwar vote. So the erstwhile Republican—the nephew of Jefferson's second-term vice president—found his strength, oddly enough, in New York and New England Federalism at least as much as in his traditional New York constituency. In the election of 1812, held in the months after Congress declared war on Britain, Clinton captured 89 electoral votes to the incumbent president's 128—one more major state and he would have been president. He felt no shame in identifying with the Federalists.

The ambiguous partisan Washington Irving, a moderate Federalist comfortable with moderate Republicans, could never have identified with the mock-Federalist Clinton, whose chief principles appeared to be self-advancement and self-congratulation. The way Clinton succeeded in alienating him was to attack in print every one of his literary friends.

The pattern began in 1811,[19] when Clinton went after Gil Verplanck for challenging the city elders, and repeated in 1814, when Clinton founded the Literary and Philosophical Society of New York and sought to make it a reserve for the truly eminent men of the town. Just as Dr. Samuel L. Mitchill's *Picture of New York* had goaded Peter Irving and gave rise to *Knickerbocker's History,* so Clinton's overly self-conscious attempt to define the contours of Manhattan's intellectual life provoked a reaction from the Irving crowd—most notably Verplanck.

Gulian Crommelin Verplanck was born in 1786 to a highly respectable family of Dutch New Yorkers. He grew up in a house on Wall Street headed by his paternal grandmother, a doting presence, but also a noted iconoclast; she enjoyed strolling conspicuously down the city streets dressed in her pink satin dress, a jeweled watch suspended from her waist. The outspoken lady had been a blatant supporter of the British during the Revolution. The precocious grandson entered Columbia College at the age of eleven—the same year Irving began to train in the law—and graduated in 1801, at age fourteen. He was the youngest person ever to graduate from Columbia.

He read in the law office of Josiah Ogden Hoffman at the same time that Irving was there. Like his friend, he did not care much for the legal profession and made little effort to attract clients. Coming from old money, linked by blood to the merchant sect, he should have been decidedly Federalist—and for a time he was. Indeed, Verplanck was too sober to devote himself to the Lads of Kilkenny, or Cockloft Hall. As the War of 1812 neared, he became a leader of the conservative Washington Benevolents, a club for budding Federalists. Still, he socialized with Paulding and the Irvings, and took an interest, as they did, in New York theater. He married Maria Fenno Hoffman's younger sister in 1811.

That same year, Verplanck took up his pen, as the fortunate "Abimelech Coody, Ladies' Shoemaker," who had won the lottery and was unsure about his next move. Dabbling in satire stimulated Verplanck's mind, and as he wrote for the pleasure of writing, he found himself doubting his Federalist principles. In 1811, he impulsively locked horns with the largely Federalist Columbia faculty amid a free speech controversy on campus. As Verplanck's politics shifted, he angered his old allies, including the irrepressible and vindictive Mayor Clinton, who tagged him "one of the ringleaders of this disorder and disgrace." Relations between the two continued to deteriorate.

As a militant nationalist during the War of 1812, Verplanck was commissioned a captain in the state militia, though, like Irving, he never saw action. In 1814, however, he fanned the flames of political conflict when he organized the American Federalist Party in opposition to the Clinton faction—the Clintonians called them "the Coodies," after Verplanck's literary alter ego. The "Coodies" were never elected to anything, but they did succeed in raising an anti-Clinton consciousness. Meanwhile, Verplanck contributed several reviews and biographies to the *Analectic Magazine,* including one on the political radical Samuel Adams.

Not to be left out, James Paulding reinforced Verplanck when the enemy was DeWitt Clinton. He also expressed his love of country with an extended sketch of the naval hero Stephen Decatur for the *Analectic.* As one who appeared constitutionally incapable of staying away from politics, Paulding contributed another political satire, this time in opposition to Great Britain's blockade of Atlantic ports, which found its way to President Madison's desk. He then volunteered for the armed services, holding the rank of major in a branch of the militia called the Independent Sea Fencibles. At the end of the war, living in the same boardinghouse as Irving and Brevoort (and for that matter, Stephen Decatur), the literary nationalist gave moral support to Verplanck's cause in opposing Clinton's cultural authoritarianism.

The lines were drawn in New York when Verplanck came out with *A Fable for Statesmen and Politicians of All Parties and Description,* mocking Clinton; and the humorless mayor replied with a petulant pamphlet titled *An Account of Abimelech Coody and Other Celebrated Writers of New-York.* Framed as a northerner's imaginative epistle to a generic southern gentleman, it is an all-out attack on Irving and his friends.

Clinton's work begins by situating New York along the American literary spectrum and claiming its superiority over Philadelphia, long "the Athens of America." What seems at first to be a celebration of the luminaries in Clinton's community very quickly becomes an indictment of certain New York upstarts for their literary mediocrity.

Adopting a cruel tone of irony, the mayor professes pride in standing on "ground trodden by the Knickerbockers and the Coodies; of the Beau and the Salmagundi, and of the Analectic Magazine." Taking up an already worn literary device, he pretends to have endured an uneasy night of sleep: "Coody approached in the darkness. . . . He was a tall man, with an angelic countenance, the genius of symetry [*sic*] had moulded his limbs." This was a personal jab at the short and dumpy physique of Verplanck. Next: "I went to the bookstores and to the literary rooms, and I obtained introduction to some of the celebrated authors."

In his roundup of New York literary competition, Clinton addresses first the accomplished Dr. Mitchill, noting that his "History of Man and of All Nations" (*Picture of New-York*) is "pronounced by good judges to contain more solid information than the History of New-York by Knickerbocker." Next, he alludes to the defeated satirist John Rodman, "whose original profession was that of an ironmonger," just to be certain that he is getting his chronology straight. At last, Clinton prepares to paint a picture of Irving:

> Incongruous as the association between the cultivation of ironmongery and literature may appear, yet it is no less true, that another celebrated author by profession, was originally concerned in a hardware store, and it is believed is still a sleeping partner. He was also brought up to the law . . . and has become the salaried editor of a Magazine.

It was standard procedure to stop short of naming names, but nothing could have been so transparent as Clinton's rebuke. He continues:

> Although his Salmagundi is upon a thread-bare plan, yet its execution exhibits some strong traits of humour, and some fine flashes of imagination. The History of New-York by Knickerbocker, independently of its broad humour, is really intolerable. The heterogeneous and unnatural combination of fiction and history is perfectly disgusting to good taste. . . . There is no doubt that this gentleman possesses a rich imagination. He has however expended the energy of his mind in pursuing ridiculous combinations, in hunting after quaint expressions, and in plundering from the stores of Le Sage and Cervantes, Rabelais and Scarron, Fielding and Smollet. As to real science and learning, his mind is a *tabula rasa:* he cannot read any of the classics in their original language; nor does he know the first elements of any science. I have spent an evening in his company, and I find him barren in conversation, and very limited in information.

In this way, Mayor Clinton spends a great deal of energy belittling Washington Irving, which shows that he recognizes the young man's ascendance among the readers of New York, and in America more broadly. It is certainly curious that a man of such power and position, who had come close to winning the presidency of the United States, could not refrain from wrangling with a writer entirely uninterested in elective office.

Revealing his torment even more transparently, Clinton dismisses all the "young and very ignorant men" who have failed to recognize that true achievement lay in securing membership to precisely those institutions with which Clinton himself has associated: "Coody, Knickerbocker, and Scottish Fiddle" have no business belittling "the Philosophical Societies of the United States." He left his best insult for Verplanck: "Of Coody it may be said, that he has a great appetite for learning, without any digestion."

Writing in the third person, the insufferably vain mayor cannot resist giving himself a God-sized pat on the back: "Mr. Clinton, amidst his other great qualifications, is distinguished for a marked devotion to science: —few men have read more, and few men can claim more various and extensive knowledge." The pamphleteer still had an eminent career ahead of him—the governorship of New York in 1817, and perennial standing as the father of the Erie Canal—but here, in early 1815, he was still feeling the need to explain why he was greater than a group of upstart writers.

Clinton's pouty pamphlet did nothing to harm any of his local detractors. In 1815, President Madison appointed Paulding secretary of the Board of Navy Commissioners. Verplanck remained a staunch nationalist; in 1818, he delivered a broad historical discourse concerning the rise of an American national culture before one of Clinton's pet institutions, the New-York Historical Society. All the while, William Irving, Jr., sat in the U.S. House of Representatives.[20]

★   ★

The author of *Salmagundi* and *Knickerbocker's History*, late editor of the *Analectic Magazine*, already had a considerable reputation as a man of letters. Without any help from DeWitt Clinton, he understood what that reputation meant—or ought to mean—at this point in his career. When Joseph Delaplaine of Philadelphia asked to include Washington Irving in his *Repository of the Lives and Portraits of Distinguished Americans*, a multivolume work that would begin publication in 1815, Irving gave him a suitably humble, and ultimately clever, reply: "I am already a little too much in the glare of notoriety for my own comfort & advantage, and have an utter repugnance to being obtruded more conspicuously on public notice." With a quip worthy of Ben Franklin, he added: "Were I even vain enough worthy a place in the biographical work you propose, I should decline the hazardous honour for I would rather that ninety nine should ask why I was *not* there, than incur the possibility of one persons asking why I *was*."[21]

Washington Irving had thus become a representative model of literary creativity among the generation of New Yorkers born during and after the

Revolution. Just as in an earlier age London literary clubs had established a fraternity of busy minds, and coffeehouse patrons argued about Sterne and emulated Goldsmith, Irving and his fellows shared their thoughts, and their written words, and so left their mark on the theater district and neighborhood taverns. Washington was a junior partner in the family business, but he was every bit his own man when it came to writing and publishing. It was he who informed his brother William and Gil Verplanck, in January 1815, that the *Analectic* would have to find a new publisher, since Moses Thomas and Bradford & Inskeep were financially ruined (Thomas would rebound, only to fail a second time in 1819). He mentioned the firm Van Winkle & Wiley as a possible alternative. This was prescient: Cornelius S. Van Winkle would become, for him, four years later, the vessel through which "Rip Van Winkle" would come to the public's attention.[22]

For now, however, Irving had ceased to write in the creative vein that had directed his *History of New York*. He had resolved to move on to discover a new talent. As peace resumed, he first thought he would sail with his friend Stephen Decatur on an expedition to the Mediterranean to intimidate the North African pirates; but he changed his mind and opted to go directly to Liverpool, where Peter was minding the family business. —

Having been unable to find the means to extend his literary voice on the "island of the Manhattoes," he sensed that he required a new immersion in Europe if he was to exert further influence as a writer. The Manhattanite prepared to exchange contexts in what would amount to an incredible seventeen-year journey. Writing to Brevoort from shipboard, he said: "I am satisfied that a little absence will be greatly to my advantage." He had no idea what he was in for, or that he would return home an international celebrity.[23]

YEARS ABROAD

CHAPTER 6

Rip Van Winkle Awakes

1815–1819

Why did I dream that sleep o'er-power'd me
In midst of all this heaven?

—John Keats, from "Endymion," 1818

A FTER A VOYAGE MARRED BY BAD WEATHER AND salvaged by the "good humour and good breeding" of his fellow passengers, Irving landed at Liverpool, where Peter ran the European operations of P & E Irving. A week later, he was off again, covering eighty-eight miles through a cultivated landscape, "a perfect garden," to the Birmingham home of his thirty-five-year-old sister Sarah (Sally) and her husband, Henry Van Wart. Van Wart, a successful businessman, was Irving's age. He had become a naturalized British subject that year. Irving arrived at night, unannounced. He so astonished his sister that it took her some time to utter even a word.[1]

He felt completely comfortable with the Van Warts, whose attractive home he nicknamed "the redoubtable castle of Van Tromp." He romped with his young nephews, and described the boys to their grandmother Sarah Irving in New York as "the most intimate friends imaginable." It was a heady summer. Napoleon was finally undone at Waterloo. Others of Irving's countrymen living in England at that moment were touting Andrew Jackson's victory over the British at New Orleans six months earlier, but Irving had no desire to participate in games of verbal swordplay with the host country. He was simply pleased to be back in England.

Peter was ill on his brother's arrival in Liverpool. Washington termed it an "inveterate rheumatic complaint." They had not seen one another for seven years, and so Peter had been unable to witness firsthand the extraordinary success of

Knickerbocker's History. The younger brother wrote home encouragingly to Ebenezer: Peter lived in "handsome furnished rooms, and keeping a horse, gig, and servant, but not indulging in any extravagance or dash." To Brevoort, he wrote that his brother was "quite unaltered." Yet Peter's physical debility persisted. When Irving realized that his brother had overbought goods for the family business, he immersed himself in the company's books: "I have no intention for the present of visiting the continent," he wrote to Ebenezer at the end of the year. "I wish to see business on a regular footing before I travel for pleasure. I should otherwise have a constant load of anxiety on my mind."[2]

In the spring of 1816, after nearly one year abroad, Irving learned from Brevoort that James Paulding was to wed the sister of their old chum Gouverneur Kemble. Contemplating his friend's rough and ready attitude toward politics and writing alike, he averred: "I am satisfied Paulding's talents will secure his fortunes with the ruling [Republican] party and he will make a good husband and be all the happier for the change of condition." In the same letter, he asked Brevoort to convey unusually warm thoughts to Serena Livingston, who was asking after him and who, like the late Matilda Hoffman, was a frail figure. "She always looked too delicate and spiritual for this rough, coarse world," Irving cooed. "She is the heroine of all my poetical thoughts where they would picture any thing very feminine and lovely." Whether or not he dared to think himself a suitable match for this daughter of an old and noble New York family, we cannot know—but Irving knew that she was being pursued by others. As things turned out, Irving's friends were slowly finding the financial means to permit them to do what he could not: Brevoort, who was born to wealth, married Laura Elizabeth Carson of Charleston, South Carolina, in the late summer of 1817; and then the long-affianced Pauldings were wed.[3]

Meanwhile, Peter's health was not restored until the spring of 1816. Washington, "harassed & hagridden by the cares & anxieties of business," assumed he would now be free to pursue artistic fancies. But the state of business remained precarious. "I have attempted to divert my thoughts into other channels, to revive the literary feeling & to employ myself with my pen; but at present it is impossible," he complained in another letter to Brevoort. "My mind is in a sickly state and my imagination so blighted that it cannot put forth a blossom nor even a green leaf." But he was reading for pleasure. The alternately sublime and devilish Lord Byron was nearing the height of his popularity on both sides of the Atlantic, and Irving suggested pieces of his poetry for Moses Thomas of Philadelphia to publish.[4]

He calculated that his future depended on the success or failure of the family business, and after a dry season with his pen he appeared to doubt that he could make ends meet as a writer. Asked by Brevoort when he anticipated returning home, he voiced his uncertainty: "I must wait here a while in a passive state, watching the turn of events." A short time earlier, he had speculated about establishing a household and finding a wife. As he divulged to Brevoort, the "when" and "how" were elusive, but the "where" was fixed: New York. England had not provided comfort enough to displace "that delightful little spot of earth" from his master plan. But now his "sober schemes" had bled into "the dreams of fairy land." This was a phrase he had previously used in his journal of 1810: "I never think on those dreams of fairy land without a confidence that there is something in store for mankind infinitely more delightful than any thing we can conceive of the kind."5

Washington Irving had made no particular mark in English literary circles—this despite the earlier legwork undertaken on his behalf by his self-appointed literary manager, Brevoort. But he continued to enjoy extended holiday respites with the lively Van Warts, playing his flute as the children danced, aware even in revelrous moments that he had left Peter to his own devices back in Liverpool. He worried about Peter, but at the same time, he was not prepared to martyr himself.

In Manhattan, the author's seventy-eight-year-old mother was entering the last year of her life. Sarah Irving reached out for news of her distant children. Her youngest, somewhat isolated in spirit as well as in geography, replied solicitously: "I hope you do not task yourself too much in writing such long letters. I know it must be a matter of trouble and weariness at your age." He assured her that Ebenezer's letters covered the same ground and that she should favor him with only "a few lines." He acknowledged that Peter was "more delicate in Constitution" these days. "For myself," he added, "I never was heartier and am only affraid [*sic*] of growing *too fat*."6

His appetite for the company of attractive women seemed undiminished. To his trusted friend Brevoort, he recounted a "ramble" with Peter at Dovedale, in Derbyshire, in January 1817, where the brothers had joined a party that included a pair of marriageable daughters: "The Miss Bathursts had that delightful frankness & simplicity of manners which I have so often remarked in the really fine women of this country." When the hike took them amid thickets and stones, the Irving brothers rose to the occasion. The awkward footing invited acts of chivalry, and a mawkish report from the younger Irving:

I had a woman, lovely woman! clinging to me for assistance & protection—looking up with beseeching weakness & dependence in the midst of difficulties & Dangers—while I in all the swelling pride of a lord of the

Creation, looked upon my feeble companion with an eye of infinite benevolence & fostering care—braved every peril of land & water—and sustained a scratched hand or a wet foot with a fortitude that called forth the
admiration of the softer sex!

Irving drooled on boyishly to complete his fairy tale: "If a Strawberry
Smotherd in cream has any consciousness of its delicious situation, it must
feel as I felt at that moment."

What sounds like a physical sensation actually resists corporeal excitement. Irving's is an engagement of the mind more than the body. His "fortitude" is not lust; he prefers the unreal. This will become more apparent as
time progresses.[7]

★   ★

In the early spring of 1817, following the unexpected loss of his wife, the sister
of Maria Fenno Hoffman, Gulian Verplanck visited Liverpool. "He seemed in
good health and tolerable spirits, though thinner than usual," Irving wrote to
Brevoort. Verplanck had spoken of the Hoffmans, prompting Irving to express
his concern that public contention would swallow up Josiah Ogden Hoffman: "I
wish he would give up political life—it is a vile tissue of petty trick & intrigue in
the State of New York, & unaccompanied by either honour or real advantage."[8]

Irving learned that Serena Livingston had married a military hero of the
War of 1812. He could not have been surprised. Aware before he sailed that
he had but a slight chance of winning her hand, Irving had persisted in viewing Serena as a shining example of feminine appeal—while, unbeknownst to
Irving and to Serena alike, her monstrously rich father, John R. Livingston,
was grooming himself to be the most successful brothel owner in New York.
The rejected author had cause to reflect again on his bachelorhood, doubtless
taking to heart his earlier words to Brevoort: "Fortune by her tardy favours
and capricious freaks seems to discourage all my matrimonial resolves." In his
mid-thirties, he was increasingly weighing the possibility that he was "doomed
to live an old Bachelor." He owned a piece of P & E Irving, but the company
was failing. And he was not publishing anything new.

In mid-1817, Irving considered returning to New York, but changed his
mind in July of that year. To Brevoort he wrote: "I have weighed every thing
pro and con on the subject of returning home & have for the present abandoned the idea." His mother had died in April, and so there was no longer a
sense of urgency—if there truly had been, while Ebenezer was nearby—of
comforting her in her old age.

At this time, with Anglo-American cultural relations in flux and critics on both sides of the Atlantic unable to predict the next phase, Irving became proactive. He contemplated a third edition of *Knickerbocker's History*, to be illustrated by his friend Washington Allston, the young American painter whom he had first met in Italy; but he also recommenced writing stories. He did not even tell Brevoort what he was doing, presuming that his immersion in a new volume would strike his friend as a "precarious" means of subsistence. He felt he was in a nearly desperate situation, he said, "cast homeless & pennyless upon the world." But he could conceive of no more productive path than the writing life. It was his one recognized talent, and the only potential source of income his brothers had ever thought he should take a financial risk on. Meanwhile, he beseeched Brevoort to pay him a visit—but his former roommate was readying himself for marriage.[9]

At this moment in Irving's postwar adventures, the door cracked open to the British world of letters. In August 1817, he was invited to dine with John Murray II, the premier publisher and bookseller of the day, at Murray's celebrated place at 50 Albemarle Street, London. The effusive Murray had already outdone his late father, an entrepreneur who had begun his publishing business in 1768, circulating among the literary elite in the age of Samuel Johnson. The son, Irving's elder by five years, was close to Walter Scott and was also the publisher of Lord Byron's hugely successful *Childe Harold's Pilgrimage*. Murray ostentatiously showed his American guest his most recent communication from Byron, who was then in Venice writing Canto IV of his heartrending poem.

Irving was flattered to be keeping such company, and was tentatively hopeful of a future collaboration with Murray. At dinner, he suggested that he help the London publisher make speedy arrangements in America, thereby circumventing those who were coming out with first American editions of his most treasured authors' works. Theirs was still an age of book piracy. Few adhered to the legal principle of international copyright, and author's rights were regularly overlooked. Irving had devised what he thought was an irresistible means of benefiting author and publisher at once.[10]

Immediately after his auspicious meeting with Murray, Irving embarked on a tour of Scotland. In Edinburgh, he called on Archibald Constable, the Scottish equivalent of Murray; and he dined with the respected literary critic Francis Jeffrey, editor of the prestigious *Edinburgh Review*, who concurred with his view of the bitterness that characterized partisan politics in America. Jeffrey had visited New York when Irving was editor of the *Analectic*, but this was their first meeting. Irving had begun a meaningful conversation with powerful men who could help him later on. The encounters with Murray, Constable, and Jeffrey made the American keenly aware that he stood to earn a good deal more by securing a British copyright for his past or future works.[11]

The book trade of Irving's early years imposed limitations on authors, and publishing opportunities were clearly spelled out: Book patrons might respond to a newspaper advertisement and subscribe in advance to a book-in-progress intended for modest distribution; an author could self-publish, bearing all costs; a publisher could agree to publish if the author paid in advance the cost of paper and incidentals, which could be recouped after sales had proceeded; or, finally, a publisher might contract with an author of some reputation, willingly undertake the risk, and wait to realize profits. This last arrangement was by no means automatic for fiction writers—indeed, there were no successful novelists in the United States. Copyright itself was fungible: The condensed version of a dictionary could be printed, for example, without compensating the original author whose text formed the substance of the abridgment; no one could mount a legal challenge.

Most American publishers made their money on pirated reprints of British works. Irving had already broken ground when he convinced Bradford & Inskeep to assume the total risk in publishing his *History of New York*. They received a 20 percent commission on sales, and he repaid their production costs only after his profits began to roll in. This experience may already have suggested to Irving, living abroad, that it was possible to negotiate for better payment and better conditions than were usual. He anticipated coordinating copyrights on both sides of the Atlantic with the help of his contacts in New York and Philadelphia. He knew, at any rate, that an *activist* middle-class author was the only kind who stood any chance of earning a living with his pen; otherwise, the field would be left to independently wealthy scions of the landed elite.[12]

These thoughts came to him at a pregnant moment in the literature of the English language. Walter Scott had recently come out with a romantic adventure, *Waverley,* and was poised to take the reading public by storm again with *Rob Roy.* For his plots, he drew on a stock of anecdotal materials taken from Scottish popular history, to great effect. In America, *Waverley* fed the taste for a new kind of narrative fiction: the historical action novel; and a new kind of hero: the adventuresome individual. With a protagonist who defied convention, Scott went beyond the prior century's colorless concern with artificial self-restraint. Irving, and even more dramatically, James Fenimore Cooper, would feel Scott's influence, and adapt.

Owing to his finances, Irving was at an uncertain, but nonetheless energetic, point in his career. His magisterial mid-twentieth-century biographer, Stanley T. Williams, insists on emphasizing the brooding and the confusion:

"In his depression gloom spread over both past and future; he could not re-member that he ever had a normal moment. He was again at Matilda's bed-side; he again took leave of his mother; he again shriveled under the business whirlwind."

It is true that the author was under a considerable strain. But Washington Irving was more complex than this long-established description suggests. A hyperbolic script that sees him "shriveling" and unable to recall a "normal moment" ignores the substance of his life experience or what it was that in-spired Irving to entertain the public. Nor, by relying on select letters, does it account for the outlet his restless correspondence with Brevoort and a few others provided. Letter writing was nothing if not a sublime appeal to friend-ship, and so Irving's openness, his confessional style, does not necessarily in-dicate a clinical depression on the scale Williams depicts. One who knew him well in the years immediately after the *Sketch Book* came out noted that he could be "oppressed with morbid feelings" at times of extreme self-judgment, only to return to his more routine conviviality, his radiant "enthusiasm," when his conversation "sparkle[d] again with wit and humor." That sounds rather like what we might call "artistic temperament."

He fretted about his professional future, and would continue to, but we want to be careful not to construct a stock portrait of the distracted, mercur-ial, haunted artist, down on his luck and wallowing in fear. For then we deny that there was any sophistication to Irving's ready observations amid his trav-els, and we overlook his incisive knowledge of the publishing trade. In truth, neither dissatisfaction nor joylessness typified him: "He has a wonderful knack at shutting his eye to the sinister side of anything," wrote the acquain-tance quoted above. He did not cease to appreciate his literary gift; nor did he fail to judge cogently where he stood among writers when he used his con-nections to secure an introduction to John Murray, or for that matter, Walter Scott, whose towering reputation he felt was fully deserved.[13]

★   ★

On August 30, 1817, during his month's travels through Scotland, Irving paid a call at Abbotsford, the still-unfinished estate Scott had built in 1812. Although Americans of the prior generation, adoring the stately columns of Greek and Roman architecture, had expressed ambivalence toward old English castles and Gothic structures, Irving partook of the mood of Scott and the budding Romantic consciousness. He saw grandeur in the formative wild, believing that enchantment lay in the age of chivalry, as the imagination might recapture it. Approaching Scott's home, Irving carried a letter of introduction from the poet

Thomas Campbell—a favor returned for the short biography Irving had contributed years before to an edition of the poet's works.

The weather had been, as Irving described it in sequential letters to Peter, "sulky and threatening," "sullen, gloomy," as he traveled in a carriage along the banks of the Tweed ("a clear stream . . . running between naked grey Hills," he wrote in his journal). Having heard only that Scott, now forty-six, was putting the finishing touches on *Rob Roy*, Irving had no idea whether he would even be seen. As the postillion of his hired coach brought Irving's letter of introduction over to the house, the passenger sat at the gate. His brief accompanying note asked politely whether Scott would be able to receive him "in the course of the day."

Then came the sound of dogs loudly barking, and a sight Irving would never forget. As he recorded in his journal that day, and wrote to Peter and to Brevoort: "Scott himself appeared limping up the hill." The great Scott was tall, well made but for his one lame leg, and wore country attire. He strolled over, with the help of a staff, to where Irving waited. Not only did the celebrated author receive the American warmly, seizing him by the hand; he insisted that Irving remain with him several more days so that he could show the promising author of *A History of New York* the surrounding lands.

"I was accordingly whirled to the portal of the cottage," Irving recounted, "and in a few moments found myself at the breakfast table." Songs wafted through the Scott house. Seventeen-year-old Sophia Scott was often present, and during his stay she more than once sang pretty border tunes for him. Converting Scott himself into a character worthy of fiction, Irving described the experience with unprecedented fulsomeness to Brevoort, who had presented *Knickerbocker's History* to the poet-novelist four years earlier:

> You know the charms of Scotts conversation but you have not lived with him in the country—you have not rambled with him about his favourite hills and glens and burns. You have not seen him dispensing happiness around him in this little rural domain. I came prepared to admire him; but he completely won my heart and made me love him. . . . I was with him from morning to night and was constantly astonished and delighted by the perpetual & varied flow of his conversation. It is just as entertaining as one of his novels, and exactly like them in style, point, humour, character & picturesqueness. I parted with him with the utmost regret.

As they had ranged over the breezy barrenness—Irving, Scott, and the hounds—the New Yorker had brought back to mind the lullabies Lizzie, his Scottish nanny, had sung to him when he was a boy living on William Street.

Perhaps never in his life would Washington Irving feel so charmed by another human being. What he did not know was how eager Scott had been to meet *him*. A knowing memoirist explained: "Scott's family well remember the delight with which he received this announcement [of Irving's arrival]—he was at breakfast, and sallied forth instantly, dogs and children after him as usual, to greet the guest, and conduct him in person from the highway to the door." Scott approached Irving without pretense or posturing—they made an immediate connection.

Listening to his host's expansive storytelling over five days, Irving must have revealed that he was moving in a new direction in his writing. His Scottish notebooks show him experimenting with a romantic formula. We can only guess at what direction Scott gave him, but it is clear that the younger man wanted advice. Irving and the famed "Border Minstrel" were of an uncommon fraternity. In 1819, the year of Irving's "Rip Van Winkle," Scott's pen produced the equally memorable romance *Ivanhoe*. They would share the limelight at the same time, and it was light enough to contain both of them.[14]

☆   ☆

While Irving wrote and studied, the family's business went bankrupt. Public notification of the failure was given in the *Times* of London on February 2, 1818. By this time, Irving was immersed in teaching himself German, reading folktales, and putting pen to paper with a lively compulsion he had not felt in years. After his return to Liverpool from Scotland in the autumn of 1817, he had learned that his eldest brother, Congressman William Irving, had talked to Henry Clay and others in an effort to find a position for him in the U.S. diplomatic service in London—an escape valve, as the family business went into decline.

His response was, in effect, "Don't worry about me." He told William: "I feel in this as in many other things deeply indebted to your affectionate care for my interests; but I do not anticipate any favors from Government, which has so many zealous and active partisans to serve." Political affairs bored him. He tried to shift attention to the two who could better use the support: "I would rather that all consideration should be given to helping up poor Ebenezer and Peter, and let me take care of myself. I feel excessive anxiety on Ebenezer's account, with such a numerous family to support [at this point five boys and three girls], and I scarcely feel less on Peter's, who is brought down at a period of life when a man begins to crave comfort and ease." As for himself, he vowed to earn what he required "by my own exertions."[15]

Next, his closest American friend in England, the painter Washington Allston, decided to return home. They had a painful parting, and Irving tried unsuccessfully to discourage his friend from going. Years later, Irving said of Allston: "He was the most delightful, the most lovable being I ever knew; a man I would like to have had always by my side—to have gone through life with; his nature was so refined, so intellectual, so genial, so pure."[16] These comments from one who was destined to go through life without a spouse tell us something important: He treated his male friends as wife substitutes. This had to do with intimacy, not sex as we understand it.

With Brevoort now married, Irving struck up a gracious correspondence with his best friend's bride so as to minimize potential feelings of jealousy. Still, Irving was becoming ever more conscious that his bachelorhood distanced him. "I am almost ashamed to say that at first the news had rather the effect of making me feel melancholy than glad," he wrote to Brevoort. "It seemed in a manner to divorce us forever; for marriage is the grave of Bachelors intimacy and after having lived & grown together for many years, so that our habits thoughts & feelings were quite blended & intertwined, a separation of this kind is a serious matter." These remarks employing the vocabulary of marital dissolution to a friendship are possibly the most personally revealing of any Irving ever wrote. Yet this did not mean that Brevoort would abandon his interest in Irving's writing; he would, in fact, have more to do with Irving's financial success in the near term than anyone else in their circle.[17]

In this generation, young bachelors off on their own were easy to typecast as morally reckless. They minimized appearing "dangerous" to society by associating closely with another male in a controlled setting. Living with his family while in his twenties, and then "graduating" to rooming with Brevoort, Irving exhibited dependability in a relationship. Then there was the matter of carnal knowledge. A woman from a genteel family was expected to be a virgin when she wed, but a bachelor at this time often resorted to sexual relations with the kind of female he would never think of marrying. His bachelor cohort tended to be aware of the occasional sexual indulgence on the part of one of their number.

When the rambunctious Peter Kemble, sometime Lad of Kilkenny and younger brother of Gouverneur Kemble, returned from a trip to England in 1811, Irving was hypercritical, going on at length to Brevoort:

We have treated Peter with great contempt, and take all possible occasions to flout him and piss upon him. I am convinced there is nothing on earth so truly *despiseable*, as a great man shorn of his power. Peter however consoles himself by courting all the little girls in town, who are under Sixteen; for you must know this old lecher has become so dainty and sickly in his palate, that nothing will go down with him but your squab pidgeons and your first weeks green pease. He has likewise become a notable leerer at buxom chamber maids and servant girls, and there is not a little bitch of a house maid that runs *proud* about the streets, but what Peter has had the nosing of her—not that the little villain tups them all, but he is one of your little gluttons whose eyes are greedier than his belly, and where he honestly Rodgers one, he dishonours a dozen with his lascivious looks.[18]

Here we can see that Irving was a man who recognized that within bachelor subculture impulses were unpredictable. He spoke a bachelor's language, understood lust, and easily recurred to the verbs "tup" and "Rodger." At the same time, he abhorred uncontrolled libertinism.[19]

In 1813, while her brother Henry was abroad, Margaret Brevoort joked that the generally upbeat Irving needed only one more thing to be complaint-free. According to her, he said "he would be perfectly happy if his wife was here." By which he had meant Henry. Forming so close a bond with Brevoort, sharing their books and their meals, Irving experienced the functional equivalent of an early nineteenth-century marriage.[20]

It is revealing, too, that upon Allston's departure, Irving filled the gap by embracing another American painter living in England, Allston's friend Charles Robert Leslie. Leslie was to contribute, along with Allston, an engraving for Moses Thomas's forthcoming new edition of the *History of New York;* Irving and he would grow extremely close in these years. The child of Marylanders, Leslie was born in London in 1794, grew up in the United States, and was apprenticed to the Philadelphia booksellers Bradford & Inskeep right around the time Irving was publishing his *History* with them. Leslie then returned to England to pursue his art career. "You came to London just when I was losing Allston," Leslie wrote to Irving, "and I stood in need of an intimate friend of similar tastes with my own." When Leslie and fellow artist Peter Powell moved in together, Irving joked: "I hope you and Peter are getting comfortable through the Honey Moon, and find housekeeping pleasant." This was what the male bond of friendship consisted of among the unmarried and upwardly mobile of Irving's generation.[21]

Living for the moment with his bachelor brother Peter, Irving would make up for the psychological loss occasioned by Brevoort's marriage and Allston's departure. He would move on, and continue his bachelor wanderings. Indeed, as his bachelor status became more and more a part of his professional identity, he would make it all seem exciting.[22]

★ ★

Having already refused his brother William's help in finding a steady job for him, Irving similarly refused the generous offer of Stephen Decatur to secure him an appointment as first clerk in the Navy Department, though the salary of $2,400 would have enabled him to "live as a prince," as William put it. "It may also be a mere stepping-stone to higher station," coaxed the congressman. "How happy I will be to see you all in a comfortable way once more." The "you all" encompassed Peter, who had similarly resolved to stay in England and eke out a living. William thought a blessing had befallen them when the celebrated Decatur proved himself such "a worthy true hearted fellow" by allowing his fondness for Washington to rub off onto the entire Irving family. But in recognizing Washington's capacity to win friends, William still could not figure him—or Peter—out: "Home has lost its charms to both the Doctor and Washington," he concluded, in a letter to Ebenezer. Washington was no less direct with Ebenezer, insisting: "I am quite unfitted for political life."[23]

As the year 1819 opened, and having relocated from Liverpool to London, Washington relied on the two men of business he most trusted, his brother Ebenezer and Henry Brevoort, to manage his new writings. To Ebenezer he sent a parcel containing an introductory essay and four stories, and asked him to convey them to Moses Thomas. His instructions: "The copy right must be taken out by the booksellers, but privately secured to me." He wanted his brother to know how much was riding on these stories: If they were well received, he had a pile more waiting. "I shall feel very anxious to hear of the success of this first re-appearance on the literary stage—Should it be successful, I trust I shall be able henceforth to keep up an occasional fire." This was the first anyone back home had heard about The Sketch Book, "a work to be continued occasionally." These test productions consisted of an "Author's Account of Himself," "The Voyage," "Roscoe," "The Wife," and "Rip Van Winkle." Irving was banking on them.[24]

A second communication with Ebenezer, meant as well for the less patient eyes of William, contains even greater insight into the youngest brother's state of mind and prescient sense of purpose: "I feel by no means satisfied to rest my reputation on my preceding writings. I have suffered [meaning: "allowed"] several precious years of youth and lively imagination to pass by unimproved, and it behooves me to make the most of what is left. If I indeed have the means within me of establishing a legitimate literary reputation, this is the very period of life most auspicious for it." Having rejected government employment, he had only this: Whatever he was to be, he was to be as a result of his pen.[25]

No sooner had he sent off his manuscript to Ebenezer than Irving received a disturbing letter from Brevoort informing him that Moses Thomas—"poor

Thomas"—had met with a financial reversal. The eager yet guarded author needed a new publisher immediately. He wrote back to his friend, who was now publishing with the reconstituted *Analectic:* "Will you," he asked Brevoort, "as you are a literary man and a man of leisure, take it under your care?"[26]

Each new piece of intelligence forced him to react. On March 3, 1819, he learned that Gulian Verplanck had delivered an address before the New-York Historical Society the previous December in which he revealed his deep disturbance over Irving's *History*, which was about to come out in a new edition. Protective of those, like himself, of Dutch heritage, Verplanck felt that Irving had gone too far in belittling his ancestors, "wasting [his] fancy on an ungrateful theme" and indulging in "coarse caricature." Irving and Verplanck had a history of friendship. They had read the law together at Josiah Ogden Hoffman's; they had come together to stare down DeWitt Clinton; and they had met up in England at the time of Verplanck's bereavement.

Rather than express agitation concerning Verplanck's public remarks, Irving was entirely conciliatory: Verplanck "said nothing of my work that I have not long thought of it myself," he wrote to Ebenezer. "He is one of the honestest men I know of, in speaking his opinion." He could not have been displeased by another of Verplanck's reasoned opinions, expressed before the same audience: "This writer [Irving] has not yet fulfilled all the promise he has given to his country." Irving was obviously in a good mood when, in a letter to Brevoort the next month, he read irony in the fact that he had seen the text of Verplanck's oration "just as I had finished the little story of Rip Van Winkle." Diedrich Knickerbocker was staging a comeback.[27]

Already known for his good business sense, Henry Brevoort surpassed Irving's expectations. He not only consented to the task of finding a publisher for the *Sketch Book* and arranging for the author's compensation but also influenced production and marketing. Securing the American copyright for Irving, Brevoort sold the first run of two thousand copies to the New York publisher-bookseller Charles Wiley. Wiley's partner, who bore the fortuitous name of Cornelius S. Van Winkle, agreed to print the serial publication. Philadelphia sales were placed in the hands of another of the "honestest" men Irving knew, the financially wounded Moses Thomas; separate deals were made with wholesalers in Boston and Baltimore. By selecting top-grade paper, Brevoort justified a higher sale price. He then advanced funds of his own—to grease the machinery, as it were—and the cover price on Irving's short pieces, which ranged from 50 to 87.5 cents, allowed for unprecedented profits: A Walter Scott novel cost $2.00 at this time, and once the seven separate installments of the *Sketch Book* (twenty-eight stories altogether) were bought, the reader would have paid more than $5.00. This was possible because of another innovation, also to be credited to Brevoort: The format would be large (octavo), on top-grade paper, in 12-point instead of the customary 8-point type.

The *Sketch Book* would be a pleasure to hold as well as to read. Britain, as a rule dismissive of American cultural trends, had long been deferred to for English-language publishing innovations. As the historian of publishing James N. Green aptly notes, "Now the world was turned upside down; an American was setting the style in book design. . . . This was the end of colonialism in literature." The Edinburgh publisher Archibald Constable, whose bookshop Irving had visited during his tour, would soon publish Scott's *Ivanhoe* in octavo, taking the cue from Irving's *Sketch Book* and upgrading the presentation of good fiction.[28]

The first paperbound *Sketch Book* sold in the United States in June 1819. As readers turned to the opening piece, "The Author's Account of Himself," they became instantly reacquainted with the Irving of *Knickerbocker* fame, except now he was "Geoffrey Crayon," a *nom de plume* that would prove as enduring as "Diedrich Knickerbocker."

Thus, *The Sketch Book of Geoffrey Crayon, Gent.* was born, and the Washington Irving who had been principally associated with a historical satire was henceforth disconnected in the popular imagination from his Manhattan roots and chiefly linked to his European productions and to an Anglo-American cultural nexus. In the minds of his countrymen back home, he would increasingly have to defend his Anglophile tendencies and his decision to remain abroad.

Opening the *Sketch Book,* then, "Crayon" introduces himself as an American with a "rambling propensity" who wandered in the imagination even as his native country—"teeming with wild fertility"—possessed all the natural scenery and endowments a person could ever ask for. He had been privileged to meet some of the "great men" of America. "But Europe," he explains, offered something else, "the charms of storied and poetical association. There were to be seen the masterpieces of art, the refinements of highly cultivated society, the quaint peculiarities of ancient and local custom." Explaining the title of his offering, Crayon observes: "As it is the fashion for modern tourists to travel pencil in hand, and bring home their portfolios filled with sketches, I am disposed to get up a few for the entertainment of my friends."[29]

In "The Voyage," the first of Crayon's longer ruminations, he describes his passage to England. The epigraph to the piece comes from an "Old Poem" about sea travel: "Hallo my fancie, whither wilt thou go?" The voyager has left his home, having "closed one volume of the world and its concerns" while preparing to open another. At sea, he meditates, "all is vacancy" but for his "day dreaming" and his "reveries." Crayon thrives on this sensibility until he learns how the imagination can move from producing good thoughts to summoning horror. He takes in the sight of a months-old shipwreck in the middle of the shapeless seascape. Before him lies a battered, nameless vessel, seaweed draped over its drifting pieces. The emotional narrator focuses on the humanity lost: "But where, I thought, is the crew!" "What sighs have been wafted after that ship, what prayers offered up at the deserted fireside of home."

Finally within sight of Liverpool after the protracted ocean crossing, Irving (for this is, no doubt, an embellished autobiographical account) peers through a telescope as he sails up the Mersey: "My eye dwelt on neat cottages with their trim shrubberies and green grass plots. I saw the mouldering ruin of an abbey over run with ivy, and the taper spire of a village church riding from the brow of a neighbouring hill." Here is the England he will honor in the later numbers of the *Sketch Book*. But for the moment, it was enough to recount the scene at the breezy port, "thronged with people." The merchant who was most eager for docking, whose livelihood was tied up in the cargo, was immediately identifiable: "I knew him by his calculating brow and restless air." Another of the greeters, an uneasy young woman, "leaning forward from among the crowd," was at last able to set aside her worries "when I heard a faint voice call her name." Her husband was a "poor sailor," his life despaired of through the voyage, who only hoped to survive this long, and who now, though weak and wasted and nearly unrecognizable, was able to be with his wife.

The Irving of *A History of New York* made light of nearly everything. The new Irving generated pathos. Having arrived in England, his American voyager stood steady as one of a crowd, yet he was a self-conscious outsider, and a bachelor: "I alone was solitary and idle . . . a stranger in the land." Everything to Irving was a human drama. He was the man of a thousand sketches, and from here forward there was to be no respite from engagement and commitment: friends and traveling companions, sights to marvel at, experiences to taste together—but, crucially, no wife, no children, no permanence.[30]

The next selection in the *Sketch Book* is "Roscoe," and here Irving offers up a portrait of a luminary of Liverpool, no longer well-known, whom Americans of this age esteemed as the author of the *Life of Lorenzo De Medici* (1795), a study of the fifteenth-century Florentine statesman and poet. William Roscoe was in his mid-sixties when Irving encountered him by chance; he was, by then, better known locally as a banker than as an "elegant" historian. Irving, who had nothing to gain by flattering Roscoe, regarded him as something of a model of what a dignified author, born without prospects—"born in a place apparently ungenial to the growth of literary talent"—could accomplish. It was not his money that sustained the author, for Roscoe had suffered a reversal of fortune, and his library of rare old books had to be auctioned off: "He is independent of the world around him. He lives with antiquity and with posterity. With antiquity, in the sweet communions of studious retirement, and with posterity in the generous aspirings after future renown." He remained, for Irving, "above the reach of pity," his life a precious example of the return one reaps in personifying decency and purity.[31]

By coincidence it would seem, for he mentions nothing of Washington Irving, the South Carolina–born Dr. Charles Caldwell, a much-published and notoriously self-important professor of medicine, made his own voyage to Liverpool in 1821, where he, too, had occasion to meet William Roscoe. Caldwell had earlier written a treatise on physiognomy, the "science" that associated facial traits with personality and intellectual capacity; so, whereas Irving was interested in the celebrated Roscoe as a man of letters, Caldwell studied him up close for his "noble countenance, and a size and form of head indicative of a high order of moral and intellectual strength and efficiency." The doctor found, through casual examination, that Roscoe "had derived from nature a good and improvable, but not a pre-eminent constitution of mind." Cultivation was one thing, naturally endowed greatness quite another. Roscoe was, in physiognomic terms, no George Washington: "In his general appearance he reminded me of Washington; but in majesty and grandeur of person, and in what constitutes strength and magnificence of head and countenance, he was greatly inferior. So, however, was every other member of the human family I ever beheld. . . . Washington stood alone." As the self-anointed arbiter of manly perfection, Dr. Caldwell could hardly have been expected to yield authority to Geoffrey Crayon. The point is that the Liverpudlian William Roscoe should have attracted all this attention.

Before we dismiss Dr. Caldwell altogether, it is worth appending his diagnosis of the host country more generally. Based on a cursory inspection of English faces when he arrived in Liverpool, Caldwell invoked national standards of beauty. English men, as well as women, were unequal to their American counterparts in measures of "elasticity, vigor, and springiness." The problem the English faced was a matter of physiological adaptation, and lay in "a want of cellular tissue." The charming doctor made it his duty to vocalize his theories in the presence of his hosts. It is, therefore, no surprise that Crayon's character sketches were better loved in England than Caldwell's.[32]

Following "Roscoe" in the *Sketch Book* is another exercise in rending hearts, this one called "The Wife." Once more, Irving seeks to give nobility to those who confront financial ruin, and then spiritually rise above it. The young wife in this maudlin little story is named Mary. She has been shielded from the knowledge that her husband's fortunes were recently overturned. George, the sullen husband, cannot bear to steal the smile from Mary's face, and so has kept her in the dark. When Crayon convinces George to come clean, and he finally does, the remarkable Mary is all aglow; she had sensed George's despair. Knowing that the real cause of it was mere money, she now embraces the tiny country cottage they were forced to move to, gathers up the strawberries, and gaily hastens down the lane to welcome her husband. George Leslie comes home to the perfect, uncomplaining wife and finds "exquisite felicity" with her. "The Wife," drafted in 1817, was meant to reflect on the experience of Washington Allston, whose wife of six years died in London in 1815; and yet, in a curious twist, the main character's surname is that of Allston's close friend, Leslie.[33]

The final piece in the initial grouping was the one that made all the difference. As the story goes—and there seems no reason to contest its essential accuracy—"Rip Van Winkle" was conceived and penned fairly spontaneously, in June 1818, after Irving had engaged in a nostalgic conversation one evening with his brother-in-law Henry Van Wart, during which the writer felt himself transported back to the Hudson Highlands. He disappeared into his room in his sister's home and composed through the night.[34] As Irving admitted whenever asked (and even inserted as a postscript in the 1848 edition), he drew upon a popular German folktale, "Peter Klaus," for the central theme of his story, but then he gave the title character and his surroundings the purely New World personality they needed to inject new life into an old tale.

Irving never tells us precisely how he came up with the name "Rip Van Winkle." Rip (alternatively "Ryp") Van Dam was a top official of colonial New York, a member of the Governor's Council for thirty-three years, and acting governor in the 1730s. Paulding refers to him in a *Salmagundi* essay as the "illustrious RYP VAN DAM . . . too modest a man ever to do any thing worthy of being particularly recorded."[35] The modest talents of Irving's Rip harmonize with that characterization. Though Cornelius S. Van Winkle became Irving's printer *after* the story was penned, he had been a mainstay of the New York publishing world for years. His office near the corner of Wall Street and Broadway could not have been more central. Moreover, the name "Van Winkle" was not uncommon in Dutch parts of New York State when Irving was growing up.[36]

Rip's story, so long familiar, has been slowly lost in Americans' historic memory. A survey of college-educated men and women born after the 1960s reveals that only about one-third could identify Rip Van Winkle at all, and most of these associated him with a television cartoon.[37] Prior to this era, Irving's story was almost universally read before high school. So perhaps some refreshing is in order.

"Rip Van Winkle" is a tale "found among the papers of the late Diedrich Knickerbocker," the author informs us. The title character is a late colonial Dutch-American who lives in a village below the Kaatskill (Catskill) Mountains of New York State, founded in the time of Peter Stuyvesant. Rip is a good-natured fellow of simple tastes, but he is a "henpecked husband." His wife nagged him because he seemed allergic to work of any kind; yet he would sit for long hours and patiently fish, and he did assist his neighbors in their most strenuous building projects. It was simply his wife whom Rip was seeking to avoid, and his own farm that he ignored. He was a particular favorite of the village children, for he played alongside them and told them ghost stories. Rip Van Winkle was "one of those happy mortals of foolish, well oiled dispositions, who take the world easy." His alter ego, his companion in idleness, was his dog Wolf. Dame Van Winkle "looked upon Wolf with an evil eye as the cause of his master's going so often astray."

One autumn day, with Wolf at his side, Rip escapes into the woods. He is carrying his gun, and on the hunt for squirrels. Feeling tired, he plops down on a hill overlooking the "lordly Hudson," and uncomfortably contemplates the next time he will have to face his wife. He comes to as a voice is calling out his name over and over, and he eventually sights a stranger lumbering up the rocks toward him, "a short, square built old fellow" with a "grizzled beard," dressed in "the antique Dutch fashion." He asks Rip to help him carry his load.

They come to an amphitheatre, where there are more quaintly dressed, grave-looking Dutchmen: "The whole group reminded Rip of the figures in an old Flemish painting." They are playing at ninepins—bowling. The balls roll, echoing through the mountains thunderously. Rip shares the men's liquor and finds it flavorful: He "reiterated his visits to the flagon so often that at length his senses were overpowered, his eyes swam in his head." He awakes recalling the experience, fearing how he is going to make excuses to his wife.

He calls for Wolf, but his dog is nowhere to be seen. He looks for his trusty fowling piece, and finds instead an old, rusty firelock. He suspects his gun has been stolen, and this poor replica left in its place. Now famished, Rip descends the mountain and returns to the village. The people he gazes at look unfamiliar, and they dress differently, too. He suddenly notices that he has grown a foot-long beard. Children congregate around him—but he does not know them either. The world seems "bewitched." He blames it on the liquor.

His house has decayed, and as he enters he realizes that his wife has gone. A stars and stripes flutters from a pole in town, and it means nothing to him. At the old village inn, the sign no longer displays "the ruby face of King George under which he had smoked so many a peaceful pipe"; George's red coat is now blue, and the head wears a cocked hat. Underneath it are the words "GENERAL WASHINGTON."

The strangers about him ask how he has voted—Federal or Democrat. The flustered Rip explains, "I am a poor quiet man, a native of this place, and a loyal subject of the King—God bless him!" Branded an old Tory, this man who has slept through the American Revolution inquires after his old neighbors. One by one, he is told that they are all either dead or have moved away. "Does nobody here know Rip Van Winkle?" he finally pleads. And now, Rip is directed to "a precise counterpart of himself" (as he remembers his own appearance), who is leaning against a tree.

"God knows," exclaimed he, at his wit's end, "I'm not myself.—I'm somebody else—that's me yonder—no—that's somebody else got into my shoes—I was myself last night; but I fell asleep on the mountain—and they've changed my gun—and every thing's changed—and I'm changed—and I can't tell what's my name, or who I am!"

His son and namesake—"an urchin begetting his own likeness" at the beginning of the story—is a grown man.

Then, as a woman pushes through the assembled crowd and takes charge, everything begins to make sense. Rip interrogates his own daughter, and finds that his wife died a short time earlier: "She broke a blood vessel in a fit of passion at a New England pedlar." His identity now established, he starts feeling better. He becomes a hit in the village every time he tells the story of the twenty-year sleep that had felt to him but a single night. He enjoys life in the "snug well furnished house" of his daughter; he thrives after having "got his neck out of the yoke of matrimony"; he adapts to being a "free citizen of the United States."

Irving concludes the story of Rip Van Winkle with another reference to the Dutch inhabitants of the village: "Even to this day they never hear a thunder storm of a summer afternoon about the Kaatskill, but they say Hendrick Hudson and his crew are at their game of nine pins." That should have been enough, but Irving is not finished until he alludes once more to the local men's fears of contracting with a shrewish wife: "And it is a common wish of all henpecked husbands in the neighbourhood, when life hangs heavy on their hands, that they might have a quieting draught out of Rip Van Winkle's flagon."[38]

So that is the story. Now for its various meanings:

Rip Van Winkle is a lazy Odysseus. No wife pines for him. As endearing a tale of escapism, alienation, and lost identity as this is, the misogynistic element in "Rip Van Winkle" goes beyond the playful satirical remarks contained in Irving's earlier writings. For the bachelor Irving, Dame Van Winkle appears to represent something truly foreboding, and Rip embodies a quality that repeats in Irving's fictional personae and among characters in his tales: a self-sustaining wanderlust, a liberated amiability (he calls it "idleness") not meant to be deterred by any human force outside himself. And then, as the psychologist Steve Rubin suggests, Rip's twenty-year sleep can be read as Irving's desire to escape normal adult relationships and resist those sexual impulses he finds uncomfortable. He has Rip return as an older man whose lusty days are buried with the colonial past.[39]

By creating for Rip a disagreeable wife—she is not even humanized with a first name—Irving furnishes him with an excuse for being that dreamy fellow seeking an alternative to his everyday reality. Rip and his creator are both natural storytellers who wish to be left alone at times of their choosing. But it goes deeper: Irving was a politically influenced writer who consistently sought to be free from contention. Thus the nagging wife in some sense symbolizes the political world that was always prodding him to declare himself.[40]

There is additional political meaning here, probably intended. The shrewish wife is the tyrant Britannia of the late colonial era; Rip's daughter Judith, who welcomes him back and takes him in, is the loving symbol of republican America, now at peace. This makes sense, because Rip is a character who really belongs to an uncompetitive age—to an America not unlike the Dutch-American dreamscape Irving had already manufactured with boyish glee in his unreal *History*. Ill-equipped to fight and lacking all ambition, Rip misses the entire Revolutionary War. After his awakening, he lives on through retellings of his story, oblivious to the politics of the 1790s, taking his village— and us—back to the gentler unknown into which he once disappeared.[41]

Let us consider other possibilities. By making Rip a whimsical creature, Irving reminds us that he is still capable of friendly "whim-whams"—never mind that he dismisses *Salmagundi* as a juvenile production, not worth republishing. But Dr. Rubin's point is also well taken: Aside from his creator's possible sexual confusion (Irving's flight response from sexual women, or refusal to accept the responsibility of marriage), the appeal of Rip is his adolescent behavior; it is what allows him to be at once startled, credulous, and alive within the dream sequence and among the gnomish Dutchmen. It is significant, too, that for all his shortcomings, Rip becomes a local celebrity, a survivor, as does the nearly broke and suddenly rediscovered Washington Irving.

As for the German antecedent for his tale, the similarities to "Peter Klaus" are unmistakable; they make "America's first short story" as connected to Europe as America's first white inhabitants were. Peter is a goatherd from a village so generic that it is named *Sittendorf,* or "Conventional Village." He goes into the mountains, where on occasion his most desirable goats, one by one, slip through a hole in a wall, never to be found. So, as Peter looks for them, a serious-appearing *"Ritter-Männer,"* or knightly man, calls to him (though not by words, exactly), and leads him to a spot of grass where others are playing at *"Kegelspiel,"* or small pin bowling. Wordlessly, again, Peter is ordered to reset the pins for the strange bowlers. He tastes their wine, finds it delicious, and falls asleep.

Upon waking, Peter Klaus notices how long his beard has grown. His goats and his dog are gone. He finds his way back to the village, sees that people are dressed unfamiliarly, and feels immediately out of place. Trees have grown in places he remembers as treeless. He can find no one he recognizes. Finally, in conversation with a woman named Marie, everything becomes clear. Who is your father? he asks. "Peter Klaus," she replies. "But it's been twenty years that we've been looking for him, day and night, because the herd came back without him." Others regard him, and one voice suddenly calls out: "Yes, it's Peter Klaus! Welcome neighbor! After twenty years, welcome!"[42]

The borrowings are obvious—the strange, silent men and their bowling game, the alcohol-induced twenty-year sleep in the mountains, the grown-up daughter who acknowledges her father. Irving's genius lies in the hypnotic charm his simple story holds, for he makes Rip a more sympathetic being than Peter Klaus.

☆　☆

In 1818, the same year Irving spent a night at the Van Warts' writing "Rip Van Winkle," the young English poet John Keats published a long poem titled "Endymion." It begins familiarly:

A thing of beauty is a joy forever:
Its loveliness increases; it will never
Pass into nothingness; but still will keep
A bower quiet for us, and a sleep
Full of sweet dreams, and health, and quiet breathing.

The allegorical device of the extended sleep is as old as Greek mythology. Endymion was a mortal, a hunter or a shepherd (depending on the telling), adored by the moon goddess, Selene. She kissed him, and caused him to fall asleep on a mountainside; there he remained, warm with life but still and ever sleeping, so that she could visit him whenever she wished.

"Peter Klaus" was just a skeleton of a story, really. After his dreamy encounters in northern Europe from 1817 to 1819, Washington Irving had plenty of inspiration beyond the one German folktale to encourage him to recover the magic he had experimented with a full decade before in his humor-filled *History*. "Rip Van Winkle" marked his own reawakening as a writer with broad public appeal.

It was easy for the reader of 1819–1820 to see that "Rip Van Winkle" was many things besides a catchy story. One of its most interesting features—the reason it belongs with the preceding pieces in the *Sketch Book*—is that it is a lament. Life's unpredictability is apparent in this story in a way that relates to the anonymous lost crew of the shipwrecked vessel in "The Voyage," or the weight borne by the accepting wife, or our empathy for Roscoe when he is ruined. With Rip, Irving leaves his reader in awe of supernatural forces as the author pines for every quality of humanity potentially lost along with the missing years. As a simple, essentially honest man, Rip is vulnerable, malleable, human. He is the perfect protagonist in a fable designed to remind us that memory—both fragile and powerful—preserves what is good in the world.

The early twentieth-century American poet Hart Crane thought of Rip as "the muse of memory," "the guardian angel of the trip to the past."[43] This is why "Rip Van Winkle" should still matter in our historical retrospection. Memory must be called back, or it disappears—an axiom Irving certainly appreciated. Playing with time, he allows for the imaginative possibility that the death of the past is a delusion. Think of it: The irony of history is that it is so overwhelming that it causes us to simplify and forget.[44]

Rival processes of awakening and forgetfulness are subsumed in the historian's art of manipulating memory. We only *think* that we remember accurately. We *presume* that we can interpret wisely. People move on, time moves on. But in "Rip Van Winkle," we don't have to accept forgetfulness because the past can communicate in such a way that its sentimental truths—our innocence, if we want—can remain with us, being made apparent through supernaturally created new memories. The memorable Rip is a part of our consciousness of all that is left behind. *Now we can lose time without losing the past!*

Beyond testing memory, beyond the subjective craft of the historian, time tricks us in other ways. There are circumstances in which our senses convey deceptions to our understanding. That is what Rip struggles with and ultimately comes to terms with: Emerging from his slumber, his beard a foot long, he returns from the mountain in a state of bewilderment. Twenty years has become, for him, a single day, and his present reality has become, overnight, a history that others have already fashioned. To belong to the new "present" he cannot trust his own inner sense of order; he has to adapt. His dreamy recollection of a past that is more distant than his chronological life, his fantastic visit with the crew of Hendrick Hudson's *Half Moon,* may or may not have occurred.

Modern Americans know very little about the year 1819. But it was an especially turbulent year, and this must have conditioned readers' reactions to the first *Sketch Book* offerings. A nationwide financial panic occurred, though Irving could not have anticipated this when he wrote "Rip Van Winkle." As a symbol of that historical moment, the story is a fair portrait of the country's adolescent charm, something that was being contested as banks across the country called in loans and caused ruin for many.

There was this reality, and there was the heightened rhetoric of national self-sufficiency that newspapers across the country sustained. If high-minded Europeans approved of some element in American culture in 1819, it was its perceived simplicity and candor and energy. Irving's story is a testament to a style of apparent effortlessness that adventure-bound Americans were touting as they revived, in the postwar years, an ideal of sympathy and moral resolve, migratory movement west, and transcendence of the ordinary. In 1819, the financial panic notwithstanding, orators and editorial writers routinely boasted "a redeeming spirit in the people." They predicted a vigorous economy, expecting to rebound from the panic without a debasement in morals. Indeed, as banks foreclosed, patriotic editors turned up the volume. The United States was "a world within itself," almost a storybook regime, with a fine climate and natural diversity. As America responded to the call—whether it is called politics of liberation or sentimental democracy—Rip's liberation, his sentimental makeup, was a part of this phenomenon. The ordinary character of Rip confirmed that new Daniel Boones were heading out again, and that westward-dreaming Americans were escaping the bounds that previously held them.[45]

Like the first frontiersmen, the commoner Rip does not always emote, and nothing is more central to his character than his "loner" identity. Yet he is not without heart. We identify with him just enough. At the same time, though, he does little to contribute. It is not until he is a graybeard that he finds real community and compassion—but he has not exactly warranted it, either. He does not live a "real" life. He lives instead through his storytelling.

How much, then, was he like Irving? Rip's personality is fashioned by the happy sensations occasioned by his having been removed from regular time and cast into a world of fiction. Before his transformation, he worked against the "regular" aspects of the life he was living, just as Irving passed up work as a lawyer, rejected job opportunities in Washington, and resisted the responsibilities of a wife and children in favor of socializing and entertaining. Once Rip made the past into something nostalgic, its difficulties no longer applied to him.

Could this be what Irving was doing, too? Was his an avoidance strategy? Being imaginative felt better than having to struggle with an obligation to raise and educate a new generation. That was Rip, too, of course. If Rip was an American misfit, Irving made him appear to be an earthy ambassador of feeling, just as a democratizing citizenry—a people going against the grain— was rhetorically being told to conceive of itself. For this reason especially, Irving's homely tale was an instant success.

CHAPTER 7

The *Sketch Book* Wins Friends

1819–1820

And all for what? To occupy an inch of dusty shelf—to have the title of their works read now and then in a future age by some drowsy churchman or casual straggler like myself; and in another age to be lost, even to remembrance. Such is the amount of this boasted immortality.

—Washington Irving, "The Mutability of Literature," in the *Sketch Book*

IRVING HAD BEEN MAKING SKETCHES—LITERALLY depicting people and places with a crayon, a waxy charcoal-based pencil— ever since he first traveled abroad, for his health, in 1803.[1] It was his habit as a writer to employ the notebooks he constantly carried with him as memory enhancers. Late in life, he described these to a young writer he admired as his "equivalent to the little thumb-sketches from which a painter makes up his larger compositions," and thus he chose to title his assembled stories a "sketch book." As "Geoffrey Crayon," he was one whose very name bespoke the instrument of his trade.[2]

Like any author, Irving on occasion questioned the durability of his talent. It had been a decade since *Knickerbocker's History* emerged as a success; he was less than wholly confident of a warm reception for his *Sketch Book* back home in America. Even as he was preparing the second, third, and fourth (of an eventual seven) paperbound installments,* he had to assume that the first

---

*We know the *Sketch Book* as a complete volume of polished stories and essays, but such a format, bound in hardcover (in two volumes), was not available in America until 1824.

installment—the first several stories, ending with "Rip Van Winkle"—would determine whether the collection succeeded or failed.[3]

The spring of 1819 went by, and summer was half gone before Irving was finally assured that part one of the *Sketch Book* was selling out in the United States. His friend James Ogilvie, the sensitive orator and educator whose reputation Irving had defended in New York, was now back in Scotland. He understood Irving's unease: "I am impatient for the arrival of the first number of your Sketch Book, because I feel assured that nothing else is wanting to restore your equipoise of mind." In late July, Irving was able to see and touch the first number, and he felt great relief that it was so handsomely made: "I cannot but express how much more than ever I feel myself indebted to you for the manner in which you have attended to my concerns," he wrote to Brevoort, who had coordinated every aspect of production. "The work is got up in a beautiful style."[4]

In August, the author received good news about sales and public approval. A gleeful letter to Brevoort found him stopping just short of gloating about the high cover price:

> If the American public wish to have literature of their own they must consent to pay for the support of authors. . . . For my part if I can succeed in writing so as deservedly to please the public and gain the good will of my countrymen it is all I care about—I only want money enough to enable me to keep on my own way and follow my own taste and inclination.

He would need money to travel and write stories of new places—but that was as much as he needed to sustain him. As the epigraph he chose to open the Crayon series read: "I have no wife nor children, good or bad to provide for."[5]

By September, Irving was calm enough to reflect on his anxious times: "We are whimsically constituted beings," he wrote to Brevoort. After so many years without publishing anything daring, and suddenly afraid to wallow in self-congratulation, he came close to doubting himself: "The manner in which the work has been received and the eulogiums that have been passed upon it in the American papers and periodical works have completely overwhelmed me. . . . I feel almost appalled by such success, and fearful that it cannot be real. . . . I begin to feel affraid [sic] that I shall not do as well again." There was truth in that. Some of the praise was not what could be called "real," because "the fix" was in: Brevoort had accepted an offer from William Coleman, the editor of New York's *Evening Post,* to praise the *Sketch Book* without naming himself or his connection to the author. "The graces of style,"

Brevoort had cooed in the *Post,* "the rich warm tone of benevolent feeling . . . and the fine-eyed spirit of observation . . . are all exhibited anew in the Sketch Book." The newspaper's commendation was then reprinted elsewhere.[6]

That same month, Brevoort gave Irving an update on production and tallied up sales. "The demand rises in every quarter," he announced cheerfully. Even without his editorial interventions, Brevoort could honestly reassure his friend: "It is a point universally agreed upon, that your work is an honor to American literature as well as an example to those who aspire to a correct & eloquent style of composition." In the same letter, he tried to straighten out the author on a subject closer to home. Brother William had not written to Washington since his refusal to accept a political appointment. The youngest brother thought the congressman was unwilling to accept his resolve. But Brevoort pointed out that William had "yielded to the justness" of his brother's objections; he was merely overworked, and therefore slow to write: "He retains his old habit of burthening himself with a world of unnecessary cares and vexations—In walking the street, he seems literally bent downward, with at least a dozen gratuitous years—yet his heart is as mellow and his sensibilities just as acute as ever." In apprehending the eldest Irving's unnatural aging, Brevoort inadvertently prophesied William's unfortunate end, at the age of fifty-five, in 1821.[7]

The second installment of the *Sketch Book* opened with "English Writers on America." Like "The Voyage," this was a transitional piece, taking the author from an American perspective to an Anglocentric one, though part of Irving's message was to fuse the two, claiming English culture as part of America's heritage. His observer persona means to establish a sympathetic connection between two long-feuding relatives so that each might acknowledge the honest dignity of the other.

We must appreciate the context. In the late 1810s, emigration to America worried some in the mother country, where social unrest continued and imagined opportunities in America only added to discontent. British travelers, who abounded in America, had been publishing accounts of their tours "intended to diffuse error, rather than knowledge," as Irving put it in "English Writers on America." In this essay, he took it upon himself to end the "literary animosity daily growing." And yet, oddly, his good offices earned him more credit in England than in America, where his undisguised Anglophilia, increasing with each installment of the serialized *Sketch Book,* resulted in considerable skepticism. New England's prestigious literary journal, the *North*

American Review, claimed: "Mr. Irving wrote better in America than in England." His peacemaking effort was not entirely appreciated, though he implicitly denied Britain any superiority over America.[8]

The question of American identity—national distinctiveness versus cultural composite—had been stewing for some time. Irving himself had presided over an Anglo-American linguistic controversy during his editorship of the *Analectic Magazine,* in 1814, when his irrepressible friend James Kirke Paulding was at the peak of his wartime nationalism. In "Americanisms," the pseudonymous writer (presumed to be Paulding) declares: "To be sure, when we subjugated the English tongue, we allowed it to retain its original name. But it is now, in the eye of national law, the American language. . . . To adopt a language, without making any alteration, is a proof of extreme poverty of intellect, as well as want of spirit."[9]

Americans were reaching for cultural independence. Somehow, Washington Irving's performance as author of the *Sketch Book* did not convince his countrymen that he was representative of that movement. In spite of the subject and tone he chose in "Rip Van Winkle," the *Sketch Book* was causing people on both sides of the Atlantic to regard him as a writer indistinguishable from English writers. If he no longer *seemed* American after five years abroad, how could he *speak* for America?

Two compositions in the *Sketch Book* are fantasies involving writers and writing: "The Art of Book Making" and "The Mutability of Literature." The first takes place in the British Museum, where the loitering Crayon notices a door that opens, now and again, for black-clad persons. His curiosity takes him into a large reading room; here, the most intense of researchers are allowed to scour old texts at will so as to manufacture new knowledge. Crayon soon falls into a reverie; now the literary pilferers turn into ragpickers who steal not worn knowledge but pieces of garments and then refashion them into odd outfits for themselves to wear. He knows what this means: "What was formerly a ponderous history, revives in the shape of a romance—an old legend changes into a modern play, and a sober philosophical treatise, furnishes the body for a whole series of bouncing and sparkling essays." He is speaking as well of his own penchant for picking apart old stories and breathing new life into them. This is how "the seeds of knowledge and wisdom shall be preserved from age to age."[10]

In "The Mutability of Literature," Irving opens again by referring to "half dreaming moods of mind" where reveries are indulged. This time the scene is Westminster Abbey, where his wandering narrator is taken through a "gloomy passage" to an interior library. Once inside and seated, Crayon accidentally loosens the clasps of an old quarto volume: "The little book gave two or three yawns, like one awakening from a deep sleep; then a husky hem, and at length began to talk." It speaks a language, "quaint and obsolete," which he is able to translate into modern English. Having sat unopened for two centuries, the forgotten book complains to him about the world's neglect: "I was written for all the world," it protests, "not for the bookworms of an abbey." After the sleep-and-awakening theme born with Rip, and the antiquarian fascination that was becoming increasingly a part of Irving's literary reveries, this essay was about the mutability of history as much as literature, and the irreverent treatment of the human consciousness by the ultimate thief—time.

Irving has attached his mind to a spiritual battle between permanence and impermanence, and makes the case for mortality:

> To reason from analogy, we daily behold the varied and beautiful tribes of vegetables springing up, flourishing, adorning the fields for a short time, and then fading into dust, to make way for their successors. Were not this the case, the fecundity of nature would be a grievance instead of a blessing. The earth would groan with rank and excessive vegetation, and its surface become a tangled wilderness.

By this measure, would creative genius "overstock the world" if not for forgetfulness?

"The Mutability of Literature" instructs us to take literature seriously, to find meaning in even the most arcane kinds of knowledge. But, it says, we cannot resist fate. The essay is thus another of Irving's lamentations. To forget and be forgotten is the law of nature: "To occupy an inch of dusty shelf. . . . Such is the amount of this boasted immortality." A book contains the stuff of someone's life; it is made from bits and pieces of a human soul. That soul has all the fixity of consciousness.

In his "half dreaming moods of mind," Irving is implicitly expressing anxiety and uncertainty about his own publications. What is to be the fate of his essays and tales? "To occupy an inch of dusty shelf" and nothing more? Will he become like William Roscoe, once prominent but increasingly remote? It is not simply that he fears posthumous anonymity, or the forgetfulness that governs the historical consciousness; he wants to introduce the new discipline of literary archaeology, to say that there is something poignant in rediscovering a thread that can lead to the restoration of lost memory, and to new knowledge that holds value in human affairs.

An author intrudes only to italicize the appeal to the reader, to say: *"This is why I write."* Try this: I am saying about Irving what Irving was saying about an obscure quarto volume and its presumptive author. I have rediscovered a largely unknown Irving, the creator of a text; I am the wandering narrator who would reawaken the uninitiated to a precious past life, lest we lose to forgetfulness something poignant and enlightening in that life.

Scanning the shelves in the recesses of Westminster Abbey, Irving has a good idea that anonymity is the constant by-product of history. Just as life went on in the village for twenty years after Rip disappeared into the mountains, the world will do without Washington Irving and almost every individual belonging to his generation. That one misty thought caused Irving to make Rip different from the rest of humankind in that, after having been presumed dead, and then forgotten, he could return home to become something he was not back in younger years—a fixture in his home village, a man well cared for and without motive to run away again. The forgotten can be reincarnated—in literature.[11]

Irving dealt with memory and imagination in a particular way. Although he paid homage to the modern chronicler seeking knowledge of the definite, that is, knowledge of a historical past that could be reliably reconstructed, he himself heeded oral (anecdotal) history as much as typographical culture. His constant goal was to give expression to a "truth" that went beyond the grand scheme of historical study, a "truth" concerned more with the poetics of memory than with precision. This preoccupation with moods is what made him a Romantic.[12]

☆   ☆

From here, the *Sketch Book* intensifies its concern with the English people, to the exclusion of American subjects. In "Rural Life in England," the admiring author makes traditional English gardening into a transcendent art: "The rudest habitation, the most unpromising and scanty portion of land, in the hands of an Englishman of taste, becomes a little paradise." Irving, the Anglophile, sounds entirely sycophantic in places: "I do not know a finer race of men than the English gentlemen," he writes. Breathing the "open air," the landed gentry acquire a "healthful tone of mind and spirits, and a manliness and simplicity of manners" that no exposure to the city can undo. It must have been a bit jarring for some of his American readers to see Irving describing the country-bred upper classes much as Thomas Jefferson famously described the American yeoman farmer. Yet both writers perceived simple virtues and a moral effect attaching to those who lived in scenic places. Indeed, for Irving, the crescendo in his essay had to come when he encountered the "ruddy faces and modest cheerfulness" of the peasantry, content with their small piece of earth.[13]

This essay is followed directly by "The Broken Heart," which can be joined with three other essays in the finished *Sketch Book*, "The Widow and Her Son," "Rural Funerals," and "The Pride of the Village." In these offerings, Irving dwells on episodes of forlorn love, death, and grieving. The first turns on gender prejudices of the time, namely: "Man is the creature of interest and ambition. His nature leads him forward into the struggle and bustle of the world. . . . But a woman's whole life is a history of the affections." He is active, she is passive, her destiny "a fixed, a secluded, and a meditative life." Declaring himself a "true believer" in heartbreak—death by disappointed love—he reflects, in the guise of fiction, on his experience at Matilda Hoffman's deathbed: "How many bright eyes grow dim—how many soft cheeks grow pale." It was a commentary on the human condition as the Romantic generation preferred to relate to it. Maria Fenno Hoffman understood what Irving meant here; she wrote to him from New York: "In your sketch of Rural Funerals, I recognized a scene which you have related in a very touching manner. It surprises me to see that your memory is as tenacious as mine."[14]

Irving proved that he was good at mingling Romantic themes. When, for instance, he encounters a lonely widow, her destitute condition somehow makes the picture of her mourning a twenty-six-year-old son the more affecting. In Irving's story, she sits beside the freshly dug grave: "Her withered hands were clasped, as if in prayer, but I could perceive by a feeble rocking of the body and a convulsive motion of her lips that she was gazing on the last relics of her son with the yearnings of a mother's heart."

Irving had a way of selecting just the right detail to produce the desired effect:

> As they lowered the body into the earth, the creaking of the cords seemed to agonize her; but when, on some accidental obstruction, there was a jostling of the coffin, all the tenderness of the mother burst forth, as if any harm could come to him who was far beyond the reach of worldly suffering.

After everyone else has gone from the churchyard, Geoffrey Crayon remains behind, watching secretly: "I could see no more—my heart swelled into my throat—my eyes filled with tears—I felt as if I were acting a barbarous part in standing by and gazing idly on this scene of maternal anguish."

In "The Pride of the Village," Crayon veers off one of the "great coach roads" and arrives at sunset at a typical English community. There he sights a funeral train moving in his direction. He learns the life story of the deceased, an only child, "the beauty and pride of the village," whose "fragile loveliness" calls up a nature metaphor: "She appeared like some tender plant of the garden, blooming accidentally amid the hardier natives of the fields." Wooed and discarded by a soldier, a "novice in seduction," she soon fades; even the soldier's moral reformation cannot save her.[15]

The observer persona is put to another use in several essays about English Christmas, and here, too, his theme is loss: a fading tradition. In Irving's longing glance, we see a world without the festive joy of Christmas, an uninspiring season—"Nature lies despoiled of every charm"—that only becomes bleaker. Americans were not yet greatly concerned with the national calendar. The Fourth of July was celebrated with tremendous pomp, but Christmas had not yet become Christmas as we know it.

There were murmurs, however. Some New England almanac makers named Christmas and saints' days in December, and children sang hymns in some places; shops in commercial Boston advertised the practice of exchanging Christmas gifts beginning in 1808. But whether marking the holiday was to be considered sacred, secular, or entirely irreligious (Episcopalians, evangelicals, and Unitarians all had different ideas), the nation as a whole could not determine. Observation was irregular at best, though frontiersmen from Lewis and Clark onward recalled Christmas as a day of feasting, and they sought (when game was available) to stage a celebration as a way of connecting with the civilization they had left behind. Otherwise, newspapers on the East Coast cared little for this unofficial holiday.[16]

Irving was making the point that Americans (his primary readership) needed more holiday amusement. He meant to infuse Christmas with meaning—not to stimulate religious zeal, as nothing could have been further from his mind; but to combine history with good fellowship, good cheer, and a vitality suited to a close-knit society. Christmas, in other words, needed a story.

Because his mind was forever alighting on a lost past, Irving would have English Christmas, like jovial Dutch New Amsterdam, rebound by force of imagination. The holiday belonged to an age he imagines in the *Sketch Book* in gendered terms, as "times full of spirit and lustihood, when men enjoyed life roughly; times wild and picturesque." In the first of his Christmas reflections he expresses his disappointment in the more "worldly" nineteenth century: "There is more of dissipation, and less of enjoyment. Pleasure has expanded into a broader but a shallower stream." He yearns to know again what Christmas had once been, "its homebred feelings, its honest fireside delights," what he conceives, somewhat idealistically, as "golden-hearted antiquity."[17]

It is hard to trace his inspiration with precision. While at the British Museum, where he came up with his nostalgic theme for "The Art of Bookmaking," Irving had copied down a poem, most likely from a pamphlet dated 1652, containing these fertile lines:

Lets dance and sing and make good chear,
For Christmas comes but once a year;
Draw hogsheads dry, let flagons fly,
For now the bells shall ring.[18]

Something of the old still remained in the English country practice, he had heard, and if that something continued to bring happiness, he wanted to see it firsthand. In the next piece in the Christmas sequence, the curious outsider Irving/Crayon goes by public conveyance to encounter the source of this gleeful preparation. As a solitary visitor, watching and learning, he describes with almost a shy anticipation the "luxuries of the holiday table," the "baskets and boxes of delicacies," and the "glossy branches of holly" set inside windows. Then, a chance meeting at a traveler's inn with "Frank Bracebridge" leads to his invitation to share in an "old-fashioned style" Christmas at the country seat of Frank's family.[19]

Here, at Bracebridge Hall, Christmas is celebrated for twelve nights, "conformably to ancient usage." Servants revel in such games as "hoodman blind, shoe the wild mare, steal the white loaf, bob apple, and snap dragon." The Yule log and Christmas candle are lit, and hanging mistletoe puts all the "pretty housemaids" in "imminent peril." Mistletoe? Irving felt it necessary to footnote the word *mistletoe,* explaining its customary function—the kissing privilege—at the bottom of the page, to educate his uninformed American readers to this quaint Christmas tradition.[20]

Christmas Day begins with family prayers, followed by a Christmas carol. Squire Bracebridge invites the neighboring poor to the house for "beef and bread and ale." It was the gentry's way of "mitigating public discontent," Irving explains, at a time when peasants "have become too knowing, and begin to read newspapers, listen to ale-house politicians, and talk of reform."[21] After this short detour into social conscience, Irving returns to what really drives his prose: the well-to-do must be seen living well. Christmas dinner follows; Squire Bracebridge presides at the table, where pheasant pie substitutes for the traditional ("authentical") peacock pie, owing to the endangered status of the brightly feathered bird.[22]

His Christmas sequence embodied Irving's lifelong theme of cultural regeneration through nostalgia. Wherever he could tap into an episode with mythic potential, a real or imagined instance, or a historical event that may or may not have happened precisely as he reconstructed it, if that episode exhibited generous spirit and soulful feelings of shared humanity he was off and writing about it.[23] As for his fascination with Christmas, Irving had chosen just the right moment to jump-start events back in New York. Christmas as he described it would start to catch hold; then gradually, over the next two decades, everything we associate with Christmas would emerge: Christmas trees, greeting cards, roaring fires, presents.[24]

To place the whole story in its proper perspective, we need to skip ahead and interweave another tale of the Hudson that only obliquely concerns Washington Irving. In December 1823, four years after the *Sketch Book* made its appearance, a Troy, New York, newspaper published "The Night Before Christmas" (also known as "A Visit from St. Nicholas"); the jaunty children's poem conveyed the imagery of Christmas in an irresistible way while introducing a jolly, jelly-bellied Santa Claus to nineteenth-century families. As in Irving's *History of New York,* Santa clenched a Dutch-style pipe in his mouth, and "stockings were hung by the chimney with care." The poem would be widely reprinted in subsequent years.

For generations, most Americans have continued to associate the reindeer-driven holiday poem and its descriptive language with Clement Clarke Moore, a professor of religious studies who was meant to have thought it up one year earlier while riding through Manhattan in an open sleigh. Recently, however, the literary detective Don Foster has credibly disproved Moore's claim of authorship and attributed the popular poem instead to Major Henry Livingston of Dutchess County, New York, a far livelier writer who was of mixed Dutch and Scottish ancestry. Whereas Moore was stern, pedantic, and largely humorless, Livingston was thoroughly infused with the spirit of Christmas from early adulthood; he delivered the lines of "The Night Before Christmas" at a gathering as early as 1807–1808, which means that he had imbibed the Dutch tradition and committed it to paper around the time Washington Irving was preparing his *History.* Although we can only speculate on the timing of the two writers' inspired attachment to St. Nicholas, we do know that Irving was an intimate of certain members of the extended Livingston clan.

In 1836, long after Gulian Verplanck had buried his disappointment over *Knickerbocker's History,* he and Irving formed the St. Nicholas Society, in part to make Christmas a more significant time for all social classes in New York. They invited Professor Moore to join. He refused them. It was seven years after this that Charles Dickens published *A Christmas Carol,* and the sentimentality of Christmas was enshrined. Major Livingston, who died before he could set history straight (and before Moore took credit for his poem), did not have his contribution to the American national holiday made evident, then, until the year 2000.[25]

The purpose of extending the story of how Christmas came to America is to give Irving the precise amount of credit that he deserves. He did not "invent" the holiday, but he did all he could to make minor customs into major customs—to make them enriching signs of family and social togetherness. Though a bachelor, he idealized family. Just as he had frolicked with the Van Wart children in Birmingham, he would help stage loving Christmases for his young New York nieces and nephews in later years.

Irving had produced two very different writings in the largely comic *History of New York* (which John Murray published in England, for the first time, in 1820) and the largely sentimental *Sketch Book.* With unprompted help from the likes of Henry Livingston, he provoked his countrymen into accepting what soon developed into a treasured holiday. Combining two distantly related December traditions that had arisen in his festive imagination, the Dutch attachment to St. Nicholas and the English remembrance of Christmas, he only had to watch as the seed germinated and the modern American Christmas grew.

✯ ✯

In the latter pages of the *Sketch Book,* Irving returned briefly to his Hudson River rambles with "The Legend of Sleepy Hollow." It is by far the longest of the *Sketch Book* tales, and owing to its association with the artful autumn institution of Halloween, is perhaps even better remembered today than "Rip Van Winkle."

The epigraph that introduces "The Legend of Sleepy Hollow" consists of four lines from Scottish poet James Thomson's 1748 work, "The Castle of Indolence."

> *A pleasing land of drowsy head it was,*
> *Of dreams that wave before the half-shut eye;*
> *And of gay castles in the clouds that pass,*
> *For ever flushing round a summer sky.*

Thomson's poem speaks to Irving's partiality for malleable nature, lazy times, pastoral slumbers, and enchantment. It opens with a quaint account of a wizard who inhabits a place noted for its "listless climate," "sleep-soothing groves," and "unnumber'd glittering streamlets." Just before the lines Irving quotes, however, are two that conjure another, more sinister picture: "A sable, silent, solemn forest stood; / Where nought but shadowy forms were seen to move." These woodlands, located in a valley, "sent forth a sleepy horror through the blood."

No wonder Irving sampled Thomson's poem to set the stage for his post-Revolutionary adventure of the hapless Ichabod Crane. All he had to do was to make one of his "drowsy heads" headless.

And so it begins:

In the bosom of one of those spacious coves which indent the eastern shore of the Hudson, at the broad expansion of the river denominated by the ancient Dutch navigators the Tappaan Zee, and where they always prudently shortened sail, and implored the protection of St. Nicholas when they crossed, there lies a small market town. . . .

This can only be an Irving tale. And indeed, it is proclaimed as one of those "Found among the Papers of the late Diedrich Knickerbocker." It presents two places of historical note: "Tarry Town," named by a set of "good housewives" because their husbands were prone to "linger about the village tavern on market days"; and the "sequestered glen" of Sleepy Hollow, where, once again a "drowsy, dreamy influence seems to hang over the land." Ancient spells still occupy the minds of the inhabitants, "causing them to walk in a continual reverie." But above all other haunted happenings, the specter of a Hessian soldier, "whose head had been carried away by a cannon ball," rules the night; his ghostly body rides time and again, we are told, toward the scene of his demise, hoping to be reunited with his lost head.

Early in the American Revolution, the British government hired a mercenary army of German-speaking troops from the principality of Hesse to supplement the British forces. To the patriots, this was an act of extreme callousness on the part of King George III, for the Hessians were alleged to be Europe's most bloodthirsty army. The Declaration of Independence pointed out the king's heartlessness in ignoring the "consanguinity" that subsisted between the motherland and its colonies by engaging this merciless force to terrorize the American countryside. John Hancock wrote that the Hessians fought "without Remorse or Compunction." In October 1776, after a skirmish not far from Tarrytown, a common soldier named Timothy Hancock (no relation) made an entry in his diary: "The Hessians took three of our men and one made his Escape and by His account they poot the other to Emediate Death as their Custom is." Some American parents believed that the Hessians would capture and eat their children. For Irving, then, the Hessian ghost was attached to a particularly frightening history.[26]

He may have formed his idea from the tragic experience of a Dutch-American in Washington's army. This militiaman, one Abraham Onderdonk, was caught up in the fighting in Westchester County, also in October 1776. In the words of one of Onderdonk's neighbors, he "was killed by a cannon ball from the enemy separating his head from his shoulders." This does not appear to be a famous episode in the annals of the war, but Onderdonk was serving under General Israel Putnam when he was killed, and Aaron Burr was, at the time, Putnam's aide de camp. So it is not unreasonable to consider that Irving might have known the details of this story.[27]

And what did the severed head mean? Irving's readers were certainly old enough to recall the use of the guillotine in the French Revolution. The head is the most defining feature of the human being; its removal is a most terrifying prospect. In that the constructed duality of body and soul has for so long dominated philosophy and literature, it is nearly impossible to conjure the soul—and the sympathetic bond that constitutes our humanity—except through the imagining eye. If the head and its beseeching eyes represent meaningful human contact, the fact that Irving's headless Hessian cannot be met by a knowing gaze is both frightful and appalling. There is no expression to connect to, no soul to encounter—argument with the Hessian is pointless. He/it defies all reciprocity of sensation. The ghost has only one mission: He must "find himself" (his head) if he is to affirm that he ever existed. And whoever crosses its path must also be painfully aware of the uncertainty of his own head, his own identity and materiality.[28]

The story of Ichabod Crane and the Headless Horseman of Sleepy Hollow takes place at about the same time that Rip Van Winkle wakes up, that is, at about the time George Washington assumes the presidency. The oddly formed Yankee teacher and singing master, whose hands "dangled a mile out of his sleeves," could be mistaken for a scarecrow from a distance. Ichabod does his utmost to spread knowledge, and yet he is peculiarly susceptible to the allure of superstitious yarns: "No tale was too gross or monstrous for his capacious swallow."

At his log schoolhouse, he rules with an iron fist, and sometimes, after school, stretches out in the clover and reads the writings of the pompous Puritan Cotton Mather, the self-anointed interpreter of Salem witchcraft. Ichabod commutes from a remote farmhouse to the center of the hollow. He passes long winter evenings with the "old Dutch wives, as they sat spinning by the fire." They impart local tales of ghosts and haunted places, and he, in turn, regales them with Connecticut stories, passed down from the previous century, concerning witches and comets and portentous sounds and visions. As he rides home in the night, Ichabod cannot help but sense a fearful presence. He shrinks from the sound of his own footsteps on the crisp ground; he imagines a "howling among the trees" or an errant ray of light to be a proximate danger—or even the headless horseman himself.

Despite his fears, he cannot resist staying into the night with the women he instructs in psalmody. For among them is one Katrina Van Tassel, the somewhat coquettish daughter of the self-sufficient, ordinarily undemonstrative but altogether thriving Baltus Van Tassel, who relishes his "snug" life "on the banks of the Hudson, in one of those green, sheltered, fertile nooks, in which the Dutch farmers are so fond of nestling." Ichabod, "the pedagogue," hungers for Van Tassel's bountiful harvest as much as he desires to possess his plump eighteen-year-old daughter. Ichabod's eyes take in the material symbols of pastoral comfort—the rows of pewterware, abundant wool for spinning, hanging strings of Indian corn and dried fruit, deep mahogany furniture, and china and silver objects on the corner cupboard. If he marries Katrina, this is what he would someday inherit.

But he has a "formidable rival" for her hand. Abraham "Brom" Van Brunt, a.k.a. "Brom Bones," is his physical as well as temperamental opposite, a resilient, fun-loving strongman, a natural leader who takes his marauding band of pranksters on horseback, galloping past farmhouses and whooping it up, just to get a rise out of the neighbors. So while Ichabod struggles to win the girl through old-fashioned psalmody, Brom Bones rivals Ichabod as a singing master by teaching "a scoundrel dog . . . to whine in the most ludicrous manner."

One fine, clear autumn day, the pitiable Ichabod rides to the Van Tassels' "quilting frolic" on a borrowed, broken-down horse named Gunpowder. He "shamble[s]" out of the gate of Hans Van Ripper's farm where he boards, and breathes in the harvesttime air. The sun is setting as he approaches the "motionless and glassy" Tappan Zee. The scene is one of magical abundance and pastoral perfection: "amber clouds," a "fine golden" horizon changing to "pure apple green," with "dark grey and purple" washing over the opposite side of the Hudson. These were the colors and sensations Irving no doubt remembered from his own early wanderings in the area.

Arriving at the Van Tassels' "mansion," Ichabod ogles the cornucopia that rests upon his host's "genuine Dutch country tea table." Baltus Van Tassel moves contentedly among his guests. A musician, an "old grey headed negro," plays his fiddle. In a revealing caricature, Irving diminishes Ichabod's pretensions as a dancer by suggesting that only unrefined blacks could find him impressive: "He was the admiration of all the negroes, who, having gathered, of all ages and sizes, from the farm and the neighbourhood, stood forming a pyramid of shining black faces at every door and window, gazing with delight at the scene, rolling their white eye balls, and showing grinning rows of ivory from ear to ear." Though Ichabod whirls his partner, the desirable Katrina, while Brom Bones sits "brooding by himself in one corner," it is not the triumph Ichabod had imagined. Indeed, not long after the festivities come to a close, after the farmers and their wagons have rumbled from the scene, Ichabod realizes the hopelessness of his cause. He rouses his steed "uncourteously" from a placid sleep, and takes to the road at this "very witching time of night."

Signs of life are few and unpromising as Ichabod rides, and "stories of ghosts and goblins" come rushing into his head. He approaches a famous spot near where the British spy Major André had fallen into American hands while he was assisting Benedict Arnold in his failed effort to sink the Revolutionary cause by conveying West Point to the enemy. (In 1821, one year after the publication of Irving's "Legend of Sleepy Hollow," the British consul in New York would undertake to exhume André from his burial site just across the Hudson in the town of Tappan and convey his remains back to England. The André affair was still very much a living memory, and a minor sticking point in Anglo-American relations.)[29]

As he aims for "Major André's tree," this "ill starred," "doleful" marker, Ichabod starts to whistle to banish his fear. Reaching the precise place where the British spy had been captured, he can feel his heart pounding. He urges his horse with a poke in the ribs, but old Gunpowder is unresponsive. Then Ichabod kicks "lustily," and finds himself moving laterally "into a thicket of brambles and alder bushes." Applying the whip only propels his troublesome steed so far; "snuffling and snorting," Gunpowder eventually reaches the bridge.

Just at this moment a plashy tramp [sound of a puddle-filled plop] by the side of the bridge caught the sensitive ear of Ichabod. In the dark shadow of the grove, on the margin of the brook, he beheld something huge, misshapen, black and towering. It stirred not, but seemed gathered up in the gloom, like some gigantic monster ready to spring upon the traveller.

"Who are you?" Ichabod stammers. He asks again, pointlessly. His tormentor, this "shadowy object of alarm," lurches up and comes down in the middle of the road, "jogging along on the blind side of old Gunpowder," who saunters on with apparent unconcern. Ichabod, helpless, cannot but think of the notorious Hessian. His determined pursuer matches his every move, speeding up and slowing down whenever he does.

Finally, the pursued man sees the speechless rider on the black steed, whose colossal figure appears "in relief against the sky," "muffled in a cloak"—

and absent his head! What should have been a head is "carried before him on the pommel of the saddle!" Nothing can disguise Ichabod's frenzied fear now. He rides as fast as he can, bending forward, his "flimsy garments" fluttering. Gunpowder still refuses to go where Ichabod directs, and in the rider's panic, Hans Van Ripper's good Sunday saddle falls off the horse, only to be trampled by the Headless Horseman. Ichabod gives Gunpowder "another convulsive kick in the ribs," and makes a final burst for the Church Bridge, where he figures he will be safe. That is when he turns and sees the "goblin" hurl something at his head:

> Ichabod endeavoured to dodge the horrible missile, but too late. It encountered his cranium with a tremendous crash—he was tumbled headlong into the dust, and Gunpowder, the black steed, and the goblin rider, passed by like a whirlwind.

The old horse is found the next day, but Ichabod is nowhere to be seen. His "worldly effects"—a bit of his clothing, his psalm book, and a pitch pipe— are what he has left behind, along with some rather disconcerting volumes on witchcraft, dreams, and fortune-telling, which Hans Van Ripper consigns to the flames. The village residents conclude that "the galloping Hessian" has carried off their teacher; and insofar as he is "a bachelor, and in nobody's debt," nobody troubles his head about him any more.

But he is not dead. A combination of things had driven off Ichabod Crane, as an old farmer later confirms: his fear that the legend is true, his concern that Van Ripper will do something to him when he discovers what has happened to his saddle, and his "mortification" over being jilted by the "heiress" Katrina Van Tassel. The unmanly Ichabod has gone elsewhere, resumed his teaching, taken up the law, and qualified himself for elective office in the provisional young republic. The more manly Brom Bones, meanwhile, has married "the blooming Katrina." Brom is known to "burst into a hearty laugh at the mention of the pumpkin," which, of course, is the projectile that felled the pathetic Ichabod.[30]

Ichabod's story, like Rip Van Winkle's and Diedrich Knickerbocker's, ridicules the gravity of history as taught by men of substance. Irving loved to assign great magnitude to silly events; by insisting always on the authority of what he was relating, he enlarged its wonderful absurdity. In "The Legend of Sleepy Hollow," he berates the self-important Cotton Mather, who wrote and published incessantly, but always as a pedantic doctrinaire. He scoffs at the innate virtues of professional politicians by graduating Ichabod from laughable schoolteacher to county jurist—an unlikely course for one so inept, but that was Irving's point. His Ichabod is one of those comic figures whose fate is determined by his failure to be intelligent and practical.

Irving, too, has been reluctant to submit to an ordinary, practical life plan. Autobiographical elements seem to jump from the pages of both "Rip Van Winkle" and "The Legend of Sleepy Hollow." Like his two characters, he feels remote from the thoughts and plans of the most stable members of society. The virginal Ichabod cannot make a young woman happy, but relies, when possible, on older, or at least domesticated, women for company and solace. Rip's chief social skill is his storytelling, and Ichabod makes inroads with the women he instructs in psalmody. Rip cannot find peace in his marriage, and Ichabod is unable to make himself sufficiently attractive to the marriageable Katrina. Brom Bones's "uncouth gallantries" have more success with Katrina than Ichabod's insinuating "advances."

What we have here, in Ichabod, is a side of Irving that senses his own impotence. He suspects attractive, available women of enjoying predatory powers—the power to mock him, to devour his manhood, to banish him. Ichabod is a man whose relationships with men seem to dissolve, a man who fails to engender sympathy. Even the shunned "Little Man in Black" warranted sympathy; but Ichabod is damned to lose that which really makes a man manly in this society.

Thus, a central theme of the story is the matter of belonging. Irving feels to some degree that he is of visitor status in the lives of those to whom he is drawn. This is the negative side of bachelorhood. The gangly, uncomfortable pedagogue Ichabod appears to be an exaggerated self-portrait—or self-satire. Long dependent on his older brothers, financially unsteady, a bachelor married to his imaginative prospects, Irving has a history of idle thoughts (if not occasional self-pity) that he must somehow move beyond.[31]

✦　✦

Encouraged by the reception of his *Sketch Book* in America, and aware that someone in England, sometime soon, would publish an unauthorized version of the tales if he did not, Irving sought out a British publisher. He approached the venerable John Murray first, in the early autumn of 1819, but Murray turned him down, uncertain about sales prospects, though he would not dismiss the value of Irving's work as literature. The "scope" of the stories Irving had sent, including "Rip Van Winkle," seemed to him to address only a limited market. Irving responded humbly to Murray, saying that he entirely understood his decision, and admitted to that "deficiency in scope" that troubled the publisher. He acknowledged "some degree of self diffidence and a want of practice and experience."

Seizing his first opportunity, Irving gamely contracted with one John Miller, who proceeded to publish a single volume of the first *Sketch Book* stories. Irving uncharacteristically agreed to assume all risks in the venture. This did not prevent him from asking Walter Scott for his "kind word in the business." Early in 1820, Miller's business collapsed, and by Irving's good fortune, Scott came to London in March to receive a baronetcy and append "Sir" to his name. While in town, the "Border Minstrel," who had recently read and raved about "The Legend of Sleepy Hollow," made it clear to Murray that he held Irving in the highest esteem, and so "induced" Murray (as Irving tells it) to change his mind. John Murray! The most important publisher of his day, the publisher of Byron, agreed to pick up where Irving's bankrupt, small-time English publisher had left off. And so began a long and fruitful literary partnership.[32]

From the London literati, Irving received many "flattering compliments," wrote the newly celebrated author to the ever-trusted Brevoort in May 1820. He now frequented the drawing room of Murray, the Prince of Booksellers, which opened to specially invited persons from the hours of two to five. And to Paulding the same month: "I am launched upon the literary world here, I find my opportunities of observation extending."[33] Just like that, he was an insider.

It was almost simple. When Murray consented to publish the *Sketch Book,* Washington Irving instantly became the talk of the town. British editions of *A History of New York* (1820, 1821) and the *Sketch Book* (1820, 1822) catapulted him to transatlantic renown. Single-handedly, Murray had made it possible for the modestly born New Yorker to overcome the powerful English prejudice against American authors. "It proves to us distinctly," wrote a British critic, a friend of Scott's, "that there is a *mind* working in America"; the *Sketch Book,* he said, was "to be classed with the best English writings of our day." Elsewhere in the British press, positive reviews reprinted long extracts from Irving's text. William Godwin, the freethinking novelist whose daughter, Mary Godwin Shelley, had just published the tour de force *Frankenstein,* wrote of the *Sketch Book:* "Everywhere I find in it the marks of a mind of the utmost elegance and refinement, a thing as you know that I was not exactly prepared to look for in an American." In the late spring and summer of 1820, as word spread through Europe and filtered back to the United States, Irving's countrymen were amazed.

It was James Ogilvie who had conveyed a copy of the *Sketch Book* to Godwin. Years before, Irving had done Ogilvie a good turn in New York by tearing apart John Rodman, the essayist who had lampooned him. Before the year 1820 was over, Irving would learn that the colorful orator had been deadening his mind with the opiate laudanum, after having earlier kicked the habit;

and now, in a moment of hopelessness, he had taken his own life. A few years later Irving recalled his sentimental Scottish friend as a "Don Quixote."[34]

The influential critic Francis Jeffrey used the pages of the *Edinburgh Review* to welcome to the British Isles the "courteous and ingenious stranger" who had authored the *Sketch Book.* Irving's "English Writers on America" had certifiably struck a chord; the time had come when American writers were to be given a fair shake. Jeffrey argued that the *Sketch Book* had been assembled "with the greatest care and accuracy, and worked up to great purity and beauty of diction, on the model of the most elegant and polished of our native writers." And here he compared Irving in particular to the respected and beloved Joseph Addison and Oliver Goldsmith in the "humorous and discursive parts" of his work, and, interestingly, to Henry Mackenzie, "in the more soft and pathetic."[35]

Mackenzie was the author of *The Man of Feeling* (1770). The principal character in this book was Harley, a young man whose altruism knows no bounds. Unmarried and seemingly not inclined to be, Harley does all he can to extend love, family unity, and true fellowship. It is not that he is a utopian, for he well understands corrupt tendencies in human nature; yet he travels around town and country, seedy as well as respectable places, trying to correct those tendencies by example. Describing scenes, inspecting countenances, asking questions, righting wrongs, he finds purpose. Like Geoffrey Crayon, wherever he roams, Harley remains a stranger among strangers, frequenting churches and graveyards, obtaining sustenance by listening to life stories and commiserating gently. Irving, as Crayon, did his share of commiserating. This American Man of Feeling had a hyperactive conscience.

Irving had now achieved all he could have hoped for, yet he never once pretended that his literary success had not come at a cost. To the married James Paulding, now a stable employee of the Navy Department in Washington and who, as Irving put it, was "not necessitated to publish for bread," he confessed that he saw himself as an odd man out: "With all my wandering habits, which are the result of circumstances rather than disposition, I think I was formed for an honest, domestic, uxorious man, and I cannot hear of my old cronies snugly nestled down with good wives and fine children round them, but I feel for the moment desolate and forlorn." He said that, at thirty-seven, he felt the time had passed to secure these blessings, and that "all the means of domestic establishment pass away like a dream." He was always negotiating with dreams. And to his other confidant: "Oh! my dear Brevoort, how much my heart warms toward you all, when I get to talking and thinking of past times and past scenes! What would I not give for a few days among the

Highlands of the Hudson, with the little knot that was once assembled there!" He wanted his oldest friends to know that he felt nothing to gloat about, and that he envied the homely informality they had seized in adhering to the proper seasons of a man's life.[36]

★   ★

Several twentieth-century Irving scholars have ruminated on Irving's bifurcated career. Martin Roth spoke for a common critique when, thirty years ago, he embraced the Irving of New York, the Irving of *Knickerbocker's History*, as the originator of a literary voice that was bold and comedic. It is this, he observed, that qualifies Irving as the progenitor of a national literature. But in his writings after going to England, the New Yorker exchanged his former boldness for a less imaginative pose, ostensibly begging for acceptance as "a naturalized son by any civilization whose cultural values seem tangible and secure." In the 1810s, argued Roth, Irving "dried up as a writer," and was never the same afterward. "Rip Van Winkle" and "The Legend of Sleepy Hollow" were all that remained of his American dream, his festive past; he had removed himself from contention when he absented himself from politics. Roth regarded Irving's invention of Diedrich Knickerbocker as a vital moment in literature, and Geoffrey Crayon's "resurrected Knickerbocker" as a "half-dead" replacement of the earlier narrator.[37]

This is how harsh some modern critics have been on Irving, despite the obvious impact he had on the literary world of his time. Paul Giles, on the other hand, sees Irving as anything but stale. Giles recently examined the interdependency of British and American literary impulses in this period, and points to Irving's subtleties in the *Sketch Book*. This was no simple sentimentalist, but a writer who combined "empathy" and "alienation," who problematized "every comfortable conception of 'home.'" Washington Irving was a romantic ironist.[38]

Had Irving abandoned the spirit of his younger years' creations only to "play it safe"? Was he becoming too conservative to be interesting, and Geoffrey Crayon excessively timid and apologetic? It is true that we may see as maudlin what Irving's readers saw as inspired. But let us exchange contexts: "America was coming to appear to Europe as a kind of cracked or crazy mirror," Giles notes trenchantly, "wherein the Old World witnessed strangely distorted representations of itself."[39] The *Sketch Book* unquestionably left a mark on Europe, as it did on America, and Irving suddenly became the model for aspiring American novelists. He had reached across the Atlantic; he had found a haven abroad. To the learned young men of his native country, this in itself was extraordinary. A select group of American painters had achieved comparable status in England, but never before a writer.

No matter how pioneering an author is, if one looks for a better example of an iconoclast, one can find it. In 1820, he was Lord Byron. Other than Scott, whom Irving continued to lionize, Byron was the literary figure who dominated the transnational republic of letters. Irving had lauded the poet in the pages of the *Analectic Magazine* in 1814, and his singularity would continue to appeal for years to come. The defiant patrician poet with a dark, debunking impulse had annoyed John Murray, his publisher, in the early years of their association, when he came over to Albemarle Street at odd moments to inspect the production of his poetry. In one notable episode, the theatrical Byron had stood amusing himself with his cane, eyeing a volume on his publisher's bookshelf, lunging at it repeatedly, as if with a sword, while his host was commenting on Byron's verse. "You think that a good idea, do you Murray?" he would rejoice, taunting and tempting without really clarifying.[40]

Byron had been in self-exile from England since 1816, and was in Italy in 1819–1820, where he continued to dangle words of passion over the page, barely repressing his carnality. He lived an almost carnivalesque life. The creator of the monumental "Childe Harold's Pilgrimage" was not only Murray's cash cow, but, like Irving, a traveler and chronicler of daily adventures. He was often smitten with country people, as Irving was, and invented equally alluring characters. Around the time Irving was writing "Rip Van Winkle," the bisexual, satirical Byron was polishing off the first canto of his ode to pleasure, "Don Juan." Just as Dame Van Winkle is a shrew, Don Juan's mother, Inez, is a righteous and unbearable know-it-all: "Some women use their tongues— she *look'd* a lecture / Each eye a sermon, and her brow a homily." Her husband is driven to seek comfort in other women's bedrooms; as a couple, they remain together while "wishing each other, not divorced, but dead." In real life, Byron used women as badly as Irving went to lengths to seek their blessing. Byron was, as he wrote of his creation Childe Harold, "the wandering outlaw of his own dark mind." He tested himself in ways Irving refused to, not the least of which was in exposing his appetites to his readers.

Through his characters, Irving feigned innocence, accepted social constraints, and seemed always surprised by events. Yet as products of the same age (Byron was five years younger), both writers saw in writing a means to challenge complacency. When they chose their subjects from the past, they wrote to recover hope from history. Byron: "And all that Hope adored and lost / Hath melted into Memory." His death at thirty-six, in 1824, occurring as he traveled alongside partisans in war-torn Greece, made him even bigger than he was in life. Beyond the power of his words, Lord Byron was all image.[41]

It is worth the digression, because Byron read and enjoyed Irving's *Sketch Book*, pronouncing on it in a letter to Murray: "Crayon is very good." The poet assured a young American visitor that he had read Irving's new work often enough to know immediately the source of any cited passage from it. Irving, who cared about literary fame more than he admitted, paid close attention to Byron's path to success. Like the poet, whom he would never meet, he took the reader into his confidence, and told the most human story he could dream up. Within a year of his becoming a Murray author, Irving eclipsed Byron as the publisher's most lucrative investment. He pleased many and offended almost no one.[42]

☆　☆

The epigraph to this chapter, taken from "The Mutability of Literature," reminds us of Irving's humanism, which was, for him, a kind of liberation. Books preserved as they generated spirit, aroused as they consoled. Irving exhorts us to cherish them, so that we might retain the spirit of every age. As the best example of recorded memory, books served as the enduring conscience of the world—our stories reflect our collective humanity.

Irving was, in this way, perfectly content to embody the softened masculinity of Harley, Mackenzie's Man of Feeling. He wrote to save us from despair. "Sleepy Hollow" is terror without rage, and "Rip Van Winkle" is consciousness without confinement—mystifying yet satisfying. Knowing how individuals can fall apart, and how societies can crumble, the author was dogged in his desire to make past and present happily coalesce. He thought he could make his readers happy by having them awaken through literature to find they had in some sense eluded death.[43]

Yet much of what he wrote was also a lamentation. He fixated on the intertwined subjects of death and memory. We may say without exaggeration that the bachelor Irving knew loneliness and feared darkness. He reveled in the company of others, which he knew brought him back and animated him. In the *Sketch Book*, he wrote *through* death and wrote *of* awakenings.

CHAPTER 8

Romantic Europe

1820–1824

We generally make love in a style, and with sentiments very unfit for ordinary life; they are half-theatrical, half romantic. By this means we raise our imaginations to what is not to be expected in human life.

—Richard Steele, *Spectator* no. 479

No woman can expect to be to her husband all that he fancied her when he was a lover. Men are always doomed to be duped, not so much by the arts of the sex as by their own imaginations.

—Washington Irving, from "Wives," in *Bracebridge Hall*[1]

O N AUGUST 17, 1820, BACHELOR ROOMMATES PETER and Washington Irving left Southampton, England, for Paris, France. Searching for an investment to give Peter one last chance to achieve financial stability, the two brothers resolved that they would put their money into a steamboat company just beginning operations along the Seine. Back home in New York, William, Ebenezer, and John Irving were not keen on the idea of a risky investment that would draw on the family's funds; nor, for that matter, did they approve any prospect that would keep Peter abroad longer.

Once established in Parisian lodgings, the rising author discovered that his new celebrity had followed him. He found himself dining regularly with America's chief representatives abroad, including the U.S. minister to France, Albert Gallatin, widely recognized as one of the most able men in the early American republic. The Swiss-born Republican, who spoke with a noticeable accent, had been a congressman from western Pennsylvania in the 1790s, before serving as treasury secretary under Presidents Jefferson and Madison. He took part in the negotiations in Ghent, Belgium, that brought the War of 1812 to an end.

Progressive, adaptable, and even-tempered, Gallatin was a veteran of several hard-fought political campaigns, and an old admirer of Aaron Burr's. He was strong-minded without being doctrinaire, and the increasingly apolitical Irving, a good-humored American man of letters, had made a conspicuous contribution to literary nationalism. This made him a welcome guest at the ambassador's quarters.[2]

Irving, a man of some stature now, reacquainted himself with the French culture. To his artist-friend Charles R. Leslie, he wrote of the "little towns of Lower Normandy," and described how the country was "peopled with an eye to the picturesque." He admired "the fine Gothic churches; the old quaint architecture of the private houses—the beauty of the common people particularly the peasantry—Their peculiar costumes, all form continual pictures." He was in high spirits.[3]

After having developed a rapport with Gallatin, Irving exchanged a bit of humorous correspondence with Gallatin's counterpart in London, Richard Rush. A son of the late Revolutionary Benjamin Rush, who had been the close friend of John Adams and Thomas Jefferson and for decades a leading Philadelphia medical authority, the younger Rush had already served his country to this point as U.S. attorney general and secretary of state during Madison's administration. Ambassador Rush was approached by the unimpeachable Lady Lyttleton (later governess to Queen Victoria's children), who needed to satisfy a nagging concern in her mind. She had deduced upon her reading of the *Sketch Book*—or, more correctly, she was made suspicious by acquaintances in the literary world—that the collection's real author was Sir Walter Scott. And so she wished to know for certain, if you please, whether Mr. Irving, an American, had actually written the sketches of rural England that she found so "admirably just."

Irving had had dealings with Rush more than once during his time in England, enough to have adopted an informal tone with him, and he surely appreciated Rush's lighthearted manner of presenting the issue: "If you do not write to me soon all that you have to say upon her letter," Rush wrote, "I shall certainly give her to understand, and perhaps under my official seal, that *you* are the author of Waverly, Rob Roy, . . . for as Sir Walter Scott is to have the credit of the Sketch Book, I can see no good reason why a portion of his laurels should not be transferred to you."

Irving happily obliged the American minister, swearing that no one had helped him write his book: "I speak fully to this point, not from any anxiety of authorship, but because the doubts which her ladyship has heard on the subject seem to have arisen from the old notion that it is impossible for an *American to write decent English.*" As to Sir Walter, Irving was explicit about the debt he felt he owed that knighted gentleman:

> I cannot help smiling at the idea that any thing I have written is deemed worthy of being attributed to Sir Walter Scott, and that I should be called upon to vindicate my weak pen from the honor of such a parentage. . . . He has always been to me a frank, generous, warm-hearted friend, and it is one of my greatest gratifications to call him such.

On receipt of this intelligence, a satisfied Lady Lyttleton invited Irving to join her family at the estate of her father, Earl Spencer, for an old-fashioned English Christmas. From Paris, Irving politely declined.[4]

These were some of the by-products of his newly won fame. Although the British were astonished by Irving's "English" prose style, the writer's former neighbors were beginning to talk, too. Henry Brevoort said that many asked whether he meant to "renounce" his country, and he urged his friend to return to New York. Irving replied defensively: "As far as my precarious and imperfect abilities enable me, I am endeavouring to serve my country—Whatever I have written has been with the feelings and published as the writing of an American—Is that renouncing my Country?" He figured that a return home at this moment would place him in a vulnerable position whereby financial considerations would once again prey upon his mind, and he would face the real pressure of succumbing to the next offer of a government appointment. This, he imagined, would effectively end his literary career.

The example of James Kirke Paulding must have influenced his thinking in this. The incisive Paulding was now a family man with a government job. He still found time to take up his pen—but with mixed results. When his reissued "Second Series" of *Salmagundi* came out in 1820, without his having consulted his chief collaborator ("I regret he had not suffered the old work to die a natural death," Irving wrote), he was unfairly criticized as an inferior writer to Irving. Yet critics could not always determine what had been Paulding's part and what was Irving's in that production. Even the twenty-nine-year-old author of the popular mock-epic *Fanny,* Fitz-Greene Halleck, denounced Paulding, from New York, as a hack, and others criticized him personally as irritable and unstable. In a warm letter to Irving, the embattled Paulding took note that some now regarded the two ancient comrades as rivals. Rivalry with Irving was, said Paulding, "a thing neither my head nor heart will sanction."

As Paulding opened himself up in letters, Irving's fondness for him enlarged. His heart was "filled to overflowing" with memories of their younger days, he said. And to Brevoort, he expressed concern about the damage lately done to Paulding's literary reputation: "There seems to be a pitiful and illiberal spirit indulged towards him," Irving wrote of his avowedly political friend. "What is the state of our literature that it can afford to treat with slight & contumely such a writer as Paulding—There is no one that has ever pourtrayed American scenery and characters with greater truth and beauty." (He was referring specifically to Paulding's poems and essays about the pioneering West.) For his part, Paulding had tried to secure a position for the unlucky Peter Irving in Washington, D.C., but without success.[5]

If Paulding's treatment irked him, Irving suffered real heartache in learning of the death of his friend and former housemate, America's foremost naval hero, Stephen Decatur. He fell not on the high seas but in a pointless duel with a disgraced naval commander over an imagined slight. Decatur had served as his comrade Oliver Perry's second in an 1818 duel on the very ground where Aaron Burr and Alexander Hamilton had met in 1804; but owing in part to Decatur's stage management, everyone had walked away alive in that instance, honor intact. His forgiving nature had prompted him to make amends with a former rival whom he now asked to serve as *his* second. There seemed no logic behind Decatur's decision at this moment to raise pistols with James Barron, at eight paces, over a thirteen-year-old argument. After both men received wounds in the hip—Decatur's the more critical—they reconciled as they lay a few feet from one another. But the bullet had torn through Decatur's intestines; he died a slow and painful death, leaving behind a wife, from whom he had kept that day's fateful plan secret. Decatur was, at the time of his death, as much of a national idol as Andrew Jackson.

Old John Adams, the ex-president, on hearing of the duel, made a reference to Walter Scott's latest novel of gallantry, which he had just finished: "Decaturs fall is an awfull [i.e., at once reverential and dreadful] event," he wrote to his daughter-in-law. "I have read Ivanhoe and there is nothing much more awfull in that." For a deeply shaken Irving, writing to Paulding, "the sad story of our gallant friend Decatur" was difficult to reflect upon. "My heart rises to my throat. . . . I can never forget how generously he stepped forth in my behalf, when I felt beaten down and broken-spirited; I never forget him as the companion of some of my happiest hours." He did not wish to think about Susan, Decatur's loving wife, who slept fitfully whenever her husband was away on a dangerous assignment, and who now existed in "absolute wretchedness." As he proved in the *Sketch Book*, Irving had spent considerable time meditating on widowhood as an emotional state.[6]

Despite this, and despite any concern related to his major investment project, the nascent steamboat company, Paris was gaiety for him. Irving was introduced to Thomas Moore, the Irish poet, wit, singing sensation, confidant of Byron, and friend of all the literati. He had had to abandon England with his family for a few years because of his association with a financial scandal. Moore, a grocer's son, who in his diary called Irving "a good-looking and intelligent-mannered man," was unusually short, but intellectually resilient. During a tour of the United States in 1804, Moore was presented to Thomas Jefferson at the President's House, but the tall Virginian mistook the little man for a boy or a servant; for this slight, he suffered Moore's barbed pen later on. The poet famously satirized Jefferson as a false republican, and touched upon his keeping of a slave concubine with the lines: "The patriot, fresh from Freedom's councils come . . . And dreams of freedom in his bondmaid's arms." This could hardly have bothered Irving, though Moore did come to regret his unfavorable remarks about America.

When Byron departed England for Italy in 1817, he wrote a farewell to the Irishman: "My boat is on the shore, / And my bark is on the sea; / But, before I go, Tom Moore, / Here's a double health to thee!" They had not begun so adoringly, however, because Byron was both sensitive and presumptuous, and at one time so was Moore. Byron had savaged Moore in an 1809 work that concerned Moore's abortive duel with the critic Francis Jeffrey of the *Edinburgh Review*. In his "English Bards and Scotch Reviewers," Byron had made Moore appear cowardly, though his real target in the piece was Jeffrey. A year and a half later, Moore wrote to open a friendlier conversation, and their misunderstanding was resolved through the intercession of the poet Samuel Rogers. A thriving alliance resulted.

Now Moore led his new American friend into his social circle. He threw an anniversary party for his wife of ten years, at which Irving danced and spread comic cheer. The sociable poet also accompanied Irving to such evocative sites as the dungeon where Marie Antoinette had spent her last days. To Brevoort, Irving reported on his time with Moore: "He is a charming joyous fellow—full of frank, generous, manly feeling." For months the two kept almost daily company, and it was Moore who then challenged Irving to write an entire book about the patriarch of Bracebridge Hall with whom Geoffrey Crayon had spent Christmas. Now that Irving had the idea put in his head of writing again, in a burst of energy he wrote a good piece of what would be *Bracebridge Hall*. He read it aloud to his diminutive Irish ally, who did not tell Irving what he really felt about the book-in-progress—that it was not the equal of the *Sketch Book*.[7]

The spring of 1821 brought rain "and cold boisterous winds," as Irving wrote to Charles R. Leslie from Paris. "The Streets are so detestable in dirty weather, that there is no walking in them." He was living near the Garden of the Tuilleries, yet his acquaintances were mostly English and Americans. He was particularly attached to Sarah and Thomas Wentworth Storrow, he being an English-born Boston merchant of considerable learning, and she something of that maternal figure he was invariably drawn to. The sincere and receptive Storrows would be like the Van Warts were to him in England, and the Hoffmans in New York.

He seemed to prefer the feeling of England and the ways of London. For this reason, perhaps, Irving kept within a narrow circle. On the other hand, he became better acquainted with John Jacob Astor, now nearing sixty, who was wintering in Paris with his family. His highly successful American Fur Company was coming to resemble a monopoly; indeed, the German-born entrepreneur had suffered only one major setback in his career, when, in 1814, he was forced to abandon his outpost of Astoria, on the shores of the Pacific Northwest. He had done so despite encouragement from the likes of Albert Gallatin, then a member of the cabinet and now America's minister to France. The noble Gallatin had then turned down a lucrative offer from Astor to be his business partner, preferring to remain in government. Astor's principal reason for being in Europe in 1821 was to see whether he could consolidate his China trade from here.

It may be that Irving never discussed his foundering steamboat venture with Astor. Upset that his New York brothers had raised suspicions concerning the viability of the project, he had turned to Astor's old employee Brevoort to front him money that he promised to repay once he received the tidy sum he expected from John Murray for the rights to *Bracebridge Hall*. He wrote to Brevoort: "The success of the Sketch Book in England has been far beyond my most sanguine expectation & any book I should now offer for sale, *good or bad*, would be sure to find a ready purchaser at a high price among the Booksellers." Peter was even more insistent that they undertake this last bid for financial independence, but he was repeatedly rebuffed by his lawyer-brother John, who agreed with William that the family should not make loans. The New York–based brothers appear to have been wiser than the Europe-based brothers, for the investment never did pay off.[8]

Irving remained in Paris, and in Moore's orbit, until July 1821, when, "rather suddenly," he felt compelled to return to London. So he recrossed the Channel, and the very next day stood alongside his painter-friends Charles Leslie and Gilbert Stuart Newton and witnessed the coronation of King George IV from outside Westminster Abbey. Irving stayed for a time with Newton, the nephew of the man who gained fame for his portraits of George Washington, and brought Newton out to Birmingham to meet the Van Warts and their now six children.

He and Newton and Leslie were inseparable now—a bachelor band resembling what Irving had known in New York in former years. Irving saw the Astors briefly as they passed through London, and he wrote a chatty letter to Moore, commenting favorably after reading Byron's just-published second canto of *Don Juan*—compared to the first, "the licentiousness is less naked and offensive." He confided to Moore that Murray "has grown amazing fond of me." He also learned at this time that Columbia College had awarded him an honorary master's degree in recognition of his literary accomplishments. He wrote in reply: "Nothing is nearer to my heart than the desire of meriting the good opinion of my countrymen; and, above all of my Townsmen." It was a triumphant summer.[9]

During the last two months of 1821, Irving grew depressed. "I am shut up from the world and suffering in health & spirits," he wrote to Leslie. At his sister and brother-in-law's in Birmingham, he was being treated for a painful condition that had left both his legs inflamed, making it nearly impossible to walk. With this illness, he was also subject to frequent fevers. Adding to his frustrations, his doctor died shortly after beginning treatment. That was when he also learned from Ebenezer of their brother William's pending death, at age fifty-five, from tuberculosis; and his sister Catharine, in Johnstown, New York, had just watched two daughters fall ill and die, including her eldest, "a fine girl of seventeen." Of his own condition, he wrote to Mrs. Storrow, in Paris, that after many weeks under two doctors' care, he had "taken medicine enough to set up a country apothecary." And, in informing her of his eldest brother's passing, he referred to William as "one who was like a father to the family."[10]

And yet he was able to get *Bracebridge Hall* into production. Murray paid him a handsome sum for the rights, even before seeing the manuscript. At the end of January 1822, back in London but still weak, and prudently remaining indoors most days, Irving sent the first volume of two to Ebenezer to make certain it was put into print before it could be pirated. This was the game now: to secure an authorized first edition quickly, and then share profits with the American seller(s). It remained that neither England nor the United States honored the other's copyright, and Irving's new work was due to be issued in London first.

Bracebridge Hall was hurried along, no doubt, to suit Murray's desire to capitalize quickly on the success of the *Sketch Book*. The author explained the concept of his new collection to Ebenezer: "It is not like a novel, but rather a connected series of tales and essays. . . . Put what price you think proper." He recommended Moses Thomas of Philadelphia as his first choice to produce the work, but Thomas was still in too weak a financial position to assume all the risk. Cornelius Van Winkle, who had moved from Broadway to Greenwich Street, would again take the lead as Irving's New York publisher, with Thomas and others involved in the publication process bearing varying fractions of financial risk.[11]

☆   ☆

Bracebridge Hall, or the Humorists, by Geoffrey Crayon, Gent., opens with the bachelor-traveler's ironic identification of himself as "a man from the wilds of America." It reminds one of the famous portrait of Benjamin Franklin in his fur hat: To the French he was a representative of American rusticity, and nothing could have been further from the truth. But Franklin let the ruse go on, and so would Crayon.[12]

Even in Irving's time, British prejudice caused some to think of the average American as closer to the American Indian than to the proper English gentleman. The author thought it coy to play off this stereotype, reminding readers of his reception by the British people when the *Sketch Book* came out: "I was looked upon as something new and strange in literature; a kind of demi-savage, with a feather in his hand, instead of it on his head; and there was a curiosity to hear what such a being had to say about civilized society." Before he is through reintroducing himself, Crayon makes it clear that England possesses nostalgic substance in the hearts of those Americans whom she too easily dismissed as "wild." He writes: "England is as classic ground to an American as Italy is to an Englishman; and old London teems with as much historical association as mighty Rome."[13]

So Crayon returns to the Hall where he had once spent Christmas, this time to attend a wedding. He encounters again the Squire, "a lingering specimen of the old English country gentleman; rusticated a little by living almost entirely on his estate, and something of a humorist." And again, we meet Simon Bracebridge, affectionately called "Master Simon," whom Irving introduced in the *Sketch Book* as "a tight brisk little man, with the air of an old bachelor," something less than a patriarch, subsisting on a small but adequate income as the Squire's "factotum"; but as a genuine relative, Master Simon is indispensable, too, as "the wit of the family" and "a complete family chronicle, being versed in the genealogy, history and intermarriages of the whole house of Bracebridge."[14]

In the new collection, Master Simon thrives in his bachelor studio on the grounds of the estate, "a perfect epitome of an old bachelor's notions of convenience and arrangement." It is replete with an "ancient elbow-chair," which Irving's fans must have found reminiscent of the thinking man's station in *Salmagundi.* Other Irving character sketches in the first volume of *Bracebridge Hall* replicate *Sketch Book* types, too: the widow ("dainty in her living, and a little of an epicure"); the lovers ("fair Julia was leaning on her lover's arm, listening to his conversation, with her eyes cast down, a soft blush on her cheek"); the old soldier ("I cannot discover, however, that the general has ever run any great risk of dying, excepting from an apoplexy, or an indigestion"); and that "old yeoman" John Tibbets, or "Ready Money Jack" ("a regular frequenter of the village inn, the landlady having been a sweetheart of his in early life").[15]

But the sporting old bachelor Master Simon is the most memorable character in *Bracebridge Hall.* Though he is "the Caesar of the village," the Squire's "busy agent" who "intermeddles" in everyone's lives, he is more than that, more than "a great man in a little world." In "A Bachelor's Confessions," Master Simon agrees to expose his vulnerability. He owns up to having given his heart to a woman who ultimately passed him up for a man of greater means. Deeply affected, he kept a lock of her hair, "which he wore in a true lover's knot, in a large gold brooch." This leads Crayon to remark that every old bachelor had to have "some confession of a delicate nature to make," some romantic adventure that he recalled with fondness and a touch of remorse. Was Irving normalizing his old bachelor, making him understandable and nonpathological, by attaching to his romantic life a trauma so overwhelming that it prevented him from ever marrying? Was Matilda Hoffman's beau doing this for self-justification? Could he be that transparent?[16]

Another essay in the collection that succeeded among readers was "The Stout Gentleman." Its derivation is known, thanks to Charles Leslie, who included it in his memoir: One day during the summer of 1821, Irving and Leslie were out and about, and Leslie remarked on a "stout gentleman" who had shared their stagecoach. His friend retorted that he liked the phrase so much that he would use it as the title for a story—all he had to do was to think up something to write about such a person. Not long after, while Leslie sketched, Irving sat on a rock and wrote, "often laughing to himself," as Leslie recorded, "and from time to time reading the manuscript to me." Irving was feeling playful again, composing the tale of a rudely demanding guest at an isolated country inn.[17]

The story takes place on a gloomy, rainy Sunday. Crayon is stuck temporarily in his room overlooking an odorous barnyard. Bored by old magazines and disappointing company, he takes undue interest in a certain unseen lodger, known to him only (by the impatient call of a waiter) as "the stout gentleman in No. 13," who was demanding that breakfast be delivered to his room. He could be anyone from a London alderman to a member of the royal family—weren't they all stout gentlemen? As the day wears on, the mystery man becomes increasingly discourteous; at one point, he makes a chambermaid tumble down the stairs. Crayon, always within earshot during these episodes, is stymied at every attempt to capture a glimpse. He is thwarted when the man does not come down to dinner. The drama builds in his mind, but his timing is invariably off whenever he conspires to make contact. Finally, when morning comes, Crayon rushes to his window and catches but the briefest sight of the man's rear—"skirts of a brown coat parted behind"—as the stout gentleman steps into the coach and whirls away. A tantalizing nonending.[18]

Most of the stories in this collection are short, but there is a lengthy one that prefigures Irving's Spanish period. It is called "The Student of Salamanca," so rough a work that Irving rewrote major portions of it later. It begins, dreamily, "Once upon a time, in the ancient city of Granada, there sojourned a young man of the name of Antonio de Castros." He is enraptured (as Irving will be in southern Spain) by "the ruins of Moorish magnificence," and is drawn to secret manuscripts, forgotten lore, a mysterious old man in a library, an "alchymist," a beautiful, dark-eyed woman, a light in a tower—this is the Irving formula. The plain-dressed student, it turns out, is of a noble lineage, but this is not apparent until he embarks on an amorous adventure involving threatened virtue, unjust allegations, near-execution, and chivalric rescue.[19]

The name of Diedrich Knickerbocker appears in volume two of *Bracebridge Hall* as the author of a truncated account of a haunted house built by early Dutch settlers near the island of Manhattan. Irving could not resist mentioning his fictional historian at least once. But only one noteworthy American tale appears in the collection of fifty-one stories that Irving calls a "medley." That is "Dolph Heyliger," the only long short story besides "Salamanca." The title character is a sprightly fellow, modestly born, and native to early eighteenth-century New York, which is still the "jolly, little old city of the Manhattoes." Dolph is the only surviving son of a beleaguered Dutch mother, a widow who dotes on him. In his youth, he was something of a free spirit, hard for her to control; to teach responsibility, she apprentices him to a learned German doctor.

But Dolph does not take to the medical profession, and so the doctor, in conjunction with his "prying gossip" of a housekeeper, spirits the young man out of the house. They relocate him to the doctor's *bowerie,* or Dutch farm, a reputedly haunted house in which the doctor himself fears spending even one night. But Dolph is enterprising; he endures night after night with the ghost, whose "tramp—tramp—tramp" he can hear in the hallways. Finally, he makes contact with the ghost, who directs him, in his dreams, toward an uncertain destiny that Dolph feels he cannot but pursue.

On supernatural instruction, more or less, he boards a sailing vessel for a voyage up the Hudson. When the craft becomes caught in a storm, Dolph falls overboard and has to swim for his life. He reaches shore, where he falls in with a famed Dutch hunter-adventurer, Antony Vander Hayden, and his Indian allies. Dolph and the hunter become fast friends. He accompanies Vander Hayden home to Albany, where he takes a liking to the man's daughter. Dolph figures that his unplanned Hudson River swim and his meeting with Vander Hayden were intended by the forces that rule his life. He now thinks he has but to attend to sensations, and, "in this loose, easy way," will find the secret to happiness.

From his bedchamber at the Vander Hayden house, he espies a Flemish portrait hanging in a "shadowy corner" of the room. It comes to life in his mind, and he realizes it is the same being as the ghost he had encountered in the doctor's haunted house. As one constantly lacking funds but desirous of marrying Marie Vander Hayden, Dolph, "with palpitating heart," follows the ghost's irresistible hints back to Manhattan, to a well on the haunted property. Here he fishes for hidden riches. Hours pass, during which he hauls up nothing but trash. He begins to lose faith. Just as he is about to give up on his dreams—"mere dreams"—he dredges up a "great silver porringer," or lidded soup tureen, which is laden with gold. Thus does Dolph Heyliger come to prosper and win his bride, "growing merrier as he grew older and wiser."[20]

Modern critics have described the character of Dolph as a middle-class hero who marries up. He is likened as well to a later creation, the roguishly appealing Huckleberry Finn, a "boyish hero, who runs away to river and wilderness and the manly company of hunters and Indians." Both are "virtual orphans" for whom the river passage involves freedom, risk, and personal attachment, getting lost and finding oneself. Like Rip, too, Dolph "wastes time, but not life."[21] Dolph's good nature helps him to succeed—another refrain that repeats throughout Irving's work. It is as if possessing a good nature is enough to ensure ultimate felicity in life, no matter how unprepared one is for a civilized job in the "real" world. Like Irving himself, Dolph adheres to his resolution to step into the unknown.

As a whole, *Bracebridge Hall* was well received. Though modeled to an extent on the happy tone of characterization and even the format of the *Sketch Book,* it did not quite match the acclaim of its predecessor. Shortly after publication, Francis Jeffrey wrote in the *Edinburgh Review* that it was "monotonous and languid" in comparison with the *Sketch Book.* But he still liked Crayon, he said, and assured him that he would not be soon forgotten; but this time, his "elegant" miscellany was too likeable, too tolerant of difference, not daring enough. Maria Edgeworth, the author of such popular novels as *Belinda* and *The Absentee,* praised Irving's new work, but qualified, "The workmanship surpasses the work. There is too much care and cost bestowed on petty objects."[22]

Among twentieth-century critics, Stanley Williams called *Bracebridge Hall* as "feeble" as the *Sketch Book* was "robust." Taking a political perspective, Pete Kyle McCarter wrote: "In *Bracebridge Hall,* [Irving] surveys the British social system from the American point of view and, again as a good Federalist, finds that class cooperation . . . offers the brightest future and the only economic salvation for England." Mary Weatherspoon Bowden has suggested that *Bracebridge Hall* may be Irving's "most complex work," achieving unity through its diversity of outlooks.[23]

For those who can get beyond its hackneyed regard for old England—an England that contemporary critics of Irving denied the existence of in 1822—*Bracebridge Hall* remains captivating. Irving's deft use of language continues to distinguish him, and his gentle brand of humor can still raise a smile. But for those who, in 1820, found the *Sketch Book* remarkable, the successor volume, in 1822, was like going back to a primitive site only to find it had become a tourist attraction; the landscape was less fresh, the sense of discovery no longer conjurable. In contrast to the *Sketch Book,* emotion in *Bracebridge Hall* seemed artificial.

Whether one responds to the sketches or not, the prevailing mood in *Bracebridge Hall* makes it revealing of Irving's purpose. Time is of the present, but is as much a backward glance. People live under a spell, or their pasts shadow them. As he did in "Rip Van Winkle," Irving invents atmospherics that project his characters into a dim netherworld. Everywhere is curiosity, inquiry, "unknown personages," "wary" looks, a "venerable manuscript," an "antiquated" mind; there are affinities in nature, errant gusts of wind, "mouldy" rooms, the sound of a ticking clock, a "bustle of anticipation." The world of Irving seems at once plausible and unreal—dreamlike.

★   ★

As he was waiting in London for *Bracebridge Hall* to appear, Irving busied himself with epistolary obligations and social dinners that placed him constantly among the most fashionable people. On one afternoon, he escorted the wife of the U.S. ambassador, Richard Rush, to a council of art lovers at the home of a countess, and dined with her on at least one other occasion a short time after. Far from abandoning his ties to the New York literary crowd, he made an attempt to find a London publisher for James Fenimore Cooper's novel *The Spy.* He wrote in March 1822 to the entrepreneurial New York publisher Charles Wiley: "The best course for Authors in America to take would be to send Manuscript copies of their works to Mr John Miller Bookseller Fleet Street & request him to dispose of them to best advantage." Miller had been his choice for the *Sketch Book* before Murray had picked it up; back on his feet after financial difficulties, Miller now chose to specialize in American authors. "He is a worthy & obliging man," Irving assured Wiley, "and disposed to do every thing to serve Americans."[24]

Writing to his old friend Brevoort, he expressed relief that his health was improving. He attributed this partial recovery to having put his work in order and sent it to the United States. Of his newest publication, "It seems to give satisfaction here," he wrote, "and I am nearly killed with kindness, for I have not a moment to myself, and am so fatigued with company and dinner & evening parties." He still felt he required rest if he was to be done with his "lameness & inflammation in the ancles, the lingering of my tedious malady." He aimed to go to Aix-la-Chappelle (today's Aachen), at the trijuncture of modern Belgium, Germany, and the Netherlands, to partake of healing waters; but it would not be for another month that he would be able to break away.

Before he left London, Irving became reacquainted with the eccentric Virginia politician John Randolph of Roanoke, whom he had met and appreciated years before in Washington. Randolph's talent for oratory had at one time caused Irving to contemplate publishing a piece about this old-fashioned planter who had a penchant for roundly criticizing whoever happened to occupy the president's chair, Federalist or Republican. (His political eccentricity was rooted in the old republican principle of distrusting a strong executive.) Randolph was attracting notice in London both because of his abnormal physical appearance and his outlandish remarks. Though he was six feet tall, his small head sat atop a thin and gawky frame; his shoulders were only nineteen inches across. Irving told Brevoort of the sensation Randolph had created: "He has been sought after by people of the first distinction. . . . For in high life here, they are always eager after every thing strange and peculiar."

It is interesting to relate Irving and the right honorable Congressman Randolph. Irving was of a political family, of course, though his writer's imagination preferred to conjure a dreamy isolation for America. No one at the time read this as alienation, nor did the more civic-minded (other than the ruthless DeWitt Clinton) shun him for his "drowsy headed" prescription for merrymaking. The unconventional Randolph symbolized a related phenomenon: He had fun with politics in the way Irving did as Diedrich Knickerbocker, treating the floor of the House as if it were Knickerbocker's stage. The old-school Virginian was an elected cut-up who lived for contention. His often shrill one-man show allowed the literary scholar and lifelong bachelor to admit his Romantic tendencies. He railed at rapid progress, and wished for a return to the fantastic isolation of the less commercial eighteenth century. Protesting America's degeneration since the Revolution, he mocked modern society with Byronic pride, impossibly pronouncing himself the descendant of an ancient Greek hero. Randolph's irrelevance to the modern world was a good part of his charm, and the ostensible reason why the appearance in London of this haughty southerner caused a stir. On another visit to the former motherland, four years later while Irving was off in Spain, the odd-looking American aristocrat would doff his hat from shipboard and call out to those on shore: "Old England and young America, united forever! Who shall divide them!" He was, indeed, as good a character as any that Irving, in his fiction, ever invented. At the close of his career, Irving would donate his portrait of Randolph to the New-York Historical Society.[25]

We know that Irving and Randolph met up several times in London, but unfortunately we know nothing of what they said on these occasions. They would meet again on English soil years later, to greater effect—that story must wait. But when they became reacquainted in 1822, Randolph was long accustomed to his quirky celebrity, and Irving was just getting used to his. Sometimes that meant long days and long, festive nights: "I have been leading a sad life lately, burning the candle at both ends, and seeing the fashionable world through one of its seasons," he wrote in a note to Peter. Presumably, this was all to keep his name—and *Bracebridge Hall*—on the minds of those with the greatest influence in London society. He had been "hand-in-glove with nobility and mobility," as he nicely put it. Now, like Sterne's character Corporal Trim, he had, he said, "satisfied the sentiment," and was ready to flee notoriety. To his good friend Stuart Newton, Irving expressed himself in comic strains the night before he boarded a steamboat for the Continent: "I expect to leave London tomorrow morning. . . . So if you want to see any thing more of me, before I am blown up, or boiled down, come & breakfast with me."[26]

He traveled by way of the Netherlands, and it is most curious that, for the second time, he had so little of interest to say about the homeland of the Knickerbockers and Van Winkles. He found nothing more notable in Amsterdam than "the queer faces." At his unsatisfactory hotel, he wrote, he heard "bad French, bad English, and worst of all, good Dutch." Perhaps there was more substance than we might want to concede to Gulian Verplanck's suspicions about Irving's lack of compassion for the real Dutch.[27]

His destination: Aix-la-Chappelle. But the healing waters proved a letdown. He remained pestered by his unnamed "cruel malady," possibly gout. It did not, however, keep him from describing the motley Europeans about the German border town where Charlemagne was born. "Everywhere you see military characters, in fierce moustaches and jingling spurs, with ribbons and various orders at their button-holes," he wrote to his sister in Birmingham. "It is extremely tantalizing to be here just on the frontiers of Germany, in the vicinity of some of the most beautiful and romantic scenery in Europe, and to be thus fettered and disabled."

Three weeks later, he was on his own in the vicinity of Wiesbaden, a hundred miles to the southeast, not only trying the "dry vapour bath of Sulphur," but enjoying public walks and gardens. The freedom was exhilarating, "as if my mind took holiday the moment it was out of the traces, like a horse turned loose in the pasture." He found the Germans "a frank, kind, well meaning people." He professed not to be thinking at all about writing. By August, though starved, he said, for an American's companionship, he had found a Russian colonel suffering from the same ailment, and was content to stay on in Wiesbaden for its expected "good remedies."[28]

In all, Irving would remain in Germany and environs for a year. He had promised his Anglo-American friends in Paris that he would be rejoining them soon, but Germany had its allure, in particular the castles along the Rhine and other such places that abounded in mysteries and hauntings. Irving wrote to his sister from the Black Forest, in October 1822, that he had seen in one old castle

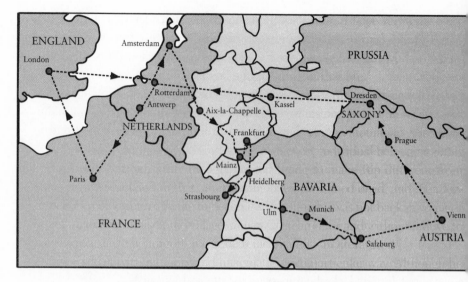

MAP 8.1   Irving's travels in Europe, 1822–1824

long galleries of pictures of all the Electors of Baden, and the heroes of its
reigning families for several centuries back, that have a most martial appearance, clad to the teeth in glistening steel. Underneath the castle we
were shown subterraneous apartments that equaled the fabrications of novelists. They were chambers where the secret tribunal held its sittings, and
where its victims were confined, and if convicted, tortured and executed.

And to Thomas Storrow, even before setting out: "I mean to get into the
confidence of every old woman I meet with in Germany and get from her, her
budget of wonderful stories." The Gothic imagination was growing in him.

As he proceeded south from Darmstadt to Heidelberg, amid disordered
references to "yawning" courtiers and "villages Spires & tracts of forest land,"
he glared at peasants in the fields, and he took an interest in the wagons,
loaded with wine, that bumped through the fertile landscape. The wanderer
prodded himself to make better sense of a historic culture by comparing and
contrasting to what was familiar. "The continual variety of romantic scenery"
and the "exuberant quantity of fine fruit" reminded him of New York State.
Trudging south along the Rhine, he enjoyed the smokiness of out-of-the-way
inns, the antiquated dress of his hostess, the stags' horns that hung on walls,
the "charming little" Bavarian capital of Munich and its "princely palaces." In
Strasbourg, he saw a French translation of the *Sketch Book* that appealed
greatly to him; a German version was soon to come from a Berlin publisher.

All he could think about were the new stories he was sure to accrue. He filled his journal with descriptions of picturesque views, the "sun and wind driving mist & clouds to their fortresses in the mountains & up the valley where they are broken up & desert in light feathery detachments."[29]

Then came the heart of Austria. Vienna perplexed him: "It is extensive, irregular, crowded, dusty, dissipated, magnificent, and to me disagreeable." The concentrations of wealth, so gaudily visible to the traveler, bore no charm for him, and the "motley" appearance of those he encountered—"Greeks, Turks, Polonaise, Jews, Sclavonians [i.e., Slavs], Croats, Hungarians, Tyroleans"—made him feel quite out of place. His ailment had now ceased to trouble him, but he continued daily footbaths just in case.

The lack of literary society convinced him to leave Vienna for Dresden, and the Kingdom of Saxony, three hundred miles to the northwest. He previewed Saxony for his sister: "a place of taste, intellect, and literary feeling," a place where he could expect to hear proper German spoken. In Dresden, then, he would seek out "winter quarters." He would put off Paris. He apologized to the Storrows for dragging his heels and not going straight to Paris to be with them. "My fate seems to be to wander," he told these fellow Americans, "or rather, it is my vocation."[30]

He made his way up to Prague in mid-November, appreciating its "fine old continental look," though his hotel was "large, dirty & rambling." He found new ways to describe the land that spread before him: A "long straight road, bordered with trees—a whitish stripe thro the brown country"; "swelling hills"; "volcanic hills"; and closing in on Dresden, "gleams of the Elbe." On arrival, he wrote to Charles Leslie: "I shall now take a master and go to work to study German. If I can get my pen to work so much the better; but it has been so long idle that I fear it will take some time to get it in a working mood." He recognized his unique pattern, evident since leaving New York seven years before: He moved about for months at a time, sometimes aimlessly, sometimes surer of the nature of his ambition; all the while he struggled to make sense of new scenes until his mind positively exploded with a new album of sketches.[31]

☆ ☆

On December 3, 1822, the day after his arrival in Dresden, Irving dined with the British and Russian ministers to the court of Saxony. He would soon be presented to envoys from France, Spain, and Prussia. He liked the size of the city (fifty thousand in population) and its air of restraint, and no doubt felt secure that he would continue to enjoy the company of fashionable men and women as he passed the long winter. But his well-being ultimately had more to do with the family of an absent British aristocrat, John Foster. Irving made their acquaintances on December 19. The Fosters, who lived just two blocks from Irving's hotel, were a doughty little English band consisting of the mother, Amelia Morgan Foster, herself the daughter of an earl, her teenage daughters, Emily and Flora, and three young sons. They had lived in the city for two years already by the time of his arrival, and they formed the hub of British society. Eighteen-year-old Emily particularly commanded Irving's attention.[32]

It is hard to decipher just when thirty-nine-year-old Washington Irving became smitten with young Emily. He made an immediate impression on the mother, no doubt, just as he had with Mrs. Josiah Ogden Hoffman and Mrs. Thomas W. Storrow. As the noted author of the *Sketch Book,* he was a curiosity wherever he went now. Though his first meal with the Fosters was undercooked, owing, he noted, to a chef who was "ill tempered & wrong headed," they were an agreeable and ready-made stand-in for his Birmingham relatives, to whom he was writing regularly. He dined with the Fosters constantly over the next months; he amused them with his stories and accompanied them when they socialized with the ambassadorial set. If he had had no motive beyond a quasifamilial closeness, all would have been effortless.[33]

But there was something about Emily. In the year leading up to Irving's arrival in Dresden, the nearly marriageable Emily had already attracted several would-be suitors. That was the situation Irving walked in on, and the atmosphere was thick with amorous competition. One was a charming and lively Italian, an art collector entirely too self-absorbed. Another was a Bavarian, the brother of a diplomat, who was more constant in his appeal (this according to Emily's diary), but apparently unready to pop the question. The third in line was an Englishman named Airey, who lived up to his name, and whom Emily seemed to consider a ridiculous, though devoted, pet. Irving had to pretend he was not one of them—his attractiveness would derive from his ability to transcend.

The loss of the Bavarian's attentions enabled Emily to form a bond with the American. She provides us a telling description of his comportment: "Mr. I— is in want of constant excitement, & support, interest & admiration of his friends seems the very food he lives on." Physically, she found him "neither tall nor slight, but most interesting, dark, hair of a man of genius waving, silky, & black, grey eyes full of varying feeling, & an amiable smile."[34]

From day one, Irving's daily routine revolved around this "head-less" family. On Christmas Day, 1822, he was presented to Frederick Augustus I, the octogenarian king of Saxony, who asked him innocently how, in logistical terms, Americans got around their big country, and then went on to comment on the perils of steamboat travel. On the 26th, the only American in town attended a "musical party" at the Prussian minister's, and spent the balance of the evening at Mrs. Foster's; he breakfasted there on the 27th, took his main meal again with the family; spent the morning of the 28th at the Fosters' once more; attended court on the 29th ("Queen a very affable old lady"); and went from the royal presence back to the Fosters' to begin rehearsal for one of the many amateur theatrical performances he and they would put together that winter. Thus the weeks flew by. The Fosters occupied rooms in a palace near the Elbe, and so had plenty of room to stage their "secret" dramas, as they called them. In attaching himself to the family, Washington Irving temporarily put aside any serious writing he might have been doing.[35]

It was Airey who had combined with the Fosters in their plays before Irving had arrived, but the Englishman was no match for the ebullient New Yorker. At one ball in town, Emily ignored Airey, dancing the waltz with her new friend, and Airey complained. According to her diary: "He must think I feel secure of *his* good graces, & want to gain Mr. Irving's." Amelia Foster tutored Irving in Italian, and Emily helped him with his French. A couple of local intellectuals took turns teaching him German.[36]

Rehearsals and evening conversations at the Fosters continued through February 1823. Irving regularly attended the Dresden theater, seeing such plays as *Hamlet* and a less impressive German comedy that he remembered as the "kissing & crying of old men and ugly women." In frequent attendance at Mrs. Foster's was her cousin (and also a friend of Tom Moore's), the very literary Colonel Barham Livius, whom Irving described to his brother Peter as bearing a likeness to the fictional Master Simon of Bracebridge Hall. One evening at the Fosters, Irving joined Livius and a group of gentlemen in a game of crambo, in which everyone takes turns adding a clever rhyming line to the one that preceded it. These activities were all pleasant enough, yet Irving was in a holding pattern.[37]

As winter turned to spring, he resolved to force the issue: He had feelings for Emily. As with the Hoffmans and, more tentatively, with the Livingstons, the Manhattan merchant's son once more expressed his interest in an alliance with an aristocratic family whose wealth and status were greatly beyond his own. At the end of April, he composed a rose-scented poem to Emily on the occasion of her birthday—"Bloom on—bloom on—frank nature's child," he wrote. He danced with her that very night at a court ball. By this time, his hopes may well already have been dashed, but he could not command himself to exit gracefully. Precise details of his suit are unobtainable, but his journal for the spring and summer of 1823 suggests a bittersweet life in Dresden amid anxious, shifting moods.[38]

It all began quite delicately. On April 3, his fortieth birthday, he rode into the countryside with the Fosters to "ramble about the Hills." That evening, Emily and Flora surprised and charmed him by acting out scenes from his three books. The next day, Irving, Livius, and the Foster family performed "The Wonder a Woman Keeps a Secret" for a select audience that included counts and countesses. On the 5th, he helped the family move into new quarters. He continued receiving Italian lessons from Mrs. Foster the next week, and he stayed late one night telling the children ghost stories. Mid-month something changed. On the 13th, his journal shows him evincing concern over an illness Emily was suffering. And on the 14th: "Mrs F scolds me for not staying to Dinner." Why would he not stay? Tuesday, April 15: "Emily looking very pretty."

It was the first time he had written these words, or anything like them. After staying at the Fosters' until eleven o'clock the next evening, he wrote dolefully on the 18th: "Read Scotts last novell—call on Livius who suffers from Toothache but is affraid of the Dentist—Am very triste—call at Fosters & take Ital Less. E still troubled with headache." And before that day ended: "Lying down when Mrs F calls on me in carriage & carries me [to her] home—take French lesson—talk with the girls—E in good spirits & listens delightfully." Something was brewing, or stewing, or had already bubbled over.[39]

Perhaps his disappointment was deepest during the latter part of April, for he wrote without explanation in his journal on the 30th that he had gone into hiding and had yet to "gather" himself "up." According to Emily's younger sister Flora, Irving did not *speak* his feelings, but offered his heart to Emily by *writing* of it to their mother: "He has confessed to my mother, as to a true and dear friend, his love for E, and his conviction of its utter hopelessness."

We do know for certain that sometime during these weeks, in response to a request, he composed a long and very personal autobiographical sketch that he presented to Mrs. Foster. He described how his essential personality had formed, how he had been all hope and happiness in youth—when "every thing was fairy land"—until life suddenly became arduous. The narrative reads self-servingly; it is by no means Irving's best work. But it is useful in highlighting how he traced the road map of his life. The author meant, as an explanation for the current state of his heart, to show Amelia Foster how his mind drew the sentimental scenes of his beloved *Sketch Book* from his personal experience.

In Irving's reconstruction of the past, the tragic dimension of his life centers on Matilda Hoffman. He writes of the time he met Maria Fenno Hoffman ("like a sister to me"), which was also, of course, when he met that "timid, shy, silent little being," Matilda. The parallel to the Fosters must have been transparent. "I don't want to make any romantic story," Irving insisted in the letter to Amelia. But that is precisely what he was doing in this tale, explaining how, on his return from Europe in 1806, he found how much he admired the "softness and delicacy" and "mantling modesty" of the teenaged Matilda. "Her shyness wore off by degrees," and he fell hopelessly in love, only to watch as she succumbed to what had first been thought an innocuous cold. "I seemed to drift about without aim or object, at the mercy of every breeze; my heart wanted anchorage," he wrote of his despondency after Matilda died. For years, he said, he "could not even mention her name." Even the unmitigated success of *Knickerbocker's History* did not restore his former spirit.

Continuing the narrative up to the present, he explained how, on the verge of being a "ruined man" financially, he had put together his *Sketch Book*. But even that did not bring him unalloyed happiness—and here he overdramatizes his pain by insisting that his brother William's death shortly after publication ("a man whom I loved better than any other man on the face of the earth") denied him a happiness he might otherwise have found. But one thing is clear: He is conscious of wanting Mrs. Foster to form a positive, not a pitying, impression of him. He reassures her that he is not a melancholy being, that he can "rise again from under severe pressures." Yet as a man who has known only struggle, he aches in the knowledge that he cannot escape those certain "shadows" that have followed him through life—a destiny ostensibly borne out by his evident unsuitability for Emily.

And so he was resigned to it: He would not have the chance of enjoying what other men did. During their months of intimacy, he had, he reminds Amelia, variously confided to her "on subjects that I recur to with excessive pain." (The statement is ambiguous: Only she knows what he is referring to here.) But it seems pointless for him to confess anything further: "Why should I trouble you [if] sympathy is of no avail." How could he expect the mother of Emily to console him? It is, all in all, a strange confession, but one that is meant to preserve his dignity.

Years later, Flora remembered Irving as charming but mood-driven: "His smile is one of the sweetest I know; but he can look very, very sad." He could be "oppressed with morbid feelings," but more often "a genial glow lights his eye and colors his cheek, and his conversation soon sparkles again with wit and humor." She also noted his "wonderful knack at shutting his eye to the sinister side of everything." Above all, she recalled him as an "admirable *relater*," a man who delighted her family with his inexhaustible stock of stories, always vivid, always enlightening. He made them feel.[40]

This was Flora's retrospective—not of this one episode, but in general. It is harder to know how her mother (more perceptive, we must suppose, and closer to Irving's age) interpreted his behavior. It seems that Irving's morbid self-appraisal of his feelings for Matilda Hoffman was meant to clarify something for Amelia first and foremost. He felt a need to acquaint her with his feelings of defeat. It was the best way he had to explain that he loved Emily and yet could not become her husband, nor probably any woman's husband.

Emily, it has been suggested, appreciated Irving as a friend but did not think of him in *that* way, as the saying goes. In her role as a sympathetic "older sister" type, Mrs. Foster might have told him, as a quieting rationale (or perhaps it was the real reason for the refusal), that her husband, still back in England, would dismiss him as a man without financial means. Regardless, Irving had a ready-made excuse of his own, on financial grounds, for why he—such an amiable person and not unattractive—was not already married: "I was not [one to] drag down any woman to his paltry circumstances, and I was too proud to tolerate the idea of ever mending my circumstances by matrimony."

He could never marry a woman of means; nor, presumably, would he marry a woman without means. But wealth and class merely represented a sideshow in his long confessional. Irving claimed that his affliction was "morbid sensitiveness" (repeating one of the words Flora was to employ in her later reminiscences) "and a quick susceptibility to any new injury." He counted on this making sense to Amelia. It is significant that he undertook the letter in response to a question *she* had unabashedly asked him, one she probably had thought about for a long time before posing it. His letter was designed to address it: *"You wonder why I am not married."*

So they agreed, Irving and Mrs. Foster. Or pretended to. "My time has now gone by," he wrote to her, assuming, perhaps, that this was the simplest way to put it. As he had written of Master Simon Bracebridge, every old bachelor had to have "some confession of a delicate nature to make," a romantic quest to recall with fondness and a touch of remorse, and Emily Foster could be tucked away in his mind as that tormented moment of rejection for him; in this way he fortified a rationale that the timeworn Matilda Hoffman story could not support alone. And just as Master Simon kept a lock of hair belonging to the woman who would not marry him, Irving would hang over the piano at Sunnyside a picture Emily had drawn for him.

And then there was his embrace of the world, like Mackenzie's Harley, the Man of Feeling. He was always doing for others, he said to Amelia, again rationalizing, and no doubt with considerable effect. He was always thinking of others, which made him a social success but not a material success. He was so busy committing to the beings he encountered in his Crayon-like travels that he shortchanged himself. That is what celibate priests did.

What he did not say was that, as Flora recognized, he craved attention and a sense of belonging. The comfort he received from Amelia probably did more for him than any communication he had with Emily. Amelia satisfied his need to feel at home, whereas Emily embodied his desire to know feminine purity and youthfulness. Both women appreciated him and let him feel that it was with them that he entertained best and shined brightest. But did he not know that Emily would not have him? Intentionally or not, Irving reserved his extraordinary thoughts of love for an unobtainable woman.

Irving fretted, and perhaps, in private, even wept, once he had written to Emily's mother. When, in late May, he traveled to Prague to escape the inner turmoil, he confessed to Amelia Foster that he should, if he were in his right mind, stay away from Dresden altogether. "And yet I think of returning! Why should I come back to Dresden? The very inclination that draws me thither should furnish reasons for my staying away." Again, a few days later: "My mind has been in a restless state of strife & indiscision.... How can I write frankly & not speak from what is uppermost in my mind."

He was tormenting himself, and she told him so. Emily, perhaps less knowing than her mother, recorded in her diary on May 19: "Our last night with Irving—before his journey—Mama suspects he meant not to return, he said he had thought of it—but that he would he could not help it." The two of them, Washington and Emily, had stood that night "on the balcony by moonlight & talked of heaven."[41]

Irving wrote to Henry Brevoort from Prague, vaguely hinting at what was on his mind by the manner in which he asked about their old New York cronies. "Harry Ogden I find is at length married and of course poor & happy." Here he invoked the trope of true love flourishing best where material comforts were absent. Yet money remained only one among several forms of rationalization for his persistent bachelorhood. He continues to Brevoort: "Where is Jack Nicholson—still making love unsuccessfully?" Nicholson was a career naval officer, the same age as Irving, whose inability to settle down might have made sense. But Irving said nothing explicit concerning his own lack of success at love.

After exchanging letters with the Fosters, Irving returned to Dresden. He accompanied Amelia and her children on a piece of the road as they headed back to England, then said a painful goodbye to the family and headed out for good, this time to Paris.

It was in the year before he met the Fosters that Irving wrote in the short story "Wives," for *Bracebridge Hall:* "Men are always doomed to be duped" in romance, not by female deception so much as "by their own imaginations." It had turned out to be a self-fulfilling prophecy. Over the months in Dresden, he had read in several languages, pursued his studies, and hobnobbed with nobility, but had come away with little more than a broken heart.[42]

✫　✫

Irving's only way out of this confused, lovelorn state was to resume writing and publishing. And so he did. But *Tales of a Traveller,* his third book in the "sketch book" format, showed little of Dresden—and little of Germany—in spite of his earlier promise to take control of a "budget of wonderful stories" there. Indeed, the work's most outspoken critic, Walter Scott's friend (and now son-in-law) John Lockhart, who had earlier extolled the comic genius of *Knickerbocker's History,* and cheered on the *Sketch Book,* lamented the new collection's lack of genuine Germanness: "He has produced a book, for aught I see, might have been written, not in three years, but in three months, without stirring out of a garret in London." And as for its stock of ghost stories, Lockhart was downright cruel. They were "with one exception, old, and familiar to everybody conversant in that sort of line." Irving now appeared to him "a man of limited reading."[43]

Murray had said he was willing to pay Irving twelve hundred guineas for the book, sight unseen. He would publish it in two volumes. Irving politely, confidently, responded that the trusting publisher ought to take a good look at the manuscript first, then determine whether it might not be worth fifteen hundred to him: "Dont think me greedy after money—but in fact I have need of all I can get just now." This makes one wonder whether Irving's Gothic turn as a storyteller might have been stimulated in some way by his and Peter's financial insecurity, and perhaps class consciousness as well. If his *Sketch Book* story of William Roscoe was in some measure an attempt to deal with issues of humiliation after the bankruptcy of P & E Irving, then the Irving of 1823–1824 was excavating a new site in his mind, and the common hysteria among his characters expressed his continuing frustration over the wandering indeterminacy of his life, even in the wake of success.[44]

From the time of the Puritans to the celebrated Levi Weeks case in the Manhattan of Irving's younger years, Gothic imagery abounded in murder pamphlets and other published reports of unexplained horrors and ambiguous deaths. As Edgar Allan Poe was to write in "Metzengerstein" (1832): "Horror and fatality have been stalking abroad in all ages. Why then give a date to this story I have to tell?" Horace Walpole's *The Castle of Otranto* (1764) contained the classic elements of the castle and cave, the subterranean labyrinth, the extinguished lamp, the hollow groan; the plot of William Godwin's *Things as They Are, or, The Adventures of Caleb Williams* (1794), a favorite of Poe's, was nothing if not a portrait of twisted reality in which the protagonist navigates the hazardous world of sensations in pursuit of (before being pursued by) a murderer. Similarly, the Philadelphian Charles Brockden Brown, in his *Wieland; or, The Transformation* (1798), featured a haunted imagination as well as an ostensibly haunted house. Stories set in darkness, amid troubled dreams and moral dilemmas, were not at all uncommon. And we know, of course, about Mary Shelley's *Frankenstein*, published a year before Irving's *Sketch Book*.[45]

Tales of a Traveller is a much-maligned collection, but it contains several charming tales, cleverly connected, that move us beyond where the author had been before. Irving presents more than just ghost stories. He strikes out anew without having to sacrifice entirely the characters and situations through which he had earlier secured his reputation. Diedrich Knickerbocker is back, as are New York scenes. The thirty-two-story collection is divided into four discrete parts: "Strange Stories by a Nervous Gentleman," "Buckthorne and His Friends," "The Italian Bandits," and "The Money Diggers."

Tales opens with a reference to "The Stout Gentleman" of *Bracebridge Hall*, linking that story to the "nervous gentleman" of the present text, a man of "shy, retiring habits," who was made uncomfortable after being identified as the one who had seen (or not quite seen) the popular man of mystery stepping into his carriage. As he had had fun weaving *Bracebridge Hall* out of the Christmas portion of the *Sketch Book*, this was Irving's way of offering a segue from one book to the next, and of extending the presumed puzzle of the stout gentleman's character. Was it, or was it not, Sir Walter Scott?

From here, he launches into a series of ghost stories, which, though mediocre, still warrant historical analysis—the genre, after all, was young. They are narrated successively by guests at a dinner for foxhunters, hosted by an "old Baronet," in whose company is Irving's "nervous gentleman." His partners for the night include a "hatchet-faced gentleman," an "inquisitive gentleman," and the "old gentleman with the haunted head": "The whole side of his head was dilapidated, and seemed like the wing of a house shut up and haunted."

In "The Adventure of the German Student," told by this last of the old gentlemen, we meet the young visionary Gottfried Wolfgang, who has taken his studies too deep into "fanciful speculations on spiritual essences," and finds himself in Paris at the time of the French Revolution. In a dream, he sees a haunting "female face of transcendent beauty." Her visage becomes fixed in his mind. One night, walking past the blood-stained guillotine at the Place de Grève, he beholds a shadowy female form and recognizes it as the woman from his dream. "I have no friend on earth!" she tells him, pointing to the guillotine. The earnest, protective Gottfried leads the pale but "dazzling" woman to his apartment. There he tells her of his dream, and they nod knowingly at the uncanny connection they share. He pledges his life to her. The next day, he leaves the apartment as his "bride" sleeps, and returns a while later to discover that she is cold—a corpse. The police arrive and confirm for him that she had been guillotined the day before. The story concludes:

> Here the old gentleman with the haunted head finished his narrative. "And is this really a fact?" said the inquisitive gentleman. "A fact not to be doubted," replied the other. "I had it from the best authority. The student told me it himself. I saw him in a madhouse at Paris."

One intriguing aspect of this story, given our discussion of Emily Foster and Irving's unrequited love, is that the main character falls for a woman he can under no circumstances marry—she is a corpse. As if Emily was not impossible enough for him to bring to the altar! Where there is love there is death, or the death of a healthy mind.

In "The Adventure of the Mysterious Picture," the "nervous gentleman" is obliged to spend the night in a room rarely occupied. He is startled awake by the horror-inducing face on the wall that stares out at him, seemingly alive. So he leaves the haunted room and sleeps on a downstairs sofa. He is the butt of jokes the next morning, until being rescued by his host, who confirms that "odd and uncomfortable sensations" are frequently produced by the picture, for which reason he had banished it to that particular room. Because his guests want to hear more, the host picks up the first-person narrative, and the next (equally unfinished, equally deficient) story, "The Adventure of the Mysterious Stranger" opens. And so on.

In his journal, on August 11, 1823, with the evolving manuscript very much in his head, Irving had jotted: "Woke at 4 oclock this morng—with a strange horror on my mind—a dread of future evil—of failure in future literary attempts—a dismal foreboding that I could not drive off by any effort of reason." It is impossible to know what part of the Tales he was working on just then, but he was certainly getting everything he had bargained for.[46]

As the author who made Ichabod's terror amusing to the reader in "Sleepy Hollow," and as the arranger of the ghost story that helped the title character acquire his fortune in "Dolph Heyliger," Irving let a series of new narrators step into Geoffrey Crayon's latest volume, all to show the silliness of letting the Gothic imagination get the better of oneself. Irving is, in the end, a critic of superstition, a writer who mocks his characters' skewed perceptions. He uses Gothicism to disrupt narrative expectation.[47]

Edgar Allan Poe, who was only fifteen at the time of publication, came to appreciate what Irving was trying to do. He called *Tales of a Traveller* "graceful and impressive," at the same time regarding Irving as an accomplished but "overrated" writer who suffered from his long exposure to Europe. When the sentimentality was sucked from Irving's tales, left behind was a core of haunted histories and petrified victims that Poe could use as a template for conveying the uncomfortable, the dark, and the dreaded. As would be true of Poe, Irving was less about the spectacle and all about the telling. Of course, Poe's writings were influenced by a different kind of insecurity and a greater degree of social estrangement.[48]

Some of the thirty-two stories in *Tales of a Traveller* work better than others. In the second of the book's four parts, the principal character is Buckthorne, "a literary man," a "young man of great expectations" (the word *buck*, as we saw in the early Irving *nom de plume* "Dick Buckram," was colloquial for "young man"). Buckthorne is something of a latter-day Tom Jones. Irving conceived him before the *Sketch Book,* when he was contemplating a full-scale novel around Buckthorne's experiences, but he ultimately had to be satisfied with a sprawling series of comic exploits within *Tales.* Here he uses his character to help him gaily spoof the English literary world:

> The land of literature is a fairy land to those who view it from a distance, but like all other landscapes, the charm fades on a nearer approach, and the thorns and briars become visible. The republic of letters is the most factious and discordant of all republics, ancient or modern.[49]

We must ask: Was Buckthorne supposed to symbolize a piece of a younger Irving? "He [Buckthorne] had seen the world, and mingled with society, yet retained the strong eccentricities of a man who had lived much alone. There was a careless dash of good humour about him which pleased me exceedingly, and at times an odd tinge of melancholy mingled with his humour and gave it an additional zest."[50] The Buckthorne sequence, replete with a miserly and unsociable old bachelor uncle, a squire's winning daughter with the sugary name of Sacharissa, and a temptress named Columbine, provides fodder for an extended biography that ends when the rambling, poetic Buckthorne achieves a modicum of respectability. Setting aside his quaint literary aspirations, he belatedly comes into his inheritance, Doubting Castle: "I've done with authorship.—That for the critics!" And is this not what Irving wants for himself? Will not the Sunnyside of his last years be his Doubting Castle?[51]

Part four of the collection, "The Money Diggers," holds together nicely. The first offering, "Hell Gate," gives Irving a chance to return to the "renowned city of the Manhattoes" and the narrow strait beside Long Island Sound where many a Dutchman's barks were smashed—or stranded for a time, as was the squadron commanded by Oloffe the Dreamer. Now, though, Hell Gate was the scene for a tale of pirate treasure featuring the "notorious" Captain Kidd.

"The Devil and Tom Walker" is meant to take place in 1727, "at the time when earthquakes were prevalent in New England." Irving's protagonist is a stingy Bostonian (just as the comparably unsympathetic Ichabod Crane hailed from Connecticut), who makes a pact with "the Black Woodsman"—also known as "Old Scratch"—so as to gain access to Kidd's treasure. In what is perhaps Irving's most pessimistic tale, Tom becomes a moneylender; shamelessly he preys on his neighbors, until the devil suddenly appears and whisks him away. He does not get far in his effort to find buried treasure, nor, once again, does the story really end; instead, we take another trail, where we meet the eponymous protagonist of one of Irving's most amiable offerings, the penultimate chapter in the volume, "Wolfert Webber, or Golden Dreams." In the cabbage-growing days of the post-Stuyvesant Dutch, Wolfert, as impoverished as a hardworking farmer can be, hears a rumor of buried money and dreams of hidden wealth. He gives up on his cabbages and goes in pursuit. Before long, he is a ruined man. At the tavern he frequents, he hears further talk suggesting that Captain Kidd once plied the Hudson. The conversation draws him deeper in.

This melts into "The Adventure of the Black Fisherman," in which "Mud Sam," a negro, is said to have witnessed, long before, some murderers digging a grave, while he was out sinking his line in the vicinity of Hell Gate. Wolfert is hooked. "Blessed St. Nicholas!" he exclaims, figuring it must be possible to "make one's self rich in a twinkling." So Wolfert pays Sam (now an old man) a visit, and convinces the fisherman to show him the site of his earlier discovery. They go off one night, and are properly spooked; back home, as Wolfert starts babbling about money to be found, his wife decides to consult a doctor—the very doctor, Irving tells us, with whom Dolph Heyliger had apprenticed. The sagacious Dr. Knipperhausen, it seems, has long specialized in mysterious ailments that relate to "seeking the short cuts to fortune," for he himself had been so afflicted since his youth in the Harz mountains of Germany. As he tackles Wolfert's case, predictably, "the doctor [catches] the malady from his patient."

The pursuit continues at an Irvingesque spot, amid the "murmuring and roaring of Hell Gate." On this night, Sam finds a chest. The moment is too much for Wolfert, and in the ensuing panic, the chest—or whatever it is—falls into the current. Are there "gnomes and spirits" guarding the treasure? All that matters is that the secret is safe. No one wins.

Wolfert resigns himself to living out his life in the manner of his forebears. By way of a postscript, we learn that, to Wolfert's delight, the city of Manhattan has expanded. He has turned his cabbage fields into rental units, and made a tidy fortune. Thus Irving ends his *Tales* on a happy note. Despite all the harbingers of doom, no one (except for the deranged German student in volume one) has been too terribly hurt.[52]

Tales was an imperfect anthology. In it, Irving created a vaguely familiar, but generally disruptive, world. He took recognizable characters from ordinary life, such as Buckthorne and the "nervous gentleman," and played havoc with them. They entered and exited and reentered the world of stories, Irving all the time pulling the strings and trying to redefine what a book could be. He unnerved.

We must recognize, too, that in 1823–1824, Irving remained at heart a social critic. (His critics did not understand this about him.) He regarded his craft as a serious one, yet did not take himself too seriously. Thus his conclusions did not have to conclude. Like "The Stout Gentleman," they did not have to provide definitive answers in order to convince *him* that they were faithful to the aim of the comic writer: undermining rational expectation.

Despite his sentimentalism, muted here in *Tales*, Irving had not abandoned satire. He aroused curiosity about a ghost story so that his narrator could hold back from finishing the tale, in this way dragging the reader to the next tale, and the next, with the hope each time that the narrator will finally be able to fill in the blanks. As in *Knickerbocker's History,* he was dissolving characters and events. Nor were Sterne's evasions in *Tristram Shandy* forgotten.

In London, Murray published *Tales* in August 1824, in two volumes. In New York, C. S. Van Winkle once again served as Irving's printer, under the supervision of Ebenezer Irving; in Philadelphia, Carey & Lea issued the book in four parts, from August to October. Then a two-volume American edition appeared in the spring of 1825. (The exact sharing of profits among the parties is not known.) It was not until 1829 that Carey & Lea, a thriving publishing house, purchased the copyright outright. After this, the partners produced several more American editions.[53]

★   ★

"I must strike out some way of my own," Irving had written to his brother Peter in September 1823, as he began to compile *Tales*. He awaited, he said, his next "inventing fit."[54] This was how he thought of himself, even while adhering to the "sketch book" formula; he was concerned that each of his books might appear too much like the last, and was therefore committed to trying something new. That is what would take him next to Spain, to the story of Christopher Columbus, and straight biography.

He had relocated to Paris in the summer of 1823, trading the Fosters for the Storrows. Over the next several months, as *Tales of a Traveller* slowly evolved, he oscillated between this family and the emotionally demanding John Howard Payne, an American dramatist eight years his junior whom he had known in New York, and with whom he had agreed to collaborate on several plays. A typical day found Irving breakfasting at a neighborhood café on coffee, bread, and butter, and then dealing with Payne's needs before returning to his own work. From time to time, his ankles swelled—the old complaint—and sometimes he simply recorded in his notebook that he was in "no mood to write." It appears that he did his best writing in December of that year; but even then he noted: "Night of troubled dreams" or "Woke early—restless and anxious—full of doubts as to literary prospects." It is clear that he wrote "Wolfert Webber" in the waning days of 1823 and the first few days of January 1824. His mind was bombarded with indefinite concerns as he prepared *Tales;* January 10: "Had vivid dream last night about the Fosters."[55]

Irving's merchant friend Thomas W. Storrow was an intimate of the Marquis de Lafayette when Irving wrote to Storrow's daughter Susan and playfully asked her about her friends, the "Laugh yets." The celebrated marquis set sail from France in July 1824 on a congressionally sponsored "homecoming" tour of the twenty-four United States, after an absence of forty years. A hero of the 1781 battle of Yorktown, and the last surviving general to have commanded forces in the Continental Army, Lafayette was delivered to New York's City Hall in a carriage drawn by four white horses at the very moment that part one of Irving's *Tales of a Traveller* was issuing from Cornelius Van Winkle's presses just blocks away. For the months Irving remained in Paris, the kindly, affluent Storrow gave over his library to his harried guest, and opened his home as well to Irving's visiting nephews, Sally Van Wart's sons. The unlucky Peter Irving arrived in November 1823 as well. Washington finished writing and editing the rest of his manuscript in the company of these friends.[56]

He was emotionally exhausted at the end. He did not yet know what to expect from the critics, but he resolved to see Murray in advance of the August 1824 publication date so that he could make timely additions and alterations to the work. Just days before Irving met with his publisher in May of that year, news of Lord Byron's death in Greece arrived, and a meeting famed in the annals of literature took place at Albemarle Street. Byron's sexually revealing autobiography, given to his friend Tom Moore for safekeeping a few years earlier, and purchased by Murray, was then and there incinerated, in the interest of the poet's posthumous reputation.

Murray's name would continue to be linked to the illustrious Byron, and—good notices or not—he was not about to abandon his favorite American author, either. When Washington Irving crossed the Channel and stepped into his publisher's drawing room, he could not miss the portrait of himself, painted in 1820 by Gilbert Stuart Newton, hanging beside Byron's likeness.[57]

CHAPTER 9

Columbus's Biographer

1824–1828

Moore and Scott have already done their best, and from the character of their productions for some years past, as compared with those of earlier date, it is evident that they will not hereafter excel or perhaps equal their past efforts.

Mr. Irving's talent seems to us, on the contrary, to be in a state of progress.... Mr. Irving is still in the vigor of life and health; and ... we are induced to anticipate the happiest results from his future labors.

—from Alexander Everett's review of *Life and Voyages of Christopher Columbus,* in the *North American Review,* 1829[1]

IN THE SUMMER OF 1824, IRVING RECONNECTED with the poets Tom Moore and Samuel Rogers and gossiped at length about the vivid life and shocking scandals of the late Lord Byron. Irving's fascination with Byron grew. He revered Byron's talents as he revered Scott's, writing of their prolific tendencies in his journal: "It is an easy thing to fly ... provided you have wings." One evening in July, he was introduced by Moore to the author Mary Shelley, who was the widow of the poet Percy Bysshe Shelley, Byron's dear friend, who had drowned two years before Byron met his death. Over the next year, Mary became enchanted with Irving's writing and, according to their mutual friend John Howard Payne, amorously inclined toward the American author; still, Irving appears to have remained ambivalent toward the widow whom Moore termed at this time "very gentle and feminine."[2]

Irving also enjoyed (or perhaps endured, for his journal reads all too matter-of-factly) a weeklong reunion with Amelia and Emily Foster, who were now at their home in Bedford. A year then passed before Irving wrote a long letter to Emily, somewhat apologetically, and somewhat defensively, taking up four sides of a folded sheet, plus a fifth. He offered her an explanation for his indifferent behavior toward her at the time: her obsession with a life of faith. She had expressed enthusiasm in her religious conviction that seemed to require evidence of a similar fervor from him—which he could not return. Religion was a subject about which he was "disposed to think rather than to talk," he rationalized in this letter. His father had forced religion on him as a child ("in its most ungracious forms"), and he had strongly resented that. But, he went on, he could see "real amiableness and beauty" in religious life when it was stripped of its ceremonial rigidity and taken out of the hands of its ministering hypocrites. And that may have been part of the problem. His letter strongly suggests that their time together was marred by the presence of religious "professionals" who made him feel, as he explained to her, "out of tune" when she was feeling, in a religious sense, "all wound up to so high a key." Apparently, the music of his passion for her died at that moment. She would go on to marry a religious "professional," the Reverend Henry Fuller, who was just slightly more mature than she—Irving being twenty-one years her elder.[3]

Returning to France, Irving took up quarters at Auteuil, "a very pleasant village in the neighborhood of Paris," near the cottage where the Storrows now resided. He wrote to his fifty-two-year-old sister Catharine, in upstate New York, whose surviving daughter would later marry the son and namesake of Thomas Wentworth Storrow. He was staying at Auteuil, Irving said, that he "might be quiet and might keep clear of the crowd & dissipation of the metropolis."

His brother Peter, holding his own at their apartment in the city, visited him on weekends. Washington had come up with a plan to occupy Peter by having him assist in compiling a multivolume edition of English literature for the publisher Galignani, whose Paris bookstore aimed to satisfy the tastes of the local British and American population. Irving often went there to read. As was true of any project that involved Peter, this one did not go very far, though apparently through no fault of Peter's. To make his own life easier, Irving also pawned off some of John Howard Payne's plays-in-progress to his brother so that their fellow New Yorker might have the benefit of two critics rather than one. By such gestures as these, Washington never let Peter feel he was in the way, or a burden. "I trust we shall continue for the future together," he wrote to their sister.[4]

Absorbing the mixed response to *Tales of a Traveller*, Irving toured the French interior with Peter that autumn, following the Loire to Tours. In November, he was back socializing with the Storrows. As winter neared, Irving characterized his mood to Henry Brevoort: "My last work has a good run in England, and has been extremely well spoken of by some of the worthies of literature, though it has met with some handling from the press."[5]

Although he took in the negative publicity with comparative unconcern, public reaction mattered to him because writing was his only regular source of income. He began taking Spanish lessons, and he studied hard into the spring of 1825. He proposed to Murray that he translate the works of Miguel de Cervantes—that is, works other than the immense *Don Quixote*. Murray gave him no definite reply. Something was drawing Irving to the Spanish culture in a profound way; certainly his previous efforts at learning languages—halfhearted attempts at French, incomplete Italian, and only slightly better German—did not compare to his immersion in Spanish. As he wrote his nephew, Ebenezer's eighteen-year-old son, Pierre Paris Irving:

> The Spanish language . . . is full of power, magnificence and melody. To my taste it excels the Italian in variety and expression—It has twice the quantity of words that the french has. I do not know any thing that delights me more than the old Spanish literature. You will find some splendid histories in the language and then its poetry is full of animation, pathos, humour, beauty, sublimity.

It possessed, he went on, an "oriental splendour," mixing "Arabic fervor, magnificence & romance" with "old Castilian pride and punctilio," chivalry, and "sensual amours"—without sacrificing virtuous feeling.[6]

In speaking up for chastity and civility, Irving prodded his nephew to be content where he was, in New York. "I am glad that you have entered into your fathers counting house," he wrote. Prosperity was a worthy pursuit, and eminently reachable if Pierre stayed put for some years: "Many of our most valuable public men have been merchants." In his next letter to the same nephew, Irving made reference to a second Pierre, his brother William's son (and his future collaborator and biographer), Pierre Munro Irving, who was four years older than his cousin Pierre. Hearing that this Pierre was bent on a European tour, Irving called such a project an idle one, an "expensive amusement" for an Irving: "No one should travel unless his fortune be made, or unless his travelling will put him in the way of making a fortune. A gaping tour of curiosity in Europe is calculated to unsettle a young man & render him unfit for regular occupation." There was nothing in the least subtle in this avuncular advice. "I speak from my own experience; having been early unsettled in all my habits by rambling abroad; and having been consequently in great risk of penury from the want of habits of business." Indeed, not learning from the failed steamboat venture, Irving had just sunk £1,000 into a Bolivian copper mine. He would lose everything.[7]

In the latter stages of his Paris period, Irving seemed to be taking stock of his life. It had been ten years since he had left Manhattan, a decade of unimagined success, but also of stinging disappointment and long-term financial insecurity for one whose only regular source of income was his writing. Writing to Brevoort, who in ten years had not visited him, he declared how much he missed New York:

> There is a charm about that little spot of earth; that beautiful city and its environs, that has a perfect spell over my imagination. The bay; the rivers & their wild & woody shores; the haunts of my boyhood, both on land and water, absolutely have a witchery over my mind. I thank God for my having been born in so beautiful a place.[8]

His New York friends remained faithful correspondents. Knowing that Irving had seen the severe reviews of *Tales of a Traveller*, James Kirke Paulding, who had left the Navy Department in 1823 and moved back to Manhattan, sent a buoying letter. "For my part I have not, like you, been sufficiently praised to feel much the want of it," he said. Paulding attributed Irving's bad reviews to "the spleen and envy of unsuccessful rivals," and reminded him of the high station he had already achieved in the world of letters, and from which he would not fall. Notwithstanding a few dissenters, America was pleased with her native son: "She is proud of you, and the most obscure recesses of the land, even Sleepy Hollow, are becoming almost classical, in consequence of the notice you have taken of them. Old Knickerbocker will last forever, as the great popular work of this country, quoted by wags for its humor, and referred to by historians for its accuracy. You know I am rather a cynic than a flatterer, and you ought to know that of all men I would not flatter you."[9]

*   *

Irving continued with his Spanish lessons, then moved (with Peter) from Paris to Bordeaux in the autumn of 1825. There he found himself "much out of order," suffering "loss of appetite, languor & great depression of spirits," which he attributed in part to climate, and in part to some "bilious" agent. "I think I should feel better both in health & spirits," he wrote to Thomas W.

Storrow, still in Paris, "if I had some literary enterprize on foot." His turbulent state of mind coalesced near the end of November, when he recorded an anxiety dream, imagining himself inside a large house as it started crumbling from within and catching fire: "[Thought] all my property & especially my Mss. were in it—rushed towards the house exclaiming I am now not worth a six pence." In the home's one untouched room sat the dependable Ebenezer Irving, arranging papers and wiping off books. By storing them in that room Ebenezer had saved everything. Some dreams do not require a licensed psychologist to interpret.[10]

Then, an opportunity appeared. On January 30, 1826, a letter arrived from a thirty-five-year-old Bostonian, Alexander Everett, protégé of, and nearly a son to, the current president, John Quincy Adams. Irving had met the experienced envoy in Paris the previous summer. Everett had been America's chief diplomat at The Hague, and was shortly to take up duties as the U.S. minister in Madrid. The letter invited Irving to assume an honorary position within the U.S. legation, where he would translate manuscripts relating to Christopher Columbus's voyages to the New World. A passport was enclosed.[11]

The embassy appointment was simply a matter of protection. Irving had requested attaché status so as to immunize himself while on the road during a time of widespread political disturbance. Spain was always unsuccessful in remaining neutral when England and France went to war, and the country had been particularly fragmented since the Napoleonic era. French armies had invaded, and though Joseph Bonaparte was a more capable ruler of Spain than King Ferdinand VII would be, an anti-French resistance rose up in the latter's name. British forces worked alongside Spanish resisters for a time, yet even Andalusia, in the south, fell to Napoleon in 1810. It was only when the French emperor's prospects in Russia worsened that the Spanish won back their country.

In 1812, a constitution produced in response to Napoleon established a mild monarchy that shared power with a unicameral republican legislature. Ferdinand VII cooperated until he was securely on the throne, but then he did all he could to discredit the idea and its proponents. In the period 1820–1822, he contended with a military revolt; the French once again intervened, taking Madrid in 1823. Ferdinand maintained his rule under the watchful eye of the French, whose troops would not consider the country safe from pro-constitution rebellion until 1828, when they finally withdrew. A healthy economy helped Ferdinand retain popularity.[12]

Everett thought Irving might want to translate the nearly complete *Colección de los viages y descubrimientos . . .* (the so-called *Voyages of Columbus*) by Martín Fernández de Navarrete, which was to appear in print shortly. John Murray had been hoping for something original from Irving's pen and was cool to the idea of publishing a straight translation. Wanting a quick fix for his financial anxiety, Irving had told his painter friend Charles Leslie prior to leaving for Madrid that he wanted him to sell Murray on the idea, or if Murray refused him, to approach another London publishing house. He was willing to accept £1,000, less than he had received for *Tales of a Traveller.* "I should have written to Murray on the subject," he complained to Leslie, "but I have had such repeated instances of his inattention to letters . . . that I wont trust to correspondence anymore, either with him or any other Bookseller." When he was in contact with Murray directly three days later, it was to convey his itinerary, and to alert him that Leslie would be paying a visit. Predictably, Murray told Leslie that he was indifferent to the project. Irving would come to agree; in time, he saw in Navarrete's work an assemblage of valuable but extraneous papers rather than a history.[13]

Upon his arrival at the U.S. legation, with brother Peter in tow, Washington Irving felt welcome. For five dollars a week, he was "comfortably situated" at the home of Obadiah Rich, former U.S. consul at Valencia, and felt there "the stillness of a cloister." Rich, who lived in Madrid with his Irish wife and their several children, was the same age as his houseguest, and, like Everett, a graduate of Harvard. Irving's debt to him was large, and not merely because of his generous hospitality. Rich was a bibliophile; his library contained some four thousand volumes, many of them on subjects related to Irving's growing interest in Columbus and the Americas.

Early in his stay with the Riches, Irving met Navarrete, now age sixty, and together they examined the Spaniard's cache of fifteenth-century documents. Navarrete was extremely fortunate for a scholar, having been assigned his task by his government, which jealously maintained the archive and allowed none but the elect to gain access. He had spent three decades on his project, without competitors, his exclusive access guaranteed and protected by the crown.[14] Some of Navarrete's connections rubbed off on Irving. After a few months of work, when the American was already deep into the life of Columbus, he went out with the Everetts to one of the royal residences, the fountains of which he compared to those of Versailles. There he accompanied the royal family on tour, with its retinue of servants and guards, and trailed by "all the motley population of the country round."[15]

It had to have been a heady feeling, knowing that he was to be the first to write the full story of Columbus in the English language, using Spanish sources long kept secret. "I am absolutely fagged and exhausted with hard work," he confided to Thomas Storrow in mid-June 1826. "I have been occupied incessantly . . . sometimes all day & a great part of the night in defiance of all the rules I had set for myself and at the risk of my health." By this time, he had already completed a seven-hundred-page rough draft. But Irving remained reticent when it came to discussing the project with Murray. By having the newspapers announce his forthcoming translation of Navarrete—before he decided to expand the book into a comprehensive history—he had seeded the ground prematurely. He wrote again to Storrow: "I do not wish to communicate with Murray on the subject until my work is compleat. He is a capricious man and sometimes neglectful; and has two or three times Given me complete checks to my undertakings, either by his silence, or his discouraging replies." Sensitive and calculating more than ever before, Irving was so involved in his work that on hearing of a quick turnaround French translation of Navarrete in the fall, he remarked, again to Storrow: "I wish to see that work & their notes [commentaries on the text] before I publish mine that I may have the last word on the subject."[16]

One interruption proved particularly satisfying. Pierre Munro Irving, William's son, unexpectedly turned up in Madrid. Pierre had grown up in a New York that rejoiced in Washington Irving's acclaim as an author, and was the son of a U.S. congressman when he attended Columbia College. He received a bachelor's degree in 1821, at the same commencement ceremony in which his absent uncle (who never attended college) was given an honorary master's. Yet having been so long away, Irving no longer felt an intimate connection with most of the younger generation of Irvings. He now had more than thirty nieces and nephews, and would have two grandnephews by the end of 1826. His only recent communication with Pierre was through Pierre's younger first cousin and namesake (Pierre Paris), and that had elicited a note of discouragement on his coming to Europe. Perhaps his lack of enthusiasm was why Irving had no knowledge of Pierre Munro's itinerary.

But all that changed. Pierre was trained in the law and had qualified to practice in New York, but unlike his late workaholic father, he was eager to see the world. Before leaving for Europe, he gave the American legation in Madrid as a forwarding address to a friend, all the while thinking his famous uncle was in Paris and would remain there. But in the spring of 1826, Alexander Everett told Washington Irving that a letter had arrived at the legation addressed to Pierre. Upon inquiry, Irving learned that his nephew had been in the south of Spain but was aiming elsewhere. So he contacted Storrow in Paris, thinking the young man would show up there next: "There can be very little chance of his being still in Spain."

Then, to his surprise, his nephew arrived in Madrid. And to Pierre's equal surprise, his uncle was there, and not in Paris! The younger Irving had roamed the city for a week before deciding to come to the legation on a passport matter. The united Irvings—Washington, Peter, and Pierre—feasted on the moment, and Washington and Pierre began a relationship that would grow into a wholesome collaboration. They established enough trust during their short time together in Madrid that on one of their walks, the uncle, though "in excellent spirits" most times, confided to his future biographer "with deep feeling" that he believed his reputation in America was being undermined by some "secret enemy" who was spreading malicious notions about him for reasons he could not understand. Pierre does not tell us whether he was able to assuage Irving's fears on that score, or whether he promised to find out more after his return to New York; but the incident does give greater insight into the author's sensitivity, and shows his sense of helplessness concerning his American reputation. And then Pierre pressed on for France, and Irving resumed his research and writing.[17]

On July 4, 1826, as the United States celebrated its fiftieth anniversary of nationhood, Irving took the day off from his labors—not celebrating, but simply "incapable of work," he recorded. The heat of these days was oppressive, and yet he made sure not to abandon his Columbus for long. His papers and Obadiah Rich's books were still spread out in Rich's private library in Madrid. "I am almost continually within doors," he wrote to Thomas Storrow, "occupying myself from morning till night among Mr. Rich's books." That fall, when the Riches moved to more spacious quarters ("Labarynths of rooms one within another," Irving wrote), they brought the Irving brothers along. They were now situated on high ground with a commanding view of the city and countryside, the interior of the house kept clean by a pair of "little old women" from the neighborhood. Irving wrote gaily of the housekeepers to young Susan Storrow, a favorite: "My brother thinks them fairies but I believe them to be witches outright, for I observe every broomstick about the house is worn to a mere stump by severe travelling."[18]

Finally, he announced to John Murray on December 21, 1826, that he had a work "nearly ready for press." It was called, he said, "The Life and Voyages of Columbus," and it encompassed not only Navarrete's choice translation but also "all the other historians in print and some in manuscript, and various documents which I have met with here." In other words, it was a legitimate work of history. He did not provide much detail to the "Prince of Booksellers," but his tone was confident. The manuscript would speak for itself. "I have worked excessively hard," he exhorted Murray, "to make this work full, particular and exact as to facts, and at the same time to make it interesting to the general reader." It was clear that he had been negotiating with himself as he wrote, facing the same dilemma that professional historians continue to tackle today: how to make a serious work of nonfiction widely accessible.[19]

Nine days after dispatching the letter to Murray, Irving summed up: "And so ends the year 1826, which has been a year of the hardest application & toil of the pen I have ever passed." It was not like Dresden or Paris, where he maintained a heavy social calendar; in Madrid, although he made friends, dined out, and attended the occasional bullfight, he concentrated more on becoming a historian. Doing so, he felt, significantly, "in better humour with myself than I have often done."[20]

On January 16, 1827, Irving heard back from Murray, who informed him that he would publish *Columbus*. Unlike before, no terms were offered; it was not a binding offer. Over the next several months, Irving engaged Thomas Aspinwall, a colonel during the War of 1812 and U.S. consul in London since 1815, as his agent in the negotiations with Murray. Finally, in July, Irving dispatched a portion of the manuscript by British courier. Businesslike, he told Murray, "I have woven into my work many curious particulars not hitherto known concerning Columbus and I think I have thrown lights about some parts of his character which have not been brought out by his former biographers." Then he made his pitch: "Considering its magnitude and the toil it has cost me I should not be willing to part with the copy right under three thousand guineas." Murray was meant to work out the specifics of the contract with Aspinwall.

After setting Irving's manuscript before Robert Southey, the poet laureate of England and no stranger to Spain, Murray came to trust his original instincts. Southey pronounced the work "likely to succeed," though he considered that there was "neither much power of mind nor much knowledge indicated in it." All Murray wanted to know was that it would succeed in the marketplace. To Aspinwall he said, "Beautiful, beautiful—the best thing [Irving] has ever written." He paid Irving's asking price.[21]

During the middle months of 1827, as Irving, in Madrid, was putting the finishing touches on his manuscript, he enjoyed the company of the twenty-one-year-old Bowdoin College graduate Henry Wadsworth Longfellow, who was "travelling for his improvement," as Irving phrased it in the several letters of introduction he prepared for the young New Englander. Longfellow, a fan of the *Sketch Book,* had met up with Pierre Munro Irving in Paris, and came well recommended; though preoccupied, Irving took time off and encouraged the young man to exercise his pen. Longfellow wrote to Irving after he left on the notoriously murderous highways of Spain, making light of his situation: "Thus far . . . no wooden crosses by the way side designated my burial place," adding, "I hope you will be as fortunate." Much later, Longfellow remarked about the busy man who had treated him so kindly in Spain: "I found the author, whom I had loved, repeated in the man. The same playful humor; the same touches of sentiment; the same poetic atmosphere; and what I admired still more, the entire absence of all literary jealousy." While he gave Longfellow his time, he did not lose his concentration: "He seemed to be always at work," recorded the future poet. "'Sit down,' he would say. 'I will talk with you in a moment, but I must first finish this sentence.'"[22]

★   ★

Irving's *Life and Voyages of Columbus* was hailed in its time on both sides of the Atlantic, and saw 175 editions, a huge number, printed between 1828 and 1900. According to a recent survey of the contents of American libraries, rural and urban alike, in the mid-nineteenth century, Irving's *Columbus* was the most commonly owned book. It undeniably influenced how American schoolchildren were taught their country's origins for the balance of the nineteenth century, and, for once, Irving's name appeared on the title page—that is, he had no objection to the use of his name in place of a clever pseudonym. By 1830, he would receive a membership in Spain's *Real Academia de la Historia* and the prestigious George IV gold medal from the Royal Society of Literature in London.[23]

To the twenty-first-century eye, Irving's *Columbus* suffers only from its author's exaggeration of Columbus's heroic qualities, and his inattention to the admiral's complicity in the wanton destruction of native culture. In the years leading up to the 1992 quincentenary of the first voyage, political activists reexamined the historical record and, not surprisingly, reached conclusions markedly different from Irving's: Discovery was really invasion. A Native American poet writing of the genocide named Columbus one of the "filthy murderers," the "liars and crooks," men who have been sold to America as discoverers, when all they did was usher in five hundred years of racist subjugation and crass opportunism. In Denver, Colorado, protesters poured blood on the statue of Columbus.[24]

Less subjective scholars now seem reasonably certain that the explorer suffered from misplaced confidence and a selective memory. He played God when he idiomatically referred to "God's manifest hand"; he claimed that his divinely inspired discoveries portended a triumphant millennium. His desire for wealth was enormous. Ethnographers have crunched the numbers, detailing precisely how it was that conquest resulted in near extinction for Hispaniola's Taino people: They were pushed into the mountains and threatened with death if they did not pay tribute in gold to the Spanish; some were driven to suicide, others converted into indentured laborers. From 1494 to 1496, according to one of Irving's sources, the rare *Historia General de las Indias,* by Fray Bartolomé de las Casas (1535), two-thirds of the natives died. Within one generation, their population plummeted from several hundred thousand to an estimated sixty thousand. A smallpox epidemic would follow in 1518.[25]

To understand Irving's contribution, we need to know how Columbus was previously memorialized by Revolution-era Americans. Yale-educated Joel Barlow published an epic poem, *The Vision of Columbus,* in 1787, the year of the Constitutional Convention, which he revised and reissued twenty years later as the *Columbiad.* New York's King's College had already adopted the patriotic name Columbia in 1784, the year after Irving was born. In 1786, the Great Seal of the United States was introduced to the American people in the pages of the *Columbian Magazine.* At the time of the tercentenary in 1792, the imagined virtues of Columbus were indissolubly linked to the sympathetic purposes of the new American nation. After discovering the New World, Columbus had, in the words of the Harvard-educated orator Jeremy Belknap, "endeavored as far as possible to treat [the natives] with justice and gentleness."[26] Columbus's example justified westward expansion. Lewis and Clark followed the Columbia River to the Pacific Ocean. Ohio attained statehood in 1803, and moved its capital, in 1816, to the centrally situated Columbus. During Irving's formative years, after all this naming, Columbus was merely mythic. So he undertook to locate Columbus the historical actor and render him flesh and blood—and yes, to paint him as a well-mannered, well-intentioned visionary.

Irving's ornamental style is immediately obvious. The biography begins:

> Whether in old times, beyond the reach of history or tradition, and in some remote period of civilization, when, as some imagine, the arts may have flourished to a degree unknown to those whom we term the ancients, there existed an intercourse between the opposite shores of the Atlantic . . . must ever remain matters of vague and visionary speculation.

The first sentence contains 105 words. In chapter one, Columbus (or Columbo, in Italian), son of a "wool comber" of Genoa, is said to have possessed "an early and irresistible inclination for the sea," a "strong passion for geographical knowledge," and "an impulse from the deity preparing him" for his destiny. He was fortunate, says Irving, to have come of age after "a long night of monkish bigotry and false learning."[27]

The biographer hides neither his purpose nor his prejudice:

> It is the object of the following work, to relate the deeds and fortunes of the mariner who first had the judgement to divine, and the intrepidity to brave, the mysteries of the perilous deep; and who, by his hardy genius, his inflexible constancy, and his heroic courage, brought the ends of the earth into communication with each other.

As a lad, Irving writes, Columbus took an interest in the unknown, yet that was not what sparked his greatness. His "nautical propensity" was "common to boys of enterprizing spirit and lively imagination brought up in maritime cities; to whom the sea is the high road to adventure and the region of romance." Columbus was special, but he had not yet given signs of that singular ability.[28]

To find proper context for Irving's biographical style and organization, it helps to compare him to another highly popular American biographer of the same period, William Wirt, whose *Sketches of the Life and Character of Patrick Henry,* first published in 1817, contained a transparent strategy to render his hero's flaws insignificant and his inspirational powers dramatic. Wirt was, like Irving, modestly born and trained in the law. He was the attorney general of the United States from 1817 to 1829, and desirous of establishing himself as a man of letters—the law merely paid the bills for him. He was an aspiring orator, standing in awe of the Revolutionary "Demosthenes" Patrick Henry, whom Wirt had never met and knew of only anecdotally. Irving had observed Wirt in the courtroom, when the Marylander served as a prosecutor at Burr's Richmond trial. Given his background, it is hardly surprising that Wirt, a self-described Romantic, easily imagined in his subject the same "hardy genius," "inflexible constancy," and "intrepidity" that Irving located in Columbus. Here is an excerpt from Wirt's depiction of the young Henry:

> I cannot say that he gave, in his youth, any evidence of that precocity which sometimes distinguishes uncommon genius. His companions recollect no instance of premature wit, no striking sentiment, no flash of fancy . . . and no indication, however slight, either of that impassioned love or liberty, or of adventurous daring and intrepidity, which marked, so strongly, his future character.

Greenwich Street in lower Manhattan, near the Hudson River, where many upwardly mobile New Yorkers kept their shops and residences in the first years of the nineteenth century. (Watercolor by Baroness Hyde de Neuville, 1810, I. N. Phelps Stokes Collection, Miriam and Ira D. Wallack Division of Art, Prints, and Photographs, New York Public Library, Astor, Lenox Tilden Foundations.)

Engraving based on John Vanderlyn's 1805 Paris portrait of twenty-two-year-old Washington Irving.

Irving finds his comic voice in the joint production, *Salmagundi*, depicting a French dancer whose feet become tangled in "a lady's cobweb muslin robe" at a New York ball. Engraving is by New Yorker Alexander Anderson, from an 1820 edition of *Salmagundi* published by Thomas Longworth, "Dusky Davy's" son.

St. Nicholas, from Diedrich Knickerbocker's perspective. Drawn by Edward W. Kemble for the 1894 Van Twiller edition of *Knickerbocker's History of New York*.

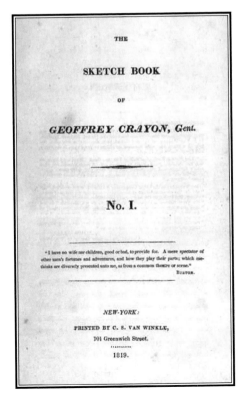

"Ah, whoreson caterpillar!" Peter Stuyvesant on the offensive during his war against the Swedes in the *History*. (From the 1897 New York edition of Irving's collected works, published by Peter Fenelon Collier.)

THE

SKETCH BOOK

OF

GEOFFREY CRAYON, Gent.

No. I.

"I have no wife nor children, good or bad, to provide for. A mere spectator of other men's fortunes and adventures, and how they play their parts; which methinks are diversely presented unto me, as from a common theatre or scene."

Burton.

NEW-YORK:

PRINTED BY C. S. VAN WINKLE, 101 Greenwich Street.

1819.

Title page of the very first issue of the serialized *Sketch Book*, 1819. It contained "The Voyage," "Roscoe," The Wife," and "Rip Van Winkle"—the first four stories in the collection that brought Irving international celebrity.

After a game of ninepins, Rip Van Winkle pours for the mysterious Dutchmen with grave faces. (Drawn by Felix O. C. Darley in 1848.)

Opening page of the first American edition of "The Legend of Sleepy Hollow," 1820.

THE

LEGEND OF SLEEPY HOLLOW.

(FOUND AMONG THE PAPERS OF THE LATE
DIEDRICH KNICKERBOCKER.)

A pleasing land of drowsy head it was,
Of dreams that wave before the half-shut eye ;
And of gay castles in the clouds that pass,
Forever flushing round a summer sky.
CASTLE OF INDOLENCE

IN the bosom of one of the spacious coves which indent the eastern shore of the Hudson, at that broad expansion of the river denominated by the ancient Dutch navigators the Tappaan Zee, and where they always prudently shortened sail, and implored the protection of St. Nicholas when they crossed, there lies a small market town or rural port, which by some

Washington Irving,
engraving after the
portrait by Gilbert
Stuart Newton, 1820.

James Kirke Paulding,
lifelong friend, prolific
author and prominent
Knickerbocker.

The Alhambra, rising above Granada, Spain, where Irving lived gloriously and let his romantic imagination soar in 1828.

Irving's Sunnyside home, beside the Hudson River, near Tarrytown and the Tappan Zee, today.

Washington Irving, circa 1849, photographed by Matthew Brady. (Library of Congress.)

William Irving, Jr., the author's eldest brother and a member of the House of Representatives from 1814 to 1819.

Businessman Ebenezer Irving, the only Irving brother to survive his celebrated sibling, in an 1850 Daguerreotype. (Given in memory of Mrs. Robert Stone Grinnell, Lawrence I. Grinnell, and Robert S. Grinnell, Jr.; Historic Hudson Valley, Tarrytown, New York.)

Joseph Jefferson III, onstage, as Rip Van Winkle, sometime in the late nineteenth century.

That was Irving's Columbus, too, who received only a "general" education in the "rudiments" of science, sufficient to prepare him for a life at sea. He had seen only "casual hours of study," having been reared instead in a "rugged school"—the lawless culture of coastal Italy. Henry was downright lazy as a scholar; as Wirt put it: "It will be seen how little education had to do with the formation of this great man's mind."

Biographies such as Irving's and Wirt's concentrated on identifying the subject's "spark," or muse, moments of inspiration and telltale signs of superior character or genius derived from nature. Indeed, as Wirt wrote of Henry: "His was a spirit fitted to raise the whirlwind, as well as to ride in and direct it." The parallel to the great admiral, who literally harnessed the wind, is irresistible: If Henry's "comprehensive view, that unerring prescience, that perfect command over the actions of men . . . qualified him not merely to guide, but almost to create the destinies of nations," Irving's Columbus established through "prescience" his "perfect command" over men and his influence over "the destinies of nations." It was axiomatic at this time that heroic biography should designate "forethought" or "foresight" (not standard knowledge) as the essential leadership quality.[29]

When Columbus arrived in Lisbon in 1470, he was an impressive physical specimen, Irving tells us, "tall, well formed, muscular, and of an elevated and dignified demeanor." (Whether this is true or not is almost impossible to know, though such characterization obviously served Irving's dramatic purpose.) His intensity caused his hair to turn gray, and then white, by the age of thirty: "His temper was naturally irritable; but he subdued it by the magnanimity of his spirit, comporting himself with a courteous and gentle gravity, and never indulging in any intemperance of language." The preceding description could as easily have pertained to a reform-minded American of the 1820s.[30]

To be that proto-republican, Columbus had to be a man of conviction—he had to suggest the idealized character of George Washington: "When Columbus had formed his theory, it became fixed in his mind with singular firmness, and influenced his entire character and conduct. He never spoke in doubt or hesitation, but with as much certainty as if his eyes had beheld the promised land"—as, of course, they eventually would. "A deep religious sentiment mingled with his meditations, and gave them at times a tinge of superstition; but it was of a sublime and lofty kind. He looked upon himself as standing in the hand of heaven, chosen from among men for the accomplishment of its high purpose." Here was the essential balance Irving had chosen to run with in his narrative—Columbus could not be completely interchangeable with a modern man of enlightenment and science because he allowed religious enthusiasm to shape his vision. But Irving minimized the ostensible flaw with frequent references to the "dignity and loftiness" of his character, invoking sublimity to soften zealotry.

In this way, Irving's Columbus retained his innate nobility. Irving had little patience with those among his own contemporaries (primarily in Europe) who chose to look at the explorer cynically and see him as a follower of others' conceptions. The protective biographer considered these "meddlesome" critics as frauds. He indicted them for "marring and mutilating" history; it was Irving's Romantic purpose "to vindicate great names from such pernicious erudition." Others had had access to the same information as Columbus, he insisted. But only Columbus was equipped to translate information into a macrocosmic campaign of renewal.[31]

★   ★

Columbus possessed not only a concept of forward progress, then, but also a political keenness that Irving endorsed. He left Portugal for the Spanish court in 1485, recognizing circumstances that favored his world-transforming mission. After a long period of domestic feuding, the kingdoms of Aragon and Castile had been united by the marriage of Ferdinand and Isabella. They acted well in concert, and had built up an awe-inspiring military force. Ferdinand's "clear and animated" eyes supported a "grave and certain" judgment; Isabella had eyes "of a clear blue, with a benign expression"—she was "one of the purest and most beautiful characters in the pages of history"; her "firmness of purpose" matched her "earnestness of spirit." By any calculation, the reader is to infer, the Spanish sovereigns, particularly the queen, would have seen the worthiness of Columbus.

Irving was constructing a familial drama with consequences for Spanish (and American) national character. A protective queen was resolute and charitable, consistent with Irving's long-held ideal of womanhood: "Her fostering and maternal care was continually directed to reform the laws, and heal the ills engendered by a long course of internal wars. She loved her people." She opposed the expulsion of the Jews and urged clemency for those of the Islamic faith as well. She promoted literature and the arts, but was personally "frugal and unostentatious." When Columbus was first presented to the king and queen (and it is not even certain that Isabella was present), he retained his "self-possession" and "unfolded his plan with eloquence and zeal." And though nothing was determined at this time, "Ferdinand was too keen a judge of men not to appreciate the character of Columbus." The narrative remained on track. The drama continued.[32]

The would-be discoverer remained in suspense until the summer of 1490, when the arms of Spain defeated the Moorish holdouts at Granada. As "the crescent was completely cast down, the cross exalted in its place, and the standard of Spain was seen floating on the highest tower of the Alhambra," the monarchs turned again to Columbus who, once more evidencing "great constancy of purpose, and loftiness of spirit," was not to be refused his dream. Of course, "the generous spirit of Isabella was enkindled" (it was her "soul" that animated the enterprise). Ferdinand, meanwhile, pondered the state of their finances at the end of a costly war. Sweetening the pot for the Christian sovereigns, a canny Columbus suggested that the riches acquired on his journey to the Indies "should be consecrated to the pious purpose of rescuing the holy sepulchre of Jerusalem from the power of the infidels." He was now in his mid-fifties, having struggled eighteen years for royal sponsorship. "His example," writes Irving, "should encourage the enterprizing never to despair." Admiral Christopher Columbus prepared to embark on "the Ocean Sea."[33]

As Irving's narrative proceeds, he focuses on Columbus's treatment of his crew as further evidence of his lofty character. Setting sail, the admiral remained brave as he ventured into the unknown, but his men were not so gallant, nor so daring. "On losing sight of this last trace of land, the hearts of the crew failed them. They seemed literally to have taken leave of the world. . . . Many of the rugged seamen shed tears, and some broke into loud lamentations. The admiral tried in every way to soothe their distress, and to inspire them with his own glorious expectations." As the voyage extended, discontent rose; along with "imagined terrors" were "boisterous murmurs," mutinous possibilities, right up to the moment when land came into view; but Columbus continued "with admirable patience" because he considered himself "under the immediate eye and guardianship of Heaven."[34]

Whether it was the Bahamas or an island attaching to Hispaniola remains open to debate even now, but the mind of Irving's admiral, in October 1492, turned to wonderment as he approached inhabited land. Irving has him pondering "whether the morning light would reveal a savage wilderness, or dawn upon spicy groves, and glittering fanes, and gilded cities, and all the splendours of oriental civilization." Delighted with the fruitful island before him, Columbus "kissed the earth and returned thanks to God with tears of joy." The crew, so long dejected and devoid of hope, could now no longer contain themselves, and "thronged around the admiral with overflowing zeal, some embracing him, others kissing his hands." Acknowledging his preeminence, they promised to obey.[35]

In his dealings with the natives of the New World, Columbus took "gentle and sage precautions." He sought to present a genial face. The responsive natives brought fruits and pure water from inland springs. In his further inspections of the region, Columbus marveled in his journal at the altruistic temperament of those whom he met: "I swear to your Majesties, there is not in the world a better nation, nor a better land." As time went on, however, a garrison was built at La Navidad, on Hispaniola, and plans were laid for colonial empire. The Spanish quest for gold led to unhealthy ambitions and "licentiousness."

Yet for Irving, the crucial moment was Columbus's leavetaking. Early in 1493, he tearfully embraced the native chiefs and sailed for Spain with his report, some gold and spices, and representative natives. Columbus urged the men he was leaving "to be circumspect in their intercourse with the natives, avoiding disputes and treating them always with gentleness and justice; and above all being discreet in their conduct towards the Indian women."[36]

Columbus received his royal welcome, took part in diplomatic discussions over the prospective division between Spain and Portugal of rights to the lands of the Ocean Sea, and made a second voyage west. Arriving back at what once was La Navidad, he found devastation. His men were apparently dead—though he could not determine whether their own transgressions or outside attack had sealed their fate. As suspicions rose, and diseases among Spanish and natives raged, relations soured. Columbus, even in Irving's account, grew anxious and more demanding. Some of his men resented the orders, and he became unpopular; the Indians, in turn, suffered under their tribute obligations to the Spanish conqueror, "obliged to grope day by day, . . . sifting their sands for the grains of gold which every day grew more scanty." Now, Irving acknowledged, "Columbus may have been too strict and indiscriminate in his regulations." Rationalizing uncomfortably: "There are cases in which even justice may be oppressive."[37]

As the Spanish presence enlarged during 1494, more of Columbus's mission became one of pacifying enemies. That was when a favorite of the admiral's, Juan Aguado, turned on his benefactor. "Puffed up by a little temporary power," "fortified with the swelling arrogance of a little mind," he ranged about collecting evidence against Columbus. The two antagonists separately resolved to return to Spain, where each would make a case for the justness of his authority.[38]

Aguado did not finish off the admiral. But indifference to his ventures back in Spain did, for a while. Though no less "lofty in spirit," in Irving's telling, the visionary was unable to excite the crown with his latest ideas for exploitation of the Caribbean. Now Ferdinand's interests lay elsewhere—in Europe. In 1498, however, Columbus was able to mount a third voyage. This time, exploring vigorously at a more advanced age, he wore himself out. "His voyages were always of a nature to wear out both soul and body." Though "parched," "consumed," "racked," and "disordered," his physical system survived because his spirit was, "as usual, superior to all bodily affliction or decay."[39]

Ferdinand and Isabella wanted the islands colonized. The problem was that their colonists expected riches to be easily obtainable. This was not Columbus's fault. Or so Irving everywhere insists. Unlike modern chroniclers, he did not see Columbus as the self-pitying man who misunderstood the other settlers. A man of "spirit, sagacity, and moderation" could not be blamed for the turbulence that was all around him.

Columbus persisted in addressing the sovereigns with an impossible idealism. Even Irving had to admit that some of what Columbus wrote might sound like "chimerical reveries." The great idealist made slaves of those taken prisoner in battle, which caused consternation in Queen Isabella. He had argued that slavery was essential to the "welfare of the colony," at least for a certain period. Ferdinand, for his part, had never regarded Columbus with, in Irving's words, "real cordiality," and so he dispatched a commission to investigate. In 1500, an "embarrassed" Columbus succumbed to the "lawless usurpation" of the court-appointed examiner, Francisco de Bobadilla. Though he "conducted himself with characteristic magnanimity, under the injuries heaped upon him," he was relieved of command by "a weak and violent man," and was sent back to Spain in chains.[40]

This was not the end of Columbus's career, but it was, in effect, the end of that period in his life when he can rationally be considered a man possessing leadership skills. Ferdinand and Isabella ceased to appreciate his campaigning psyche. Though he wrote incessantly in an effort to vindicate himself, the disgraced admiral never regained his stature. His zeal sounded less and less reasonable, and more confrontational. He became, in fact, a pest, going so far as to pen an appeal to the pope, listing his grievances and fantasizing the biblical geography of the New World.[41] Irving did not see the fanaticism in this; he recounted the approach to the pope merely as a respectful salute, noting only in passing Columbus's remark that he was "impeded" in his holy enterprise "by the arts of the devil."[42]

Irving's Columbus (he of a "loyal heart") had to be vindicated. And who was his unshakable ally in this, Irving's cause? The "sincere" and "noble-minded" Isabella, of course, who "beheld this venerable man approach, and thought on all he had deserved and all he had suffered." He saw tears in her "benign" eyes, which rendered him speechless, but for the "violence" of his own tears, as he knelt before her. We are to believe that she recognized the "intemperance of his enemies," and judged that Columbus's worst offense was "inexperience in government."[43]

Irving did not show Columbus to have been arbitrary in his conduct at any time while in a position of command. Instead, he used words that connoted pragmatism, or good common sense. Nor did Irving pick apart the brooding mysticism, extreme reliance on faith, or the self-justifications in what Columbus wrote. In describing Columbus's particular brand of piety—"religion mingled with the whole course of his thoughts and actions"—Irving saw that it was infused and ultimately tainted with what he called "superstition." Superstition caused Columbus to exhibit "bigotry" toward those too obstinate to accept Christianity; he recommended "the severest punishments" for nonbelief. But in his persecution of Indians, he was "goaded on by the mercenary impatience of the crown, and by the sneers of his enemies." In this way, the essentially decent Columbus became a scapegoat for all failures; he had been unfairly charged with incompetence, shorn of all "rights and dignities" owed him, and slandered by men far baser than himself.

In so concluding his biography, Irving defended Columbus against the historical charge of excess ambition: "The charge is inconsiderate and unjust," the author asserts. "He aimed at dignity and wealth in the same lofty spirit in which he sought renown." That is, he wanted nothing that his energies did not justify. "His ardent, imaginative, and mercurial nature was controlled by a powerful judgement, and directed by an acute sagacity." "His conduct as a discoverer was characterized by the grandeur of his views, and the magnanimity of his spirit." He was a practical man, "constantly defeated by the dissolute rabble which he was doomed to command; with whom all law was tyranny."

Suddenly, it becomes clear that Irving has fashioned Columbus into a moderate Federalist, "magnanimous" and "lofty in spirit," because he was naturally superior and conscious of the hazards inherent in a society lacking proper regulation of the "rabble," those ungrateful, "worthless" men who blindly groped for more power.[44]

★　　★

Life and Voyages of Columbus would bring Irving many happy returns. Before he died, it would be translated into Spanish, Dutch, French, German, Greek, Italian, Polish, Swedish, and Russian.[45] Few books in modern times have had such a reach, or such an impact. Irving's *Columbus* may be hagiographic to the point of exasperation for today's historian; but neither is ours a time that can claim freedom from subjectivity. Of importance to our study of Irving, *Columbus* showed once again that he could reinvent himself as a writer. The mastermind behind *Knickerbocker's History*, a ridiculous spoof of the seventeenth century, had produced a substantial, intrinsically valuable nonfiction history of the fifteenth century without forgetting how to write popularly.

Irving's friend Thomas Storrow had predicted early on that *Columbus* would not be profitable enough to warrant all the labor the author was putting into it, and Irving was happy to remind Storrow of his faulty prediction. At the end of 1827, he did not yet know how the public would receive his massive biography, though he was starting to feel optimistic: "If it takes with the public it will be more advantageous for me than any work of mere imagination that I could have produced."[46]

In February 1828, as the four-volume *Columbus* was coming off the presses in London, Irving prepared to leave Madrid for points south. Before heading out, he conveyed to his old and trusted friend Henry Brevoort his innermost hopes for *Columbus*. But these were couched in repressed and uncertain language: "It will give me satisfaction if my present work, by its success, replies to some of the cavilling that has been indulged against me; but I fear I can never regain that delightful confidence which I once enjoyed of, not the good opinion, but the *good will* of my countrymen. To me it is always ten times more gratifying to be liked than to be admired." In a rare confessional moment, he let it be known why he often hesitated to publish: The personal attacks that his success had elicited from jealous critics brought him sadness. Still, a grand curiosity was luring him to the south of Spain, and he could not think of returning home until he had experienced the place of Moorish ascendancy, and had written of it.[47]

At this time, he also received a visit from one of Ebenezer's sons, Theodore, who was only eighteen. "He does not appear to have the talent of his cousin Pierre Munroe [*sic*], but he is as yet very young. . . . I was highly pleased with Pierre Munro and only regretted that I could not See more of him and have him longer with me." It had been a year and a half since Pierre's visit, and Irving's words indicated that he had come to trust his future literary collaborator. Pierre had already seen parts of the south, his European journey having begun when the vessel he had boarded in New York, notably named the *Columbia*, docked at Gibraltar. From there, he and a traveling companion had visited Cádiz and Seville. But his uncle did not have to hear of dreamy garden landscapes from Pierre; he would find them on his own.[48]

Irving was feeling robust. "The pure dry climate of Spain agrees with me," he wrote to his sister Catharine, in upstate New York. The frail lad who had first traveled to Europe for his health was now middle-aged and beginning to put on weight that he would be unable to take off. Peter, on the other hand, was ailing again. Though helpful as a researcher, he had been suffering from incapacitating headaches and other undiagnosed ills: "His constitution is generally enfeebled and requires care and quiet." And so Washington Irving would be making the journey to Granada without family, though he would have the company of two members of the Russian legation in Madrid.[49]

He arranged for Peter and Theodore Irving to book passage to Paris, and under sunny skies, left Madrid in a diligence, or stagecoach. It was the first day of March 1828. The following day, he opened a new journal notebook, writing: "Morning early—one of the great plains of La Mancha—reddish earth—ridge of hills to south—Moon sinking behind hills on east—sun about to rise." Already he was whirling back through the historical imagination, stopping his pen after these words: "In sight of the blue Hills at the foot of which is Puertolapiche where Don Quixote was knighted." He was off on another nostalgic adventure.[50]

CHAPTER 10

The Alhambra's Writer in Residence

1828–1832

We are no half-way admirer of the former writings of Crayon, Knickerbocker, and Jonathan Old Style. We have been led by the same warm and gentle heart, the same refined and cultured mind, the same soft and melting, yet disciplined imagination for many a year long gone by. . . . now, indeed it is pleasant to keep still onward with such a companion, over distant and more strange scenes, to the banks of the streams of Spain; by her mountains, topped with silver; to her old cities and romantic towers. We are there actually, while reading the Alhambra.

—Review of *The Alhambra*,
in the *New-York Mirror*, 1832[1]

IN 1481, WHEN FERDINAND AND ISABELLA WERE solidifying their hold on Spain, the southern province of Granada was the last corner of the south that remained in Moorish hands. An annual tribute to the Christian rulers was all that prevented a final, inevitable conquest. But in the closing days of that year, the sultan Muley Aben Hassan decided that the best defense was a good offense. He recklessly stopped the payments, and struck first, advancing from his capital, the centuries-old fortress of Alhambra that towers above the city of Granada. His target was the weakly defended Christian fortification at Zahara, situated in the mountains more than a hundred miles to the west. Victorious, the Moor returned home to the Alhambra, confident he had made his point.

Around that time, we are told, a cave-dwelling *alfaqui,* a religious sage and recluse, came out of hiding and predicted the end of the Moorish empire. The sultan rejected his prophecy, but beyond the Alhambra, within the city of Granada, people were deeply worried. Christian forces were already poised to take revenge. In February 1482, they stormed the city of Alhama, just twenty miles from Granada. Twice, Muley Aben Hassan attempted to retake Alhama, but failed. His people held him accountable for waking the hungry Christian giant, and they deposed him. His son Boabdil was put on the throne of Granada. In the streets of the Moorish city, a cry was heard: "Woe is me, Alhama!"[2]

In 1816, a good dozen years before Washington Irving went to Granada, took up residence in the Alhambra, and retold this story, Lord Byron had already found romantic anguish in the matter of Alhama and the Alhambra, and the prophetic speech of "old Alfaqui" that forecast ruin. In Byron's poem, Granada's unrepentant ruler, Muley Aben Hassan, silenced the white-bearded messenger of bad tidings by ordering his head cut off. Inside the Alhambra fortress, all sensed the beginning of the end:

> *And men and infants therein weep*
> *Their loss, so heavy and so deep;*
> *Granada's ladies, all she rears*
> *Within her walls, burst into tears.*
> *Woe is me, Alhama!*[3]

★　★

Washington Irving received his first close-up look at the Alhambra on March 10, 1828. Church bells rang around him, and he saw "a superb sunset." The next day, he called on the governor of Granada, met the archbishop, and was moved to enter the chapel where on January 2, 1492, the last Moorish king, "the unfortunate" Boabdil, ceremonially surrendered the keys to the city to Ferdinand and Isabella. It was at the Alhambra, in April of the same year, in the tiled *Salón de Embajadores,* or Hall of the Ambassadors, that the Christian king and queen handed Christopher Columbus the official documents sanctioning his first voyage.

Irving was living out a fantasy. He visited the tombs of the two sovereigns who had sponsored the discoverer of the New World, and he took an evening walk along the river that runs past the Alhambra. He met Mateo Ximenes (Jiménez) for the first time—the seventeen-year-old peasant who was to serve as an indispensable guide on his subsequent visit to the palace. Mateo's stock of stories would inspire Irving's renowned *Tales of the Alhambra.*

MAP 10.1 Irving's travels in Spain, 1826–1829

By March 17, he had begun writing notes to himself, thinking how he might develop something out of the romance already in his head:

Sunrise Seated on the Monte de los Martyros. The Alhambra on my right— The Vega [plain] before me—Bells sounding from the city. . . . Alhambra reddening in the sunshine—Sound of running water—Cocks crowing— Smoke rising from various parts of the city. . . . Sun begins to gleam along the vega and light up spires & houses. Alhambra guarded by old men who can hardly shoulder their muskets.[4]

Irving was still unsettled in his plans. He did not yet know that he would be returning for a longer visit, or what it would entail. He could not imagine that the Alhambra palace would become his temporary home, as he collected the oral histories that would eventually comprise the durable volume many would regard as his "Spanish *Sketch Book*."

On March 20, he left Granada along a congested road, heading for Cádiz and Seville, by way of Málaga, Ronda, and Gibraltar. As he rode west, he kept noting in his journal, "Moorish village," "Moorish looking towers," "lonely Moorish watch tower." At all times, he, or someone in his party, carried a carbine for protection against the bandits and *contrabandistas* who roamed Spain.

The American author plainly enjoyed the sense of danger as he traveled the rugged Andalusian countryside. He was comforted by the thought that his guards were as rapacious as anyone else on the route who might eye him as prey. They repaired to dirty inns, and they navigated mountain passes that Irving called "savage." He described the air as "perfumed." He was well on the way toward completing his next book, begun when he was living in Madrid: *Chronicle of the Conquest of Granada,* a chivalric history of the years 1478–1492. Only after this work would he return to pure storytelling, and *Tales of the Alhambra.*

Irving was entirely charmed. Where he tracked and stumbled, they must have, too, those fifteenth-century fighters. In Málaga, a fertile valley beside the Mediterranean, he marveled at "the wild and melancholy grandeur of naked mountains" that he could see simply by looking up. When he peered deep into the faces of the people there, he saw history written on them: "In the meanest hovels are to be found models of manly grace and beauty," he wrote to David Wilkie, one of his artist friends. "Many of the women too mingle the Moorish feature and complexion with those of the European." As he left the valley, ascending to where Spanish armies once spied the Moorish town, he confirmed the conditions he would write about in *Conquest of Granada:* "steep slippery," "toilsome," "winds along precipice." He turned his head, and glimpsed again, from above, the enchanting Málaga.[5]

He moved on to Gibraltar by way of what he termed "the circuitous route" through the mountains of Ronda. Strangers' faces continued to stir him, life stories promised in each furrowed mien, and all he had to do was ask. Then, as he arrived in the tiny British colony of Gibraltar, the scene shifted. The streets had English names. At breakfast over the next several days, he enjoyed the company of the U.S. vice consul, Richard McCall, one of his old New York buddies from Lads of Kilkenny days. Wide world, small world. The road west to Cádiz was less tricky than the road whence he had come, but he continued to delight in it, remarking on fragrant blossoms and sweet scents in the air—"aromatic plants—nightingales singing," "oranges and citrons in fruit & flower . . . the fields enameled with flowers of various kinds beautiful blue ones—vermillion—yellow &c."

Signs of civilization were not always welcome. In Cádiz, for example, he found, instead of history, social disruption: "One is continually reminded that all the outward gaiety and splendour of its snow white and spacious mansions, cover internal poverty, ruin and wretchedness." This was a port of call, not a destination. On April 14, he gave up the horse and took a daylong steamboat trip to the old and alluring city of Seville; there, Irving would make a temporary home for himself, conduct important archival research through the summer, and remain, on and off, for the better part of a year.[6]

When he was not writing, he was constantly being entertained. The library of the Cathedral of Seville, containing the books that had belonged to Columbus's son Fernando, was open to him. David Wilkie was there as he arrived, and tarried long enough to complete a portrait of Irving that shows him keen-eyed and refreshed. Others of the British community invited him to dinner. He took fruitful walks along the romantic, narrow streets.

One of Irving's favorite correspondents at this time was a Russian friend from Madrid, Prince Dmitri Ivanovich Dolgorouki, to whom he wrote of his joy in happening upon unique examples of religious art "in an obscure convent seldom visited by the foot of a traveller." The process of discovery more than amused Irving: He pretended that his little jaunts were conspiratorial visits, and treated the "delicious" unknown paintings he had happened upon as though they were his mistresses: "I carry on a kind of intrigue with them, visiting them quietly and alone, and I cannot tell you what delightful moments I pass in their company; enhanced by the idea of their being so private and retired." Once he heard that one was taken out and shown in a public gallery, the soft conspiracy was over for him, and his "Virgins" lost their appeal—they were "not ladies for my money." His own fixation with virginal young women—Matilda Hoffman, Emily Foster—and his apparent lack of interest in more mature women (or available widows?) must by now raise eyebrows for some readers.

His fixation on the Moorish inheritance continued unabated, and the Andalusians seemed distinct from all other Europeans. To Dolgorouki, he wrote: "They belong more to Africa in many of their traits and habitudes; and when I am mingling among them in some of their old Country towns, I can scarcely persuade myself that the expulsion of the Moors has been any thing more than nominal." The lore of the "dark and flashing eyes" of the women of Seville did not attract him; he noticed, instead, their sunburned skin and declared them "void of bloom." When he was not exploring the surrounding country (as, for example, his visit to the port of Palos, from which Columbus had sailed in 1492), he spent much of his time among the English, and met up with the occasional American.

He found a particular friend in John Nalder Hall, who had come to southern Spain for his health. To cope with the summer heat, and to afford the writer inspiration, Irving and Hall rented a country cottage on a hilltop just outside Port St. Mary (above Cádiz) from New Yorker Richard Hackley, a former U.S. consul.[7] Irving had by now become used to traveling everywhere with his trunks of research and, this time, a nearly complete original manuscript. In October, from Cádiz, he "put up parcels," one to London and one to New York, with final drafts of *Conquest of Granada*, detailing, in separate letters to his London agent, Colonel Thomas Aspinwall, and to his brother Ebenezer, what his demands were with respect to copyright arrangements.

By late November, his friend Hall was dead, an already delicate system ravaged as the result of a fall from a horse. Irving wrote of the loss of the "amiable & interesting" Hall in a letter to Brevoort: "I cannot tell you my dear Brevoort how mournful an event this has been to me. It is a long while since I have lived in such domestic intimacy with any one but my brother. . . . I could not have tho[ugh]t that a mere stranger in so short a space of time could have taken such a hold upon my feelings." Some years later, Irving told his nephew Pierre of a conversation he and Hall had had about the possibility of life after death. It was Hall, feeling the precariousness of his own life, who had brought up the subject, soberly asking Irving whether he would mind a "visit" from him after he died. "Why, Hall," Irving had said, "we have lived so amicably together, I don't know why I should fear to welcome your apparition, if you are able to come." So they made a compact, and Hall said: "If I can solve the mystery for you, I engage to do it." After December, Irving tried repeatedly to call up the spirit of his friend, but to no avail.[8]

Nevertheless, the year 1828 ended, Irving confided to his journal, as "one of the most tranquil in spirit" of his life. Because *Columbus* was such an unmitigated success, he could expect to remain free of "the gloom that has sometimes oppressed me." By then, he had returned to Seville, and while there attended a performance of Rossini's comic opera *The Barber of Seville*. He waited out the winter months for news of the publication of *Conquest of Granada*, which he was careful to describe to Dolgorouki as a different kind of story of chivalry than was ordinarily related: one, he insisted, without love or gallantry. It was meant to be "the chivalry of actual life, as it existed at the time, . . . daring enterprizes and rough hard fighting." He had depicted the war as he found it in the old chronicles, "a stern, iron conflict, more marked by bigotry than courtesy."[9]

Though as history *Conquest of Granada* was quite respectable, we would still today call it a romance; for in it soldiers "behold" and "stagger," approach "by stealth," and reach destinations "faint and aghast." It was a more self-consciously literary exercise for the author than the historically detailed *Columbus* had been.

✹   ✹

It was, indeed, a different sort of book. Irving introduces his *Chronicle of the Conquest of Granada* with an invented author, as he did his satirical *History of New York* and his three "sketch books." His successor to Diedrich Knickerbocker is "Fray Antonio Agapida," a Catholic, who is "deeply and accurately informed of the particulars of the wars between his countrymen and the Moors." The somewhat smug—even perverse—Agapida injects himself into the narrative at various places, usually to give a boost to the Catholic cause.

Considering the sober research and determined historical writing that the book stands for, Irving's decision to lighten the opening few pages and mar the subsequent narration seems unusual, until we consider Irving's sensibility: He may now have become a "legitimate" historian, but he remained guarded, evasive. He was not simply testing the waters with his invention of Agapida; he was calculating on the fickleness of the reading public. He never forgot that Murray had rejected the *Sketch Book* until its sales under a minor publisher whetted his appetite for it. He presumed that the public would certainly have tired of him by now had he not varied his perspective. "One must prose [*sic*] and be tedious at times," he explained to Thomas Aspinwall, "to get a name for wisdom with the multitude, that ones jokes may afterwards pass current." That is what *Columbus* had achieved for him—a reputation for scholarship; and why he invented Agapida for *Conquest of Granada*—a slight twist, so as not to repeat the style of *Columbus*. He intentionally made his second Spanish history something "between a history and a romance."[10]

Conquest of Granada begins when Muley Aben Hassan defies Ferdinand and launches the ill-conceived attack on Zahara; then comes Ferdinand's reprisal at Alhama, "the richest town in the Moorish territory." Irving evokes the thriving ballad from which Byron's poem derived its inspiration: "Woe is me Alhama!" was in every mouth, he writes. In his version of "old Alfaqui" the cave-dwelling hermit, "a voice rose from the midst of the obsequious crowd" to indict the sultan, but Irving the historian does not assess the moment; instead, the "indignant Fray Antonio" tells of the hoary prophet as a Catholic of the time might, calling him "one of those fanatic Infidels possessed by the devil." Irving is expansive in narrating Aben Hassan's military response to Alhama, but he leaves out the seer's beheading. It is not clear what is history and what is mere song.[11]

Irving does tell of the prophecy made upon the birth of Aben Hassan's son, Boabdil. The court astrologers, in casting their horoscope, were "seized with fear" in establishing "that this prince shall sit on the throne of Granada, but that the downfall of the kingdom shall be accomplished during his reign." For this, Boabdil was known as "El Zogoybi" (the unfortunate), and more simply as "El Chico" (the younger). His Moorish mother was the beauty Ayxa; but Aben Hassan had also taken as wife Fatima, or La Zoraya ("light of dawn"), a Christian who had been taken captive when younger. The rival sultanas battled over their respective sons' futures. Granada's fate hung in the balance.[12]

The plot revolves around military strategy. The Spanish protagonist is the generally cautious, but ultimately decisive Don Roderigo Ponce de Leon, Marques de Cádiz. "While all Andalusia was thus up in arms, and pouring its chivalry through the mountain passes of the Moorish frontier," this red-haired chief was "sharing every hardship and being foremost in every danger; exemplifying that a good commander is the vital spirit of an army." His success is, for all intents and purposes, foreordained.[13]

His opposite was Muley Abdalla el Zagal "the valiant," younger brother of Muley Aben Hassan. El Zagal led Moorish forces to a much-needed victory over the Christian army west of Málaga, temporarily restoring confidence. But el Zagal had to fight on two fronts: A civil war loomed over the right to the throne at Granada. As Muley Aben Hassan took ill and died, a struggle for succession ensued. Would el Zagal wrest the Alhambra, once and for all, from his nephew Boabdil? Or would the Marques de Cádiz, proud cavalier in the service of Ferdinand and Isabella, prevail?

Boabdil was elevated to the throne at Granada, but proved unequal to the task. He rode at the head of a large army, hoping to prove himself a fit commander, only to snatch defeat from the jaws of victory. Taken captive at Lucena and treated with all the respect due a monarch, he struck a deal with Ferdinand in which he obtained peace and his safe return to Granada in exchange for a subservient relationship to the Spanish crown.

When the Christian army attacked Moorish Loxa, "the wavering Boabdil el Chico" went back on his promise to Ferdinand and fought back. "When he had once made up his mind, he acted vigorously," writes Irving of his unlucky hero. "The misfortune was, he either did not make it up at all, or he made it up too late." Boabdil put on his armor, led on his men "with impetuous valor," and suffered two wounds in his first encounter. The contest raged on without him. After a two-day "shower of missiles," crossbow arrows, and charges from handheld "arquebus" guns, Boabdil accepted his familiar role as "the unfortunate," and negotiated the surrender. He was forced to yield his right to Granada.[14]

The only victory he secured was over his uncle, el Zagal, and no doubt to the delight of Ferdinand. Boabdil had weakened el Zagal's force, which might otherwise have saved Málaga for the Moors. Boabdil sent word of his triumph to the Spanish sovereigns, and showered silks and perfumes on Queen Isabella. Profiting by the death of his father and the defeat of his uncle by Christian forces, he came into full and uncontested possession of the Alhambra palace—but for how long? He stayed in the palace and awaited Ferdinand's final success. From his window, Irving writes floridly, Boabdil and his councilors "could behold the Christian squadrons glistening through clouds of dust, as they poured along the vega."[15]

Moorish cavaliers continued to fight Ferdinand's army, but they had little to hope for anymore. With his usual bad timing, Boabdil felt the impulse to take the field in person, rallying an infantry that "was never to be depended on." His people were approaching starvation. Granada capitulated, and the Moors were granted a kind of limited autonomy; Boabdil and his family were permitted to leave with their precious possessions.

Boabdil conveyed the keys to the city to Ferdinand, and with that, his unhappy reign came to an end. From the hill that afforded him one last view of Granada, the departing Boabdil exclaimed to Allah, "When did misfortunes ever equal mine?" Of no less tragic significance, his rival el Zagal sought refuge in North Africa, only to be imprisoned by the king of Fez, who held him responsible for the fall of Granada.[16]

☆ ☆

Irving's fascination was more than mere infatuation, for Granada was more than simply a political and religious battleground. There was something peculiarly promising about the cultures that mingled on the Moorish-Christian frontier, and it seems that Irving picked up on this sense of possibility with all the time he spent in archives. During the fifteenth century, as recent scholars have emphasized, an official truce, sustained by peacekeeping mechanisms, allowed meaningful transfrontier alliances to form. In instances of accidental border crossings, Moors appealed to Christian authorities on the basis of an accepted theory of "good neighborliness." When no reparation was made to the aggrieved family in Moor-on-Christian or Christian-on-Moor murder, the subsequent revenge killing did not always have to inflame the other side. Men known as *alfaqueques* crossed back and forth with diplomatic immunity, arranging ransoms, exchanges, and returns of missing persons. Transfrontier violence occurred, but a regular flow of information calmed the air, and the sense of frontier gradually diminished. Apparently, this condition, as much as conditions of chivalry, drew Irving to his subject: Civility and hope had persisted for a long time, despite the bloody slaughter that succeeded. The lesson of history, to him, was that of lost opportunity.[17]

Granada was in the hands of Irving the historian. Boabdil was in the hands of Irving the artist. We have seen Boabdil before. He is a less mysterious version of "The Little Man in Black," a man fated to be misunderstood by his compeers and only retrievable through imaginative history. He is related to the Aaron Burr whom Irving pitied when he visited him in the Richmond jail. Irving gravitated to those figures in the public eye who had been somehow placed in untenable positions, who could find no way to do what was right, but wanted to nonetheless. Irving adopted the incompetent Boabdil, as he had earlier adopted the indolent Rip Van Winkle. He loved the underdog.

Conquest of Granada was published in Philadelphia by Carey & Lea, in April 1829, and by Murray in London the following month. According to contract, Irving was due $4,750 and £2,100 respectively—quite princely sums. Speaking of which, in mid-April, the author was joined in Seville by his friend Prince Dolgorouki, the son of a poet and currently secretary to the Russian legation in Madrid.[18] Days later, Irving received his first copy of Murray's product. He apprised Peter of its "beautiful style," his only disappointment being that his publisher had decided, on his own, to add the name "Washington Irving" to the title page, when the author had wanted his "Fray Agapida" to lay claim to the "literary mystifications" of the contents.[19]

Irving would conclude his years in Spain with another literary-historical escapade worthy of publication, but it could come from only one place. And so, on the first of May, with one more book launched into the world, Irving, now forty-six, and the indefatigable Russian, Dolgorouki, thirty-two, saddled their horses and went over the mountains and into Granada, taking a mere five days. They had a single escort, who carried only an unloaded musket. But they arrived without incident in the historic city.[20]

Well, not exactly without incident. Just as the *Sketch Book* opens with "The Voyage," *Tales of the Alhambra* opens with "The Journey," the author's first-person account of those five days. These were mountains "destitute of shrub or tree," yet with verdant valleys "where the desert and garden strain for mastery." Walled towns, "built like eagles' nests among the cliffs," existed to help the traveler recall a romantic past; ascents and descents, "resembling the broken steps of a staircase," challenged the horses on which they rode. One recognized in the worn mountainscape the "haunts of banditti," and could not but wonder whether "the eye of some lurking bandolero" was upon him at any given moment: "As our proposed route to Granada lay through mountainous regions, where the roads are little better than mule paths, and said to be frequently beset by robbers, we took due travelling precautions"—not only "stout steeds," but "a sturdy Biscayan lad" as valet and guide.[21]

Each mountain town presents an occasion for banter and braggadocio. Irving employs cigars and grandiloquence, guitar playing and big black whiskers, "buxom damsels" and sumptuous storytelling, to add anticipation to every page. And every few paragraphs the reader is reminded again of the threat from known robbers. There are strong, swaggering males, a young widowed innkeeper whose "dark eye was full of fire." The air is thick with secrets. It is a world suspended in time, in which Don Quixote is thought a real historical personage. Otherworldly scenery magnifies Irving's vagabond fantasy: an "arched bridge," a "ruined tower," the "dim light of a lamp," a "bubbling rivulet," a little salt lake "reflecting like a mirror the distant mountains." Eventually, "this wild and intricate country, with its silent plains and valleys intersected by mountains," feeds into Granada: the end of one dream, the beginning of another.[22]

In the chapter that follows, Irving describes the Alhambra fortress itself, "the royal abode of the Moorish kings," where Islam made its last stand for empire in Spain. Since he had just told the story at great length in *Conquest of Granada,* he is content to continue drifting from the plainly historical into the artistically inspired. Dolgorouki rooms with him for a few days and is then "summoned away by the duties of his station," as Irving reports in the text. In this manner, he remains "for several months, spellbound in the old enchanted pile," and gets to time-travel all by himself.

The *Alhambra* stories, in general, symbolize Irving's idealization of the past. It is no accident that before sketching the contours of the sprawling ruddy fortress, he announces that the historical and poetical are "inseparably intertwined in the annals of romantic Spain."[23] We then meet his rediscovered companion and guide, young Mateo Ximenes, *"hijo de la Alhambra,"* a self-described son of the Alhambra whose family has lived there for countless generations. Together, they explore all within the red dust-stained stone walls of the palace complex, including the renowned Court of Lions:

> In the centre stands the fountain famous in song and story. The alabaster basin still sheds their diamond drops; the twelve lions which support them, and give the court its name, still cast forth crystal streams as in the days of Boabdil.[24]

The Court of Lions has been described in modern accounts as "a Moorish cloister," a site where medieval Muslims prayed and studied—a *madrasa.*[25] It is "elegance" more than "grandeur"—the whiteness of the marble pillars— that strikes Irving in this section of the palace: "It is difficult to believe that so much has survived the wear and tear of centuries." Of course, to be of meaning to one such as Irving, the place must have legends attached to it. At nighttime, it is said, "a low confused sound, resembling the murmuring of a multitude," resonates through the Court of Lions. These are reputedly the souls of murdered cavaliers.[26]

On they tramp, through portals and into halls, where more stories are suggested. In "The Author Succeeds to the Throne of Boabdil," Irving appears almost to be giggling as he tells of "negotiations" with the governor that lead to his temporary residence in the Alhambra palace. He expresses amazement when he learns that the governor lives in town when so perfect a residence is afforded him. It is a mere matter of "convenience," the governor explains, because his daily business takes place down the mountain. "But," the official smiles, "if you think a residence there is so desirable . . ." The governor's invitation appears at first to be a Spaniard's customary politeness—and Irving knows better than to accept outright—until it turns out to be a sincere summons.[27]

As he lives out his dream, Irving continues with a first-person story that involves the staff of the palace. "The good Tia Antonia" is his innkeeper, overseeing meals. The "merry-hearted little Dolores" sweeps up. A "tall, stuttering, yellow-haired lad, named Pépe," works in the gardens and brings flowers to the suite. Fearing competition from these people, the ragged, talkative, good-humored—everyone in the Alhambra dreamscape is good-humored—Mateo Ximenes conspires to "weave himself" into all of Irving's plans. As the author stands before a balcony in the rose-scented palace and gazes upon Granada, with a far-reaching view of the vega, he doubts his own senses: "I am almost tempted to fancy myself in the paradise of Mahomet, and that the plump little Dolores is one of the bright-eyed houris, destined to administer to the happiness of true believers." Again, the appeal to him of the sweet virgin.[28]

In "Mementos of Boabdil," Irving once more pursues the unlamented last king of the Moors. With Mateo at his side, he tries to retrace Boabdil's steps. He thinks he might finally have located the elusive gate from which Boabdil exited the Alhambra, the gate that was closed to honor his "last wish." It lay amid the rubble beneath the Tower of the Seven Floors, a place famous for "strange apparitions and Moorish enchantments." Sacred only to Irving at this point, it had been blasted with French gunpowder just a few years before.

From here, Irving and his humble aide descended into a "rugged ravine beset by thickets of aloes and Indian figs, and lined with caves and hovels swarming with gypsies." They rode out to the summit where the exiled king took in Granada for the last time—it still bore the name given it in 1492: *el ultimo suspiro del Moro,*" or "the last sigh of the Moor." This was where Ayxa, his mother, reproached Boabdil for his failure to be a man. As one might expect of the creator of the indolent Rip Van Winkle, Irving's attitude toward the incompetent ruler is far more generous: "Throughout the whole of his brief, turbulent, and disastrous reign, he gives evidence of a mild and amiable character."[29]

Of the many stories that follow, "Legend of Prince Ahmed Al Kamel, or the Pilgrim of Love" and "Legend of the Three Beautiful Princesses" encapsulate the spirit and tone of the "Spanish Sketch Book." In the first, Irving begins at the white-walled Generalife, the hilltop citadel that looms above the Alhambra. Here the promising Prince Ahmed (as he was anointed by the astrologers) has spent his early years. His father has raised him in seclusion within the walls of this palace known for its cypress-lined garden. He was to know nothing of "the allurements of love" until he arrived at full maturity.[30]

Prince Ahmed is educated by an Egyptian sage who adores antiquarian objects and shuns living beauty. The black slaves who attend Ahmed are "hideous mutes" who know "nothing of love." When the prince cannot help himself from exhibiting sentimental tendencies, he is confined to a tower. There he becomes acquainted with a hawk, "pirate of the air," an owl that talks "something of astrology and the moon," and a "restless, bustling" swallow, too often on the wing to be a satisfying conversationalist. When the prince hears the birds' mating chants in the springtime, he seeks to learn the secret of "this thing called love."

His teacher tries to dissuade him from acquiring the forbidden knowledge. But the inquisitive occupant of the tower hears one morning from a lonesome dove what it means to be separated from the partner of one's heart; and so he conspires with the trusted bird to communicate by letter with a princess, "innocent and unspotted," whom the dove has identified for him. The letter is addressed "to the unknown beauty, from the captive Prince Ahmed." It is delivered by air. Sadly, the messenger dove is struck by a "wanton" archer's arrow on its return flight; it expires at the prince's feet, leaving the princess's whereabouts unknown.

Ahmed escapes from the palace. The keen owl, an expert in topography, leads him to Seville, where a gray-headed raven uses "palmistry" to assess the prince's fate, and directs him next to a palm tree in Cordova. There, a voluble bright green parrot, with "pragmatical eye," identifies the object of his love as a princess named Aldegonda, the daughter of a Christian king of Toledo. On the orders of her father—"to guard her from the tender passion"—she is not to be seen by any man until her seventeenth birthday. Though the owl and the parrot bicker constantly, they successfully directed the pilgrim of love to Toledo. His princess has just come of age, and is about to be exposed to the world for the first time. She will be given to the knight who proves strongest and most adept with his weapon.

Ahmed, untutored in military arts, is disheartened. But the owl brings him to a cave where magic armor, a lance, and an Arabian steed are hidden, and the prince prepares for the tournament. On the appointed day, as an unknown Muslim, Ahmed is denied entrance to the competition—only Christian princes can take part: "Rival princes surrounded him with haughty and menacing aspects." He stands his ground; his "demoniac" horse suddenly charges, and his magic lance scatters the opposition. The king protests the irregularity, but Ahmed is only partly in control of what is happening: "He was born full tilt against the king, and in a moment the royal heels were in the air." (Shades of a scene from Peter Stuyvesant's war against the Swedes.) The Arabian steed then bears the prince back across the plain to the cave.

The parrot returns with the city's gossip. The princess, unnerved, has been taken to her couch: "All Toledo was in consternation." The tender prince finds himself at the heart of no small drama. Taking time to think things through, he returns to the city disguised in simple garb and appears at the palace claiming to have a cure for the princess. He sits within earshot of her chamber and plays a tune on his "pastoral pipe"; he chants from the lyrical letter the ill-fated dove had delivered. The princess, in tears, recognizes the words and lifts her head. The king reads her silent wish, and authorizes Ahmed to enter the room. Color is restored to her cheek, and a "dewy light" appears in her eyes. The ineffective court physicians who watch all this are overwhelmed, and the king offers Ahmed the highest rank among his physicians. But Ahmed wants one thing only: a relic, a sandalwood box containing a silk carpet. It is produced, and he now reveals himself to be the "Pilgrim of Love," whom the beautiful Aldegonda adored. Together they sail away on the magic carpet. Ahmed becomes king at Granada, and his bride, now sultana, is permitted to uphold her Christian faith. Peace reigns at the Alhambra.[31]

In "Legend of the Three Beautiful Princesses," Irving tells a tale of the embattled King Mohamed, "the Left-handed." He is an aging monarch (and the father of Ayxa, the mother of Boabdil), who cannot resist a particular "beautiful damsel, richly attired," whom his men had taken prisoner at a frontier fortress. After some negotiation, his Christian captive surrenders to his wishes and bears him triplets: Zayda, Zorayda, and Zorahayda. They come into the world three minutes apart, but recognize seniority among themselves— Zayda, the eldest, is "intrepid," and takes the lead in curiosity; Zorayda is conscious of beauty, and exhibits taste; Zorahayda is "timid" and "sensitive," and becomes easily lost in reverie.

Raised in a distant castle, separated from the opposite sex, the young women become interested in three young Spanish cavaliers who had been taken prisoner. Though enslaved, the gallant trio bear themselves with dignity, manly pride, and high-mindedness, which deepens their appeal to the princesses. Eventually, however, they are ransomed back by their wealthy families. The princesses, each in love with one of the cavaliers, are downcast by this news—having been born to a Christian woman, they can conceive of Christian husbands as easily as Muslim ones. But their father the monarch sees that they remain under his control.

The unyielding father moves the princesses back to the Alhambra, where they are guided by "the discreet Kadiga," their late mother's duenna—their governess. Kadiga makes secret arrangements with the cavaliers, and at midnight on the appointed day, lowers a rope ladder from the princesses' balcony apartments to the garden below, enabling escape. The elder two manage to descend the ladder, but Zorahayda fatefully hesitates. Just then, drums and trumpets let the escapees know that their plot has been discovered, and so the two sisters hurry on to the subterranean passage that is to take them to freedom.

From this time on, Zorahayda remains under guard in the tower. It is reported that she regrets her weakness: "Now and then she was seen leaning on the battlements of the tower, and looking mournfully towards the mountains." She dies young.[32]

The Alhambra was made for a malleable history. From the stillness of his room in a remote sector of the enchanted palace, Irving had nothing but the sound of flowing fountains, nightingales, and the "humming of bees" to disturb his thinking and writing. As he wrote to Peter: "It is a singular good fortune to be thrown into this most romantic and historical place, which has such a sway over the imaginations of readers in all parts of the world." Given this hyperconsciousness of the literary potential arising from his circumstances, Irving descended into Granada "but rarely," and enjoyed quiet strolls where lemon trees scented the air. He wrote from the Alhambra through the middle months of 1829, and in July began to think it might be time for him to return to Peter's side, and to pay a visit to the Van Warts in Birmingham.[33]

It was then that Irving received word that his services were desired—by his government.

☆ ☆

For quite a while now, he had lived as a man who crossed borders, an American collecting friends and stories along with passports, a "citizen of the world." Through Alexander Everett in Madrid, he was occasionally apprised of political intelligence. In February 1829, a few weeks before Andrew Jackson's inauguration, Irving learned from Everett that the rough-hewn general had defeated the incumbent John Quincy Adams, Everett's mentor. "I was rather sorry when Mr. Adams was first raised to the presidency," the author admitted, "but I am much more so at his being displaced; for he has made a far better president than I expected, and I am loth to see a man superseded who has filled his station worthily." The wavering ex-Federalist and Burr sympathizer now ventured a constitutional opinion: "These frequent changes in our administration are prejudicial to the country; we ought to be wary of using our power of changing our Chief Magistrate when the welfare of the country does not require it." His reason for saying this was to show empathy for Everett, who was no Jacksonian, and who was being recalled.

At the same time, in desiring to see his country ruled by prudent men, Irving preferred to reflect on Jackson's "*hickory* characteristics," which he thought might make the Tennessean "a sagacious, independent, and high-spirited president." He was pleasantly surprised to learn next that his old Kilkenny friend Samuel Swartwout, though marred by his connection to the discredited Burr, had been resurrected; he would return to the political arena, by dint of a patronage appointment, as Jackson's collector at the port of New York. "I am rejoiced," wrote Irving to Henry Brevoort from the Alhambra. "Sam Swartwout has at length come uppermost in the political wheel. What a whirligig world we live in!"[34]

Another of his old friends, Jack Nicholson, a naval officer, an inveterate bachelor, and now reputedly a round-bellied man, was close to the upstate New Yorker Martin Van Buren. Van Buren was to come into the administration as President Jackson's secretary of state and would soon prove to be his top political aide. Nicholson had in turn suggested Irving's appointment as secretary of legation at the embassy in London. He would be of second rank, reporting to the incoming U.S. minister, Louis McLane, who until recently had been a U.S. senator from Delaware. Irving, resistant to political appointment up to this time, finally acquiesced. It would be a singular way of reestablishing himself in London.

The appointee shot off a series of letters confirming the news—to Alexander Everett, to Thomas Aspinwall, and to McLane. He wrote incredulously to his brother Peter: "That I should have that fat, jolly little tar, Jack Nicholson, for a patron! . . . Little Jack has had a kind of dogged, determined kindness for me now for about twenty-five years, ever since he took a liking for me on our getting tipsy together at Richmond, in Virginia, at the time of Burr's trial. It is a proof of the odd way in which this mad world is governed." As it turned out, James Paulding was in Washington at just the right moment, and had seconded Nicholson's nomination of Irving for the post.[35]

No matter that he felt unprepared for the position he had accepted, Irving pressed on toward London. The irony in this move was that he had intended to return to America that autumn. Fate had intervened, and he would remain in England for the next two and a half years.[36]

He was obliged to depart Granada in the midst of its hottest season. He bade farewell to Tia Antonia and little Dolores, and had as his traveling companions a musket-bearing Portuguese and a young Englishman named Ralph Sneyd. Sneyd's family history sparked his interest: His older cousin had been the betrothed of Major John André of Revolutionary War fame. For some reason, Miss Sneyd had second thoughts about the handsome officer—this was in England, some years before his foray along the Hudson. She went on to marry Richard Edgeworth, widower-father of the immensely popular sentimental novelist Maria Edgeworth.[37]

On the road north, twelve days after his departure from the Alhambra, Irving and Sneyd reached the port city of Valencia, where Irving wrote a letter to Brevoort and repeated a familiar refrain: "I do not think I am fitted for public life." Being of two minds, he had his last look at Granada not quite as the defeated Boabdil at the *ultimo suspiro del Moro* but as "a sailor who has left a tranquil port to launch upon a stormy and treacherous sea."[38] This was metaphorical, of course, because he went overland through southern France. Rather than proceed straight to London, he stopped for a time in Paris to visit with Peter, whose haggard face had filled out, and who seemed much restored. He could not convince Peter to accompany him to London, for Peter had few positive memories of that place now. Sneyd did not wait for Irving, but crossed the channel by himself, where he took ill and died a short time later. Chance collisions produced companions of the road—short-lived friendships. Irving registered the deaths of John Nalder Hall and Ralph Sneyd and then went on. It was a way of life for the nineteenth-century traveler.[39]

He arrived at the U.S. legation in late September 1829, and went right to work: "How from being a loitering author, dreaming in the Alhambra, I was suddenly hurried away to the stir & bustle of diplomatic life in London." He continued to interact regularly with the literary community of Britain, celebrating Murray's publication of Tom Moore's *Life of Byron,* just a month after arriving in town. He wrote promptly to Ebenezer, asking him to find an American publisher for the work and to obtain the best agreement possible for his great friend. Moore was hurting financially, and Irving made it clear to his brother: "I am deeply interested in his welfare, and for the ease and comfort of his amiable family." Ebenezer acted quickly, before the book could be pirated, and chose the young firm of Harper Brothers, in New York, which had offered $1,500. Moore might have been a little jealous at the greater sums his friend was being paid for his writings; but this did not put a strain on their relationship, nor did it keep the famously spirited little man from joining Irving at dinner parties—at the McLanes' one evening, he entertained the mixed company with his beautiful singing voice.

As he was reading Moore's biography of Byron, Irving showered the author with praise. From the beginning, he said, he was "moved and delighted"; he judged the work "not merely one of the most fascinating pieces of biography extant, but one of the most splendid documents of the human mind and the human heart. . . . It has all the variety of Scene, passion and incident of the most romantic novel, with all the potent charm of truth." Irving hoped that Moore's book would rescue Byron's personal reputation; for the poet, though he was well loved for his work, was most remembered for his flamboyance, his rakish confidence, and his way with women.[40]

Irving corresponded several times with the novelist William Godwin, the father of Mary Shelley. Godwin was in his mid-seventies, and still spinning out tales. He had recently declared bankruptcy, and a new novel, *Cloudseley,* was designed to improve his lot. Back in 1794, *Caleb Williams* had been an international best seller, mixing a critique of arbitrary power with a call for heightened humanity; it continued to find readers a generation later. Godwin had, nonetheless, dug himself a hole.

Even before reading the manuscript, Irving offered his services—actually Ebenezer's services—in locating an American publisher for it, citing "the fame of your former productions." On his first sight of the novel, Irving told Godwin that its "scenes of domestic distress" moved him. Unfortunately, despite systematic efforts, Ebenezer was unable to find the eighteenth-century radical a willing publisher. On a related front, Tom Moore, speaking for Godwin's widowed daughter, repeatedly appealed to Irving to agree to a tripartite dinner—John Howard Payne had represented Mary Shelley in a similar bid once before. Finally, on June 7, 1830, Irving and Mary dined together. Whether the result was in the least romantic we can only guess, though it hardly seems likely.[41]

In the midst of this mediation work on behalf of authors, Irving dashed off a short letter to Peter, telling him, "I have abandoned the idea of the History of the United States"—a work he had apparently not discussed with many others—"but have determined immediately to undertake . . . a Life of Washington." He was not to commence the work until the final decade of his life;

but his excitement at this moment, as he grew comfortable with his diplomatic post, suggests that he was enjoying what he described to his brother as "scenes and affairs of high interest." Life in London was motivating him to undertake "higher intellectual labors." His current salary from the U.S. government, $2,000 annually, contributed to his sense of ease. And as one might have predicted, he became fast friends with his superior, McLane, and McLane's amiable wife. Their domestic establishment became a second home, a pattern we have seen repeated elsewhere.[42]

Officially, he participated in discussions that resulted in an expansion of American rights to trade with British possessions in the West Indies. This was a major coup, long sought by the United States and long withheld by the former mother country, which was destined to mark a shift in Anglo-American relations. Irving had no further complaints about government service.

Meanwhile, there was his relationship with John Murray to renew. They had remained cordial, but were now mainly businesslike in their dealings. Murray's son had joined the firm, which helped the situation because he and Irving got on well. Irving had returned from Spain with trunks of notes, and he had hammered out another volume, *Voyages and Discoveries of the Companions of Columbus,* well before *Tales of the Alhambra* was ready for the presses. His abridgement of its predecessor, the Columbus biography, had sold ten thousand copies, which made Murray very happy. But Murray figured that Irving was squeezing out all he could from his Spanish notes, and that *Companions of Columbus* was not going to see significant sales; he offered Irving five hundred guineas, to which the author reluctantly agreed. This was, nevertheless, a substantial work, in the manner of *Columbus,* which the author described in his introduction as the voyages of "disciples of the admiral, who, enkindled by his zeal, and instructed by his example, sallied forth separately in the vast region of adventure to which he had led the way." These "disciples" included the so-called discoverer of the Pacific Ocean, Vasco Nuñez de Balboa, and—recalling Irving's longtime interest in unmarried men as literary characters—"The Bachelor Martin Fernandez de Encisco."

Prince Dolgorouki, reassigned to London, joined Irving's social circle. Then in the fall of 1830, Henry Brevoort visited, and the two friends took time off their respective labors to navigate the smoke and fog of London and catch up in person after fifteen years apart. The record is scant, but we can imagine that Brevoort saw a physically different Washington Irving, to judge by a letter Irving sent to their old chum Gouverneur Kemble, still a bachelor businessman and now in charge of a foundry on the Hudson River, near West Point. The diplomat Irving told Kemble: "I have a villainous propensity to grow round and robustious, and I fear the beef and pudding of England will complete the ruin of my figure."

Also that season, Virginia's John Randolph returned to London, affording Irving one more taste of the half-mad congressman, lately President Jackson's choice as U.S. minister to Russia. Irving had first become acquainted with Randolph at Burr's Richmond trial in 1807, and had right away appreciated his animated conversation. They had crossed paths again in 1822, in England. Now, in 1830, Randolph reported to Irving that he had second thoughts about accepting the diplomatic post. He had been unable to withstand the Russian climate for more than six weeks—and it was summer! Not only that, in appearing to bow comically at the time of his presentation to the tsar, he had created an international controversy. But, as he explained to Irving, the cause of the gaffe was his physical imbalance, and he did not depart St. Petersburg before having taught the tsarina to laugh well.

Irving tried to smooth things out for Randolph in London. Accompanying him to court, he tried to give the odd-looking Virginian some tasteful advice as to dress; but Randolph insisted on getting up in his trademark manner: antiquated knee buckles, white stockings, and shoes with gold buckles. The Duke of Sussex asked Irving, "Who's your friend, Hokey Pokey?" Writing of the incident to Peter, Irving referred to John Randolph as a "rare bird." He could have compared him to the lean and distracted Ichabod Crane—but that might have been to insult his beloved Ichabod. After sailing home to Virginia, the unpredictable Randolph took to using opium. He died in 1833. His legend did not burn out for years thereafter, for he was an iconoclastic character in the panorama of early American politics. And Irving, who continued his life on the frontiers of history and fiction, was always able to appreciate characters.[43]

★   ★

These were stimulating times for Irving. Not above complaining that his official position represented a sacrifice of literary reputation, the middle-aged writer nonetheless had come to understand (and take to) diplomatic protocol. In June 1830, he received an honorary doctorate of laws in a ceremony at Oxford. There is some irony in this: A biographical dictionary published in New York for a list of subscribers, in 1825, and containing a section on "eminent living characters," claimed that the "eminent" Washington Irving had been "educated at Columbia College"—which he was not. And to further the fiction, he was now an "L.L.D." as well, simply for taking his own road.[44]

King George IV, the eldest son of George III, died after a ten-year reign, and was succeeded by his younger brother, William IV. The psychological distance from the time of the American wars had lengthened, and Irving could write mischievously to Peter of the new, sixty-five-year-old monarch: "The king keeps all London agog; nothing but sights, parades, and reviews. He is determined that it shall be merry old England once more." At a royal dinner, he noted, "Mr. McLane and the king became so thick that some of the *corps diplomatique* showed symptoms of jealousy." The rotund and affable king had served in the Royal Navy and was especially taken that America's minister had begun his career as a midshipman, and had first taken to the sea with a young and untried Stephen Decatur. Irving predicted that William IV would be "the most popular king that ever sat on the English throne." In fact, his seven-year reign was to be fairly uneventful, and he would be succeeded by his niece, Queen Victoria.[45]

Irving was naturally attentive to political "combustion," as he called it, in Spain, where a succession crisis loomed; and in France, as well, where Charles X, a Bourbon, was deposed in the July Revolution of 1830. Irving stood firmly by the deliberative Louis McLane, whose negotiating efforts he described in nearly chivalric terms in his correspondence with the congressional leadership back home. In mid-1831, the McLanes returned to America, where the hardworking diplomat was now to join Jackson's cabinet as secretary of the treasury. Irving was temporarily placed in charge of the legation, pending the arrival of the new minister, the Dutch-American Martin Van Buren, favorite son of Kinderhook, New York—Irving's onetime retreat—and a good friend of McLane's. Van Buren, Jackson's first-term secretary of state, would be biding his time in London, as things turned out, until the president's reelection effort in 1832, when he would return to Washington as vice president of the United States.

For the time being, then, Irving kept his focus on Europe, where fears of further upheaval did not materialize. As a temporary chargé d'affaires, he acquitted himself well. Fortunately for him, he had no ambition to enter the confused political world of Washington. It was a time of cabinet shuffling and bruised egos, of disunionist threats and personal vendettas, and it would continue to be so for the remainder of Andrew Jackson's turbulent presidency. The independent-minded McLane himself would leave Treasury, refusing on principle to carry out the president's banking policy; and though he would succeed to the State Department, he would leave there after a year in opposition to the administration's aggressive approach toward France. Unlike most who disagreed with the hot-tempered Jackson, however, McLane and the president would part as friends.

In the candid Van Buren, the son of a tavern keeper and an early Burrite,[46] Irving found much to admire. Van Buren and Irving were born just a few months apart, and both grew up in large families. Upon his fellow New Yorker's arrival in London in September 1831, Irving arranged for him to be presented to Lord Palmerston, the foreign minister, and to the attentive King William. Anglo-American relations had never been warmer, and Van Buren seemed relaxed. He wrote of Irving to President Jackson not long after their acquaintance began: "He cherishes a most devout and sincere respect for your character and is I have no doubt a man of the most perfect purity and in every respect truly estimable." And after another month of frequent association, again to Jackson: "I was mistaken in supposing, that his literary occupation had given his mind a turn unfavourable to practical business pursuits, and as I am not sure that you did not entertain the same impression, I think it but just to correct the error." Avowing that "a better American, or a more honest man does not live," Van Buren went so far as to suggest to the president that Irving be made chargé d'affaires in Madrid, where he and his writings had already made "a marked impression upon the favourable feelings of the men who constitute the Court."[47]

The future president, along with his son John, joined Irving in December 1831 for a rambling tour of the English countryside. Irving found the Van Burens to be excellent traveling companions; he was able to retrace some of the roads he had taken and places he had stopped at that were made famous in the *Sketch Book*. Accompanying the Van Burens first on a visit to Shakespeare's birthplace, and then to a traditional Christmas at a merry mansion, he arranged for the three of them to stay at Newstead Abbey, home of the late Lord Byron. After a few days there, Van Buren felt he should return to London, and Irving stayed on alone to absorb the abbey's mysteries and memories. He would later describe the experience in a romantic essay.

During his fortnight at Newstead Abbey, he wrote letters to his sister Catharine, his brother Peter, and his painter-friend Charles R. Leslie. Byron was not buried at Newstead, though he had wished to be. Irving nonetheless found much to contemplate, such as the ivy-covered front of a ruined Gothic church, and a garden with terraced walkways and fishponds. "You may easily imagine the charms of such a residence," he told his sister, "connected with poetical associations with the memory of Lord Byron." The neighboring peasantry already had a stock of "superstitious fables," whether or not they had directly enjoyed the dead poet's society.[48]

Not long thereafter, in February 1832, Van Buren received catastrophic news. The Senate belatedly (and narrowly) rejected the president's nomination of him for the post in London. He had not been at his station for much longer than the eccentric John Randolph had lasted in St. Petersburg, but he would be returning home. Irving was with Van Buren when he received this news, and smartly encouraged him to explain events to the British in such a way as to represent the Jackson administration as stable; that is, to explain the nature of political partisanship in Jacksonian America. This Van Buren did, with good results.

Van Buren had been a widower for many years. Although sexually linked at one point (accurately or not, we do not know) to Stephen Decatur's widow, the father of four sons was fortunate in keeping his personal life out of the newspapers. But his visibility as Jackson's right-hand man cost him in other ways. He was constantly hounded by those who felt they had been slighted by the common man who was the sitting president. Most prominent among the Jackson haters was his estranged first-term vice president, John C. Calhoun, who had the distinct pleasure, as president of the Senate, of casting the deciding vote against Van Buren, his rival for the president's ear.

Van Buren immediately recognized Calhoun's tactical error. He had played into Jackson's hands by making the Dutch New Yorker a martyr. Van Buren had, since 1803, hobbled along as a Burrite, then Lewisite, then anti-Clintonian, and only belatedly a Jacksonian; he had served as state legislator, state attorney general, U.S. senator, New York governor (briefly), and U.S. secretary of state. He was a veteran of the same topsy-turvy political alignments that Irving had known firsthand until he left his native state in 1815. Martin Van Buren was a political survivor. And now he would receive enough sympathy votes to make him vice president—and Jackson's successor.[49]

On Washington's Birthday, 1832, Irving wrote to Louis McLane: "It is with deep concern that I have heard the rejection of Mr Van Burens nomination, not from any harm it will do him; as I have no doubt it will extend and strengthen his popularity, but because it is calculated to impair the dignity of our highest legislative body, and to injure our national character by this reckless act of party violence." These were probably the most bitter words Irving ever wrote with regard to American politics that were not couched in satirical language.[50]

At long last, Washington Irving became an advocate. Ironically, he did so as a Jacksonian Democrat. While Van Buren remained in London, they strategized together, encouraged by those at home who wanted Van Buren to "throw himself into the Senate, and attack his foes sword in hand," as Irving put it in a letter to Peter. "We had long talks on the subject," the author-diplomat added, helping the not-quite-minister decide how he would finish out his stint in London. With Irving as his protector, Van Buren appeared, head held high, at several official functions; and when the *London Times* reported that the unaccredited envoy's acts, to date, would be voided until the Senate autho-rized them, Irving demanded and received a retraction from the newspaper. The British—in particular the royal family—treated Van Buren with sympa-thy. Irving, who believed that "this vote in the Senate goes far towards ulti-mately elevating him to the presidential chair," probably hinted as much to his British contacts. "The more I see of Mr. V. B. the more I feel confirmed in a strong personal regard for him," he told Peter in March. "He is one of the gentlest and most amiable men I have ever met with." Irving did his best to look for the tender side in everyone.[51]

Van Buren sailed at the beginning of April, and as Irving planned likewise, he realized he first needed to find a home for *Tales of the Alhambra,* his Span-ish "Sketch Book." The previous fall, he had tried to convince John Murray that "the miscellaneous work," as he was generically calling it, would stimu-late new sales of *Conquest of Granada.* Even Irving, it seems, did not appre-ciate the full potential of the tales. After coolly taking on another Irving production, his unexceptional *Life of Mahomet,* for a modest five hundred guineas, Murray was feeling pessimistic about sales prospects; and so the two were unable to come to terms on what would prove to be one of Washington Irving's most unforgettable productions.

In the end, the London firm of Colburn and Bentley paid Irving a thousand guineas, and published *Alhambra* in May 1832, giving "Geoffrey Crayon" as its author. The next month, Carey and Lea, of Philadelphia, issued the book in the United States, in two duodecimo volumes, also assigning it impersonally to "the Author of the Sketch Book."[52] But neither publisher appears to have an-ticipated the enduring appeal of Spain's storied Andalusia. From today's per-spective, the "miscellaneous work" has proven nearly as durable as the red fortress itself. It launched an interest in Spanish tradition in England and America that would be sustained for decades after Irving's death.[53]

Within days of *Alhambra*'s U.S. publication, a Baltimore newspaper gushed: "The Alhambra displays the characteristic excellencies of Mr. Ir-ving—the easy, natural narrative, the smooth and elegant diction, the pithy humor." Though some critics hesitated, the British overall adored the book—it was, to many of them, a perfect companion to the original *Sketch Book.* Ir-ving's painter-friend David Wilkie, who had visited him in Spain and urged the project on Irving, and to whom *Tales of the Alhambra* was dedicated, claimed in 1833 that the work had become so popular that Irving was now considered "the founder of a school."

That might be something of an exaggeration. It is more accurate to say that *Tales of the Alhambra,* over time, has been resilient rather than a turning point in literature. Where "Rip Van Winkle" and "The Legend of Sleepy Hollow" became almost instantly intermeshed with American culture, *Alhambra* has remained in print as a collector's item, a charming gift book, a travel companion, and a quirky example of Irving's romantic imagination.[54]

☆   ☆

He had traveled far, and not simply in miles, in the years since he arrived in England and gradually fashioned his perspective on life into the *Sketch Book.* He had tarried in France and Germany, but it was in Spain that he found true motivation. In Spain, he refined his romantic style and magnified his escapism. In the *Sketch Book* and *Tales of a Traveller,* he had communed some more with his old friend Diedrich Knickerbocker. But in Spain, he succeeded to a new persona.

As a satirist (at his core, Irving never stopped being a satirist), his politics concerned the folly of overconfidence. This began when he took the side of the colorful early Dutch against the odds-on favorites—the uppity English. He continued in this vein when he showed the Indians of the New World to be a contented, generous people who were ruined by the complexities of life that the pushy Spanish settlements brought to them; they, like his unappreciated Columbus, suffered from a purity of purpose. It was true again when he wrote of the Moors, who created beautiful architecture, valued learning, and exhibited tolerance; and of Boabdil, who could not decide between peaceful coexistence and the value of chivalry, and who endured banishment from southern Europe. Each time, Irving pointed to the unwarranted confidence of those who were customarily anointed the victors in standard histories. Proud ideologies were unquestioning ideologies, and generally intolerant ideologies. Irving refused to celebrate the victors uncritically.[55]

Like many a satirist, he wanted the world to be right. Not that he expected much. Literature provided Irving what was missing in his political reality. And so he identified with the defeated in history—the disappearing Dutch influence in New York, the Indians of the Spanish Caribbean, the "unfortunate" Moor Boabdil. Despite his sudden comfort with Jackson's men, he was no radical, no Jeffersonian democrat. He still favored rule by the enlightened set rather than the fictive "people." He viewed the rising star of the New Yorker Martin Van Buren as a less tainted version of the Aaron Burr whom his brother Peter had championed. It is worth noting, then, that Burr's stated favorite for the presidency, as early as 1816, was Andrew Jackson. The much-abused former vice president was back in New York, his fugitive status behind him, a practicing attorney scrupulously steering clear of the political limelight.

Burrite stalwart Sam Swartwout was a prominent Jacksonian. Even a son of the arch-Federalist Alexander Hamilton was now Jackson's intimate, and had been the acting secretary of state in 1829, until Van Buren's arrival in Washington.

The political landscape had evolved; alliances had noticeably shifted. The word *democracy*, once associated with "the rabble," now meant simply, and more broadly, American-style governance. The first president to call the country a "representative democracy" was the early Federalist John Quincy Adams. In all this confusion, Washington Irving became something different from before. Certainly he was not the reactionary those of his countrymen imagined him when they interpreted Geoffrey Crayon's embrace of old England (and English aristocrats) as a betrayal of American ideals.

This can be proven simply. In 1829, after having heard secondhand that Gilbert Stuart Newton thought his friend had been too long out of England and should return there, Irving wrote to Thomas Aspinwall from Seville. "I have no ambition of currency in the circles of bluestocking gossips," he contested. "And as to a residence in England, I believe both English authors and English painters injure one another by herding so much together and copying each other's faults. As to myself, being an American, Spain is as much entitled to my study as England, and at present has more novelty to repay the Student." Being an American—and he had never ceased to feel American—he consistently aimed to secure his independence.[56]

He had not seen his native New York for seventeen years. It was time for Washington Irving to return home, if not to defend himself against those who doubted his "Americanness," then simply to recharge himself, to reawaken. He had been abroad for very nearly the same amount of time that Rip Van Winkle had spent sleeping.

REPATRIATION

CHAPTER 11

Knickerbocker New York

1832

Thank you for your favor of the 2d [with] the paper describing the festive welcome given to the return of Mr. Irving. The distinguished honour done him was due to his genius, and the literary fruits of it, which his Country may well be proud of.

—James Madison to Le Roy de Chaumont,

June 9, 1832[1]

B Y 1832, MANY OF THOSE MEN WHO HAD DOMINATED the New York scene during Irving's formative years as a writer were now dead. His brother William was one, having left behind a family of four sons and two daughters. So was the overachieving and famously satirized professor, U.S. senator, and author of *A Picture of New-York*, Dr. Samuel L. Mitchill, who died in the autumn of 1831. The acerbic DeWitt Clinton collapsed suddenly in 1828, at the age of fifty-eight, after having first delivered the goods, literally, as chief promoter of the Erie Canal, already profitable upon its completion in 1825. Clinton would go down in history not as the surly critic of "Abimelech Coody" and "Diedrich Knickerbocker" but as a model state executive who made possible the "marriage of waters"—Lake Erie and the Atlantic Ocean. The Erie Canal would assist America's Romantic transformation by facilitating visits to the most radiant sight on the continent: Niagara Falls.

Irving's old set had been joined by a rising breed of younger writers. To be a Knickerbocker in 1832 was to be a New York literary personality. While abroad, Irving had inadvertently given his pet name to a movement, a good-natured, Romantic-historical, and subtly satirical school of thought. To the original Dutch Knickerbockers James Kirke Paulding and Gulian Verplanck were added the energetic novelist James Fenimore Cooper and two New England–born poets, William Cullen Bryant and Fitz-Greene Halleck.

Paulding remained during Irving's years in Europe one of his most trusted friends. Their letters were refreshingly unguarded. As it was with all of the former Lads of Kilkenny, Irving did not, in his middle years, discount the early bond formed at "Cockloft Hall," nor did he allow the young bachelors' clever banter in the taverns near the Park Theater to fade entirely from memory. *Salmagundi* was the stuff of a different era, but it made for a brand of good fellowship that anchored Irving. No matter how far he traveled, he always had time for the businessman Gouverneur Kemble and fat Jack Nicholson, the navy man, both of whom, like Washington and Peter Irving, had kept to their bachelor habits. Paulding and Brevoort were married, but the group was still an extended family. Recall that Paulding, whose sister had married William Irving, himself married Kemble's sister; and while in Washington, D.C., they lived in the Pennsylvania Avenue house they purchased from Commodore Stephen Decatur, who had earlier been Irving's New York housemate. The Pauldings' first son was named Peter Kemble Paulding; the second, William Irving Paulding.

As an author, Paulding had struggled to equal Irving's success, and was fated to be considered a jealous competitor of Irving's whether or not it was true. While Brevoort and Ebenezer Irving were tending to American editions of the highly successful *Sketch Book*, Paulding sputtered, capitalizing on his younger friend's sudden marketability by instigating a reissue of their *Salmagundi*. The unforgiving critics said that Paulding had too few new ideas. But in 1824, the year of Irving's *Tales of a Traveller*, Paulding's *Koningsmarke, the Long Finne* put an end to all that.

An historical satire that took its cue from Henry Fielding's *Tom Jones* and Sir Walter Scott's historical romances, with a touch of *Knickerbocker's History* thrown in, *Koningsmarke* was set in a seventeenth-century Swedish community in Delaware. With entertaining digressions and several lively characters, the book had some serious things to say about "what might have been" concerning the Indians' treatment by white colonists. Paulding was conscious of the effect that Cooper's historical novels were already having, and his posthumous reputation would suffer for appearing to be a follower of Scott and Cooper, as well as Irving—in a creative sense, always a bridesmaid. Nevertheless, this was the first of Paulding's works to gain him a reputation in England, where the reviews were no less favorable than in his native country.

Koningsmarke opens comically, its introductory chapter explaining itself as "forbidden to our female readers, as containing secrets worth knowing." And then, the narrator declares, in the spirit of Fielding, or *Salmagundi*, that "it is much better for an author to commence his work, without knowing how it is to end, than to hamper himself with a regular plot, a succession of prepared incidents, and a premeditated catastrophe." Paulding will have nothing to do with common sense. He goes on to mock book critics (so often his nemeses) for their "horrible propensity to wickedness, in mauling and cutting up innocent authors, with as little remorse as if they were so many cabbages or pumpkins." Such imagery marked the Knickerbocker style. It retained its links, and recognized its debt, to eighteenth-century drollery.[2]

Paulding's older brother William, a lawyer, former congressman, and former militia general, became mayor of New York in the mid-1820s. James returned from Washington at this time and struck up a lifelong friendship with the poet Bryant, whose influence on the New York scene would eventually rival Irving's. With Irving still in Europe, Paulding continued to test the waters. He published *John Bull in America* in 1825, a satire that centered on the unpleasantness of the English, a race of men he had first molested in print in the lead-up to the War of 1812. It was followed by a collection of short stories, *The Merry Tales of the Three Wise Men of Gotham,* and a play, *Lion of the West,* with its popular Davy Crockett character, "Nimrod Wildfire." *Lion of the West* was staged in London in 1832, while Irving's distinctly positive legacy at the U.S. legation was still fresh in people's minds.

His pen unable to pause for long, Paulding also produced two more novels that served to solidify his reputation: *The Dutchman's Fireside* (1831) and *Westward Ho!* (1832). *The Dutchman's Fireside,* like Cooper's classic *The Last of the Mohicans* (1826), takes place largely in upstate New York during the French and Indian War of the late 1750s. Its handsome hero, Sybrandt Westbrook, as rustic in his manners as he is honorable in his aims, is scholarly, awkward, and antisocial. His love interest is his well-bred cousin Catalina Vancour, who occasionally exhibits coquettish qualities but is otherwise appealing.

Catalina is flattered by the attentions of a colonel who possesses "the truly Irish propensity to falling in love extempore." The sensitive Sybrandt assumes his chance of winning her love has dissolved. Yet she truly, quietly, prefers her cousin in his "snuff-colored clothes" to the scarlet-suited officer. The war ("a higher duty") is all that prevents a duel between the rivals, meant to take place on the Palisades, near where Burr would later kill Hamilton. Instead, Sybrandt enters the service of Sir William Johnson and his Mohawk allies— all of this taken from a page in history. Lovelorn, Sybrandt nearly decides to forfeit his life in battle, but the experienced Sir William dissuades him: "Disgust of life is an ignoble impulse to heroic actions."

The would-be lover dares to infiltrate the enemy camp, refuses to flinch before an uplifted tomahawk, and learns the enemy's plans. In a clash with hostile Indians, he saves the life of his rival for Catalina's love, who requires, but refuses, the amputation of one leg. The dying man tells Sybrandt that Catalina had earlier confessed her love for him—for her shy cousin in the "snuff-colored" outfit. Through a series of mix-ups that begins with a letter misdirected, Sybrandt is presumed dead. It is only months later that he is able to appear before an ailing Catalina, and revive her with the truth of his constant love. The couple join, and are happy.[3]

The Dutchman's Fireside was Paulding's one enduring work, though *Westward Ho!* also sold well. It, too, was a romance, and featured a family of Virginia pioneers as they settled in Kentucky. Paulding had never been to the trans-Allegheny West, and although Henry Clay refused to censure him for lack of authenticity, other westerners were less supportive. Not only was Paulding a chronicler of the New West who did not know it firsthand, he was a U.S. naval official who had never been to the Old World. He was no Irving, the constant traveler who had mined Europe for its history and character. Without the slightest sense of shame, Paulding would tell a Richmond bookseller in 1834 that he had devoted his life to encouraging American genius, "and, most especially, to draw[ing] its attention and its efforts toward our own history, tradition, scenery, and manners, instead of foraging in the barren and exhausted fields of the Old World."[4]

Gulian Verplanck, in the more than ten years since he had visited Irving in England, continued to straddle politics and literature. In 1820, he entered the New York State Assembly, where he championed educational reform and did his best, as he had before, to pass judgment on DeWitt Clinton. He was elected to Congress in 1824, and served until 1832, a Jackson Democrat right up until the president declared war against the Bank of the United States, when he could no longer support the administration. He went home to New York just as Irving was returning from England.

As a writer, Verplanck helped to establish the *New-York American,* a successful newspaper of the 1820s, for which he wrote occasional verse. His 1829 story, "Gelyna," was, like Cooper's and Paulding's novels, set in the French and Indian War. It concerns an heiress in the neighborhood of Albany who possesses "an air of romantic and original beauty." Visiting Manhattan, she meets "the hero of her visions," an army major, and watches him go off to war. He dies, and Gelyna's spirit sinks. Refusing to accept his death, she succumbs to a delirium that lasts weeks. Her health restored, she learns to endure, but declines to marry. These many decades later, as "a venerable old lady," she still sometimes retreats in her mind to the year 1758, and flies to the window, to stand lookout for the return of her missing major. Verplanck summarizes, Irvingesque: "I have told the story with scrupulous adherence to the facts as they were related to me. . . . But it is worthy of some more eloquent pen. Oh [British poet Thomas] Campbell, Irving, Allston! had I your genius, I could desire no higher subjects for the canvas, for poetry or pathos, than might be drawn from this simple story of faithful, unfaltering, undoubting love."[5]

★　★

Washington Irving and James Fenimore Cooper should have met sooner. In 1832, Cooper was in Europe. He had quit New York for England six years before, when Irving was already in Spain. Irving wrote from Madrid to Henry Brevoort: "I left Paris a considerable time before the arrival of Mr. Cooper, and regret extremely that I missed him. I have a great desire to make his acquaintance, for I am delighted with his novels." He particularly liked the way Cooper wrote of life at sea. In the 1810s, before he turned to writing, Cooper had lived in Westchester, but he and Irving never crossed paths. Cooper's rise to national fame coincided with the extraordinary success of Irving's *Sketch Book*. The two authors, so often compared, seem to have tramped through similar territory for years, sharing interests and correspondents, without meeting.

In 1822, at the height of his popularity in London, Irving had asked John Murray to take on Cooper's *The Spy*, but Murray declined. He would contract for *The Pioneers*, Cooper's next, while Irving was in Germany; thus, if Irving did not directly benefit Cooper, his earlier recommendation may have helped soften up Murray. Cooper wrote to Irving from New York, thanking him for his efforts. Yet Cooper was also heard to disparage his fellow New Yorker—in part because he believed Irving too much subject to Old World influences, and in part, some say, out of jealousy over Irving's greater success.[6]

Cooper was to the manor born—in the American fashion. He was the son of a poorly educated Pennsylvanian, a Quaker, who became a wealthy Federalist after developing large tracts of land in central New York State at the end of the American Revolution. William Cooper became a judge. His son—like Irving, a youngest son in a large family—was born in 1789, briefly attended Yale, and upon his expulsion for vandalism went off to sea for the adventure of it. He sailed on a merchant ship to Europe in 1806, and spent three years as a midshipman in the American navy; but he always retained a sense of his father's experience as the developer of an interior wilderness.

James Cooper inserted his mother's maiden name of Fenimore into his authorial signature, and incorporated his perspective on nature—the site of rustic beauty and imperial violence—into his best-known works. The bucolic sur-roundings of central New York, especially memories of frontier-era Coopers-town and Lake Otsego, were for Cooper what the lower Hudson was for Irving. Both men knew the forests and waterways of the state, and both could judge the character of the ordinary people who inhabited the region.

Cooper was most often compared to Sir Walter Scott, whose Waverley nov-els, from 1815, ushered in the genre of historical romance. The inventive Scott had started what Cooper perfected: chivalric tales of heroes and villains, adventures and rescues, always involving real events from a distant past. But Cooper did not consider himself an imitator, and in his own mind he was the democrat to Scott's aristocrat. In the way they managed their subjects, this may have been true, but Cooper was an American aristocrat by breeding.[7]

Yet that identity began to fall apart. At virtually the same moment as the firm of P & E Irving collapsed in Liverpool, Cooper's land inheritance disap-peared; within three years, everything he owned was handed over to his cred-itors. As his status in New York precipitously dropped, Cooper wrote his way out of debt. With The Spy, he recovered an identity—he was no longer merely William Cooper's son. This occurred as Washington Irving was recap-turing his own fading celebrity with the Sketch Book.

Though he insisted on the originality of his first literary triumph, Cooper must have done more than just lightly peruse the work of Scott when he wrote The Spy, his novel of the American Revolution. The story takes place in the "neutral ground" of Westchester, between the encampments of the British and American troops. For his patriot readership, Cooper reworked the tale of Major John André and his captors, among whom, it should be recalled, was John Paulding.[8]

In a sense, Cooper was the anti-Irving. He increasingly wrote to distin-guish American literature from the styles of Europe, whereas Irving increas-ingly wrote to enable America to join world literature. It is understandable, then, that Cooper was never at ease with his sobriquet, "The American Scott." He did not like being compared on the basis of their common theme: manly characters staging confrontations across an untamed expanse. Similarly, if he was classed by others as a Knickerbocker writer, it did not suggest to him that he was part of Irving's set. They had never really shared Manhattan: When Ir-ving was growing up there, Cooper was living upstate; it was not until Irving had been in Europe for some years that Cooper moved to Greenwich Street. He established "the Den" in the back room of publisher Charles Wiley's bookstore, in 1823, and then inaugurated the weekly Bread and Cheese Club, which met at the Washington Hotel at Broadway and Chambers Street. Cooper's intellectual circle included the younger William Cullen Bryant and

Fitz-Greene Halleck, as well as Irving's acquaintances John Wesley Jarvis and the ubiquitous Verplanck.[9]

After *The Spy,* Cooper was successful again with *The Pioneers* (1823); and in early 1826, a few months before he left for seven years in Europe, *The Last of the Mohicans* was released. Immediately upon its U.S. publication, he wrote to John Miller in London, the small-scale British publisher who had first attempted the *Sketch Book* before Murray took over. He explained that the book was already tremendously popular, and that he was confident it would prove more successful "than any of its predecessors." He was right. But, like Irving, Cooper was irritated by the lack of international copyright protection; he commented to Miller that he had a friend in Congress, "Verplanck (the Author)," who was going to do something about that. Miller would publish *The Last of the Mohicans,* but was unable to extend to Cooper the sums Irving had been commanding.[10]

Before he left New York, unlike the more reticent Irving, Cooper appealed directly to New York Governor DeWitt Clinton to intercede, if possible, and find him a consular post in Europe. "I should prefer to be on the waters of the Mediterranean, or near them," he wrote. Cooper needed the money that a government appointment would afford. His family remained financially strapped, despite the success of his fiction. While abroad, he learned how Irving was able to negotiate for rights in both the U.S. and England and near-simultaneous publication. It is questionable whether Cooper ever did as well.[11]

Late in 1826, when Paris was his base, Cooper had a surprising encounter on the stairway of the building he was living in. As he told the story to a close friend in New York, "From something in his countenance, . . . I thought he was coming to see me. Indeed, I fancied I knew the face, though I could not remember the name." It was none other than Sir Walter Scott. They spent an hour talking, and breakfasted together the next two days before Sir Walter returned to London. "He treated me like a younger brother," said Cooper, a remark reminiscent of the thrill Irving had had in Scotland some nine years before.

After this, Cooper conveyed to the publishers Carey and Lea what he had learned from the open and approachable Scott: Sir Walter had long enjoyed an advantageous copyright arrangement on both sides of the Atlantic, whereas an American author was harder pressed to negotiate for a just contract that would be applicable in England. Cooper wanted publishers on both sides to cooperate, through agents. He may not have enjoyed being called a junior version of Scott, but he seemed to approve of Scott the man.[12]

Cooper was a sociable individual, though he did not share Irving's reputation for geniality. To be a writer is, almost by definition, to be sensitive to criticism, and a healthy ego probably bought Cooper even more criticism than he would otherwise have earned. On the one hand, he considered James Paulding his friend; on the other, he could barely conceal his disdain for parts of *The Dutch-man's Fireside*. "Did you publish Paulding's book?" he inquired of Carey and Lea from Paris, in 1831. "I have just read it, and I think it quite good—Some parts excellent, but very unequal." Cooper was particularly critical of how Paulding had integrated Sir William Johnson into the plot. He knew "a good deal . . . by report" of the colony's celebrated superintendent of Indian affairs, having grown up in the right circles in central New York. From his father's friends he had heard "an infinity of anecdotes of Sir William, who was a very different sort of person from what Paulding has him." In fact, he said, Paulding's Sir William was no closer to the real man "than Gen. Jackson is like your Father in God the Pope."[13]

In the spring of 1832, the increasingly thin-skinned Cooper wrote from Paris to the veteran New York playwright William Dunlap that he thought he was not getting a fair shake. "I do not know why it is so," he grumbled, but "I rarely see my name mentioned even with respect in any American publication. . . . There may be better writers than I in the country, but there certainly is no one treated with so little deference." Irving had his own concerns about his treatment from fellow Americans during his long absence, but they did not rise to the level of Cooper's consciousness of censure.[14]

Also at this time, Cooper was exchanging letters with another in Irving's circle, the well-off, easygoing Henry Brevoort. Despite Cooper's lukewarm feelings toward Irving, whom he still had not met, he and Brevoort seemed to get on well. Nevertheless, on learning of Irving's imminent return to New York, Cooper began to express feelings of jealousy again, suspecting that he did not fare as well as he should when comparisons were made. Irving had been so long in Europe, affiliated with two embassies, and yet, by his accommodationist manner, was demonstrably less of an America patriot than Cooper thought himself.[15] Cooper had gone on record, in his 1828 *Notions of the Americans*, with an uncompromising defense of his national culture, praising developments in American politics and manners. Could Irving say he had done as much?[16]

★   ★

William Cullen Bryant, perhaps the most precocious figure among America's literary crowd, retained the goodwill of both Cooper and Irving. Born in the hills of western Massachusetts in 1794, he published for the first time, at fourteen, a satire on Jefferson's embargo. As the years passed, Bryant would come to see Jeffersonian democracy as a good thing. He attended Williams College, but found it uninspiring and the library too small. He did Greek translations there, beginning with Anacreon's ode to spring, which had been famously rendered by Tom Moore. The junior class at Williams, seeing the two anonymously placed side by side, judged Bryant's the superior version. In "Fanny" (1819), Fitz-Greene Halleck would call "Anacreon Moore," as Irving's Irish friend was popularly known, "England's prettiest bard." In coming years, Bryant and Halleck both would be placed in the same category as the celebrated Europeans.

Toward the end of 1811, Bryant read *Knickerbocker's History*, and found it highly entertaining. Then, amid what he later described as "solitary rambles in the woods," he dashed off the poem "Thanatopsis," a nature-worshipping picture of life and a powerful interrogation of death, which he would be able to use as a calling card in the writing profession. Bryant had not thought of publishing it, and more than five years passed before his father found it in a drawer and submitted it to the *North American Review*. "Thanatopsis" wowed a generation.

As the War of 1812 unfolded, Bryant immersed himself in the study of law, practicing in the town of Great Barrington until 1824, when he visited New York and met, among others, James Fenimore Cooper, and was inspired to return to writing in earnest. Acting on the advice of Jared Sparks, then the editor of the *North American Review*, Bryant gave up his law practice ("this beggarly profession") and relocated to Manhattan, where he took charge of a new literary magazine, the *New-York Review and Athenaeum Magazine*. Congressman Gulian Verplanck told him he had made the right decision.

Bryant got a lift by publishing in the pages of his magazine Fitz-Greene Halleck's poem "Marco Bozzaris," concerning a champion of the Greek resistance to Turkish rule—that fashionable romantic enterprise of the mid-1820s that had drawn in Lord Byron and sealed his fate the year before. Bryant was now attending Cooper's famous lunches at Wiley's bookstore, where he befriended the young artist (later inventor) Samuel F. B. Morse, and the soon-to-be-heralded landscape painter Thomas Cole, who at this time occupied the garret of his father's house on Greenwich Street. Bryant, recognizing Cooper's prickliness, was loath to review Cooper's *Last of the Mohicans;* he wrote privately to fellow editor Richard Henry Dana of the imposing Cooper: "Ah, sir! he is too sensitive a creature for me to touch. He seems to think his own works his own property, instead of being the property of the public."

When Cooper left for Europe in mid-1826, his Bread and Cheese Club was unable to survive without him, and Bryant, along with Cole, established the Sketch Club to take its place. Meanwhile, William Coleman, founding editor of the *New York Evening Post*, at the job since 1801, was in ill health and needed help, so Bryant came on as assistant editor. Aside from his regular managerial duties, he wrote poetry for the onetime Federalist paper, which he now gave a Democratic political slant. In 1829, Coleman died, and Bryant took over as editor—a position he would retain through the Civil War era, and for the rest of his long life.

In 1827, in the context of praising Cooper, Irving had written to Brevoort: "I have been charmed likewise with what I have seen of the writings of Bryant and Hallack [sic]. Are you acquainted with them. I should like to know something about them personally—their vein of thinking is quite above that of ordinary men and ordinary poets and they are masters of the magic of poetical language." In 1831, when Bryant was, arguably, America's most distinguished poet, he assembled his poems into a single volume. Hoping to gain a readership abroad, he sent his collected poems to John Murray, and told Irving what he was doing. Verplanck followed with a letter in support of Bryant's aim of obtaining "an honorable publication in Europe." Irving answered Bryant, in early 1832, from Byron's Newstead Abbey, saying that he was sorry Bryant had gone directly to Murray, "who has disappointed me grievously in respect to other American works entrusted to him. . . . I shall however Write to him about your work."

As anticipated, Murray was unresponsive. Irving then found Bryant a London publisher who agreed to divide profits with the poet. Irving generously wrote an introduction to the English edition, thinking he could promote Bryant more effectively by likening his perspective to that of Cooper:

> The British public has already expressed its delight at the graphic descriptions of American scenery and wild woodland characters, contained in the works of our national novelist, Cooper. The same keen eye and fresh feeling for nature . . . will be found to characterize this volume, condensed into a narrower compass and sublimated into poetry.

Beyond Irving's sturdy confidence in Bryant, the stark contradiction between Irving's unbounded praise for Cooper and Cooper's stinginess with regard to Irving is underscored in these lines.

Bryant's work received its first review in the British Isles in *Blackwood's Edinburgh Magazine* in the spring of 1832, just as Irving was boarding the vessel that would bring him home. No poet could have wished for a better review. "Bryant's genius," it said, "consists in a tender pensiveness, a moral melancholy, breathing all over his contemplations, dreams, and reveries." The poet-editor heard from his friend Dana, who must have had Irving in mind as well, when he wrote: "Our men of real genius must send abroad for their good names."[17]

The other New York–based poet Irving admired, Fitz-Greene Halleck, was born in Guilford, Connecticut, in 1790. His mother was directly linked to the early Puritans, and his father was a country merchant known for his manners and merriment—and, less admirably, for support of the king during the Revolution. Their son received his entire formal education in conservative Guilford, moving to the freer world of New York City at the age of twenty-one, where he went to work as a store clerk and bookkeeper in a financial concern. He wrote bits of poetry at that time, revealing the influence, it is said, of Tom Moore.

Halleck was gay. Among the bachelors on the New York literary scene who remain sexually indescribable, his sexuality alone cannot be doubted. During the War of 1812, he served with Irving intimates Henry Brevoort and Samuel Swartwout in the Iron Greys unit, which paraded menacingly and saw no action. His most important early friendship was with Joseph Rodman Drake, members together in the ironically named Ugly Club, whose associates were conscious of their mental talents. Drake was described as the handsomest man in the city; he possessed, as Halleck told his sister, "a face like an angel—a form like an Apollo."

Halleck was the best man at Drake's 1816 wedding. But unlike Irving and Brevoort during the same period, Halleck never got over his loss of Drake to marriage and fatherhood, even as the pair of Halleck and Drake collaborated on the notorious "Croaker" poems, which appeared in Coleman's *Evening Post* in 1819. Coleman told Bryant that he was quite taken when the "Croakers" (anonymous when they submitted their work to the paper) finally revealed themselves to him: "Drake looked the poet; you saw the stamp of genius in every feature. Halleck had the aspect of a satirist." "Croaker" was a latter-day *Salmagundi*.

"Fanny" was Halleck's satire on the nouveau riche. It was published that same year by Charles Wiley, who had only months earlier joined forces with Cornelius Van Winkle to publish Irving's *Sketch Book*. Wiley told Halleck that he was "the only writer in America, Irving excepted," whose works he would risk publishing. Virginia's John Randolph adored "Fanny," and carried his copy on a voyage to England, presenting it to the novelist Maria Edgeworth.

When Drake took ill and died in 1820, Halleck, understandably, was crushed. His eulogistic tribute began memorably:

> *Green be the turf above thee,*
> *Friend of my better days!*
> *None knew thee but to love thee,*
> *Nor named thee but to praise.*

Through the decade of the 1820s, Halleck continued to earn a living as an aide to men of business, while rising in esteem as America's premier versifier—certainly the equal of Bryant. The final chapter epigraph in Cooper's *Last of the Mohicans,* on courage and death, is taken from Halleck's "Marco Bozzaris." Halleck was an active member of Cooper's luncheon club.

His fame held steady throughout the decade of the 1820s, and in February 1832, when he traveled to Washington, Fitz-Greene Halleck dined on two occasions with President Jackson. Then, on May 15, literally days before Irving docked in New York, the tycoon John Jacob Astor hired the poet as his private secretary. Halleck lived on his employer's Hellgate estate at the same time as he undertook to edit the first "complete edition" of the works of Lord Byron.[18]

A New York attitude had grown in Irving's absence, one that owed "Diedrich Knickerbocker" more than it owed to "Geoffrey Crayon." Halleck preferred *Knickerbocker's History* to the *Sketch Book*—late in life, he said so. Of the Knickerbocker writers, Halleck was, stylistically, the most like Irving (even more so than Paulding). Like Irving, too, he was a charmer who was often a loner.

What all the Knickerbocker writers had in common was their "edge," their abstract energy. A mixture of sentiment and irony made their cause meaningful and distinctive in its day. They embodied something called "manly" sentiment. What was not pure amusement in it was remotely political. Theirs was a critique of insincerity and lack of imagination. The Knickerbockers mocked predictable behaviors. They challenged orthodoxies.

At the same time as Knickerbockerism flourished, a novelistic style emerged, inspired by Sir Walter Scott, which Cooper pioneered and Paulding drew upon. This style did not represent Irving to any great degree, for he gravitated to the short story—that is, until he sought to extend his reputation by graduating to scholarly history. Still, it was Halleck, the American Byron, who, more than any of the others, carried forward the mode of wit that Irving left behind when he departed New York in 1815. He and Irving were practical-minded men, versatile, sociable men, adept at the business of life. But they lived in another world, too: the fantasy world in which they invested their hearts.

*   *

These were the personalities, then, who, by 1832, had come to rule the literary community in New York City: Paulding, Verplanck, Cooper, Bryant, and Halleck. There were others, of course, but these five were the most remarkable. And now, with the notable exception of Cooper, they, along with city officials, delighted in welcoming Washington Irving home.

He would find the Manhattan of 1832 almost unrecognizable. It was, for one, a place where money ruled the day. Approximately half the city's wealth was in the hands of the top 4 percent of the taxable population. The 1820s had seen a population explosion: Now more than two hundred thousand people lived on the island of Manhattan, and more than a half million residents of New York State who had not been there in 1815 were counted in the 1830 census. Banking, transportation, shipbuilding, insurance, and other industries had grown decisively. Broadway and Greenwich Street (Manhattan's west side) remained the better addresses; but northward expansion meant that Greenwich Village, known in Irving's younger days principally for Newgate prison and Aaron Burr's Richmond Hill mansion, was fast becoming a respectable middle-class community. In 1831, Burr's mansion, now in Astor's hands, was hoisted up and log-rolled downhill, where it was rechristened as a theater. A poetry competition was held, the winner's poem to be read at the theater's dedication: It was master of ceremonies Gulian Verplanck who recited the poem, first breaking open the envelope so that he could read out the name of the winning entry for all to hear—and it was Halleck.[19]

John Jacob Astor had not only bought the Burr property but also a good deal more of the Village. He was making a killing, buying up long-term land leases, subdividing, and building residences on them. A man born in 1816 said that as a child he had faltered whenever he walked over to Canal Street, "in dread of imaginary savages" to the north of that line, "or of the press gangs that stole little boys and carried them off to sea." Now, everything above Canal was civilized; the regular beat of a decent life prevailed in Greenwich Village.

This new New York was a place that cried out for speculation. Gentlemen's agreements traditionally reached at the Tontine Coffee House, at the corner of Wall and Water Streets, paled in comparison to what now transpired at the formal New York Stock & Exchange Board, organized in 1817. Steamboats vied with wind-powered craft; commercial traffic moved inland via the Hudson River and the Erie Canal, and up and down the coast. On February 23, 1832, the day after New Yorkers marked the grand centennial of George Washington's birthday, the Harlem Railroad broke ground at Murray Hill. Four-horse teams led omnibuses at regular intervals, taking more than a dozen passengers at a time along up- and downtown routes. The city was wide awake.[20]

When word reached New York that Irving was heading home onboard the *Havre*, the weekly *New-York Mirror* printed a lengthy front-page sketch of the eclectic author whose works varied more in character "than those of any other living writer." He who combined "fine wit" (*Salmagundi*) with "touching pathos" (*Sketch Book*) and "broad and irresistible burlesque" (*Knickerbocker's*

History) was also one whose personal life was "destitute of romantic interest, unless such as some prolific fancy may conjure up from the fact that one so highly gifted with the power of describing the tender and amiable in others, should have himself preferred the secluded path of celibacy."

What a seemingly strange, taunting statement to be made amid such unmitigated praise! The author of the article, claiming intimacy with the Irving family, qualified: "From near shades of character, and anecdotes of private friendship, delicacy would forbid our withdrawing the veil." The unrevealed secret may have been an allusion to the presumed effect of the Matilda Hoffman deathbed scene, the traditional rationale behind Irving's reluctance to marry. But the writer's choice of the word *celibacy* (which at this time could still mean, generically, "single") still raises questions. By 1832, public morals were beginning to demand an explanation for a sustained bachelor existence. Whatever the truth may have been, to write "the secluded path of celibacy" sounded better in this environment than to leave open the possibility that Irving was whoring around Europe, where sex was notoriously public.[21]

★   ★

As a boy, Washington Irving had often watched ships come into the bustling port of Manhattan after an Atlantic crossing. Now, he was a passenger—one could almost say he was a professional traveler. Since he had last set eyes on his native New York, he had come and gone through countless European ports. This time, leaving England, he was in his fiftieth year, no longer a young man. The first half of the forty-day transit was rather wintry; but when the captain steered a course south toward Bermuda, smoother seas prevailed.

Spring sights appeared before him. He surveyed the New York landscape with deep emotion. "A thousand sails of all description" dotted the sunny horizon. To one side, he noted, the green forests of Brooklyn had been supplanted by village features. Greeted by as many unfamiliar as familiar structures extending from the waterfront, there was no doubt left in his mind: In the seventeen years since he had gazed on it, New York City had grown into a "vast commercial emporium." He came ashore without fanfare, but all that was to change when the news spread that he was back.

The day was May 21, 1832. At the end of more than a month on the high seas, his first stop after docking was Ebenezer's home on Bridge Street, near the Battery. But he was unable to rest much. Local officials and old acquaintances dropped by when they heard he was home. On May 23, he dined with James Paulding, Captain Jack Nicholson, Josiah Ogden Hoffman's oldest son Ogden (presently district attorney of New York), and the former mayor Philip

Hone, who wrote in his diary three days later: "The return of Geoffrey Crayon has made old times and the associations of early life the leading topics of conversation amongst his friends."

Before Irving could blink, a public dinner was arranged by the city's new elite, expressly to pay tribute to the man who had done an unprecedented amount of good for the literary reputation of New York. At the top of the list of the ad hoc welcoming committee was Lad of Kilkenny Sam Swartwout, Burr's former aide, who for the past three years had held the lucrative post of collector of customs revenues at the port of New York. Overwhelmed by the hospitality he was receiving, Irving agreed to submit, and the date of May 30, a Wednesday, was set.

It was well chosen, a clear and mild day sandwiched between two days of rain. The Irving banquet took place at the City Hotel on Broadway, above Trinity Church, where in 1815 DeWitt Clinton had boldly declared that he would build the Erie Canal, and where, in 1824, the long-absent war hero Lafayette was fêted. The event was attended by three hundred citizens skimmed from New York's top layer. Chancellor James Kent, nearing seventy, and for decades the most esteemed jurist in the state, presided. Paulding sat at Irving's right, a willing second fiddle now that a slew of his American stories had made his, more or less, a household name. The painters Gilbert Stuart Newton and John Trumbull were wedged in nearby. There, too, were Hoffmans, and the distinguished statesman Irving had known as minister to France, Albert Gallatin. These days, the Swiss-born Pennsylvanian was a bank president and an adopted New Yorker. Another with ties to politics past was Le Roy de Chaumont, French-born, a prosperous New York investor, who sent a newspaper clipping of the event to James Madison, the oldest living ex-president.

Others who would have liked to attend the banquet, such as Bryant and Verplanck, were in distant parts. The City Hotel was decked out. "It was a regular Knickerbocker affair," observed Philip Hone. "There were old New Yorkers and their descendants in goodly numbers, who are seldom seen at such places." Many had come simply to scrutinize the founder of a school of prose writing—who was no longer as thin as they remembered him.

Irving was the talk of the town. Unforced laughs, impassioned speeches, and long toasts—one to "the Dutch Herodotus, Diedrich Knickerbocker!"— filled the banquet hall. Chancellor Kent expressed gratitude to Irving "for the exalted rank to which he has raised the literary reputation of this country." Before Irving happened on the New York scene, he said, "taste and manners were greatly in need of improvement." What Irving did in *Knickerbocker's History,* his first great composition, was to combine "sentiment and pathos" with undeniable "good feeling," "good temperament," and "humanity"—all of it "written in the finest strain of burlesque gravity." With the "liberal moral, and pathetic reflections" of the *Sketch Book* and its successors, he remained an "American genius," even while living abroad. "On English ground," he had matched "the grace and elegance" of the most moving of the British writers: Joseph Addison, Oliver Goldsmith, and Henry Mackenzie.

The *Morning Courier,* one of several newspapers to publish reports, printed a text of Irving's speech, noting the many moments when he was interrupted by cheers. It did not seem to matter that the man of the hour had admitted to several people that he was nervous—or perhaps his nerves did not show.

Gazing out at the tables before him, Irving paid homage to the friends of his youth, and to others he did not recognize but knew as "sons of the patriarchs of my native city." Surprisingly, given Chancellor Kent's eulogium—and perhaps without premeditation—he made reference to the feelings of hurt that hounded him while overseas: "I had been led, at times, to doubt my standing in the affections of my countrymen," the *Morning Courier* transcribed his remark. "Rumors and suggestions had reached me [here Mr. I. betrayed much emotion] that absence had impaired their kind feelings—that they considered me alienated from my country." He acknowledged that pride had kept him from writing home to "vindicate" himself from the charge of alienation (which was, after all, a composite of rumor, a couple of reviews, and his own imagination); "nor should I have alluded to it at this time, if the warm and affectionate reception I have met with on all sides since my landing . . . had not proved that my misgivings were groundless."

Applause interrupted him. A bit later: "It has been asked 'Can I be content to live in this country?' Whoever asks that question, must have but an inadequate idea of its blessings and delights." And here, surprisingly he spoke disparagingly of the "gloom" of the Old World, where he had felt so comfortable for so long, saying now that its "doubt and danger" were easy to contrast with the "life and animation" of a burgeoning America:

> Is this not a city by which one may be proud to be received as a son? Is this not a land in which one may be happy to fix his destiny, and his ambition— if possible—to found a name? (A burst of applause, when Mr. Irving quickly resumed:)—I am asked how long I mean to remain here? They know but little of my heart or my feelings who can ask me this question. I answer, as long as I live.

As long as I live. All those assembled roared, and waved their handkerchiefs. Though he had not planned an exit strategy, he seized this moment, and terminated his speech then and there. Washington Irving had come home to a hero's welcome.[22]

⋆ ⋆

One who would have liked to have been present was William Irving's son Pierre Munro, who was instead in rural Northampton, Massachusetts, confronting the slow death of his wife of three years—he had thought that the cool air would help to cure her of what was likely consumption. She would be gone by October, at the age of twenty-three. As it was, not more than a month after Irving's return, the cholera that he had seen in London had swept south from Canada. Fourteen confirmed cases (eleven of them fatal) were all it took to force cancellation of that year's Fourth of July parade in New York City. People knew what was coming, and hundreds, then thousands, fled to the countryside. By August, when the crisis began to ease, there would be 3,500 New York fatalities.[23]

Irving politely refused a ceremonial banquet invitation from Philadelphia, similar to the one in New York, and traveled to Washington, D.C., in June, outracing the cholera. He was bound for the nation's capital ostensibly to settle the accounts he had maintained as chargé d'affaires in London, though curiosity no doubt fueled some part of his plan. The length of time spent in journeying there was half what it had been twenty years earlier; this time he went by steamboat and railroad, two new forms of transportation.

Upon arrival in Washington, he paid a call on a family he had become intimate with in London, that of the current secretary of the treasury, Louis McLane. "McLane stands the fatigue and annoyance of his station much better than I had anticipated," he wrote to Peter in Paris, recurring to his axiom that no political appointment ever came without a threat to one's personal serenity. And then he went to the White House to meet his employer, as it were, President Andrew Jackson. Again to Peter: "I have been most kindly received by the old general, with whom I am much pleased as well as amused. As his admirers say, he is truly an *old Roman*—to which I would add, *with a little dash of the Greek;* for I suspect he is as *knowing;* and I believe he is *honest.*"[24]

The "Roman" was noble and forceful, in the shorthand of the day, but the "Greek" impressed others by his stock of knowledge. Jackson's qualities were widely associated with a Roman's take-charge stubbornness; yet Irving, somewhat idealistically, preferred to detect in the president a kind of intelligence with which the poorly educated, highly emotional frontier lawyer, judge, and general was rarely credited.[25]

At this very moment, Jackson was gearing up to bring down the Bank of the U.S.—the "monster bank," as he saw it—for its monopolistic, antidemocratic tendency. His two nemeses in this battle were the bank's director, Nicholas Biddle (a member of whose family was among those proposing to honor Irving in Philadelphia), and Senator Henry Clay. Before he left Washington, the politically moderate Irving, unabashed admirer of Jackson, was also able to revive his old acquaintance with Clay, whom he had first met and liked in 1811. The popular Kentuckian was challenging the president's reelection bid that season by highlighting the justness and viability of the national bank Jackson anathematized.

His party, the Whig, was designed around its opposition to the power, real and symbolic, of a single man: Andrew Jackson. The dissident Whigs, who would not win a national election until 1840, favored strong institutions and a federal government that could be granted a reasonable amount of power as a moral watchdog; many Whigs approved antislavery agitation. The Democrats, in principle, embraced economic opportunity for ordinary folks, declared an anti-elitist individualism, and mildly sympathized with southerners' sensitivities concerning states' rights. In New York City, the erstwhile Jacksonian Democrat Gulian Verplanck would switch sides, leave Congress, and run unsuccessfully for mayor in 1834 as a Whig because of the president's imprudent, destabilizing stance against banks. After his defection, opposition Democrats would predictably berate him as an elitist.[26]

As we have repeatedly seen, the politics of New York were never easy to define. By 1832, old and unsteady alliances bore less resemblance than ever to the new pro- and anti-Jackson configuration. So, one must wonder, how did the sons of Federalists, select Hoffmans and Hamiltons, grow to be Jacksonians?

The Federalist Party of George Washington, Alexander Hamilton, and Josiah Ogden Hoffman was no more. For some time now, old Federalists had not known where to turn for the strong executive leadership to which they ordinarily gravitated. Few career politicians warmed to the unsociable John Quincy Adams; though an outstanding patriot, the aloof and opinionated New Englander judged issues as they arose, and did not produce a definable ideology around which conservative forces could rally. William Coleman, Alexander Hamilton's handpicked editor at the *Evening Post* in 1801, grew tamer in his Federalism as the years went by, and ardently supported the strong-willed Jackson over Adams (mostly on personal grounds). James Alexander Hamilton, Alexander Hamilton's son, was a close aide to Jackson, and a staunch supporter of the president's bank policy, though the very idea of a national bank had been his father's, forty years earlier.[27]

This gradual transformation occurred after the War of 1812, when Jefferson was out of the picture and Anglo-American relations did not so starkly divide the parties anymore. Former Federalists accommodated themselves to the accession to power of a younger generation. Those of their children who did service in the War of 1812 imbibed the military ideal of respect and devotion to a proven leader. These were chivalric days (as magnified in the tales of Cooper and Irving), in which Jackson, a mighty hero in that war, was seen as a decisive figure, his words plain and undisguised, his behavior untainted by backroom dealing.

While in 1828 Jackson symbolized a fresh start, after 1832, there were a good number like Verplanck who lost faith. For this reason, Jackson scheduled a visit to New York to reclaim (or avoid alienating) his Knickerbocker followers. But as his behavior began to appear more impulsive and less rational, defense of the aging, haggard president started to tax more of his better-educated supporters. Some of his closest friends would defect to the Whigs and one, fellow Tennessean Hugh Lawson White, would campaign for president against Martin Van Buren, Jackson's handpicked successor.

This being the case, how did Washington Irving, a onetime Federalist, make himself comfortable with the party created by "William the Testy," Thomas Jefferson? The answer to this question is less complicated. If in the early days of the century, Irving was afraid of the *idea* of the democratic rabble, an uneducated mass exercising the franchise, by the period 1829–1832, he felt willing to take a chance. He liked the minds of men such as Louis McLane and Martin Van Buren: If they could work comfortably with Jackson, and were not afraid of his message, then perhaps Irving did not have to fear the rugged Tennessean's thunderous style either. Irving had never been an ideologue; his flexible nature may have softened him up for a tentative romance with Jacksonian democracy.

It is hard to know precisely what Irving meant by "true" when, in 1833, he told the New Jersey–born playwright and oft-called "Father of American Drama," William Dunlap, that *"democracy is the only true system."* Irving was comparing life in America to the caste-based society he had witnessed in Europe; but he was probably also reflecting the notion shared by 60 percent of New York voters in 1832 that the United States had been energized by the coming of Jackson. Dunlap, who had known a teenaged Irving, was now nearing seventy. He pressed the author for his political perspective by acknowledging that he himself had always been a Democrat (in the partisan sense), dating back to Jefferson's time. He was proud, he said, that the U.S. governing system was designed not to bring down the few but to exalt the many. What did Irving think? "He was convinced of it," Dunlap penned in his diary. "His feelings & political creed was changed."[28]

Irving now felt confident that the laws put in place at the time of the nation's founding had not been sacrificed to demagoguery. That was how he was able to change his view of popular sovereignty. Insular southerners had ruled the union before; northern merchant capital directed the present, even with a southerner in the White House. Irving was at ease with the internal operations of the political system that had evolved.

★   ★

The year 1832 presented multiple signposts of change. As Irving said his goodbyes to friends and associates in England, he must have figured that, at his age, he might not ever sail the Atlantic again.

Some months before his voyage home, he had had a poignant interview with his first sponsor, Sir Walter Scott, now sixty, to whom he owed so much. Over a quiet dinner in London, as he gazed upon this old friend, Irving could see how fatigued Scott was. In contrast, Scott saw Irving as the picture of health. "Ah, my dear fellow," he said, taking him by the hand, "time has dealt lightly with you." But Scott, who lost his wife in 1826, and had then suffered serious financial losses when a printing firm he was a partner in failed, had now lost his step. He had begun—for the first time—to write for money. Physically worn the day he broke bread with Irving, the beloved novelist left on a voyage on the Mediterranean in the hope of repairing his health; but his friends were not surprised when he returned, and died, at Abbottsford, in the early autumn of 1832.[29]

His death marked the end of an era in British letters. It was the beginning of the age of Thomas Carlyle, another son of Scotland, a new preserver of memory. In recalling his countryman, five years later, as the best example of British manhood, Carlyle wrote with more than a little nostalgia: "Alas, his fine Scotch face, with its shaggy honesty, sagacity and goodness. . . . We shall never forget it; we shall never see it again."

It was, indeed, then, the end of an era. The 1832 Reform Act in the House of Commons was about to bring a more representative government to Great Britain, as industrialization altered the physical landscape. Political liberty, the full emancipation of slaves, and the enhanced manufacturing economy were going forward hand in hand. It was the age of coal, iron, and steam. The year Irving left, everything was beginning to change.

It was time for Washington Irving to direct his focus once again to American subjects.

CHAPTER 12

A Tour on the Prairies

1832–1834

With the great, he feels sufficiently acquainted—He desires most to ramble among the natural actions of men—He watches every spring and looks with microscopic eye into the hidden wheels that move men along, on the common walks of life. His mode of recording events, is not to confide much to the memory, but to sketch in a little book every occurrence worthy of remembrance.

—Henry L. Ellsworth, on Washington Irving,
Fort Gibson, Oklahoma, November 17, 1832[1]

The American father, who can afford it, and does not buy a copy of Mr. Irving's book [A Tour on the Prairies], *does not deserve that his sons should prefer his fireside to the bar-room.*

North American Review, July 1835

ON HIS WAY BACK FROM WASHINGTON IN LATE JUNE 1832, during that season of cholera, Irving stopped in Philadelphia and saw half a performance of *Macbeth*. He noted that he was part of a "very thin" audience. Though he continued to affect unconcern as he returned to Manhattan, he was soon steaming up the Hudson with Paulding and two gentlemen whom he had met aboard the *Havre:* Charles Joseph Latrobe and Comte Albert-Alexandre de Pourtalès.

Latrobe was thirty-one, English, and the nephew of a well-known architect, Benjamin Henry Latrobe, who had helped design the President's House when Jefferson was its occupant. A scholar as well as avid traveler, Charles J. Latrobe met the Pourtalès family while mountain climbing in the Alps. On this extended journey through America, he was the tutor/chaperone to the nineteen-year-old Pourtalès, who was Swiss, and, it was said, sent by his parents to exercise (and exorcise) a spirit of adventure that Europe could not contain.

Irving began his tour with these "most agreeable travelling companions" in Manhattan. They arrived at West Point after a steamboat trip of four hours. Gouverneur Kemble's barge, outfitted with an awning, was waiting for them—Kemble's foundry on the opposite shore of the Hudson, at Cold Spring, cast guns for the army. At Kemble's bachelor cottage, nestled in a cove enveloped by tress, they stayed a few days "lolling on the grass" and finding relief from the heat in the cool, clear waters of the Hudson River. From here, they steamed upriver to Catskill; next a stagecoach delivered them into the mountains, and to a hotel where they communed with Irving's past—for these were (as he recounted the trip in a letter to Peter) "the veritable haunts of Rip Van Winkle."[2]

Following a brief stay in Manhattan (presumably at Ebenezer's house) to answer his mail, Irving went by boat to Boston, where he checked into the much-touted Tremont Hotel. There he enjoyed the company of his former London chum Gilbert Stuart Newton, who was shortly to marry a Bostonian. Taking the overland route, Latrobe and Pourtalès met Irving at the Tremont. All this was merely phase one of what Irving projected as a passage west with his brother John, now a judge in Manhattan. Things would change—for one, Jack Irving would not make the trip. And Irving would diverge greatly from his initial plan to see only as much of the frontier as Ohio, Kentucky, and Tennessee.

We can try to imagine Irving's daily existence, but it is hard to appreciate fully the kind of nomadism he had become accustomed to under the conditions of travel that prevailed in the nineteenth century. The toll on the body had to be considerable. During the first six months after his return to the United States, in the wake of a forty-day Atlantic crossing, he was on the seas or on the road more—much more—than he was in any fixed place. Now, with Latrobe and Pourtalès, he traveled up to Concord, New Hampshire, skirted the crystal lakes of the center of the state, trudged through the White Mountains, and hiked up Mount Washington with the experienced climber Latrobe. He wrote of the "grand, savage, and striking" peaks, and said he found this part of New England "beautiful beyond expectation."

As the European pair went in for more mountaineering in Vermont, Irving returned to New York via the Connecticut River. Noting the persistence of the deadly cholera in Manhattan, he joined Ebenezer and family at Tarry-town, and found "a great part of the family forces . . . collected" at a small cottage. This included his fifty-eight-year-old sister Catharine, a favorite corre-spondent while he was in Europe, her husband Daniel Paris, and a teenage daughter named Sarah whom he had not met before, but who would become the fondest of his nieces.

It was a short stay, but he received a good dose of family. On his last day with them, Washington went on a wagon ride with Ebenezer and two nephews to the Saw Mill River, and in mid-afternoon hopped on a mail wagon for the ride past Peekskill to the Hudson River landing, where he boarded an overnight steamboat. Next stop was Albany, even more of a traffic hub since the dawn of the canal era. Irving had arranged to meet up again with Latrobe and Pourtalès at Saratoga Springs, which was now accessible by rail out of Schenectady. They enjoyed the fishing at Saratoga before starting west.

The stage carried them parallel to the Mohawk River. Why they chose not to travel the Erie Canal is uncertain. But they did more or less track along the canal route, staying at Rome and riding out to visit the nearby Oneida Indi-ans. They passed through the "thriving town" of Seneca Falls, and the even more promising one of Rochester, soon to be incorporated as a city. The three travelers arrived at Niagara Falls on August 23, 1832, thirteen days out of Saratoga.

It was sunset when Irving first viewed the northern border spectacle. He descended to the bottom of the American Falls the next morning, watching the swallows "playing about in the mist." Later, from his notes: "Beautiful transparency of the water bright feathery look of water." There are certainly more awestruck commentaries from those who have seen the Niagara Falls. Judge William Cooper recorded in 1810: "Sense dwells upon the image— thought wanders obscurely after something which it cannot grasp, and the be-holder is lost in ecstasy as I am in description." And Daniel Webster in 1825: "Water, vapor, foam, & the atmosphere are all mixed up together in sublime confusion." For Irving, a relative latecomer, it was as noteworthy that there were already "great yawning Hotels overlooking the falls." Perhaps not all forms of progress tickled him equally.[3]

A most fortuitous meeting then took place. Aboard a steamboat on Lake Erie, en route from Buffalo to Detroit, the Irving party met Henry Leavitt Ellsworth of Windsor, Connecticut. Ellsworth was a Yale graduate, a lawyer, and the son of the Federalist mainstay Oliver Ellsworth, a delegate to the Constitutional Convention who later served as chief justice of the Supreme Court during the John Adams administration. The younger Ellsworth had a twin brother who was married to Noah Webster's daughter, and who was cur-rently a member of Congress—with Whig sympathies. Their Federalist father many years dead now, Henry Ellsworth had recently received an important appointment from President Jackson to head up a commission designed to evaluate the lands and prospects of the Indian Territory and to organize the resettlement of Indians west of the Mississippi River. He was not the administration's first choice, or its second, but was considered only after a couple of more likely Jacksonians, Tennesseans, had first declined. It was a momentous assignment.[4]

Andrew Jackson, of course, had first earned fame as an Indian fighter in Alabama Territory during the War of 1812. As early as 1820, he had charged: "It is high time to do away with the farce of treating with Indian tribes." One of his first acts after coming into office in 1829 was Indian removal. This was a controversial resolve at the time of Irving's return from Europe, for the Supreme Court had ruled that Indians were "domestic dependent nations"; it was the federal government's responsibility to protect their territorial rights. As president, Jackson could have spoken up for the Creeks and Cherokees, who were the tribes most immediately affected. He could have ordered Georgia to honor the High Court's decree. But that was not his position. The least charitable view shows Jackson standing aside and making way for the forced relocation of assimilated eastern Cherokees along the horrific Trail of Tears, in 1838.[5]

Irving was more than a little interested in the subject. Back when he was writing for the *Analectic Magazine* during the War of 1812, he had published two pieces on Indians, modified versions of which were later included in the English printing of the *Sketch Book*. "Traits of Indian Character," as originally drafted, obliquely criticized Jackson's war against the Creeks, and warmly defended native culture on grounds of its essential humanity and rationality. It explained how Indians' so-called barbarous behavior could be an understandable reaction to white violence, hypocrisy, and injustice. Indians, Irving wrote, were a people "dispossessed of their hereditary possessions by mercenary and frequent wanton warfare" whose collective character was "traduced by bigoted and interested [i.e., having something to gain] writers."

Moving from an editorial to a biographical style, Irving's essay "Philip of Pokanoket" was an interpretation of a tragic piece of history. The seventeenth-century New England leader Metacom (also known as King Philip) had acculturated into white society, only to rebel against his supposed benefactors in protest over a miscarriage of justice. He paid for it with his life—betrayed by a "renegade" Indian. For Irving, the story was largely one of Euro-American obstinacy and oppression, fed by prejudice. An Indian on the loose evoked exaggerated stories of terrorism—and placed Philip outside the bounds of

Christian compassion—all because he had tried to avoid being humiliated. Irving shows how Philip's persecution became clear only with historical hindsight.

The allegorical power of Irving's writing has endured, but would he be ready to draw a connection between Philip's cause and the Cherokees of his own time? The full impact of Jackson's removal policy was not yet apprehended in 1832, when Irving and Ellsworth met up. A missionary to the Cherokees, Samuel Worcester, had decried what was happening, and it was his case that reached the Supreme Court. "They have followed our counsel with the docility of children," William Wirt, the former attorney general, argued on behalf of the Indians. "We asked them to become civilized, and they became so." The resort to such unpalatable, patronizing language indicates how far in the past this episode is. The president, meanwhile, professed to fear for the destiny of decent Cherokees if they continued to live among southern whites. Removal, he claimed, was best for all.[6]

Irving, so long abroad, was no expert in the politics of Indian removal. Nor was he ever predisposed, in spite of his political connections, to commit to internal policy debate. Indeed, it was quite the opposite with him. He was unlikely to contest the will of Andrew Jackson, that honest "old Roman" with "a little dash of the Greek," whom he preferred to see as a man who wished all people well.

There on Lake Erie, not knowing what to expect, Irving snatched the chance to accompany Ellsworth on his fact-finding mission. Later he wrote to Peter: "The offer was too tempting to be resisted: I should have an opportunity of seeing the remnants of those great Indian tribes, which are now about to disappear as independent nations, or to be amalgamated under some new form of government."[7] There is a tone of nostalgia here, a consciousness of his being witness to a historic shift; but the tone and the consciousness are of inevitability more than disappointment.

Irving's neutral position was not then untenable. The modern scholarly view is that the compounded failures of several administrations to act fairly in the face of whites' land hunger was the cause of most of the Indians' problems. But this was not the prevailing view in the summer of 1832. Even within the Cherokee nation, leaders were unable to agree on what constituted a prudent course. The War Department was hoping that Ellsworth would confirm what it had already assured the Indians living east of the Mississippi: that the lands west of Arkansas Territory were highly desirable.

☆　☆

Latrobe and Pourtalès had been intending to go on from Detroit into Canada, but Ellsworth's invitation to their party changed everything. As Irving put it while they were yet in Ohio, Latrobe and Pourtalès were "delighted with the idea of travelling on horseback through the forests and praries, camping in tents at nights, and hunting Deer, Buffalos & wild turkeys."

They had docked in Ashtabula and followed the lakeshore road to Cleveland, still a small town. Its subsequent growth would come as a result of its position as the northern terminus of the Ohio-Erie Canal. As the Irving party had done in crossing upstate New York by stage rather than canal barge, they did the same, with Ellsworth, on their southerly swing toward the Ohio River boomtown of Cincinnati. The drive was partly through woods, partly through open country, and Irving noted "rich loamy soil—noble trees" in the central portion of the state. Columbus, the capital, was a "neat flourishing," though, like Cleveland, still a "small place." Five days after departing Cleveland, they arrived in Cincinnati.[8]

Irving wrote to his sister Catharine explaining why he preferred the open road to the city. He always traveled under his own name, and people in populated places made a scene once they identified him. Attending the theater his first night in Cincinnati, for example, he sat as the manager came onstage between acts and announced his presence. All eyes turned. "I remain as brief a time as possible in towns & cities, for the attentions I meet with are often rather irksome & embarrassing than otherwise," he vented. "[I] have induced my companions to hasten our departure, that I may escape all further importunities of the kind." He explained to his sister that he did not mean to be standoffish, but that it was hard to be famous: "I have a shrinking aversion from being made an object of personal notoriety that I cannot conquer." He had earlier understood the necessity of being gracious and accommodating when he sat through the public welcome at the City Hotel in his hometown of New York, back in May, but that was the exception.[9]

From Cincinnati, where hundreds were employed in the steamboat construction business, the four men boarded a medium-sized (130-ton) steamboat for the daylong transit to Louisville, where they transferred to the steamboat *Illinois*. Mechanical problems delayed their departure for St. Louis, and Irving ended up paying a call on the mayor of Louisville, who happened to be a former New York neighbor back when he and Brevoort were living together in a boardinghouse on lower Broadway, in 1811. Sometimes America could still feel like a fairly intimate place.

Kentucky reminded Irving that he was in the slave-owning South. He jotted in his journal in the language of the day: "Old negro Stewart very black with bright madrass handkerchef on head—large feet, gold ear rings—Shirt collar up to his ears"; "fat Negro wenches drying apples & peaches"; "chorus of Negro boat men"; and "old negro steward scolding young negros for lying." As they returned to the water, Irving described his fellow passengers, leaving out no antebellum stereotype: "From every part of Union—mercht from N York, smug, dapper a calculating Yankee. Reckless boastful Virginian." He was enlisted as the translator for a French-speaking Canadian, and had his first moonlight glimpse of the mighty—and muddy—Mississippi River.[10]

Parts of the journey demanded patience. To stay alert and occupied, Irving kept his journal. The young Count Pourtalès killed time by shooting ducks from the deck. Having run aground on the Ohio several times, they were a full week out of Louisville when they finally landed in St. Louis, even then thought of as gateway to the romantic West.

They did not arrive without incident, however. On their last night on the water, the sound of splintering wood informed them that their boat had been struck by a larger steamboat. In the confusion, female passengers broke out sobbing, until being assured that the damage would not sink them. Pourtalès explained: "Since our vessel had not suffered much damage, the crew merely cursed the pilot of the other boat with the strong oaths which usually season the speech of western Americans." In his journal, begun at St. Louis, he conveyed his energy: "I am about to die of excitement."[11]

They were there only a couple of days, but they were busy days. Irving and his companions met with the territorial governor, William Clark, of the famous pair of Lewis and Clark, at the governor's farm. Irving described the legendary explorer as a "fine healthy robust man," "frank and intelligent," with long, flowing gray hair. Clark arrived home on horseback, toting a rifle—the perfect picture of a western man. His guests dined alfresco in a fine orchard, attended by black servants; the meal consisted of "good, but rustic" fare: fried chicken, bison, and roast beef, with potatoes and tomatoes—the last being an uncommon ingredient in American cooking before the Civil War. Over the fireplace in Clark's cottage, Irving glimpsed a long-stemmed Indian pipe, or calumet, which he fancied. The West was still new to him.

The next day, Irving and his companions took a ten-mile detour south along the Mississippi to an army barracks, where he met a famous prisoner. Chief Black Hawk of the Sac tribe, a man in his late sixties, was considerably less formidable than his reputation painted him. The Black Hawk War had been sparked only months earlier, when the chief led his people back to their Rock Island, Illinois, lands, and contested their occupation by whites. For a time successful in resisting the Illinois militia (which then included a twenty-three-year-old Abraham Lincoln, who saw not a single Indian), Black Hawk was picked up on the western banks of the Mississippi, in Iowa, and brought south to the spot where Irving encountered him—a defenseless old Indian, his arms and ankles chained. It was only days after his capture when Irving stood face-to-face with the Sac chief.

Assessing him first as an anthropological specimen, the author listened to a doctor who was "given to craniology" describe how Black Hawk's small head and aquiline nose indicated "the organ of benevolence strongly developed." (This was meant as living proof of the "noble savage" parable.) Turning to the political implications of what he was seeing, Irving wrote to his sister Catharine: "I find it extremely difficult, even when so near the seat of action, to get at the right story of these feuds between the White & the red man and my sympathies go strongly with the latter." He could not have predicted that the following year the beaten old war chief would be paraded before urban crowds on the East Coast, and witness a balloon ascension and fireworks display over New York harbor. Black Hawk would meet there, too, an old acquaintance from John Jacob Astor's American Fur Company, one of the whites "who treats our people right."

The symbolic power of certain staged events tells us a great deal about the nation's past. The parallel histories of Indian America and white America, and the privileged position given to the latter group in teaching texts, is crystallized in Black Hawk's route, coinciding as it did with the reelected president's northern tour. Both were spectacles. And at a couple of points, the two spectacles poetically united. The old Indian brought out crowds no less impressive than those generated by the old Indian-fighter, President Jackson. When their tours intersected in Baltimore, the celebrated Sac chief received an audience with the tough-talking Jackson. The president made sure to remind him (should he need reminder) of the power of white America. The message was always the same: peace on Washington's terms, or war and destruction.

In dictating his autobiography, Black Hawk made it perfectly clear that no member of his nation had ever killed a white woman or child. After seeing the northeast, and being seen, the erstwhile prisoner returned to the north-central Mississippi region as a free, peace-loving man, and made his home in a lodge of peeled bark near the Iowa River.[12]

In his novels of the prior decade, *The Pioneers* and *The Last of the Mohicans,* James Fenimore Cooper, like Lydia Maria Child in *Hobomok,* had done much to make the American Indian a fetish. But the early 1830s were even more critical years in the literary construction of frontiersmen and noble savages. Questions loomed: Were Indians innocents to be molded into Christians, or innocents whose inherent decency would necessarily decay when exposed to Euro-American culture? That is, were their cultures so distinct that they could not thrive alongside whites under any circumstances? It is important to qualify that Irving's *Sketch Book* piece on Philip/Metacom does not project a future of cross-cultural harmony so much as it mines the sentimental drama in the Indian's fight to the death. Both Black Hawk's life as a celebrated captive and the dutiful Ellsworth investigative team that Irving tagged along with belonged to—what shall we call it?—the mockery of diplomacy that assured the western Indians of a future as relics and curiosities.[13]

Irving and his tourist friends left Black Hawk's side to gather supplies: wagons, tents, and horses. They then started across Missouri toward Indian country. They were accompanied by Antoine Deshetres, better known by his nickname "Tonish," who would achieve renown in Irving's *A Tour on the Prairies* similar to that of Mateo Ximenes in *Alhambra*. Irving referred to this "swarthy, meagre, wily," and irrepressible Creole, who was about forty years old, as "our little Frenchman." Prior to accepting employment with their party, Tonish had served as guide for the Seneca tribe (originally from the western part of New York State) in their migration to what would later be called Oklahoma.

Tonish performed as the expedition's cook, and a groom for the horses. He spoke not only French and English but also Osage, a Siouan dialect—and sometimes, one has the impression, he spoke all at once, for he spoke volubly. Irving joked that his true language was "Babylonish." The difference between Tonish and Mateo, besides their ages, was captured in the former's boast of having "a wife in every tribe." He could hardly open his mouth without "gasconading" about his various exploits as a hunter and warrior; his lies were so elaborate, and so meandering, that it became a game among the elders in the party to keep track of them. Tonish took a particular liking to Pourtalès, and promised to teach the impressionable young count how to catch a wild horse. Latrobe referred to Tonish as "our scape-grace," or rascal, probably thinking that the incorrigible Creole would only encourage Pourtalès to more outrageous actions than he would have undertaken on his own.[14]

At Independence, a common point of embarkation for pioneering parties, Irving paused again to write a letter to his sister Catharine for distribution among family members. Relating his tour on horseback through the sparsely populated country, he called Independence "a straggling frontier village," and predicted an even rougher time when he reached the hunting grounds of the

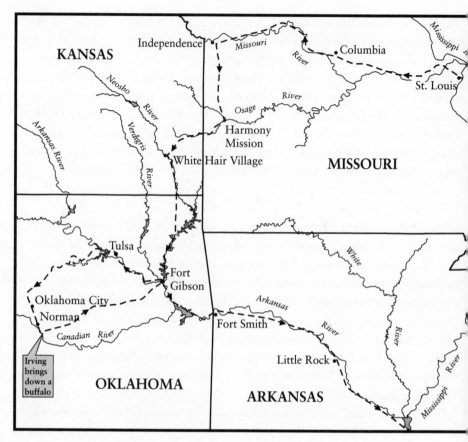

MAP 12.1   Irving's tour on the prairies, September–November 1832

Osage tribe, where he expected to chase buffalo—the oft-spoken goal of his trip. But then, incongruously, or perhaps revealing his age, Irving back-tracked, telling Catharine that he really yearned to be in New York, "to feel myself once more really at home."[15]

Pourtalès, too, awaited the wide unknown after "oceans of enameled greenery" that was Missouri. He had enjoyed their trek across the new state, and the tall, thick grass bursting with brilliant flowers. In Independence, he tells us, Irving shared his ambition to write *two* books about their adventure.[16] Anticipation mounted. Traveling south through eastern Kansas, and sleeping in bearskin, Irving made observations about the Osages and other tribes, whose character he wished to study. For, at Independence, he had met a missionary to the Arkansas Osages known as "White Hairs,"[17] who told him that southern tribes were "more shrewd and intelligent" than northern. At the

Harmony Mission, where they spent a full day, he learned that Osage children were skilled writers, and students of geography.

Day by day, Irving continued taking down stories about Indians and the western life. On October 3, he sketched the world that he woke to: "Beautiful morng Breakfast Scene—men round pans and Kettles—groups of little hounds looking on—growling & snapping of large dogs. . . . Indian gets up mounts his horse & away—Osages never eat early in the morning when travelling." October 4, at a White Hair village, where he visited a monument to a recently deceased Osage chief: "Mound on a hill surrounded by railing—three poles with flags—trophies—a scalp—scalping Knife &c—He had killed four Pawnees."[18]

Who were these Osages that so fascinated him? They had traditionally inhabited portions of the states of Missouri, Kansas, Arkansas, and Oklahoma, but had also ventured into Texas and Colorado. Throughout the eighteenth century, their warring abilities were everywhere touted. Jefferson recognized the Osages as the greatest potential adversary in the vast Louisiana Territory, one that required a tactful approach: "They are the great nation south of the Missouri," he wrote. "With [them] we must stand well, because in their quarter we are miserably weak." Previously, the Osages had pretty much had their way with the Spanish between the Missouri and Arkansas Rivers, preventing the sale of guns to rival tribes. But they were also avid traders, and had come to relish their commercial ties with the Americans, helped along by the Chouteau family, French businesspeople connected with the founding of St. Louis, who had long lived among them.[19]

One of Irving's party since St. Louis was Colonel Auguste Pierre Chouteau, a West Point graduate close to his own age, onetime aide to the controversial General James Wilkinson (Irving's "General Jacobus von Poffenburgh," in *Knickerbocker's History*), and son of the Jefferson administration's agent to the Osages. Colonel Chouteau did a good amount of business with the Osages, amassing bearskins, deerskins, beavers, and otters for shipment to New Orleans and beyond. "He speaks all imaginable languages," wrote Pourtalès, "with a command of their nuances and shades of meaning as varied as the colors of the rainbow." Pourtalès was impressionable, and tickled by it all. He had by now exchanged his dress for the local look, including leather shirt and moccasins: "I do not know how I shall become reaccustomed to civilization."[20]

The monotony of this stretch of prairie ended as they neared Fort Gibson, erected in 1824 at the confluence of the Arkansas, Verdigris, and Neosho Rivers. It was built, in part, because of Osage-Cherokee discord, the sort of problem Ellsworth was meant to evaluate for the U.S. government. Fort

Gibson was constructed of logs, plastered with mud, and already in disrepair when Irving visited. Rooms were dark, as windows were small.[21]

Here, on the morning of October 10, 1832, Irving met the inscrutable Sam Houston, a large, "well formed fresh looking man" wearing boots with brass spurs, who had the habit of expressing himself in a military mode. In 1829, he had resigned as governor of Tennessee and gone to live with his surrogate Cherokee family. He had established himself at the "Wigwam Neosho," a few miles above Fort Gibson, where he speculated in Osage land and hoped to engage in trade on a large scale as a semiofficial liaison between the Indians and his trusted friend and political mentor, Andrew Jackson. This tough-minded (some said vulgar) westerner would leave shortly for Texas, and greater renown; but for now, Governor Houston, as he was still known, was an entrepreneur, much as Chouteau was. Yet there was something larger than life about him. He was, as Irving noted in his journal, "given to grand eloquence."[22]

*   *

It is at this point in the journey that the adventure comprising *A Tour on the Prairies* really opens. The Ellsworth-Irving party arrived at Fort Gibson at a good time: Some army rangers had left not long before on an excursion into a part of the territory that the Pawnees used, and which no whites had yet, as Irving wrote, "penetrated." Two fleet and reliable Creek Indians were sent out to catch up with the rangers and instruct them that they should wait for Commissioner Ellsworth and Irving to join them.

October 11, 1832. In his published text, Irving contrasts the Creeks with the Osages, the former "gaily dressed . . . in calico hunting-shirts of various brilliant colors, decorated with bright fringes"; the latter "stately fellows; stern and simple in garb and aspect . . . and their poverty prevents their indulging in much luxury of apparel." Osages had "fine Roman countenances"—a reminder of the simply formed warrior Jackson?—"and broad deep chests; and as they generally wore their blankets wrapped round their loins, so as to leave the bust and arms bare, they looked like so many noble bronze figures." He wants to say that the Creeks are the more fanciful dressers but that he prefers the poorer Osages, in whom he detects stoic nobility.[23]

In fact, though, the descriptive Irving was a standoffish observer in comparison to the young Pourtalès, who never published but left an impulsive vignette of what it meant to strike up an instant friendship with an Osage. He explains in his journal that "Beautiful Bird" (*Bel Oiseau* to the French) was sixty years old, and like many of the Osages, eager to forge warm relations with the whites. The two of them communicated at length "in pantomime Osage," and exchanged gifts: a calumet pipe for a powder horn. Then, writes the Swiss count, "we left each other sworn to friendship, probably only to meet again in the next world."

The animated Pourtalès, constantly amazed at the cordiality of the Osages, had goals somewhat at variance from his fellow travelers. He was in search of a "temporary" Indian wife, having heard that one could be easily bargained for. He also was quick to make fun of Commissioner Ellsworth, who could not make sense of cultures that were foreign to his staid New England primness, and who pronounced among the Osages

> with patriarchal simplicity, and with the good-fellowship of the Quakers that Uncle Sam had sent him to get them to shake hands with their enemies the Pawnees. He asked them with the same anodyne unctuousness not to kill the Pawnees. Thereupon the young, the old, the male, and the female Osages burst into laughter. The Lord Commissioner took this as a sign of approbation and visible emotion.

Irving, it seems, stood somewhere in between Ellsworth and Pourtalès, talkative and companionable, but more reserved before the Indians. Perhaps not perceiving, or perhaps to avoid embarrassing Ellsworth in his published text, Irving wrote of the commissioner's impromptu speech that it "seemed to have a most pacifying effect upon the multitude."[24]

It was fifty miles through unpoliced Indian country to the spot where the larger party of forward rangers awaited them. For defensive purposes, they rode one after another, Indian-style, "leaving but one narrow well trampled track to mark their course" so as to conceal their real number. They gazed fearfully into the distance as they followed the Trail of the Osage Hunters until they finally met up with the rangers, whose commander, Captain Jesse Bean, led them on a bee hunt. The effusive Tonish, meanwhile, rolled up his sleeves to cook wild turkey, no doubt accented with honey dug from the hollow of a tree. They were in the neighborhood of modern Tulsa, a place as yet empty of inhabitants.[25]

After the bee hunt, Irving encountered "a scene of the greatest hilarity" back in camp, where some of the rangers were having a shooting contest, while others wrestled and played games. Their youth and vigor stimulated his pen, and gave him another opportunity to state his preference for American over European life:

I can conceive nothing more likely to set the youthful blood into a flow than a wild wood life of the kind and the range of a magnificent wilderness abounding with game and fruitful of adventure. We send our youth abroad to grow luxurious and effeminate in Europe; it appears to me that a previous tour on the prairies would be more likely to produce that manliness, simplicity and self dependence most in unison with our political institutions.[26]

To cap off the evening's entertainment, Pourtalès got fed up with a plaintive owl, and shot it with his rifle. It fell right on Irving's tent.[27]

The next morning, the bugle sounded early, and Tonish prepared venison fritters, "fried in the fat of salt pork," along with Turkish coffee. This softened Ellsworth's normally critical pose, and he complimented Tonish broadly: "A good cook—a fine hunter—a stranger to fear, and as fleet as a deer." Ellsworth could not bear coffee, or black tea, due to his nerves, so Tonish began collecting goldenrod. Both Ellsworth and Irving found the plant stimulating—"in large quantities it is laxative." Irving asked to have some sent to New York, and Pourtalès did likewise for Switzerland.[28]

Ahead lay precipitous hills. The captain and others stretched out on the grass, Irving tells us, and consulted their map of the frontier. An experienced Osage hunter was called over to verify their course. Then the entire company moved out, forming "a line of upwards of half a mile in length." Finding the banks too steep where they had originally planned to cross the Arkansas River, they plunged into dense forest for a time until they could locate a fordable spot. Supplies were towed, Indian-style, on a dried buffalo-skin minibarge. When Irving himself was placed on top of a pile of luggage and sent across the Arkansas in this way, he was inspired to write, with obvious reference to his early days as a burlesque author: "It appeared to me pretty much like the wise men of Gotham who went to sea in a bowl." When Irving had crossed successfully, Ellsworth was taken over on the same conveyance.[29]

Scenery brightened the trek. Irving took in an "undulating country, of 'oak openings' where the eye stretched at times over wide tracks of hill and dale"; there was "a beautiful peninsula made by the windings and doublings of a deep, clear and almost motionless brook"; a smoky haze that "tempered the brightness of the sunshine into a golden tint"; and many more such descriptions. Irving liked to reshape the physical world at every turn, to "build castles in the clouds," as he put it. He reveled, too, in "rural repose," favoring imagery that gave the American prairie greater promise than it had before. It seems hardly a coincidence that William Cullen Bryant echoed Irving's praise for the prairie that same year, with these nationalistic lines:

There are the Gardens of the Desert, these
The unshorn fields, boundless and beautiful,
For which the speech of England has no name.

Elevating the picturesque was characteristic of the Jacksonian moment.[30]

When he ran out of description, Irving listened to the men tell stories of earlier Indian encounters. Tonish, meanwhile, took advantage of some green recruits and sounded the "oracle" among them, claiming to know of Pawnees who could match any white marksman with their deadly bows and arrows. As Irving retells it in *Tour,* "the Pawnee, according to Tonish, could shoot with unerring aim three hundred yards, and send his arrow clean through and through a buffalo; nay he had known a Pawnee shaft pass through one buffalo and wound another."[31]

Anticipation intensified as they approached Indian hunting grounds. Latrobe wrote: "As to the Buffalo, our eagerness to fall in with him increased day by day."[32] If not, there was the wild horse—remnants, Irving presumed, of the Andalusian breed brought over by Spanish discoverers. And then someone cried out, "Buffalo!" as three or four of the rugged creatures pulled within view of Irving's party. Captain Jesse Bean and his hunters gave chase across the parched landscape, but the animals escaped. The following morning, one ranger had better luck, and returned to camp with a nice slab of buffalo draped across his horse. But it was not the same as being there.

There was a momentous false alarm in the midst of all this, an incident that Irving left out of his accounts. When one of their party spotted some Pawnees, the news spread through camp that there might be five hundred of them, poised to attack at any moment. Shots were heard over the next hill, and someone said that several of the rangers had been killed already. Panic ensued. "Oh! the confusion," Ellsworth recorded. "Mr. Irving could only find one *Leggin,* and he was calling through the camp loud, and louder still, for his odd leggin, of mighty little consequence in a battle—He was as *pale* as could be, and much terrified." Ellsworth, who was writing to his wife, explained how calm and determined he himself had remained, thus implying that the famous literary adventurer Washington Irving was really a coward. Instead of preparing to take part in his own defense, all Irving could think about was the lost half of a pair of leggings. Whether Ellsworth was telling the truth or embellishing, it turned out that a couple of hatless rangers, hunting for game, had been mistaken for five hundred hostile Indians.[33]

A couple of days passed. Every mounted man was on the lookout. The captain was the next to wound a buffalo. (Latrobe hailed Jesse Bean as one of the best shots on the expedition.) Irving was armed with a couple of single-shot pistols, which was all he had been issued, and found a perch where he quite nearly finished off the captain's quarry; but then the wounded bull "plunged forward, dashing and crashing along with neck or nothing fury, where it would have been madness to follow him." Still no luck.

Just then, Irving was treated to a sublime experience. Ascending a hill, he surprised a wild black mare and ceased for the moment to fixate on buffalo:

> At sight of me she started back, then turning, swept at full speed down into the valley and up the opposite hill, with flowing mane and tail and action free as air. I gazed after her as long as she was in sight, and breathed a wish that so glorious an animal might never come under the degrading thralldom of whip and curb.

Faced with this perception of the wonder of nature, our hero seemed content to let others seek trophies.[34]

It was over two subsequent days, October 29–30, outside of present-day Norman, that, according to Latrobe's account, the tourists found the adventure they had come seeking. The rangers had split into small groups, and Irving's group happened to go in a likely direction. He constructs his story with a different kind of deliberation now—with a reflective wisdom, with remove, cautioning the reader who might think buffalo hunting merely a race over level land that hurtling across the prairie entails negotiation around rifts and ravines, while avoiding the burrows of small animals. And then he proceeds to narrate the climax of his time as a buffalo hunter: Slowly, and with a careful circumvention, his team had gained on a scattered herd. Irving takes the first shot—both pistols miss. Latrobe, his horse less fleet, had lost some ground, but he pulls up, aims his double-barreled gun, and brings his bull to the ground. Irving borrows Latrobe's weapon and charges after the thundering herd. He gets close enough, fires, and in that split second equals Latrobe's achievement.

And then Irving has to contend with his conscience, for the animal he has shot is still alive and in great pain. He approaches it, primes one of his pistols, and contemplates the final act—which gives him pause: "To inflict a wound thus in cool blood I found a totally different thing from firing in the heat of the chase." But he does so, and a more experienced huntsman comes over and slices off the buffalo's tongue, presenting it to Irving as a trophy of the hunt.

The young and impetuous Pourtalès, meanwhile, had kept on charging after buffalo on his own, refusing to stop until he had bagged one. Occasional shots rang out, but he and the retreating herd he was pursuing finally disappeared into the horizontal distance. Irving and Latrobe grew anxious for his safety, but could do little. In the twilight, buglers sounded their notes, hoping to guide Pourtalès back to camp. Eight buffaloes had been killed that day, and the campfires were roasting them.

During the night, wolves were attracted to the carcasses, and melancholy howlings overtook the midnight air. Still no sign of Pourtalès. By morning, worries for the Swiss adventurer mounted. He was, as Irving wrote, "liable to fall into the hands of some lurking or straggling party of savages." A dozen rangers set out to look for him, and Irving went along. At one point, a lone horseman was sighted on a distant hill, and one of the searchers cried out, "It is the Count!" But he was mistaken. A second horseman appeared beside the first, and they were presumed Pawnee scouts, causing even greater worry that their comrade had fallen into the hands of hostile forces. Suddenly, Pourtalès appeared from another direction, shouting out to the search party. He had indeed become disoriented under a darkening sky, and had spent the night in a tree, nestled between forked branches in his comfortable saddle. Fully expecting to be haunted during his lonesome night on the prairie, he somehow slept until sunrise, dreaming of Switzerland. Irving ends the chapter with a single line: "So closed the events of our haphazard buffalo hunt."[35]

After this, they headed back east in the direction of Fort Gibson. Several days of cloudy and windy weather caused them to pick up their pace; after "weary wayfaring," as Irving puts it, and pangs of hunger, they at last sighted the colorful Creeks, and realized that they were close to base. For Irving, it would be a relief to exchange his traveling pencil for a solid table and pen and ink at Fort Gibson. Yet, as he reports in the pages of *Tour*, "having been accustomed to sleep in the open air, the confinement of a chamber was, in some respects, irksome."[36]

☆   ☆

It is not noted in *A Tour on the Prairies*, but Washington Irving served as secretary for the expedition. The colonel who was selected to assist Commissioner Henry Ellsworth did not arrive at Fort Gibson on time, and so Ellsworth made an ad hoc appointment. Then, after the monthlong mission ended, he indicated to Secretary of War Lewis Cass that Irving was uninterested in further federal appointment—at least, nothing that "would detain him from the literary pursuits." And although he did not expect to be paid for his official duties, Irving said that he would accept government reimbursement for the cost of his horse.[37]

Ellsworth had spent a good many weeks traveling with the author. They had exchanged opinions on various subjects. Irving revealed, for instance, how fame disturbed him, how embarrassed he became when put on public display, as when Oxford had conferred an honorary law degree on him and he had to listen to a half hour of greetings and praises in Latin, and shouts of *"Sketch Book!"* and *"Knickerbocker!"* from the appreciative crowd. Writing to his wife, Ellsworth made observations about Irving's finances and personal habits—some of which he seems to have coaxed out of Irving during long days spent in close quarters. He had asked Irving point blank just how much money he was earning as a professional writer, and Irving detailed what Murray and his American publishers had paid him in advance of publication for copyright authority in several instances. Irving said he had, at this point, from $25,000 to $30,000 in ready cash, which made him financially comfortable. "He is a batchelor and wants no money," wrote Ellsworth, "but for his relatives several of whom are dependent on him—His affections are strong for his family connections." He could not read letters from his sister Catharine "without tears."

As to Irving's personal habits, Ellsworth's remarks are again noteworthy. In a time when members of the same sex still had the option to "bundle" in sleep without embarrassment—to share a bed or a tight blanket for warmth through the night—Irving preferred to sleep apart, even when they lodged in a room together that had only one bed. Ellsworth stated that his traveling companion had a particular concern with cleanliness: He shaved every day, changed his clothing more often than most, and was what we today call a "neat freak." In the commissioner's words: "Before he sits down to write his sketches or other works, he always washes himself up nice, and with everything clean on him and around him, he says his ideas flow properly—but when he is dirty, the power of association dries up every literary pore."[38]

Irving was finished with the prairie. "We led a complete hunters life, subsisting upon the produce of the chase," he wrote to Catharine on November 16, from southeastern Arkansas, at the junction of the Arkansas and Mississippi Rivers. Out in the wild, he had had plenty of time to ruminate about the future. He wanted a home. Responding to something in a letter he had received from Catharine at Fort Gibson, he said that he wished to purchase a piece of land in Tarrytown, adjacent to that owned by his nephew Oscar, his late brother William's thirty-two-year-old son. It had a "little cottage" on it, and overlooked the Hudson. This is the first indication of his plan to acquire "Wolfert's Roost," the future Sunnyside, which he had first spied so many years before when hiking along the Hudson with Jim Paulding. The place would have to be bought from "the Dutchman," as Irving called its present owner. "I am willing to pay a little unreasonably for it," he wrote, betraying his eagerness.[39]

Beginning the long journey home, he went by steamboat down the Mississippi to Vicksburg, where the vessel paused overnight. Though shy of publicity, as he so often claimed, Irving allowed the locals to corral him into a late evening "Wine Party." Back on board, he steamed on to New Orleans, "one of the most motley and amusing places in the United States," he commented in a letter to Peter, with reference to its mixed flavor of French, Spanish, and Indian cultures. The remainder of his route north was overland, by mail stage, and apparently bumpy and unremarkable. He passed through Alabama, Georgia, and the Carolinas, finally arriving in Washington, D.C.

There, he took comfortable quarters near the McLane family, and ate his meals at their home—not unlike his custom in Dresden with the Fosters. He intended to stay in town just a few days, but ended up passing the entire winter of 1832–1833 in the nation's capital, attending a number of the debates in Congress. It was rumored, meanwhile, that he was involved with the treasury secretary's daughter Rebecca. It was untrue.

One source of that rumor was Baltimore's John Pendleton Kennedy, the author of a popular novel that any discriminating reader could recognize as a tribute to Irving's style. *Swallow Barn* has been described by many as a Virginia version of *Bracebridge Hall*, portraying the southern gentleman as Irving had the English gentleman. It was published in May 1832, just as Irving arrived home, and the two authors became friends during Irving's Washington winter. Kennedy was a dozen years Irving's junior, and his genial personality matched Irving's; he, too, wove in and out of the worlds of business and politics, but preferred the literary life to all else. In attempting to find Kennedy a London publisher, Irving touted him as "a particular friend" and "one of the most desireable authors to be secured in this country."[40]

While making new friends, Irving and his old gang stayed close—Verplanck, for one, was in Congress. The former Lads of Kilkenny knew they could always appeal to one another, and so it was no burden to Irving when he received a "redhot letter" from his "warmhearted friend" Sam Swartwout that concerned fears for Paulding's tenure in office as navy agent in New York. Irving took the case first to Martin Van Buren, and then, just after New Year's Day, 1833, visited with President Jackson to iron out what proved to be a false rumor concerning Paulding's refusal to cough up money for a Jacksonian cause. Reassuring Paulding that his job was safe, Irving reiterated his sentiments about the president: "The more I see of this old cock of the woods, the more I relish his game qualities." He took the opportunity to quash that other rumor, telling Gouverneur Kemble that no, he was not going to marry Rebecca McLane: "I thought that such an ancient gentleman as myself might play the part of uncle to a young belle, without being suspected of being her beau." She would go on to marry one of the late Alexander Hamilton's sons.[41]

So long professing a lack of passion for politics, Irving finally admitted to his brother Peter in the early spring of 1833 that he had become addicted to Capitol Hill. "I heard almost every speech, good and bad, and did not lose a word of any of the best." This was the age of oratory, and none could top Daniel Webster of Massachusetts, Henry Clay of Kentucky, and John C. Calhoun of South Carolina, collectively known as "the Great Triumvirate." The related issues of a protectionist tariff and South Carolina's threat to nullify an act of Congress inspired some of the finest speechmaking of the antebellum decades. The president threatened South Carolina, Calhoun's state (as well as the state in which he himself was born), with a federal invasion—an armed takeover. Irving embraced Jackson's tough-talking stand against disunion.[42]

By the end of March 1833, Irving was back in Manhattan, arriving in town only to find that more honors awaited him. A letter from President Josiah Quincy of Harvard, a relative of the Adamses, the former mayor of Boston, and before that a member of Congress, informed him that during his romp through Indian country he had been awarded an honorary doctorate of laws from Harvard. Living for a time at Ebenezer's, he was able to enjoy family again; but, even so, Irving proved he could not stay put for long. He embarked on another southern tour, accompanied this time by the son and namesake of his brother the judge, John T. Irving.[43]

With his knack for making himself part of living history, Washington Irving arrived in Fredericksburg, Virginia, just after President Jackson had been accosted by a navy lieutenant whom he had ordered dismissed from the service for theft. The president was on a steamboat, reading a newspaper and smoking his pipe, when the man entered and said, "You have injured me," then slapped him in the face. The old frontier duelist, now infirm and unable to stand without pain, bled from his cheek. Irving met up with the injured party at Fredericksburg, and reported to Peter: "I saw a good deal of the president that evening, and the next morning. The old gentleman was still highly exasperated. . . . It is a brutal transaction, which I cannot think of without indignation, mingled with a feeling of almost despair, that our national character should receive such crippling wounds from the hands of our own citizens." Irving was feeling an intense loyalty to Andrew Jackson, and a sense of being personally bound to the fate of Jackson's America. From Fredericksburg, he made a brief stop in Charlottesville, at the University of Virginia, and returned to New York in time to be part of Jackson's postinauguration visit to the city. Van Buren was there, and so was McLane—Irving's key associates in the administration. Old Hickory's popularity could be read on the faces of the crowd that lined Broadway to cheer him. And Irving considered himself part of the inner circle.[44]

He was at nephew Oscar's place below Tarrytown in July, and at Saratoga Springs after that, taking the healing waters and socializing. Heading back to Manhattan, he stopped at the home of his old friend Knickerbocker—the "real," now retired, ex-Congressman Herman Knickerbocker—outside Albany. "He received me with open arms," Irving wrote to Peter. Then, for half of September, Irving took to the road with Martin Van Buren, accompanying the vice president to his hometown of Kinderhook and beyond. At Kinderhook, the nostalgic Irving saw another old acquaintance, the schoolteacher Jesse Merwin, whom he had spent time with in 1809 and later transformed into Ichabod Crane.

Van Buren and Irving traveled comfortably in an open carriage, conscious that this was to be enjoyed as a thoroughly Knickerbocker excursion: to Rip's Catskills, Poughkeepsie, and south along the west bank of the Hudson to Tappan, where in October 1780, under orders from George Washington, the wartime spy John André was hanged, and where now, Irving noted in his journal of the trip, there were "women with Dutch Sun bonnets—people talk dutch." From Tappan, they continued on to Hackensack and to good old Communipaw. Then, in early October, Irving made "a rapid move"—his words—and returned to Washington; there he would advise McLane on a course of action once the treasury secretary resolved to leave the administration in protest against the combative president's imprudent bank policy. Jackson was destined for a grueling second term. He figured he required a cabinet that would not disagree with him.

Irving had placed himself squarely in the middle of these negotiations, taking a "family dinner" with President Jackson, worrying about the old man's health, and entreating Van Buren to "be at his elbow" as a restorative. Though he professed to Van Buren that he wanted to stay out of politics and "amuse" himself again with "literary occupations," the one thing Irving was not doing in these months was writing anything of consequence, or even preparing his western travel notes for publication.[45]

He finally began to take up that project on his return from Washington in the final weeks of 1833. It would be a year, however, before he was ready to release *A Tour on the Prairies*, his first book since sailing from Europe. In the interim, his nephew John T. Irving, Jr., had completed his own tour of the West—to Pawnee country, north of the Ellsworth-Irving expedition. Eventually, uncle and nephew would both have books out on similar subjects, John's to be titled *Indian Sketches*.

More Americentric literature was emerging from Irving's circle. That same year, 1835, Charles Fenno Hoffman would publish *A Winter in the West*. He was not just any writer to Irving, but the son of Josiah Ogden and Maria Fenno Hoffman, in his cradle while Irving was most often at the Hoffman home reading to the ill-fated Matilda. New Yorkers now recognized Hoffman as a newspaperman (writing for the *New York American*) and a contending Knickerbocker poet and author.[46]

★   ★

Once more, Irving settled in at Ebenezer's place near the Battery. One of his nieces wrote an absent brother that "Uncle Washington has got us in the habit of dancing every evening." As he was polishing off *A Tour on the Prairies*, he received a curious offer from John Jacob Astor. It made him think of his thirty-one-year-old widower nephew, Pierre Munro Irving, whose visit to him in Madrid some years back had produced feelings of attachment.

Pierre was at this moment attempting a new life in Jacksonville, Illinois. William Cullen Bryant had visited a year before Pierre moved there, and found it depressing. But the town was growing, and already had a small college. A new generation's rising stars thought Jacksonville a town with a bright future. Not only Pierre, but also another promising attorney, the future presidential hopeful Stephen A. Douglas, practiced there. Pierre had purchased a number of town lots and was dabbling in land speculation. He also participated in various community activities—which usually involved dancing and drinking. He protested one "abomination" of the frontier life: the religious revival, which he saw as trickery, "evil . . . in the garb of good." Like his uncle, he was tolerant of most forms of religion, but reacted against that which demanded the surrender of reason.[47]

In the early autumn of 1834, Pierre received a letter from his uncle informing him that John Jacob Astor wished to commission a history of his disbanded Pacific Coast settlement of Astoria. The curmudgeonly Astor, now in his seventies, wanted to shape his legacy. Since many of the early leaders of the Oregon venture had kept diaries, there was ample material on which to draw. "The old gentleman has applied to me repeatedly," Irving wrote to Pierre, "offering . . . to pay liberally for time and trouble. . . . I am so much engrossed with other plans, that I have not time for the examination of papers, the digesting of various materials, etc." Believing his nephew might be amenable to reconsidering his own western settlement plan, Irving suggested to Astor that they invite Pierre back to New York to assist. "The old gentleman caught at the idea," promising Pierre employment for at least a year. Astor was "an early friend of your father [William], for whose memory he retains high regard," Irving reminded his nephew; "and he has always been on terms of intimacy with your uncle Peter and myself."[48]

Pierre gave his uncle an encouraging response. He knew that in the 1790s, before entering politics, his late father had opened his career in business in the fur trade of the Mohawk region of New York State, just when Astor was amassing his fortune and conceiving his American Fur Company. Irving followed up: "I have since had a definite conversation with Mr. Astor, and fixed your compensation at *three thousand* dollars." This was decidedly more than a Jacksonville, Illinois, lawyer was likely to earn in a year, and a third more than Pierre had asked for. Still, the young man figured on returning to Illinois after his year with Astor was up to pursue further speculation in western lands.

Astor's only demand was that the accomplished Washington Irving put his "finishing hand" on the book. This would make it a true collaboration between uncle and nephew. Lest his nephew remain under any misapprehension, Irving clarified that Pierre was to prepare the Astoria book in crude form only. As a work for hire, "it is a *sine qua non* with Mr. Astor that my name should be to the work." Once he had compiled the research, Irving would take over, "take it in hand, and prepare it for the press." Finally, it was agreed that Pierre would live with Astor at his residence in Manhattan, where he would enjoy as well the company of Fitz-Greene Halleck—"a very pleasant companion," Irving assured—the esteemed poet who had, by then, served as Astor's private secretary for over a year.[49]

As the year 1834 came to a close, Washington Irving had irons in the fire. He had done a favor for a talented nephew who had suffered setbacks; and *A Tour on the Prairies* was in the hands of two publishers with whom he had a track record. They were Carey, Lea, and Blanchard in Philadelphia and John Murray—a man he had thought he was finished with—in London. Through the intercession of his London agent, Thomas Aspinwall, Irving had struck a bargain with a newly receptive Murray, who agreed to bring out Irving's reminiscences of Sir Walter Scott and Lord Byron (*Abbotsford* and *Newstead Abbey*), along with *Tour*, under the group title *The Crayon Miscellany*. The title page bore the words "by the AUTHOR of the SKETCH BOOK." Murray paid £400 for *Tour* alone, an equal sum for the pair of *Abbotsford* and

Newstead Abbey, and saw fit to publish a British edition of John T. Irving's *Indian Sketches.* A year later, he would add the less original *Legends of the Conquest of Spain* to the mix, bringing *The Crayon Miscellany* to three volumes. Meanwhile, the Philadelphia firm agreed to pay Irving $1,500 for a first run of five thousand copies of *Tour,* and $300 for each additional thousand copies printed. *A Tour on the Prairies* would remain in print throughout the nineteenth century.

Over the years, the firm of Murray paid Irving nearly £10,000 for copyrights, the most profitable of which, for Irving, was his biography of Columbus. Any unpleasantness that remained in Irving's thoughts of the businessman he had once called "the Prince of Booksellers" was balanced by memories of their shared successes. Owing to Murray's magnetic power, Irving had become the darling of London's literary elite at a time when British poets and authors were at the height of their popularity in America. Irving never minimized the impact of that fact on the direction of his career.

Resettled in America, he had only so many notes from his years abroad that remained unpublished and could be reworked. Despite his unexpected involvement in affairs of state—Jacksonian Democrats even urged him to run for a seat in Congress in 1834, which Irving, of course, refused—President Jackson's intimate no longer had his mind on politics. He would now be looking for more American subjects to interest his pen. Yet, as odd as it sounds, at the age of fifty-one, Washington Irving still had not found himself a permanent home anywhere.[50]

CHAPTER 13

Sunnyside

1835–1845

I can live cheaper here than else where, and benefit my "Kith and Kin" into the bargain.

—Washington Irving, from Sunnyside, 1838[1]

I really believe that when I die I shall haunt it: but it will be as a good spirit, that no one needs be affraid of.

—Washington Irving, on Sunnyside, 1843

IN THE EARLY SPRING OF 1835, PIERRE WAS HARD AT work at Astor's Broadway mansion and, by his own account, eating the millionaire's oysters and drinking his champagne. His uncle, meanwhile, was realizing a vision. It had been two years since he wrote to his sister from Arkansas that he had his mind's eye set on a run-down cottage near the Tarrytown property of Pierre's older brother Oscar. "Uncle Washington . . . has a good right to spend his money on one hobby or another, and I expect he will find great amusement in improving the place," the author's business-minded brother Ebenezer told his son William.

Washington Irving now made the purchase of close to fifteen acres, including that stone house in the old Dutch style, which had once belonged to Wolfert Eckert, an advisor to Peter Stuyvesant. From Eckert it had descended to Jacob Van Tassel, namesake of the well-to-do family in "The Legend of Sleepy Hollow." Its new owner was perfectly content to call the place "the Roost" (i.e., Wolfert's Roost) for a few years, when the expanded residence became known as "Sunnyside."[2]

Names mattered to Irving, the storyteller, as did genealogy. Without these, he could not so easily have accomplished a reconstitution of the past to serve and entertain the present. So it matters that the house he bought was in the Van Tassell family until 1802, when the surrounding 150 acres were deeded to the Ferris family. Benson Ferris was the clerk of the Old Dutch Church, which had existed in the neighborhood since 1685 or thereabouts, and Ferris, in turn, was the husband of Maria Acker, a direct descendent of Wolfert Eckert.

Here was a country setting, where the old names still had meaning. To go back even further, the name "Tarrytown" may have derived from a common surname on early Long Island, Tarry, rather than being the more colorful notion of a place where a traveler might "tarry." Earlier than that, the area was inhabited by an Algonquian people related to the Mohicans, called Weekquaesqueeks (Anglicized as "Wickers Creeks"). In 1835, when Irving acquired his retirement home, Tarrytown was not yet an incorporated village, but belonged to the township of Greenburgh.[3]

Irving's place, three miles south of historic Tarrytown, was a secluded site, and, needless to say, there was as yet no village of Irvington either. He described it to Peter in mid-1835 as "a beautiful spot, capable of being made a little paradise." He elaborated: "I have had an architect up there, and shall build upon the old mansion this summer. My idea is to make a little nookery somewhat in the Dutch style, quaint, but unpretending. It will be of stone." He expected his retreat to be not only a peaceful place in the country where he could write, but also a place where Ebenezer and his large family could "ruralize during the pleasant season of the year."[4]

All in all, it was a promising season for Irving. Having apparently undergone a health crisis, Henry Brevoort was back New York following a stay in Europe, "regaining his good looks and good condition rapidly." Peter had finally expressed his intention of returning home as soon as his erratic health stabilized long enough to make a sea voyage possible. There would be room for him in Tarrytown, less than twenty-five miles north of the city as the Hudson flowed.[5]

Irving also kept up his correspondence with his new friend in Baltimore, the writer John P. Kennedy, delighting in the release of his *Horseshoe Robinson*, a novel of the American Revolution that takes place, as Kennedy's writing typically does, in the South. Receiving an advance copy, Irving did not realize that he was supposed to keep mum about the contents. "I was so tickled with some parts of it," he gleefully reported to the author, "that I could not for the life of me help reading them to some of my cronies among the brokers and jobbers of Wall Street." Living at Ebenezer's, practically around the corner from the financial exchange, he had returned to investing.[6]

Kennedy's publisher was Irving's, the increasingly influential Carey, Lea & Blanchard. Though he was already wealthy and did not have to rely on writing to supplement an income, *Horseshoe Robinson* would prove his best-selling book. In fact, the generous Kennedy had recently begun to patronize a penniless former West Point cadet named Edgar Allan Poe. The son of a Baltimorean, Poe had been drifting from place to place, and vocation to vocation, during an unstable youth, until Kennedy recognized his talent and gave his work public recognition. He would shortly secure Poe a position at the *Southern Literary Messenger* in Richmond, where the poet would open a notorious career as a reviewer, attacking men of letters—including a few whom Irving wished to promote, such as Longfellow and Halleck. Poe made occasional criticisms of Irving himself, at first hailing the appearance of *A Tour on the Prairies*—"A book from the pen of Washington Irving, is a *morceau*, which will always be eagerly sought after"—before wearying of the "monotony" of the literary journey and nitpicking about Irving's style. Only Kennedy, it seemed, was completely immune to his barbs. Poe had the Byronic tendency to criticize roundly and personally, though he was thin-skinned with regard to criticism of his own work. None of this would interfere with the growing friendship between Kennedy and Irving, and in their few personal encounters later on, Irving always maintained a cordial posture with regard to Poe.[7]

The prickly Poe notwithstanding, Irving must have been pleased overall by the reviews of *A Tour on the Prairies*, praised for its narrative style and realism. The *North American Review* cooed: "It is a sort of sentimental journey." The *Western Monthly Magazine* did a roundup of his career, explaining why it was that Irving never disappointed: His *Columbus* would always appeal to the "scholar and statesman," and his humor and fiction entertained "the great mass of English readers." His writing combined "beauty" and "decorum" with fabulous invention—classic American characters who were unforgettable: "Rip Van Winkle, Ichabod Crane, and the Little Gentleman in Black, belong to American literature and to Washington Irving." Delighting in the novelty of *A Tour on the Prairies*, the reviewer congratulated Irving for his deliberative restraint and self-respect: "Mr. Irving has not been ashamed of his country, or of his mother tongue, and has not been seduced by bad models, or deluded by the popularity which his genius gained for him in the fashionable circles of London." At this moment, Washington Irving's popularity (and prospects) appeared more secure than at any previous time in his life.[8]

★　★

In August 1835, he took up residence at Astor's summer retreat at Hellgate, on the opposite shore of the East River from Manhattan, in modern (what else would it be called?) Astoria, Queens. Here, along with Pierre and fellow lodger Fitz-Greene Halleck, he gazed out at the rumbling waters, worked with Pierre's notes, and hammered out *Astoria*. He called the temporary quarters, not surprisingly, "a bachelor resort." The poet Halleck was not writing much, primarily because Astor, who was investing more than $100,000 in New York real estate annually and operating as a private banker, kept him busy. Irving reported him gone most days, and home evenings.[9]

With few distractions, the two Irvings made good progress on their collaborative venture. In periodic reports to Peter, Washington was always upbeat about the work. Beginning in April 1835: "Pierre Munroe is busily engaged gathering together materials. . . . I have not taken hold of the subject yet, but I have no doubt I shall be able to make it a rich piece of mosaic." In May: "I am now engaged in the work on the subject of Mr. Astor's great enterprise; and I am much mistaken if I do not make it a very rich, curious, and unique work." In October: "I finished my first draught of the Astor work [after] a long and successful fit of writing. I have much yet to do to it, but it will be merely in the way of enriching it by personal anecdotes. . . . I feel sanguine as to the work proving interesting to the general reader." Of those who visited the home of John Jacob Astor during this period, Irving took a special interest in Captain Benjamin Bonneville of the U.S. Army, the son of a French-born New Yorker, who, Irving would later write, "strangely ingrafted the trapper and hunter upon the soldier." Bonneville was just back from three years in the Rocky Mountains; his expeditions would result in Irving's next western-oriented narrative after *Astoria*.[10]

Work at the future Sunnyside proceeded apace. Irving figured he would pay for improvements on the house by writing "a legend or two about it." A stone was laid in, of Irving's design, over the entrance door to Wolfert's Roost, marking the date of its origin, 1656; his own name was added to the stone: "Washington Irving / anno 1835." He sketched the design elements he was intent on seeing included, and attended to the masonry, windowpanes, recessed rooms, and wallpapering. He told Peter that he was building him "a delightful little nest . . . on the banks of the Hudson," and a private room where he could take his meals, if he chose, and where no one would disturb him. One is led to think that Peter had privacy issues, just as Washington required a clean room and a clean body when he worked.[11]

Anticipating Peter's return home after twenty-seven years abroad, Irving meant to completely spoil his brother, now sixty-three and the eldest of the six surviving Irving siblings. He adored the generous, practical, hardworking

Ebenezer, who continued to handle many of the details in Washington's relations with American publishers. But he remained most intimate with the less fortunate Peter, whose life had become one of hesitation and disappointment. His downturn occurred, curiously enough, right at the moment his younger brother struck literary gold with *Knickerbocker's History,* a project they had begun in tandem. Before *Jonathan Oldstyle,* Peter was the Irving brother whom insiders expected to succeed in the world of literature. No less a judge than the triumphant New York playwright William Dunlap had termed him "a gentleman of the first talents."[12]

The chronically unhealthy Peter Irving did not start a family, and he did not attain financial security, but he never resented his brother's success. He, more than anyone else, was present to witness his younger brother's toil. For the better part of seventeen years, while Washington was abroad, Peter remained by his side as an informal adviser, when not actually assisting in research.

December 1835 found Washington at Hellgate with Pierre, who had spent the autumn recovering from a mild case of smallpox, and whose portion of the work on *Astoria* was essentially done. Still unpaid and too proud to ask for an advance, Pierre had little to do at this point but to entertain his super-rich employer with a morning game of billiards. Then, the entire city of New York went into shock: On December 16–17, a freezing, gusty night, Manhattan's financial district went up in flames, shattering the local economy. Fortunately for Ebenezer, who had the most to lose, his Bridge Street home was not touched, and he had recently, presciently, moved his business offices from the affected area. John T. Irving, the judge, had accumulated a fortune over the years, and so his estimated losses of $41,000 could be absorbed. "Poor" Henry Brevoort also lost $50,000 in investments, but he was extremely wealthy and could bear it easily. Irving himself lost the $3,000 he had invested in an insurance company that failed. Others, of lesser means, lost everything.

Some thirteen acres and 674 buildings were destroyed in the Great Fire, as it became known. The trading records at the New York Stock & Exchange Board were rescued just in time, as flames lurched up Wall Street and burned out a portion of William Street, the long-vibrant wholesale and retail area where Washington Irving had come into the world. Nevertheless, he was able to celebrate Christmas at "the Hive," as he was calling Ebenezer's house on Bridge Street. In this tight-knit family, one gets the impression that the celebrated author could do no wrong. One of his nephews wrote to another earlier that year: "Uncle Wash in good spirits, full of fun and doing a little more good every day. . . . Whenever anything is wanting, Uncle speaks and it is got. . . . egad if he were only rich we might live like fighting cocks."

As to Christmas, there were grandchildren now, and the once obscure holiday that Washington Irving had done so much to promote was so ingrained that he was able to report to Peter that their grandnieces were in good hands, "Santa Claus having filled their stockings with presents." In the coming year of 1836, Irving would help found a new society in New York, the St. Nicholas Society, and serve as its secretary through 1841. The selection of its first president, Peter G. Stuyvesant (a direct descendant), made clear that the society was entrusted with the Dutch-American legacy to prevent the city from being overrun by those latecomers who looked fondly to their New England Yankee traditions. Emerging from the ashes of the Great Fire, Irving's New York was once again trying to paint a joyful picture of its past.[13]

While *Astoria* was in gestation, Irving's literary allies continued to prosper. In a short space of time, Paulding published *The Book of St. Nicholas: A Life of Washington* (for juvenile readers) and *Slavery in the United States*, this last, in retrospect, an embarrassing apology for the South's peculiar institution. He coupled an interest in writing for children with an intensified commitment to the Democratic Party—his partisan newspaper pieces would win him appointment as President Van Buren's secretary of the navy. Even Verplanck weighed in with a volume of fanciful stories, under the title *The Fairy Book,* which Paulding would then try to copy.

Meanwhile, Longfellow's first collection of essays, *Outre-Mer* (i.e., Beyond the Sea), came out before the end of 1835, and was seen by many as a *Sketch Book* imitation. Its author had been professor of modern languages at Bowdoin since his return from Spain, and, as a poet of some renown by this time, was taking up a new post as professor of belles-lettres at Harvard. Like Irving, he was becoming famous for an "irreproachable gentility," as one critic has termed it, whose poems soothed broad segments of American society. Also in 1836, Irving embraced the work of John James Audubon, on whose behalf he wrote warm letters of introduction to Benjamin F. Butler (Jackson's attorney general) and Martin Van Buren. He was hoping that the government would show favor to the pioneering ornithologist's "magnificent work," and underwrite his further travels.[14]

Irving finally got the present he wanted in June 1836—Peter's return. With that, he contentedly focused his energies on the forthcoming publication of *Astoria* and his new Westchester residence. He sent Pierre a note while his nephew-collaborator was in Toledo, Ohio, inspecting new land investment opportunities. "I am printing my book," the note read, "and completing my cottage slowly, and hope the former will contribute toward defraying the accumulated expense of the latter." He was still waiting for furniture, without which Peter's room was uninhabitable; and he was also preparing to invest his publishing earnings in property, piggybacking with Astor on some parcels in Green Bay and sanctioning Pierre to find him promising Toledo lots. As usual, he would be lucky to break even.[15]

Irving's Philadelphia publisher paid him $4,000 for *Astoria*. London would come through with another £500. Irving apparently took nothing from Astor, except to ensure that the money promised to Pierre for his arrangement of the mass of original documents was finally conveyed. And then he gave Pierre an additional $1,000 from his own pocket, separate from the money he made available for any investment opportunity Pierre found.[16]

When it came to publishing, at least, Irving seemed to have consistent good fortune. *Astoria* was greeted with serious interest, and Irving (whose real name—not a pseudonym, and not simply "By the Author of the *Sketch Book*"—appeared on the title page) was given credit for his ability to process the facts of the fur trader's mission without losing the sprightliness of narrative. The book was presented as a history, and in that sense did not greatly differ from the style of his Spanish productions, in which romance and anecdote accentuate a national tradition.

Astoria introduced colorful characters and scenes of adventure reminiscent of *A Tour on the Prairies*, and even the Spanish tales. As we meet the western type, around whose lives romantic stories are told, we are tempted to recall their predecessors in Irving's work. The "voyageurs" could just as easily have roamed the mountains of southern Spain in the company of *contrabandistas*:

> The "voyageurs" form a kind of confraternity in the Canadas like the arrieros, or carriers of Spain, and like them, are employed in long internal expeditions of travel and traffic . . . prone to pass their time in idleness and revelry about the trading posts or settlements, squandering their hard earnings in heedless conviviality, and rivaling their neighbors, the Indians, in indolent indulgence and an imprudent disregard of the morrow.[17]

In Irving's narrative, Mr. Astor is a man with a "great scheme of commerce and colonization" and, in contradistinction to the rugged types in his employ, a benign patriarchal figure. As the guiding spirit of the Astoria project, who has the ear of Presidents Jefferson and Madison, he proves himself consistently to be a man of caution and calculation. From 1810 to 1814, in order to advance the American fur trade, he must underwrite both continental and seafaring expeditions. Amid great trials—business as well as human—he persists for as long as is prudent.

The book, all in all, is a tale of hardships. It describes how the fledgling settlement, a "lonely fort" at the mouth of the Columbia River, on the northern Pacific coast, contended with Indian raids and tauntings and, ultimately, the might of the British navy. In one notable encounter north of the settlement, Astor's ship *Tonquin* suffers an attack from Indians, and is lost. Astor has urged his employees to be cautious about allowing dangerous numbers of Indians to come onto his ships; but in this instance, unarmed Indians "thronged" the *Tonquin*. They were unarmed, for the most part, but they had come to purchase knives, and it was with those knives that "the savages rushed upon their marked victims."

Astor had confidently purchased the *Tonquin* for $38,000. He was impressed with the ninety-four-foot-long, three-masted vessel with a twenty-two-gun capacity, which was built in New York in 1807. It had already sailed twice to China. There were twenty-three of Astor's men onboard at the time of its fatal encounter. Irving had known its captain, Jonathan Thorn of Schenectady, New York, in their younger years; but he judged Thorn now, from correspondence, to have become a "peevish" and "headstrong" man, unskilled at diplomacy, who needlessly provoked the Indians. When his ship came under siege, the ill-fated captain vigorously fought off his attackers, "dealing crippling blows to right and left, and strewing the quarter deck with the slain and wounded"—it sounds a bit like the tragic stand of Colonel William B. Travis at the Alamo mission in Texas, which heroic event occurred as *Astoria* was in production.

But Thorn was no hero, at least in Irving's narrative. From an Indian interpreter who survived the *Tonquin* attack, the transactions of that day were recorded. It appears that the captain was clubbed from behind and killed as he tried to fight his way to the cabin where firearms were stored. In the end, only four of the crew escaped death. A mortally wounded ship's clerk, still alive the morning after, waved invitingly to several reconnaissance canoes, luring the Indians back to see what plunder might yet be had. When a sizeable number had climbed aboard, he set off a suicidal explosion, taking with him some of his dead comrades' enemies.[18]

Faced with such adversity, even before the outbreak of the War of 1812, Anglo-American hostilities deepened Astor's problem of sustaining a distant commercial experiment. Amid hazards and repeated harassment, Astoria had no choice but to fold. Most important, it lacked an armed force of sufficient power to challenge those who would confront it.

Irving's graphic history caught the attention of readers on both sides of the Atlantic. Three years after publication, its authenticity was called into question by an Irish reviewer who had visited the area—Irving, of course, had not traveled west of Oklahoma.[19] What strikes us today, however, is Irving's position with respect to the future of the Indians of North America. In his appendix to *Astoria*, he endorses a view advanced by Captain Bonneville, which can only be seen as a 180-degree shift from his earlier sentimental writings.

When Irving returned east from Osage lands at the end of 1832, emphasizing in the pages of *A Tour on the Prairies* the good fellowship possible in Indian country, he demonstrated ambivalence about the U.S. government's Indian policy. Though he related the rangers' fears of confrontation with the Pawnees, no disputes of any significance took place while Irving was present. And as a Man of Feeling, he was bound to find lamentable the compulsory relocation of assimilated eastern tribes. After writing the history of Astoria, however, Irving expressed the opinion that a strong federal presence was needed to stabilize internecine feuds, calm tensions, and encourage a healthy trade with the tribes who roamed the vast and mountainous middle of the western country (if not the Pacific Northwest as well). He imagined the West as a place where the United States might serve as an honest broker.

Bonneville believed that the "restless and wandering hordes" he had seen in the Rocky Mountain region needed to see a permanent armed presence if they were to be persuaded not to prey, steal, and murder. Indians had a tradition of demonstrating skill and daring by raiding (not trading) for horses, which mere "philanthropy" could not counteract, he said. Well-armed trading posts, garrisons situated closer to the Great Plains than the current entrepôt of Spanish-held Santa Fe, in the Southwest, would go far toward routinizing commerce and extending U.S. control. Irving called Bonneville's suggestions "excellent."[20]

Here was the change: Instead of confining his opinions to the very personal stories he was best known for, Irving suddenly felt the need to adopt the cause of a willful U.S. government. The documents under consideration in *Astoria* were mostly two decades old when Irving saw them, yet it was (at least in part) the experience of Astor's vanguard that now caused him to feel something new—to feel that concern or compassion for Indian peoples was not sufficient in itself to establish U.S.-Indian relations on a firm footing or to afford a remedy for the unpredictability that certain of the tribes exhibited.

He had become a government man. What most of white America saw as a lack of provocation in its attitude toward skeptical Indians, those closest to the encircled native peoples unquestionably saw as a relentless pattern of dispossession that made rational the taunts and instigations meant to embarrass the government's armed representatives and turn back the ever-expanding power of official Washington. The Trail of Tears was deplorable policy, but "Philip of Pokanoket" remained literature, and not a guideline for decisionmakers. With

Astoria, the influential author had separated Philip's dignity and Osage affability from the fashioning of future Indian policy.[21]

Enamored with Bonneville's story, Irving bought the rights to the army officer's papers and moved directly from *Astoria* to *The Adventures of Captain Bonneville,* which was published in Philadelphia and London in mid-1837. *Bonneville* is a romance. It depicts the manly trapper as a daring "Robin Hood" in leather garb and ostentatious leggings; stock Indians (one stupid and unsympathetic, another courageous and ingenious); a buffoon of a "raw" Irish cook; and a sublime American landscape. Most important, Irving's fearless captain is a reasoner, that superior being who proves his mettle as he surveys the perilous wild from atop his lusty steed. American reviewers tended to praise the book for reasons of nationalism as much as literary merit, whereas British reviewers disliked it as an expression of American vulgarity and acquisitiveness.[22]

Bonneville is a vehicle for Irving to celebrate a man's finding his manhood on the frontier. He de-emphasizes the humanity of the Crow and Blackfeet tribes, but praises the decency and piety of the "inoffensive" Nez Perce people, who owed their morals to the influence of white men; he glamorizes the longhaired trappers' "proneness to adopt savage habitudes" and "discard everything that may bear the stamp of civilized life," down to copying the Indian's walk. As bachelors (Irving's word), the trappers lavish attention on their horses; and when they take an Indian bride, delicate and bejeweled to their taste, they outfit her horse with even more decoration. The American trappers are his "cavaliers of the mountains."[23]

The alacrity with which this book was prepared has provoked modern literary scholars to demean *Bonneville* as an expansionist government's propaganda—a "fur-trapping" expedition actually engaged in the reconnaissance of British and Mexican movements—and quite possibly the worst writing Irving ever did. It smells of a book written simply for money: Irving was paid $3,000 by his American and £900 by his British publishers. But one discerning critic professes to understand Irving's strategy: "As a romantic Western historian," writes Richard H. Cracroft, "he reserved the right to take facts from the prosaic limitations of laconic journalese and to let them soar through his filigree toward what he hoped would be the proud, romantic, national literary tradition. For a country with little or no past, this was the best he could do."

The question seems to be whether Irving, as a nineteenth-century writer, is due his license, or whether he owed posterity the hard truth about the struggle over the trans-Mississippi West. He had gone in his career from lighthearted critic of the so-called enlightened theorist to unabashed romancer of manly conquerors. Something had moved Irving to construct an exaggerated definition of rugged American masculinity whereby Indians were no longer praised for their fortitude, and women were reduced to ornaments. Irving diminished the "softer, more self-indulgent" French-Canadian trapper who must have an Indian wife, comparing him unfavorably to the American trapper who needed only the wilderness in which to prove himself. It was that intrepid discoverer who had his own "technical language" and who fully appreciated the picturesque surroundings; and it was, similarly, the dedicated captain who appeared most worthy as he stood before the glistening peaks.

Why did Irving do this? In short, it was how he believed an American epic had to be presented: strong, exotic personalities, definable codes of behavior for his white heroes, and a demanding landscape on which to stage epic exploits. His admiration for the pioneer seems to presage the "resistless restless race" of Walt Whitman's "O Pioneers!"[24]

☆ ☆

As Irving was seeing *Astoria* through to publication, he wrote in a jesting but revealing tone to Pierre, in Toledo: "I am printing my book and completing my cottage slowly, and hope the former will contribute toward defraying the accumulated expenses of the latter." In the final months of 1836, the move to Sunnyside was completed. Irving entertained "a brace of nieces" in September. Astor, thrilled by the reception of their book, paid a visit to Tarrytown in November. By Christmas, Peter was living there permanently. Irving even added a pet pig to his menagerie, named Fanny, which took occupancy of the barn on the property.

It was his "dear bright little home," as he wrote to his niece Sarah Paris, Catharine's resilient twenty-three-year-old, who resided temporarily at Ebenezer's. It was a place where he could concentrate on his writing, if he chose, or just escape the commotion of the city. He wanted his family there, as many of them and as often as possible, for they apparently occupied themselves well enough that he did not have to adjust his pattern. He needed an excuse to emerge from the room where he wrote. "Old bachelor though I be," he said to Sarah, "I cannot do without womankind, about me." What he wanted, and eventually got, was to feel like the kindly patriarch of an eighteenth-century sentimental novel, or a lovable eccentric.[25]

As the year 1837 opened, Tappan Bay was all ice; snow glistened from the distant hills, and a good fire warmed the cottage. Peter was feeling in better health for the moment, and was quite cheery. At any given time, one or another of the nieces helped the bachelors keep house. The author, unaccustomed to domesticity, entertained himself by sliding on the ice of the Hudson. From time to time, he went into Manhattan, generally to commune with the writing and publishing world; on one occasion during his first season at "the Roost," he attended a booksellers' banquet, along with Paulding, Bryant, and Halleck. There he proposed a toast to his old acquaintance, the septuagenarian English poet Samuel Rogers, who had just written to him in praise of the poems of Halleck: "They are better than anything we can do just now on our side of the Atlantic." Byron lacked a successor as the poetic genius of the English-speaking world, and the charitable Irving had proposed his recent housemate Halleck.[26]

Irving's impact on Europe was not soon forgotten. That spring, Louis Napoleon, the future French emperor, visited the author's Tarrytown cottage. Irving found his guest merely quiet, and without noticeable ability. Peter, meanwhile, grew uncomfortable. It is hard to pinpoint just how this happened. In February, Irving had written of the two of them as "cosey & comfortable as heart can wish"; in March, he supposed that his brother's health was still good, as Peter sat "surrounded by books and buried to the chin in News papers of all countries." But it was not to last. Peter moved back to Ebenezer's, where there was more, apparently, to keep him entertained, as his health, once again, gave signs of deterioration.[27]

Nationalist though his western adventures had made him, politics held no more charm for Irving. His friend of six years, his sometime traveling companion Martin Van Buren, was inaugurated as president in March 1837. An even older friend, Gouverneur Kemble, was now a congressman, and very much a Washington fixture; he tried to coax Irving to visit the capital and look in on the state of national politics. But Irving demurred: "I have a love of ease and tranquility growing upon me that makes even the bustle of gay society irksome, and which quite incapacitates me for the turmoil and excitement of a great political metropolis in a high state of fermentation." He allowed that he felt the days of Jacksonian brusqueness were—or should be—gone, and he hoped that an era of compromise, befitting the popular will, would follow. Whether Van Buren as president could effect this he did not know.

So much had happened in America's national life that the world of their political youth—Irving's and Kemble's—had to have seemed remote and irrelevant. The banking system was in disarray, and on the minds of everyone even remotely concerned with the health of the country. There were more and more poor crowded into cities like New York, while small-scale artisan communities were becoming harder to sustain. Factories were proliferating, and business-minded people were increasingly restless. In the autumn of 1836, a symbol of turn-of-the-century New York, the able and often inscrutable Aaron

Burr, died at the age of eighty, with nary a word spoken among Irving's old crowd—at least as far as we know. Van Buren, the recipient of just over 50 percent of the popular vote that year, had practiced law and was once Burr's co-counsel. Some thought he was Burr's political—and still others claimed, biological—offspring. His presidency was greeted without the excitement that accompanied General Andrew Jackson's accession to office.

Van Buren understood the political game as well as anyone. But his term coincided with a moment of—as Irving put it—"financial perplexity." The first New Yorker to serve as president was swallowed up by the depressing circumstances he inherited from the outgoing president, and it would take him the better part of his four years to stabilize the economy. Ebenezer took it hardest: The Panic of 1837 broke up the credit system and forced him to shut down his import business. He sold his Bridge Street home, and his daughters went to live with their uncle in Tarrytown.

At this moment, with many Americans suffering financially, Irving enjoyed abundant literary capital, a reputation for levelheadedness, and all-around goodwill. He was beloved by an ever-growing number of readers, now spanning two generations. In the autumn of 1837, he received a long, beseeching letter from Catharine Wirt of Richmond, the daughter of William Wirt, the former attorney general and the biographer of Patrick Henry who had more recently argued successfully on behalf of the Cherokees before the Supreme Court. Wirt had died in 1834, leaving behind a trove of letters and manuscripts, public and private papers.

"He never wrote for posthumous fame," she contended, establishing the virtues of her late father. But hers was no ordinary appeal. Catharine Wirt had grown up around men of letters, yet it was Irving alone whom she deemed right for recapturing her father's spirit. She attributed to Irving the qualities she revered in her father:

> I know you through that mirrored self which you have held up to the world in your imperishable writings—and the perception which they have given me of the head and heart of their author has emboldened me to speak thus freely of a Father between whom and Yourself I trace a striking resemblance and congeniality in many of the most admirable and winning qualities.

She had thought of attempting the biography herself, but realized it needed an unbiased pen. Irving did not accede to her request, but John P. Kennedy did. Whether it was as a result of Irving's urging or intercession we can only speculate.[28]

Somehow, Washington Irving's name came up on several levels as a man to help steer past the threatening currents set in motion by the Panic of 1837. But despite his relationship with the president, no political office would claim him. He was offered the position of secretary of the navy in April 1838, and was happy when his refusal caused the secretaryship to fall to Paulding. How could the un-ambitious resident of a rural "roost," before whose window birds sang each morning, possibly say yes to the embattled president? A short while before, Ir-ving had rejected overtures (presented "unanimously and vociferously") that he accept the mayoralty of New York. The language he used in both refusals had something in common: In saying no to Van Buren, he allowed that it would take "but a short carreer of public life at Washington to render me mentally and phys-ically a perfect wreck." To Kemble, he referred to their native city in its present state as "a perfect political Hellgate." So much for "perfection."[29] Irving's quin-tessential comments on his unsuitability for a politically active life were issued in mid-1838 to Gouverneur Kemble, one from whom he never held back:

> You seem to think I may have some idea of running for Congress. I must run mad first. I have kept clear of politics in my younger, more stirring and ambitious years, and am now too old, and unambitious and lazy, and wise, and philosophical and magnanimous, to be drawn into the scuffle.[30]

In mid-March 1838, the upright Judge John T. Irving died. He was, in Pierre's words, "a martyr to an overtaxed mind." Then, in late June of the same year, Peter died. Washington had Peter's body transported north by steamer from Manhattan to Westchester, for burial in a temporary grave until a regular Irving family plot could be arranged. It was the beginning of a mournful interlude in the life of the extended family. Catharine was suffering from painful rheumatism, and could scarcely sleep. Beyond the loss of Peter, which he did not speak of easily, Irving missed seeing his old friend from Paris, Thomas Wentworth Storrow, who paid a surprise two-day visit to Tar-rytown only to arrive when Irving was in Manhattan.

It took him nearly three months after Peter's death to write of his feelings to his sister in England, Sally Van Wart. And then he poured out his soul.

> That great bereavement, following so soon after the death of brother John has affected me most dismally. My health, for years so uninterrupted and excellent, has given way under it. . . . Every day, every hour I feel how com-pletely Peter and myself were entertwined together in the whole course of our existence.

It was, he openly acknowledged, their bachelorhood that cemented their bond. The rest of the family had produced families of their own, which necessarily served "to weaken the fraternal tie," Irving continued to sister Sally, "but we stood in the original, unimpaired relation to each other, and . . . we grew more and more together." Peter knew his raw writings better than anyone else. During his years in Europe, Peter had followed him from place to place, providing him with an emotional link to his past at times when he might otherwise have felt detached, directionless, adrift. None of his other relatives could take Peter's place—he admitted this to Sally—no matter how affectionate their concern. "Since our dear mothers death," he added, in a rare disclosure, "I have had no one who could so patiently and tenderly bear with all my weaknesses and infirmities."

And what of Peter's weaknesses and infirmities? No one has been able to explain why he never achieved anything, given his innate ability. Three-quarters of a century ago, the Irving biographer Stanley Williams was vague about Peter: "What is not set down is the physical and spiritual blight which had halted his talents and consigned him to aimless exile in Europe. Irving knew the secret of this, and was silent; now, in fact, did not care. Peter was dead; that was enough." All we do know for certain is that in the last months of his own life, Washington Irving continued to speak of Peter to his Peter-substitute (his nephew Pierre), designating the two of them as the ones he could always rely on.[31]

To add life to his surroundings after Peter's death, and to bolster his spirits, Irving saw to it that his nieces and nephews stayed with him as much as possible. "My little cottage is well stocked," he wrote to Sally in October 1838. "I have Ebenezers five girls, and himself also, whenever he can be spared from town." To the same sister, five weeks later: "My cottage is a rallying spot, and place of refuge I may say for some branches of the family." He was learning to live in a circumscribed way, keeping to a budget, severely limiting his travel, and yet, somehow, never wholly convinced that the public would continue to welcome new writings from him. Again to Sally: "I begin to hope there is yet some stuff in me unworked, and which I may be able to work out successfully. If so, life will still have its occupation and motive, and I may continue to live to some purpose." This was not exactly the language of youthful exuberance that had long radiated from his pen.[32]

☆   ☆

No matter what he did, Washington Irving could not win any praise but the most grudging from the second name in American letters, James Fenimore

Cooper. Back in 1826, just as his classic *The Last of the Mohicans* was enjoying brisk sales and glowing reviews, Cooper had proposed Irving, who was living abroad, for membership in New York's Bread and Cheese Club. But that spirit of camaraderie did not last. In Europe from 1826 to 1833, Cooper showed off his republicanism at every opportunity, renewing his glorious dedication to the Revolutionary past in recurring walks with Lafayette at the old general's estate of La Grange. On his return from seven years in Europe, Cooper was given no particular welcome, which served to reopen the old wound—presuming that he was thought to be of less value to the national literature than the Anglophile author of the *Sketch Book*. Cooper's criticisms of Irving were known to many of the literati.

Irving retaliated with kindness. Upon reading Cooper's *The Pathfinder* (1840), one of the Leatherstocking tales, the theme of which revolves around both wilderness and seagoing adventure, Irving let all who cared—and that included Bryant and Halleck—know how impressed he was with the book's depth and gripping prose. Cooper's works would live on, he insisted, whether or not his own did. But Cooper, even after hearing of Irving's tribute, did not bend: "My opinion has been independent of what that gentleman might have said of me, or my writings, or character. . . . A published eulogy of myself from Irving's pen could not change my opinion of his career. . . . I have never had any quarrel with Mr. Irving, and give him full credit as a writer. Still, I believe him to be below the ordinary level, in moral qualities, instead of being above them, as he is cried up to be." In sum, the censorious Cooper considered Irving a hypocrite, whose love of country was thin, and who schemed to advance his career and have everybody love him.[33]

Cooper's judgment is contradicted by a telling exchange that took place between Irving and the historian William Hickling Prescott at the beginning of 1839. While conducting research at the New York Society Library, Irving was informed by the librarian that both he and Prescott of Boston appeared to be working on the subject of the conquest of Mexico. Prescott had written the picturesque and highly respected *History of Ferdinand and Isabella* (1837), and had since turned to the American theme. Irving, without hesitation, instructed the librarian to inform Prescott that he would yield the subject. At that point, Prescott introduced himself to Irving by letter, which began:

My dear Sir:
    —If you will allow one to address you so familiarly, who has not had the pleasure of your personal acquaintance, though he feels as if he had known you for a long time.

The New Englander explained how he had come to his subject, and the state of his research. He was touched by Irving's gesture: "I accept your proffered courtesy in the same cordial spirit in which it was given." Irving answered that though he had for several years thought about writing a proper history of Mexican civilization, and was "determined to dash into it at once," he could not do so now. "The manner in which you have executed your noble history of Ferdinand and Isabella gave me at once the assurance that you were the man to undertake this subject; your letter shows that I was not wrong in the conviction." Having, in all likelihood, gotten further than Prescott in his writing, he promised to supply needed materials to his fellow author and historian.

Prescott responded with conventional humility: "Your relinquishing the ground seems to impose on me an additional responsibility to try to make your place good, from which a stouter heart than mine may well shrink. I trust, however, in you I shall find a generous critic." When his *History of the Conquest of Mexico* was published in 1843, Prescott saluted Irving, in his preface, for his unselfishness.[34]

The immediate project thus abandoned, the creator of the faux-historian Diedrich Knickerbocker became a salaried writer of sketches for the *Knickerbocker Magazine,* a monthly literary journal named after Irving's character that was representative of the sentiment and wit of those New Yorkers (and adopted New Yorkers) who regularly alternated between Romantic themes and healthy satire. His *Knickerbocker* sketches (many drawn from Irving's earlier notebooks) would be collected and published separately, in 1855, under the title *Wolfert's Roost.*

As a new decade arrived, Irving had grown attached to his routine on the banks of the Hudson at Tappan Bay, and by early 1841 had renamed his place "Sunnyside." During what he termed the "genial months of the year," he lived very much out of doors, in a "free and unceremonious style." He was nowadays an avid birdwatcher. A previously elusive calm settled over him when the weather was fair. Even in the winter, he said, sunshine often prevailed in the skies over Tarrytown. He told his sister Sally that his move from the city had occasioned new interest in the area, and a number of New Yorkers had already established themselves nearby. When he required company, there were frequent gatherings he could attend, with music and dancing. One of his neighbors was James Alexander Hamilton, a Jackson aide and son of the preeminent Federalist. As time passed, the neighbors became better and better friends. Irving tried to paint a picture for his sister of picnics beside the river and "carriages glistening through the woods." He accompanied his family on rides through "his" Sleepy Hollow. When the sun shone, Irving worshipped:

"In no climate within the range of my experience is sunshine more beautiful in its effect on landscape than in this." Neither Spain nor Italy compared, he said. He was home.

When he felt like venturing into the city, he tried not to accept invitations that would feel burdensome. He was tickled, though, in forwarding invitations to his six nieces to attend "the Great Brevoort Fancy ball, which is convulsing the whole fashionable world." Five hundred guests crowded the Brevoorts' Fifth Avenue mansion, and Irving proposed that Ebenezer's eldest, Kate, come in "a primitive dutch dress and go as Katrina Van Tassel just from the Van Tassel cottage." If he had his way (and he did, of course), Uncle Washington's literary creations would carry meaning to the next generation, and the next after that.[35]

His finances were increasingly unsteady, however, and he had no new major writing project in mind. His land investments had gone decidedly nowhere, and he was, once again, nervous. At the same time, a favorite niece, Catharine's daughter Sarah Paris, married the son and namesake of Thomas Wentworth Storrow; and in 1841, the former Miss Paris moved to—Paris. It was hard for her uncle to let her go, harder still for her mother to say goodbye to her only surviving daughter: "Their very existences are woven together," Irving wrote. He himself could not bear to accompany Sarah to her oceangoing steamboat. The anticipation was intense, but the parting occurred. Sarah stopped in Birmingham, England, to visit with the aunt she had never known, Sarah Irving Van Wart, and then went on to France.

One whom Irving called an "eccentric but excellent fellow," by the name of Van Bibber, tried to perk up the kindly author, whom he had seen in the company of his nieces at Sunnyside. "My only wish," the man wrote, in a letter dripping with honey, "is, that your own orchard may shower down its choicest blossoms on your head, and that, during all this merry springtime, you may have sweet thoughts, pleasant dreams, and frequent visits from the muses." But the muses were not descending. Moreover, a barricade was going up to shield Sunnyside from the "surges of the Tappan Sea," and, more fearfully, from a railroad under construction, which would speed right past Irving's property most hours of the day. During this trying season, both modernity and Romantic melancholy crept up on him. The wife of James Paulding (who was also the sister of Gouverneur Kemble) died. Irving went upriver to pay a condolence visit to Kemble at Cold Spring. He continued five miles past Kemble's to see Henry Brevoort and family, who now resided in the Hudson Highlands, and who, owing as much to good investments as a good inheritance, was upgrading his city mansion at Fifth Avenue and Ninth Street.[36]

Irving was buoyed by a sudden prospect. He had received a letter from a writer he admired. Charles Dickens was coming to America! The exclamation mark is from Irving's letter on the subject to his niece Sarah. "I look forward to shaking hands with you," Dickens had written expectantly. "There is no living writer, and there are very few among the dead, whose approbation I should feel so proud to earn." The twenty-nine-year-old Dickens was at this time known principally for his 1836 *Sketches of Boz,* even more so than for *Oliver Twist* (1839). He had paid homage to Irving by visiting the places made famous in the *Sketch Book.* He had even fantasized about accompanying Irving on his ramblings. In his words: "I should like to travel with you . . . down to Bracebridge Hall." He had read the Spanish writings, too, and shared Irving's compassion for the "poor, unhappy Boabdil." And, lest Irving doubt it, "Diedrich Knickerbocker I have worn to death in my pocket, and yet I should show you his mutilated carcass with a joy past all expression." Irving had a testimonial of real meaning to savor.[37]

He took some time to complete a little book that amounted to a favor for a distraught mother who had buried seven of her nine children. Her most talented, the prolific Margaret, had succumbed to tuberculosis at the age of fifteen, leaving behind a collection of her poetry. "Her whole life was one dying day,—one long heartbreak," wrote William H. Prescott to a young female (the most obvious, if not intended, reader of Irving's treatment). *Biography of the Late Margaret Miller Davidson* (1841) was a weepy volume, and in an age when sentimental literature flourished, Irving, who had known the bright child and her "poetical effusions," could not but be moved to find among her poems one that he had inspired: "Boabdil El Chico's Farewell to Granada." He accorded the copyright and profits from the book to the child's grieving mother.[38]

Here was Irving again expressing his deep feelings for pure, young, dead females, replaying his emotions after the demise of Matilda Hoffman. He was not the only writer to do this—the genre of publishing the drawn-out deathbed scenes of young women was a staple of Christian literature. Agnes Wirt, a daughter of William, was the same age as Margaret Davidson when she died in 1830, claiming to have heard "sweet . . . heavenly music" in her final days. Aggie's dismal story was related in a short, sentimental pamphlet.[39] Perhaps Irving had not responded to the tender appeal of her older sister Catharine, who had adored and lost her sister and her father and would have been greatly succored by an animated volume in the Irving mode; yet he agreed to give the world *Biography of the Late Margaret Miller Davidson.* For him, there was nothing more fetching than a female child whose poetry was tender and promising, and who would in fact and memory always remain pious and pure and never grow into a carnal woman.

Around this time, too, he began the project he had contemplated years earlier but had shrunk from its magnitude—a life of George Washington. He would have made real progress on it, too, had he not been galvanized by a call from President William Henry Harrison's (and, by inheritance, John Tyler's) secretary of state, the great clarion of the Senate in its heyday, Massachusetts's Daniel Webster. How this came about is extraordinary.

In the pivotal election of 1840, Irving unexpectedly defected from the incumbent Van Buren. The Dutch-descended Kinderhook native he had taken such a liking to had let Irving down in a way the author could not forgive. Earlier that year, Irving had taken up his pen to write an uncomfortable letter. It began: "My dear Sir, I am about to appeal to your friendship in a way I once little dreamt of doing, by asking a favor in which my own personal interests are involved." Ebenezer was in deepening financial distress, and the president had the power to appoint him to a finance post in New York City. Irving laid out the case in all its particulars, citing "the vicissitudes of the times," his own dried-up income, his brother's "spotless integrity and thorough worth," and a "charming family of daughters" who now shared Irving's Sunnyside cottage with him, and presumably would suffer if their father did not receive a lucrative job.

Time passed, and Irving received no reply. He felt increasingly awkward after Paulding spoke to the president on Ebenezer's behalf. The author wrote without self-censoring to Gouverneur Kemble: If Ebenezer should be denied a salaried position at this point, "it will be a humiliation that will grind my spirit for the rest of my days." Still the president failed to act, and Irving told Kemble on the eve of the national election that he felt Van Buren had "betrayed heartlessness in friendship and lowmindedness in politics." In this scenario, the president had ostensibly come under the control of a faction of "low demagogues" who were greedily interested in controlling appointments.

The decision to ignore Ebenezer's plight appeared one of political expediency. Irving's old friend Jack Nicholson, now a commodore in the navy, and every bit a Van Buren partisan, wrote to the president and described Irving's apostasy to the Whig Party as that of "a pure and honest man . . . throwing himself away." It appears that neither Irving nor Van Buren was able to understand the pressures the other felt, and the result was a personal split that had political ramifications.[40]

Irving gave his support to Van Buren's opponent, the Virginia-born William Henry Harrison. With Harrison's death from pneumonia just a month into his term, the celebrated citizen of Sunnyside found himself in the good graces of the administration of another Virginian, John Tyler, the tenth U.S. president—and, it is worth noting, the first president to have been born *after* Washington Irving. Tyler was an anti-Jackson Democrat who had found temporary quarters among the Whigs, and, like Irving, he espoused a political view that was becoming increasingly difficult to categorize. At this awkward moment in the political life of the nation, even Daniel Webster, a onetime Federalist, was tentatively embracing a states-rights southerner in Tyler.[41]

After Secretary of State Webster submitted the nomination of Washington Irving for the post of U.S. minister to Spain, the nominee jotted a note to Ebenezer, expressing his surprise: "Nothing was ever more unexpected. It was perfectly unsolicited." And then, realizing how his routine would be upset: "It will be a severe trial to absent myself for a time from dear little Sunnyside; but I shall return to it better enabled to carry it on comfortably."

He went to Washington to meet with President Tyler, thus adding to the list of his presidential acquaintances. "A very good-hearted, fine-tempered man," he estimated the new chief executive. He found himself seated at supper at the President's House next to Tyler's daughter-in-law, who just happened to be the daughter of Mary Fairlie, the "Sophie Sparkle" of *Salmagundi.* It must have been somewhat surreal for the fifty-eight-year-old bachelor.

Irving told Pierre that the appointment, universally applauded in Congress, was "the crowning honor" of his life. He left his Tarrytown home in Ebenezer's hands, coaxing him with the following: "You will find, in my little library, books about gardening, farming, poultry, &c., by which to direct yourself. The management of the place will give you healthful and cheerful occupation."[42]

He had been spending considerable sums to maintain his farm: wages for his hired labor; garden implements; turnip, cucumber, and lettuce seed; wagon (and sleigh) repairs; oats and shoes for his horses; mouse and rat traps. He supported family members, and often liked to update his wardrobe. But he expected to line his pockets as a diplomat, and to return to Sunnyside with enough funds "to put up as many weathercocks as I please." Meanwhile, he was able to handpick his Madrid aides: J. Carson Brevoort, the twenty-four-year-old son of his dear friend, and Alexander Hamilton, Jr., the twenty-six-year-old son of his Tarrytown neighbor and grandson of the Revolutionary.[43]

Not long before he left for Europe, Irving was at last able to shake hands with Charles Dickens, when the latter was banqueted in New York in February 1842. Halleck was there, and Bryant, too, and Irving was talked into presiding. Always uncomfortable in speechmaking, he fumbled through a simple toast—a hurtful event for him, though others appear not to have taken much notice. And the whole Dickens business appears to have been something of a letdown anyway. As much as he had looked forward to their meeting, and as much as Dickens relished it, Irving appears to have been a bit disappointed in Dickens the man, who was less refined than the educated Englishmen he had grown accustomed to. Yet, as he prepared for his journey, Irving received one more ecstatic letter from the English novelist: "Wherever you go, God bless you!" Dickens gushed. "What pleasure I have had in seeing and talking with you, I will not attempt to say. I shall never forget it as long as I live."[44]

It had already been ten years since Irving's grand reception at the City Hotel, welcoming him home from Europe. The anniversary did not escape the notice of his friends. On the eve of his departure, a deputation of leading citizens, led by Philip Hone and including Bryant and Verplanck, proposed to give Irving a festive send-off before his "honorable mission" to Spain. This time, he begged off, protesting that he had already been "paid, and overpaid, and paid again for all the little good I may have effected in my somewhat negligent and fortuitous career." There was no banquet.

When the month of May arrived, Washington Irving was back in London, visiting with the erudite Edward Everett, present U.S minister to England and brother of Alexander Everett, the man he had last known as minister to Spain. And then he saw Murray, and the artist Charles R. Leslie, and the long-lived poet Samuel Rogers. He shook hands again with the always engaging Tom Moore, and implored his Irish friend to help him avoid all ceremonial dinners. He explained to Moore how he had broken down in attempting to say a few words on behalf of Dickens in New York—he kept on shaking his head in recalling his embarrassment. "That *Dickens* dinner," Moore recounted in the pages of his diary, "which he always pronounced with strong emphasis, hammering all the time with his right arm. . . . 'that *Dickens* dinner' still haunted his imagination."

Irving stayed in England just long enough to make the rounds briefly. He was presented to the young ("acquits herself with grace and ease") Queen Victoria, and he saw his sister Sally in Birmingham. And, thinking ahead to the final history he would undertake as an author, he researched the family background of George Washington by going on an expedition to Northamptonshire in search of the original manor of the first president's English forebears.[45]

★ ★

He held up well, still the hearty traveler. En route to Madrid, he spent precious time in Paris with another of his regular correspondents, his niece Sarah (Paris) Storrow. Since her departure, he had written her long letters, some of the longest he ever wrote, each teeming with affection: He mentioned in one that every time he passed a spot of scenery they had traversed together, he would grow sad, and be reminded of "what I have lost in losing you." In Paris, he had a reinjection of the love he had missed for fourteen months.

The traveler's old habits returned. He continued collecting stories and bits to use in stories. On one of the many days he spent touring with Sarah, they visited the chapel where Napoleon now reposed. In a gilt box at the foot of the sarcophagus was the emperor's preserved heart; on top of it, his sword; and under glass, "his famous little Cocked hat." The day after this experience, the in-transit minister was presented to the current ruler of France, King Louis Philippe, his queen, and their family, at the royal country residence of Neuilly-sur-Seine. Yet to his sister Catharine, the reconstituted diplomat wrote something surprising—he said that Europe no longer compelled him in the manner it had formerly. He felt homesick: "It is possible I may have gathered wisdom under the philosophic shades of Sleepy Hollow, or may have been rendered fastidious by the gay life of the cottage; it is certain that, amidst all the splendors of London and Paris, I find my imagination refuses to take fire, and my heart still yearns after dear little Sunnyside." And similarly, to Pierre and Helen Irving (the widower Pierre having remarried to his first cousin): "I am spoiled by the life I led at Sunnyside, and have not, during the whole time that I have been in Europe, had one of those right-down frolicsome moods that I have enjoyed at the cottage."[46]

As much as he delighted in the companionship of Sarah, now the mother of an infant, he associated Paris with the late Peter Irving. He could not help but remember Peter "at every step," as he informed his sister Sally: "He is continually present in my mind since my return to Europe." There was much "melancholy" in places where previously there had been as much "joyous excitement." Crossing the threshold into one particular garden that was Peter's favorite, he wrote: "I felt my heart completely give way." Nor did he feel particularly eager to assume his ministerial duties, or "the great tide of public and fashionable life."

The emotions were running hot. When he quit Paris in July 1842, at least he had diversion. For he was joined then by fresh blood, two aides who had not seen Europe before: Brevoort the younger and Hamilton the younger. Irving wrote meaningfully to the father of the former: "He seems like a new link in our old friendship." The three travelers enjoyed picturesque scenery along a southwestern route, stopping in Tours and Bordeaux, though Irving continued, he said, to feel Peter's presence beside him.

Gradually Irving adapted to his situation. As he prepared to ascend the Pyrenees, he was able to write that his carriage was comfortable and his traveling companions "young and fresh and buoyant." Upon arrival in Madrid, he was established in one wing of a palace. Reality came upon him all at once, and he shuddered at the thought of his sudden importance: "It seems strange to me to find myself all at once the master of a new house; walking from room to room all having the look of a long established abode; strange servants running at my call and bowing to me with profound respect."[47]

Spain was experiencing yet another political transition. Upon the death of King Ferdinand VII in 1833, his twenty-seven-year-old widow, Maria Cristina, a niece of Louis Philippe of France, became regent queen for her daughter Isabella, who would not attain marriageable age until 1846. The succession was opposed by the late king's brother, whose armed followers eyed Madrid from the provinces and occasionally threatened the capital. When Irving met Louis Philippe in Paris, the unpopular regent queen had abdicated and fled to her uncle's side; she was eventually conducted back to Spain by General Baldomero Espartero, one of three generals now contending for power. As regent when Irving crossed the Pyrenees, Espartero was the man to whom the U.S. minister presented his credentials. Irving pronounced his "sincere desire to draw more and more closely the ties of amity" between Washington and Madrid. After this, he was received by the twelve-year-old future queen.

He endured the summer heat and the ceremonial visits, enjoying his evening walks along the nearby Prado, or grand public walk, and his talks with young Hamilton in which he reminisced about "the glorious sunsets of the Hudson and the purple outlines of its Western hills"—this he recounted in a letter to Sarah Storrow in Paris. "In fact," he went on, "the more I think of home the more it assumes the tints and colorings of romance to me; and I deck out sweet little Sunnyside with all the ideal charms the imagination of a lover bestows upon his absent mistress." It was a curious choice of metaphor—something out of an aging bachelor's fantasy world.

Irving bore a special concern for young Isabella, on whom so much of the nation's attention was focused. Reformers and hard-line monarchists vied with one another to see what more stable form of government might be put in place, what taxes and tithes revised—and above all, whom the queen would marry, with or without foreign interference, when she attained her majority. She had "light hair and light eyes," Irving reported to his sister Catharine, her face "not handsome" but "agreeable" (he had said much the same about Queen Victoria), and marred by a skin condition that gave her a "rough and somewhat *mealy* look." He guessed that, with frequent baths, she would outgrow this condition. She appeared to him, above all, young and innocent—

and he could not help taking an interest in young and innocent women, whether royal or merely of genteel breeding.

His aide expressed a different compulsion. In the spirit, perhaps, of his womanizing grandfather, Irving's Alexander Hamilton found Madrid disappointing in that he was not meeting any likely young women. "He is fond of society and especially of ladies society, and anticipated much delight among the dark eyed Señoritas of Spain," Irving confided to Sarah. "His romance, therefore, is completely at fault; and he looks back with repining to the flirtations he was accustomed to enjoy in the United States."

In November 1842, four months after his assumption of official duties, and after having moved to a sunny mansion that was more to his liking, Irving was witness to the coup that replaced General Espartero with an ad hoc coalition, under whose auspices Isabella would come into power when she attained her majority. Throughout this period, Britain and France would carry on negotiations in an attempt to decide that most important question in a royal female's life, the marital union, needed to sustain the balance of power on the Continent. Fortunately for Irving, his tour would end shortly before these negotiations produced a new wave of misunderstanding and disorder. He monitored the rumors and machinations of all the parties, and kept Secretary of State Webster regularly apprised.[48]

The responsibilities of his office made it impossible for him to do any meaningful work on his prospective *Life of George Washington*. As a diligent and effective advocate for U.S. commercial interests, he appealed to the Spanish foreign minister to remedy a situation in which existing duties and regulations made it unprofitable for American ships to do business at the ports of Barcelona, Cádiz, or Málaga; he pointed out that the United States imported vast amounts of goods from Spanish Cuba and Puerto Rico—$14 million, "nearly as much," he argued, "as Spain herself imports from the whole world." That "golden stream of revenue" was but a small percentage of what it could be if Spain were to enter into new commercial negotiations. Cuba would occupy much of his attention during his ambassadorship: Ever since John Quincy Adams's tenure as secretary of state under President Monroe, Washington had been concerned about Britain's designs against the island. Should a weakened Spain countenance a British move on Cuba, America would not stand idly by.[49]

The active envoy had a rich epistolary life. He stayed close to his Sunnyside family, writing home with the occasional "peep" into the world of the royals and "the whipt syllabub of diplomacy"; he took apart "the petty machinery of the Great world," and commented on all the "sage representatives of governments, bowing with profound reverence and conjuring up nothings to say to a couple of little girls"—the sympathetic, isolated queen and her younger and far better-looking sister. From his palatial "bachelor's nest," Irving did his best to imagine what he was missing at Christmastime at Sunnyside. He ate his holiday dinner, replete with plum pudding and minced pie, in the company of his British counterparts, at their embassy.[50]

The year 1843 brought him his first health crisis in many years—the same inflammation of the legs (gout-like) that had plagued him in Europe twenty years before. It was the result, his nephew Pierre figured, of overwork and lack of physical exercise. His physician told him to stop writing, and the patient grumbled: "The Doctor, would also, if he could, put a stop to my almost incessant reading, as he thinks any fixed attention for a length of time wearies the brain and in some degree produces those effects on the system which originated my complaint." So Irving put aside his *Life of Washington,* and would not pick it up again until his return to Sunnyside. He could hardly recognize himself, he wrote to niece Sarah, "so listless and inert." To official correspondents, he apologized for delays in writing by referring obscurely to "a harassing and protracted indisposition." Young Hamilton monitored his health closely, and tried to get the patient's mind off his aches by reading Sir Walter Scott's novels to him. In his more lighthearted letters home, Hamilton reported on his highly satisfying life with "uncle Geoffrey" (Crayon).[51]

Though not a politically cunning individual, Irving was knowledgeable enough, when physically robust, to perform his duties with ease. His naturally tolerant personality and his romantic engagement with Spanish history and legend earned him a host of friends. His presence in Madrid called up former associations, notable among which was the restoration of his correspondence with Prince Dolgorouki, the Russian diplomat with whom he had traveled overland from Seville to the Alhambra. The prince was now minister to the court of the Kingdom of Naples. It seems that Irving's prairie companion Count Pourtalès was in Dolgorouki's vicinity as well, so he conveyed best wishes to the onetime "buffalo hunter."

Dolgorouki apparently appreciated female beauty in the manner Irving did, for the author regularly wrote to the Russian on this subject. In renewing their correspondence, the never-married American picked up where he had left off fifteen years before. There was a young woman of Madrid they (especially Irving) had marveled at, whom Irving had found again. He was still "struck" by her, he said, but the effect was quite different. In 1827: "She was young, recently married, fresh and unhackneyed in society, and my imagination decked her out in every thing that was pure, lovely, innocent and angelic in womanhood."

And now:

> She was pointed out to me at the theatre shortly after my arrival in Madrid. I turned with eagerness to the original of the picture that had ever remained hung up in *sanctity* in my mind. I found her still handsome, though somewhat matronly in her appearance, seated *with her daughters* in the box of a fashionable nobleman, younger than herself, rich in purse but poor in intellect; and who was openly and notoriously her *caviliere Servante*. The charm was broken—the picture fell from the wall—She may have the customs of a depraved country and licentious state of society to excuse her; but I can never think of her again in the halo of feminine purity and loveliness.[52]

What we find in the letter writer, now nearly sixty years old, is a man with a reverential view of womanhood. He reminded the prince that his way was, and had always been, to stand back as a spectator—not to be part of the "gay world," not generally to memorize faces or recollect ordinary people. But this woman had been different in his mind. You recall, don't you, Dolgorouki?

The incident reveals something about Irving that may not have been sufficiently clear before. For so long indefinite in his stated attractions, the self-conscious bachelor did not express hunger for women; rather, he sought innocent perfection in them. Only the teenagers Matilda Hoffman and Emily Foster, so far as we know, had so drawn him that he could fantasize about marrying them. Is this not odd? "Time dispells charms and illusions," he tells Dolgorouki now. The charm was broken for him whenever the fantasy creature became something his imagination did not wish to conjure. The "halo of feminine purity and loveliness" had dissolved. "Sanctity" was preserved, he said, only in his mind.

Meanwhile, Irving continued to pour forth in letters to America. To George Ticknor of Harvard, who took a particular interest in Spanish literature, he wrote of that other New Englander, William H. Prescott, whose *Conquest of Mexico* was now nearing completion: "I shall be very impatient to read the work," Irving reached out. "I was very much gratified with making his acquaintance just before my departure from the United States. He is one of those few authors who do not disappoint in personal intercourse the high expectations they raise by their works." Whether or not because of Cooper's barbs, Irving conscientiously avoided giving any author a reason to call him selfish. The next year, he would congratulate Prescott on "the applause and admiration [your work] has excited throughout the whole republic of letters. . . . You have done full justice to the singularly poetic and romantic nature of your subject." Irving missed the writing life as much as he missed the family circle at his Tappan Bay sanctuary.[53]

He continued to think about "the little Queen," as he referred to Isabella, who was beginning "to look somewhat womanly." Frequent letters to and from his sister Catharine and niece Sarah led him to take a personal interest in the affairs of Ebenezer's daughter Kate, who had been engaged since 1841 to James Paulding's nephew Phil. She had recently suffered an emotional setback owing to Phil's faithless behavior; without breaking off the engagement, the young man had begun to court Mary Hamilton, the daughter of Irving's Tarrytown neighbor James Alexander Hamilton, and sister of his dependable aide Alexander. Irving was uncharacteristically severe in calling Phil a "miserable animal" and "a selfish driveling dolt" who mingled "mental imbecillity" with abject "meanness." Kate was better off without him, he said, and should replace her former affection with due contempt. He was a protective uncle, and a traditional moralist, and glad to learn (by way of a letter from Mary to her brother) that Phil had received a proper upbraiding from everyone in the well-knit Irving-Paulding-Hamilton network.

Almost automatically, he ended letters home by wistfully imagining himself at Sunnyside again: "My heart dwells in that blessed little spot; and I really believe that when I die I shall haunt it: but it will be as a good spirit, that no one needs be affraid of." Spain was in the midst of political combat, which spilled into the streets of Madrid. To Daniel Webster, he wrote: "We are threatened with that state of anarchy and civil war, which appears to have been the persevering aim of secret influences both within and without the Country." If we discount his concern for the "little Queen," Ambassador Irving, even under a state of siege, had no obvious anxiety beyond his yearning to be back in a happy house with Ebenezer, Catharine, and the family.[54]

To alleviate the condition in his legs that kept him housebound, he rode in a carriage all the way to Paris in September 1843, figuring that a respite from work, in the company of his adored niece Sarah, would restore his health. He did see some improvement in what he now referred to as his "obstinate malady," but continued political unrest compelled him to return to Madrid earlier than he would have preferred. To Sarah, he wrote in December: "I am deeply concerned to see the poor little Queen drawn into the vortex of political dissension. Her situation is full of peril and uncertainty."[55]

Hamilton, who had proven to be an outstanding second-in-command at the U.S. legation, left Irving's diplomatic family in 1844 to return home. It was a tremendous loss, for Irving had grown exceedingly fond of him. He was replaced by Jasper Livingston, the son of the late Brockholst Livingston, the

Supreme Court justice in whose New York law office Irving had labored in 1801, just before entering the firm of Josiah Ogden Hoffman. Young Livingston was "genteel," Irving reported, and "politely accomplished." He spoke excellent Spanish. A new generation with intimate links to the ambitious names of post-Revolutionary New York was now serving the nation; and Washington Irving, with stories in his head going back to the 1790s, knew all the players: fathers, sons, and now grandsons.[56]

While he remained in Spain, his ankles would never quite return to normal. A second visit to Paris in the autumn of 1844, after a three-week detour to his sister's in Birmingham, England, did not cure the condition. He would be back again a year later. Stateside, Irving's former aides had moved on. Alexander Hamilton, who had come to Spain with an eye for the ladies, married Angelica Livingston, who had fancied him before his departure, and had exercised patience by throwing off "two or three rich offers" during his absence. Henry Brevoort's son Carson found a mate as well, a Long Island heiress.

The one person Irving could unload on during these years was his niece Sarah, now the mother of two. Writing to her on March 27, 1845, he was deeply reflective:

> I am now at that time of life when the mind has a stock of reccollections on which to employ itself; and though these may sometimes be of a melancholy nature, yet it is a "Sweet Souled Melancholy," mellowed and softened by the operation of time; and has no bitterness in it. My life has been a checquered one, crowded with incidents and personages, and full of shifting scenes and sudden transformations; all these I can summon up and cause to pass before me, and in this way can pass hours together in a kind of reverie.

Memory took the place of imagination, as he wandered about the Prado and watched the "passing throngs."[57]

Lest it be suggested that his melancholy meant more than it did, a letter to Sarah one week later—April 3, 1845—found him quite buoyant on his birthday:

> I reccollect the time when I did not wish to live to such an age, thinking it must be attended with infirmity, apathy of feeling; peevishness of temper. . . . yet here my Sixty-second birthday finds me in fine health; in the full enjoyment of all my faculties; with my sensibilities still fresh, and in such buxom activity, that, on my return home yesterday from the Prado, I caught

myself bounding up stairs, three steps at a time, to the astonishment of the porter; and checked myself, reccollecting that it was not the pace befitting a Minister and a man of my years. If I could only retain such health and good spirits I should be content to live on to the age of Methuselah.[58]

Still, there was little left to excite him in Madrid. He breakfasted alone these days, called for Jasper Livingston when he felt like talking—Livingston was less companionable than Hamilton had been—and from time to time attended social gatherings at other embassies. Thinking ahead, he wrote to the publisher George P. Putnam in New York, announcing that although he had no volume in preparation, he planned to revise his complete works, and wished to negotiate a copyright agreement with his firm. The so-called Author's Revised Edition was to require four years of work before it became available from Putnam, but it would be to Irving's satisfaction.[59]

After James K. Polk of Tennessee succeeded John Tyler in the spring of 1845, Irving waited a bit to see what would happen, and then resigned his office. He did so from Paris, addressing his letter to Secretary of State James Buchanan, the fourth cabinet executive he had been in contact with during his three years abroad. He was driven, he wrote, by "an earnest desire" to return to his country and "actuated by no party feeling."[60]

Queen Isabella II was officially on the throne, the first Spanish queen since the Isabella who had championed Christopher Columbus. There had been so many twists and turns, and now Maria Cristina, the oft-exiled mother of the queen, was back in the palace and exercising power. Irving approved of her. The question of fifteen-year-old Isabella's marital future lay at the center of that year's political drama. Uncertainty reigned.[61]

All Irving could do was to continue to send reports to Washington. This he had always done skillfully and, especially when the appreciative Webster was reading his dispatches, with literary flair. But he learned that some of his later expenses were not to be reimbursed by the government, and this slight, which he deemed intentional, irked him. Besides, he was being obliged to wait at his post until his successor was chosen, and was doing so for longer than he would have liked, and without adequate updates from the Polk administration.

CHAPTER 14

In the Shadow of George Washington

1846–1859

I have just read your fourth volume with intense interest and the highest satisfaction. To me it surpasses all the others. . . . You are securing for yourself what Milton looked forward to achieve by lofty aspirations, meditative thought and patient labor–"an immortality of fame."

–Washington Irving to George Bancroft, author of the
ten-volume *History of the United States*, March 1852[1]

I did not go to bed till I had finished all the last half of the [fifth and final] volume; and my first moment this morning is to tell you with what delight, and, in all soberness, emotion, I read it. . . . The throbbings of your heart are as marked and perceptible along the pages as anything you ever wrote.

–Bancroft to Irving, giving his impressions of
Life of George Washington, May 1859[2]

AS THINGS TURNED OUT, HIS EXTENDED PRESENCE in Europe made it possible for Irving to participate, with his old friend Louis McLane, in key negotiations with the British over the most pressing foreign policy issue of the day—the disposition of Oregon Territory. He was already schooled in its history because of his writing of *Astoria*. Washington Irving was to give more of himself to his country before being allowed to retire for good.

When he left the United States in 1842 to assume his duties in Madrid, the future of Texas, then an independent republic, was yet uncertain. President Tyler very much wanted to annex it, but presidential hopefuls Henry Clay and Martin Van Buren opposed him. They expected Texas statehood to lead to war with Mexico, which had held the land until Sam Houston's 1836 offensive in response to the Alamo bloodbath. Since then, Mexico had neither recognized Texas independence nor attempted to reacquire the land. A tense Senate vote went against annexation in 1844, but when James K. Polk came into office, the cause of "manifest destiny" prevailed, and Texas joined the Union in December 1845. Border tensions rose, as expected, and war with Mexico loomed.

American settlement was changing the landscape in Oregon Territory as well as in Texas. This time, the foreign challenge came from Great Britain. As the year 1846 opened, Polk threatened the British with a renunciation of the 1818 treaty of joint occupation if American terms were not accepted and a proper border established between the United States and western Canada. He meant to set the boundary at the 49th parallel, though he hinted that a British delay in agreeing to terms would cause the issue to erupt into something bigger.

Fortunately for Louis McLane of Delaware, U.S. minister to Great Britain for the second time, the well-respected Washington Irving, formerly his attaché in London, was now a seasoned diplomat, temporarily residing in nearby Paris, attending to his "obstinate malady." Before going to England, Irving wrote to his nephew Pierre Munro that he was of one mind with President Polk in the matter of Oregon, and did not believe that an aggressive policy would "create any *flare-up* in England." Yet if war came as a result of English intransigence, American consciences would be clear: "I am . . . of the opinion that we have the right on our side, and that the world will ultimately think so."[3]

In January 1846, he was reunited with his "invaluable friends" Louis and Catherine Mary McLane, staying under their roof as he got down to the business of negotiating with the British. In that the *London Times* fanned the flames of war (as did passion-filled American newspapers that reached England), official talks had to ignore public outcry if peace was to prevail. This is where Irving's presence, and his social relationships with members of the British government, made a difference in the tone of the discussions. After two weeks, the Oregon question was on the road to resolution. McLane told Irving that his presence was "quite a god send." The stumbling block had been possession of the Columbia River, "one of the great outlets of our empire," as Irving proudly referred to it.[4]

He still had a job to do, however. The erstwhile minister to Spain felt it requisite that he return to Madrid, clean up shop, and await his successor. For four years, he had made sense of the intrigue at the Spanish court. His valedictory speech before Queen Isabella II, in March, was brief. He wished her, he said, "from the bottom of my heart," a long and happy life, and a glorious reign. When his replacement finally arrived in July, Irving hastened to leave. The Mexican War was under way, and Spain was remaining neutral. It was a war that Irving believed could have been avoided with more skillful diplomacy on both sides.[5]

His earlier writings aside, Irving left behind in Spain a legacy best summarized in the remarks of a Spanish gentleman, which William Cullen Bryant recorded a decade later: "Why does not your government send out Washington Irving to this court?" the Spaniard probed, though by this time Irving was in his mid-seventies. "I assure you, it would be difficult for our government to refuse anything which Irving should ask."[6]

☆   ☆

Though he had nested at the McLanes' for most of his stay in London, Irving could not stay completely invisible. An old acquaintance, Emily Foster's younger sister Flora, now married, had discovered his whereabouts and contacted him. More than twenty years had gone by since the winter Irving had spent with the Fosters in Dresden. "Your letter [its contents lost to us] called up delightful recollections of past times," he answered graciously, updating her on what was most important to him at that moment: "I built me a pretty cottage on the banks of the Hudson in a beautiful country, and not far from my old haunts of Sleepy Hollow." Though it was "well stocked with nieces and enlivened by visits by friends and connexions," such a state of bliss was "too happy to last." Diplomatic duty had taken him from his utopia, and he was eager to return to it.

He kept repeating the same note. Madrid had made him long for Tarrytown. As soon as he was "relieved from the duties and restraints of office," he would hurry back, "where every thing is ready for my reception and where I have but to walk in, hang up my hat, kiss my nieces, and take my seat in my elbow chair for the remainder of my life." And that is, in essence, what finally occurred in September 1846. As a bonus, Sarah Storrow, her husband, and their two children paid a visit to Sunnyside, as though to help Uncle Washington readjust.[7]

And so he became a New Yorker again. He visited with a frail John Jacob Astor, who had aged noticeably during Irving's four years abroad—"bowed down and almost helpless," he wrote. The millionaire fur trader had continued

to amass a fortune in railroads and canals, state and city bonds, financial institutions and life insurance companies, and revenues from the Astor House
Hotel, near City Hall. He had groomed his son William to take over family operations; meanwhile, though his private secretary, Fitz-Greene Halleck, stayed
on, Astor hired a new special adviser, the former Harvard librarian Joseph
Green Cogswell. According to Henry Brevoort, the old man began to take a
decided interest in the possibility of an afterlife, too.

In these years, Cogswell was championing a pet project with his employer:
the Astor Free Library. It had still not moved from the design to construction
stage because the man with the money was slow in parting with it while alive,
even as he warmed to the idea of so noble a bequest to the city. In 1839, the
ex-librarian had convinced Astor to proceed, and Irving (whom Astor had already made an executor of his estate in 1836) was named an uncompensated
trustee of the prospective library, along with Cogswell, Brevoort, Halleck, and
William Astor. Irving had great respect for Cogswell, and would have made
him his secretary of legation in Madrid had Astor not vetoed the plan so as to
retain the services and companionship of his learned aide. Now that Irving was
back in New York, discussions about the library resumed.[8]

Astor had his Halleck and his Cogswell, and Irving had his nephew Pierre,
now living in Manhattan, whom he kept in charge of his mostly sluggish investments, as he had during his time in Europe. As he turned his attention to his literary property, he turned again to Pierre, whom he liked to have around
whenever possible so he could think out loud. Irving's Philadelphia publisher was
no longer printing his works, and he had not yet finalized a deal with Putnam.[9]

His greatest effort went into repairing and enlarging Sunnyside. A windfall
from Pierre's investments spurred him on, and from late 1846 through the
spring of 1847, he oversaw building. One consequence of his stepped-up activity was a recurrence of his swollen ankle, apparently aggravated by his time
outdoors in the cold and wet; it would be many months before he would feel
in full health again.[10] Yet this was when he tacked on to Sunnyside the signature "pagoda" top of the "make shift little Mansion," as he gaily described the
original house to Gouverneur Kemble of Cold Spring, who had seen its outline
as he plied the Hudson in his boat but had not yet had an up-close tour. Irving
could now boast of "one of the most complete snuggeries in the country." The
pagoda tower featured a weathercock imported from Holland, purchased by a
local entrepreneur known familiarly as the "King of Coney Island." It had been
detached from a windmill near Rotterdam that was to be demolished.[11]

Irving fervently hoped that his private peace would not be demolished either when the new railroad running along the Hudson brought noisy locomo-

tives past his door. The trees along the riverbank provided the only barricade between ironclad modernity and his precious elbow-chair. Pierre wrote later of his uncle's first "paroxysm of annoyance": "If the Garden of Eden were now on earth, they would not hesitate to run a railroad through it," Irving had cried out. But he gradually acquiesced to the inevitable, and accepted the $3,500 compensation that was offered him for permitting construction crews to dig up his neighborhood. The offenders sympathized, and wrote him a polite letter acknowledging that "the derangement of rural taste and retirement" he had to suffer was greater than that of "any other proprietor . . . below the Highlands." This would not stop Irving from complaining to Gouverneur Kemble in 1850 of the "infernal alarm" of the "railroad steam trumpet" that woke him one midnight and left him with "shattered nerves." Owning the mind of a logical man, he thought it not inappropriate to suggest that "some signal less coarse and brutal" than the train whistle could be devised. In the end, he made the best of the situation by striking a deal by which he or his family members could flag down any train and board it from the Sunnyside property.[12]

During his first year back home—the first year of his official retirement—Irving wrote of his new station in life with hope. "I am a complete rustic," he commented quintessentially to a friend in Spain. "Live almost entirely at home . . . and though within five and twenty miles of New York, with rail road and steam boat conveyances, have suffered between four and five months to elapse without visiting it. I am surrounded by my family of nieces, who are like daughters and most affectionate daughters to me." To Sarah Storrow, who was back in France: "My own place has never been so beautiful as at present . . . and I am never tired of sitting there in my old Voltaire chair, of a long summer morning, with a book in hand, sometimes reading, sometimes musing on the landscape, and sometimes dozing and mixing all up in a pleasant dream." The dream mode had crept back into his prose for the first time in quite a while. This was how almost everyone preferred to picture Geoffrey Crayon as a retiree.[13]

In March 1848, Astor died. Irving was a pallbearer at his funeral in Manhattan, and an executor of his will, for which he was to receive approximately $10,500. Many who considered Astor a miser felt he should have given more to charity than the 6 percent of his fortune that he directed for public purposes. Predictably, perhaps, Irving's old antagonist James Fenimore Cooper, no fan of Astor's either, wrote to his wife on hearing the news: "J. J. Astor goes to the tomb. . . . Irving is an executor and report says with a legacy of $50,000. What an instinct that man has for gold!" It was not true, of course. Almost immediately after Astor's funeral, work accelerated on the Astor Library, and in 1849, Irving was elected to serve as its first president of the board. He made the effort to attend nearly every one of its monthly meetings, regardless of health. The library opened to the public five years later, with eighty thousand volumes, livening up Lafayette Street (just below Astor Place).[14]

Also in the critical year of 1848, Irving concluded arrangements with George Putnam to publish his complete works, in fifteen volumes, over the next two years. The author did a considerable amount of editing, sometimes updating while composing introductions and conclusions for such works as the *Sketch Book* and *Alhambra* that were not a part of earlier editions. In writing the new preface to *A History of New York*, "The Author's Apology," he began by eulogizing "my brother the late Peter Irving," who had helped him to conceive the parodic book. *Knickerbocker's History*, in fact, was the first volume of the Putnam collection to appear, in September 1848, and its sales were strong enough to bring about a second printing after one month. An astounding 350,000 copies of the Author's Revised Edition by Putnam would be sold over nine years, earning its author $80,000. In that time, individual volumes were sold separately and reprinted as needed.[15]

Irving's productivity at Sunnyside was altogether stunning. He started out in 1847–1848 by putting into publishable form some of his notes from the 1820s. These emerged as two volumes, *Mahomet* and *Mahomet's Successors*, in 1849 and 1850. Drawing on his years as a student of Spanish history and creative champion of the defeated Moors, and giving credit to a recent work in German, Irving synthesized what he considered a history of the prophet appropriate for "a family library." *Mahomet* is a period piece, straightforward in many of its details, and inherently critical of the culture of violence. This becomes even more apparent in *Mahomet's Successors*, a largely political history in the manner of the *Conquest of Granada*.[16] Meanwhile, he arranged for the publication of a single-volume biography of Oliver Goldsmith and a patchwork volume of already published stories, *A Book of the Hudson*, both in 1849.[17] He did all this without abandoning the *Life of Washington*, at this point a bundle of notes destined to comprise five volumes and to be his longest work.

The Goldsmith biography is of particular interest because of what Goldsmith meant to Irving growing up. This volume was "a labor of love," as Irving wrote in his preface, for he considered Goldsmith a charming character as well as a compelling stylist. "There are few writers for whom the reader feels such personal kindness as for Oliver Goldsmith," Irving declares. "We read his character in every page, and grow into familiar intimacy with him as we read." His accessibility was owing to a combination of "artless benevolence" and "whimsical, yet amiable views of human life." It was, for Irving, a matter of seeing literature as a communion of author and reader.

The Irish-born Goldsmith (1728–1774) was a high-minded poet and novelist whose fame, like Irving's, grew but gradually. "He had not those brilliant though fallacious qualities which flash upon the public, and excite loud but transient applause," wrote his American admirer. Yet he was a member of England's most exclusive literary club, its discriminating gatekeeper being the illustrious Dr. Samuel Johnson, who was responsible for helping Goldsmith to place his brilliant *The Vicar of Wakefield* with a publisher. Johnson's acolyte, the morbid and gossiping James Boswell, a man of "ludicrous ambition," according to Irving, sought to diminish Goldsmith's reputation. A defense of the literary underdog naturally appealed to Washington Irving.

Because of his trials and misadventures, Goldsmith's life could be told as a picaresque tale, bringing Irving back to his roots as a satirist who did his research well. Nor could Irving resist quoting Goldsmith's portrait of the Dutch, so obviously indebted to it was his own mock-history: "The downright Hollander is one of the oddest figures in nature. Upon a lank head of hair he wears a half-cocked narrow hat, laced with a black ribband; no coat, but seven waistcoats and nine pair of breeches, so that his hips reach up almost to his armpits." Goldsmith was known for his full optimism and his empty purse—exactly the sort of individual whose qualities we can imagine Irving hungering to write about. Indeed, nothing made Irving so happy as being able to celebrate a man's decency along with his talent.[18]

✫ ✫

Entering his last decade of life, though his patience for the turbulence of New York City had declined, Irving entertained regularly, and even seemed not to mind visits to Sunnyside from friends of his friends. In the summer of 1851, an unannounced visitor presented him with a letter of introduction. It was the nephew of one whose name must always have compelled a smile from Irving. Herman Knickerbocker of Schaghticoke, New York, signed the letter "your ever to be remembered and true friend." That same year, *Harper's New Monthly Magazine* anointed Irving "the Patriarch of American Letters." Though he could not have been pleased by the Tarrytown carriage owner who brought sightseers to Sunnyside, he politely shook hands with strangers, and did his best to respond to written requests for his autograph when they came from young people.

His Sunnyside was no longer the retreat he had planned in the mid-1830s—the noisy locomotive was the least of his interruptions in the 1850s. He could not escape the life of celebrity. And so he resigned himself to a certain amount of performing. He was a spellbinding host, according to numerous visitors, and a ready conversationalist who turned on his best Geoffrey

Crayon impression just to give the people what they wanted. But he did so artfully; the "real" Irving—a very private person—remained hidden from view. He avoided public notice as much as possible; he told the Irving Literary Society, for example, that he would not speak to the group, though its sole purpose was to celebrate his career: "I have an insuperable repugnance to public speaking," he explained.[19]

Around this time, there was one devotee whom Irving cultivated, a writer by the name of Donald Grant Mitchell, who wrote as "Ik Marvel." Best known for his *Reveries of a Bachelor* (1850) and *Dream Life* (1851), Mitchell was not quite thirty when he and Irving struck up an acquaintance. He was an essayist very much in the Irving tradition. One need only read the first paragraph of the preface to *Reveries of a Bachelor* to make the comparison:

> This book is neither more, nor less than it pretends to be; it is a collection of those floating Reveries which have, from time to time, drifted across my brain. I never yet met with a bachelor who had not his share of just such floating visions; and the only difference between us lies in the fact that I have tossed them from me in the shape of a Book.[20]

Mitchell and Irving were introduced at Lafayette Place, in New York, by Lewis Gaylord Clark, who had been editor of the *Knickerbocker Magazine* since 1834. Mitchell asked Irving whether *Dream Life* might be dedicated to him, and Irving replied:

> Though I have a great disinclination in general to be the object of literary oblations and compliments, yet in the present instance I have enjoyed your writings with such peculiar relish and have been so drawn toward the author by the qualities of head and heart evinced in them, that I confess I feel gratified by the dedication.

He only objected to the "LL.D." that Mitchell intended to append to Irving's name (referring to the degree Oxford had conferred on him in 1830), which Irving regarded as "a learned dignity" to which he had "never laid claim."[21]

In that the opening epigraph in *Dream Life,* from Shakespeare's *The Tempest,* reads: "We are such stuff / As dreams are made of; and our little life / Is rounded with a sleep," it would seem as though the fabulous Rip Van Winkle had a re-creator on his hands. Irving wrote of his sudden intimacy with Mitchell in a letter to Sarah Storrow. "He is a very gentleman like amiable little fellow and I have taken a great liking to him both as an author and a man."[22]

It was a friendship in marked contrast to Irving's touchy relationship with the prolific James Fenimore Cooper, who died at the age of sixty-two in September 1851, at Cooperstown. In February 1852, a commemoration for the deceased author was held in New York, at which the former senator and former secretary of state Daniel Webster presided. Though Cooper would probably have preferred otherwise, Irving was placed at the head of the organizing committee.[23]

At the event itself, the awkward speaker Irving made himself heard—as he self-deprecatingly reported to John P. Kennedy—for only one minute, with "but one break down, but the pangs of delivery were awful." William Cullen Bryant gave the keynote address, during which he alluded to the "unhappy coolness" that subsisted between Cooper and Irving. Irving made no public display of his discomfort with the statement, but he did say to his nephew Pierre afterward that the coolness was "all on Cooper's side; that he had never been conscious of any cause of difference between them." He had last seen Cooper at the offices of George Putnam—their "common literary resort"— and recalled thinking then that the somewhat younger Cooper was "in full vigor of mind and body, a very 'castle of a man'" who, Irving thought, was "apparently destined to outlive me." They had both achieved fame because of invented characters who were in some way disruptive of the social order. Yet the two authors could not socialize.

There was a passing of the torch in the early 1850s, in this and many ways. Old warhorses such as Webster, Clay, and Calhoun were dying off—Webster only months after his Cooper eulogy. Men born during the Revolution, who had lived to reshape the republic, were yielding to others. Not long after the Cooper commemoration, Irving learned of another passage that caused him sadness, and reawakened old memories. This time it was the Irish songster Tom Moore, four years his elder. Moore's death was not unexpected, for the poet's mind had, Irving said, "suffered eclipse." Irving was part of a dying generation.[24]

He, too, was interrupted by illness; but, like a brittle old farmer driving his mule, he prodded his Washington biography along. He did not deny that writing was taking a toll on him. "When a man is in his seventieth year, it is time to be cautious," he wrote to Sarah Storrow. In July 1852, and again in July 1853, he traveled to Saratoga Springs for the healing baths ("though I believe that all I require is a good spell of *literary abstinence*"). In the first instance, he fortuitously met up with John P. Kennedy and his wife Elizabeth, having no idea they would be there. The epicure now had ideal dinner companions.

It had been fifty years since he had come here as a young Manhattanite— a law clerk with weak lungs and a washed-out look. The baths were of secondary importance to Saratoga now, because society flourished with or without them. New York's wealthiest had staked out claims; the literati were entertained at watering holes of a different sort. Saratoga was a reminder of the history Irving had lived through. In 1809, Julia Stockton Rush, the wife of the Revolutionary medical authority Benjamin Rush, had happened on the healing waters, and she helped promote the area as a social destination as well as a health spa. In the 1820s, keen on the beautiful natural surroundings, Cooper was staying there when he conceived the landscape for *The Last of the Mohicans*. By mid-century, with the advent of railways, luxurious hotels lined Broadway in Saratoga Springs. Foreigners flocked there as well. And as things turned out, Donald G. Mitchell was around, too, and just a few doors from where Irving roomed. As they took morning walks together, the young writer plied the elderly author with questions about the "humors of writing," and how he had brought the *Sketch Book* to life. Irving had become a teacher by example, and Mitchell treasured his *"bonhomie."*[25]

When Irving returned to Saratoga the next summer, he arranged to meet up with Kennedy. It was on this occasion that he accompanied his fellow author—whom he affectionately called "Horseshoe," after Kennedy's novel *Horseshoe Robinson*—on a voyage up Lake Champlain, and thence by rail across northernmost New York State to Ogdensburg, on the Oswegatchie River, where he had not been since his rough overland trek with the Hoffmans and Ogdens in 1803. Regaling his nieces Sarah (i.e., the daughters of Catharine and Ebenezer) with remembrances of a half-century past, he was the more sentimental in writing to the Parisian Sarah:

> There were still some rocks where I used to sit of an evening and accompany with my flute one of the ladies who sung—I sat for a long time on the rocks summoning Reccollections of byegone days and of the happy beings by whom I was then surrounded—All had passed away—all were dead and gone; of that young and joyous party I was the sole survivor—they had all lived quietly at home and out of the reach of mischance—yet had gone down to their graves—while I, who had been wandering about the world, exposed to all hazards by sea and land—was yet alive.[26]

As if to acknowledge that he was tempting fate with these thoughts, Irving reported in the same letter that he had made certain arrangements upon his return to Tarrytown. As lower Manhattan was being transformed and Beekman Street was to be widened, he had rescued his parents from the Irving vault in the Beekman Street churchyard. In what their son called a "solemn and sacred duty," William and Sarah Irving were deposited in undisturbed earth next to the

Old Dutch Church in Sleepy Hollow. He had purchased a family plot, shaded by oaks, and erected an iron railing around it, removing the family, he said, from "that restless city where nothing is sacred." As the historian Thomas Connors recently explained, this was Irving's chance to bury the mother he so adored for the first time, having been in England at the time of her death.

He had been thinking about the rural cemetery for at least ten years when he wrote to Ebenezer about bringing the remains of their late brother Peter to this place. So he now felt a sense of relief. "There I have seen the remains of the family gathered together and interred where they cannot be again disturbed," he told Sarah Storrow. "I have marked out my resting place by my mothers side, and a space is left for me there." In what Connors refers to as Irving's "sentimental geography," the bachelor brothers were to be interred directly beside their parents (Peter was next to William, Sr.); the married sons, along with their spouses, fanned out from there. Significantly, Pierre Munro Irving was to be buried at his uncle's feet, and Irving's beloved nieces above his head.[27]

Meanwhile, aiming to preserve his life a little longer, Irving had taken on a homeopathic physician, John C. Peters. Peters was trying to convince him that he needed to eat more sensibly. He "has my head in his hands," the patient joked with John P. Kennedy, "and is poisoning me into a healthy state of the brain."[28]

★ ★

From his home in the country, Irving had less and less to say about national politics, though he seemed familiar with just about everyone in high office. He judged officers of the government for their character more than their party affiliation—this is what he had always done. In 1852, Franklin Pierce of New Hampshire was elected president, and William Rufus King of Alabama vice president.

Irving counted King as a friend. Both bachelors, they had first met in 1817, in Liverpool, when King, then thirty-one, was en route home from a stint at the U.S. legation in Russia. Then, as Irving headed for Madrid in 1842, he spent time with King in Paris, when King was the U.S. minister to France. Learning of King's election as vice president, Irving called the Alabama Democrat "an upright honorable man; a gentleman in spirit and deportment." He wished that roles were reversed, and King the chief executive—so long as a Whig could not win the presidency. The only Alabaman ever elected vice president (nor has any been president), King was also the shortest-serving. He died at his home in the early spring of 1853, without ever presiding over the Senate.

As for Pierce, a staunch Jacksonian and brigadier general in the Mexican War, Irving knew him, but not well. Intending to do research on George Washington at the State Department archives, and living at the home of John Pendleton

Kennedy (then secretary of the navy), he attended Pierce's inauguration, enjoyed a private conversation with him, and was touched by how the incoming president was taking care of Nathaniel Hawthorne. They had been college classmates at Bowdoin, and Hawthorne had written Pierce's official campaign biography after having published *The Scarlet Letter;* now, the writer would be gainfully employed as the U.S. consul in Liverpool. For Irving, no one who patronized writers could be all bad. He wrote to the "quiet and gentleman-like" President Pierce only once, it appears—to request a consular appointment for his writer friend Donald G. Mitchell. The letter had its intended effect: Mitchell was named U.S. consul in Venice.[29]

These days, Irving was most interested in Revolutionary politics. It was in 1847 that he had begun the Washington biography in earnest, that is, writing something every day. He allowed his other, smaller book projects to divert him, but faithfully returned to his Washington each time. In 1853, after Pierce's inauguration, he toured the western part of Virginia with Kennedy, covering ground that his subject had trodden at the time of the French and Indian War. Over that year and the next, a first volume came together, and a second, taking the soldier up to his darkest moments, in the fall of 1776, when the Continental Army was nearly decimated at the battle of Long Island. Meanwhile, as Washington Irving toiled, the small village just south of Sunnyside, sustained by a railroad stop and called Dearman, was renamed Irvington.

Wolfert's Roost was published in 1855, just before the first volume of *Life of Washington.* These desultory stories, published in the *Knickerbocker Magazine* at least a dozen years before, were new to many readers, and so Irving realized both belated praise and unexpected sales. As a good bit of it was drawn from notebooks of the 1820s, Geoffrey Crayon returned to charm a younger set of readers. The introductory offering, the title tale of "Wolfert's Roost," which first appeared in the *Knickerbocker Magazine* in 1839, was vintage Knickerbocker, and semiautobiographical. It recalled "the fabulous days" of the Dutch mariners along the lower Hudson, the "great Mediterranean Sea of the New-Netherlands" known as the Tappan Zee, and Irving's own inheritance from those days, "The Roost." In the story, Wolfert Acker goes to war at the behest of William the Testy, and serves as "privy counsellor" to Peter Stuyvesant before retiring to his stone mansion beside the Hudson that was allegedly "harassed by Yankee witchcraft." There are suggestions that Wolfert's wife was of the enemy and that she "used to ride on a broomstick to a witches' Sabbath in Sleepy Hollow" while her husband lived. Wolfert's ghost had since haunted his apple orchard in the moonlight.[30]

In September 1855, after some years of estrangement, Irving responded to an invitation from former President Martin Van Buren to visit him in Kinderhook. Van Buren was now residing at Lindenwald, the estate previously owned by the Van Ness family, where Irving had gone to mourn Matilda Hoffman and where he had written a portion of *Knickerbocker's History*. Presumably he made the trip north along the Hudson by rail, taking the opportunity to see Gouverneur Kemble in Cold Spring; possibly he even took Kemble with him to Van Buren's. The record is scanty here, but reconciliation was certainly in order.[31]

Irving had known almost all the chief executives of his lifetime. He had cast his eyes on the strapping figure of George Washington when he was six, and after attending the Burr trial he had an audience with Jefferson in the President's House. Madison consistently showed him respect; Jackson and Van Buren both treated Irving as a confidant; and Tyler had sent him to Madrid. And through his friend Kennedy, Irving had met Millard Fillmore and Franklin Pierce. Now he returned to the first of them all, a man whose singular place in American history led Irving to feel that a serious biography would be the proper culmination of his long career of image making.

Realizing the amount of work his multivolume *Life of Washington* entailed, he officially hired his nephew Pierre as his full-time assistant in 1855, at a monthly salary of $135. He did so to help him preserve energy, as much as anything. Pierre's job, in theory, was to compile information and write preliminary chapters, as he had done for *Astoria*. This would allow his uncle to devote more of his time to the art of narrative.[32] *Life of Washington* was to be a thoroughgoing narrative history, as opposed to that other popular format of the nineteenth century, the "Life and Letters" biography, which featured the subject's letters with only minimal annotation and commentary. The "Life and Letters" arrangement filled in chronological blanks and led the reader from one letter to the next.

The most accomplished writer-editor in America was Jared Sparks (1789–1866), who had worked largely with New England authors for the previous twenty years in compiling short, popular biographies, primarily of New York and New England heroes and statesmen of the colonial and Revolutionary age, for his Library of America series. Sparks was a graduate of Harvard, and he had succeeded Edward Everett as president of that institution in the early 1850s. His projects included multivolume editions of the writings of George Washington and Benjamin Franklin, in twelve and ten volumes respectively, as well as a two-volume treatment of Washington.[33]

Another prominent figure in American history writing was George Bancroft (1800–1891), also from Massachusetts. In that odd juxtaposition of creative pens and military bureaucracy, Bancroft, like Paulding under Van Buren and Kennedy under Fillmore, had served as Polk's secretary of the navy. Just as Irving completed his tour as U.S. minister to Spain in 1846, Bancroft assumed the post of U.S. minister to England, where he remained for three years. He had completed the first volume of his massive *History of the United States* in 1834; and in 1855, he had published the sixth of what would eventually be ten volumes—this was the volume that covered the American Revolution, and would have been of particular interest to Irving as he wrote of General Washington's trials amid war. Irving told Bancroft, a few days before they were to dine together, that he had found it "graphic" and "dramatic," "vigorous" and "concise."[34] He admired the exertions of Sparks, as he admired the skill of Bancroft. Sparks and Bancroft were learned men and lifelong friends, and they recognized Irving as a compeer.

Irving's *Life of Washington* relied closely, as the best histories of the antebellum period did, on public documents. His preface to volume one states up front: "Though a biography, and of course admitting of familiar anecdote, excursive digressions, and a flexible texture of narrative, yet, for the most part, it is essentially historic. Washington, in fact, had very little private life, but was eminently a public character." Of course, no biographer today would make such a statement, believing as we do that private considerations, or self-fashioning, invariably have an impact on an individual's public performance. Irving, however, goes on to say that his role as biographer is mainly to show how a "great drama" (American nationhood) was essentially indistinguishable from "the principal actor" who was George Washington. In the tradition of Sparks and Bancroft, he appeals to "good authority," chiefly Washington's letters—and here Irving specifically mentions his time in the State Department archives, fortifying his reliance on the Washington correspondence published by Sparks.

In fact, Irving did not limit his research to these sources. He consulted British and French writings, the journals of the Continental Congress, Chief Justice John Marshall's five-volume biography (1804–1807, the first to draw on Washington's personal records), the memoirs of various Revolutionary War generals, and the *Annals of Congress*, which reported, often verbatim, the content of virtually every speech made in the national legislature. Altogether, the modern editors of Irving's *Life of Washington* have located some 180 volumes, or sets of volumes, that they believe Irving used.[35]

Sparks was a professional historian, but Irving had the advantage of being one of the smoothest and most elegant writers in America. Marshall's *Washington* suffered from being a partisan document, designed to promote the Federalist cause, and its manner of expression had been superseded by a younger generation's taste for more evocative and engaging language. Still, like

Marshall, who owed his own rise in Federalist circles to the first president, Irving tended to protect his subject from full exposure, refraining from telling all he had gleaned about the general's petulance and irritability. The result is a well-researched, highly energetic, and still-accessible biography that does not, however, go much beyond the predictable portrait of a man of morals and unselfish commitment. Irving keeps coming back to Washington's "inherent probity . . . on which he regulated all his conduct," or "characteristic firmness, caution and discrimination"—a patriotic perspective that had become cliché.[36]

Two key episodes will serve to illustrate the tenor of Irving's *Life of Washington*. The August 1776 retreat of American forces from Long Island was a test of generalship as well as of character. The British had landed without opposition, and Washington's army, to avoid capture, rowed to Manhattan to regroup. All of New York City would fall into enemy hands soon after. This sequence of events marked a low point in Washington's military career. The commander had allowed his army to be cornered, but then saw large numbers ferried across the East River without detection, helped along by a change in wind direction in the middle of the night and by a thick morning fog. Irving tells it dramatically:

> Never did retreat require greater secrecy and circumspection. Nine thousand men, with all the munitions of war, were to be withdrawn from before a victorious army, encamped so near, that every stroke of spade and pickaxe from their trenches could be heard. The retreating troops, moreover, were to be embarked and conveyed across a strait three quarters of a mile wide, swept by rapid tides. The least alarm of their movement would bring the enemy upon them.

With the army temporarily safe in Manhattan, Irving accords Washington credit, though what really happened was that the commander initially acted too slowly, then relied on faulty intelligence, and luckily profited from the opposing general's refusal to follow the recommendations of his aggressive battalion commanders. Yet Irving writes: "This extraordinary retreat . . . was one of the most signal achievements of the war, and redounded greatly to the reputation of Washington, who, we are told, for forty-eight hours . . . scarce closed his eyes, and was the greater part of his time on horseback." The key to Irving's narrative was his subject's resilience and determination.[37]

Later in the war, Washington was faced with the betrayal of his friend Benedict Arnold, an event traditionally taught as an archetypal morality play in the republic's history. The crucial role played by James Paulding's cousin

John in André's capture near Tarrytown, which led to Arnold's discovery, gave the unraveling of Arnold's plot more meaning to Irving than it did to most; therefore, in relating the story of the conspiracy to surrender West Point, the author supplies plentiful detail: the river patrols, the delicate spy game, a "nocturnal proceeding full of peril," a "midnight negotiation," the color of André's coat—everything.

The setting is the "Tappan Sea," which the author of the story knew all too well. And when André, carrying a passport with Arnold's signature, is taken prisoner in the so-called Neutral Ground between the British and American lines, Irving offers his credentials, by inference, in the authority with which his narrative voice proceeds:

> The one in refugee garb who brought André to a stand, was John Paulding, a stout-hearted youngster, who, like most of the young men of this outraged neighborhood, had been repeatedly in arms to repel or resent aggressions, and now belonged to the militia. He had twice been captured and confined in the loathsome military prisons where patriots suffered in New York. . . . Both times he had made his escape.

He had been wearing a "refugee" (Tory) uniform, given to him while in prison, and it was the coat that convinced André he was a friend; and thus the spy had revealed himself. A footnote pronounces Irving's expertise: "Stated on the authority of Commodore Hiram Paulding, a son of the captor, who heard it repeatedly from the lips of his father." It was Paulding who found incriminating papers in André's boot and exclaimed, "My God! He is a spy!"[38]

Irving maintains a sprightly pace throughout the five volumes. He provides a sort of valedictory at the opening of the final volume when he states that the *Life of Washington* has been "the crowning effort" of his literary career. Here, too, he gives proper credit to Pierre for his assistance, and thanks the reading public for its "kindly disposition" toward the previous four volumes. Then he proceeds to take George Washington from the presidency to his grave.

The historical Washington was, by most accounts, the least approachable of warm-blooded beings. Irving chooses to present a well-balanced demeanor: "The character of Washington may want some of those poetical elements which dazzle and delight the multitude, but it possessed fewer inequalities, and a rarer union of virtues than perhaps ever fell to the lot of one man." A litany of saccharine virtues proceeds from here, meant to justify Irving's final declaration: "The fame of Washington stands apart from every other in history; shining with a truer luster and a more benignant glory."

Seeing how Irving constructs the intellectually modest Virginian as a superior creature, one is reminded of the biographer's treatment of another sober being, a man to whom he attributes "a quick apprehension, a retentive memory, a vivid imagination, and an inventive genius": the historic Mohammad (Mahomet). "Owing but little to education, he had quickened and informed his mind by close observation." In both, we might say, Irving was writing about the founder of a religion. His five volumes depicting the life of Washington consequently warrant the designation "Romantic biography." No one could share the sunlight with this Washington, but could stand only in his shadow.[39]

★   ★

Irving was at peace. As he wrote to John P. Kennedy's wife Elizabeth: "The life I lead in my little nest at Sunnyside is what Byron stygmatised as a 'mill pond existence' without events or agitations." The always contentious Byron had had an unsuccessful marriage, which stirred things up at a certain juncture in the "mill pond existence," but Irving did not have a wife that he could even imagine nagging him: "My bachelor lot affords no variety of the kind; and if my womankind have any fault in their management, it is that they make things too smooth around me; so that I float quietly along without a ripple to fret or to write about." His old friend Paulding, destined to outlive him only by months, wrote that he hoped Irving was "sliding smoothly down the hill" of life. Irving's reply was a reiteration of what he had said to Elizabeth Kennedy: "I am better off than most bachelors are, or deserve to be. I have a happy home; the happier for being always well stocked with womankind, without whom an old bachelor is a forlorn dreary animal."[40]

In December 1856, *Harper's New Monthly Magazine* printed a copiously illustrated piece on Washington Irving's Sunnyside that enlarged its already romantic status in American literary lore. While Irving lived, his dream world on the riverbank was already a relic; or, as the article reads, "a home amidst the altars upon which [Irving] has devoutly offered up the love and worship of a long life, and upon which he has reverently placed many of the sweetest fruits of his genius."

The *Harper's* piece was an invitation to worshippers. At almost any hour of the day, it said, Sunnyside cottage was but an hour's train ride from the city, and a short walk from Irvington station. "To see the setting of this sparkling little jewel of a home properly, though, you should properly make your approach by water"—that is, by steamer. To visit Tarrytown was to visit scenes of the Revolution still imaginable—"a region of stirring incident and interest." Remember where the "timely arrest" of Major André took place, and just across the water, in "old Tappantown," where that same soldier-spy was hanged. The reader's appetite properly whetted, the article offers a "peep" into the secluded cottage where Washington Irving even now reigned over a tree-encircled farm—he is quoted saying just that: "Yes, I'm monarch of *all* I survey!"

The open, sunlit lawn, the rustic paths, the "dreamy atmosphere"—this was only a surface impression. The compliment to Sunnyside and its monarch continued: "In its very modest yet well-balanced proportions we see his figure of healthful manliness, though scarcely reaching to the middle stature. There is, too, about the odd little mansion, an air of quiet, true dignity, mingled with a feeling of sly mischievousness; unconscious yet observant; dreaming yet wide-awake." Dreaming, yet wide awake. A fit retirement, one must suppose, for one who would live out the life of Rip Van Winkle.[41]

Perhaps a dreamy sentiment settled over Irving as he opened a letter that had needed twenty-four years to be undertaken: "I think I ought to begin by telling you who is writing to you—Emily Foster, now Emily Fuller." They had last seen one another in 1832. She was writing in the hope that her eldest son, who intended to settle in the United States, would meet her old author friend. "I have lately been reading over my old Dresden journal," she told him, "where you are a part of our daily life, and feel it all over again so completely, I cannot believe all the time since has really passed." She had also been engaged with Irving's works, that is, she and her children, taking turns reading aloud from *Alhambra, Bracebridge Hall,* and *The Sketch Book.* "I could see you, your *own self,* as we read, and your very smile." Irving sent her a long and generous reply in which he invited her son to visit and informed her of his "quiet life in a little rural retreat." His neighbors and nieces, he wrote, "almost make me as happy as if I were a married man." He let the mother of five know that he spoke of her often with his nieces, and that a picture she had long ago painted hung over the piano in his drawing room.[42]

In his last years, he pondered the significance of where he had traveled, both in the world and in his mind, giving thought to younger writers' contributions to what he directly called "our national literature." He continued to hear from Dickens, who told him outright "how often I write to you, individually and personally, in my books." He complimented the historian John L. Motley, whose *Rise of the Dutch Republic* he had read with "unflagging interest." He entertained the essayist and wit Oliver Wendell Holmes, who had recently published *The Autocrat of the Breakfast-Table.* Irving read it, Pierre reports, "with great zest."[43]

His health took a turn for the worse in 1858, and throughout 1859, he seemed to know that his time was limited. He had asthma. He coughed and had trouble breathing, especially in the cold weather. His physician, John C. Peters, prescribed treatments based on the patient's sleeping habits, appetite, and moods. The homeopath, who noted that the author was coping with an enlargement of the heart, retained Irving's confidence until the end; Irving tended to feel that the five-volume *Washington*, this and nothing else, was his undoing.

His married niece and nephew, Helen and Pierre, moved up from the city to reside permanently at Sunnyside from December 1858 on. Pierre must have been thinking at this time of the understanding he and his uncle had reached some time before—that he would write the authorized biography of Washington Irving—for this was when he began a daily journal of his uncle's activities and offhand comments. Pierre had already prepared a draft of the early period, at least through 1820. Trusting in Pierre's ability, Irving had written into his 1850 will that if he should die prematurely, his *Life of Washington* would be managed by his nephew.[44]

During the spring and summer of 1859, Irving gathered strength, but not enough to resume a normal routine. Pierre described April 3, Irving's seventy-sixth birthday, as a "dull, cheerless day," though his uncle received flowers from Sunnyside's gardener and from a neighbor, the wife of a New York newspaper editor. Muttered Irving, as Pierre transcribed: "Beautiful flowers to a withered old man." The bouquets kept coming. Meanwhile, the author started using a glass inhaler prescribed by Dr. Peters, which contained "olive tar."

His breathing was inconsistent. He tended to have good days and bad nights. "Pestered to death with letters, applications for autographs, presents of books for libraries, &c. &c.," he complained to Pierre. "I wish there were no post office." One morning at breakfast, realizing that Pierre had spent the entire night beside him, he became choked up as he sought to express how his nephew's devotion made him feel. On May 22, when he was having difficulty getting rest, Helen asked him how he was. "Miserable, miserable, miserable," he returned. "Ah, if I could only die at once and not live to be a burden to myself and others!"[45]

On May 23, the very next day after wishing to be rid of age, Irving took the train to New York and delighted in an exhibition of Frederic Church's large canvas, *The Heart of the Andes*. Two days later, he attended a board meeting of the Astor Library. On May 30, he was back in the city, this time to visit his doctor—and his tailor! If he thought he was dying, why get measured for a new suit?

As the weather improved, so did Irving's spirits. One day in mid-June, Pierre found him "playful and facetious." Later that month, on receiving a letter from an irate southerner who thought that his *Washington* failed to chastise the first president for having opposed slavery in his last years, he reacted: "Did you ever know such fools, willing to incur the opprobrium of the whole world for their accursed slavery?" Around the same time, he offered a final impression of Aaron Burr: "Burr full of petty mystery—made a mystery of every thing." Apparently, the discredited vice president had a habit of whispering to people when others were in the room, which Irving had found, even at the time, disconcerting. Then again, part of the charm of Irving's "Little Man in Black" was the air of mystery that surrounded him.[46]

As autumn came on, his shortness of breath intensified. That intimate of his late years, the writer-politician John P. Kennedy, was in New York at the end of October; he wrote an affectionate note to his friend Irving to say that he would try to visit him at Sunnyside. "Now that you have laid Washington up in his five immortal volumes and have nothing more to tempt you to outwork your health, I hope to find you enjoying the reward of a well spent life in the contentment of a comfortable and hearty old age." He visited Sunnyside on Halloween, and saw a man who looked "wretchedly altered."[47]

On November 7, a day of rain and clouds, Irving received a visit from Theodore Tilton of the New York *Independent,* who stayed for just thirty minutes—long enough to write an article about Sunnyside on a day without sun. He asked the author which of his books he looked back on with the most pleasure. "I scarcely look with full satisfaction upon any," Irving answered, "for they do not seem what they might have been. I often wish that I could have twenty years more, to take them down from the shelf one by one, and write them over." He acknowledged that his moods conditioned how (and how often) he wrote, recalling having marveled at Sir Walter Scott, who could get writing done at any time. He said that he himself went weeks without being able to lift his pen, and then, without knowing quite how, he would be writing nonstop.

While still on the subject of Scott and his literary circle, the newspaperman ventured the suggestion that Irving write one more book.

"What is that?"

"Your reminiscences of those literary friends."

"Ah," he exclaimed. "It is too late now! I shall never take the pen again."

Tilton then described Irving's study, a small room with a "great writing table," its walls hung with pictures and neatly arranged bookshelves, and "not a speck of dust upon carpet or cushion." As the newspaperman was leaving, the darkness of the day made space for a shaft of sunlight; it fell on the author, who stood wrapped in his Scottish shawl. The symbolism was unmistakable.[48]

Another visitor in November 1859, one William Dix, was equally imbued with nostalgia, and found in Irving's face something glowing and tender. His smile was endearing, and his voice "tremulous partly with infirmity but more with emotion." To encounter Irving, it seemed, was to imagine some sublime feeling directed to oneself—every such fortunate soul felt he was meant to memorialize meeting a fading star. These overwrought eulogia were, alas, Irving's recompense for a career of writing feelingly about the human spirit.

Toward the end of his life, Irving treated Pierre, his constant companion, to frank opinions. Because Dr. Peters could not attend his patient as often as he needed attention, Pierre doubled as a physician's assistant. As he read aloud to his uncle, they struck up conversations about the people who had made an impact on Irving's life. Verplanck, whom he still reckoned as "just, upright, honorable," Irving also described as "abrupt, cold, not companionable," despite those better qualities. He expressed his disappointment in Dickens—the man, not the writer. One Knickerbocker he consistently complimented was William Cullen Bryant, whose poems, he said, were "perfect gems." And he continued to insist that Cooper's Leatherstocking novels were exceptional, and would live on and on. Just days before he died, he read Cooper's *The Deerslayer,* which he had somehow skipped. On finishing it, he qualified his praise of the author, charging that there was "an immense deal of twaddle" in the drone of dialogue. This was his last comment on Cooper, which, although disapproving, was still nothing compared to the invective that had poured from Cooper with regard to him.[49]

These nuggets come largely from Pierre Munro Irving's unpublished notes, and they serve to remind us that Pierre exclusively conveyed his uncle's kinder, gentler side in his hagiographic, yet indispensable, biography. What other less appealing traits have been buried we will never know. For instance, we glean from "The Legend of Sleepy Hollow," and a few uncensored letters, that Irving referred stereotypically to African-Americans' habits, casting blacks as humble in intelligence and devoid of taste. He did not make the kinds of repulsive comments that many other northern satirists or proponents of polygenesis (multiple creations, one for each race) did, but neither was he as sensitive as the modern mind demands. And we know, too, that, in the 1840s, he wrote condescendingly about the Irish laborers who were employed nearby in the construction of a new system of water delivery to Manhattan. When "a colony of Patlanders," as he called them, were encamped in the vicinity of Sleepy Hollow, he was charmed to learn that the hard-drinking Irish started seeing apparitions—"misshapen monsters . . . invariably without heads." For Irving this was, of course, life imitating art.[50]

Irving had not visited Sleepy Hollow cemetery for more than a year, Pierre happened to note in his journal on November 24, 1859. That Sunday, November 27, the ailing author attended church. Pierre jotted: "Asthma apparently abating." Irving seemed well enough that Pierre left him, and went to town on the 8:39 train on Monday morning, returning as the family was finishing up dinner. His uncle had had wine, and was telling a story about wine tasting.

Evening found Irving in a cheerful mood. Pierre recalled that the sunset was uncommonly beautiful. Looking west across the Hudson, he wrote that the sky was "hung with clouds of the richest crimson." Uncle Washington several times remarked on this spectacle of nature. Preparing for bed at 10:30 p.m., he was joined by his niece Sarah—Ebenezer's Sarah—who heard him announce suddenly: "I feel so dreadfully depressed." And then: "I must arrange my pillows for another weary night." He paused, and spoke again, saying either, "If this could only end" or "When will this end?" She could not be sure of the precise words. At that instant, he grabbed his left side, and fell backwards.

Sarah cried out, and Pierre ran upstairs from the parlor. Niece and nephew could both tell that there was no avail. They went through the motions of bathing his arms and feet, to stimulate him. But he was already gone. The local physician, Horace Carruthers, rushed over, but all he could do was to pronounce Washington Irving dead.[51]

The funeral took place on Thursday, December 1, at Christ Church, Tarrytown. Donald G. Mitchell ("Ik Marvel") was present, and was reminded of the "beaming expression" in Irving's eyes when they had last seen one another. He was moved to look on Irving's countenance again, but as he approached the coffin, he realized what death was. The casket was open, but the eyes of the corpse had been closed: "It seemed to me that death never took away more from a living face."[52]

At some point—no one knows precisely when—Henry Wadsworth Longfellow visited Irving's simple grave in Sleepy Hollow cemetery, and in 1876 composed a poem to record the experience:

> *Here lies the gentle humorist, who died*
> *In the bright Indian Summer of his fame!*
>
> *Living, to wing with mirth the weary hours,*
> *Or with romantic tales the heart to cheer;*
> *Dying, to leave a memory like the breath*
> *Of summers full of sunshine and of showers,*
> *A grief and gladness in the atmosphere.*[53]

CHAPTER 15

The Future of
Rip Van Winkle

Take my word for it, the only happy author in this world is he who is below the care of reputation.

—Washington Irving, from *Tales of a Traveller*[1]

Rip Van Winkle! There was magic in the sound of the name as I repeated it.

—Joseph Jefferson III, star of the
popular play *Rip Van Winkle,* 1889[2]

I N MANY WAYS, WASHINGTON IRVING WAS TO THE nineteenth century what Benjamin Franklin was to the eighteenth. Each had a copious capacity for wit, and each owed his success to the printing press. Satirists and humorists, national symbols who charmed multitudes, they come down to us as agreeable and resourceful men who tried to sound humble and antiheroic as they reached out to an ever-widening community. Franklin gave us homilies, Irving told us stories. They were, furthermore, youngest sons in large families without land or inherited wealth. The improbability of their celebrity is part of what makes them so interesting as historical actors and biographical subjects.

Most do not realize that America was accepted as a world player only in stages. As was said of Franklin, it was said of Irving, too, that before he crossed the Atlantic, his nation was assumed savage and his countrymen simple. Franklin and Irving were—and not only in their diplomatic roles—two of

America's most successful ambassadors to the Old World. As the first was adored by the French, the second cast a spell over the Spanish. Europe as a whole hailed them as autonomous beings who transcended their parochial origins; yet they each contributed something unique to the ripening American personality.

If he were merely a sober moralist, Ben Franklin would not be the same "character" for us three hundred years after his birth. So it was with Washington Irving. He helped to establish a Manhattan attitude, built on parody, which crystallized as Knickerbocker New York. As he grew older, the playful writer carried the colonial-Revolutionary mindset to a new place: a more sensuous imagination and a more tender preoccupation with life's art. Irving created a national literature where there was thought to be none, just as Franklin before him had proved that the colonies were capable of producing "genius." Both became caught up in politics simply by getting noticed.

★　★

Franklin was the wealthier man. He knew how to convert ideas into capital, and he retired from the printing business at the age of forty-two. Irving struggled financially. If we add up his earnings across four and a half decades of active writing, Irving accrued about a quarter of a million dollars. By today's standards, he died "comfortable" but not rich. Although he proved it possible to support oneself by writing fiction, for most of his career he had to write for money. He was never quite satisfied, never financially independent, until the last decade of his life, in the windfall provided by Putnam's republication of his complete works. Up to the Civil War, no American author could call himself wealthy solely on the basis of his publishing history.

Washington Irving has always been portrayed as a genial, almost carefree individual. But we now know better. He worried, he grumbled. Donald G. Mitchell came clean on April 3, 1883, in Tarrytown, at the centennial celebration of Irving's birth: "At times—rare times, it is true—I have seen this most amiable gentleman manifest a little of that restive choler which sometimes flamed up in William the Testy,—not long-lived, not deliberate,—but a little human blaze, of impatience at something gone awry."[3] Had he been angelic, his literary productions could only have been boring.

In an 1810 notebook entry, Irving gave expression to his suspicions about living authors' treatment by the critical public. "Of departed authors," he wrote, "we judge merely by their works. Here then we see nothing but the most fair & luminous parts of their character. . . . But living authors are constantly before the public eye and exposed to the full glare & exposure of scrutinizing familiarity, . . . subject to the weakness & follies of other men."[4] These were the thoughts of the twenty-seven-year-old author of *Knicker-bocker's History*, who was not yet the author of the *Sketch Book*, not yet a biographer or a serious historian, and not yet so meanly reviewed as to justify his cynicism. But he already understood the world of New York politics when he wrote these lines, and he understood the state of literary criticism. In reflecting on the death of James Fenimore Cooper in 1851, he issued an addendum to his 1810 jottings in a letter he wrote to Lewis G. Clark, editor of the *Knickerbocker Magazine:* "When an author is living, he is apt to be judged by his last works. . . . When an author is dead, he is judged by his best works." Clearly, Irving had ideas about literary reputation; he also saw the vicious trends in human psychology all around him, which may have made him a better writer in the long run.[5]

Washington Irving's somewhat diminished reputation among modern literary critics and his slow recession from the national historic memory during the last century shows us how ideologies change as history slips away. It says, too, that no aspect of an author's legacy is sacrosanct. Modern culture, increasingly voyeuristic, operates on the principle that it is equally valid to seek the foibles of the person as to comprehend the mastery of the artist, whether living or dead.

As such, Irving becomes a more interesting biographical subject when we finally overturn the silly assumption that prevailed for at least a century after his death: that his love for Matilda Hoffman explains his lifelong bachelorhood—a love so enduring that he refused to marry. The intensity of his friendships with men was no less crucial to his outlook and temperament and writing. One need only recall his anguish following the death of his roommate John Nalder Hall at the cottage they shared in southern Spain: "It is a long while," Irving told Brevoort, "since I have lived in such domestic intimacy with any one but my brother," or since another man "in so short a space of time could have taken such a hold upon my feelings." And what of Peter, that other lifelong bachelor? Were the Irving brothers' bachelor quarters anything other than a surrogate spousal arrangement, with a relatable level of affection? Men fulfilled needs for him—emotional, and we should not presume physical—that were ordinarily fulfilled by a wife.

Irving does not seem asexual. But what, then, was he? In these pages, we have discovered that he took a powerful interest in virgin innocence. Unless all his letters and stories lie, once carnal knowledge was attained, a woman no longer appealed to him, except as a desexualized, generally maternal friend. He was decidedly uncomfortable with mature female sexuality; that is, sex with a woman was a dangerous prospect. Given his need for order and clean-liness, or the attention he paid to personal hygiene and a dirt-free environ-ment without which he could not be productive as a writer (as attested by Henry Ellsworth on the Oklahoma prairie), we might conclude that Irving lived by a "pollution taboo," and that it had sexual ramifications.

But in other respects, Irving's view of womanhood was quite conventional. Throughout his publishing career, he idealized the untouchable female, ele-vating the virtuous widow or some other woman in mourning. For Irving, a connoisseur of female beauty, the "best" women were adorable but sexless. Whether he had sex with women or not, then, there was more to his sexual outlook than a quiet commitment to remaining the eternal beau of a girl who died in 1809.

What exactly did all his romantic longing mean? Did he, in fact, go through life in love with eighteen-year-old virgins who would not have him as a hus-band? To put it another way, was his real life akin to that of Prince Ahmed, "The Pilgrim of Love" in one of the *Alhambra* tales, who dreamt of a princess he had never seen, and wrote her passionate poetry? Did Irving visit prosti-tutes, as the majority of men in his situation did? In America, as in Europe, men could generally do so without recrimination. He plainly enjoyed the company of women. He confided in them easily, even if he showed little in-terest in a sustained physical relationship with any of that gender.

On the other hand, even if we ignore the cultural calculus that a boy with a distant father who is close to his mother has a fair chance of growing up to be gay, recent scientific studies have persuasively linked homosexuality in men to the number of older brothers they have: The progressive immuniza-tion of mothers to male-specific antigens with each pregnancy affects sexual differentiation in the brain for each subsequent male fetus. Each older brother a man has increases his likelihood of being gay by 33 percent.[6]

Did Irving, with four older brothers (seven, if we include the three who did not survive infancy), hide from posterity his sexual activity with women, or his sexual activity with men? Or was he just an impossible dreamer?

He may have been gay, without acting on the impulse. This is possible, but we cannot make the assertion without speculating unduly. His bache-lorhood does raise interesting questions, but it is best understood in the context of nineteenth-century bachelorhood, which does not replicate all of the sexually driven prognoses of the modern age. In the past, one could be accepted as a bachelor if he were to find some useful role in society that made up for the failure to procreate conventionally; his personal habits be-came curiosities, as they were for Irving's character Master Simon, in *Brace-*

bridge Hall, who sits in his bachelor "nest" and plays plaintive old tunes on his fiddle. In his public role as the Squire's factotum, Simon is always "full of bustle; with a thousand petty things to do, and persons to attend to, and in chirping good-humor." Irving could be regarded as a Man of Feeling (the Mackenzie model) who generally subsumed libidinous desire in his commitment to literature. He became that bachelor known as social, but non-threatening. In Irving's time, one need not be embarrassed to have lived a bachelor's life.[7]

★   ★

If no exposé has emerged from this quarter, then, another exposé style blossomed in the 1930s, when Stanley T. Williams of Yale produced his demeaning two-volume Irving biography—the twentieth-century standard. We must ask ourselves why he went to such lengths to undermine Irving's reputation. Williams's Irving was a blundering sentimentalist who "beat his brains, and scribbled in notebooks"; a "superficial romantic" who "loved scraps of culture" instead of "erudition"; a mediocre man who unequivocally adored great men. Whenever he gave Irving the benefit of the doubt, Williams fell to pitying the man. He yawningly emphasized the "age-old legends" from which "Rip Van Winkle" was cribbed, crediting Irving's uniting of his reading and his personal experience only so as to link his "pilferings" to his "importunate moods." Williams had little to say about "The Legend of Sleepy Hollow" other than vaguely to acknowledge it as one of a few *Sketch Book* stories that "still retain their hold on the imagination."

Overall, the *Sketch Book* was "tepid," said Williams, "too varied," and laden with "trite emotion." It washed over him, a sloppy flood of words that "overflows, lacking form, into a delta, with sands of sentiment and pools of quiet thought. In these last," Williams resolved, "Irving is persuasive, but sand predominates." It would seem that the biographer was accusing the author of the *Sketch Book* of kicking sand in his face. He nonetheless claimed to appreciate Irving's "long, indolent sentences, and select vocabulary," which is, ironically, what his own sprawling critique suggests to today's reader.[8]

Williams cast a long shadow. Few disputed his contention that Irving's writings lacked real originality—that it would be more accurate to call the author an amateur entertainer. Thirty years after Williams, responding to this downgrading, an Irving enthusiast wrote words that still make sense: "Modern detractors of Irving, like modern detractors of Longfellow, have generally been distressed over the fact that he was not Herman Melville or Ernest Hemingway. This much is undeniable, but why it should occasion so much distress is not quite clear. That he was a 'genteel' writer admits of no doubt, but in his time 'genteel' was not a dirty word."[9]

Rather than engage in the same kind of debate, this book has tried to show something else: Born into a merchant's family in a still uncity-like, though not quite sylvan, lower Manhattan, and unlikely at birth to become an influential citizen of the world, Washington Irving did, by force of personality, bring important changes to culture. If, in the current literary canon, he does not have the prominence he once had, he certainly led one of the most public lives in the nineteenth century. Nothing about it was commonplace. Thus (and it warrants emphasis), *for the cultural historian, even more than for the literary critic, Washington Irving looms large.*

✦   ✦

The world Irving entered was Benjamin Franklin's and George Washington's. It used language to constitute social authority, to uphold an ideal temperament and a certain definition of masculine and feminine virtue grounded in universal nature. But that world was limited in imagination.[10] The world Irving died in was Abraham Lincoln's, a world marked by deep divisions, to be sure, but also stimulated by a less homogeneous and plainly sentimental approach to history and the human spirit. In between, Washington Irving reconceived the individual as someone creative and responsive. He helped to make language more liberating. Along with subtle characterization, private thoughts and traits grew in conviction in the writings of the age of Irving.[11]

The early nineteenth century was transformative in literary history for many reasons. The literary marketplace mattered more to society than it had before, and perhaps more than it does now. It was where one sought out new insights and new freedoms, and discovered genius. In the twenty-first century, when poetry no longer inspires on a grand scale and only a vague and unreliable nostalgia for the roots of heroic democracy connects us to the early American republic, the life of Irving stands to remind us of every generation's need to isolate a soul in the republic's origins. Irving is one of our best guides to the informal personality of that generation of coastal Americans, born at the time of the nation's founding, who were able to define the national identity through literary models.

Both as cultural critic and purveyor of pure affection, Irving shows us how his countrymen sought to capitalize on their professions of humanity—which is, after all, how progress is declared in a democracy. Whether his subject was the western trapper of his day, or the imagined Dutch of the past, or the even earlier Columbus, he gave his country the epic historical romances it craved.

The durability of Irving's books through the early twentieth century drama-tized Americans' faith in what was—and is yet touted as—an "authentic" American creed. He celebrated an at-once vigorous, amusing, and oppor-tunistic people.

Speaking of authentic Americans, what might we say about Rip Van Win-kle, post-Irving? To begin, even those who thought that Irving's reputation was undeserved insisted that "Rip Van Winkle" was a great piece of writing—they merely said that it was the last great writing Irving did. Its reach is un-deniable. More than a half-century before H. G. Wells's time machine gave industrial expression to a similar kind of fantasy, Rip Van Winkle became an unlikely hero in the collective imaginations of Americans and others around the world. And he remained so. Rip was left unscathed by time. And was that not Irving's point?

The story transcended cultures. In France, as *Le Flacon de Rip* (1867) and *Rip la légende du dormeur* (1891), it was extracted from the *Sketch Book* and published separately. The Dutch first published the *Sketch Book* in 1823, but "Rip Van Winkle" endured so long that it was published by itself in 1906. A Yiddish translation of the story appeared in New York in 1923. The first fully illustrated edition of "Rip Van Winkle" was also published in New York, in 1848, with drawings by Felix O. C. Darley; a London version emerged two years later. In all, nine stand-alone editions of an illustrated "Rip Van Winkle" were published in the nineteenth century, and another seven (including French, Italian, and German productions) between 1900 and 1910.[12]

Drawing upon his private fascination with the Hudson region of New York State, and his compulsion to resuscitate "old" New Netherland, Irving amplified—though, technically, he did not introduce—what would become an enduring fascination with time displacement and time travel. At the same time, he left a mark on the imaginations of Europeans that enlarged in the decades after his death, despite the uncontested fact that the central premise of his tale dated from the ancient Greeks and could be found in a variety of texts, including the modern German, that were popular when Ir-ving wrote.[13]

Plays based on "Rip Van Winkle" were performed in America from as early as 1829. Joseph Jefferson III toured the country for years after the Civil War, playing Rip onstage, and was a recognized authority on the story. If a twenty-year sleep were merely unlikely, he wrote in his autobiography, "there would be room for argument pro and con; but as it is an impossibility, I felt that the audience would accept it at once."

The actor gave a lot of thought to his performance:

> From the moment *Rip* meets the spirits of Hendrik Hudson and his crew I felt that all colloquial dialogue and commonplace pantomime should cease. It is at this point in the story that the supernatural element begins, and henceforth the character must be raised from the domestic plane and lifted into the realms of the ideal.

In the minds of many awestruck theatergoers, Joe Jefferson was endowed with the spirit of Rip Van Winkle. They spoke to him as though he could bring them closer to a being with a sublime purpose. Harriet Beecher Stowe went out of her way to meet with the actor, and she expressed her opinion that the meeting between Rip and his daughter near the end of the story mirrored an encounter between King Lear and Cordelia.

And so, almost as an apostle, Jefferson felt he was under a high obligation to give a correct interpretation of the Rip he had resurrected for late nineteenth-century Americans. Through this one actor, who said he never tired of the role, Rip continued to challenge the ordinary construct of time. After one performance in the town of Catskill, New York, Jefferson attended a reception sponsored by the Rip Van Winkle Club, where the nervous master of ceremonies introduced him as "Washington Irving." Joe Jefferson's father had been a mainstay of American theater in its infancy—a young Irving had seen him perform at New York's Park Theater in the late 1790s—and the son lived long enough to star as Rip in a silent film, early in the twentieth century. As late as 1928, visitors to the Catskills were stopping to ask directions to Rip Van Winkle's grave! As often happens, history and fiction had become indistinguishable.[14]

Classic movies that Americans have come to love dwell on the themes that grow out of "Rip Van Winkle." In Frank Capra's *It's a Wonderful Life* (1946), an unlikely angel, Clarence Oddbody, treats the main character, George Bailey, to an alternative perspective on his past. As much as the device reminds us of Charles Dickens's *A Christmas Carol* (1843), it reflects the time-bending experience of the earlier "Rip Van Winkle" as well. Sentimental truths emerge from supernaturally created new memories.

In Woody Allen's comic fantasy *Sleeper* (1973), the Rip figure is a pathetic New Yorker who goes into the hospital for a routine surgery and wakes up two hundred years later in a society that is technologically advanced but as absurd as anything Irving contrived in *Knickerbocker's History;* and the more recent classic *Field of Dreams* (1989) evokes Irving's engagement with nostalgic sentiment and paranormal communication. In the film, the main character, Ray Kinsella, hears voices and builds a baseball diamond for long-dead baseball players (rather than Dutch bowlers), for whom time and physical decease are no longer barriers to re-experiencing the pleasures of the world. Kinsella, like Rip, is a social outcast, and his field a wasted plot of land, until his cornfield is transformed into a ball field, and his myth attains the status of plausibility.

The "field of dreams" is a sacred historic site, just as Rip, a kind of tourist attraction in his dotage, lives out his years as proof that, every once in a while, people who are willing to imagine beyond the accepted logic of time can tap into a cherished historical moment and find magic, if not fulfillment, in escaping the ordinary. Perhaps the most significant lesson, though, is this: In *Field of Dreams,* as in Rip's tale, we can lose time without losing the past. This is the fantasy of all antiquarians, and Irving is nothing if not an antiquarian. Somehow we emerge feeling safe while still feeling vulnerable. Without rejecting what is real, we come as close as we want to touching eternity.

It is axiomatic to say that memory makes the past meaningful every day of our lives. In that sense, we are constantly trying to reorient ourselves. The film *Memento* (2000), a tale of revenge as seen through the experience of a man whose short-term memory constantly disappears, represents the violent underside of the question Irving considered. The character Leonard works against the clock (his injured and inadequate brain) in a desperate bid to recover his memory and so resolve his obsession concerning his wife's death. His world is one of lost knowledge and overpowering ambiguity—it is "Rip Van Winkle" on steroids, moving backwards, and it raises the larger, fundamental question: How much of our present is occupied with concerns about the past?[15]

In the first work of popular literature in the twenty-first century to bring "Rip Van Winkle" forward, Audrey Niffenegger features a protagonist whose involuntary movement through time wears down his physical body while elevating his capacity to feel and to love. In her ingenious novel, *The Time Traveler's Wife* (2003), Henry DeTamble, like Rip, is a bit of an idler; but the author deftly compels us to identify with his time-bending adventures. He seems immortal, yet he embraces his mortal destiny; he tampers with history just so much that he manages to ensure that he is not quickly forgotten. As Joe Jefferson said about "Rip Van Winkle," Niffenegger enables us to believe her tale precisely because it is beyond imagining.

★ ★

One hundred years ago, in the decades before Stanley Williams came along, Irving's tale of "Rip Van Winkle" was at the peak of its power, in part because

America and Europe were then mourning a loss of innocence. The industrial age had unleashed an unprecedented level of cynicism with regard to outward progress. Politics and empirical histories were deterministic, and less stable than they appeared; fiction and poetry offered solace. While citizens coped with bold headlines, modern psychology, and modern warfare, Irving's welcoming world was one place to turn to that many could still remember as safe and nurturing.

In moral terms, the state of mind today is not as different as we would like to think. In technological terms, we have entered a world with unprecedented potential for change: The very future of the book is uncertain, given the ease, arresting style, and immediacy by which electronic images are disseminated. It is too soon to predict what will happen to the form typographical culture has traditionally taken, but perhaps Irving's creations still have a future—and not just as vague cultural symbol, as suggested in a recent headline about a long-comatose Arkansan: "A Real Rip Van Winkle Story: Man Recovers after 20 Years."[16] As the historian of early America Perry Miller noted back in 1961, Rip Van Winkle has long provided those Americans who reject our Puritanism with a lovable antihero. Miller drew an irresistible comparison between the Catskill Mountain wag and his Old West progeny: "A whole people committed to unremitting industriousness embraced the shiftless Rip, just as they would later let their thwarted longings for vagabondage take them down the Mississippi with Huckleberry Finn." They are America's innocent mischief makers, lost souls who are accepted by a country otherwise too serious about its inherent greatness.[17]

We all know what it means to feel stuck in a less than stirring reality and to want to escape it. As another literary critic pointed out, "Rip has no dreams at the beginning and would probably never have any did he not step accidentally into the realm of fabulous time." His otherworldly adventure provides "the wonder of letting go."[18] This is one reason why we dream. The neurological phenomenon of wakefulness is both relatable to, and separable from, consciousness. This is where the unscientific Irving is at his most playful. His admitted "half dreaming moods of mind," like the "drowsy, dreamy" character of Sleepy Hollow, are transient worlds. Dreams that still exist in memory at the moment of awakening tell us that internal stimuli, as aids to the conscious imagination, represent a part of us that we need not dismiss as irrelevant: The paraconsciousness in Irving's stories may make a muddle of ordinary time, but it can also deepen who we are.[19]

Rip Van Winkle's republic is a pastoral utopia for men. Time is gentle, adolescence perpetual. In Rip's republic, the imagination governs. No one gets bullied anymore; political contention is muted; women do the meaningful work while men lounge and form bonds among themselves. Through Rip's eyes, the past that is gone is harmless, and in the present there is nothing to do. The slacker who eluded death lives on as a celebrity. His sensational stories soothe. Rip's republic, in short, is men at play.

Irving takes escapist fantasy (streams of thought and feeling and perception) and uses it to shift attention from the ordinary flow of reality. He never even tells us how old Rip Van Winkle is. His aim, in this way, is to entertain by bending, or extending, time. Yet he is not overly simplistic, either. He does not ignore the problems that can arise in altered states: He relates how in moments of sensory impairment, as in Rip's twenty comatose years, identity can be compromised. How does the self turn on and turn off? he asks. That question, which persists in Irving's Gothic tales, remains today at the root of our attempt to qualify the meaning of Rip's experience.

☆　☆

Irving as historian cannot be regarded in quite the same way. In *Columbus* and *George Washington*, he relishes time as a softener of emotions. Architect of the historical imagination, Irving is today part of the ebb and flow of American historiography. Even if, to nineteenth-century minds, history meant sweeping change and grandiose occasions, Irving understood the crucial importance of the archive, and of the primary source. Whether or not one chooses to believe that he was rigorous enough in his research, or sufficiently conscious of the role ideology plays in every historical text, he was a historian, and not merely a weaver of tales.

But what kind of a historian was Irving? He had a jaunty, sometimes starry-eyed, way of telling history. It is undeniable that when he wrote he was thoroughly caught up in the romance of history. He could not help but re-create it imaginatively. He was that kind of historian, because he was Geoffrey Crayon, who started out life as a "rambler" and went on to become a world traveler. History preeminently concerns dispersals, removals, migrations, and adventures—disruptions and renewals in patterns of belonging. Irving experienced movement across oceans and continents that helped him to imagine history in this way.

To be a coherent historian is to separate one's self from the past, to prioritize issues, and to evaluate culture as part of the atmosphere surrounding events. Irving sought to do all of these things—but then he was sure to deliver breathless beauty along with logic. He refused to sacrifice beauty. It is what separates him from the professionally trained historian of our time.

It is for this reason that Irving's influence can be found among a host of authors who applied the style both of his Hudson River legends and *A Tour on the Prairies* when they took up western subjects. Modern interpreters of the tradition find borrowings in the works of William H. Prescott, Nathaniel Hawthorne, and Bret Harte, among others. In the words of one: "Irving was the first American writer to discover a literary bonanza in the trans-Mississippi West." And not only that: "His Western works were well known among the wagon trains along the Oregon Trail." Thus, the genre of writing about the West, in fiction and nonfiction alike, owes a significant debt to Washington Irving. He understood what the West (and western manhood) meant to America—the interaction of romance and reality would always belong to its history. In a broader sense, he perfected the art of enlivening history through the invocation of exotic personalities and codes of cultural behavior in a picturesque landscape, a style that typified nineteenth-century historiography.[20]

To Irving and the Romantics, the study of history was expansive, stirring, impressionistic, and declarative. The preceding age had described the march of civilization in more fixed terms, with taxonomic models and ultimate causation—it was constantly recommending moral correctives for unenlightened self-interest. The Romantics differed in that, relatively speaking, they accepted chaos; they took refuge in a consciousness of the energetic and unfixed, and of history's fertility—that is, its capacity to mutate and to modify.

To Irving's mind, and to ours, time is constituted by memory, and history is about forgetting. If the historian's role is to slow the process of forgetting, the role of the Romantic historian was to apply nostalgia to this slowing of forgetfulness. The ideal, the unreal, was as much a part of history as recorded events. The Gothic Irving, meanwhile, saw history in the shadows and confronted it there. For the repressed bachelor that he was, it is remarkable how honestly he depicted the forces that shape memory. He wanted to illustrate how letting go of superstition could bring back the lost beauties of the past.

Though not explicitly philosophical, he explored the nature and uses of power. In his treatment of the Spanish and the Moors he succeeded where some modern historians still fail: He accommodated conflicting truths. His empathy for the defeated was purposeful—this is a common attribute of modern historians, too. Earlier histories were more pious than Irving's; his were indulgent and agreeable, intended to provide a deep calming effect, both for the reader and for himself. He was, as many have claimed over the years, a genteel historian, no less than he had been an insurgent satirist before that. And perhaps there is no great contradiction in his having been both.

✷   ✷

We have left only to weigh the changes that took place in Irving as the decades passed. Over the course of his writing life, he moved from toying with the foibles of men and women, to a more serious treatment of the human heart, to expositions of broad, sweeping forces of history. By the time he was fifty, women had ceased being of any real importance to his work, as he eagerly embraced the robust lives of *voyageurs*, adventurers—real men.

How do we capture the essence of Washington Irving? Was he a remarkably versatile artist, a writer in search of new experiences who was able to do much with multiple literary genres, and whose tastes adjusted in rational ways as he grew? Or was he an uneasy chameleon who could never quite fit in, and so kept changing from one thing to another? The choice, really, should not be so arbitrary. Here, in sum, was how Irving's career evolved, and what he ultimately prescribed:

He began as a satirist, writing with hilarity while living in the thick of New York politics.

He went to England, and quickly grew enamored with English gentility, assuming the pose of the curious stranger sent to observe English habits and tastes.

In Spain he became a true Romantic, living out a fantasy of time travel during his residency at the Alhambra, resurrecting the myths of a lost culture.

Returning to the United States, he was transformed into a supernationalist, living for some months as a "tourist pioneer," then transcribing the *Adventures of Captain Bonneville*, a largely overlooked work, which celebrated expansionism as a modern romance of legitimate conquest. This was when he stopped mourning the Indian's sacrifice to America's destiny.

He capped off his career with two biographies: a compact account of the "ideal" writer, Oliver Goldsmith, who symbolized the humanity and wit of the world Irving had entered, and a magisterial life story of George Washington, the foremost founder, the nearly perfect patriarchal president, symbol of the conservative nation. If *Columbus* represented the blood link between the Old World and the New, *Life of Washington* reminded the Union of its debt to a dignified Federalism.

In his politics, Irving had come full circle. He wished to resettle the unsettled and restore good sense, coping with time as he finally acquiesced to it. But he did not do so simply to write happy endings. That was never his goal.

Both as a storyteller and as a historian, Irving re-created a past that he could populate and direct, a past that was bigger than the quotidian struggle he knew in his own life. He gave his country something that republican government, with its precious parchment and marble pillars, did not confer: access to the pleasures of the imagination. Putting it simply, when he awakened Rip Van Winkle, Washington Irving bequeathed the great American folktale. We are all curious to know how life will go on without us. Rip found out.

Acknowledgments

When I began collecting Irvingiana, I did not know that I would embark on this project. Long before I became a historian, though, I attended Hackley School in Tarrytown, New York, which is Washington Irving territory. I was at Hackley for eight years, graduating in 1970. The school, which has been offering a well-rounded education since 1899, sits on a hilltop above the Hudson River, about a mile from what Irving called the "Tappan Sea." On my youthful "rambles," to use another Irving word, I had occasion to visit Sunnyside, and to hang out in Sleepy Hollow.

If four undergraduate years at Columbia University didn't make a Manhattanite out of me, then the next eight surely did, when I worked at the site of the Tontine Coffee House, at the corner of Wall and Water Streets. It was the center of New York's trading culture in Irving's day, and a place the Irving clan knew well. Fast-forward to the year 2000, when I arrived in Tulsa, Oklahoma. I have been living a block from the Arkansas River, close to where Irving went on a bee hunt during his colorful "tour on the prairie." So even when my mind was elsewhere, I have been following Irving around.

I have written interpretive treatments of early American figures before, but this is the first to take the form of biography. I felt that Irving, a giant of the nineteenth century, deserved a twenty-first-century biographer, his reputation having taken a bit of a tumble in the century between. In giving him a fresh look, I have made it a priority to situate Irving in the political world that animated his writing. At the same time, I have eagerly read the work of literary scholars. So as to make the text reader-friendly, I have largely relegated to endnotes my engagement with that scholarship.

In my labors, I had valuable assistance from individuals and institutions I wish to credit: James N. Green, John Van Horne, Phil Lapsansky, and the rest of the excellent staff of the Library Company of Philadelphia; the Huntington Library, in San Marino, California, one of the most grand and picturesque research facilities anywhere; Alderman Library and Special Collections at the University of Virginia (not neglecting my favorite haunt, Heartwood Books) in Charlottesville; the Wisconsin State Historical Society, the libraries of the University of Wisconsin, and Paul's Books on State Street, Madison; Catalina Hannan and the good folks at Historic Hudson Valley and Sunnyside, the home of Washington Irving; the New York Public Library; and the New-York Historical Society. My thanks as well to Andy Lupardus, Rita Howell, and the other supportive people in McFarlin Library at the University of Tulsa.

I was given encouragement and direction by historians, literary scholars, Irving admirers, and world travelers. I especially wish to thank Karen Kelleher, Ana Carreño, John and Karen Shea, Michael and Suzanne Wallis, Kristin Hahn and Charles Stringer, Frank Shuffelton, Peter S. Onuf, James P. Ronda, Jay H. Geller, T. J. Stiles, J. Christoph Hanckel, Steve Kluger, Tom Connors, Laura Stevens, Susan Dixon, David Goldstein, Suzy Akin, Cabell Smith, Cathy Myers, and Steve Rubin—with moral support from Val and Eldon Eisenach, Beebie Isenberg, and Josh Burstein.

At Basic, I have had the good fortune to work with Liz Maguire on two books. Liz was generous as a person and conscientious as an editor; her unexpected death in April 2006 was a blow to many, myself included. Jo Ann Miller took charge and took excellent care of the manuscript, for which I am deeply grateful. Assistant editor Chris Greenberg was a helpful advocate, too. Susan Leon presented a thousand good ideas for streamlining the manuscript. In the production of two books now, Jennifer Blakebrough-Raeburn has been a spectacular copy editor. And I could not do without my literary agent, Geri Thoma, who joins sincere concern to a keen mind.

As always, my zeal to recover the mind of early America could not have generated as much heat without the goodness and steadiness of my dearest friend, Nancy Gale Isenberg.

Notes

ABBREVIATIONS

CW-Journals   *The Complete Works of Washington Irving: Journals and Notebooks.* Edited by Nathalia Wright and others. 5 vols. (Madison and Boston: University of Wisconsin Press and Twayne Publishers, 1969–1981).

CW-Letters   *The Complete Works of Washington Irving: Letters.* Edited by Ralph M. Aderman and others. 4 vols. Boston: Twayne Publishers, 1978–1982.

CW-Misc.   *The Complete Works of Washington Irving: Miscellaneous Writings 1803–1859.* Edited by Wayne R. Kime and others. 3 vols. Boston: Twayne Publishers, 1981.

PMI   Pierre M. Irving. *The Life and Letters of Washington Irving.* 4 vols. New York: G. P. Putnam's Sons, 1862.

STW   Stanley T. Williams. *The Life of Washington Irving.* 2 vols. New York: Oxford University Press, 1935.

CHAPTER 1

1. *CW-Journals*, 2:287.

2. Edwin G. Burrows and Mike Wallace, *Gotham: A History of New York to 1898* (New York: Oxford University Press, 1999), 21; Samuel L. Mitchill, *The Picture of New-York; or the Traveller's Guide Through the Commercial Metropolis of the United States* (New York: I. Riley, 1807), 1–2.

3. Paul Wilstach, *Hudson River Landings* (Indianapolis: Bobbs-Merrill, 1933), chaps. 1 and 3.

4. The foregoing discussion draws mainly upon these sources: Sidney I. Pomerantz, *New York, an American City, 1783–1803* (New York: Columbia University Press, 1938), chaps. 3 and 4; Judith L. Van Buskirk, *Generous Enemies: Patriots and Loyalists in Revolutionary New York* (Philadelphia: University of Pennsylvania Press, 2002); Burrows and Wallace, *Gotham*, chaps. 16 and 17; Martha J. Lamb, *History of the City of New York: Its Origin, Rise and Progress* (New York and Chicago: A. S. Barnes, 1877–1880), vol. 3.

5. PMI, 1:26–27.

6. Ibid., 1:20–23, 37. Since the Presbyterians tended to support the patriot cause, the British looked upon them with suspicion.

7. Ibid., 1:35–36.

8. Pomerantz, *New York,* 286–291, 304–306; Mitchill, *Picture of New-York,* 64, 69; Burrows and Wallace, *Gotham,* 356–360; Thomas A. Janvier, *In Old New York* (New York: Harper & Brothers, 1894), 40, 192–194.

9. Before the Revolution, more than 50 percent of the Dutch-speaking population in America lived in New York, and another 20 percent lived in neighboring parts of New Jersey. See A. G. Roeber, "'The Origin of Whatever Is Not English Among Us,'" in Bernard Bailyn and Philip D. Morgan, eds., *Strangers Within the Realm: Cultural Margins of the First British Empire* (Chapel Hill: University of North Carolina Press, 1991), 236.

10. PMI, 1:28–30.

11. Ibid., 1:32–33, 4:352.

12. The Pauldings' patriotism was severely tested when history was rewritten. John Paulding was defamed in Congress for allegedly having questionable motives in the André affair; and James's father, after supplying the Revolutionary forces on credit, was never reimbursed because he had provisioned the army without "official" authorization. He was stripped of his property and sent to debtor's prison. Paulding's maternal grandfather, Nathaniel Ogden, suffered permanent brain damage when he was slashed across the head by a vindictive British soldier. The author long retained in his mind an image of this pathetic old man as he walked along the shore of the Hudson talking to himself. Larry J. Reynolds, *James Kirke Paulding* (Boston: Twayne Publishers, 1984), 1–3; concerning the controversy that surrounds André's capture and John Paulding's role, see Otto Hufeland, *Westchester County During the American Revolution, 1775–1783* (White Plains, NY: Westchester County Historical Society, 1926), 346–353.

13. John Larson, *Internal Improvements: National Public Works and the Promise of Popular Government in the Early United States* (Chapel Hill: University of North Carolina Press, 2001); on the significance of the Post Office Act of 1792, see Richard R. John, *Spreading the News: The American Postal System from Franklin to Morse* (Cambridge, MA: Harvard University Press, 1995), esp. 35–41.

14. Ralph M. Aderman and Wayne R. Kime, *Advocate for America: The Life of James Kirke Paulding* (Selinsgrove, PA: Susquehanna University Press, 2003), 25, 30. Washington was impressed that his friend had published poetry (at fourteen!) in the *New-York Magazine,* which was widely subscribed to in the literate city. In fact, as many shopkeepers and artisans as merchants and lawyers read it. David Paul Nord, "A Republican Literature: A Study of Magazine Reading and Readers in Late Eighteenth-Century New York," *American Quarterly* 40 (March 1988): 42–64. *The New-York Magazine* remained in circulation from 1790 to 1798.

15. PMI, 1:40–42. As to the black crew, with slavery beginning to disappear from the northern states, a seaman's life remained the choice of many free blacks.

16. *Longworth's American Almanack, New-York Register, and City Directory* (New York: John C. Totten, 1799), passim.

17. WI to Moses Thomas, May 8, 1815, *CW-Letters,* 1:391; PMI, 3:156; Joseph A. Scoville, *The Old Merchants of New York City* (New York: Carleton, 1863), 1:76.

18. R. H. Kampmeier, "Peter Irving (1771–1828): Physician, Litterateur, and Burrite Polemist," *Pharos* (Summer 1987): 15–18.

19. Estelle Fox Kleiger, *The Trial of Levi Weeks, or the Manhattan Well Mystery* (Chicago: Academy Chicago Publishers, 1989); *Longworth's American Almanack, New-York Register, and City Directory* (1799), 132–135.

20. *Diary of William Dunlap, 1766–1839* (New York: New-York Historical Society, 1930), 1:254; Richard A. Harrison, *Princetonians, 1769–1775* (Princeton, NJ: Princeton University Press, 1980), 403–404. During the same month as the Weeks trial, Livingston and Burr combined to represent the interest of Benjamin Rush, Philadelphia physician and signer of the Declaration of Independence, in a suit against a libelous Federalist publisher, William Cobbett.

21. Records do not show which of the three ambitious (but apparently, in this instance, unpaid) attorneys carried out most of the dramatic cross-examinations. See David Longworth, *A Brief Narrative of the Trial for the Bloody and Mysterious Murder of the Unfortunate Young Woman, in the Famous Manhattan Well* (New York: Longworth, 1800), 3–5, 10; Nancy Isenberg, *Fallen Founder: The Life of Aaron Burr* (New York: Viking Penguin, 2007).

22. Kleiger, *The Trial of Levi Weeks,* esp. 201–204.

23. See, for example, the work of one anonymous poet who "fictionalized" the murder, having "Curvin," the cowardly villain, hire a professional criminal to emerge from the shadows, at the appointed hour, near the Manhattan Company well. As the seducer watches, the assassin squeezes all life from the beautiful victim. "The Manhattan Tragedy or Curvin and Elma: An Historical Ballad," manuscript dated 1799, New-York Historical Society.

24. See Julia Stern, "The Politics of Tears: Death in the Early American Novel," in Nancy Isenberg and Andrew Burstein, eds., *Mortal Remains: Death in Early America* (Philadelphia: University of Pennsylvania Press, 2003), 108–119.

25. This is an essential theme in Isenberg, *Fallen Founder.*

26. The three pamphlets were, in order of issue: Longworth's *A Brief Narrative of the Trial for the Bloody and Mysterious Murder of the Unfortunate Young Woman, in the Famous Manhattan Well*; James Hardie, *An Impartial Account of the Trial of Mr. Levi Weeks, for the Supposed Murder of Miss Julianna Elmore Sands*; William Coleman, *Report of the Trial of Levi Weeks, on an Indictment for the Murder of Gulielma Sands.* All were issued in 1800. The Furman genealogy is hard to document with certainty: Aside from the printer, Longworth's directory for 1799 shows two local officials (who were militia officers as well) with the same surname, as well as a Water Street merchant named Furman.

27. Until now, biographers and others have largely accepted Irving's professed comfort with the Federalists at face value and have formulaically repeated his one or two softly expressed statements on the subject. This is only half the story: One has to appreciate the complexity of New York politics with which the closely knit Irving brothers were centrally concerned. The lack of a political edge in his stories during his heyday as an author has led history to forget that Washington Irving's writings up to the mid-1810s served as a political lightning rod. See below.

28. As to commerce, Jefferson warned citizens against imitating the "depravity" of a European manufacturing system that he feared and expected rapid growth in trade would bring about. If this occurred, he said, Americans would adopt such manners as would erode the virtues of an agrarian-based republican society. Jefferson deeply feared the social disease of urban decay. The Federalists, on the other hand, did everything to encourage a commercial republic. See especially Drew R. McCoy, *The Elusive Republic: Political Economy in Jeffersonian America* (New York: W. W. Norton, 1980).

29. Donna Hagensick's 1969 observations are remarkably nuanced for the period in which she was writing. She accepts Stanley Williams's generalization that the Irving

family, with its merchant profile, was "generally conservative in its outlook," and she states, less convincingly, that support of Burr was a convenient means to attack Jefferson; still, she is pointedly correct in her suggestion that understanding Irving requires our understanding his class aspirations, and she recognizes that "the transition from Federalist to Burrite Republican was not a difficult one to make in New York" in 1802–1803. Donna Hagensick, "Irving: A Litterateur in Politics," reprinted in Ralph M. Aderman, ed., *Critical Essays on Washington Irving* (Boston: G. K. Hall, 1990), 178–191, quote at 181; also Edward Wagenknecht, *Washington Irving: Moderation Displayed* (New York: Oxford University Press, 1962), 107. The always perceptive William L. Hedges attempts to make sense of the confused circumstances of New York politics, erring only in accepting too easily the historical consensus that Burr, to gain Federalist support, had to have sold out his Republican "doctrine"; his "doctrine" did not change, but his commitment to commercial growth made him increasingly appealing to those distrustful of the Jefferson-Clinton alliance. Hedges comes closer to the truth when he characterizes the anti-Jefferson sentiment in New York during the embargo, at the time of Irving's *History of New York;* and he is careful to cite Henry Adams's observation that Irving was closer to the definition of Burrite than of Federalist. William L. Hedges, *Washington Irving: An American Study, 1802–1832* (Baltimore: Johns Hopkins University Press, 1965), 59–64. Williams points out Irving's whitewashing of his family's connection to Burr, in STW, 1:35, 388n62.

30. It is in these terms that the following episode makes sense: When Peter was in the nation's capital at the end of 1802, two months after establishing his Burrite newspaper, the *Morning Chronicle,* his younger brother Washington filled in as general editor. The latter wrote at this time to an upstate lawyer of his acquaintance: "I feel in a curious situation, manager of a paper, with the principles of which mine do not much accord." An anonymous hand, seemingly knowledgeable and contemporaneous, and perhaps that of the recipient of the letter, explains in the marginalia that Irving preferred the Federalist view of the world (original spellings retained): "His brother is edidor of the Cronicle Express [the periodical version of the daily *Morning Chronicle*]—I now take that paper— it is democratic and Washinton is Federal." WI to Amos Eaton, December 15, 1802, *CW-Letters,* 1:5, 7n. In the same letter, Irving commented that he preferred creatively writing to laboriously managing, and he used the metaphor of being thrown off a horse—for that is what he feared might happen as a result of Peter's having vested editorial authority in one so inattentive as he.

31. PMI, 3:204, 313; Carl Van Doren, *Benjamin Franklin* (New York: Viking Press, 1938), chap. 2; J. A. Leo Lemay, *The Life of Benjamin Franklin,* vol. 1 (Philadelphia: University of Pennsylvania Press, 2006), 205–206.

32. *Letters of Jonathan Oldstyle, Gent.,* #4, December 4, 1802, 14–15; Burrows and Wallace, *Gotham,* 375.

33. *Spectator* (Philadelphia: Crissy and Markley, 1851), no. 17, 1:110.

34. Washington took his cue from his brother Peter, too, though he had more to give. A few years earlier, Peter had written some criticism of New York plays, recommending an often-disparaged genre to an upwardly mobile clientele. He wrote in service to the playwright-promoter William Dunlap, who had long been arguing against the traditional prejudice that associated the theater's popularity with dissipation or a loss of social virtue (the same strictures against novel reading as a genre that unduly excited the mind had currency well into the nineteenth century). If Peter's was a liberal critique, his younger brother had something different in mind: having as much fun with the audience as with

the performance, which was the whole point of the Oldstyle essays. On Dunlap, see Joseph J. Ellis, *After the Revolution: Profiles of Early American Culture* (New York: W. W. Norton, 1979), 129–133.

35. *Letters of Jonathan Oldstyle, Gent.*, #4, December 4, 1802, 14–15; Hedges, *Washington Irving*, 27–28. The stereotype would persist. In frontier Nashville in the 1820s, another place struggling with its social identity, a new "Jonathan" would visit the local theater. An unpolished vocabulary again matched his country ways: "Did y'ever go to the Playhouse? / O lauks, what a nation fine place." Once more, it would be the size of the curtain that caused Tennessee's Jonathan to wonder out loud how many shirts might be sewn together if more practical use were made of the material. See Andrew Burstein, *America's Jubilee* (New York: Knopf, 2001), 224–225.

36. *Letters of Jonathan Oldstyle, Gent.*, no. 3, December 1, 1802; no. 4, December 4, 1802, 8–12. The management of the theater did try to encourage civilized behavior—if it could not silence the eaters, it did urge the audience not to smoke. See George C. D. Odell, *Annals of the New York Stage* (New York: Columbia University Press, 1927; reprint, AMC Press, 1970), 2:162–163.

37. Walter A. Reichart, "Washington Irving and the Theatre," in Aderman, *Critical Essays on Washington Irving*, 166–178; Mitchill, *The Picture of New-York*, 155; Odell, *Annals of the New York Stage*, 2:1–7; Burrows and Wallace, *Gotham*, 404.

38. The literary scholar Paul Giles writes: "Irving's mode is not so much that of subversion but of perversion; his work does not radically undermine conventional values, but rather holds them in suspension . . . dignity and buffoonery, civility and disorder, are brought into a dangerous juxtaposition." See Giles, *Transatlantic Insurrections: British Culture and the Formation of American Literature, 1730–1860* (Philadelphia: University of Pennsylvania Press, 2001), 143.

39. If we want, we can even find in *Spectator*'s pages a prototype of sorts for Ichabod Crane's scare in Irving's "The Legend of Sleepy Hollow": "As I was walking in this solitude, where the dusk of the evening conspired with so many other occasions of terror, I observed a cow grazing not far from me, which an imagination that was apt to startle might easily have construed into a black horse without a head; and I dare say the poor footman lost his wits upon some such trivial occasion." For *Spectator*, belief in the haunted house and assorted tales of apparitions made more sense than nonbelief—an opinion, the authors underscore, that was favored by "the historians, to whom we may join the poets, and likewise the philosophers of antiquity." Prophecies abound in *Spectator*'s pages, as they do in Irving's later Gothic writings. See *Spectator*, no. 110, 3:16–17.

40. Hugh Blair, *Lectures on Rhetoric and Belles Lettres* (Philadelphia: Troutman & Hayes, 1852), esp. Lecture 18. First published 1783.

41. *Spectator*, no. 9, 1:69–72. There was also the "Club of Duellists," which admitted as members only those who could give evidence of having "fought his man"; and the celebrated "Kit-Cat Club," named after a pastry chef called Cat who baked mutton pies that the club members devoured. See also no. 72, 2:95–98, on the "Everlasting Club."

42. Van Doren, *Benjamin Franklin*, chap. 4; Lemay, *Benjamin Franklin*, 1:332–356; Verner W. Crane, "The Club of Honest Whigs: Friends of Science and Liberty," *William and Mary Quarterly* 23 (April 1966): 210–233.

43. An offshoot of the Calliopean was the short-lived but productive Drone Club, which attracted James Paulding, and in the mid-1790s saw its poetry disseminated through the *New-York Magazine*. Brother John T. ("Jack") Irving was a member of the Belles Lettres club, in addition to the Calliopean. Later literary clubs in New York, inspired by the satiric

bent of many members, would devise comical or ironic names, such as the Ugly Club, which featured some of the more attractive and creatively accomplished men about town. (*Spectator* no. 17 introduced an "Ugly Club" in which "no person whatsoever shall be admitted without a visible queerity in his aspect.") Eleanor Bryce Scott, "Early Literary Clubs in New York City," *American Literature* 5 (March 1933): 3–16; Thomas Bender, *New York Intellect* (New York: Alfred A. Knopf, 1987), 27–36; John W. M. Hallock, *The American Byron: Homosexuality and the Fall of Fitz-Greene Halleck* (Madison: University of Wisconsin Press), 6, 48–49.

44. Andrew Burstein, *Sentimental Democracy: The Evolution of America's Romantic Self-Image* (New York: Hill & Wang, 1999), 210–211, 220; David Simpson, *The Politics of American English, 1776–1850* (New York: Oxford University Press, 1986), 42–43, 46–50.

CHAPTER 2

1. Theodore Corbett, *The Making of American Resorts: Saratoga Springs, Ballston Spa, and Lake George* (New Brunswick, NJ: Rutgers University Press, 2001).

2. Introduction to the Ogden Family Papers, William L. Clements Library, University of Michigan.

3. August 3, 1803, *CW-Journals,* 1:7–8.

4. August 7–11, 1803, ibid., 1:10–17; PMI, 1:48–51.

5. August 13–16, 1803, *CW-Journals,* 1:19–27.

6. PMI, 1:57–59. He referred to the trappers in his 1837 *Adventures of Captain Bonneville.*

7. John Denis Haeger, *John Jacob Astor: Business and Finance in the Early Republic* (Detroit: Wayne State University Press, 1991), 52–56.

8. PMI, 1:59–60, 4:157–158.

9. The identity of Quoz was long assumed to be either Peter Irving, James K. Paulding, or Henry Brevoort; but Bruce I. Granger, an editor of the *Letters of Jonathan Oldstyle, Gent.* (Boston: Twayne Publishers, 1977), explains that it is "probable" that Quoz is none of the above, but rather a friendly drama critic named Elias Hicks, who was associated in some way with Peter Irving and the *Chronicle.* See Editorial Appendix 46 and WI to Elias Hicks, May 4, 1805, *CW-Letters,* 1:181, 187n.

10. Another definition for *buckram* was "strong linen cloth stiffened with gum" (a material used in bookbinding). Samuel Johnson, *A Dictionary of the English Language* (Philadelphia: Johnson & Warner, 1813), n.p. In Letter 6 of "Jonathan Oldstyle," Oldstyle volunteers advice "to the actors—less etiquette—less fustian—less buckram," wherein "fustian," like "buckram," was a *double entendre* for cotton linen and "bombast."

11. *CW-Misc.,* 1:3–7.

12. January 29, 1804, in Mark Van Doren, ed., *Correspondence of Aaron Burr and His Daughter Theodosia* (New York: Covici, Friede, 1929), 149. It is not clear whether Burr sent Theodosia the most recent "Dick Buckram" essays or a complete collection including all of the "Jonathan Oldstyle" pieces.

13. Nancy Isenberg, *Fallen Founder: The Life of Aaron Burr* (New York: Viking Penguin, 2007), chap. 7; Wayne R. Kime, "Pierre M. Irving's Account of Peter Irving, Washington Irving, and the *Corrector,*" *American Literature* 43 (March 1971): 108–114.

14. *CW-Misc.,* 1:8.

15. PMI, 1:62.

16. Wayne R. Kime, *Pierre M. Irving and Washington Irving: A Collaboration in Life and Letters* (Waterloo, Canada: Wilfrid Laurier University Press, 1977), 219.

17. STW, 1:41–42; WI to Ann Hoffman, August 10, 1807, *CW-Letters*, 1:246.

18. A second passport, issued by police authorities, varied only in its characterization of Irving's eyes (blue, not gray) and nose (middling, not long). PMI, 1:75; see also various passport descriptions in Irving travel notes, *CW-Journals*, 1:461.

19. Ibid., 1:81, 92–95; WI to Cathalan, September 15, 1804, *CW-Letters*, 1:76–77. Translation: "You are English, monsieur?" said he—"Excuse me," replied I, "I am from the United States of America"—"Well—*it's the same thing!*"

20. *CW-Journals*, 1:39; WI to William Irving, Jr., August 14, 1804, *CW-Letters*, 1:53.

21. Laurence Sterne, *A Sentimental Journey Through France and Italy* (London: T. Beckett and P. A. De Hondt, 1770), 2:10; see extended portraits of Sterne in Wilbur L. Cross, *The Life and Times of Laurence Sterne* (New Haven, CT: Yale University Press, 1925); David Thomson, *Wild Excursions: The Life and Fiction of Laurence Sterne* (New York: McGraw Hill, 1972); and Arthur H. Cash, *Laurence Sterne: The Later Years* (London: Methuen, 1986). Irving, like Thomas Jefferson (and, no doubt, others) before him, carried Sterne's slender, duodecimo volume with him on his first exploration of the French and Italian countryside. Irving may have found him objectionable as president, but Jefferson, too, embraced a decidedly Sternean sensibility when he tried to love the world and its people during his time in Europe. He wrote from Marseilles, during the spring of 1787, in the third person, constructing himself as a Sternean "traveller" confined to the small room of a country inn: "Charmed by the tranquillity of his little cell, he finds how few are our real wants, how cheap a thing is happiness, how expensive a one pride." Jefferson repeated this passionate script to several correspondents, at various moments during his journey. See Andrew Burstein, *The Inner Jefferson: Portrait of a Grieving Optimist* (Charlottesville: University Press of Virginia, 1995), chaps. 2 and 3.

22. Sterne, *A Sentimental Journey*, 1:27–28, 86–87; *CW-Journals*, 1:86.

23. *CW-Journals*, 1:88–89; WI to William Irving, Jr., September 20, 1804, *CW-Letters*, 1:91.

24. WI to Alexander Beebee, September 18, 1804, *CW-Letters*, 1:79–80. Jefferson wrote from Paris that he feared a young American coming there would find sexual experimentation irresistible: "He is led by the strongest of all the human passions into a spirit for female intrigue destructive of his own and others' happiness, or a passion for whores destructive to his health." Jefferson to John Banister, Jr., October 15, 1785, in Merrill D. Peterson, ed., *The Portable Thomas Jefferson* (New York: Viking Penguin, 1975), 393.

25. *CW-Journals*, 1:96–101 and passim; WI to Beebee, September 18, 1804; to William Irving, Jr., September 20, 1804, *CW-Letters*, 1:86, 89–90.

26. WI to William Irving, Jr., October 27, 1804, *CW-Letters*, 1:105–106.

27. Washington Irving and Samuel Swartwout were the same age. Sam and his older brother John, a state assemblyman, were among the staunchest of Burrite political operatives, and closely associated with the *Morning Chronicle*. The Swartwouts acted as Burr's couriers, from time to time, and would become deeply involved in Burr's subsequent adventure in the West. William Peter Van Ness, Burr's second at the duel, was indicted; John Swartwout went into hiding, temporarily, as Sam Swartwout led Burr south, and out of harm's way. On the Swartwouts, see B. R. Brunson, *The Adventures of Samuel Swartwout in the Age of Jefferson and Jackson* (Lewiston, NY: Edwin Mellen Press,

1989), chap. 1. For a better sense of the composition of the Burrite conclave, from its enemy's point of view, see "Burr Meeting," in the *American Citizen,* March, 7, 1804, in which, along with the Swartwouts, William Irving is identified as "the *auctioneer*," and Peter as simply "the Editor."

28. WI to William Irving, Jr., August 1 and October 27, 1804, *CW-Letters,* 1:43, 48–49, 105–106. Before word of the Burr-Hamilton duel had reached him, Irving had written from Bordeaux, urging Peter on. The *Morning Chronicle* continued to hammer at inconsistencies and injustices on the New York political scene—"malevolent passions" of a "merciless faction," to repeat the words a friend of Washington's had written in the *Chronicle* on the eve of the vote. But in the aftermath of the duel, Irving's feelings were more mixed, as these letters to his brother reveal.

29. WI to William Irving, Jr., October 27, 1804, *CW-Letters,* 1:107.

30. WI to Furman, October 24, 1804, ibid., 1:111.

31. *CW-Journals,* 1:103–110; WI to William Irving, Jr., October 27, 1804, *CW-Letters,* 1:103–104.

32. *CW-Journals,* 1:111, 119–123; WI to William Irving, Jr., October 24, 1804, *CW-Letters,* 1:105.

33. Departure from Genoa in December 1804 prompted him to record these thoughts: "It was with the deepest regret I left this city . . . where I had found a friend particularly dear to me . . . but this is the grand misfortune of traveling—no sooner have we become acquainted in any place and began to form an agreeable circle of friends—but we are obliged to tear ourselves away and again in a manner become alone in the world." *CW-Journals,* 1:119–120, 141; WI to William Irving, Jr., November 16, 1804, *CW-Letters,* 1:136.

34. WI to "Andrew Quoz," January 1, 1805, *CW-Letters,* 1:165–169.

35. *CW-Journals,* 1:148–152.

36. Ibid., 1:195–209.

37. WI to William Irving, Jr., April 4 and 12, 1805, *CW-Letters,* 1:172–174, 178–179; *CW-Journals,* 1:251–252, 277–278.

38. *CW-Journals,* 1:290.

39. Ibid., 1:305–309, 321.

40. PMI, 1:139–140.

41. WI to William Irving, Jr., May 31, 1805, *CW-Letters,* 1:189–190; *CW-Misc.,* 1:149.

42. He wrote of differences among cultures: "A frenchman is apt to turn everything into a jest or bon *mot*—an Italian always agrees to the truth of what you say resigning his real opinion out of politeness—An Englishman hears you with impatience when you contradict him, and opposes you with positiveness and obstinacy—the Swiss on the contrary listens to you with attention—weighs the justice of your remarks and the truth of your arguments and makes his reply accordingly with manly politeness and freedom." *CW-Journals,* 1:389.

43. Irving found himself at this bizarre moment arguing with a Frenchman in favor of the purer American way of conducting a romance. To the inquisitive merchant from Lyons, he explained that the fair sex in America were "remarkable for their affectionate fidelity to their husbands." In an exchange that took place in French, the merchant turned and exclaimed, "Mon dieu, what an unhappy country for *les garçons*." "Indeed," the romancing Cabell interjected, "*il faut se marrier là*." One must marry there. *CW-Journals,* 1:407; Cabell's notes of this day mention their companions and the pleasing country views, but nothing of his own flirtatious behavior. Richard Beale Davis, "Wash-

ington Irving and Joseph C. Cabell," in *English Studies in Honor of James Southall Wilson* 5 (1951): 11–12.

44. *CW-Journals,* 1:399–400.

45. Ibid., 1:422–425; WI to William Irving, Jr., May 31, 1805; to Peter Irving, July 15, 1805; to Alexander Beebee, August 3, 1805, *CW-Letters,* 1:190–192, 196, 201.

46. *CW-Journals,* 1:445, 449–452, 455–456.

47. Ibid., 1:579–580.

CHAPTER 3

1. *Salmagundi,* ed. Bruce I. Granger and Martha Hartzog (Boston: Twayne Publishers, 1977), no. 8, 164.

2. PMI, 1:164–172; STW, 1:74–78. Swartwout is not usually included in Irving biographers' list of the "Lads of Kilkenny," but Irving identifies him as such in a letter of introduction sent to Joseph Gratz of Philadelphia. See WI to Gratz, July 8, 1806, *CW-Letters,* 1:221.

3. Richard Beale Davis, "Washington Irving and Joseph C. Cabell," in *English Studies in Honor of James Southall Wilson* 5 (1951): 14–19.

4. The twentieth century's foremost Irving critic, Stanley T. Williams of Yale's English Department, gave it a mixed review: "Some bubbles of this wine still rise lightly to the surface," he wrote in the 1930s. "Yet, too often, instead of wisdom, there is adage; instead of wit there is flippancy; instead of characters there are labels." STW, 1:81. It should be added that Williams rarely had anything positive to say about an Irving composition.

5. Joseph J. Ellis, *After the Revolution: Profiles of Early American Culture* (New York: W. W. Norton, 1979), chap. 6. On the other hand, Webster was astute enough to sell licenses for the right to print his work, sometimes by auction. Leon Jackson, *The Business of Letters,* chap. 1, forthcoming, seen in manuscript.

6. PMI, 1:175–176; Ralph M. Aderman and Wayne R. Kime, *Advocate for America: The Life of James Kirke Paulding* (Selinsgrove, PA: Susquehanna University Press), 38–42, 48; *Salmagundi,* Editorial Appendix, 319, 379, 401–402.

7. PMI, 1:168–169; *CW-Letters,* 1:217–218.

8. PMI, 1:171; *CW-Letters,* 1:219.

9. John Irving to John Furman, July 16, 1807, in Leonard Beach, ed., *Peter Irving's Journals* (New York: New York Public Library, 1943), 9n.

10. John Lambert, *Travels Through Canada and the United States of North America in the Years 1806, 1807, & 1808* (London: Baldwin, Cradock, and Joy, 1816), 2:90.

11. *Salmagundi,* no. 1, 75–76. Irving was not aping Sterne out of a lack of originality. He was playing off a familiar idiom to which readers automatically related. Sterne's art was the art of the digression, the art of fixation, and Irving, at this early stage in his writing career, was getting mileage out of both. "Digressions, incontestably, are the sunshine,—they are the life, the soul of reading," writes Sterne. "Take them out of this book, for instance, you might as well take the book along with them." Laurence Sterne, *Tristram Shandy,* ed. Ian Watt (Boston: Houghton Mifflin, 1965), vol. 1, chap. 22. As to the relative importance of Sterne in Irving's search for a style of burlesque, see, generally, Martin Roth, *Comedy and America: The Lost World of Washington Irving* (Port Washington, NY: Kennikat Press, 1976).

12. Sterne, *Tristram Shandy,* vol. 3, chap. 1; *Salmagundi,* no. 1, 76–77.

13. Lambert, *Travels Through Canada and the United States of North America*, 2:91.

14. *Salmagundi*, no. 1, 76. Sterne discourses on customs, too, invoking classical authorities for ridiculous theories, as Irving would do in *A History of New York*. Though the French take themselves seriously, Sterne refuses to: "The French are certainly misunderstood:—but whether the fault is theirs, in not sufficiently explaining themselves . . . I shall not decide." And he notes: "The French have a *gay* way of treating everything that is Great; and that is all that can be said about it." See *Tristram Shandy*, vol. 7, chap. 18. In Irving's next foray as a *Salmagundi* author, he insists on his universal respect for foreigners. *Salmagundi*, no. 3, 89–90.

15. Ibid., no. 1, 77.

16. *Universal Biographical Dictionary, Containing the Lives of the Most Celebrated Characters of Every Age and Nation* (New York: n.p., 1825), 342. The English satirist John Wolcot (1738–1819) wrote under the pseudonym "Peter Pindar," and presumably the Irving brothers knew of his work as well. Other Evergreen-Pindar exchanges on "young belles" who "dance out their days" and "who freeze with a frown, and who thaw with a sigh" are found in *Salmagundi*, nos. 3 and 4, 93–95, 98–100.

17. Ibid., no. 11, 195–200.

18. Ibid., no. 6, 130.

19. Irving did for "whim-whams" what Sterne did for noses, buttonholes, and whiskers. According to Sterne, *whiskers* was a word, and an aesthetic, that held sway briefly in the world as soon as the Queen of Navarre heard its mellifluous sound. It "stood its ground," until one day the irresistibly handsome Sieur de Croix rode by, whiskerless, and the entire idea lost all decency. Sterne, *Tristram Shandy*, vol. 4, chap. 32; vol. 5, chap. 1; *Salmagundi*, no. 6, 129–132. The most immediate explanation for *Salmagundi*'s adoption of "whim-wham" in the title derives from Isaac D'Israeli's *Flim-Flams! or, the Life and Errors of My Uncle, and the Amours of My Aunt*, published in London in 1805. See William L. Hedges, *Washington Irving: An American Study, 1802–1832* (Baltimore: Johns Hopkins University Press, 1965), 46. One of Samuel Johnson's definitions for *whim* is "an irregular motion or desire"—thus *whim*, in the vocabulary of Irving's day, still had a strong connotation of "a thing turning round" in addition to being "an odd fancy." Johnson's *Dictionary*, alike in editions of 1755 (London) and 1813 (Philadelphia).

20. Remarkably, there really was a "Mustaffa," captain of the "Ketch *Abdullah*," who had been captured off the coast of North Africa and brought to New York aboard the USS *John Adams* while Irving was abroad; he was even entertained at the Park Theater. *Salmagundi*, Explanatory Notes, 343n.

21. Oliver Goldsmith, *The Citizen of the World: or, Letters from a Chinese Philosopher, Residing in London, to His Friends in the East* (Albany, NY: Barber and Southwick, 1794), 13–14; *Salmagundi*, no. 3, 90–91. For a thorough comparison of Goldsmith's Chinese visitor and *Salmagundi*'s Mustapha, see Ralph M. Aderman, "Salmagundi and the Outlander Tradition," *Wisconsin Studies in Literature* 1 (1964): 62–68.

22. *Salmagundi*, no. 7, 142–144.

23. Ibid., no. 11, 189–191; Sterne, *A Sentimental Journey*, 2:45.

24. WI to Mary Fairlie, May 2, 1807, *CW-Letters*, 1:231–232.

25. References to "Gotham" in *Salmagundi*, nos. 3, 7, and 17, pp. 96, 162, 272–277. On the English origins of Gotham, both a real town and a fabled place known for the mad antics of its inhabitants, see Edwin G. Burrows and Mike Wallace, *Gotham: A History of New York to 1898* (New York: Oxford University Press, 1999), xii–xiv.

26. Peter Irving made an obscure reference in his journal in 1807 suggesting that he accompanied Burr on either the 1805 or the 1806 trip west, though what his purpose might have been is unclear: All we know about Peter paints him as a sweet dreamer, not a knight of the frontier. Beach, *Peter Irving's Journals*, 115. Peter says of a Scottish scene: "It resembles those I recollect to have seen near Marietta [Ohio]," which is where Burr traveled as he made contacts toward putting his filibuster plan in motion.

27. B. R. Brunson, *The Adventures of Samuel Swartwout in the Age of Jefferson and Jackson* (Lewiston, NY: Edwin Mellen Press, 1989), chaps. 2–4.

28. New York Senator Samuel L. Mitchill, who like Jefferson bought Wilkinson's story, wrote of Burr without any sympathy at all: "By what means he will get out of this scrape I do not know . . . but he is full of cunning and subterfuge, and will reserve for himself a hole to creep out at." Nancy Isenberg, *Fallen Founder: The Life of Aaron Burr* (New York: Viking Penguin, 2007), chap. 8; Andrew Burstein, *The Passions of Andrew Jackson* (New York: Alfred A. Knopf, 2003), chap. 3; Royal Ornan Shreve, *The Finished Scoundrel* (Indianapolis: Bobbs-Merrill, 1933); Walter Flavius McCaleb, *The Aaron Burr Conspiracy and a New Light on Aaron Burr* (New York: Dodd, Mead, 1903; reprint, Argosy-Antiquarian, 1966), esp. chaps. 6 and 12; Dumas Malone, *Jefferson the President, Second Term* (Boston: Little, Brown, 1974), 261.

29. Isenberg, *Fallen Founder*, chap. 8.

30. WI to Mary Fairlie, May 13, 1807, *CW-Letters*, 1:234–236.

31. Davis, "Washington Irving and Joseph C. Cabell," 20; PMI, 1:190.

32. WI to Maria Fenno (Mrs. Josiah Ogden) Hoffman, June 4, 1807, *CW-Letters*, 1:237–238.

33. WI to Paulding, June 22, 1807, ibid., 1:239–240.

34. Thomas Perkins Abernathy, *The Burr Conspiracy* (New York: Oxford University Press, 1954); Hay to Jefferson, May 31, 1807, Jefferson Papers, Library of Congress, cited in Dumas Malone, *Jefferson the President: Second Term, 1805–1809* (Boston: Little, Brown, 1974), 311, 328–329; Francis F. Beirne, *Shout Treason: The Trial of Aaron Burr* (New York: Hastings House, 1959).

35. WI to [Mary Fairlie?], July 7, 1807, *CW-Letters*, 1:244; PMI, 1:202–203.

36. Hay to Jefferson, August 11, 1807, cited in Malone, *Jefferson the President: Second Term*, 335.

37. Davis, "Washington Irving and Joseph C. Cabell," 20.

38. *Salmagundi*, nos. 8 and 18, pp. 162, 277–283. Though affectingly told, the story would perhaps have been more solemnly received in the fall of 1807, were "Linkum Fidelius" not the nonsensical philosopher whose epigraphs (for example, "STYLE, is— style") are scattered throughout the *Salmagundi* series. He was, allegedly, "once lord mayor" of Gotham.

39. WI to Kemble, July 1, 1807, *CW-Letters*, 1:242.

40. *New-York Mirror, and Ladies' Literary Gazette*, November 5, 1825, 119.

41. It is entirely possible that Irving, in his story and in his letters from Richmond, captured more of the "inner" Burr than did illustrious biographers. The two most often cited nineteenth-century authorities are James Parton and Henry Adams. Parton's *The Life and Times of Aaron Burr* (New York: Mason Brothers, 1857) acknowledged that he considered his subject "a baffling enigma!" and went on to describe with journalistic flair and oversimplification a "gallant," but not a statesman. His Burr could stoically "accept the inevitable without repining," and as an Epicurean consider it "a weakness to mourn, and wisdom to enjoy." Parton, *Life and Times of Aaron Burr* (Boston and New York:

Houghton Mifflin, 1892), quote at 2:250; Scott E. Casper, *Constructing American Lives: Biography and Culture in Nineteenth-Century America* (Chapel Hill: University of North Carolina Press, 1999), 225–228. Asked to write a Burr biography for the American Statesman series in 1881, Adams betrayed his prejudice, saying: "Burr is the type of charlatan pure and simple, a very Jim Crow of melodramatic wind-bags." Ernest Samuels, *Henry Adams: The Middle Years* (Cambridge, MA: Harvard University Press, 1958), 185.

42. WI to Ann Hoffman, November 17, 1807, *CW-Letters*, 1:250–252.

43. The interpretive skill of Mary Weatherspoon Bowden has made it abundantly clear just how political *Salmagundi* was. See Bowden, "Cocklofts and Slang-whangers: The Historical Sources of Washington Irving's *Salmagundi*," *New York History* 61 (April 1980): 133–160. Morgan Lewis appeared, in 1807, a political changeling. The son of a Welsh merchant of the colonial era (a signer of the Declaration of Independence), he had defeated Burr for governor in 1804 as the Clinton-Livingston candidate. In refusing to be swallowed up in Clinton's statewide power grab, he played nice with some of the Federalists, including Josiah Ogden Hoffman. But he lacked the authoritative manner to maintain the political balance he was trying to achieve.

44. *Salmagundi*, no. 8, 152–157. I take my identification of "Langstaff" as Lewis from Bowden's analysis. Not every one of her connections between *Salmagundi* characters and real New York politicians is expressed with the same degree of certainty; but in this particular case, the Langstaff-Lewis connection strikes me as accurate. A truce of sorts had been called between Clintonians and Burrites in early 1806, complicating Lewis's position, so that as Irving was writing, he must have felt unable to predict what New York politics would present next. On this situation, see Evan Cornog, *The Birth of Empire: DeWitt Clinton and the American Experience, 1769–1828* (New York: Oxford University Press, 1998), 73–78.

45. Goldsmith's "man in black" was mentioned in different contexts across the pages of his epistolary work, *The Citizen of the World,* as "an humourist in a nation of humourists," who tried to portray himself as curmudgeonly, while actually being quite generous. "He takes as much pains," writes Goldsmith, "to hide his feelings, as any hypocrite would to conceal his indifference; but on every unguarded moment the mask drops off, and reveals him to the most superficial observer." The "man in black" shows up one last time at the end of the book, to offer his well wishes to the Chinese philosopher. *Citizen of the World: or, Letters from a Chinese Philosopher, Residing in London, to His Friends in the East* (Albany, NY: Barber and Southwick, 1794), 93, 455–456.

46. The editors of the modern edition of *Salmagundi* have catalogued the various assignments of authorship over the years. In some essays, it is easy to detect Washington Irving's imagination and writing style; in other cases, Paulding's or William Irving's hand is apparent; elsewhere, joint authorship seems possible. See *Salmagundi*, 327–329.

47. "Ordinary" was another name for "pub." Longworth was always looking for this kind of attention. In addition to *Salmagundi*, he published, in 1807, a farce called "The Farm House." He thrived on his eccentricity, insisting, in some of his publications, on spelling cities in lowercase, as "new-york" or "philadelphia," apparently for no reason other than to challenge the norm. STW, 1:80.

48. PMI, 1:194; *Salmagundi*, textual commentary, 383–387. Paulding assumed that Longworth was making more than he should (and the authors less than they should), whereas Irving seems to have had no problem with the business arrangements. Long-

worth himself asserted that he had paid the three contributors "handsomely." James N. Green of the Library Company of Philadelphia explored the matter in "Author-Publisher Relations in America up to 1825," an unpublished manuscript presented at the American Antiquarian Society, Worcester, Massachusetts, 1994, cited with the author's permission. Earlier, Thomas Paine, the author of the best-selling Revolutionary pamphlet *Common Sense,* argued with his original publisher over printers' ethics and profit sharing. See Michael Everton, "The Would-be Author and the Real Bookseller," *Early American Literature* (2005): 79–110.

49. As to the long-term impact of *Salmagundi,* we have the testament of the Massachusetts editor (and soon to be congressman) Edward Everett, in 1822: "Mr. Irving has long been one of the most popular writers our country has produced. . . . We all remember the success of Salmagundi, to which he was a large and distinguished contributor; with what rapidity and to what extent it circulated through America; how familiar it made it with the local pleasantry, and the personal humors of New York." From a review of *Bracebridge Hall,* in *North American Review* (July 1822): 206.

CHAPTER 4

1. Thomas A. Janvier, *In Old New York* (New York: Harper & Brothers, 1894), 40, 50, 152, 206, 214–215; R. W. G. Vail, *Knickerbocker Birthday* (New York: New-York Historical Society, 1954), 4–8; Nancy Isenberg, *Fallen Founder: The Life of Aaron Burr* (New York: Viking Penguin, 2007), chap. 5.

2. *Longworth's American Almanack, New-York Register, and City Directory* (New York: John C. Totten, 1799); edition of 1800 spells "Almanac" without the "k," and shows the publisher as Longworth & Wheeler; subsequent editions through 1806 show D. Longworth as sole publisher.

3. PMI, 1:233.

4. Ibid., 1:222–227; STW, 1:87–89, 102–107.

5. WI to Ann Hoffman, November 17, 1807; to Joseph Gratz, March 30, 1808; to Henry Brevoort, May 9 and June 11, 1808, *CW-Letters,* 1:250–258; George S. Hellman, *Washington Irving, Esquire* (London: Jonathan Cape, 1925), 71.

6. Rollin G. Osterweis, *Rebecca Gratz: A Study in Charm* (New York: G. P. Putnam's Sons, 1935), 108 and passim.

7. PMI, 1:229–230; STW, 1:105; Hoffman Family genealogy, Clements Library, University of Michigan; Osterweis, *Rebecca Gratz,* 116.

8. WI to Brevoort, May 11, 1809; to William P. Van Ness, December 18, 1809, *CW-Letters,* 1:263–264, 281; STW, 1:408n. There is some question as to whether Merwin was really Irving's model for Ichabod, though there is little doubt that Merwin himself thought so. Pierre M. Irving, however, thought to deny the connection. PMI, 4:80–81; Wayne R. Kime, *Pierre M. Irving and Washington Irving: A Collaboration in Life and Letters* (Waterloo, Canada: Wilfrid Laurier University Press, 1977), 257. Suffice it to say that Merwin of Kinderhook appears to have given Irving at least some inspiration for the portrait. The two remained in touch until late in Irving's life.

9. Jarvis subsequently did an interpretive portrait of "Diedrich Knickerbocker," which Irving, in his last years, recalled without enthusiasm: "Jarvis tried, but failed to embody my conception of Diedrich Knickerbocker," he told his nephew Pierre. "My idea was that he should carry the air of one profoundly impressed with the truth of his own History." PMI, 4:242–243.

10. One might imagine that partisan principle in the post-Revolutionary period was expressed in deeply philosophical tones, given what we think we know about the Constitutional Convention of 1787, and the republican discourse that emanated from it. In fact, though, newspapers of the 1790s and early 1800s achieved the most effect through barbed humor and downright insult. (James Cheetham's *American Citizen*, in its attacks on Aaron Burr and his editor Peter Irving, is just one example of this tendency.) Thus, a critic's merit was more often linked to satirical talent than to legal knowledge. Knowledgeable readers wanted to be "in on" the taunt or tease. Here is where Irving would shine.

11. Samuel L. Mitchill, *The Picture of New-York; or the Traveller's Guide Through the Commercial Metropolis of the United States* (New York: I. Riley, 1807), 1–5, 64–65, 69, 93–94, 128–129.

12. PMI, 1:219–220.

13. WI to Brevoort, October 23, 1809, *CW-Letters*, 1:274; PMI, 1:234–235.

14. Irving made an entry in his personal journal, in 1810, underscoring his opinion of the New-York Historical Society: "There is in this city a Society composed of several highly respectable gentlemen called the NYHS. They meet once a quarter to talk over what they have not done & what they ought to do." *CW-Journals*, 2:30. An advertisement for the book in James Cheetham's pro-administration, anti-Burr *American Citizen* is another ironic twist given the transparent lampoon of Jefferson in the text.

15. Herman Knickerbocker in *Biographical Directory of the American Congress, 1774–1949* (Washington, DC: United States Government Printing Office, 1950), 1422.

16. PMI, 1:236–237, 257–258; Joseph A. Scoville, *The Old Merchants of New York City* (New York: Carleton, 1863), 1:75–76.

17. *A History of New York*, ed. Michael L. Black and Nancy B. Black (Boston: Twayne Publishers, 1984), 30.

18. Ibid., 35–36.

19. Irving insisted that he randomly selected the Dutch surnames he used in his fiction and did not intend to mock the living. "It was a confounded impudent thing in such a youngster as I was," he told nephew Pierre, "to be meddling in this way with old family names; but I did not dream of offence." PMI, 1:247.

20. *A History of New York*, 52–77. So taken was he with the idea of the unchanging, unobserved village that Irving returned to it in an 1839 article, "Communipaw," for the *Knickerbocker Magazine*. He updated life in the seat of Old Dutch civilization to show what strategies were being used to prevent the descendants of "Oloffe the Dreamer" from being tainted by the nearby Yankee influence. See *CW-Misc.*, 2:122–129. Note that the chapter containing Oloffe's dream was added in 1812, when Irving revised the book for its second printing.

21. From the 1625 *Nieuwe Wereldt* by Johannes de Laet, in J. Franklin Jameson, ed., *Narratives of New Netherland, 1609–1664* (New York: Charles Scribner's Sons, 1909), 45; characterization of Minuit is in Ellis Lawrence Raesly, *Portrait of New Netherland* (New York: Columbia University Press, 1945), 58.

22. Oliver A. Rink, *Holland on the Hudson: An Economic and Social History of Dutch New York* (Ithaca, NY: Cornell University Press, 1984), 119, 131, 225.

23. *A History of New York*, 93.

24. Ibid., 130.

25. Ibid., 131.

26. Ibid., 148–151.

27. Ibid., 136–138, 154–155, 161–163.

28. Jameson, *Narratives of New Netherland*, 310–311; *A History of New York*, 78. Irving, of course, cannot restrain himself from absurdly twisting the derivation of "Manhattan" to describe "a custom among the squaws, in the early settlement, of wearing men's hats."

29. *A History of New York*, 133–134.

30. It was not only Federalists who opposed the embargo—the president's own secretary of the navy called it "this mischief-making busybody." What Jefferson saw as "peaceable coercion" caused distress to numerous American merchants and traders. Leonard D. White, *The Jeffersonians: A Study in Administrative History, 1801–1829* (New York: Macmillan, 1951), chap. 29; Dumas Malone, *Jefferson the President, Second Term, 1805–1809* (Boston: Little, Brown, 1974), chaps. 25 and 26. Jefferson's move was unpopular, but it also had a logic, one that Irving refused to see. "The ocean," wrote Jefferson, "like the air, is the common birthright of mankind"; the cessation of trade with belligerent nations had become a "moral obligation," designed to restore a sense of the law of nations. "To the Society of Tammany, or Columbian Order No. 1, of the City of New York," in Merrill D. Peterson, ed., *The Portable Thomas Jefferson* (New York: Viking Penguin, 1975), 328–329.

31. Among interpreters of the *History*, and Irving's treatment of Jefferson in it, there is a range of thinking. At one end is Mary Weatherspoon Bowden, *Washington Irving* (Boston: Twayne Publishers, 1981), which goes against the grain and states up front that Irving was, in spite of everything, "throughout his life a staunch Jeffersonian"; Michael L. Black and Nancy B. Black, as co-editors of the modern edition, call Diedrich Knickerbocker a "fanatical anti-Jeffersonian," *A History of New York*, xviii; William L. Hedges, *Washington Irving: An American Study, 1802–1832* (Baltimore: Johns Hopkins University Press, 1965), 62–64, emphasizes economic interests as the overriding explanation for Irving's Federalism; and Robert A. Ferguson, "Hunting Down a Nation: Irving's *A History of New York*," *Nineteenth-Century Fiction* 36 (June 1981): 22–46, suggests that Irving felt "intimidated" by Jefferson's worldview, and was but an "adolescent daydreamer" weakly contending with the superior legal mind of an Enlightenment intellectual. Stanley Williams and others have stressed Jefferson's exceptional frugality when it came to military expenditures, and his failure to prepare adequately for the coming War of 1812, as reasons for Irving's sensitivity. Williams adds to this critique Irving's evident discomfort with the coarseness of democracy. See STW, 1:92–94, 118, 2:268. On the Dutch, see Edwin G. Burrows and Mike Wallace, *Gotham: A History of New York to 1898* (New York: Oxford University Press, 1999), 62.

32. *A History of New York*, 194–198; on the real Colonel Butler, see Andrew Burstein, *Passions of Andrew Jackson* (New York: Alfred A. Knopf, 2003), 65–67, 75.

33. Because he wished to leave the country a balanced budget, Jefferson did not want to spend on strengthening the navy. Irving refers to "the fatal word Economy, the stumbling-block of William the Testy." See *A History of New York*, 271.

34. Ibid., 167–168.

35. Burrows and Wallace, *Gotham*, chaps. 4 and 5; Rink, *Holland on the Hudson*, 260–263.

36. *A History of New York*, 201–202, 228–230, 236–242.

37. Ibid., 285, 292.

38. See *A History of New York,* 74; also Townsend Percy, *Appleton's Dictionary of New York and Vicinity* (New York: D. Appleton, 1880), 99. Irving's notes, pasted into an 1854 G. P. Putnam *History of New-York,* at the Huntington Library, San Marino, California; Edwin T. Bowden, comp., *Washington Irving: A Bibliography* (Boston: Twayne Publishers, 1989), 102. Even the early French, Irving reported, referred to this place as *"Porte d'Enfer."*

39. It was Dr. Mitchill who, with scholarly gravity, provided a first idea of the means to relate the local nomenclature: "The principal market in New-York is the *Fly-Market,*" he wrote. "This is an uncouth name to a stranger, who is naturally led to expect from it, a market swarming with flies." Patiently offering a correction, he identified a place, southeast of Pearl Street, "originally a salt meadow, with a creek running through it, from where Maiden Lane now is, to the East River; forming such a disposition of land and water as was called by the Dutch *Vlaie,* a valley or wet piece of ground; when a market was first held there, it was called the *Fly,* or *Vlaie Market,* the Valley or Meadow market." Deadpan, Mitchill concludes: "This name certainly ought to be rejected and a better one adopted." Mitchill, *Picture of New-York,* 131; *A History of New York,* 163, 213, 219.

40. Andrew Burstein, *Sentimental Democracy: The Evolution of America's Romantic Self-Image* (New York: Hill & Wang, 1999), 102, 248, and passim. The most developed Freudian analysis of the infant motif and Irving's "regression" is Jonathan A. Cook, "'Prodigious Poop': Comic Context and Psychological Subtext in Irving's *Knickerbocker's History,*" *Nineteenth-Century Literature* 49 (March 1995): 483–512.

41. *A History of New York,* 86–87.

42. In addition to Irving, the civic-minded Republican John Pintard, a founder of the New-York Historical Society (among his many philanthropic activities), was a particular enthusiast of the Dutch patron saint. As early as December 6, 1793, his diary notes the occasion of St. Nicholas Day. He was a proponent of establishing Washington's Birthday and Fourth of July holidays, too. Concurrent with Irving's publication of *Knickerbocker's History,* Pintard funded Alexander Anderson's engraving of the solemn-looking fourth-century Bishop of Myra, who tended to the sick and suffering and later became St. Nicholas. The Historical Society distributed Anderson's rendering as a broadside. Charles W. Jones, "Knickerbocker Santa Claus," *The New-York Historical Society Quarterly* 38 (October 1954): 357–383; Stephen Nissenbaum, *The Battle for Christmas* (New York: Alfred A. Knopf, 1996); Burrows and Wallace, *Gotham,* 462–463. Irving's subsequent contributions to America's Christmas holiday will be discussed at greater length in chapter 7.

43. *A History of New York,* 41, 222.

44. It should also be said that Irving's narrative style in the *History,* Knickerbocker's need to explain himself and work toward benefiting the reader, and the intent focus on meanings, real or fabricated, are all decidedly Sternean traits. See especially Max Byrd, *Tristram Shandy* (London: Unwin Hyman, 1985), chap. 4.

45. Hedges, *Washington Irving,* 76–77. The first to see (or, at least, record) the strong connection to Swift was Walter Scott, who in 1813 praised Irving's cleverness; Scott also detected "some touches" that reminded him of Sterne. PMI, 1:240.

46. PMI, 1:240; Ralph M. Aderman, *Critical Essays on Washington Irving* (Boston: G. K. Hall, 1990), 35.

47. In this vein, see James E. Evans, "The English Lineage of Diedrich Knickerbocker," *Early American Literature* 10 (1975): 3–13; and Ferguson, "'Hunting Down a Nation.'"

CHAPTER 5

1. Richard Beale Davis, "James Ogilvie and Washington Irving," *Americana* 35 (July 1941): 437–442; Dumas Malone, *Jefferson the President, Second Term* (Boston: Little, Brown, 1974), 130–131; *The Family Letters of Thomas Jefferson,* ed. Edwin Morris Betts and James Adam Bear, Jr. (Charlottesville: University Press of Virginia, 1986), 331.

2. *CW-Misc.,* 1:xxv–xxvi, 39–49, 288–291; *Fragment of a Journal of a Sentimental Philosopher, During His Residence in the City of New-York, to Which Is Added, a Discourse upon the Nature and Properties of Eloquence as a Science* (New York: n.p., 1809); STW, 1:125.

3. WI to Maria Fenno Hoffman, February 12 and February 26, 1810, *CW-Letters,* 1:282–284.

4. PMI, 1:255–258.

5. WI to Brevoort, January 13 and February 7, 1811; WI to William Irving, February 16, 1811; to Moses Thomas, October 13, 1813, *CW-Letters,* 1:295–298, 300–302, 305–306, 359–360; *CW-Journals,* 2:263. Just as Irving seemed to relish the company of Dolley more than James Madison, he warmed to Hannah Gallatin, wife of Treasury Secretary Albert Gallatin, more than to the husband.

6. Brevoort to WI, June 28, 1811, and March 1, 1813, *Letters of Henry Brevoort to Washington Irving,* ed. George S. Hellman (New York: G. P. Putnam's Sons, 1916), 32–33, 72–74; WI to Brevoort, May 15, 1811, and March 17, 1812, *CW-Letters,* 1:316–320, 334–335; PMI, 1:281–282. In a letter of introduction Irving wrote on Brevoort's behalf to an acquaintance who was serving the U.S. diplomatic effort in France, he called Brevoort "one of the dearest friends I have, with whom I have been for years on terms of the closest & most confidential intimacy." WI to David B. Warden, March 7, 1812, *CW-Letters,* 1:334.

7. Brevoort to WI, March 1, 1813, *Letters of Henry Brevoort to Washington Irving,* 82; George S. Hellman, *Washington Irving, Esquire* (London: Jonathan Cape, 1925), 85; PMI, 1:239–240, 300, 306; STW, 1:417n.

8. *Salmagundi,* Textual Commentary, 397–400.

9. PMI, 1:285–286.

10. WI to John E. Hall, September 26, 1810, *CW-Letters,* 1:290.

11. "Hector Bullus," *The Diverting History of John Bull and Brother Jonathan* (New York and Philadelphia: Bradford & Inskeep, 1812), esp. 3–4, 15–22, 67–70, 90, 98, 134.

12. WI to William P. Van Ness, February 20, 1811, *CW-Letters,* 1:307.

13. WI to Peter Irving, December 30, 1812, ibid., 1:350–351.

14. Robert J. Allison, *Stephen Decatur: American Naval Hero, 1779–1820* (Amherst: University of Massachusetts Press, 2005), chaps. 12 and 13, New York episodes at 123–125.

15. "Biographical Memoir of Commodore Perry," *Analectic Magazine* (March 1814); *CW-Misc.,* 1:92–105.

16. Tompkins had long favored a strong state militia, writing one militia general in mid-1812: "I feel a confidence that we shall make ourselves masters of Canada by militia only." He had even made egalitarian noises with respect to the composition of state forces, conscripting a range of young men, so that the poor would not fill the ranks by themselves. See Daniel D. Tompkins, *Free Trade & Sailor's Rights! An Address to the Independent Electors of the State of New York* (Albany, NY: Office of the *Argus*, 1813), quotes at 6, 10, 12; Ray W. Irwin, *Daniel D. Tompkins: Governor of New York and Vice*

President of the United States (New York: New-York Historical Society, 1968), 178–181; C. Edward Skeen, *Citizen Soldiers in the War of 1812* (Lexington: University of Kentucky Press, 1999), 151.

17. See John W. M. Hallock, *American Byron: Homosexuality and the Fall of Fitz-Greene Halleck* (Madison: University of Wisconsin Press, 2000), 50–51; Wayne R. Kime, *Pierre M. Irving and Washington Irving: A Collaboration in Life and Letters* (Waterloo, Canada: Wilfrid Laurier University Press, 1977), 188.

18. J. C. A. Stagg, *Mr. Madison's War: Politics, Diplomacy, and Warfare in the Early American Republic* (Princeton, NJ: Princeton University Press, 1983), 182–183, 240–242, 402–407, 433–434; PMI, 1:312–316, 321–325; Irwin, *Daniel D. Tompkins,* 186–191.

19. "I would be sorry to see you drawn into their vortex," William Irving wrote of the Clinton political machine to former Burrite William Peter Van Ness, in 1811. "Rest well assured that DeWitt has not 100 friends in this City." William Irving, Jr., to Van Ness, February 7 and March 23, 1811, Clifton Waller Barrett Collection, Special Collections, University of Virginia Library.

20. The preceding section draws on Robert July, *The Essential New Yorker: Gulian Crommelin Verplanck* (Durham, NC: Duke University Press, 1951); Ralph M. Aderman and Wayne R. Kime, *Advocate for America: The Life of James Kirke Paulding* (Selinsgrove, PA: Susquehanna University Press, 2003), chap. 3; James Kirke Paulding, *The Lay of the Scottish Fiddle: A Tale of Havre de Grace* (New York and Philadelphia: Bradford & Inskeep, 1813); DeWitt Clinton, *An Account of Abimelech Coody and Other Celebrated Writers of New York, in a Letter from a Traveller, to His Friend in South Carolina* (New York: n.p., January 1815), quotes at 3–5, 7–8, 12–15.Clinton's reluctance to show appreciation for Irving's talent is curious in light of nationalistic words he spoke in the inaugural address he gave before the Literary and Philosophical Society, as its first president, in 1814: "In Europe, there is a literary corps who are authors by profession. Here we have scarcely any person of this description, and we have not much vernacular literature. . . . America leans for literary support on Europe, and we have been too much in the habit of estimating the value of books by the place of their origin. The time will surely arrive when an eminent American author shall be no longer considered an anomaly, deriving his celebrity more from his singularity, than the merit, of his productions." He obviously found Irving guilty by association. As Irving lightheartedly attested to Verplanck, "I shall regularly have my doublet dusted every month or two; as I find I always am inculpated in your iniquities. This comes of a mans keeping bad company." Clinton, *An Introductory Discourse, Delivered Before the Literary and Philosophical Society of New-York, on the Fourth of May, 1814* (New York: Van Winkle and Wiley, 1815), quote at 26–27; WI to Verplanck, January 17, 1815, *CW-Letters,* 1:386.

21. WI to Delaplaine, August 10, 1814, *CW-Letters,* 1:364.

22. WI to William Irving, January 15, 1815; to Gulian Verplanck, January 17 and January 21, 1815, ibid., 1:385–388.

23. WI to Brevoort, May 25, 1815, ibid., 1:394.

CHAPTER 6

1. WI to Sarah Irving, July 4, 1815; to Henry Brevoort, July 5, 1815, *CW-Letters,* 1:395–397; STW, 1:146, 418n; PMI, 1:333–334.

2. PMI, 1:333, 341–342, 346; WI to Brevoort, July 5, August 23, and December 28, 1815; to Ebenezer Irving, August [?] 1815, *CW-Letters,* 1:397, 418, 421, 430.

3. WI to Brevoort, March 15, 1816, *CW-Letters*, 1:433–434. With what reads for us almost as pained resignation, and what for his class and his generation probably amounts to a common trope, Irving commented to Brevoort on the institution of marriage: "It is what we must all come to at last. I see you are hankering after it, and I confess I have done so for a long time past. We . . . shall both come to it sooner or later."

4. WI to Thomas, May 3, 1816; to Brevoort, May 9 and July 16, 1816, ibid., 1:444–449; PMI, 1:357; STW, 1:150.

5. WI to Brevoort, July 16, 1816, *CW-Letters*, 1:450; Notebook of 1810, *CW-Journals*, 2:36.

6. WI to Sarah Irving, August 31 and October 18, 1816, *CW-Letters*, 1:454–456.

7. WI to Brevoort, January 29, 1817, ibid., 1:466–468.

8. WI to Brevoort, May 20, 1817, ibid., 1:476–477.

9. PMI, 1:361–369; M. A. Weatherspoon, in "1815–1819: Prelude to Irving's *Sketch Book*," *American Literature* 41 (January 1970): 566–571, highlights a crude deception perpetrated upon Irving by his ostensible rival for Serena Livingston, Virginian Henry Lee; Edwin G. Burrows and Mike Wallace, *Gotham: A History of New York to 1898* (New York: Oxford University Press, 1999), 484; WI to Brevoort, December 9, 1816, June 7 and July 21, 1817; to Allston, May 21, 1817, *CW-Letters*, 1:463, 477–479, 482, 486–487.

10. Ben Harris McClary, ed., *Washington Irving and the House of Murray* (Knoxville: University of Tennessee Press, 1969), introduction and 3–9.

11. "*Constable, the Bookseller's Shop*," he inscribed in his journal of the trip, "a dark, low, dingy shop—I passed it at first without noticing it, expecting to find a spacious, striking book shop." And then, reflecting on the phenomenon: "*Murrays shop* is equally unimposing tho' more fashionably situated & elegant in its air." August 26, 1817, *CW-Journals*, 2:98–99.

12. William Charvat, *Literary Publishing in America, 1790–1850* (Philadelphia: University of Pennsylvania Press, 1959); James N. Green, "Author-Publisher Relations in America Up to 1825" (unpublished paper, 1994). Green engages with Charvat's argument and points out its deficiencies. I was also able to review the book manuscript of Professor Leon Jackson, of the University of South Carolina, whose *The Business of Letters* will shed new light on the business of authorship in nineteenth-century America.

13. STW, 1:153–155. The early decades of the nineteenth century were an especially poignant time in the history of letter writing, the much-honored craft of literary self-confession. Williams supposes that the inconsolable Irving had somehow learned during episodes of persistent melancholy to write so as to "tame this mood" and "cleanse that marsh in his mind." We are meant to understand that this is how and why he took up the German language, read German folktales, and ultimately produced "Rip Van Winkle." This is, indeed, one possible interpretation of what Williams terms the "prenatal period" of Irving's *Sketch Book*. But it seems too obviously bent on finding an easy-to-digest explanation for Irving's failure to publish during his first years in England, when his financial concerns were real and ever present. Yet Williams goes on to picture Irving in overly dramatic terms, making his way through the London crowds, "one of the thousands uncertain of a livelihood, sauntering aimlessly about the city, with unstrung nerves." Ibid., 157. "Unstrung nerves" seems rather an embellishment, given the limitations on extant evidence. The acquaintance who wrote knowingly of Irving's moods was Flora Foster Dawson. See PMI, 4:353 (appendix). Also note Irving's explanation for his period of literary inactivity, as discussed with the writer Donald G.

Mitchell in the 1850s. Irving stated that he found himself "bereft of all the fancies" he had ever had for "weeks" (not months, not years), before he was able to write the *Sketch Book* stories. Irving added of the critical public: "If a man does a thing tolerably well in his happy moods, they see no reason why he should not always be in a happy mood." This does not equal a sustained or clinical depression. See the preface of 1863 to "Dream Life: A Fable of the Seasons," in *The Works of Donald G. Mitchell* (New York: Charles Scribner's Sons, 1907), xiii. On the emotional content of the epistolary tradition as understood in the eighteenth and nineteenth centuries, see Howard Anderson and others, eds., *The Familiar Letter in the Eighteenth Century* (Lawrence: University Press of Kansas, 1966); Bruce Redford, *The Converse of the Pen: Acts of Intimacy in the Eighteenth-Century Familiar Letter* (Chicago: University of Chicago Press, 1986); Karen Lystra, *Searching the Heart: Women, Men, and Romantic Love in Nineteenth-Century America* (New York: Oxford University Press, 1989); and Andrew Burstein, *Inner Jefferson: Portrait of a Grieving Optimist* (Charlottesville: University Press of Virginia, 1994), esp. chap. 4.

14. Visit with Walter Scott, *CW-Journals*, 2:117; WI to Peter Irving, August 26, September 1 and 6, 1817; to Brevoort, August 28, 1817, *CW-Letters*, 1:490–504. Since it contains references to the August 30 visit to Abbotsford, the letter to Brevoort dated August 28 was begun on that day and continued after several days. For analysis of Irving's essay "Abbotsford," see esp. William Owen, "Reevaluating Scott: Washington Irving's 'Abbotsford,'" in Stanley Brodwin, ed., *The Old and New World Romanticism of Washington Irving* (Westport, CT: Greenwood Press, 1986), 69–78. In 1835, three years after the death of Sir Walter Scott, Irving finally commemorated their first encounter with the publication of "Abbotsford."

15. WI to William Irving, December 23, 1817, *CW-Letters*, 1:514–515; George S. Hellman, *Washington Irving, Esquire* (London: Jonathan Cape, 1925), 101; PMI, 1:394–395.

16. PMI, 1:405.

17. WI to Brevoort, October 10, 1817, *CW-Letters*, 1:508–509.

18. WI to Brevoort, June 8, 1811, ibid., 1:322. A subsequent letter to Brevoort indicates that Peter Kemble had contracted a venereal disease. See July 8, 1812, ibid., 1:337–338.

19. In his Paris notebook a few years later, when he was forty, he would write for his own amusement: "An irish lady & her nice fresh daughter came in [to his friend's home] & sat some little time—one that a man would feel no compunction in begetting children upon—." This kind of bawdiness shows Irving capable of a devilish spirit when it came to fantasizing about particular women. See *CW-Journals*, 3:317.

20. Hellman, *Washington Irving, Esquire*, 80–81.

21. *Autobiographical Recollections by the Late Charles Robert Leslie*, ed. Tom Taylor (Boston: Ticknor and Fields, 1860), 16; PMI, 1:405–406; WI to Brevoort, September 27, 1818; to Leslie, November 2, 1821, *CW-Letters*, 1:534, 654.

22. There is much recent literature on masculinity in nineteenth-century America, but little that directly offers insight into Irving's life. The best exposition of Irving's sexual world is Bryce Traister, "The Wandering Bachelor: Irving, Masculinity, and Authorship," *American Literature* 74 (March 2002): 111–137. For readings that touch on the subject of bachelorhood and sexuality in the context of Irving's New York experience, see in particular Howard P. Chudacoff, *The Age of the Bachelor* (Princeton, NJ: Princeton University Press, 1999), and Timothy J. Gilfoyle, *City of Eros: New York City, Pros-*

titution, and the Commercialization of Sex, 1790–1920 (New York: W. W. Norton, 1992). Michael Warner's interpretive essay situates Irving in the "transitional period between patriarchy and modern heterosexuality." Warner argues impressively with regard to Irving's sensitivity on issues of families and inheritance, and he notes that Irving fails to develop meaningful female characters in his fiction. In his stories, Irving is wistful for a happiness rooted in the time before his friends were of marriageable age. See Warner, "Irving's Posterity," *ELH* 67 (Autumn 2000): 773–799.

23. PMI, 1:409–410; William Irving to WI, October 24, 1818, in the Berg Collection, New York Public Library.

24. WI to Ebenezer Irving, March 1, 1819, *CW-Letters*, 1:539. In suggesting a first printing of three or four thousand copies, Irving demanded discretion. "Don't show the Mss. to any one," he pleaded with his brother, "nor say any thing about it."

25. WI to Ebenezer Irving, March 3, 1819, ibid., 1:540. Consistent with his overall theme of an Irving who struggles with his own middling capacities, Williams dramatizes the relationship between Irving and his older siblings, probably overinterpreting the family dynamic. "So long had the brothers done his thinking for him," he writes, "that to act alone was a wrench. . . . Nor could Washington, throughout his life, be quite independent of the fear of fraternal disapproval. It may be doubted whether the brothers ever looked upon him as an adult." William Irving, Jr., to be sure, treated his writer-brother with a certain amount of paternalism; but Washington Irving was far from the incompetent here conjured. STW, 1:171.

26. WI to Brevoort, March 3, 1819, *CW-Letters*, 1:542.

27. PMI, 1:240–242; WI to Brevoort, April 1, 1819, *CW-Letters*, 1:545.

28. Green, "Author-Publisher Relations in America."

29. "The Author's Account of Himself," in *Sketch Book,* ed. Haskell Springer (Boston: Twayne Publishers, 1978), 9–10.

30. "The Voyage," ibid., 11–15. As a literary scholar who applies psychological methods, Jeffrey Rubin-Dorsky sees Irving's recent emotional history in the stories he chooses to tell. Thus, Crayon/Irving in "The Voyage" is "a tentative man for whom fixed points of social reference continually dissolve." There is "a surface layer of anticipated satisfaction" in his experience that "camouflages a subterranean level of gnawing doubt." For Irving's persona, the ideal of transcendence is never sustained too long, for he is frequently brought back to reality. Rubin-Dorsky, *Adrift in the Old World: The Psychological Pilgrimage of Washington Irving* (Chicago: University of Chicago Press, 1988), 42.

31. "Roscoe," in *Sketch Book,* 16–19.

32. *Autobiography of Charles Caldwell, M.D.,* ed. Harriot W. Warner (Philadelphia: Lippincott, Grambo, 1855; reprint, New York: Da Capo Press, 1968), 365–366, 371–372.

33. STW, 1:182, 429n; *Sketch Book,* Explanatory Notes, 308.

34. STW, 1:168–169.

35. *Salmagundi,* no. 17, 272.

36. There is one other possible meaning conjured by the title character's name: R.I.P. popularly stands for "rest in peace," as used on grave markers; its true derivation is the Latin *requiescat in pace.* "RIP" would seem the right moniker for one who fell into a long sleep and was imagined to have disappeared and died; yet this reference appears a less likely influence on Irving than those already mentioned—R.I.P. is more widely associated with the later nineteenth century.

37. Washington Irving himself was often misidentified as an "African-American scientist" or abolitionist, probably confused with another historical figure named after the first president, George Washington Carver.

38. *Sketch Book,* 28–41.

39. The remarks of Dr. Rubin, professor emeritus at Whitman College, were made in a private communication with the author.

40. Irving's misogyny is modest in the context of traditional literary female-bashing. Women had provided an easy target for two centuries by this point, painted by medical thinkers and writers alike as neurologically delicate, subject to moods and fits, and, as wives, prone to folly when not properly "handled" by their men. Female intellectualism was mocked again and again in comedies of the seventeenth and eighteenth centuries; wit supposedly "intoxicated" the "feeble" female brain—women were seen as pretenders. Irving certainly did not go as far as this in his depiction. One of his favorite authors, Oliver Goldsmith, took the same approach female conduct manuals adopted, maintaining that a woman must live to cheer and comfort a man, while accepting male enforcement of her performative boundaries. She was meant to stabilize domestic life and not to aspire to much more. Women who moved outside "the narrow limits of domestic offices," Goldsmith wrote, "move eccentrically, and consequently without grace. . . . But how are they changed, and how shocking do they become, when the rage of ambition, or the pride of learning, agitates and swells those breasts, where only love, friendship, and tender care should dwell!" Women who refused to assume their "natural" position as society's most cordial and most tender deserved to be mocked as distortions of nature. This is not Irving's purpose. The aggressive character of Dame Van Winkle can be seen as nothing more than a literary device allowing Irving to present Rip as her opposite: evasive, even cowardly, and one who consistently tries to stay out of trouble (and then, of course, keeps getting into trouble). See Katharine M. Rogers, *The Troublesome Helpmate: A History of Misogyny in Literature* (Seattle: University of Washington Press, 1966), chap. 5, Goldsmith quotes at 185–186; Felicity A. Nussbaum, *The Brink of All We Hate: English Satires on Women, 1660–1750* (Lexington: University of Kentucky Press, 1984).

41. Terence Martin has written epigrammatically that Irving's world is a world removed, "a region of greater imaginative latitude" that we choose to make familiar. See "Rip, Ichabod, and the American Imagination," *American Literature* 31 (May 1959): 137–149, quote at 141.

42. The story of Peter Klaus, as related in Johann Carl Christoph Nachtigal Otmar, *Volks-Sagen nacherzählt von Otmar,* published in Bremen in 1800, a volume easily accessible when Irving was reading German in 1817–1818. See the analysis of Herbert A. Pochmann, "Irving's German Sources in the *Sketch Book,*" in *Studies in Philology* 27 (July 1930): 477–507; also "The Genesis of the Rip Van Winkle Legend," *Harper's New Monthly Magazine* (September 1883): 617–622. I thank Jay H. Geller for assisting me with the German translation.

43. Cited in Philip Young, "Fallen from Time: The Mythic 'Rip Van Winkle,'" in James W. Tuttleton, ed., *Washington Irving: The Critical Reaction* (New York: AMS Press, 1993), 70.

44. It was Walter Shear who first evaluated the meaning of the death of the past in Irving's craft. See Shear, "Time in 'Rip Van Winkle' and 'The Legend of Sleepy Hollow,'" *Midwest Quarterly* 17 (1976): 158–172. Robert A. Ferguson reads the story practically as one that acts out the tensions inherent in *generational* time. "Rip Van Winkle" en-

dures, he says, because its fantastic elements put time "in our favor," allowing Rip to get away with his bad habits while still shining a light on the failure of Rip fully to appreciate his having abandoned his family; in old age, he is cared for by the child (now mother) Judith, whom he deserted. It is as if he had disappeared on a twenty-year alcoholic binge. But Irving, "as part of the twist in his humor," refuses to be direct, or realistic, in pointing out what would have been the more likely explanation for Rip's disappearance if it had occurred in Irving's day. (The temperance movement in America got into full gear just after the publication of the *Sketch Book.*) In the end, Rip escapes, and allows the reader to escape, "the torments of existence" through the hope of experiencing the same "timely good fortune" that he does. See Ferguson, "Rip Van Winkle and the Generational Divide in American Culture," *Early American Literature* 40 (2005): 529–544.

45. Yet it is not in his relationship with family or friends, but in his impulse toward his dog Wolf that Irving shows us this sentimental quality in Rip. In the woods, "he would sometimes seat himself at the foot of a tree, and share the contents of his wallet with Wolf, with whom he sympathized as a fellow-sufferer in persecution." Upon which, Irving raises the level of sympathetic understanding: "Wolf would wag his tail, look wistfully in his master's face, and if dogs can feel pity, I verily believe he reciprocated his feeling with all his heart." See Andrew Burstein, *Sentimental Democracy: The Evolution of America's Romantic Self-Image* (New York: Hill & Wang, 1999), chaps. 8 and 9, quotes at 262, 266, 309–310.

CHAPTER 7

1. In Irving's day, a sketching crayon was closer in its chemical composition to a pastel than to a modern pencil. I am grateful to art historian Susan Dixon for this clarification. The word *pencil* was defined in Johnson's *Dictionary* as (1) "A small brush of hair which painters dip in their colors" (thus, a paintbrush); (2) "A black lead pen, with which, cut to a point, they write without ink"; and (3) "Any instrument writing without ink." The word *crayon*, more simply, was "A kind of pencil; a roll of paste to draw lines with." *Dictionary of the English Language* (Philadelphia: Johnson & Warner, 1813).

2. Preface of 1863 to "Dream Life: A Fable of the Seasons," in *The Works of Donald G. Mitchell* (New York: Charles Scribner's Sons, 1907), xii.

3. Modern editions of the *Sketch Book* are adapted from the 1848 edition, containing Irving's later revisions. The substance varies noticeably from the original, but does not alter essential meanings. The "Postscript" to "Rip Van Winkle," for instance, was not added until 1848.

4. PMI, 1:423; WI to Brevoort, July 28, 1819, *CW-Letters*, 1:551.

5. PMI, 1:423; WI to Brevoort, August 12, 1819, *CW-Letters*, 1:554. The epigraph was from the recluse Robert Burton (1577–1640), who was known for his humor as well as for his *Anatomy of Melancholy*. Burton was also a favorite of Laurence Sterne.

6. WI to Brevoort, September 6, 1819, *CW-Letters*, 1:559–560; Brevoort's review, in Ralph M. Aderman, ed., *Critical Essays on Washington Irving* (Boston: G. K. Hall, 1990), 46. Irving was not without negative publicity; a peevish pamphlet reminiscent of DeWitt Clinton's earlier diatribe was printed in December 1819, titled *Brief Remarks on the "Wife" of Washington Irving*, which compared the author of the *Sketch Book* to "a boy moving *awkwardly* on stilts." The author was Egbert Benson, age seventy-three, who had served as a New York State judge and attorney general, and as president of the New-York Historical Society from its founding in 1804 until 1816. See STW, 1:433n142.

7. Brevoort to WI, September 9, 1819, *Letters of Henry Brevoort to Washington Irving*, ed. George S. Hellman (New York: G. P. Putnam's Sons, 1918), 109–113.

8. Matthew J. Pethers, "Transatlantic Migration and the Politics of the Picturesque in Washington Irving's *Sketch Book*," *Symbiosis* 9 (October 2005): 135–158; *North American Review* 15 (July 1822): 223. The author of the piece was the future Massachusetts congressman Edward Everett.

9. *Analectic Magazine* (May 1814): 405–406. David Simpson writes, with reference to the leading English lexicographer, that "it was to prove more difficult to declare independence from Samuel Johnson than it had been to reject George III." Simpson, *The Politics of American English* (New York: Oxford University Press, 1986), 33, 127–128.

10. "The Art of Book Making," in *Sketch Book*, 63.

11. "The Mutability of Literature," ibid., 100–108. As the Irving scholar Mary Weatherspoon Bowden puts it, in "The Mutability of Literature . . . we are presented with the paradox of Crayon fleeing merriment, being buried, while still asserting that it is only those who are closest to human life and nature who will be able to escape oblivion." See Bowden, *Washington Irving* (Boston: Twayne Publishers, 1981), 64. Jeffrey Rubin-Dorsky reads "self-directed irony" into the seriocomic essay, and Irving's fears for his own "legitimacy" as an author. See Rubin-Dorsky, *Adrift in the Old World: The Psychological Pilgrimage of Washington Irving* (Chicago: University of Chicago Press, 1988), 57–58.

12. For a pertinent discussion, see Patrick H. Hutton, *History as an Art of Memory* (Hanover, NH: University Press of New England, 1993), chap. 8, "History at the Crossroads of Memory."

13. "Rural Life in England," in *Sketch Book*, 50–55; Thomas Jefferson, *Notes on the State of Virginia*, ed. Frank Shuffelton (New York: Penguin Books, 1999), Query XIX, 170. Jefferson, of course, was romanticizing those free men who labored in the fields, and who looked up to no social superior; whereas Irving was more interested in the calm that prevailed over rural society, owing to the ordinary inhabitants' comfort with the traditional social hierarchy.

14. PMI, 1:431.

15. "The Pride of the Village," in *Sketch Book*, 257–263.

16. Stephen W. Nissenbaum, *Christmas in Early New England, 1620–1820: Puritanism, Popular Culture, and the Printed Word* (Worcester, MA: American Antiquarian Society, 1996); Nissenbaum, *The Battle for Christmas* (New York: Alfred A. Knopf, 1996); J. M. Golby and A. W. Purdue, *The Making of Modern Christmas* (Athens: University of Georgia Press, 1986), chaps. 2 and 3; Penne L. Restad, *Christmas in America* (New York: Oxford University Press, 1995), 22–25. On the comparative importance of the Fourth of July, see Matthew Dennis, *Red, White, and Blue Letter Days: An American Calendar* (Ithaca, NY: Cornell University Press, 2002), chap. 1.

17. "Christmas," in *Sketch Book*, 149–151.

18. See *The Vindication of Christmas*, a 1961 Christmas production of Cornelia and Waller Barrett, from Irving's notebook pages in their possession, Special Collections, University of Virginia Library.

19. "The Stagecoach," in *Sketch Book*, 153–158.

20. "Christmas Eve," ibid., 159–162.

21. "Christmas Day," ibid., 169–179.

22. "Christmas Dinner," ibid., 180–183.

23. William L. Hedges has succinctly described Irving's Crayon as "a go-between," mediating moods and attempting to unite competing British and American cultures. He characterizes Irving's narrator as "the shy spectator who wishes he had close friends or relatives, the aging bachelor who would half like to be married, the American in England searching for a past, the traveler trying to get to something like home. Crayon," he concludes, "is a prompter of good feeling among others, who finds it impossible to get himself settled. Hedges, *Washington Irving: An American Study, 1802–1832* (Baltimore: Johns Hopkins University Press, 1965), 129. Of the spiritual quality Irving seems to be reaching for in his nostalgic journey into the English past and his mixed reception in this regard, see Richard V. McLamore, "The Dutchman in the Attic: Claiming an Inheritance in *The Sketch Book of Geoffrey Crayon*," *American Literature* 72 (March 2000): 31–57.

24. Golby and Purdue, *Making of Modern Christmas*, 43.

25. Don Foster, *Author Unknown: On the Trail of Anonymous* (New York: Henry Holt, 2000), chap. 6. Foster, a Shakespeare scholar whose talents have been employed by the FBI, prosecutes his case against Moore on the basis of internal evidence in the writings of Moore and Livingston. Not all scholars uncritically accept Foster's findings, prominent among them Stephen Nissenbaum, whose *The Battle for Christmas* highlights the role of Moore in the Americanization of Christmas. The mystery is again deepened when we consider Irving's ambiguous connections to the players in this drama. Recall that Irving was an intimate of Serena Livingston, of the Clermont line of the Livingston family. He was earlier associated with Robert Swift Livingston of the Manor line of the Livingstons while at Josiah Ogden Hoffman's law offices, and before that worked for Henry Brockholst Livingston, who was of the same line. Henry Livingston was of the Gilbert line. All Livingston lines lived and owned properties both in New York City and along the Hudson south of Albany. See Joan Gordon, "The Livingstons of New York, 1675–1860: Kinship and Class" (PhD diss., Columbia University, 1959).

26. John Hancock quote in John Ferling, *A Leap in the Dark: The Struggle to Create the American Republic* (New York: Oxford University Press, 2003), 158–159; Timothy Hancock quote in Andrew Burstein, *Sentimental Democracy: The Evolution of America's Romantic Self-Image* (New York: Hill & Wang, 1999), 115; Michael C. C. Adams, *Echoes of War: A Thousand Years of Military History in Popular Culture* (Lexington: University Press of Kentucky, 2002), 65.

27. Adrian C. Leiby, *The Revolutionary War in the Hackensack Valley: The Jersey Dutch and Neutral Ground, 1775–1783* (New Brunswick, NJ: Rutgers University Press, 1962), 53.

28. See Regina Janes, *Losing Our Heads: Beheadings in Literature and Culture* (New York: New York University Press, 2005).

29. Michael Meranze, "Major André's Exhumation," in Nancy Isenberg and Andrew Burstein, eds., *Mortal Remains: Death in Early America* (Philadelphia: University of Pennsylvania Press, 2003), 126–131.

30. "The Legend of Sleepy Hollow," in *Sketch Book*, 272–297.

31. See David Greven, "Troubling Our Heads About Ichabod: 'The Legend of Sleepy Hollow,' Classic American Literature, and the Sexual Politics of Homosocial Brotherhood," *American Quarterly* 56 (March 2004): 83–110, and Rubin-Dorsky, *Adrift in the Old World*, 104–106.

32. WI to Scott, October 30 and November 20, 1819, *CW-Letters,* 1:567–570; Ben Harris McClary, ed., *Washington Irving and the House of Murray* (Knoxville: University of Tennessee Press, 1969), 17–20; PMI, 1:451–453; textual commentary, in *Sketch Book,* 353.

33. PMI, 1:453–455.

34. STW, 1:190; Richard Beale Davis, "James Ogilvie and Washington Irving," *Americana* 35 (July 1941): 447–449.

35. "Review of *The Sketch Book* by Geoffrey Crayon," in Aderman, *Critical Essays,* 52–55. Similar to Jeffrey, Godwin was taken aback that an American could be so perceptive with respect to English rural scenes, wondering why no British author had ever been inspired to write on country life in such a manner. See PMI, 1:422.

36. WI to Brevoort, August 12, 1819, *CW-Letters,* 1:555; PMI, 1:457, 463.

37. Martin Roth, *Comedy in America: The Lost World of Washington Irving* (Port Washington, NY: Kennikat Press, 1976), xi, 156.

38. Paul Giles, *Transatlantic Insurrections: British Culture and the Formation of American Literature, 1730–1860* (Philadelphia: University of Pennsylvania Press, 2001), 142–149.

39. Ibid., 149.

40. Benita Eisler, *Byron: Child of Passion, Fool of Fame* (New York: Alfred A. Knopf, 1999), 314.

41. From "Don Juan," Canto I, and "Childe Harolde's Pilgrimage," Canto III.

42. It was in 1821 that Byron engaged in a long conversation about Irving with Joseph Coolidge of Boston, who would soon after marry the most literary-minded of Thomas Jefferson's granddaughters. Byron said that Irving's writings were his "delight" and that he knew the *Sketch Book* nearly by heart. See PMI, 2:25–26. In acknowledging the influence Byron's work exerted on Irving, Stanley Williams still could not be deterred from his persistent need to belittle Irving, whom he considered "a superficial romantic . . . dead to the deeper impulses of romanticism." In the *Sketch Book,* he averred, Irving was "unshaken by the glory of romanticism's introspection or its philosophic thought." STW, 1:178–179. As to Irving's coming to eclipse Byron, Ben Harris McClary writes that "when Byron's decline came as Irving's public reputation was in the ascendancy, even Murray cooled to the romantic poet." McClary, *Washington Irving and the House of Murray,* 39.

43. Jeffrey Rubin-Dorsky writes compellingly: "Although Ichabod acts as a force of destruction, he is an anomaly in his environment. Primarily, Sleepy Hollow is a safe place. When the supernatural, so often discussed and debated, finally appears, we are not frightened. . . . But in 'Rip Van Winkle,' we can never be sure that we understand what took place in the Catskill Mountains; we will always be awed, mystified, and continually disturbed by Rip's expression of overwhelming loss on returning to his native village." Rubin-Dorsky, *Adrift in the Old World,* 118.

CHAPTER 8

1. "Wives," in *Bracebridge Hall,* ed. Herbert F. Smith (Boston: Twayne Publishers, 1977), 46.

2. PMI, 2:13–18. The Albert Gallatin Papers at the Library of Congress are rich and revealing. There is still no better general treatment of Gallatin than Henry Adams's biography, now well over a century old.

3. WI to Leslie, November 30, 1820, *CW-Letters,* 1:607.

4. WI to Rush, October 28 and December 6, 1820, ibid., 1:600–601, 609–610; PMI, 2:19–24.

5. *Salmagundi*, Historical Note, 323–324, Textual Commentary, 401; WI to Brevoort, March 27, 1820, *CW-Letters*, 1:579–580; Ralph M. Aderman and Wayne R. Kime, *Advocate for America: The Life of James Kirke Paulding* (Selinsgrove, PA: Susquehanna University Press, 2003), chaps. 3 and 4.

6. Robert J. Allison, *Stephen Decatur: American Naval Hero, 1779–1820* (Amherst: University of Massachusetts Press, 2005), 3, 102, 200–215; PMI, 1:457–458.

7. STW, 1:198–202; PMI, 2:33–39; WI to Brevoort, March 10, 1821, *CW-Letters*, 1:615; Jan Ellen Lewis and Peter S. Onuf, eds., *Sally Hemings and Thomas Jefferson: History, Memory and Civic Culture* (Charlottesville: University Press of Virginia, 1999), 138, 199–200; "To Thomas Moore," in *The Works of Lord Byron* (Ware, England: Wordsworth Editions, 1994), 100; Benita Eisler, *Byron: Child of Passion, Fool of Fame* (New York: Alfred A. Knopf, 1999), 309–312.

8. WI to Leslie, March [?] 1821; to Brevoort, April 14, 1821; to Peter Irving, September 6, 1821, and March 24, 1822, *CW-Letters*, 1:617–618, 622–626, 646, 672; John Denis Hager, *John Jacob Astor: Business and Finance in the Early Republic* (Detroit: Wayne State University Press, 1991), chaps. 7 and 8.

9. PMI, 2:52–56; WI to William Harris, August 6, 1821; to Moore, August [?], 1821, *CW-Letters*, 1:637, 644. Harris, an Episcopal clergyman and Harvard graduate, was Columbia's president at the time.

10. WI to Ebenezer Irving, September 28 and November 1, 1821; to Leslie, October 25, November 2, and December 8, 1821; to Mrs. Thomas W. Storrow, December 10, 1821, *CW-Letters*, 1:647, 650, 653–654, 657, 659–660.

11. WI to Ebenezer Irving, January 29, 1822, ibid., 1:661–662; Introduction to *Bracebridge Hall*, xxiv.

12. Carl Van Doren, *Benjamin Franklin* (New York: Viking Press, 1938), 570–571. Franklin intentionally dressed down for effect. "Think how this must appear among the powdered heads of Paris," he wrote.

13. "The Author," in *Bracebridge Hall*.

14. "The Hall," in ibid.; "Christmas Eve," in *Sketch Book*, 164–165.

15. "The Busy Man," "The Widow," "The Lovers," "An Old Soldier," and "Ready Money Jack," in *Bracebridge Hall*, 11, 21, 23, 31, 36, 38.

16. "A Bachelor's Confessions" and "Village Worthies," ibid., 163–165, 178.

17. *Autobiographical Recollections by the Late Charles Robert Leslie*, ed. Tom Taylor (Boston: Ticknor and Fields, 1860), 43; PMI, 2:56.

18. "The Stout Gentleman," in *Bracebridge Hall*, 49–56.

19. "The Student of Salamanca," ibid., 100–154.

20. "Dolph Heyliger," ibid., 251–300.

21. See esp. William Hedges, *Washington Irving: An American Study, 1801–1832* (Baltimore: Johns Hopkins University Press, 1965), 182–188.

22. Maria Edgeworth was a marvelous satirist and arguably England's most accomplished sentimentalist of this period. Even Scott said he felt himself in her debt. Jeffrey's review in Ralph M. Aderman, ed., *Critical Essays on Washington Irving* (Boston: G. K. Hall, 1990), 58–62.

23. STW, 1:207–211; Pete Kyle McCarter, "The Literary, Political, and Social Theories of Washington Irving" (PhD diss., University of Wisconsin, 1939), 476; Mary Weatherspoon Bowden, *Washington Irving* (Boston: Twayne Publishers, 1981), 79.

William Hedges has observed that while the book is conventional in its sentimental depiction of the harmonious domestic scene, Irving does not surrender to the Squire's
benevolent despotism without exposing, on some satiric level, the patriarch's absurdity.
In defense of his position, Hedges explains Irving's nonending: "Instead of finally representing a social *order*, the book simply delights in disorder." Hedges, *Washington Irving*,
171–176.

24. WI to Wiley, March 6, 1822; to Richard Rush, June 5 and 14, 1822, *CW-Letters*,
1:667–668, 674, 681.

25. WI to Brevoort, June 11, 1822, ibid., 1:676–678; *CW-Journals*, 2:263; on Randolph's personality and antics, see Andrew Burstein, *America's Jubilee* (New York: Alfred A. Knopf, 2001); Luther Bradish to WI, May 19, 1858, Berg Collection, New York
Public Library.

26. WI to Peter Irving, June 30, 1822; to Newton, July 5, 1822, *CW-Letters*, 1:689,
690.

27. PMI, 2:90–91.

28. WI to Sarah Irving Van Wart, August 2 and 19, 1822; to Thomas W. Storrow, August 20, 1822, *CW-Letters*, 1:694–697, 699–701.

29. *CW-Journals*, 3:23–28, 46–48; WI to Storrow, July 11, 1822; to Sarah Irving Van
Wart, September 18 and October 3, 1822, *CW-Letters*, 1:692, 704–709.

30. *CW-Journals*, 3:66; WI to Sarah Irving Van Wart, October 27, 1822; to Storrow,
November 16, 1822, *CW-Letters*, 1:717–719, 723–724.

31. *CW-Journals*, 3:75, 85, 87–88; WI to Leslie, December 2, 1822, *CW-Letters*,
1:725.

32. *CW-Journals*, 3:94, 97; WI to Thomas Storrow, December 22, 1822, *CW-Letters*,
1:728.

33. Walter A. Reichart, *Washington Irving and Germany* (Ann Arbor: University of
Michigan Press, 1957), 83–86; *CW-Journals*, 3:97.

34. Stanley T. Williams and Leonard B. Beach, eds., *The Journal of Emily Foster*
(New York: Oxford University Press, 1938), 70–71, 98, 110–111, 118, and passim.

35. *CW-Journals*, 3:101–103.

36. Williams and Beach, *Journal of Emily Foster*, 114–115; *CW-Journals*, 3:108, 112.

37. Ibid., 3:123–125; WI to Peter Irving, March 10, *CW-Letters*, 1:732.

38. *CW-Misc.*, 1:157–158; *CW-Journals*, 3:143.

39. *CW-Journals*, 3:134–140.

40. PMI, 4:353, and passim.

41. WI to Amelia Foster, April/May [?] 1823, May 23 and 28 and June 1, 1823, *CW-
Letters*, 1:737–744, 752, 754, 759; Williams and Beach, *Diary of Emily Foster*, 138–139;
Reichart, *Washington Irving and Germany*, 93. For a provocative assessment of this
episode in the context of Irving's attitude toward marriage in general, see Jenifer S.
Banks, "Washington Irving, the Nineteenth-Century Bachelor," in Ralph M. Aderman,
ed., *Critical Essays on Washington Irving* (Boston: G. K. Hall, 1990), 253–265.

42. WI to Brevoort, June 6, 1823; to Emily Foster, June 23, 1823, *CW-Letters*, 1:762,
767. In describing the episode as a failure of the imagination, Jeffrey Rubin-Dorsky also
compares Irving to Ichabod Crane, as one who could "neither satisfy nor win his Katrina.
Manhood had escaped him." He goes on to contend that the "three most powerful stories" in *Tales of a Traveller* reveal Irving's "howl of protest" over Emily Foster's rejection
of him, having "silenced his hopes for marriage and heterosexual legitimacy." These are
speculative but certainly interesting arguments. See Rubin-Dorsky, *Adrift in the Old*

World: The Psychological Pilgrimage of Washington Irving (Chicago: University of Chicago Press, 1988), 158–159, 195. Jenifer Banks considers "Wives" as a piece of the evidence that leads her to argue that Irving endured a "lifelong struggle between the appeal and the threat of women." See Banks, "Washington Irving, Nineteenth-Century Bachelor," 254–255.

43. Review of *Tales of a Traveller*, in *Blackwood's Edinburgh Magazine* (September 1824), reprinted in Aderman, *Critical Essays on Washington Irving*, 64.

44. WI to John Murray, March 25, 1824, *CW-Letters*, 2:41–42; David Anthony, "'Gone Distracted': 'Sleepy Hollow,' Gothic Masculinity, and the Panic of 1819," *Early American Literature* 40 (2005): 111–144.

45. Daniel A. Cohen, "Blood Will Out: Sensationalism, Horror, and the Roots of American Crime Literature," in Nancy Isenberg and Andrew Burstein, eds., *Mortal Remains: Death in Early America* (Philadelphia: University of Pennsylvania Press, 2003), 31–55; Donald A. Ringe, *American Gothic: Imagination and Reason in Nineteenth-Century Fiction* (Lexington: University Press of Kentucky, 1982), 18; Allan Lloyd-Smith, *American Gothic Fiction: An Introduction* (New York: Continuum, 2004).

46. *CW-Journals*, 3:209.

47. See discussion in Donald A. Ringe, "Irving's Use of the Gothic Mode," *Studies in the Literary Imagination* 7 (Spring 1974): 51–66; for a long-range perspective, see Judith Richardson, *Possessions: The History and Uses of Haunting in the Hudson Valley* (Cambridge, MA: Harvard University Press, 2003).

48. Hedges, *Washington Irving*, 194–206; on Poe's overall critique of literary nationalism, and his implicit discomfort with Irving's European-influenced thinking, see J. Gerald Kennedy, "'A Mania for Composition': Poe's Annus Mirabilis and the Violence of Nation-building," *American Literary History* 17 (Spring 2005): 1–35. Yet Poe also believed in what Kennedy terms a "Republic of Letters ruled by an aristocracy of intellect." And he employed parodic devices not unlike Irving. Mary Weatherspoon Bowden calls *Tales of a Traveller* Irving's "least gentle, most despairing" work, in *Washington Irving*, 96; John Clendenning credits him with having given us "one of the first examples of psychological gothicism," while "mirthfully help[ing] to destroy all that was crude in gothic fiction. See "Irving and the Gothic Tradition," *Bucknell Review* 12 (1964): 98.

49. "The Poor Devil Author," in *Tales of a Traveller*, ed. Judith Giblin Haig (Boston: Twayne Publishers, 1987), 92.

50. "A Practical Philosopher," ibid., 94.

51. "The Strolling Manager," ibid., 145; William Hedges interpolates from the critical failure of *Tales of a Traveller*, and Irving's discouraging remarks to his nephew (brother Ebenezer's eldest, now eighteen) about a career in writing, that Buckthorne's message to posterity was his own. See Hedges, *Washington Irving*, 218–219n.

52. "The Devil and Tom Walker," "Wolfert Webber," and "The Adventure of the Black Fisherman," in *Tales of a Traveller*, 217–264.

53. Textual commentary, ibid., 285–288.

54. WI to Peter Irving, September 4, 1823, *CW-Letters*, 2:5–6.

55. *CW-Journals*, 3:254–270 and passim.

56. WI to Susan Storrow, February 26 and December 28, 1826, *CW-Letters*, 2:186, 214; A. Levasseur, *Lafayette in America in 1824 and 1825* (Philadelphia: Carey and Lea, 1829 [New York: Research Reprints, 1970]), 14–16; STW, 1:256.

57. Ben Harris McClary, ed., *Washington Irving and the House of Murray* (Knoxville: University of Tennessee Press, 1969), 51–53.

CHAPTER 9

1. *North American Review* 28 (January 1829): 103–134, reprinted in Ralph M. Aderman, ed., *Critical Essays on Washington Irving* (Boston: G. K. Hall, 1990), 87–88. Everett was by no means an objective critic of Irving's work, as will become apparent in the present chapter.

2. *CW-Journals*, 3:337–338, 342, 366, 410; STW, 1:287–288. Moore accompanied Mary Shelley to Gilbert Stuart Newton's, where she met Irving. See Paula R. Feldman, "Mary Shelley and the Genesis of Moore's *Life* of Byron," *Studies in English Literature* 20 (Autumn 1980): 611–620. Byron's recent biographer remarks that the poet had been kind to the intellectually assertive Mrs. Shelley after the death of her husband, but prior to that "had never been fond of Mary; he preferred women in conventional roles: playful, pious, or tenderly protective, an unthreatening hybrid of sexualized child and nurturing mother." Benita Eisler, *Byron: Child of Passion, Fool of Fame* (New York: Alfred A. Knopf, 1999), 694. Payne was in love with Mary Shelley, but she lost whatever interest she had in him, and presumably convinced him to pursue Irving on her behalf.

3. *CW-Journals*, 3:358–366, 667–668; WI to Emily Foster, August 23, 1825, Clifton Waller Barrett Collection, Special Collections, University of Virginia Library, and *CW-Letters*, 2:128–131; STW, 1:448n. In Dresden, where Emily sometimes recognized coquettish tendencies in herself, she had noted in her diary, in French: "Independence is a dream—but not the happiness in life." Stanley T. Williams and Leonard B. Beach, eds., *The Journal of Emily Foster* (New York: Oxford University Press, 1938), 92. In an undated journal entry some six or more months after his letter to her, Irving mused: "The clergy being disabled from taking part in political affairs—should keep themselves untaintd by the passions of the world"; and in the very next entry, pontificating on "Marriages—early," he considered that young married females ought to remain detached from all contentions: "They must not be worldly." As suggestive as these statements are, both hers and his, they are not unequivocal. Irving's views on religion, like his views on women, are too complex to be described categorically.

4. WI to Catharine Irving Paris, September 20, 1824, *CW-Letters*, 2:75–76; STW, 1:454n, and *CW-Journals*, 3, passim.

5. *CW-Journals*, 3:430; WI to Brevoort, December 11, 1824, *CW-Letters*, 2:90.

6. Irving clarified further that Spanish and German literature were both "free from licentiousness," and could be read by women; the Spanish drew on a tradition of "manly honour and female virtue"; and the German was young, and put together "under the restraints of modern decency." WI to Pierre P. Irving, March 29, 1825, *CW-Letters*, 2:106–109. On Irving's reading in Spanish history and literature at this time, and its impact on his thinking, see Pete Kyle McCarter, "The Literary, Political, and Social Theories of Washington Irving" (PhD diss., University of Wisconsin–Madison, 1939, 187–190); on his reading in foreign languages generally, see Edward Wagenknecht, *Washington Irving: Moderation Displayed* (New York: Oxford University Press, 1962), 60–63.

7. WI to Pierre P. Irving, August 29, 1825, *CW-Letters*, 2:132; *CW-Journals*, 3:488.

8. WI to Brevoort, December 11, 1824, *CW-Letters*, 2:90.

9. PMI, 2:239.

10. WI to Storrow, October 31, 1825, *CW-Letters*, 2:146; *CW-Journals*, 3:546.

11. PMI, 2:245–252; WI to Everett, January 12 and 31, 1826, *CW-Letters*, 2:165, 168. When younger, Everett had been Adams's private secretary when Adams was U.S. minister to Russia, residing in St. Petersburg in the lead-up to the War of 1812.

12. Louis Bertrand and Sir Charles Petrie, *The History of Spain* (New York: D. Appleton-Century, 1934), part 2, chap. 6; Jean Descola, *A History of Spain* (New York: Alfred A. Knopf, 1963), 365–369.

13. WI to Leslie, February 3, 1826; to Murray, February 6, 1826, *CW-Letters*, 2:169, 173.

14. WI to Leslie, February 23, 1826; to Thomas Storrow, April 14 and July 9, 1826, ibid., 2:178, 192–194, 205n; John Harmon McElroy, "The Integrity of Irving's Columbus," *American Literature* 50 (March 1978): 3–4; STW, 1:303–305.

15. WI to Thomas Storrow, August 31, 1826, *CW-Letters*, 2:209.

16. WI to Thomas Storrow, June 12, July 12, and October 26, 1826, ibid., 2:199, 206, 211; estimate on the length of the rough draft, in *The Life and Voyages of Christopher Columbus*, ed. John Harmon McElroy (Boston: Twayne Publishers, 1981), xlii.

17. Wayne R. Kime, *Pierre M. Irving and Washington Irving: A Collaboration in Life and Letters* (Waterloo, Canada: Wilfrid Laurier University Press, 1977), 3–14; WI to Thomas Storrow, June 12, 1826; to Mrs. Storrow, July 9, 1826, *CW-Letters*, 2:198–199, 204; PMI, 2:253.

18. *CW-Journals*, 4:40; WI to Thomas Storrow, July 9, 1826; to Susan Storrow, December 28, 1826, *CW-Letters*, 2:205, 214–215.

19. WI to Murray, December 21, 1826, ibid., 2:213.

20. *CW-Journals*, 4:63.

21. Ben Harris McClary, ed., *Washington Irving and the House of Murray* (Knoxville: University of Tennessee Press, 1969), 85–95.

22. Longfellow to WI, September 24, 1827, Berg Collection, New York Public Library; PMI, 2:265–266.

23. Scott E. Casper, *Constructing American Lives: Biography and Culture in Nineteenth-Century America* (Chapel Hill: University of North Carolina Press, 1999), 79–80, 351n; Carla Rahn Phillips and William D. Phillips, "Christopher Columbus in United States Historiography: Biography as Projection," *History Teacher* 25 (February 1992): 119–135; Thomas J. Schlereth, "Columbia, Columbus, and Columbianism," *Journal of American History* 79 (December 1992): 937–968. One near contemporary openly disparaged the work, a Maryland lawyer who in a series of essays in the *Southern Literary Messenger* in the early 1840s accused Irving of having plagiarized Navarrete's research. Enough people learned of the charge that Irving felt the need to assure his nephew Pierre of the falsity of it so that Pierre could defend him in good conscience: "If you ever hear again of my having practised any disingenuous artifice in literature, to advance myself or to injure others, you may boldly give the charge a flat contradiction." Nevertheless, in the first half of the twentieth century, Irving's most influential biographer, Stanley Williams, embraced the Marylander's attack on Irving as "well reasoned," and indicted him for "near-plagiarism." Williams disregarded the fact that Navarrete himself attested to the integrity of Irving's *Columbus*—Irving, sensitive to criticism, appended Navarrete's laudatory letter to the book's preface after 1831. STW, 2:302–303. In 1978, English professor John Harmon McElroy offered persuasive evidence that Irving's scholarship was consistent with the best history of the nineteenth century. He provided several solid reasons for his conclusion: A source Irving cited more often than Navarrete was Fernando Colón's *Historia del Almirante Don Cristobal Colón*, written by the illegitimate son of Columbus. But in recognizing its less than ideal provenance—the only extant edition being a flawed Italian translation—Irving compared this text with a series of other works (forty-three altogether) before committing his book to the printer. This

act showed the marks of an alert historian. Additionally, Irving drew extensively upon two other sources: *Historia General de las Indias* (1535), by Fray Bartolomé de las Casas, and an official government history with the same title dating to the early seventeenth century. According to McElroy's count, Irving cited his four most important sources 511 times, and the next five in importance 135 times. He also cited 141 other minor sources 254 times. This pattern certainly suggests a careful researcher, not one looking for shortcuts. WI to Pierre M. Irving, November 12, 1842, *CW-Letters,* 3:391–394; McElroy, "The Integrity of Irving's Columbus," 5–16. Late nineteenth-century Columbus scholars, most notably the Columbus critic Henry Harisse, were big enough to credit Irving with having written a "more than literary" work: "It is a history written with judgment and impartiality." On Williams's side is John Boyd Thacher, whose Columbus biography of 1903 contained a lament over the obscurity of the productive Navarrete, meanwhile claiming that Irving took "nearly every thread" of his book from Navarrete (ibid., 10–12). For a thorough analysis of the nineteenth-century reviews of Irving's Columbus biography, see *Life and Voyages of Columbus,* lxxxviii–xcvii.

24. Matthew Dennis, *Red, White, and Blue Letter Days: An American Calendar* (Ithaca, NY: Cornell University Press, 2002), 152–157. On the quincentenary, in general, see Stephen J. Summerhill and John Alexander Williams, *Sinking Columbus: Contested History, Cultural Politics, and Mythmaking During the Quincentenary* (Gainesville: University Press of Florida, 2000).

25. Felipe Fernandez-Armesto, *Columbus* (Oxford: Oxford University Press, 1991), 23–24, 39, 118; Noble David Cook, "Sickness, Starvation, and Death in Early Hispaniola," *Journal of Interdisciplinary History* 32 (Winter 2002): 349–386; Massimo Livi-Bacci, "Return to Hispaniola: Reassessing a Demographic Catastrophe," *Hispanic American Historical Review* 83 (2003): 3–51.

26. Dennis, *Red, White, and Blue Letter Days,* 131–139, quote at 137; see also Schlereth, "Columbia, Columbus, and Columbianism."

27. *Life and Voyages of Columbus,* 9–13. Europe had gone dark, Irving qualifies, while science had "taken refuge in the bosom of Africa" among the "Arabian sages," and did not revive in the maritime community of Genoa until Columbus's century.

28. Ibid., 10, 12.

29. William Wirt, *The Life of Patrick Henry* (Hartford, CT: S. Andrus & Son, 1832), 23–25, 137; for two extensive portraits of Wirt, see Casper, *Constructing American Lives,* 46–61, and Andrew Burstein, *America's Jubilee* (New York: Alfred A. Knopf, 2001), chap. 2. Casper traces the "life and character" model of biography to Samuel Johnson, the essayists Joseph Addison and Richard Steele, and as far back as Plutarch. It is also worth speculating as to whether Irving had the model of his late friend Stephen Decatur in his mind.

30. *Life and Voyages of Columbus,* 22.

31. Ibid., 30–31.

32. Ibid., 42–47.

33. Ibid., 57, 62–69. Lest we imagine Irving was making all this up, the most recent American researcher, citing the same Spanish sources, as well as new ones, captured the drama as Irving did. In his 2005 *Dogs of God: Columbus, the Inquisition, and the Defeat of the Moors,* James Reston, Jr., writes: "Queen Isabella's capitulation was a testament to Columbus's unshakable persistence, to his single-mindedness, to his certainty in the correctness of his vision. . . . He suddenly stood taller than any sea captain in Spain." Both authors also emphasize the importance of the supportive Luis de Santángel, respected

financier of Aragon, who interceded with Isabella at the final stage of negotiation, just when Columbus's appeal was conclusively denied and he was about to give up and leave Spain. Irving on Santángel: "He did not restrain himself to entreaties, but mingled almost reproaches, expressing astonishment that a queen who had evinced the spirit to undertake so many great and perilous enterprizes, should hesitate at one where the loss could be so trifling, while the gain might be incalculable. He reminded her what might be done for the glory of God." And Reston: "Upon hearing of Columbus's departure, he rushed into the queen's presence to launch a passionate protest. He was surprised and disappointed that so great and high-minded a queen had dismissed this man of quality when his project involved so little risk to the crown, and yet, if successful, would bring such glory to Spain and to the Church." Only Reston explains that Santángel was Jewish, a *converso* (convert), whose family would be immune from the terror of the Inquisition because of the financier's special relationship with the crown and the Columbus mission. James Reston, Jr., *Dogs of God: Columbus, the Inquisition, and the Defeat of the Moors* (New York: Doubleday, 2005), 249, 251; *Life and Voyages of Columbus*, 64.

34. A modern historian assesses the situation differently, preferring to highlight Columbus's self-satisfaction with his role as "lone manipulator," a man who will falsify the ship's log to allay fears: "He positively enjoyed the cybernetics of deception." See Fernandez-Armesto, *Columbus*, 79.

35. *Life and Voyages of Columbus*, 77, 84–93.

36. Ibid., 99, 125–126, 130–135. Note Irving's repetition of the same two words, *gentleness* and *justice*, which Jeremy Belknap used in his briefer Columbus treatment in the prior century. In this section of the biography, Irving establishes what he imagines to have been the explorer's Edenic vision, so that the biography as a whole can be read as Romantic regret—for white "civilization" ruined Columbus's dream of starting the world over with a gentle race. John D. Hazlett believes that Irving was, in this way, interested in praising an anti-imperialist Columbus. Irving's problem, Hazlett says, is that in disassociating Columbus from "intentional wrong-doing," he still allows him to be responsible for Eden's destruction through his "quixotic delusions" and overall innocence. See Hazlett, "Literary Nationalism and Ambivalence in Washington Irving's *The Life and Voyages of Christopher Columbus*," *American Literature* 55 (December 1983): 560–575.

37. *Life and Voyages of Columbus*, 232–233, 291–293.

38. Ibid., 301–303.

39. Ibid., 341–342.

40. Ibid., 343, 414–415, 422–425.

41. Fernandez-Armesto, *Columbus*, 160–161.

42. *Life and Voyages of Columbus*, 450.

43. Ibid., 427–429, 432–433.

44. Ibid., 564–568.

45. Ibid., lxxxvi.

46. WI to Storrow, December 1, 1827, *CW-Letters*, 2:256; McCarter, "The Literary, Political, and Social Theories of Washington Irving," 191, noting that Irving considered his *Columbus* as a dignified work, and thus "a better foundation on which to build a literary reputation" than belles-lettres.

47. WI to Brevoort, February 23, 1828, *CW-Letters*, 274–276.

48. Kime, *Pierre M. Irving and Washington Irving*, 12–13.

49. WI to Catharine Irving Paris, February 17, 1828, *CW-Letters*, 2:270–271.

50. *CW-Journals*, 4:135.

CHAPTER 10

1. Reprinted in Ralph M. Aderman, ed., *Critical Essays on Washington Irving* (Boston: G. K. Hall, 1990), 95.

2. Ahmed ibn Mohammed al-Makkari, *The History of the Mohammedan Dynasties in Spain*, vol. 2, trans. Pascual de Gayangos (London: Routledge Curzon, 2002 [1840, 1843]), 370–373; Anwar G. Chejne, *Muslim Spain: Its History and Culture* (Minneapolis: University of Minnesota Press, 1974), chaps. 5 and 6; James Reston, Jr., *Dogs of God: Columbus, the Inquisition, and the Defeat of the Moors* (New York: Doubleday, 2005), 84–89.

3. "A Very Mournful Ballad on the Siege and Conquest of Alhama," 1816, in *The Works of Lord Byron* (Ware, England: Wordsworth Editions, 1994), 97–99. Writing on Alhama in *The Story of the Moors in Spain* (first published in 1837), Stanley Lane-Poole noted Byron's inaccuracies in his translation of the popular Spanish ballad.

4. *CW-Journals*, 4:144–148; WI to Antoinette Bolviller, March 15, 1828, *CW-Letters*, 2:281–283; Claude G. Bowers, *The Spanish Adventures of Washington Irving* (Boston: Houghton Mifflin, 1940), 35–36.

5. *CW-Journals*, 4:162–171; WI to Prince Dmitri Dolgorouki, March 29, 1828; to David Wilkie, April 2, 1828, *CW-Letters*, 2:288–289, 297.

6. WI to Alexander Everett, April 15, 1828, ibid., 2:298–300; *CW-Journals*, 4:184–188; Bowers, *The Spanish Adventures*, 64.

7. Hackley had been able to secure his official position through connections: His wife was the sister of Thomas Jefferson's son-in-law.

8. WI to Prince Dmitri Dolgorouki, May 18 and July 21, 1828; to Alexander Everett, August 20, 1828; to _____ (Hall's relative), December 5, 1828; to Brevoort, December 20, 1828, *CW-Letters*, 2:310–311, 323–324, 329, 359–360, 367; Bowers, *The Spanish Adventures*, 74–75, 90–91, 94; *CW-Journals*, 4:234, 240; PMI, 2:359–360.

9. *CW-Journals*, 4:243, 245; WI to Prince Dolgorouki, January 10, 1829, *CW-Letters*, 2:375.

10. WI to Aspinwall, April 4, 1829, ibid., 2:395–397; Loretta Sharon Wyatt, "The Charm of a Golden Past: Iberia in the Writings of Washington Irving and Antonio Gonçalves Dia," in Stanley Brodwin, ed., *The Old and New World Romanticism of Washington Irving* (Westport, CT: Greenwood Press, 1986), 105–106.

11. *A Chronicle of the Conquest of Granada*, ed. Earl N. Harbert and Miriam J. Shillingsburg (Boston: Twayne Publishers, 1988), 12–14, 18–23.

12. Ibid., 30–32.

13. Ibid., 27–28.

14. Ibid., 132–137.

15. Ibid., 183–185.

16. Ibid., 264–269, 288–291.

17. Ian Macpherson and Angus MacKay, *Love, Religion and Politics in Fifteenth Century Spain* (Leiden, Netherlands: Brill, 1998), 17–18, 157–161. Irving was invariably critical of religious extremism in *Conquest of Granada*, just as he had been in *Columbus*. MacKay details "acts of savagery" spurred by the "holy undertaking" of Spanish reconquest; it was "common practice for frontier Christians to return from their forays with the severed heads or the sliced-off ears of their defeated Moorish opponents." Ibid., 166–167.

18. On Dolgorouki's career, see STW, 1:481n, and "Unpublished Letters of Foreign Writers of the 18th and 19th Centuries from Leningrad Manuscript Collections" (Moscow: Academy of Sciences, 1960), 272–275, in Russian.

19. WI to Peter Irving, April 10, 1829, *CW-Letters*, 2:400.

20. WI to Peter Irving, May 9, 1829, ibid., 2:411.

21. "The Journey," in William T. Lenehan and Andrew B. Myers, eds., *The Alhambra* (Boston: Twayne Publishers, 1983), 6–7.

22. Ibid., 8–24.

23. On Irving's repetitive language of romance and enchantment—the "Oriental supernatural"—in this text, see Pete Kyle McCarter, "The Literary, Political, and Social Theories of Washington Irving" (PhD diss., University of Wisconsin–Madison, 1939), 194–197.

24. "Palace of the Alhambra," in Lenehan and Myers, *The Alhambra*, 25, 30.

25. Robert Irwin, *The Alhambra* (Cambridge, MA: Harvard University Press, 2004), 89.

26. "Palace of the Alhambra," in Lenehan and Myers, *The Alhambra*, 31.

27. "The Author Succeeds to the Throne of Boabdil," ibid., 35.

28. Ibid., 36–39.

29. "Mementos of Boabdil," ibid., 93–96.

30. "Generalife" and "Legend of Prince Ahmed," ibid., 127–130; Irwin, *The Alhambra*, 59–62, 75. The Generalife was probably built in the early to mid-fourteenth century; one of Irving's windows faced it.

31. "Legend of Prince Ahmed," in Lenehan and Myers, *The Alhambra*, 131–151.

32. "Legend of the Three Beautiful Princesses," ibid., 176–192. In an undated version of his table of contents, Irving placed "Legend of the Three Beautiful Princesses" at the very end of volume one, perhaps believing it a compelling tale that whets the appetite for volume two. That was its position in the first edition, though Irving's other plans for chapter positioning were changed and titles were abandoned before publication. See "Outline for the Description of the Alhambra," Clifton Waller Barrett Collection, in Special Collections, University of Virginia Library.

33. WI to Peter Irving, June 13 and July 4, 1829; to Catharine Irving Paris, June 16, 1829, *CW-Letters*, 2:436, 441–442, 446.

34. WI to Alexander Everett, February 14, 1829; to Brevoort, May 23, 1829, ibid., 2:381–382, 425. Disturbed by the "pique, passion, and caprice" that went along with criticisms of Adams, Irving was consoled by the fact that Jackson won handily; for this, to him, promised greater calm than a closer contest, whereby "nearly balanced parties" would more or less equally divide the country into two warring camps. Again, his greatest desire was for stability.

35. WI to Peter Irving, July 18, 1829, ibid., 2:447; PMI, 2:397, 399.

36. WI to Ebenezer Irving, July 22, 1829, *CW-Letters*, 2:451.

37. Bowers, *The Spanish Adventures*, 128–129; WI to Catharine Irving Paris, August 10, 1829, *CW-Letters*, 2:463, 467; PMI, 2:412–413.

38. WI to Brevoort, August 10, 1829, *CW-Letters*, 2:460–461.

39. WI to Catharine Irving Paris, August 10, 1829, ibid., 2:466.

40. WI to Johann Nikolaus Bohl von Faber, September 29, 1829; to Ebenezer Irving, November 6, 1829; to Moore, November 17, 1829, ibid., 2:468, 477, 480–481; Moore to Irving, PMI, 2:420–422; STW, 2:16–17.

41. WI to Godwin, October 14 and November 14, 1829, January 16 and 30, 1830; to Mary Shelley, May 28, 1830, *CW-Letters,* 2:472, 480, 498, 505, 525.

42. WI to Peter Irving, December 18 and (late December?) 1829, ibid., 2:494–495.

43. WI to Congressman Churchill C. Cambreleng, August 30, 1830, and March 2, 1831; to Kemble, January 18, 1830; to Peter Irving, October 19 and 22, 1830, *CW-Letters,* 2:500–501, 542–545, 555–556, 558, 596; Ben Harris McClary, ed., *Washington Irving and the House of Murray* (Knoxville: University of Tennessee Press, 1969), 132–140; PMI, 2:440–442; Andrew Burstein, *America's Jubilee* (New York: Alfred A. Knopf, 2001), 298; *Collected Letters of John Randolph of Roanoke to Dr. John Brockenbrough, 1812–1833,* ed. Kenneth Shorey (New Brunswick, NJ: Transaction Books, 1988), 134–136. Although the *Oxford English Dictionary* does not list the term *hokey pokey* before 1847, giving it as a cousin of *hocus pocus,* meaning a "deception," it is clear that the appellation was meant to diminish the oddly dressed Randolph as one out of place and not to be taken seriously.

44. *Universal Biographical Dictionary, Containing the Lives of the Most Celebrated Characters of Every Age and Nation* (New York: n.p.), 432.

45. PMI, 2:430–433, 442–443; WI to Peter Irving, July 27, 1830, *CW-Letters,* 2:535–536.

46. Van Buren was a junior member of Burr's political band, until for reasons of expediency he switched allegiance to Morgan Lewis in the governor's race of 1804. Still, he thought highly of the unlucky Burr, and after the exiled New Yorker returned from Europe in 1812, Van Buren attempted to secure him belated compensation for his Revolutionary War service; the two then served as co-counsel in an 1819 court case. Van Buren was often compared with Burr in terms of their physical stature, overall character, legal skills, and political acumen. See Jerome Mushkat and Joseph G. Rayback, *Martin Van Buren: Law, Politics, and the Shaping of Republican Ideology* (DeKalb: Northern Illinois University Press, 1997).

47. Van Buren to Jackson, September 21 and November 25, 1831, in John Spencer Bassett, ed., *Correspondence of Andrew Jackson* (Washington, DC: Carnegie Institute, 1929), 4:352, 378.

48. WI to Peter Irving, January 20, 1832; to Catharine Irving Paris, January 20, 1832, *CW-Letters,* 2:680–681, 683–685.

49. John Niven, *Martin Van Buren: The Romantic Age of American Politics* (New York: Oxford University Press, 1983), 162–163, 295–296.

50. WI to McLane, February 22, 1832, *CW-Letters,* 2:692–693.

51. WI to Peter Irving, March 6, 1832, ibid., 2:695–698.

52. Edwin T. Bowden, comp., *Washington Irving: Bibliography* (Boston: Twayne Publishers, 1989), 362–386.

53. In Spain, the book was immediately translated. Fourteen editions would appear over the ensuing century—indeed, tourists' affinity for Spanish romance has been a mark of pride in that country ever since Irving. The introduction to an illustrated English-language edition of *Tales of the Alhambra,* published in Granada recently, states: "Spain and Granada in particular have always evoked the fervour of the Romantics. . . . If, for the Northern European on the one hand, the Spaniard has always been a figure of romance, daring and passion, the Spaniard in his turn has conjured up similar visions of the Granadine Moors." R. Villa-Real, introduction to *Tales of the Alhambra,* ed. Miguel Sánchez (Granada, Spain: n.p., 1994), 8. Irving's collection was also published in Paris, in 1832, by the Galignanis, with the title *The Alhambra, or the New Sketch Book.*

54. McClary, *Washington Irving and the House of Murray,* 157–167; PMI, 3:17–18; STW, 2:317–319; Lenehan and Myers, *The Alhambra,* xxxii–xlix.

55. This is essentially the conclusion reached by Richard V. McLamore, in "Postcolonial Columbus: Washington Irving and *The Conquest of Granada,*" *Nineteenth-Century Literature* 48 (June 1993): 26–43.

56. WI to Aspinwall, April 29, 1829, *CW-Letters,* 2:409. Similarly, in random writings in a notebook of 1825, he had declared: "I profess no false enthusiasm as concerning my country—I know her faults & imperfections but I know from all that I have seen of this land that she has within her the most munificent & magnificent place for human Successes." *CW-Journals,* 5:327. This notebook is referred to as a commonplace book, strewn with quotations from ancient and modern writers, and liberally peppered with Irving's own aphorisms. Though the editors date it as 1825, when he was in Europe, many of his comments relate to his feelings of attachment to America.

CHAPTER 11

1. Letter in Special Collections, University of Virginia Library. Madison was in retirement at his estate of Montpelier, in central Virginia. The French-born Chaumont, an American citizen and land speculator whose father had known Benjamin Franklin in Paris many years before, had come to reside in New York.

2. James Kirke Paulding, *Koningsmarke, or, Old Times in the New World* (New York: Harper & Brothers, 1834), 3–6, 191–193.

3. James Kirke Paulding, *The Dutchman's Fireside,* ed. Thomas F. O'Donnell (New Haven, CT: College & University Press, 1966), 47–50, 182, 207, 216, 226, 242–243, 253.

4. Aside from direct quotes from the texts of *Koningsmarke* and *The Dutchman's Fireside,* my overall understanding of Paulding in this period is gleaned from the biography by Ralph M. Aderman and Wayne R. Kime, *Advocate for America: The Life of James Kirke Paulding* (Selinsgrove, PA: Susquehanna University Press, 2003), chaps. 5–9. Paulding's remark to the bookseller is at page 169.

5. "Gelyna: A Tale of Albany and Ticonderoga," reprinted in Kendall B. Taft, *Minor Knickerbockers* (New York: American Book Company, 1947), 72–90.

6. PMI, 2:73–74, 259–261; Cooper to WI, July 30, 1822, in *The Letters and Journals of James Fenimore Cooper,* ed. James Franklin Beard (Cambridge, MA: Harvard University Press, 1960), 2:75; Stephen Railton, *Fenimore Cooper: A Study of His Life and Imagination* (Princeton, NJ: Princeton University Press, 1978), 60–61, 121. Irving had also written to Thomas W. Storrow: "I have not seen Coopers last work [*The Last of the Mohicans*], but I hear it well spoken of. I am glad he is coming to Europe. It will be of great Service to him." WI to Storrow, July 12, 1826, *CW-Letters,* 2:206.

7. George Dekker, *James Fenimore Cooper: The American Scott* (New York: Barnes & Noble, 1967), chap. 2.

8. For an analysis, see Michael Meranze, "Major André's Exhumation," in Nancy Isenberg and Andrew Burstein, eds., *Mortal Remains: Death in Early America* (Philadelphia: University of Pennsylvania Press, 2003), 123–135. Also compelling is Bruce A. Rosenberg, *The Neutral Ground: The André Affair and the Background of Cooper's The Spy* (Westport, CT: Greenwood Press, 1994).

9. Railton, *Fenimore Cooper,* 163; Edwin G. Burrows and Mike Wallace, *Gotham: A History of New York to 1898* (New York: Oxford University Press, 1999), 469–470; Charles H. Brown, *William Cullen Bryant* (New York: Charles Scribner's Sons, 1971), 136.

10. Cooper to Miller, February [7–12?], 1826, in *Letters and Journals of James Fenimore Cooper,* 1:127–128.

11. Cooper to Clinton, February 9, 1826; to Henry Colburn, October 17, 1826, ibid., 129, 166–167.

12. Cooper to Mary (Mrs. Peter Augustus) Jay, November [7–13?], 1826; to Carey and Lea, November 9, 1826, ibid., 169–174.

13. Cooper to Carey and Lea, November 6, 1831, ibid., 2:149–151.

14. Cooper to Dunlap, March 16, 1832, in *Diary of William Dunlap* (New York: New-York Historical Society, 1930), 3:606.

15. *Letters and Journals of James Fenimore Cooper,* 1:231.

16. For revealing examples of British reactions to Cooper's *Notions of the Americans,* see George Dekker and John P. McWilliams, eds., *Fenimore Cooper: The Critical Heritage* (London: Routledge & Kegan Paul, 1973), 148–154. One of these concludes: "Let Mr. Cooper stick to his novels and romances, if he does not wish to discredit the land of his birth, and make himself a common laughing-stock." Ibid., 152. Cooper's need to distinguish his political purpose from Irving's masks their common literary posture. The critic Allen Guttman wrote: "Irving stands with Cooper in that both men were divided between the attractions of the new and the steady appeal of the old. Both were committed *explicitly* to an ordered and hierarchical agrarian society." Their famous characters, Cooper's Natty Bumppo and the Indian Chingachgook, like Rip Van Winkle and Brom Bones, "are American heroes who would be as unwelcome in the council rooms of the Federalist Party as in the chambers of Bracebridge Hall." See Guttman, "Washington Irving and the Conservative Imagination," *American Literature* 36 (May 1964): 173.

17. The foregoing discussion is drawn largely from Brown, *William Cullen Bryant.* Quotes at 44, 52, 78–79, 103, 112, 122, 131, 136, 197–199; WI to Bryant, January 26, February 14, and March 6, 1832, *CW-Letters,* 2:687, 691, 694; PMI, 2:472–475; Verplanck to WI, December 31, 1831, in Hellman Collection, New York Public Library; Dekker and McWilliams, *Fenimore Cooper,* 37. On Bryant as a poet, see also Richard Ruland and Malcolm Bradbury, *From Puritanism to Postmodernism: A History of American Literature* (New York: Viking, 1991), 74–77.

18. Nelson Frederick Adkins, *Fitz-Greene Halleck: An Early Knickerbocker Wit and Poet* (New Haven, CT: Yale University Press, 1930), 5–6, 23–24, 32–42, 67, 87, 99, 103, 253; John W. M. Hallock, *The American Byron: Homosexuality and the Fall of Fitz-Greene Halleck* (Madison: University of Wisconsin Press, 2000), 55–59, 106–108; Taft, *Minor Knickerbockers,* 96, 102, 116. It is worth noting that the question of whether Joseph Rodman Drake was bisexual or exclusively heterosexual has never been resolved. As the modern literary scholar Hallock (a descendant) notes, Halleck convinced himself that Drake had only married for financial reasons.

19. Adkins, *Fitz-Greene Halleck,* 246–247.

20. Burrows and Wallace, *Gotham,* 445–448, 455–457, 460; Brown, *William Cullen Bryant,* 138; John Denis Haeger, *John Jacob Astor: Business and Finance in the Early Republic* (Detroit: Wayne State University Press, 1991), chap. 9; *Diary of Philip Hone,* ed. Bayard Tuckerman (New York: Dodd, Mead, 1889), 1:46. The Englishwoman Frances Trollope, a visitor in the months before Irving's return, commented on the attractive gray granite buildings and the flagstone streets of lower Manhattan. "At night," she wrote, "the shops, which are open till very late, are brilliantly illuminated with gas, and all the population seem as much alive as in London or Paris." Battery Park remained

stylish, but the sheer numbers of people who packed the roadways (not to mention the garbage-devouring pigs that strayed from the poorer sections of town) meant that there had to be more desperate types visible in the mushrooming city than were present at the end of the War of 1812, when Irving was last here. Trollope, *Domestic Manners of the Americans* (New York: Dodd, Mead, 1927 [1832]), 311.

21. "Sketches of Distinguished Characters: Washington Irving," *New-York Mirror*, March 3, 1832; on the tenor of the times, see Helen Lefkowitz Horowitz, *Rereading Sex: Battles over Sexual Knowledge and Suppression in Nineteenth-Century America* (New York: Alfred A. Knopf, 2002).

22. PMI, 2:486–492; STW, 2:35, 334n; Burrows and Wallace, *Gotham*, 459, 465; B. R. Brunson, *The Adventures of Samuel Swartwout in the Age of Jefferson and Jackson* (Lewiston, NY: Edwin Mellen Press, 1989), 66; Aderman and Kime, *Advocate for America*, 165; *Memoirs and Letters of James Kent, LL.D.* (Boston: Little, Brown, 1898), 230–234; entries of May 22, 23, 26, and 30, 1832, in *Diary of Philip Hone*, 1:53–55. Stuart Newton wrote of the extravaganza the next day to the absent Peter Irving: "His delight seems to be boundless, and it ought to be so, for I do not know how either his pride or his affections could be more gratified than by the enthusiastic and kind reception he meets with—it is really an era in this place!"

23. *Diary of William Dunlap*, 3:602–606; Burrows and Wallace, *Gotham*, 589–593.

24. WI to Peter Irving, June 16, 1832, *CW-Letters*, 2:705; PMI, 3:21–22.

25. Former New York mayor Philip Hone expressed the Jackson detractors' overall view in similar terms: "His flatterers, the sycophants who crawl beneath his feet, impose upon his weakness and flatter his vanity; they persuade him that his obstinacy is firmness, and his vengeance Roman dignity." See entry of December 30, 1833, in *Diary of Philip Hone*, 2:86. On Jackson's personality generally, see Andrew Burstein, *The Passions of Andrew Jackson* (New York: Alfred A. Knopf, 2003).

26. The fear of Jackson's anti-bank alliance was that New York's financial juggernaut was being controlled by a group of private individuals, the select shareholders of the Philadelphia-based Bank of the United States, who controlled government deposits—this was the most obvious definition of elite privilege. Instead, they would redistribute the government's money among trusted state banks. The problem was that Jackson did not, as a rule, negotiate incremental reform; he would pounce on Biddle's bank, taking out too much too soon, thus forcing Biddle to constrict credit and destabilize the economy. Money became scarce, and financial panic loomed. Biddle took action to reduce the immediate costs of credit tightening; but a panic occurred anyway in 1837, and it spoiled Van Buren's one-term presidency.

27. Another example of what happened to the old Federalists is the Sedgwick family: Theodore Sedgwick was a devoted Hamiltonian, who believed in the politics of deference, and served as Massachusetts congressman and senator. He was sidelined by the democratic upsurge in the early 1800s; his four sons, one of whom was a close friend to William Cullen Bryant, all grew to be vocal Jackson supporters. Gilman M. Ostrander, *Republic of Letters: The American Intellectual Community, 1775–1865* (Madison, WI: Madison House, 1999), 113; on Coleman's shifting politics, see Brown, *William Cullen Bryant*, 159, 168–169. It should be noted that there was dissension within the Jackson ranks, as concerned New York: James A. Hamilton and Van Buren, for example, deeply distrusted Irving's old friend Samuel Swartwout.

28. *Diary of William Dunlap*, 3:746–747.

29. PMI, 2:458–460.

CHAPTER 12

1. Henry Leavitt Ellsworth, *Washington Irving on the Prairie, or a Narrative of a Tour of the Southwest in the Year 1832*, ed. Stanley T. Williams and Barbara D. Simison (New York: American Book Company, 1937), 71.

2. WI to Peter Irving, July 9, 1832, *CW-Letters*, 2:709–710.

3. *CW-Journals*, 5:4–23; Andrew Burstein, *Sentimental Democracy: The Evolution of America's Romantic Self-Image* (New York: Hill & Wang, 1999), 231–232, 281–282.

4. John Francis McDermott, ed., *The Western Journals of Washington Irving* (Norman: University of Oklahoma Press, 1944), 9.

5. Jackson to Secretary of War John C. Calhoun, September 2, 1820, *Papers of Andrew Jackson*, ed. Sam B. Smith and others (Knoxville: University of Tennessee Press, 1980), 4:388. For a more detailed analysis of Jackson's aggressive tendencies toward Indians and others, see David S. Heidler and Jeanne T. Heidler, *Old Hickory's War: Andrew Jackson and the Quest for Empire* (Baton Rouge: Louisiana State University Press, 1996).

6. The Supreme Court case, *Worcester v. Georgia,* concerned the state's claim to sovereign jurisdiction over Cherokee lands within its boundaries. Anthony F. C. Wallace, *The Long Bitter Trail: Andrew Jackson and the Indians* (New York: Hill & Wang, 1993); John Ehle, *Trail of Tears: The Rise and Fall of the Cherokee Nation* (New York: Anchor Books, 1988), Wirt quote at 241.

7. WI to Peter Irving, December 18, 1832, *CW-Letters*, 2:733–734.

8. *CW-Journals*, 5:25–34. On the commercialization of Ohio in the 1820s, canal building, and the position of Cincinnati in particular, see Andrew Burstein, *America's Jubilee* (New York: Alfred A. Knopf, 2001), chap. 5.

9. WI to Catharine Irving Paris, September 2, 1832, *CW-Letters*, 2:718.

10. *CW-Journals*, 5:42–48, 53.

11. George F. Spaulding, ed., *On the Western Tour with Washington Irving: The Journal and Letters of Count de Pourtalès* (Norman: University of Oklahoma Press, 1968), 21–23.

12. WI to Catharine Irving Paris, September 13, 1832, *CW-Letters*, 2:722–723; *CW-Journals*, 5:57–66; Donald Jackson, ed., *Black Hawk: An Autobiography* (Urbana: University of Illinois Press, 1964).

13. On the reassessment of the Indian in histories and novels during this period, see Richard Slotkin, *Regeneration Through Violence: The Mythology of the American Frontier, 1600–1860* (Middletown, CT: Wesleyan University Press, 1973), 354–359.

14. *A Tour on the Prairies,* in *The Crayon Miscellany,* ed. Dahlia Kirby Terrell (Boston: Twayne Publishers, 1979), 11–14; Charles Joseph Latrobe, *The Rambler in Oklahoma: Latrobe's Tour with Washington Irving,* ed. Muriel H. Wright and George H. Shirk (Oklahoma City: Harlow Publishing, 1955), 2–5; Spaulding, *Journal and Letters of Count de Pourtalès,* 25. On Tonish's role in the narrative as a stock comic character, see William Bedford Clark, "How the West Won: Irving's Comic Inversion of the Westering Myth in *A Tour on the Prairies,*" *American Literature* 50 (November 1978): 335–347.

15. WI to Catharine Irving Paris, September 26, 1832, *CW-Letters*, 2:725–726.

16. Spaulding, *Journal and Letters of Count de Pourtalès,* 34–36.

17. The original "White Hair" was a chief whose Osage name was "Paw-Hiu-Ska," or "Pawhuska." Of the band's history, see *CW-Journals*, 5:73n; Latrobe, *Rambler in Okla-*

homa, 10–11n; and John Joseph Mathews, *The Osages: Children of the Middle Waters* (Norman: University of Oklahoma Press, 1961).

18. *CW-Journals,* 5:72–87; on Irving's observations, from the Osage perspective, see Mathews, *The Osages,* chap. 47, "On the Prairie."

19. Colin G. Calloway, *One Vast Winter Count: The Native American West Before Lewis and Clark* (Lincoln: University of Nebraska Press, 2003), 374–383, 428–431. The original White Hair and several other Osages visited Jefferson in Washington; see Mathews, *The Osages,* 539.

20. *CW-Journals,* 5:59; Grant Foreman, *A History of Oklahoma* (Norman: University of Oklahoma Press, 1942), 6–8; Spaulding, *Journal and Letters of Count de Pourtalès,* 39–40.

21. The most detailed description is given in Ellsworth, *Washington Irving on the Prairie,* 4.

22. Foreman, *A History of Oklahoma,* 9–10; Andrew Burstein, *The Passions of Andrew Jackson* (New York: Alfred A. Knopf, 2003), 181; *CW-Journals,* 5:171. The journal entry is undated, but makes the most sense here. Additional background on the contours of the emerging Indian territory can be found in Gaston Litton, *History of Oklahoma* (New York: Lewis Historical Publishing Company, 1957), 78–89.

23. *A Tour on the Prairies,* 12–15; *CW-Journals,* 5:105. In his rough notes, he marvels at first sights—"Oriental look—like Sultans on the Stage. . . . They look like fine birds of the Prarie," he observes of the Creeks. In the polished published version of *Tour,* he tends to reach for what would be taken for anthropological correctness.

24. Spaulding, *Journal and Letters of Count de Pourtalès,* 38, 45–46; *A Tour on the Prairies,* 24–26.

25. *A Tour on the Prairies,* 19–23, 28–31; Ellsworth's description of the bee hunt is as good as Irving's; he watches as a metaphor comes to life, and the trapped swarm flies in a *"Bee line"* to its hive. Ellsworth, *Washington Irving on the Prairie,* 30.

26. *A Tour on the Prairies,* 32. Although Irving found the rangers' outdoor activities charming and playful, Latrobe noted that the men evidenced little interest in anything but "swopping." He tells the story of one enlistee who swopped his horse so many times that when their party finally returned to Fort Gibson he had the same horse he had started out with; see Latrobe, *Rambler in Oklahoma,* 47–48. In his defense of American ways, Irving had made a complete turnaround. Back in 1785, Thomas Jefferson, as American minister to France, had written an almost identical caution, for the sake of a young Virginian—well before there was any "tour on the prairie" as a masculine outlet. Using the generic third person, Jefferson predicted what would happen to an impressionable American in England or on the Continent: "He acquires a fondness for European luxury and dissipation and a contempt for the simplicity of his own country. . . . It appears to me then that an American coming to Europe for education loses in his knowledge, in his morals, in his health, in his habits, and in his happiness." Like the longtime Anglophile Irving, Jefferson was thought by some of his countrymen to have imbibed too much of Europe—in his case France. So both had sought ways to assert their nationalism. Jefferson to John Banister, Jr., October 15, 1785, in Merrill D. Peterson, ed., *The Portable Thomas Jefferson* (New York: Viking Penguin, 1975), 392–394. In an undated notebook, probably of 1825, Irving wrote: "I really don't See the propriety of sending our young men abroad to study foreign follies and foreign fopperies." *CW-Journals,* 5:320.

27. *CW-Journals,* 5:116; Spaulding, *Journal and Letters of Count de Pourtalès,* 50.

28. Ellsworth, *Washington Irving on the Prairie*, 17, 32.

29. *A Tour on the Prairies*, 32, 36, 39–41. Latrobe, too, tells of the day's events and the river crossing with considerable flair; see his *Rambler in Oklahoma*, 37–41.

30. For a good discussion of Irving's use of picturesque description and the genre it belongs to, see Beth L. Lueck, *American Writers and the Picturesque Tour: The Search for National Identity, 1790–1860* (New York: Garland Publishing, 1997), 91–102. In the chapter preceding this discussion, Lueck deals at length with Irving's friend Paulding—the comparison of the two men's attitudes and styles is helpful.

31. *A Tour on the Prairies*, 48–53. For an analysis of contradictory elements—of rhetoric versus reality—in Irving's portrayal of his experience in Indian territory, see Heiner Bus, "Geoffrey Crayon 'Lighting Out for the Territory' and for Cultural Nationalism: A Reevaluation of Washington Irving's Western Writings," in Udo J. Hebel, ed., *The Construction and Contestation of American Cultures and Identities in the Early National Period* (Heidelberg, Germany: Universitätsverlag, 1999), 155–179. On Irving's specific contributions to Americans' understanding of a western vocabulary, through his own experience and his communications with fur trappers and army rangers, see Wayne R. Kime, "Washington Irving and Frontier Speech," *American Speech* 42 (February 1967): 5–18.

32. Latrobe, *Rambler in Oklahoma*, 47.

33. Ellsworth, *Washington Irving on the Prairie*, 93.

34. *A Tour on the Prairies*, 66–67, 72–77, 88; Latrobe, *The Rambler in Oklahoma*, 54; Spaulding, *Journal and Letters of Count de Pourtalès*, 70–71.

35. *A Tour on the Prairies*, 97–108; Latrobe, *Rambler in Oklahoma*, 70–79. Irving has Beatte, a half-Indian member of the party, cry, "It is the Count!" when the horseman on the hill is sighted. In Latrobe's telling, an anxious Tonish exclaims, "Qu-qu-qu'il est là!" Latrobe states the number of hours of sleep Pourtalès received—ten.

36. *A Tour on the Prairies*, 118–122.

37. Ellsworth to Cass, November 18, 1832, in Latrobe, *Rambler in Oklahoma*, 91.

38. Ellsworth, *Washington Irving on the Prairie*, 70–71, 79–80. In a commonplace book of 1825, Irving wrote: "Cleanliness costs nothing and it is [so] near a virtue that in many countries it has been made a part of religion." *CW-Journals*, 5:329. Though he was by no means a creative writer, Ellsworth reveals Irving in the mode of the sentimental bachelor common to Irving's stories, especially *Bracebridge Hall*. For an analysis of this, and of masculine sentiment and masculine autonomy in *A Tour on the Prairies*, see Bryce Traister, "The Wandering Bachelor: Irving, Masculinity, and Authorship," *American Literature* 74 (March 2002): 111–137.

39. WI to Catharine Irving Paris, November 16, 1832, *CW-Letters*, 2:731–732.

40. WI to Citizens of Vicksburg, November 17, 1832 (these are Irving's comments, as published four days later in the Vicksburg *Advocate & Register*); to Peter Irving, December 18, 1832; to Richard Bentley, January 7, 1834, *CW-Letters*, 2:733–737, 785; Kennedy repeated the rumor about Irving and Miss McLane in a letter to his wife, as noted in STW, 2:46.

41. WI to Paulding, January 3, 1833; to Kemble, January 4, 1833, *CW-Letters*, 2:743–744, 777n.

42. Merrill D. Peterson, *The Great Triumvirate: Webster, Clay, and Calhoun* (New York: Oxford University Press, 1987), chap. 4.

43. On the eve of the War of 1812, when he first saw Congress in action, Irving had found the old Federalist Quincy to be a powerful orator—"like a lion, lashing his sides

with his tail!" He had paid Quincy a call during his brief stay in Boston in the summer of 1832. Edmund Quincy, *Life of Josiah Quincy of Massachusetts* (Boston: Fields, Osgood, 1869), 285–286; WI to Josiah Quincy, April 3, 1833, *CW-Letters*, 2:757.

44. Robert V. Remini, *Andrew Jackson: The Course of American Democracy, 1833–1845* (Baltimore: Johns Hopkins University Press, 1984), 60–61, 72; PMI, 3:51–52.

45. PMI, 3:52–54; WI to Van Buren, October 5, 1833; to Peter Irving, October 28, 1833, *CW-Letters*, 2:773–774, 779; *CW-Journals*, 5:183, 194.

46. In the first months of 1833, Hoffman served as inaugural editor of a periodical, to be known, once it began prospering, as *The Knickerbocker Magazine*. But his tenure there was short-lived, and over the course of that year he journeyed to Cleveland, Detroit, nascent Chicago, and St. Louis, from which he derived his 1835 volume.

47. Wayne R. Kime, *Pierre M. Irving and Washington Irving: A Collaboration in Life and Letters* (Waterloo, Canada: Wilfrid Laurier University Press, 1977), 28–31, 37n.

48. WI to PMI, September 15, 1834, *CW-Letters*, 2:798–799.

49. WI to PMI, October 29, 1834, ibid., 2:801–802; PMI, 3:62; Kime, *Pierre M. Irving and Washington Irving*, 32–35.

50. PMI, 3:67–68; *Washington Irving and the House of Murray*, ed. Ben Harris McClary (Knoxville: University of Tennessee Press, 1969), 169–172, 196; *Crayon Miscellany*, xxviii–xxx.

CHAPTER 13

1. WI to Catharine Irving Paris, March 22, 1838, *CW-Letters*, 2:925.

2. Ebenezer Irving to William Irving (his son), November 22, 1834, Historic Hudson Valley collection; Wayne R. Kime, *Pierre M. Irving and Washington Irving: A Collaboration in Life and Letters* (Waterloo, Canada: Wilfrid Laurier University Press, 1977), 40; Alvah P. French, ed., *History of Westchester County, New York* (New York and Chicago: Lewis Historical Publishing Company, 1925), 2:938–939.

3. J. Thomas Scharf, *History of Westchester County, New York* (Philadelphia: L. E. Preston, 1886), 2:232–235; French, *History of Westchester County, New York*, 688–691, 706–708.

4. WI to Peter Irving, July 8, 1835, *CW-Letters*, 2:835–836.

5. WI to Peter Irving, May 25, 1835, ibid., 2:825.

6. WI to Kennedy, June 5, 1835, ibid., 2:829.

7. Kenneth Silverman, *Edgar A. Poe: Mournful and Never-Ending Remembrance* (New York: HarperCollins, 1991), 117–122; Nelson Frederick Adkins, *Fitz-Greene Halleck: An Early Knickerbocker Wit and Poet* (New Haven, CT: Yale University Press, 1930), 261; "Critical Notices," in the *Southern Literary Messenger* (April 1835): 456. Irving continued to champion Halleck, as evidenced in letters to the poet Samuel Rogers and the critic John Lockhart, both in England (February 3 and 4, 1836, *CW-Letters*, 2:852–854).

8. PMI, 3:66–67; *Crayon Miscellany*, xxxi; *Western Monthly Magazine* for June 1835, in Ralph M. Aderman, ed., *Critical Essays on Washington Irving* (Boston: G. K. Hall, 1990), 103–107.

9. An edition of Halleck's collected poems, effectively a reprint of an 1827 edition, emerged at the end of 1835. It is hard to know what Halleck was like as a housemate during these months. He received a boost when Poe requested an original poem for the

Messenger, and John Quincy Adams (the former president, now a congressman) lauded his work on the floor of the House. Irving wrote to Thomas Aspinwall in London, praising Halleck and suggesting that a "small collection" of his poems might be published in England. Nothing came of the effort. Although the correspondence of Washington and Pierre says little, others among Halleck's acquaintances remarked on his cynicism, if not despondency, at this time. Though Astor paid his salary, he was something of a purist; the general preoccupation with "stocks and lots and speculations" in New York caused him to shun society. WI to Aspinwall, May 20, 1835, *CW-Letters,* 2:818, 821–823, 843; Adkins, *Fitz-Greene Halleck,* 257, 260, 264, 266, 272; John Denis Haeger, *John Jacob Astor: Business and Finance in the Early Republic* (Detroit: Wayne State University Press, 1991), chap. 9.

10. WI to Peter Irving, April 17, May 16, and October 8, 1835; *CW-Letters,* 2:818, 821–823, 843; Bonneville quote from the "Introductory Notice" to Irving's *The Adventures of Captain Bonneville, U.S.A.*

11. Kime, *Pierre M. Irving and Washington Irving,* 45–46; WI to Peter Irving, October 8 and December 25, 1835; to Ebenezer Irving, October 16, 1835; to George Harvey (whom Irving adjudged "architect"), November 23, 1835, *CW-Letters,* 2:843–847.

12. Stanley T. Williams classified Peter as "a Knickerbocker Socrates." STW, 1:25.

13. Theodore Irving to William Irving, January 17, 1835, Historic Hudson Valley collection; WI to Peter Irving, December 25, 1835, *CW-Letters,* 2:846–848; Edwin G. Burrows and Mike Wallace, *Gotham: A History of New York to 1898* (New York: Oxford University Press, 1999), 452–455, 596–598.

14. Ralph M. Aderman and Wayne R. Kime, *Advocate for America: The Life of James Kirke Paulding* (Selinsgrove, PA: Susquehanna University Press, 2003), 178–189; Larry J. Reynolds, *James Kirke Paulding* (Boston: Twayne Publishers, 1984), 14–15; Matthew Gartner, "Becoming Longfellow: Work, Manhood, and Poetry," *American Literature* 72 (March 2000): 59–86, quote at 67; WI to Butler, October 19, 1836; to Van Buren, October 19, 1836, *CW-Letters,* 2:877–878; STW, 2:277.

15. PMI, 3:89–90.

16. Ibid., 3:86–87; on the Irving-Astor relationship at this juncture, see Andrew Myers, "Washington Irving and the Astor Library," *Bulletin of the New York Public Library* 72 (June 1968): 380–381.

17. *Astoria, or Anecdotes of an Enterprize Beyond the Rocky Mountains,* ed. Richard Dilworth Rust (Boston: Twayne Publishers, 1976), chap. 4.

18. Ibid., chap. 11; James P. Ronda, *Astoria and Empire* (Lincoln: University of Nebraska Press, 1990), 94–95. Ronda's is a systematic study of the incident, and of the Astoria enterprise generally, relating Irving's *Astoria* to more recent interpretations. See ibid., 235–237.

19. Later critics, with several decades of added perspective, found fault with the author's methods. But Irving has had his share of supporters over the years. Many distinguished modern historians of the frontier West choose to laud him for his impartiality. Most recently, James P. Ronda has credited Irving with integrity as a scholar, while acknowledging his compulsion to dramatize. *Astoria,* xxxi–xxxiv; Ronda, *Astoria and Empire,* 340.

20. *Astoria,* 370–374.

21. In his *Tales of Adventurous Enterprise: Washington Irving and the Poetics of Western Expansion* (New York: Columbia University Press, 1990), chap. 3, Peter Antelyes examines the satirical elements of Irving's treatment of the fear of Indians, focusing

primarily on *A Tour on the Prairies*. See also the assessment of Irving's attitude toward Indians in Edward Wagenknecht, *Washington Irving: Moderation Displayed* (New York: Oxford University Press, 1962), 110–113.

22. *The Adventures of Captain Bonneville*, ed. Robert A. Rees and Alan Sandy (Boston: Twayne Publishers, 1977), chaps. 1 and 2.

23. Ibid., chaps. 7, 31, and 47.

24. Ibid., xxx–xxxi, xxxv–xxxix; Mary Weatherspoon Bowden, *Washington Irving* (Boston: Twayne Publishers, 1980), 163–165; Richard H. Cracroft, *Washington Irving: The Western Works* (Boise, ID: Boise State University, 1974), 38; others who see value in Irving's *Bonneville* are Bernard DeVoto and Andrew B. Myers. I am grateful to James P. Ronda for supplying the Cracroft piece. Irving's egregious depictions of Indian behavior culminate in his characterization of a romantic feud between one of the trappers and the Shoshone males over "a pert little Eutaw wench" in chapter 47 of *Bonneville*. There is everything "dashing and heroic" in the trapper, in the eyes of the Indian girl, and only "caprice" in her erstwhile Indian husband, who already had taken another wife.

25. PMI, 3:90–97; WI to Gouverneur Kemble, September 28, 1836, *CW-Letters*, 2:875.

26. PMI, 3:98–99, 113–117; WI to Sarah Paris, January 11, 1837, *CW-Letters*, 2:890–891.

27. PMI, 3:116–117; WI to Thomas Aspinwall, March 16, 1837, *CW-Letters*, 2:903.

28. Catharine G. Wirt to WI, October 28, 1837, in the Hellman Collection, New York Public Library. Kennedy and Wirt were both Marylanders, and were acquainted. The two-volume biography was titled *Memoirs of the Life of William Wirt*, published in Philadelphia by Lea and Blanchard.

29. WI to Kemble, January 10 and March 12, 1838; to Catharine Irving Paris, March 22, 1838, *CW-Letters*, 2:918–921, 923, 925; Kime, *Pierre M. Irving and Washington Irving*, 59.

30. WI to Kemble, June 2, 1838, *CW-Letters*, 2:929.

31. WI to Sarah Irving Van Wart, September 22, 1838, *CW-Letters*, 2:936–937; STW, 2:93.

32. PMI, 3:125; WI to Sarah Irving Van Wart, October 24 and December 1, 1838, *CW-Letters*, 2:939–944.

33. STW, 2:54–57; Van Wyck Brooks, *The World of Washington Irving* (New York: E. P. Dutton, 1944), 334–335. Cooper had continued to author volumes that were critical of the British, most notably his 1837 *Gleanings in Europe: England*. As for Irving's prediction, he was correct insofar as Cooper's novels clearly outsell Irving's stories in today's U.S. market.

34. PMI, 3:133–146.

35. WI to "My Six Nieces," February 4, 1840; to Sarah Irving Van Wart, November 25, 1840, *CW-Letters*, 3:40–42, 61–62.

36. PMI, 3:162, 167–168; WI to Sarah Irving Van Wart, April 30, 1841, *CW-Letters*, 3:85–86; *CW-Journals*, 5:197n.

37. PMI, 3:164–165.

38. *Biography of the Late Margaret Miller Davidson*, ed. Elsie Lee West (Boston: Twayne Publishers, 1978), xxxvii–xliii.

39. Andrew Burstein, *America's Jubilee* (New York: Alfred A. Knopf, 2001), 300.

40. WI to Van Buren, January 13, 1840; WI to Kemble, February 4 and October 31, 1840, *CW-Letters*, 3:34–35, 38–39, 58–59.

41. Webster wrote of Tyler: "My hope is that he will consider himself instructed, not by one single State, but by the *Country*." On Webster's choices, see Merrill D. Peterson, *The Great Triumvirate: Webster, Clay and Calhoun* (New York: Oxford University Press, 1987), 302–303. For an inside account of the politics of the Harrison-Tyler succession in 1841, see Henry A. Wise, *Seven Decades of the Union: The Humanities and Materialism, Illustrated by a Memoir of John Tyler* (Philadelphia: J. B. Lippincott, 1872), chap. 9.

42. PMI, 3:176–182; WI to Ebenezer Irving, February 17 and March 16, 1842, *CW-Letters*, 3:183–184, 192–193; Bowden, *Washington Irving*, 147.

43. PMI, 3:180, 182; Account Books, in *CW-Journals*, 5:462–473.

44. PMI, 3:182–187; STW, 2:116–117; Kime, *Pierre M. Irving and Washington Irving*, 160. Dickens wrote critically of America after his visit, and Irving subsequently behaved with restraint toward Dickens, admitting his displeasure only much later in his life. For a clearheaded analysis of the evidence that Irving did not entirely reciprocate Dickens's warm feelings for him, see W. C. Desmond Pacey, "Washington Irving and Charles Dickens," *American Literature* 16 (January 1945): 332–339.

45. PMI, 3:188–201; *CW-Journals*, 5:199–204, 215–216.

46. *CW-Journals*, 5:223–225; WI to Sarah Paris Storrow, July 31, 1841; to Catharine Irving Paris, June 10, 1842; to Helen Dodge Irving, June 26, 1842, *CW-Letters*, 3:142, 237, 240.

47. WI to Sarah Irving Van Wart, June 8, 1842; to Catharine Irving Paris, June 20 and July 25, 1842; to Henry Brevoort, July 1, 1842, *CW-Letters*, 3:233–234, 241–242, 252, 254–255.

48. Claude G. Bowers, *The Spanish Adventures of Washington Irving* (Boston: Houghton Mifflin, 1940), chap. 7; Louis Bertrand and Sir Charles Petrie, *The History of Spain* (New York: Appleton-Century Company, 1934), 467–475; WI to Secretary of State Daniel Webster, August 2 and November 5, 1842; to Sarah Paris Storrow, August 12, September 26, and October 10, 1842; to Catharine Irving Paris, September 2 and November 20, 1842, *CW-Letters*, 3:263–264, 281, 307–316, 338–339, 353, 373–379, 403–410. Irving's September 2 letter to Catharine is a perfectly lucid account of Spanish politics of the decade leading up to his ambassadorship.

49. WI to Count Almodóvar, November 8, 1842, *CW-Letters*, 3:381–386; STW, 2:182–183.

50. WI to Charlotte Irving, September 16, 1842; to Catharine Irving Paris, November 20, 1842, *CW-Letters*, 3:330–331, 407; PMI, 3:276.

51. PMI, 3:276–277; WI to Catharine Irving Paris, June 21, 1843; to Sarah Paris Storrow, June 24, 1843, *CW-Letters*, 3:541, 543; Alexander Hamilton (son) to James Alexander Hamilton (father), March 10, 1843, Historic Hudson Valley Collection.

52. WI to Dolgorouki, October 18, 1842, *CW-Letters*, 3:355–357.

53. WI to Ticknor, January 11, 1843; to Prescott, October 15, 1844, *CW-Letters*, 3:462, 821.

54. WI to Catharine Irving Paris, March 25 and June 21, 1843; to Sarah Paris Storrow, April 13 and July 18, 1843; to Secretary of State Daniel Webster, June 22, 1843, *CW-Letters*, 3:497, 513, 543–544, 546, 559.

55. WI to Sarah Paris Storrow, December 2, 1843; to Secretary of State Upshur, January 19, 1844, *CW-Letters*, 3:623, 654.

56. WI to Sarah Irving, January 19, 1844; to Sarah Paris Storrow, March 8, 1844, *CW-Letters*, 3:649, 691.

57. PMI, 3:363–364; WI to Sarah Paris Storrow, March 27, 1845, *CW-Letters*, 3:922–925.

58. WI to Sarah Paris Storrow, April 3, 1845, *CW-Letters*, 3:929.

59. WI to George P. Putnam, August 13, 1845, *CW-Letters*, 3:1020–1021.

60. WI to Secretary of State Buchanan, December 12, 1845, *CW-Letters*, 3:1038–1039.

61. Bowers, *Spanish Adventures of Washington Irving*, chaps. 10–14.

CHAPTER 14

1. *CW-Letters*, 4:301.

2. PMI, 4:281.

3. WI to Pierre Munro Irving, December 29, 1845, *CW-Letters*, 3:1041.

4. WI to Sarah Paris Storrow, January 15 and February 2, 1846; to Pierre M. Irving, February 3, 1846, *CW-Letters*, 4:6, 10–11. Irving did experience a certain frustration with McLane. He confided to Sarah that, in spite of their friendship, there was something self-serving in McLane's approach to him, and that he had learned over the years to expect to encounter this blind side, or lack of sensitivity, in McLane: "I am accustomed to be disappointed in him, when the business in hand did not exactly meet his views or serve his purposes." Specifically, Irving had sought to publish an article on the Oregon question that would explain the U.S. position in a reassuring manner, but McLane had not supplied all of what he needed to complete this peacemaking treatise. When he felt he had done all he could in London, Irving decided to return to Paris en route to Madrid.

5. Claude G. Bowers, *The Spanish Adventures of Washington Irving* (Boston: Houghton Mifflin, 1940), chap. 14.

6. STW, 2:199.

7. WI to Flora Foster Dawson, February 5, 1846, *CW-Letters*, 4:13–14.

8. WI to Sarah Paris Storrow, October 18, 1846, *CW-Letters*, 4:98; John Denis Haeger, *John Jacob Astor: Business and Finance in the Early Republic* (Detroit: Wayne State University Press, 1991), 264–279; Andrew Myers, "Washington Irving and the Astor Library," *Bulletin of the New York Public Library* 72 (June 1968): 378–399.

9. PMI, 3:395–396; Wayne R. Kime, *Pierre M. Irving and Washington Irving: A Collaboration in Life and Letters* (Waterloo, Canada: Wilfrid Laurier University Press, 1977), 93–94.

10. Irving joked to Pierre's wife, Helen, that the time he was obliged to spend indoors would render him "rusty and crusty." WI to Helen Dodge Irving, February 14, 1847, *CW-Letters*, 4:113.

11. WI to Kemble, July 8, 1847, ibid., 4:138–139.

12. PMI, 4:37–38; WI to Kemble, August 7, 1850, *CW-Letters*, 4:215; Kime, *Pierre M. Irving and Washington Irving*, 116.

13. WI to Sarah Paris Storrow, August 23, 1847; to Sabina O'Shea, September 18, 1847, *CW-Letters*, 4:144, 151.

14. Haeger, *John Jacob Astor*, 282–284; Cooper's letter to his wife, April 1, 1848, cited in STW, 2:210; see also Myers, "Washington Irving and the Astor Library," 386–388.

15. WI to Charles R. Leslie, October 19, 1848, *CW-Letters*, 4:184; PMI, 4:237. *Wolfert's Roost* (1855) was added as volume 16, and the *Life of Washington* (1855–1859)

as volumes 17–21. See Edwin T. Bowden, comp., *Washington Irving: Bibliography* (Boston: Twayne Publishers, 1989), 744.

16. Further discussion of these works can be found in Mary Weatherspoon Bowden, *Washington Irving* (Boston: Twayne Publishers, 1981), 170–175.

17. *A Book of the Hudson* contained some *Knickerbocker Magazine* pieces, including an extensively revised "Communipaw"; also "Rip Van Winkle" and "The Legend of Sleepy Hollow," "Dolph Heyliger" and "Wolfert Webber." Bowden, *Washington Irving: Bibliography*, 456. Adding to the author's popular exposure, *The Irving Gift*, a "selection of gems," emerged in 1852, through an arrangement between Putnam and Phinney in Buffalo; this illustrated assemblage of famous passages contained portions of *Salmagundi*, including "The Little Man in Black"; *Knickerbocker's History;* and "The Legend of Sleepy Hollow."

18. Quotes are from *Oliver Goldsmith: A Biography*, ed. Elsie Lee West (Boston: Twayne Publishers, 1978), chaps. 5 and 13.

19. Knickerbocker to WI, June 17, 1851, Hellman Collection, New York Public Library; WI to the Irving Literary Society (Maryland), December 11, 1848, *CW-Letters*, 4:186; Kime, *Pierre M. Irving and Washington Irving*, 147–157.

20. Donald G. Mitchell ("Ik Marvel"), *Reveries of a Bachelor: Or a Book of the Heart* (New York: Baker & Scribner, 1851), v.

21. WI to Mitchell, November 15, 1851, *CW-Letters*, 4:277; "Dream Life: A Fable of the Seasons," in *The Works of Donald G. Mitchell* (New York: Charles Scribner's Sons, 1907), x.

22. WI to Sarah Paris Storrow, November 10, 1852, *CW-Letters*, 4:335.

23. Fitz-Greene Halleck was secretary of the memorial committee that Irving headed. Irving suggested that a "noble" statue of Cooper be erected, showing him as he was in his prime; Halleck, ever respectful of Cooper, and throughout his life outwardly nonpartisan (though, in his heart, he was an elitist who sneered at democracy), concurred. Halleck understood Cooper—a man who set himself apart, set himself above, and carried on. Nelson Frederick Adkins, *Fitz-Greene Halleck: An Early Knickerbocker Wit and Poet* (New Haven, CT: Yale University Press, 1930), 288–290, 319.

24. WI to Rufus W. Griswold, September 18, 1851; to Lewis G. Clark, October 6 and 15, 1851; to John P. Kennedy, December 20, 1853, *CW-Letters*, 4:260–263, 457; PMI, 4:103–104.

25. WI to Catharine Irving, July 17, 1852; to Sarah Paris Storrow, July 29, 1853, *CW-Letters*, 4:318–319, 422; Theodore Corbett, *The Making of American Resorts: Saratoga Springs, Ballston Spa, and Lake George* (New Brunswick, NJ: Rutgers University Press, 2001), 219–226; "Preface of 1863," in *The Works of Donald G. Mitchell*, xi–xvii. When Mitchell visited Sunnyside, Irving took him for a ride through Sleepy Hollow, pointing out the sights that figured in "The Legend of Sleepy Hollow."

26. WI to Sarah Irving, August 12, 1853; to Sarah Paris Storrow, September 19, 1853, *CW-Letters*, 4:427, 435–437.

27. Thomas G. Connors, "The Romantic Landscape: Washington Irving, Sleepy Hollow, and the Rural Cemetery Movement," in Nancy Isenberg and Andrew Burstein, eds., *Mortal Remains: Death in Early America* (Philadelphia: University of Pennsylvania Press, 2003), 187–203.

28. WI to Kennedy, December 20, 1853, *CW-Letters*, 4:457.

29. PMI, 3:343–344; WI to Sarah Paris Storrow, March 28, 1853; to Pierce, April 21, 1853, *CW-Letters*, 4:385, 395. Mitchell's purpose in traveling to the Mediterranean was to research an historical work, again suggesting how Irving was a role model.

30. *Wolfert's Roost*, ed. Roberta Rosenberg (Boston: Twayne Publishers, 1979), 3–7; PMI, 4:185–188.

31. WI to Martin Van Buren, September 4, 1855, *CW-Letters*, 4:549.

32. Kime, *Pierre M. Irving and Washington Irving*, 132–133.

33. As a Massachusetts Unitarian, Sparks was interested in promoting a judicious Whig view of society; as a documentary historian, he was a champion of "authentic" rather than oral or anecdotal accounts of great men. See Scott E. Casper, *Constructing American Lives: Biography and Culture in Nineteenth-Century America* (Chapel Hill: University of North Carolina Press, 1999), 135–148. One of Sparks's prospective authors in the Library of America plan was Gulian Verplanck, meant to write on New Yorker Robert R. Livingston.

34. WI to Bancroft, October 27, 1854, *CW-Letters*, 4:504. Note that it was during Bancroft's term as secretary of the navy that the U.S. Naval Academy was established at Annapolis.

35. *Life of George Washington*, ed. Allen Guttmann and James A. Sappenfield (Boston: Twayne Publishers, 1982), 1:xxxix–xlv. The review of volumes 1–4 in the *North American Review* (April 1858) points to Irving's effective use of primary sources; see Ralph M. Aderman, ed., *Critical Essays on Washington Irving* (Boston: G. K. Hall, 1990), 142–152.

36. This is not to say that Irving was less discriminating than he should have been—it would be unfair to apply the rules that govern today's scholars. He is careful to couch information he cannot authenticate in such phrases as "Tradition gives us an interesting picture of . . ."; and he fills in blanks cautiously by suggesting that an event "could not but have had" such and such an effect. He does give his readers drama, as expected of him: "At the eleventh hour the mother's heart faltered" or, "Yet, at this very moment, a lurking spirit of rivalry between Jefferson and Hamilton was already existing," as he looked at controversies within Washington's cabinet. Here, he is careful not to rely on Marshall's biased perspective alone, though he interprets Jefferson's response to arch-Federalist Hamilton as overreaction; thus, when Irving offered his "this is what Hamilton probably meant," to say that Jefferson mistook his policy prescription for an anti-republican or monarchical one, he did so only after analyzing two separate editions of Jefferson's papers. *Life of George Washington*, 1:17, 3:273, 5:328. Quotes are from chap. 2 of Irving's vol. 1, chap. 31 of vol. 4, and chap. 8 of vol. 5. (The Twayne edition combines Irving's five volumes into three.)

37. Ibid., 3:470–474 (Irving's chap. 32 of vol. 2). Compare Jared Sparks, in his two-volume treatment, writing of the same moment: "The retreat, in its plan, execution, and success, has been regarded as one of the most remarkable military events in history, and as reflecting the highest credit on the talents and skill of the commander. So intense was the anxiety of Washington, so unceasing his exertions, that for forty-eight hours he did not close his eyes, and rarely dismounted from his horse." Though Irving dramatizes the action of the retreat and Sparks is more prosaic, the essentials are repeated in this instance. Sparks, *Life of George Washington* (Boston: Tappaan and Dewet, 1845), 1:239–240. For a good brief account by a modern historian of Washington's plight on Long Island, see John E. Ferling, *The First of Men: A Life of George Washington* (Knoxville: University of Tennessee Press, 1988), 164–168.

38. *Life of George Washington*, 3:59–71 (Irving's chap. 9 of vol. 4).

39. Ibid., 3:469–475 (Irving's chap. 34 of vol. 5); *Mahomet*, chap. 39. In an effort to humanize his subject, Irving draws on James Paulding's earlier, much simpler biography

for an anecdote about the founding father's final days, quoting one of Washington's nephews: "I have sometimes thought him decidedly the handsomest man I ever saw; and when in a lively mood, so full of pleasantry, so agreeable to all with whom he associated, that I could hardly realize he was the same Washington whose dignity awed all who approached him."

40. WI to Elizabeth Kennedy, February 8, 1855; to Paulding, December 24, 1855, *CW-Letters,* 4:525, 568.

41. "Sunnyside, the Home of Washington Irving," *Harper's New Monthly Magazine* 79 (December 1856): 1–21. The article gives, nearly word for word, the account of Irving's encounter with George Washington that would appear in Pierre M. Irving's 1862 four-volume biography, adding: "As Washington was the political, so his namesake is the literary Father of his country."

42. PMI, 4:217–220.

43. PMI, 4:220, 264; WI to Motley, July 17, 1857; to Holmes, January 4, 1859, *CW-Letters,* 4:630, 671. Holmes's son, of course, was the distinguished twentieth-century Supreme Court justice.

44. Kime, *Pierre Irving and Washington Irving,* 119, 145, 173–180, 252–254.

45. Pierre was to write: "Those nights, when I look back on them, seem a strange mingling; for between the paroxysms of distress, he would seize on anything to divert his own thoughts, or what he feared must be the weariness of those who were watching with him." Ibid., 186–199; PMI, 4:278–280, 285.

46. Kime, *Pierre Irving and Washington Irving,* 200–211. Once again, on August 4, Irving referred to Burr's "petty mysteries," adding that he was "a man of *large views* and paltry means—arts—to accomplish them." Ibid., 219.

47. Kennedy to WI, October 23, 1859, Hellman Collection, New York Public Library; Kime, *Pierre Irving and Washington Irving,* 162; PMI, 4:315.

48. PMI, 4:318–323.

49. Kime, *Pierre Irving and Washington Irving,* 194, 234, 238, 326; PMI, 4:324–325.

50. WI to Lewis G. Clark, March 17, 1840, *CW-Letters,* 4:48–49; on racial theories and standards current at the time of Irving's writings, see Elise Lemire, *"Miscegenation": Making Race in America* (Philadelphia: University of Pennsylvania Press, 2002).

51. PMI, 4:326; Kime, *Pierre Irving and Washington Irving,* 239.

52. "Preface of 1863," in *The Works of Donald G. Mitchell,* xvii–xviii.

53. Henry Wadsworth Longfellow, "In the Churchyard at Tarrytown," in Andrew B. Myers, ed., *A Century of Commemoration on the Works of Washington Irving* (Tarrytown, NY: Sleepy Hollow Restorations, 1976), 39.

CHAPTER 15

1. "The Poor Devil Author," in *Tales of a Traveller,* ed. Judith Giblin Haig (Boston: Twayne Publishers, 1987), 92.

2. Jefferson later wrote that the idea of playing the part he became famous for struck him while living in "a queer old Dutch farmhouse" in the Poconos. *The Autobiography of Joseph Jefferson* (New York: The Century Company, 1889), 224–229, and Introduction to *Rip Van Winkle as Played by Joseph Jefferson* (New York: Dodd, Mead, 1899), 10–11.

3. "Address," in Andrew B. Myers, ed., *A Century of Commemoration on the Works of Washington Irving* (Tarrytown, NY: Sleepy Hollow Restorations, 1976), 57.

4. *CW-Journals*, 2:10.

5. WI to Clark, October 6, 1851, *CW-Letters*, 4:262.

6. Among the numerous studies that confirm this phenomenon, and that typically involve ten thousand or more subjects, see Ray Blanchard, "Quantitative and Theoretical Analyses of the Relation Between Older Brothers and Homosexuality in Men," *Journal of Theoretical Biology* 230 (September 2004): 173–187; Blanchard, "Fraternal Birth Order and the Maternal Immune Hypothesis of Male Homosexuality," *Hormones and Behavior* 40 (September 2001): 105–114; and Anthony F. Bogaert, "Interaction in Older Brothers and Sex-Typing in the Prediction of Sexual Orientation and Men," *Archives of Sexual Behavior* 32 (April 2003): 129–134. The number of older sisters has been shown to be irrelevant in predicting a man's sexual orientation.

7. From "The Busy Man," in *Bracebridge Hall*. On the social position of the mid-nineteenth-century bachelor, see also Vincent J. Bertolini, "Fireside Chastity: The Erotics of Sentimental Bachelorhood in the 1850s," *American Literature* 68 (December 1996): 707–737.

8. STW, 1:45, 156–157, 178, 184–187. "As literature," Williams wrote, "at least a half-dozen [*Sketch Book*] essays are worthless; twice that number bear the stigma of mediocrity." And he was just warming up. His comments about Irving's subsequent books were no more complimentary.

9. Edward Wagenknecht, *Washington Irving: Moderation Displayed* (New York: Oxford University Press, 1962), 188.

10. In general, see David Simpson, *The Politics of American English, 1776–1850* (New York: Oxford University Press, 1986), chap. 1. Kurt Müller takes note of Irving's departure from the Franklin model for fashioning a personal identity. He terms Franklin's "progressive" and Irving's a "conservative counter-model," focusing on generational differences: Irving resisted the universal Enlightenment ideas of perfectibility and unlimited progress in favor of an agrarian communalism and Rip Van Winkle–like aversion to the Puritan-capitalist work ethic. This may sound ironic, given Irving's long pursuit of financial security and his early comfort with commercial interests in New York. Still, Müller's argument is compelling in its assessment of the cultural significance of Irving's response to Franklin. Müller, "'Progressive' and 'Conservative' Concepts of American Identity: Washington Irving's Response to the Franklinesque Model," in Udo J. Hebel, ed., *The Construction and Contestation of American Cultures and Identities in the Early National Period* (Heidelberg, Germany: Universitätsverlag, 1999), 137–153.

11. Although eighteenth-century models persisted, Irving's generation not only expanded the American vocabulary but also enthroned colloquialism. H. L. Mencken dubbed this a "gaudy era." Circumventing more orthodox literary scholarship, Michael West describes a satirical, seriocomic Irving as one whose words always contain more than meets the eye, and whose contribution to fiction and the American language can be seen as "an expanded pun." Mencken, *The American Language* (New York: Alfred A. Knopf, 1938), chap. 4; West, *Transcendental Wordplay: America's Romantic Punsters and the Search for the Language of Nature* (Athens: Ohio University Press, 2000), 291–296.

12. *Washington Irving: A Bibliography*, comp. William R. Langfeld (New York: New York Public Library, 1933), 67–68, 82–84. Similarly, in Spain, Irving's *Alhambra* remains in vogue; as recently as 2003, *El Embrujo del Sur* (Sorcerer of the South), a Spanish animation feature, was drawn from the collection, with one actor supplying the voice of Washington Irving.

13. Philip Young treats the various legends at length in "Fallen from Time: The Mythic 'Rip Van Winkle,'" in James W. Tuttleton, ed., *Washington Irving: The Critical Reception* (New York: AMS Press, 1993), 67–84.

14. *The Autobiography of Joseph Jefferson,* 228–229, 452–453, 458–460; George C. D. Odell, *Annals of the New York Stage* (New York: Columbia University Press, 1927; reprint, AMC Press, 1970), vol. 2, passim; PMI, 4:253; "Old Rip, a Whiskered Peter Pan Lives On," in *The New York Times Magazine,* April 1, 1928. I thank Catalina Hannan, librarian of Historic Hudson Valley, for bringing the *Times* article to my attention. Washington Irving more than once saw Joseph Jefferson II onstage at William Dunlap's Park Theater. In September 1858, a year before his death, the lifelong theatergoer was impressed when he saw the son and namesake perform in a comedy—once again, in New York City. Joe Jefferson was told that Irving was in the audience. They never met in person.

15. Melissa Clarke, "The Time-Space Image: The Case of Bergson, Deleuze, and *Memento," Journal of Speculative Philosophy* 16 (2002): 167–181.

16. Associated Press story, as reported in the *Ithaca (NY) Journal,* July 4, 2006.

17. Perry Miller's "Afterword," in the Signet Classic edition of *The Sketch Book of Geoffrey Crayon, Gent.* (New York: New American Library, 1981), 377. Robert A. Ferguson speculates on Rip's relevance to our time. "We value Rip most," he writes, "because we find something of our own foibles in him." He manages to solve problems we cannot, dying and returning to life "on his own terms." See Ferguson, "Rip Van Winkle and the Generational Divide in American Culture," *Early American Literature* 40 (2005): 529–544.

18. Walter Shear, "Time in 'Rip Van Winkle' and 'The Legend of Sleepy Hollow,'" *Midwest Quarterly* 17 (1976): 161.

19. On this subject, see Antonio Damasio, *The Feeling of What Happens: Body and Emotion in the Making of Consciousness* (New York: Harcourt, 1999).

20. Richard H. Cracroft, *Washington Irving: The Western Works* (Boise, ID: Boise State University, 1974), 40–41; *The Adventures of Captain Bonneville,* ed. Robert A. Rees and Alan Sandy (Boston: Twayne Publishers, 1977), xxxii. On Irving's consciousness of the marketability of the western adventure, see Peter Antelyes, *Tales of Adventurous Enterprise: Washington Irving and the Poetics of Western Expansion* (New York: Columbia University Press, 1990), 81–84.

Selected Bibliography

Note: References in the text to Irving's fiction and histories are to the Twayne editions, in the *Complete Works*, published between 1977 and 1988. I have also consulted, when possible, other nineteenth- and twentieth-century editions to get a feel for different presentations of Irving's prose.

Aderman, Ralph M., ed. *Critical Essays on Washington Irving*. Boston: G. K. Hall, 1990.

———. ed. *The Letters of James Kirke Paulding*. Madison: University of Wisconsin Press, 1962.

———. ed. "Salmagundi and the Outlander Tradition." *Wisconsin Studies in Literature* 1 (1964): 62–68.

Aderman, Ralph M., and Wayne R. Kime. *Advocate for America: The Life of James Kirke Paulding*. Selinsgrove, PA: Susquehanna University Press, 2003.

Adkins, Nelson Frederick. *Fitz-Greene Halleck: An Early Knickerbocker Wit and Poet*. New Haven, CT: Yale University Press, 1930.

Allison, Robert J. *Stephen Decatur: American Naval Hero, 1779–1820*. Amherst, MA: University of Massachusetts Press, 2005.

Antelyes, Peter. *Tales of Adventurous Enterprise: Washington Irving and the Poetics of Western Expansion*. New York: Columbia University Press, 1990.

Anthony, David. "'Gone Distracted': 'Sleepy Hollow,' Gothic Masculinity, and the Panic of 1819." *Early American Literature* 40 (2005): 111–144.

Barnes, Homer F. *Charles Fenno Hoffman*. New York: Columbia University Press, 1930.

Bassett, John Spencer, ed. *Correspondence of Andrew Jackson*. Vol. 4. Washington, DC: Carnegie Institute, 1929.

Beach, Leonard, ed. *Peter Irving's Journals*. New York: New York Public Library, 1943.

Bender, Thomas. *New York Intellect*. New York: Alfred A. Knopf, 1987.

Bertrand, Louis, and Sir Charles Petrie. *The History of Spain*. New York: D. Appleton-Century, 1934.

Blair, Hugh. *Lectures on Rhetoric and Belles Letters*. Philadelphia: Troutman & Hayes, 1852 [1783].

Bowden, Edwin T., comp. *Washington Irving: A Bibliography*. Boston: Twayne Publishers, 1989.

Bowden, Mary Weatherspoon. "Cocklofts and Slang-whangers: The Historical Sources of Washington Irving's *Salmagundi*," *New York History* 61 (April 1980): 133–160.

———. *Washington Irving*. Boston: Twayne Publishers, 1981.

Bowers, Claude G. *The Spanish Adventures of Washington Irving.* Boston: Houghton Mifflin, 1940.

Brodwin, Stanley, ed. *The Old and New World Romanticism of Washington Irving.* Westport, CT: Greenwood Press, 1986.

Brooks, Van Wyck. *The World of Washington Irving.* New York: E. P. Dutton, 1944.

Brunsen, B. R. *The Adventures of Samuel Swartwout in the Age of Jefferson and Jackson.* Lewiston, NY: Edwin Mellen Press, 1989.

Burrows, Edwin G., and Mike Wallace. *Gotham: A History of New York to 1898.* New York: Oxford University Press, 1999.

Burstein, Andrew. *America's Jubilee: How in 1826 a Generation Remembered Fifty Years of Independence.* New York: Alfred A. Knopf, 2001.

———. *The Passions of Andrew Jackson.* New York: Alfred A. Knopf, 2003.

———. *Sentimental Democracy: The Evolution of America's Romantic Self-Image.* New York: Hill & Wang, 1999.

Byrd, Max. *Tristram Shandy.* London: Unwin Hyman, 1985.

Caldwell, Charles. *Autobiography of Charles Caldwell, M.D.,* ed. Harriot Warner. Philadelphia: Lippincott, Grambo, 1855. Reprint, New York: Da Capo Press, 1968.

Calloway, Colin G. *One Vast Winter Count: The Native American West Before Lewis and Clark.* Lincoln: University of Nebraska Press, 2003.

Casper, Scott E. *Constructing American Lives: Biography and Culture in Nineteenth-Century America.* Chapel Hill: University of North Carolina Press, 1999.

Charvat, William. *Literary Publishing in America, 1790–1850.* Philadelphia: University of Pennsylvania Press, 1959.

Chejne, Anwar J. *Muslim Spain: Its History and Culture.* Minneapolis: University of Minnesota Press, 1974.

Chudacoff, Howard P. *The Age of the Bachelor.* Princeton, NJ: Princeton University Press, 1999.

Clark, William Bedford. "How the West Won: Irving's Comic Inversion of the Westering Myth in *A Tour on the Prairies.*" *American Literature* 50 (November 1978): 335–347.

Clendenning, John. "Irving and the Gothic Tradition." *Bucknell Review* 12 (1964): 90–98.

Clinton, DeWitt. *An Account of Abimelech Coody and Other Celebrated Writers of New York, in a Letter from a Traveller, to His Friend in South Carolina.* New York: n.p., 1815.

———. *An Introductory Discourse, Delivered Before the Literary and Philosophical Society of New-York, on the Fourth of May, 1814.* New York: Van Winkle and Wiley, 1815.

Cook, Noble David. "Sickness, Starvation, and Death in Early Hispaniola." *Journal of Interdisciplinary History* 32 (Winter 2002): 349–386.

Cooper, James Fenimore. *The Letters and Journals of James Fenimore Cooper.* Edited by James Franklin Beard. Vol. 2. Cambridge, MA: Harvard University Press, 1960.

Corbett, Theodore. *The Making of American Resorts: Saratoga Springs, Ballston Spa, and Lake George.* New Brunswick, NJ: Rutgers University Press, 2001.

Cracroft, Richard H. *Washington Irving: The Western Works.* Boise, ID: Boise State University, 1974. (Boise State University Western Writers Series, No. 14.)

Crane, Verner W. "The Club of Honest Whigs: Friends of Science and Liberty." *The William and Mary Quarterly* 23 (April 1966): 210–233.

Davis, Richard Beale. "James Ogilvie and Washington Irving." *Americana* 35 (July 1941): 435–458.

———. "Washington Irving and Joseph C. Cabell." *English Studies in Honor of James Southall Wilson* 5 (1951): 7–22.

Dekker, George. *James Fenimore Cooper: The American Scott.* New York: Barnes & Noble, 1967.

Dennis, Matthew. *Red, White, and Blue Letter Days: An American Calendar.* Ithaca, NY: Cornell University Press, 2002.

Dunlap, William. *Diary of William Dunlap, 1766–1839.* New York: New-York Historical Society, 1930.

Ehle, John. *Trail of Tears: The Rise and Fall of the Cherokee Nation.* New York: Anchor Books, 1988.

Eisler, Benita. *Byron: Child of Passion, Fool of Fame.* New York: Alfred A. Knopf, 1999.

Ellis, Joseph J. *After the Revolution: Profiles of Early American Culture.* New York: W. W. Norton, 1979.

Ellsworth, Henry Leavitt. *Washington Irving on the Prairie, or a Narrative of a Tour of the Southwest in the Year 1832.* Edited by Stanley T. Williams and Barbara D. Simison. New York: American Book Company, 1937.

Evans, James E. "The English Lineage of Diedrich Knickerbocker." *Early American Literature* 10 (1995): 3–13.

Everton, Michael. "The Would-be Author and the Real Bookseller." *Early American Literature* 40 (2005): 79–110.

Ferguson, Robert A. "Hunting Down a Nation: Irving's *A History of New York.*" *Nineteenth-Century Fiction* 36 (June 1981): 22–46.

———. "Rip Van Winkle and the Generational Divide in American Culture." *Early American Literature* 40 (2005): 529–544.

Fernandez-Armesto, Felipe. *Columbus.* Oxford: Oxford University Press, 1991.

Foreman, Grant. *A History of Oklahoma.* Norman: University of Oklahoma Press, 1942.

Foster, Don. *Author Unknown: On the Trail of Anonymous.* New York: Henry Holt, 2000.

Gartner, Matthew. "Becoming Longfellow: Work, Manhood, and Poetry." *American Literature* 72 (March 2000): 59–86.

Giles, Paul. *Transatlantic Insurrections: British Culture and the Formation of American Literature, 1730–1860.* Philadelphia: University of Pennsylvania Press, 2001.

Gilfoyle, Timothy J. *City of Eros: New York City, Prostitution, and the Commercialization of Sex, 1790–1920.* New York: W. W. Norton, 1992.

Golby, J. M., and A. W. Purdue. *The Making of Modern Christmas.* Athens: University of Georgia Press, 1986.

Goldsmith, Oliver. *The Citizen of the World: or, Letters from a Chinese Philosopher, Residing in London, to His Friends in the East.* Albany, NY: Barber and Southwick, 1794.

———. *The Vicar of Wakefield.* New York: New American Library, 1961.

Gordon, Joan. "The Livingstons of New York, 1675–1860: Kinship and Class." PhD diss., Columbia University, 1959.

Green, James N. "Author-Publisher Relations in America up to 1825." Unpublished paper presented at the American Antiquarian Society, Worcester, MA, 1994.

Greven, David. "Troubling Our Heads About Ichabod: 'The Legend of Sleepy Hollow,' Classic American Literature, and the Sexual Politics of Homosocial Brotherhood." *American Quarterly* 56 (March 2004): 83–110.

Guttman, Allen. "Washington Irving and the Conservative Imagination." *American Literature* 36 (May 1964): 165–173.

Haeger, John Denis. *John Jacob Astor: Business and Finance in the Early Republic.* Detroit: Wayne State University Press, 1991.

Hallock, John W. M. *The American Byron: Homosexuality and the Fall of Fitz-Greene Halleck.* Madison: University of Wisconsin Press, 2000.

Hazlett, John D. "Literary Nationalism and Ambivalence in Washington Irving's *The Life and Voyages of Christopher Columbus.*" *American Literature* 55 (December 1983): 560–575.

Hebel, Udo J., ed. *The Construction and Contestation of American Cultures and Identities in the Early National Period.* Heidelberg, Germany: Universitätsverlag, 1999.

Hedges, William L. *Washington Irving: An American Study, 1802–1832.* Baltimore: Johns Hopkins University Press, 1965.

Hellman, George S., ed. *Letters of Henry Brevoort to Washington Irving.* New York: G. P. Putnam's Sons, 1916.

———. *Washington Irving, Esquire: Ambassador at Large from the New World to the Old.* London: Jonathan Cape, 1925.

Hoffman, Daniel G. "Irving's Use of American Folklore in 'The Legend of Sleepy Hollow.'" *PMLA* 68 (June 1953): 425–435.

Horowitz, Helen Lefkowitz. *Rereading Sex: Battles over Sexual Knowledge and Suppression in Nineteenth-Century America.* New York: Alfred A. Knopf, 2002.

Hutton, Patrick H. *History as an Art of Memory.* Hanover, NH: University Press of New England, 1993.

Innes, J. H. *New Amsterdam and Its People.* Port Washington, NY: Ira J. Friedman, 1969. First published 1902 by Charles Scribner's Sons.

Irving, Washington. *The Adventures of Captain Bonneville.* Edited by Robert A. Rees and Alan Sandy. Boston: Twayne Publishers, 1977.

———. *The Alhambra.* Edited by William T. Lenehan and Andrew B. Myers. Boston: Twayne Publishers, 1983.

———. *Astoria, or Anecdotes of an Enterprize Beyond the Rocky Mountains.* Edited by Richard Dilworth Rust. Boston: Twayne Publishers, 1976.

———. *Bracebridge Hall.* Edited by Herbert F. Smith. Boston: Twayne Publishers, 1977.

———. *A Chronicle of the Conquest of Granada.* Edited by Earl N. Harbert and Miriam J. Shillingsburg. Boston: Twayne Publishers, 1988.

———. *The Crayon Miscellany.* Edited by Dahlia Kirby Terrell. Boston: Twayne Publishers, 1979.

———. *A History of New York.* Edited by Michael L. Black and Nancy B. Black. Boston: Twayne Publishers, 1984.

———. *Letters of Jonathan Oldstyle, Gent.* Edited by Bruce I. Granger and Martha Hartzog. Boston: Twayne Publishers, 1977.

———. *The Life and Voyages of Christopher Columbus.* Edited by John Harmon McElroy. Boston: Twayne Publishers, 1981.

———. *Life of George Washington.* Edited by Allen Guttmann and James A. Sappenfield. Boston: Twayne Publishers, 1982.

———. *Mahomet and His Successors.* Edited by Henry A. Pochmann and E. N. Feltskog. Madison: University of Wisconsin Press, 1970.

———. *Oliver Goldsmith: A Biography; Biography of the Late Margaret Miller Davidson.* Edited by Elsie Lee West. Boston: Twayne Publishers, 1978.

———. *Salmagundi.* Edited by Bruce I. Granger and Martha Hartzog. Boston: Twayne Publishers, 1977.

———. *Sketch Book.* Edited by Haskell Springer. Boston: Twayne Publishers, 1978.

———. *Tales of a Traveller.* Edited by Judith Giblin Haig. Boston: Twayne Publishers, 1987.

———. *Wolfert's Roost.* Edited by Roberta Rosenberg. Boston: Twayne Publishers, 1979.

Irwin, Ray W. *Daniel D. Tompkins: Governor of New York and Vice President of the United States.* New York: New-York Historical Society, 1968.

Irwin, Robert. *The Alhambra.* Cambridge, MA: Harvard University Press, 2004.

Isenberg, Nancy. *Fallen Founder: The Life of Aaron Burr.* New York: Viking Penguin, 2007.

Isenberg, Nancy, and Andrew Burstein, eds. *Mortal Remains: Death in Early America.* Philadelphia: University of Pennsylvania Press, 2003.

Jackson, Andrew. *Papers of Andrew Jackson.* Edited by Sam B. Smith and others. Knoxville: University of Tennessee Press, 1980.

Jackson, Donald, ed. *Black Hawk: An Autobiography.* Urbana: University of Illinois Press, 1964.

Jameson, J. Franklin, ed. *Narratives of New Netherland, 1609–1664.* New York: Charles Scribner's Sons, 1909.

Janes, Regina. *Losing Our Heads: Beheadings in Literature and Culture.* New York: New York University Press, 2005.

Janvier, Thomas A. *In Old New York.* New York: Harper & Brothers, 1894.

Jefferson, Joseph. *"Rip Van Winkle": The Autobiography of Joseph Jefferson.* London: Reinhardt & Evans, 1949.

Jenkins, Stephen. *The Greatest Street in the World: The Story of Broadway, Old and New, from the Bowling Green to Albany.* New York: G. P. Putnam's Sons, 1911.

Jones, Charles W. "Knickerbocker Santa Claus." *The New-York Historical Society Quarterly* 38 (October 1954): 357–383.

Jones, Howard Mumford. *O Strange New World.* New York: Viking Press, 1964.

July, Robert W. *The Essential New Yorker: Gulian Crommelin Verplanck.* Durham, NC: Duke University Press, 1951.

Kampmeier, R. H. "Peter Irving (1771–1828): Physician, Litterateur, and Burrite Polemicist." *Pharos* (Summer 1987): 15–18. (Note: Peter Irving died in 1838—title contains a misprint.)

Kime, Wayne R. *Pierre M. Irving and Washington Irving: A Collaboration in Life and Letters.* Waterloo, Canada: Wilfrid Laurier University Press, 1977.

———. "Washington Irving and Frontier Speech." *American Speech* 42 (February 1967): 5–18.

Kleiger, Estelle Fox. *The Trial of Levi Weeks.* Chicago: Academy Chicago Publishers, 1989.

Lamb, Martha J. *History of the City of New York: Its Origin, Rise and Progress.* New York and Chicago: A. S. Barnes, 1877–1880.

Lambert, John. *Travels Through Canada and the United States of North America in the Years 1806, 1807, & 1808.* London: Baldwin, Cradock, and Joy, 1816.

Latrobe, Charles Joseph. *The Rambler in Oklahoma: Latrobe's Tour with Washington Irving.* Edited by Muriel H. Wright and George H. Shirk. Oklahoma City: Harlow Publishing, 1955.

Leiby, Adrian C. *The Revolutionary War in the Hackensack Valley: The Jersey Dutch and Neutral Ground, 1775–1783.* New Brunswick, NJ: Rutgers University Press, 1962.

Lemay, J. A. Leo. *The Life of Benjamin Franklin.* 2 vols. to date. Philadelphia: University of Pennsylvania Press, 2006.

Leslie, Charles Robert. *Autobiographical Recollections by the Late Charles Robert Leslie.* Edited by Tom Taylor. Boston: Ticknor and Fields, 1860.

Letters About the Hudson River, and Its Vicinity. New York: Freeman Hunt, 1837.

Livi-Bacci, Massimo. "Return to Hispaniola: Reassessing a Demographic Catastrophe." *Hispanic American Historical Review* 83 (2003): 3–51.

Longworth, David. *Longworth's American Almanack, New-York Register, and City Directory.* New York: John C. Totten, 1799; Longworth & Wheeler, 1800; D. Longworth, 1801–1806.

Lueck, Beth L. *American Writers and the Picturesque Tour: The Search for National Identity, 1790–1860.* New York: Garland Publishing, 1997.

Macpherson, Ian, and Angus MacKay. *Love, Religion and Politics in Fifteenth Century Spain.* Leiden, Netherlands: Brill, 1998.

Malone, Dumas. *Jefferson the President, Second Term, 1805–1809.* Boston: Little, Brown, 1974.

Mathews, John Joseph. *The Osages: Children of the Middle Waters.* Norman: University of Oklahoma Press, 1961.

Mathews, Mitford M. *The Beginnings of American English.* Chicago: University of Chicago Press, 1931.

McCaleb, Walter Flavius. *The Aaron Burr Conspiracy and a New Light on Aaron Burr.* New York: Argosy-Antiquarian, 1966. First published 1903 by Dodd, Mead.

McCarter, Pete Kyle. "The Literary, Political, and Social Theories of Washington Irving." PhD diss., University of Wisconsin–Madison, 1939.

McClary, Ben Harris, ed. *Washington Irving and the House of Murray.* Knoxville: University of Tennessee Press, 1969.

McDermott, John Francis, ed. *The Western Journals of Washington Irving.* Norman: University of Oklahoma Press, 1944.

McLamore, Richard V. "The Dutchman in the Attic: Claiming an Inheritance in *The Sketch Book of Geoffrey Crayon.*" *American Literature* 72 (March 2000): 31–57.

———. "Postcolonial Columbus: Washington Irving and *The Conquest of Granada.*" *Nineteenth-Century Literature* 48 (June 1993): 26–43.

Mitchell, Donald G. "Dream Life: A Fable of the Seasons." In *The Works of Donald G. Mitchell.* New York: Charles Scribner's Sons, 1907.

———. ("Ik Marvel.") *Reveries of a Bachelor: Or a Book of the Heart.* New York: Baker & Scribner, 1851.

Mitchill, Samuel L. *The Picture of New-York; or, the Traveller's Guide Through the Commercial Metropolis of the United States.* New York: I. Riley, 1807.

Mott, Frank Luther. *History of American Magazines, 1741–1850.* Cambridge, MA: Harvard University Press, 1957.

Murray, Laura J. "The Aesthetic of Dispossession: Washington Irving and Ideologies of (De)Colonization in the Early Republic." *American Literary History* 8 (Summer 1996): 205–231.

Mushkat, Jerome, and Joseph G. Rayback. *Martin Van Buren: Law, Politics, and the Shaping of Republican Ideology.* DeKalb: Northern Illinois University Press, 1997.

Myers, Andrew B., ed. *A Century of Commentary on the Works of Washington Irving.* Tarrytown, NY: Sleepy Hollow Restorations, 1976.

———. "Washington Irving and the Astor Library." *Bulletin of the New York Public Library* 72 (June 1968): 378–399.

Nissenbaum, Stephen. *The Battle for Christmas.* New York: Alfred A. Knopf, 1996.

———. *Christmas in Early New England, 1620–1820: Puritanism, Popular Culture, and the Printed Word.* Worcester, MA: American Antiquarian Society, 1996.

Niven, John. *Martin Van Buren: The Romantic Age of American Politics.* New York: Oxford University Press, 1983.

Odell, George C. D. *Annals of the New York Stage.* New York: Columbia University Press, 1927. Reprint, AMC Press, 1970.

Osterweis, Rollin G. *Rebecca Gratz: A Study in Charm.* New York: G. P. Putnam's Sons, 1935.

Ostrander, Gilman M. *Republic of Letters: The American Intellectual Community, 1775–1865.* Madison, WI: Madison House, 1999.

Pacey, W. C. Desmond. "Washington Irving and Charles Dickens." *American Literature* 16 (January 1945): 332–339.

Parton, James. *Life and Times of Aaron Burr.* Boston and New York: Houghton Mifflin, 1892. First published 1857 by Mason Brothers.

Paulding, James Kirke. *The Diverting History of John Bull and Brother Jonathan.* New York and Philadelphia: Inskeep & Bradford, 1812.

———. *The Dutchman's Fireside.* Edited by Thomas F. O'Donnell. New Haven, CT: College & University Press, 1966. First published 1831 by J. & J. Harper.

———. *Koningsmarke, or, Old Times in the New World.* New York: Harper & Brothers, 1834.

———. *The Lay of the Scottish Fiddle: A Tale of Havre de Grace.* New York: Inskeep & Bradford, 1813.

———. *Stories of Saint Nicholas.* Syracuse, NY: Syracuse University Press, 1995.

Peterson, Merrill D. *The Great Triumvirate: Webster, Clay, and Calhoun.* New York: Oxford University Press, 1987.

Pethers, Matthew J. "Transatlantic Migration and the Politics of the Picturesque in Washington Irving's *Sketch Book.*" *Symbiosis* 9 (October 2005): 135–158.

Pochmann, Herbert A. "Irving's German Sources in the *Sketch Book.*" *Studies in Philology* 27 (July 1930): 477–507.

Pomerantz, Sidney I. *New York, an American City, 1783–1803.* New York: Columbia University Press, 1938.

Raesly, Ellis Lawrence. *Portrait of New Netherland.* New York: Columbia University Press, 1945.

Railton, Stephen. *Fenimore Cooper: A Study of His Life and Imagination.* Princeton, NJ: Princeton University Press, 1978.

Reichart, Walter A. *Washington Irving and Germany.* Ann Arbor: University of Michigan Press, 1957.

Restad, Penne L. *Christmas in America: A History.* New York: Oxford University Press, 1995.

Reston, James Jr. *Dogs of God: Columbus, the Inquisition, and the Defeat of the Moors.* New York: Doubleday, 2005.

Reynolds, Larry J. *James Kirke Paulding.* Boston: Twayne Publishers, 1984.

Richardson, Judith. *Possessions: The History and Uses of Haunting in the Hudson Valley.* Cambridge, MA: Harvard University Press, 2003.

Ringe, Donald A. *American Gothic: Imagination and Reason in Nineteenth-Century Fiction.* Lexington: University Press of Kentucky, 1982.

———. "Irving's Use of the Gothic Mode." *Studies in the Literary Imagination* 7 (Spring 1974): 51–66.

Rink, Oliver A. *Holland on the Hudson: An Economic and Social History of Dutch New York.* Ithaca, NY: Cornell University Press, 1984.

Rip Van Winkle, as Played by Joseph Jefferson. New York: Dodd, Mead, 1899.

Rogers, Katharine M. *The Troublesome Helpmate: A History of Misogyny in Literature.* Seattle: University of Washington Press, 1966.

Ronda, James P. *Astoria and Empire.* Lincoln: University of Nebraska Press, 1990.

Roth, Martin. *Comedy and America: The Lost World of Washington Irving.* Port Washington, NY: Kennikat Press, 1976.

Rubin-Dorsky, Jeffrey. *Adrift in the Old World: The Psychological Pilgrimage of Washington Irving.* Chicago: University of Chicago Press, 1988.

———. "The Value of Storytelling: 'Rip Van Winkle' and 'The Legend of Sleepy Hollow' in the Context of 'The Sketch Book.'" *Modern Philology* 82 (May 1985): 393–406.

Ruland, Richard, and Malcolm Bradbury. *From Puritanism to Postmodernism: A History of American Literature.* New York: Viking Penguin, 1991.

Scharf, J. Thomas. *History of Westchester County, New York.* 2 vols. Philadelphia: L. E. Preston, 1886.

Schlereth, Thomas J. "Columbia, Columbus, and Columbianism." *Journal of American History* 79 (December 1992): 937–968.

Scott, Eleanor Bryce. "Early Literary Clubs in New York City." *American Literature* 5 (March 1933): 3–16.

Scoville, Joseph A. *The Old Merchants of New York City.* New York: Carleton, 1863.

Shear, Walter. "Time in 'Rip Van Winkle' and 'The Legend of Sleepy Hollow.'" *Midwest Quarterly* 17 (1976): 158–172.

Shirk, George H. "A Tour on the Prairies Along the Washington Irving Trail in Oklahoma." *Chronicles of Oklahoma* 45 (Autumn 1967): 312–331.

Simpson, David. *The Politics of American English, 1776–1850.* New York: Oxford University Press, 1986.

Skeen, C. Edward. *Citizen Soldiers in the War of 1812.* Lexington: University Press of Kentucky, 1999.

Slotkin, Richard. *Regeneration Through Violence: The Mythology of the American Frontier, 1600–1860.* Middletown, CT: Wesleyan University Press, 1973.

Spaulding, George F., ed. *On the Western Tour with Washington Irving: The Journal and Letters of Count de Pourtalès.* Norman: University of Oklahoma Press, 1968.

Spiller, Robert E. *The American in England During the First Half Century of Independence.* New York: Henry Holt, 1926.

Stagg, J. C. A. *Mr. Madison's War: Politics, Diplomacy, and Warfare in the Early American Republic.* Princeton, NJ: Princeton University Press, 1983.

Sterne, Laurence. *A Sentimental Journey Through France and Italy.* London: T. Becket and P. A. De Hondt, 1770.

———. *Tristram Shandy.* Edited by Ian Watt. Boston: Houghton Mifflin, 1965.

Taft, Kendall B., ed. *Minor Knickerbockers.* New York: American Book Company, 1947.

Tompkins, Daniel D. *Free Trade & Sailor's Rights! An Address to the Independent Electors of the State of New York.* Albany, NY: Office of the *Argus*, 1813.

Traister, Bryce. "The Wandering Bachelor: Irving, Masculinity, and Authorship." *American Literature* 74 (March 2002): 111–137.

Tuckerman, Bayard, ed. *Diary of Philip Hone.* 2 vols. New York: Dodd, Mead, 1889.

Tuttleton, James W., ed. *Washington Irving: The Critical Reaction.* New York: AMS Press, 1993.

Universal Biographical Dictionary, Containing the Lives of the Most Celebrated Characters of Every Age and Nation. New York: n.p., 1825.

Vail, R. W. G. *Knickerbocker Birthday: A Sesqui-Centennial History of the New-York Historical Society, 1804–1954.* New York: New-York Historical Society, 1954.

Van Doren, Carl. *Benjamin Franklin.* New York: Viking Press, 1938.

Van Doren, Mark, ed. *Correspondence of Aaron Burr and His Daughter Theodosia.* New York: Covici, Friede, 1929.

Voorsanger, Catherine Hoover, and John K. Howat, eds. *Art and the Empire City: New York, 1825–1861.* New Haven, CT: Yale University Press, 2000.

Wagenknecht, Edward. *Washington Irving: Moderation Displayed.* New York: Oxford University Press, 1962.

Wallace, Anthony F. C. *The Long Bitter Trail: Andrew Jackson and the Indians.* New York: Hill & Wang, 1993.

Warner, Michael. "Irving's Posterity." *ELH* 67 (Autumn 2000): 773–799.

Weatherspoon, M. A. "1815–1819: Prelude to Irving's *Sketch Book*." *American Literature* 41 (January 1970): 566–571.

White, Leonard D. *The Jeffersonians: A Study in Administrative History, 1801–1829.* New York: Macmillan, 1951.

Williams, Stanley T., and Leonard B. Beach, eds. *The Journal of Emily Foster.* New York: Oxford University Press, 1938.

Wilson, James Grant. *Bryant and His Friends: Some Reminiscences of the Knickerbocker Writers.* New York: Fords, Howard & Hurlbert, 1886.

———. *The Memorial History of the City of New York and the Hudson River Valley.* 4 vols. New York: New-York History Company, 1892–1893.

Wirt, William. *The Life of Patrick Henry.* Hartford, CT: S. Andrus & Son, 1832.

Wise, Henry A. *Seven Decades of the Union: The Humanities and Materialism, Illustrated by a Memoir of John Tyler.* Philadelphia: J. B. Lippincott, 1872.

Index

409